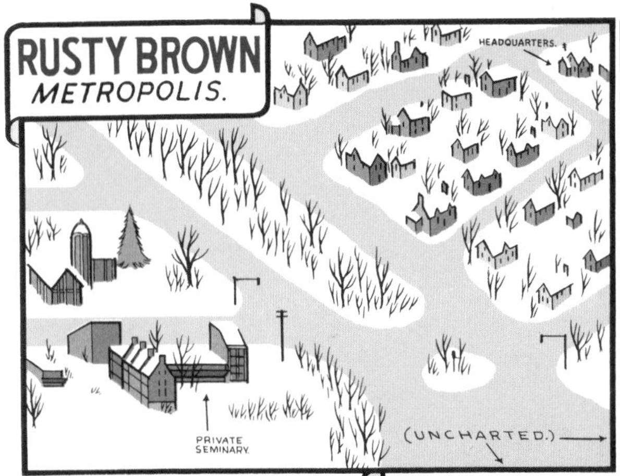
RUSTY BROWN
METROPOLIS.
HEADQUARTERS.
PRIVATE SEMINARY.
(UNCHARTED.)

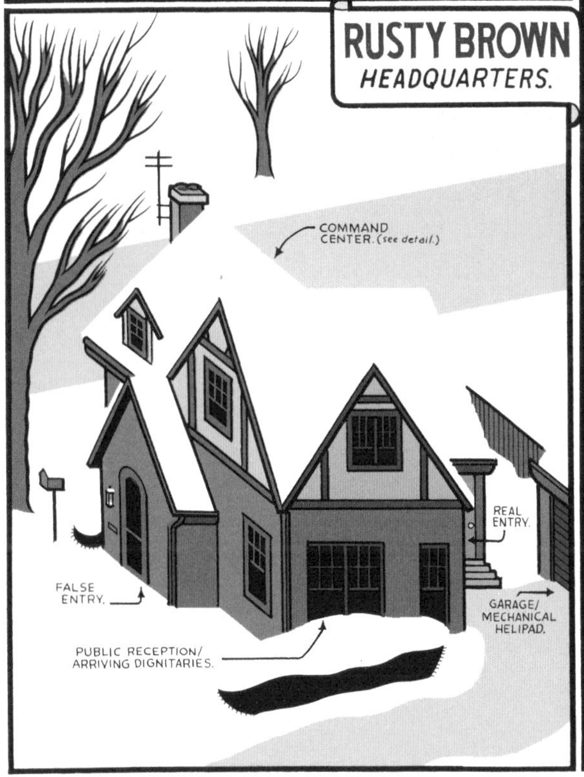
RUSTY BROWN
HEADQUARTERS.
COMMAND CENTER. (see detail.)
REAL ENTRY.
FALSE ENTRY.
GARAGE/ MECHANICAL HELIPAD.
PUBLIC RECEPTION/ ARRIVING DIGNITARIES.

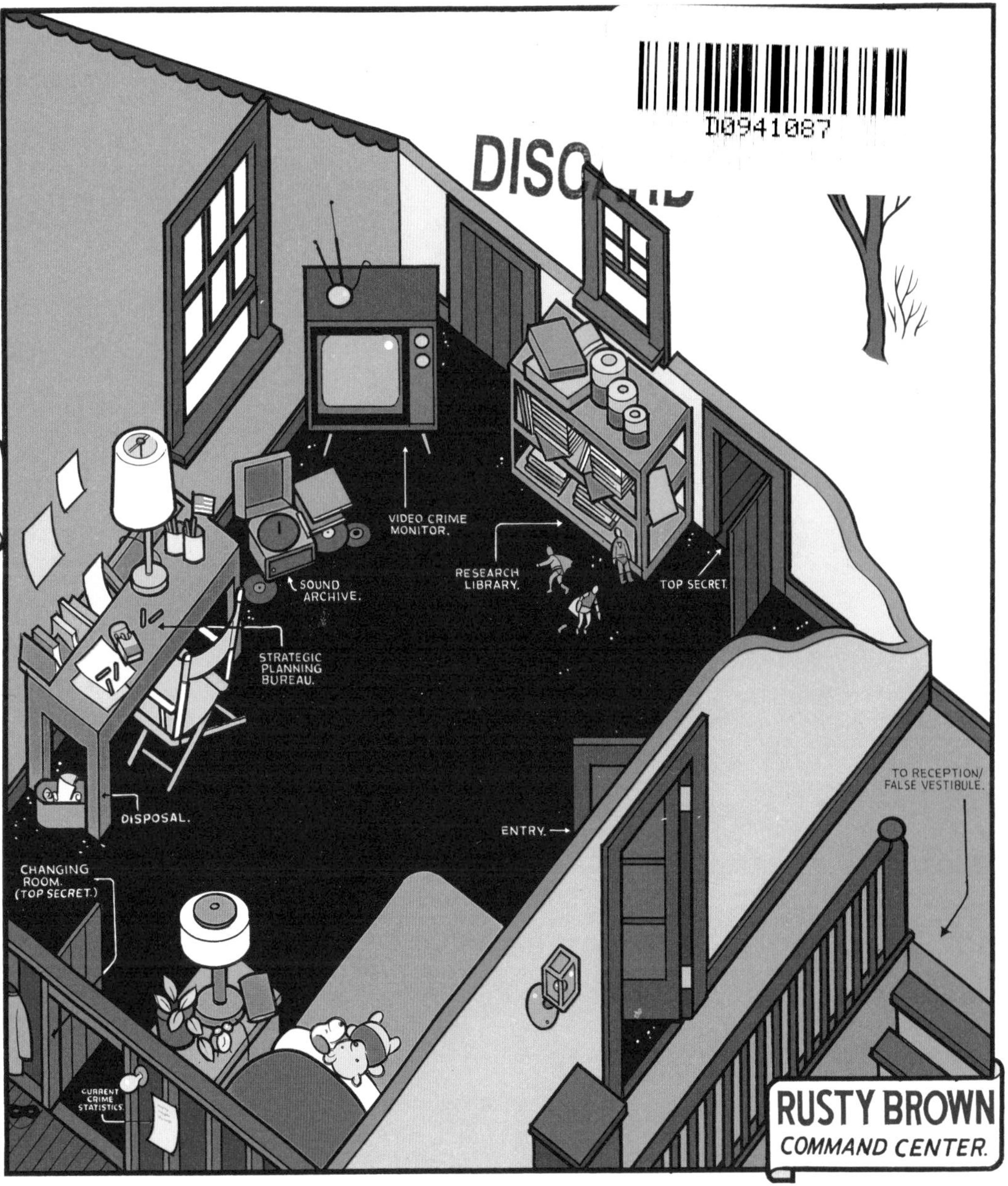
VIDEO CRIME MONITOR.
SOUND ARCHIVE.
RESEARCH LIBRARY.
TOP SECRET.
STRATEGIC PLANNING BUREAU.
DISPOSAL.
ENTRY.
TO RECEPTION/ FALSE VESTIBULE.
CHANGING ROOM. (TOP SECRET.)
CURRENT CRIME STATISTICS.
RUSTY BROWN
COMMAND CENTER.

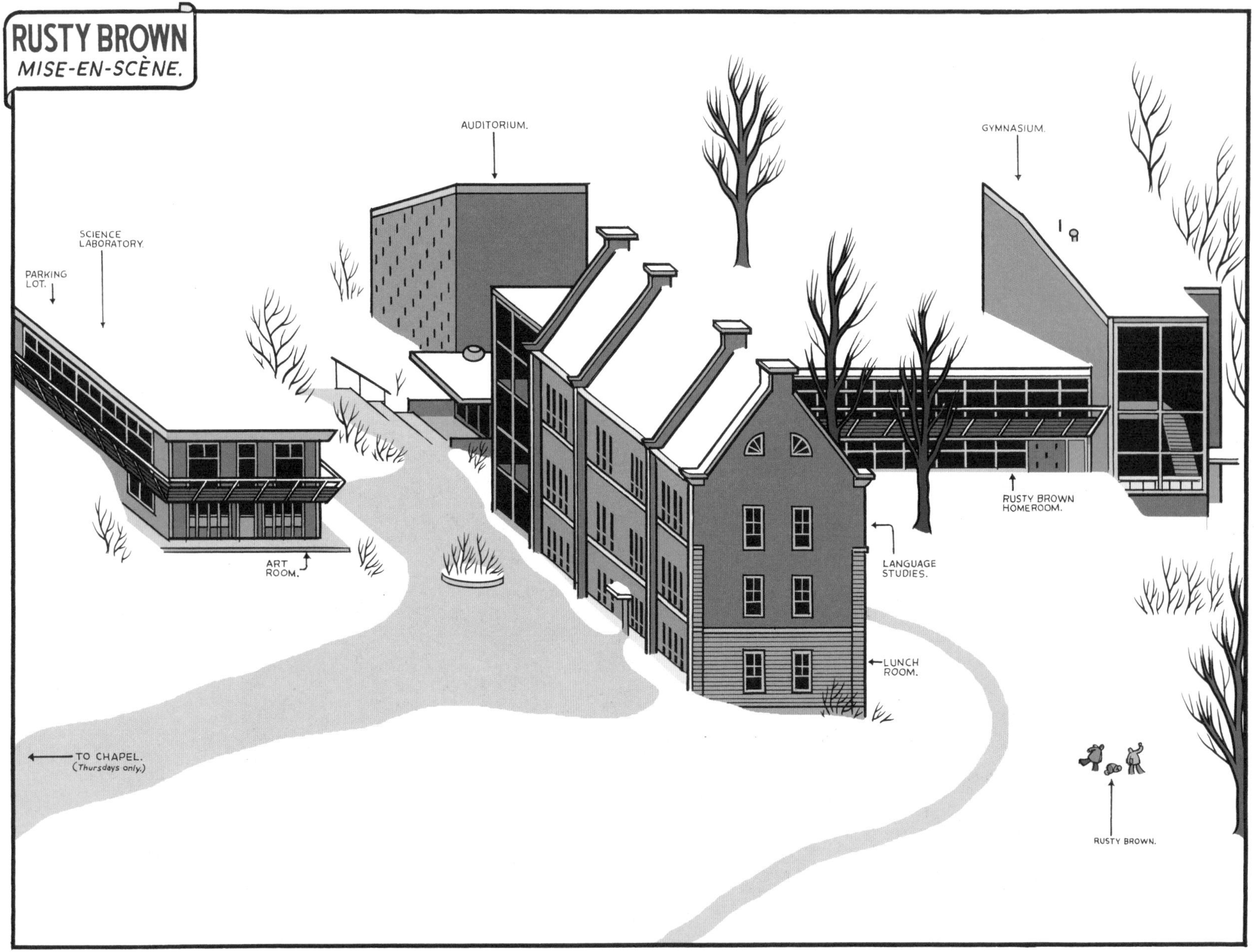
RUSTY BROWN
MISE-EN-SCÈNE.
AUDITORIUM.
GYMNASIUM.
SCIENCE LABORATORY.
PARKING LOT.
ART ROOM.
RUSTY BROWN HOMEROOM.
LANGUAGE STUDIES.
LUNCH ROOM.
TO CHAPEL.
(Thursdays only.)
RUSTY BROWN.

"No two are alike,"
any schoolchild will tell you.

And indeed, of the few thousand snowflakes
captured on paper or film since man began
studying them roughly three centuries ago,
no true matches have been found.

But what of the billion trillion or so
that haven't been seen — or, more properly, won't ever be seen?
Isn't it possible that at least two of them
might be somewhat similar?

In 1655, the scientist Robert Hooke first tried to sketch
what René Descartes had described as the "little roses" or
"wheels with six teeth" that collected around him
in mounds and drifts.

Peering as closely as he could with one of the world's first microscopes, Hooke's subjects nonetheless melted away as he drew them, his pictures more the product of memory than of direct observation. Fortunately, however, with the precise photographic techniques available to us today, scientists are now able to "stop in time" the natural evaporation of snowflakes so that we all may study their beauty for as long as we like.

While a snowflake on a finger lingers only a second before resolving back into a drop of water, freezing that drop of water will not produce a snowflake— it will only produce a little bead of ice.

The exquisite, miraculous shape of a snowflake is a result of the singular path it takes through utterly unique conditions of cloudiness, temperature, and humidity, a veritable picture of its whole life from its birth as a speck of dirt to its end as a fragile miniature crystal flower.

Like the growing rings of a tiny hexagonal tree, billions of water molecules spin around and around, each finding the closest, easiest, and most comfortable bond (just as people, who seek the companionship of like minds and bodies, cannot simply be thrown together and expect to thrive) until, with no room left to fall, the whole finds its way to your snowshovel, glove, or TSSHHT

RUSTY

Peering as closely as he could with one of the world's first microscopes, Hooke's subjects nonetheless melted away as he drew them, his pictures more the product of memory than of direct observation. Fortunately, however, with the precise photographic techniques available to us today, scientists are now able to "stop in time" the natural evaporation of snowflakes so that we all may study their beauty for as long as we like.

While a snowflake on a finger lingers only a second before resolving back into a drop of water, freezing that drop of water will not produce a snowflake— it will only produce a little bead of ice.

The exquisite, miraculous shape of a snowflake is a result of the singular path it takes through utterly unique conditions of cloudiness, temperature, and humidity, a veritable picture of its whole life from its birth as a speck of dirt to its end as a fragile miniature crystal flower.

Like the growing rings of a tiny hexagonal tree, billions of water molecules spin around and around, each finding the closest, easiest, and most comfortable bond (just as people, who seek the companionship of like minds and bodies, cannot simply be thrown together and expect to thrive) until, with no room left to fall, the whole finds its way to your snowshovel, glove, or TSSHHT

RUSTY

BROWN

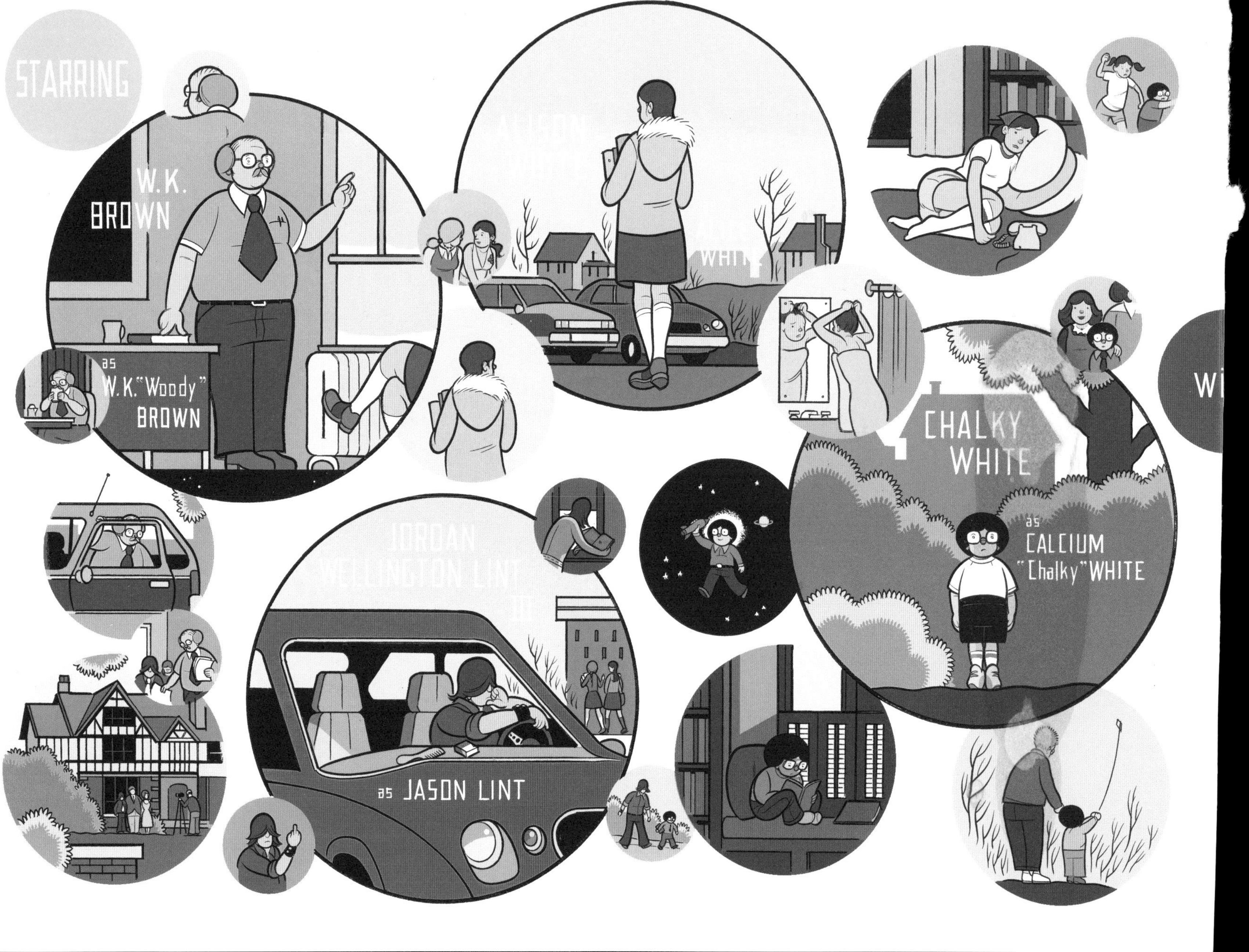
STARRING
W.K. BROWN
as W.K. "Woody" BROWN
JORDAN WELLINGTON LINT III
as JASON LINT
CHALKY WHITE
as CALCIUM "Chalky" WHITE

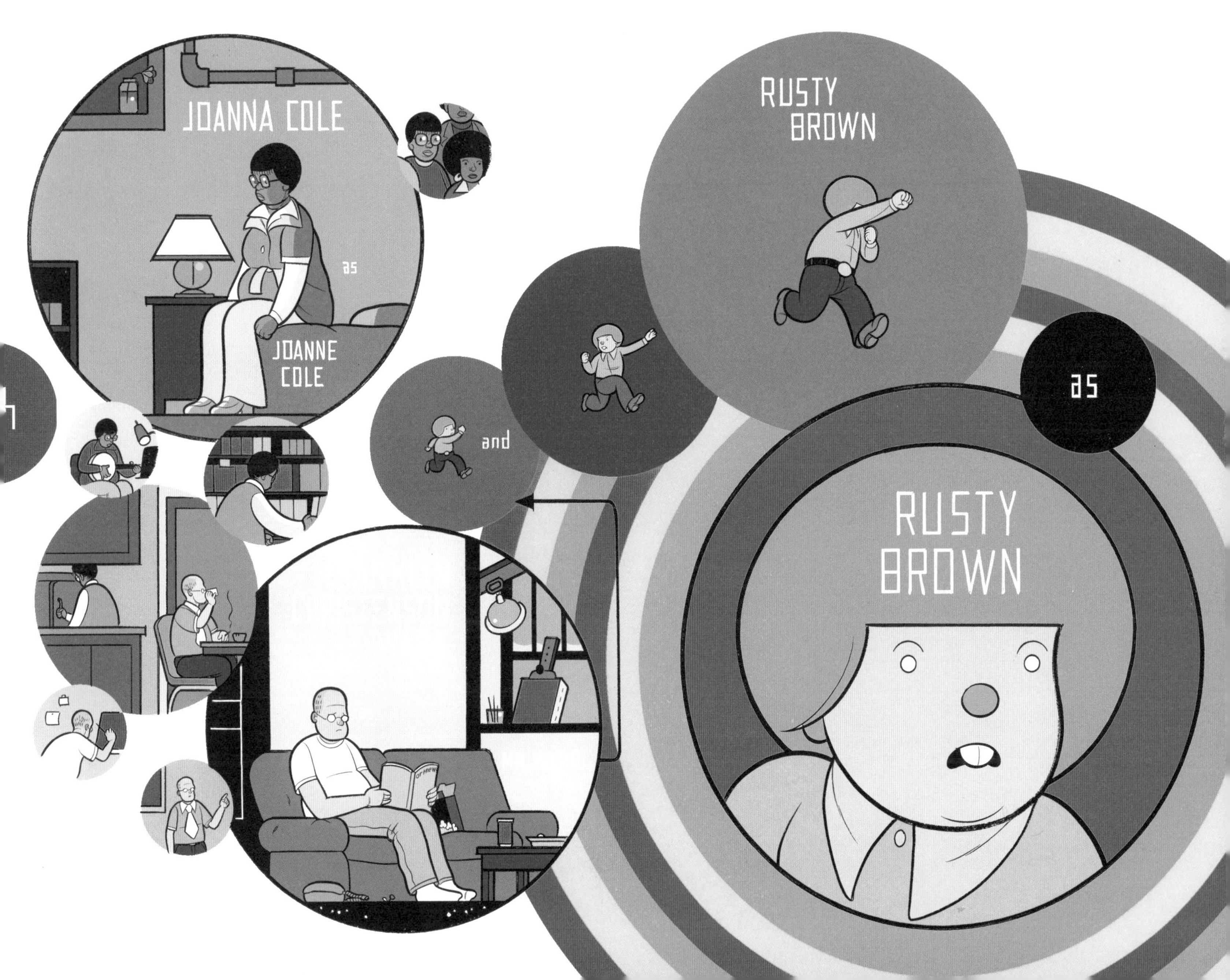
JOANNA COLE
as
JOANNE COLE
and
RUSTY BROWN
as
RUSTY BROWN

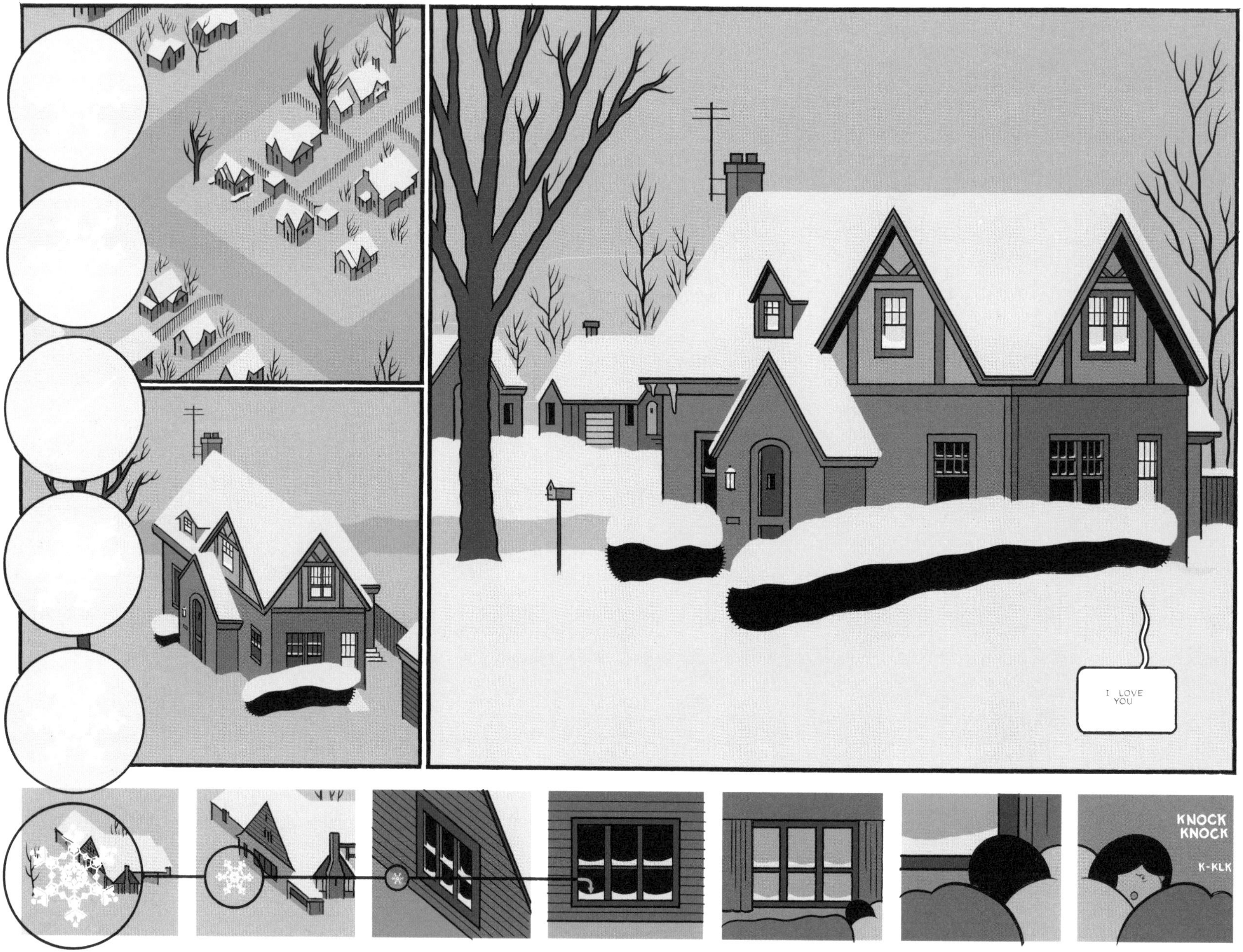
I LOVE YOU
KNOCK KNOCK
K-KLK

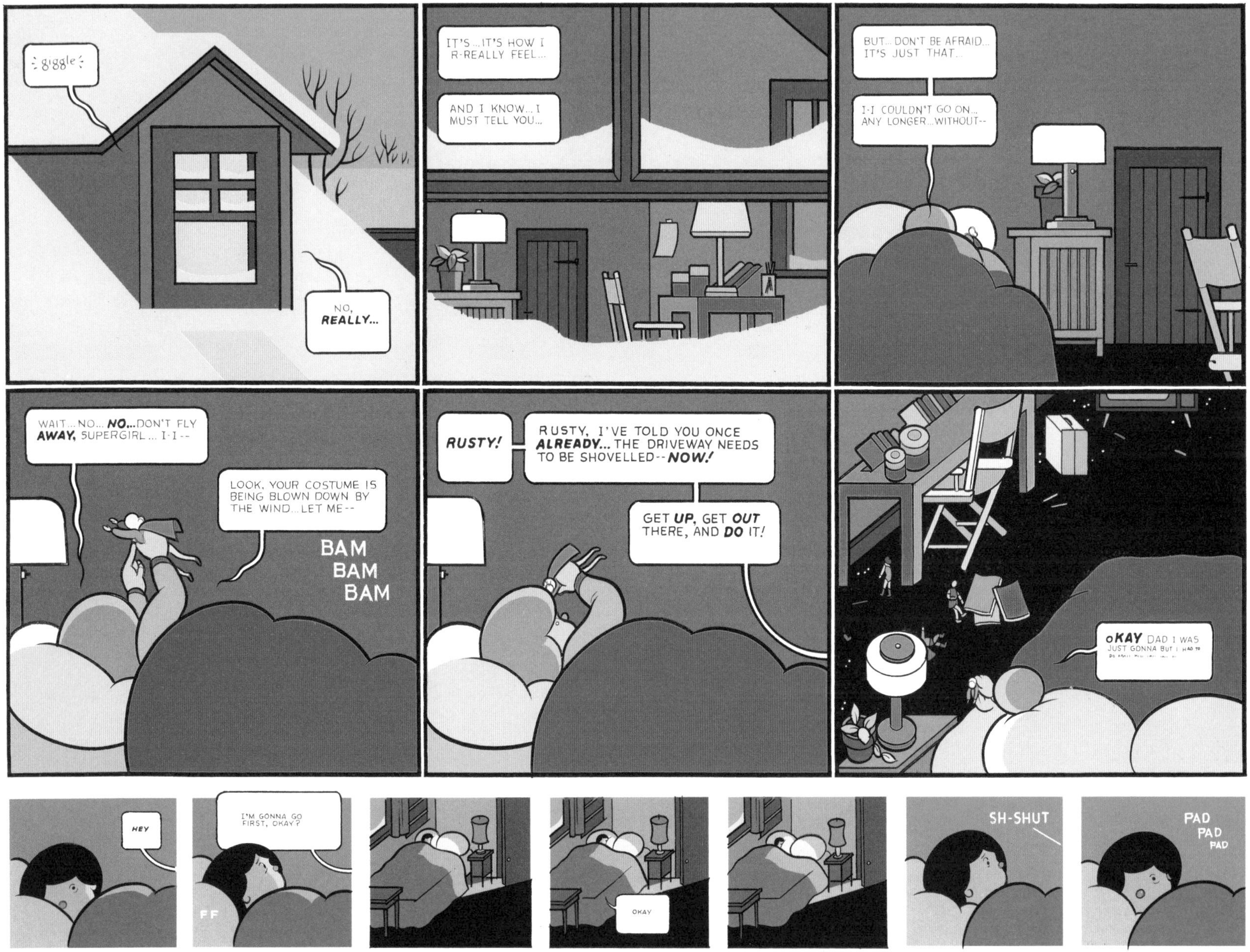
giggle
NO, REALLY...
IT'S ...IT'S HOW I R-REALLY FEEL...
AND I KNOW... I MUST TELL YOU...
BUT... DON'T BE AFRAID... IT'S JUST THAT...
I-I COULDN'T GO ON... ANY LONGER... WITHOUT--
WAIT... NO... NO... DON'T FLY AWAY, SUPERGIRL... I-I--
LOOK, YOUR COSTUME IS BEING BLOWN DOWN BY THE WIND... LET ME--
BAM BAM BAM
RUSTY!
RUSTY, I'VE TOLD YOU ONCE ALREADY... THE DRIVEWAY NEEDS TO BE SHOVELLED--NOW!
GET UP, GET OUT THERE, AND DO IT!
OKAY DAD I WAS JUST GONNA BUT I HAD TO
HEY
I'M GONNA GO FIRST, OKAY?
FF
OKAY
SH-SHUT
PAD PAD PAD

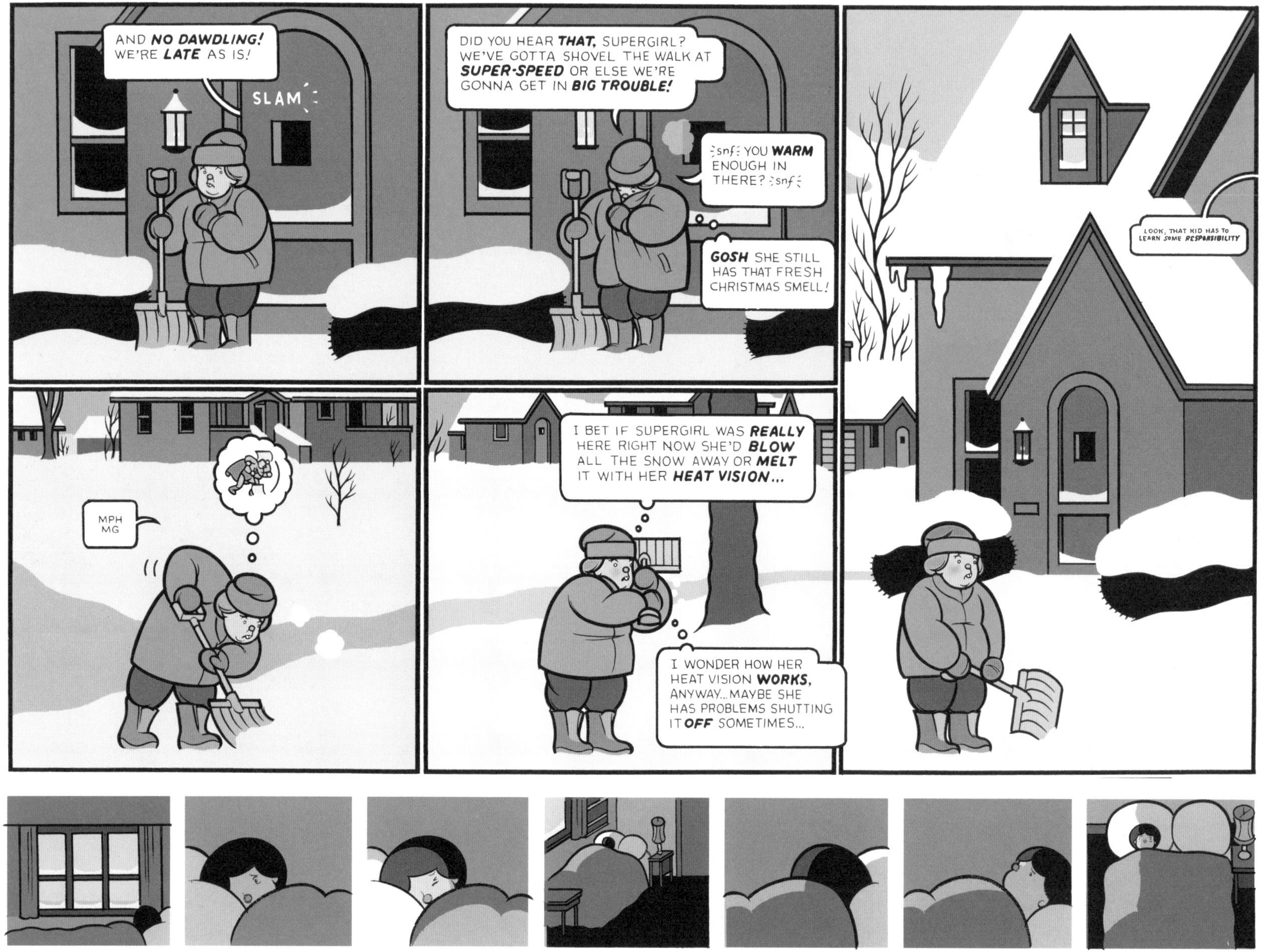
AND NO DAWDLING! WE'RE LATE AS IS!
SLAM
DID YOU HEAR THAT, SUPERGIRL? WE'VE GOTTA SHOVEL THE WALK AT SUPER-SPEED OR ELSE WE'RE GONNA GET IN BIG TROUBLE!
snf YOU WARM ENOUGH IN THERE? snf
GOSH SHE STILL HAS THAT FRESH CHRISTMAS SMELL!
LOOK, THAT KID HAS TO LEARN SOME RESPONSIBILITY
MPH MG
I BET IF SUPERGIRL WAS REALLY HERE RIGHT NOW SHE'D BLOW ALL THE SNOW AWAY OR MELT IT WITH HER HEAT VISION...
I WONDER HOW HER HEAT VISION WORKS, ANYWAY... MAYBE SHE HAS PROBLEMS SHUTTING IT OFF SOMETIMES...

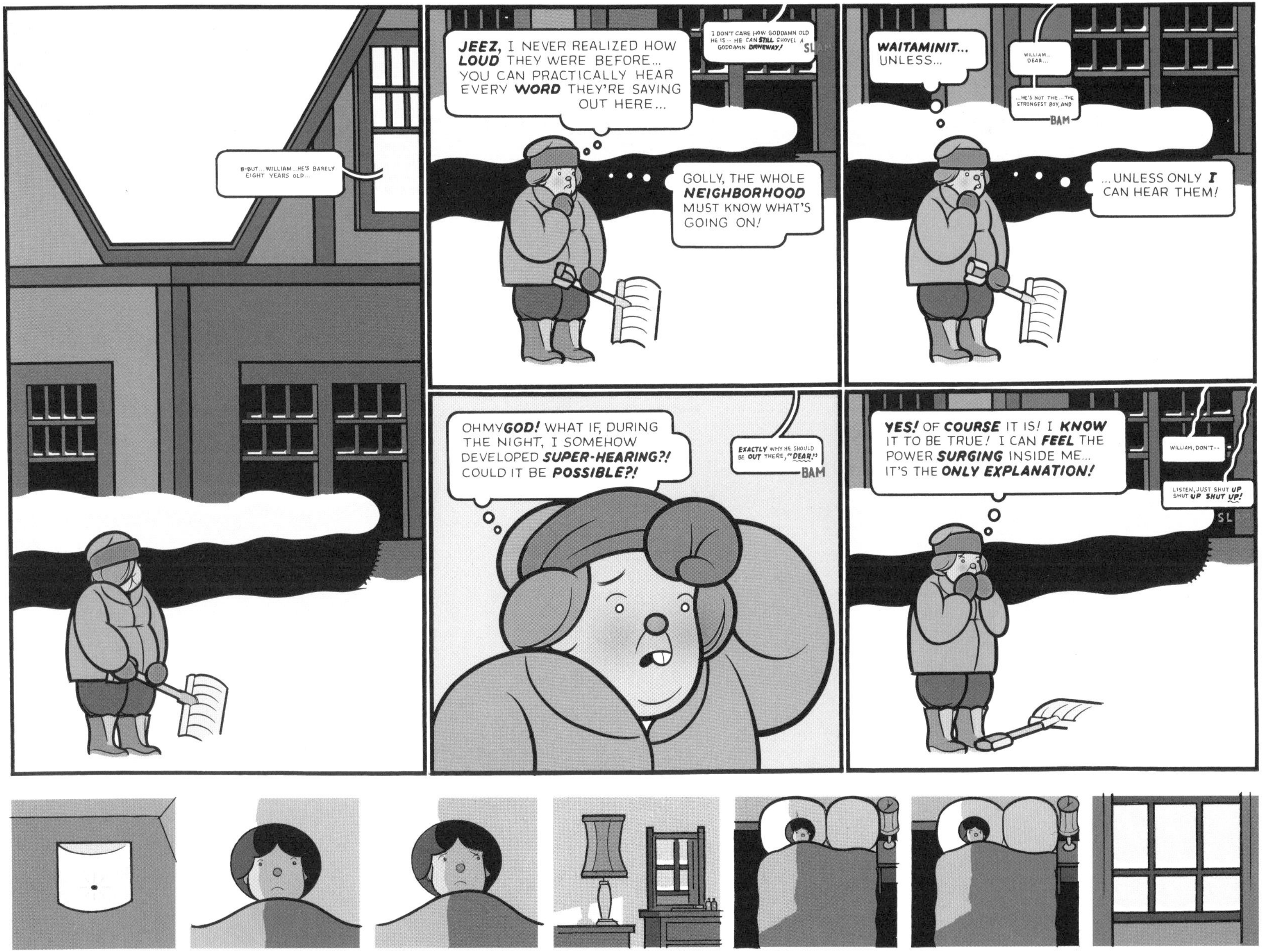
B-BUT... WILLIAM... HE'S BARELY EIGHT YEARS OLD...
JEEZ, I NEVER REALIZED HOW **LOUD** THEY WERE BEFORE... YOU CAN PRACTICALLY HEAR EVERY **WORD** THEY'RE SAYING OUT HERE...
I DON'T CARE HOW GODDAMN OLD HE IS -- HE CAN **STILL** SHOVEL A GODDAMN **DRIVEWAY!**
SLAM
GOLLY, THE WHOLE **NEIGHBORHOOD** MUST KNOW WHAT'S GOING ON!
WAITAMINIT... UNLESS...
WILLIAM... DEAR...
...HE'S NOT THE... THE STRONGEST BOY, AND
BAM
...UNLESS ONLY **I** CAN HEAR THEM!
OHMY**GOD!** WHAT IF, DURING THE NIGHT, I SOMEHOW DEVELOPED **SUPER-HEARING?!** COULD IT BE **POSSIBLE?!**
EXACTLY WHY HE SHOULD BE **OUT** THERE, "**DEAR.**"
BAM
YES! OF **COURSE** IT IS! I **KNOW** IT TO BE TRUE! I CAN **FEEL** THE POWER **SURGING** INSIDE ME... IT'S THE **ONLY EXPLANATION!**
WILLIAM, DON'T--
LISTEN, JUST SHUT **UP** SHUT **UP SHUT UP!**
SLAM

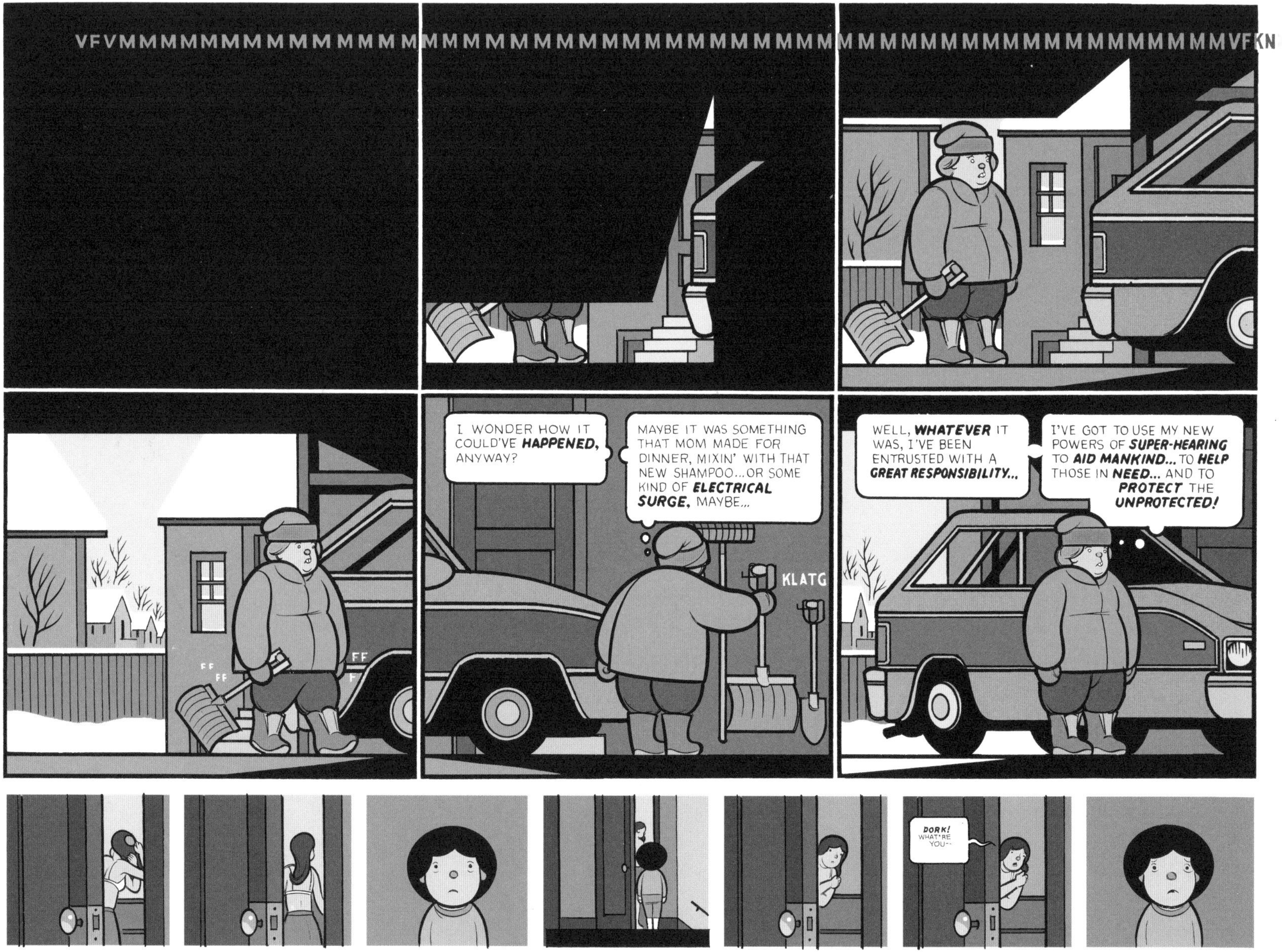

VFVMMMMMMMMMMMMMMMMMMMMMMMMMMMMMMMMMMMMMMMMMMMVFKN
FF FF
FF F
I WONDER HOW IT COULD'VE **HAPPENED,** ANYWAY?
MAYBE IT WAS SOMETHING THAT MOM MADE FOR DINNER, MIXIN' WITH THAT NEW SHAMPOO...OR SOME KIND OF **ELECTRICAL SURGE,** MAYBE...
KLATG
WELL, **WHATEVER** IT WAS, I'VE BEEN ENTRUSTED WITH A **GREAT RESPONSIBILITY...**
I'VE GOT TO USE MY NEW POWERS OF **SUPER-HEARING** TO **AID MANKIND...** TO **HELP** THOSE IN **NEED...** AND TO **PROTECT** THE **UNPROTECTED!**
DORK! WHAT'RE YOU--

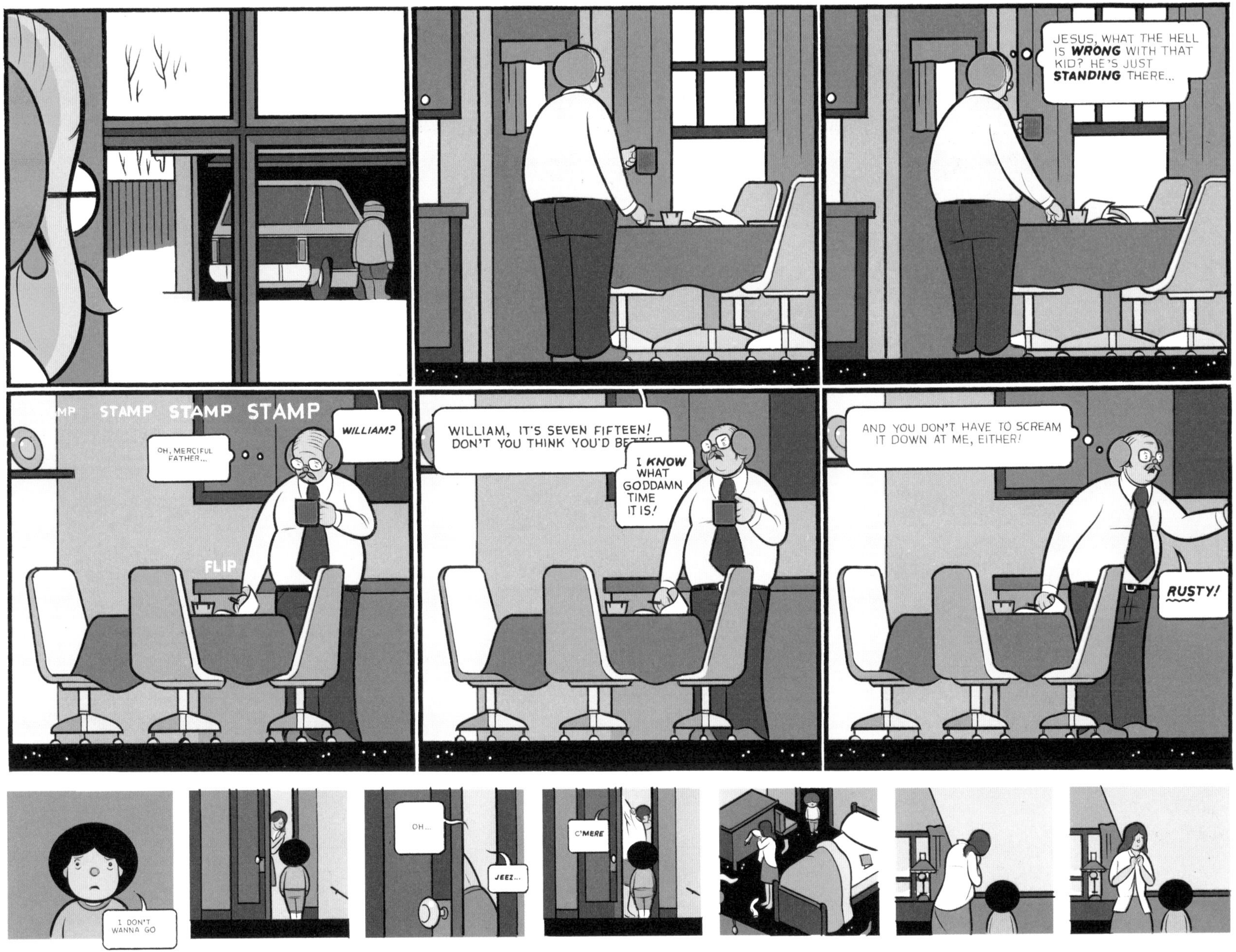

JESUS, WHAT THE HELL IS WRONG WITH THAT KID? HE'S JUST STANDING THERE...
STAMP STAMP STAMP
OH, MERCIFUL FATHER...
WILLIAM?
FLIP
WILLIAM, IT'S SEVEN FIFTEEN! DON'T YOU THINK YOU'D BE
I KNOW WHAT GODDAMN TIME IT IS!
AND YOU DON'T HAVE TO SCREAM IT DOWN AT ME, EITHER!
RUSTY!
I DON'T WANNA GO
OH...
JEEZ...
C'MERE

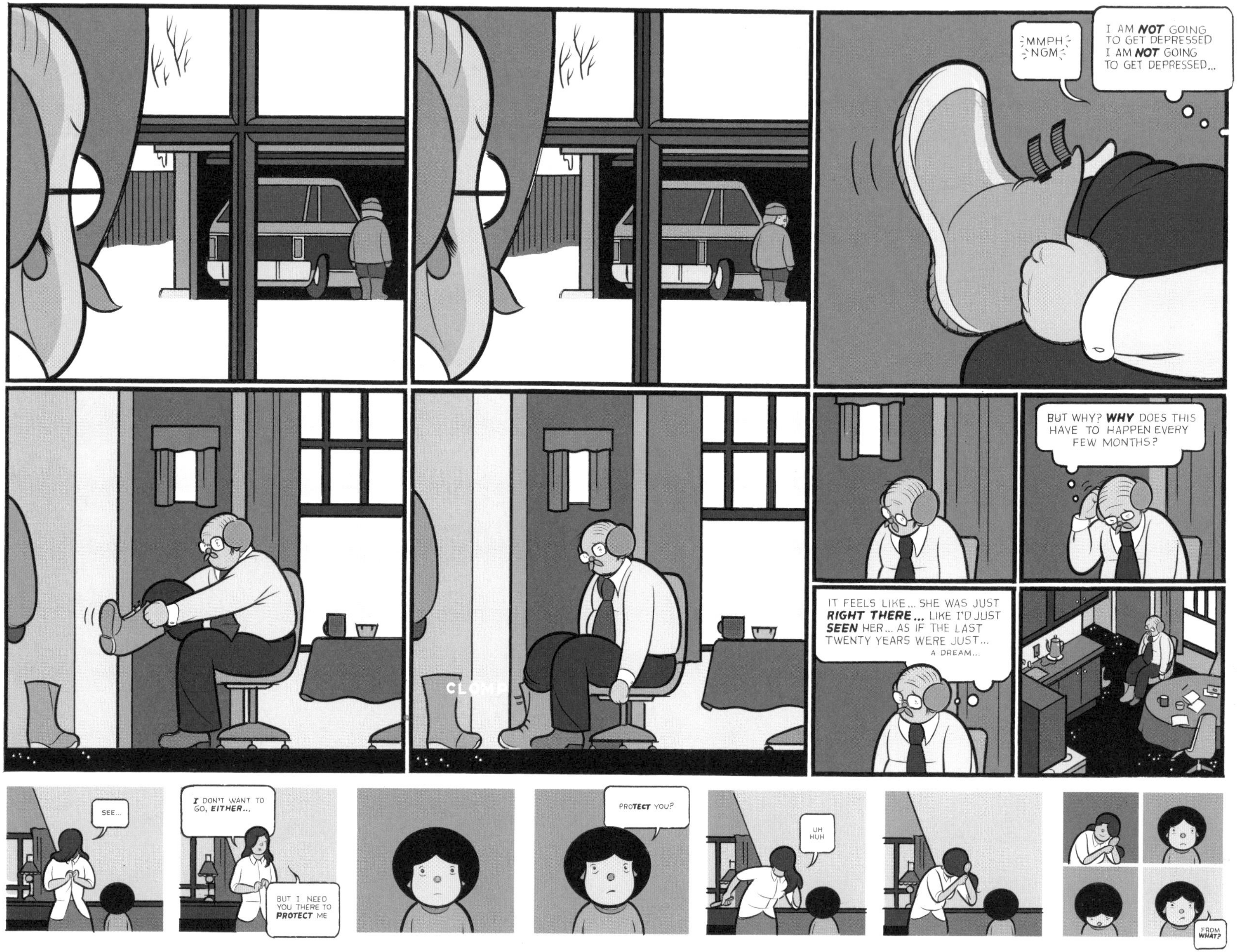
MMPH NGM
I AM NOT GOING TO GET DEPRESSED I AM NOT GOING TO GET DEPRESSED...
CLOMP
BUT WHY? WHY DOES THIS HAVE TO HAPPEN EVERY FEW MONTHS?
IT FEELS LIKE... SHE WAS JUST RIGHT THERE... LIKE I'D JUST SEEN HER... AS IF THE LAST TWENTY YEARS WERE JUST... A DREAM...
SEE...
I DON'T WANT TO GO, EITHER...
BUT I NEED YOU THERE TO PROTECT ME
PROTECT YOU?
UH HUH
FROM WHAT?

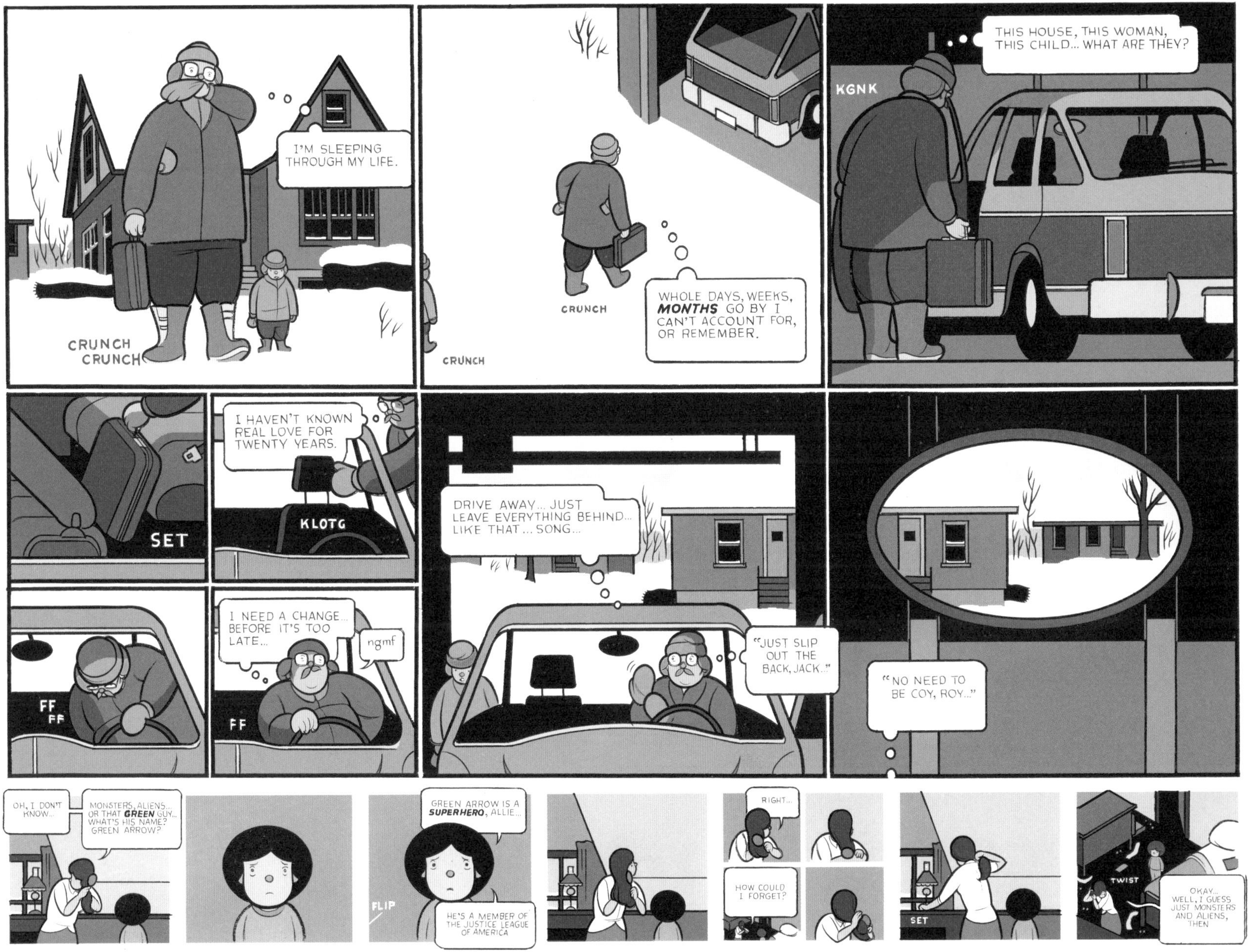

I'M SLEEPING THROUGH MY LIFE.
CRUNCH CRUNCH
CRUNCH
CRUNCH
WHOLE DAYS, WEEKS, **MONTHS** GO BY I CAN'T ACCOUNT FOR, OR REMEMBER.
KGNK
THIS HOUSE, THIS WOMAN, THIS CHILD... WHAT ARE THEY?
SET
I HAVEN'T KNOWN REAL LOVE FOR TWENTY YEARS.
KLOTG
FF FF
I NEED A CHANGE... BEFORE IT'S TOO LATE...
ngmf
FF
DRIVE AWAY... JUST LEAVE EVERYTHING BEHIND... LIKE THAT... SONG...
"JUST SLIP OUT THE BACK, JACK..."
"NO NEED TO BE COY, ROY..."
OH, I DON'T KNOW...
MONSTERS, ALIENS... OR THAT **GREEN** GUY... WHAT'S HIS NAME? GREEN ARROW?
GREEN ARROW IS A ***SUPERHERO***, ALLIE...
FLIP
HE'S A MEMBER OF THE JUSTICE LEAGUE OF AMERICA
RIGHT...
HOW COULD I FORGET?
SET
TWIST
OKAY... WELL, I GUESS JUST MONSTERS AND ALIENS, THEN

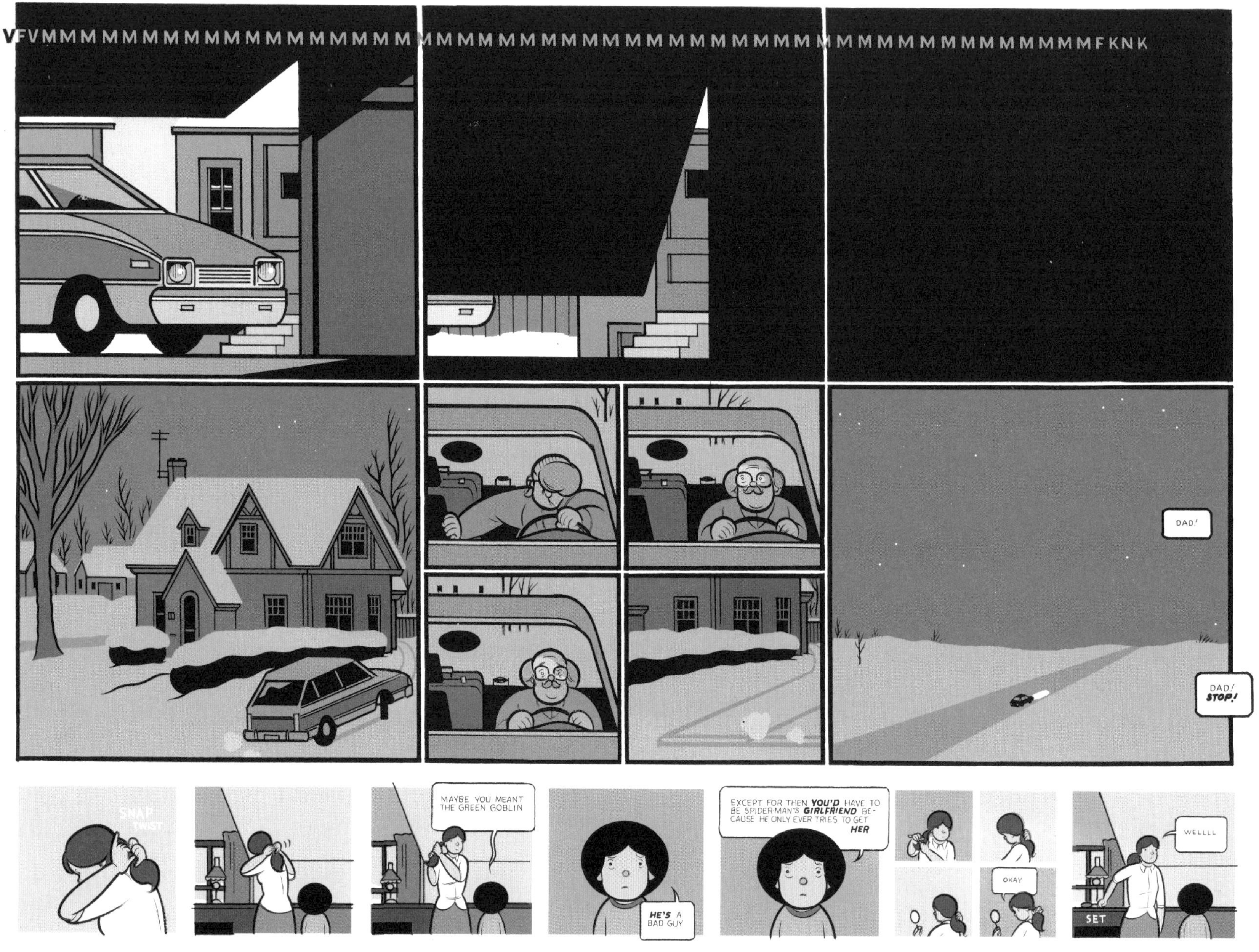
VFVMMMMMMMMMMMMMMMMMMMMMMMMMMMMMMMMMMMMMMMMMMMMMMMMMMMFKNK
DAD!
DAD! STOP!
SNAP
TWIST
MAYBE YOU MEANT THE GREEN GOBLIN
HE'S A BAD GUY
EXCEPT FOR THEN YOU'D HAVE TO BE SPIDER-MAN'S GIRLFRIEND BE-CAUSE HE ONLY EVER TRIES TO GET HER
OKAY
WELLLL
SET

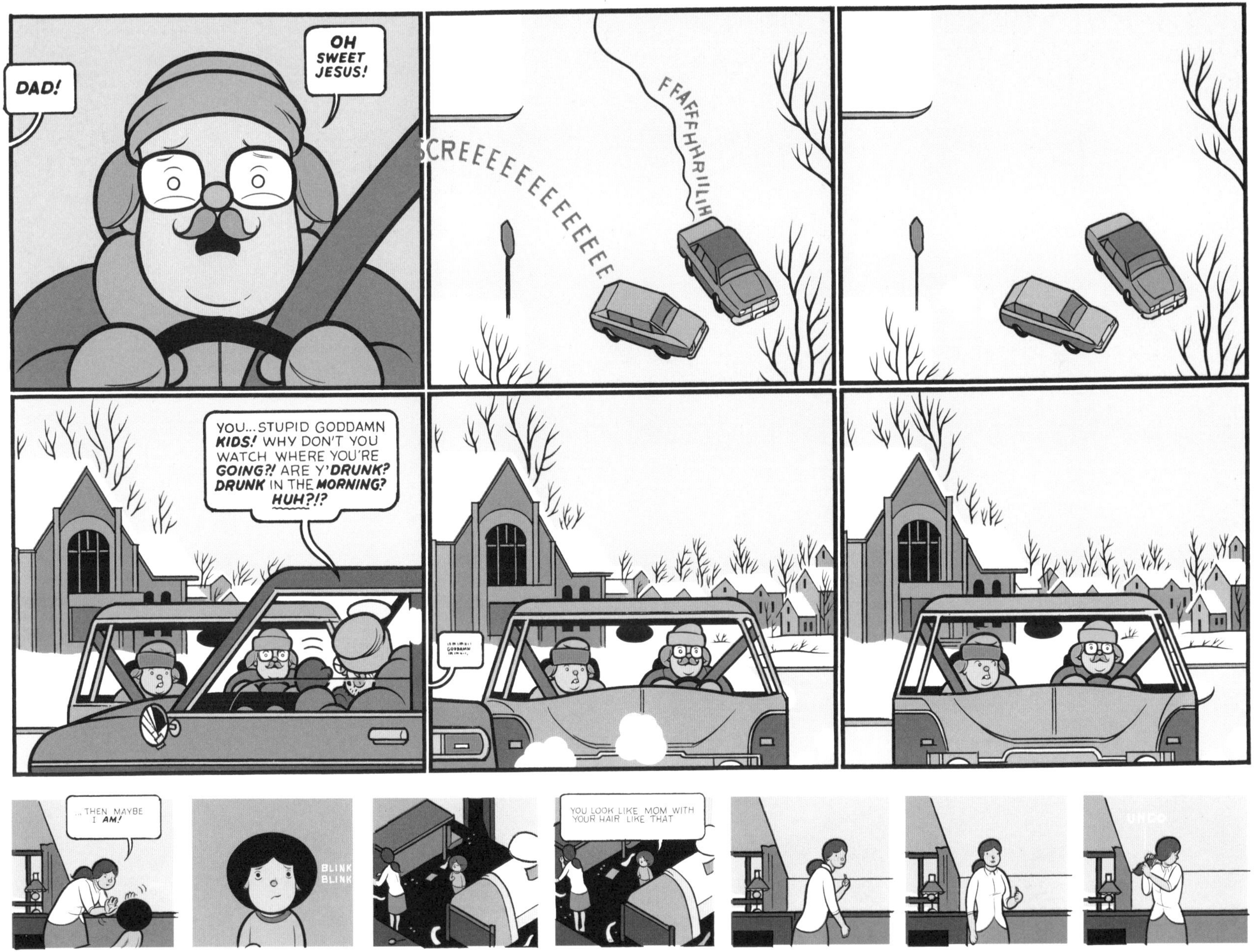
DAD!
OH SWEET JESUS!
SCREEEEEEEEEEEEEE
FFAFFHHRIILIH
YOU... STUPID GODDAMN KIDS! WHY DON'T YOU WATCH WHERE YOU'RE GOING?! ARE Y'DRUNK? DRUNK IN THE MORNING? HUH?!?
GODDAMN
...THEN MAYBE I AM!
BLINK BLINK
YOU LOOK LIKE MOM WITH YOUR HAIR LIKE THAT

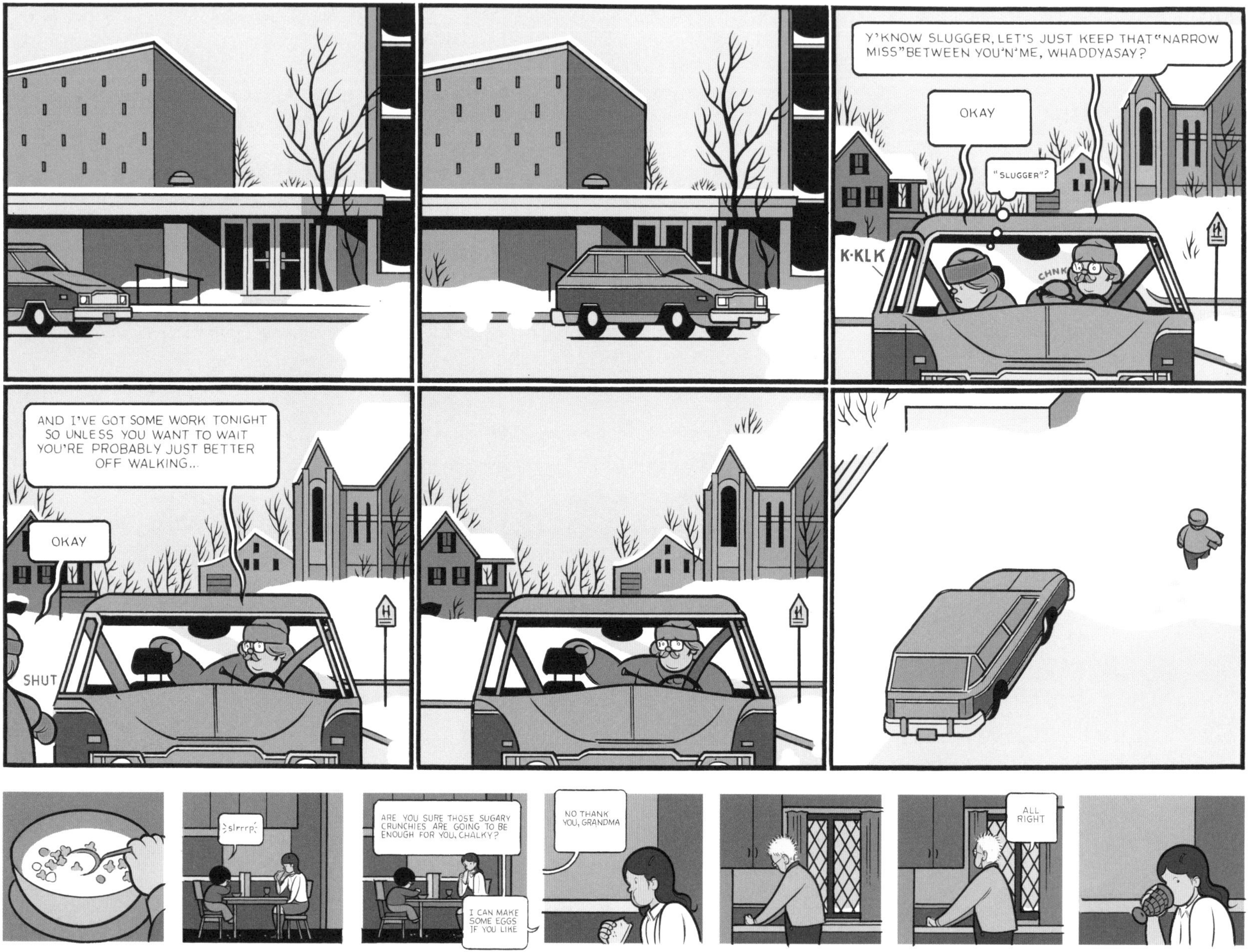
Y'KNOW SLUGGER, LET'S JUST KEEP THAT "NARROW MISS" BETWEEN YOU'N'ME, WHADDYASAY?
OKAY
"SLUGGER"?
K·KLK
CHNK
AND I'VE GOT SOME WORK TONIGHT SO UNLESS YOU WANT TO WAIT YOU'RE PROBABLY JUST BETTER OFF WALKING...
OKAY
SHUT
slrrrp
ARE YOU SURE THOSE SUGARY CRUNCHIES ARE GOING TO BE ENOUGH FOR YOU, CHALKY?
I CAN MAKE SOME EGGS IF YOU LIKE
NO THANK YOU, GRANDMA
ALL RIGHT

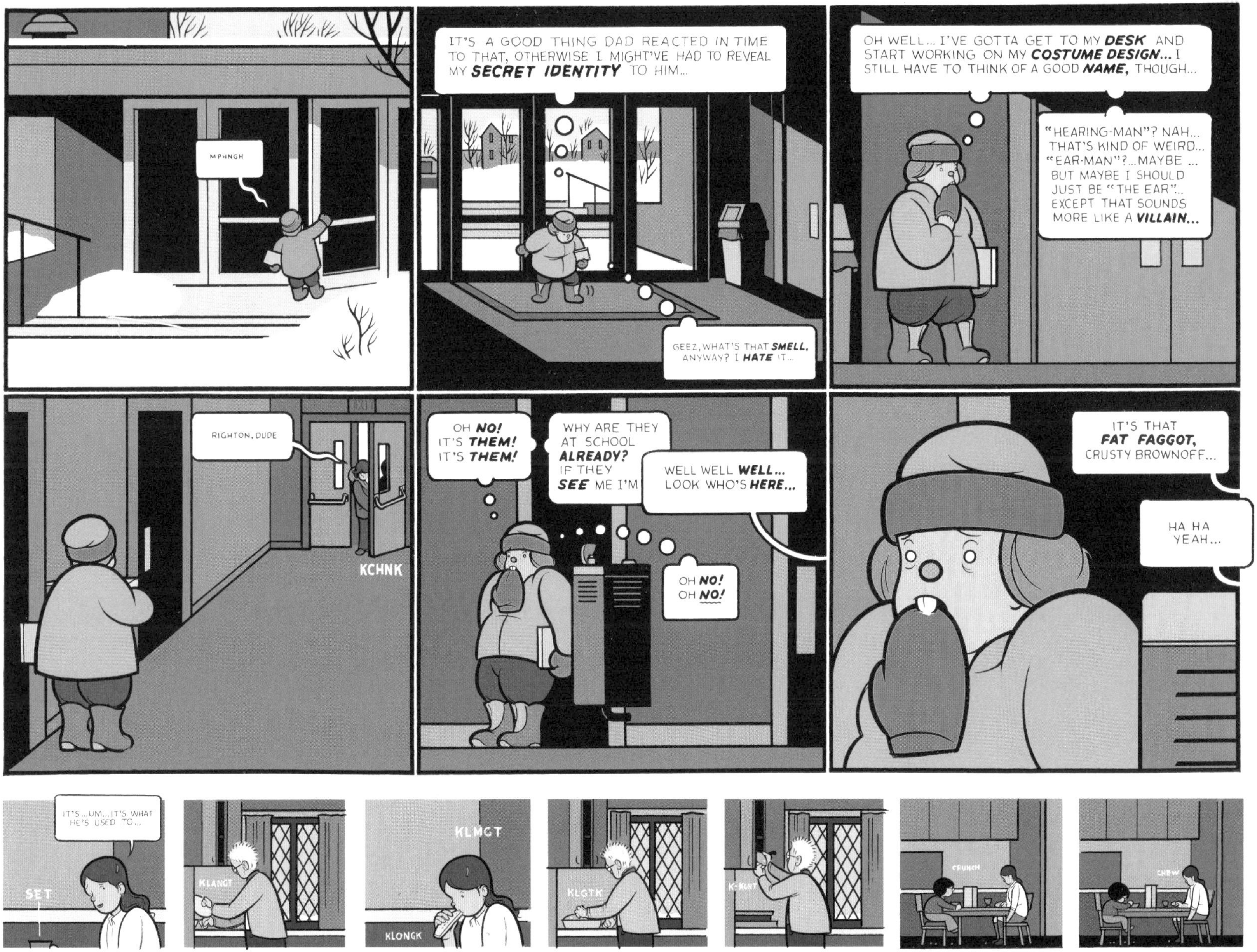
MPHNGH
IT'S A GOOD THING DAD REACTED IN TIME TO THAT, OTHERWISE I MIGHT'VE HAD TO REVEAL MY **SECRET IDENTITY** TO HIM...
GEEZ, WHAT'S THAT **SMELL**, ANYWAY? I **HATE** IT...
OH WELL... I'VE GOTTA GET TO MY **DESK** AND START WORKING ON MY **COSTUME DESIGN...** I STILL HAVE TO THINK OF A GOOD **NAME**, THOUGH...
"HEARING-MAN"? NAH... THAT'S KIND OF WEIRD... "EAR-MAN"?...MAYBE ... BUT MAYBE I SHOULD JUST BE "THE EAR"... EXCEPT THAT SOUNDS MORE LIKE A **VILLAIN...**
RIGHTON, DUDE
KCHNK
OH **NO!** IT'S **THEM!** IT'S **THEM!**
WHY ARE THEY AT SCHOOL **ALREADY?** IF THEY **SEE** ME I'M
WELL WELL **WELL...** LOOK WHO'S **HERE...**
OH **NO!** OH **NO!**
IT'S THAT **FAT FAGGOT,** CRUSTY BROWNOFF...
HA HA YEAH...
IT'S...UM...IT'S WHAT HE'S USED TO...
SET
KLANGT
KLMGT
KLONGK
KLGTK
K-KGNT
CRUNCH
CHEW

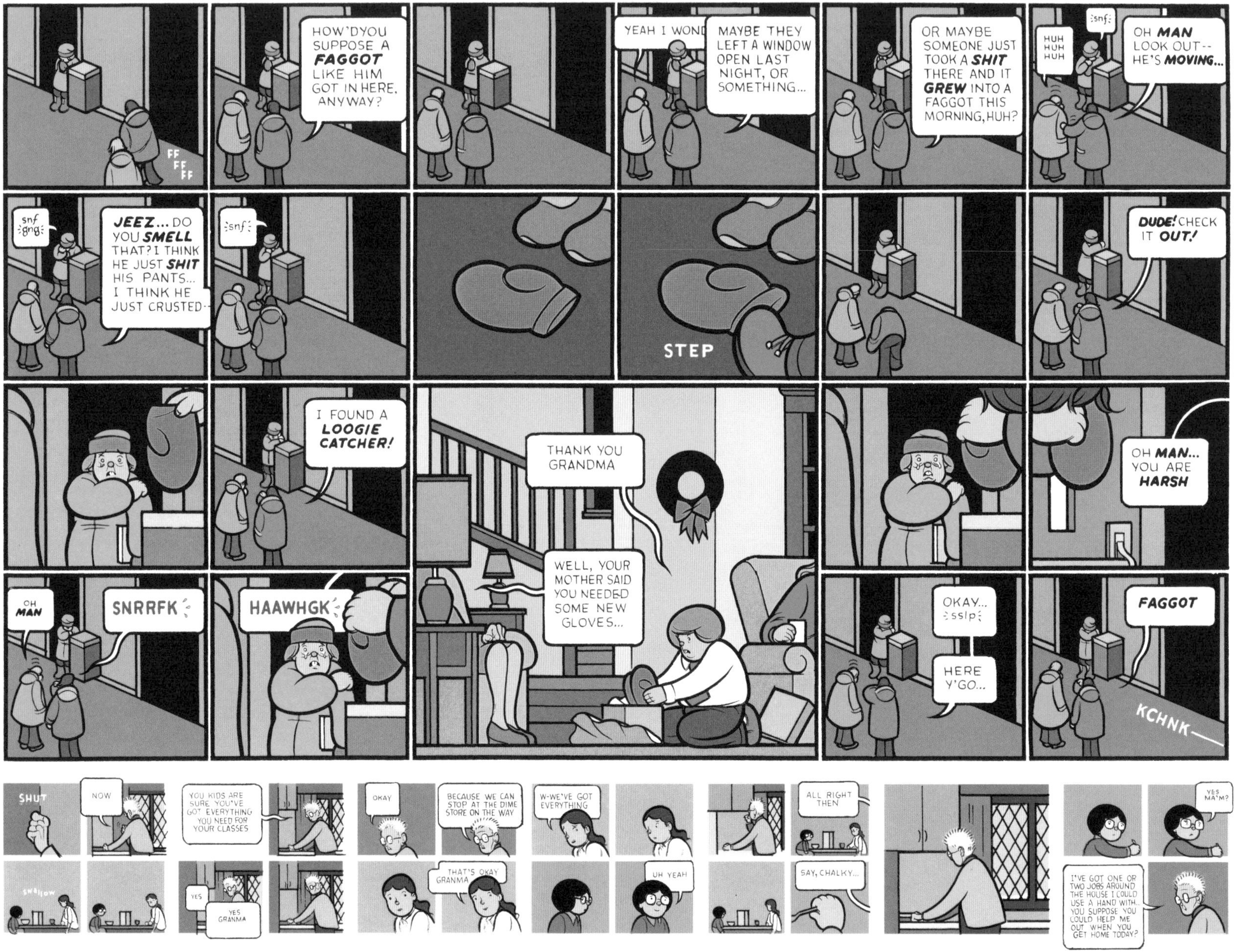
FF FF FF
HOW'DYOU SUPPOSE A FAGGOT LIKE HIM GOT IN HERE, ANYWAY?
YEAH I WOND
MAYBE THEY LEFT A WINDOW OPEN LAST NIGHT, OR SOMETHING...
OR MAYBE SOMEONE JUST TOOK A SHIT THERE AND IT GREW INTO A FAGGOT THIS MORNING, HUH?
HUH HUH HUH
snf
OH MAN LOOK OUT-- HE'S MOVING...
snf gng
JEEZ... DO YOU SMELL THAT? I THINK HE JUST SHIT HIS PANTS... I THINK HE JUST CRUSTED--
snf
STEP
DUDE! CHECK IT OUT!
I FOUND A LOOGIE CATCHER!
THANK YOU GRANDMA
WELL, YOUR MOTHER SAID YOU NEEDED SOME NEW GLOVES...
OH MAN... YOU ARE HARSH
OH MAN
SNRRFK
HAAWHGK
OKAY... sslp
HERE Y'GO...
FAGGOT
KCHNK
SHUT
NOW
swallow
YOU KIDS ARE SURE YOU'VE GOT EVERYTHING YOU NEED FOR YOUR CLASSES
YES
YES GRANMA
OKAY
BECAUSE WE CAN STOP AT THE DIME STORE ON THE WAY
THAT'S OKAY GRANMA
W-WE'VE GOT EVERYTHING
UH YEAH
ALL RIGHT THEN
SAY, CHALKY...
YES MA'M?
I'VE GOT ONE OR TWO JOBS AROUND THE HOUSE I COULD USE A HAND WITH... YOU SUPPOSE YOU COULD HELP ME OUT WHEN YOU GET HOME TODAY?

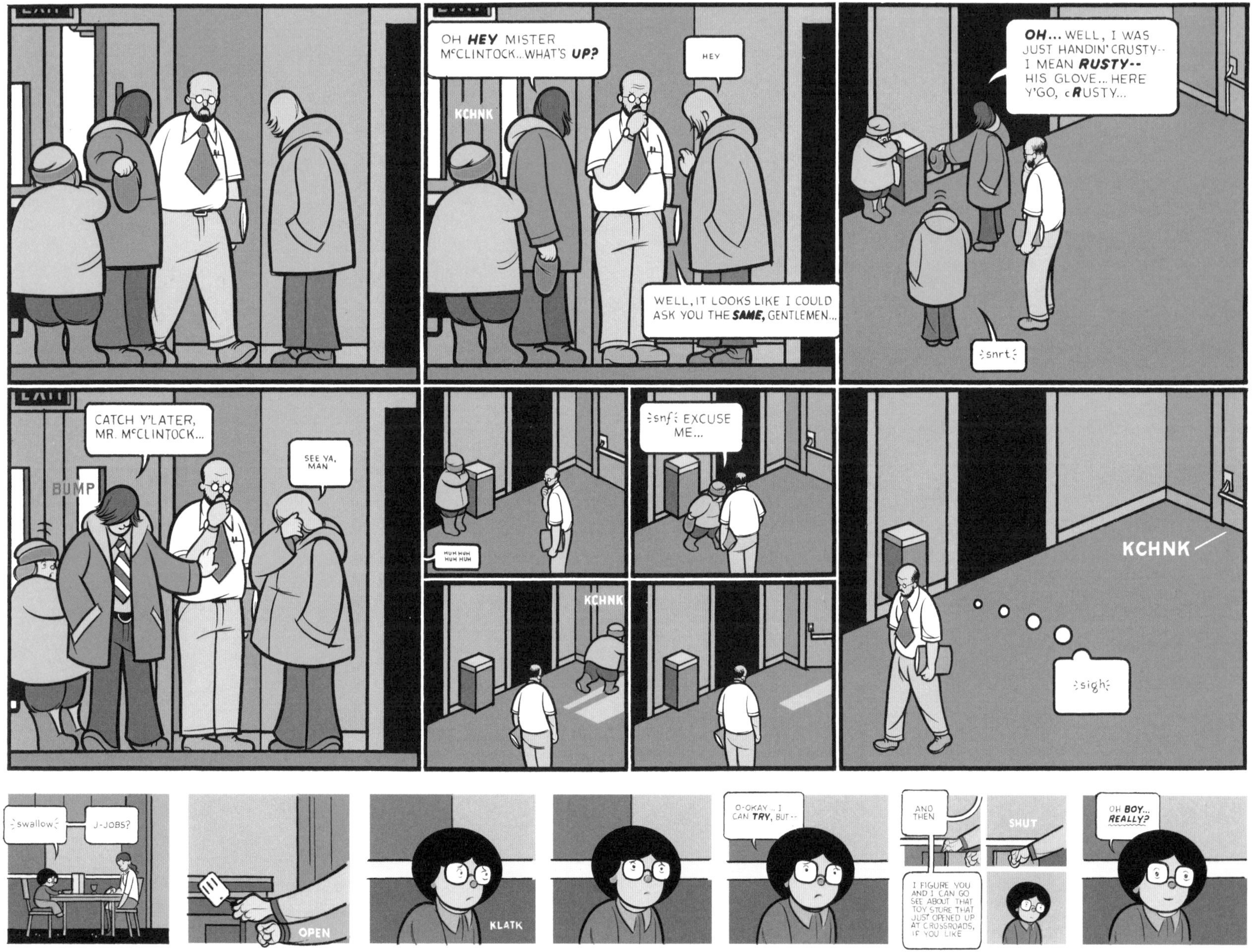

KCHNK
OH HEY MISTER McCLINTOCK... WHAT'S UP?
HEY
WELL, IT LOOKS LIKE I COULD ASK YOU THE SAME, GENTLEMEN...
OH... WELL, I WAS JUST HANDIN' CRUSTY-- I MEAN RUSTY-- HIS GLOVE... HERE Y'GO, cRUSTY...
snrt
BUMP
CATCH Y'LATER, MR. McCLINTOCK...
SEE YA, MAN
HUH HUH HUH HUH
snf EXCUSE ME...
KCHNK
KCHNK
sigh
swallow
J-JOBS?
OPEN
KLATK
O-OKAY... I CAN TRY, BUT--
AND THEN
I FIGURE YOU AND I CAN GO SEE ABOUT THAT TOY STORE THAT JUST OPENED UP AT CROSSROADS, IF YOU LIKE
SHUT
OH BOY... REALLY?

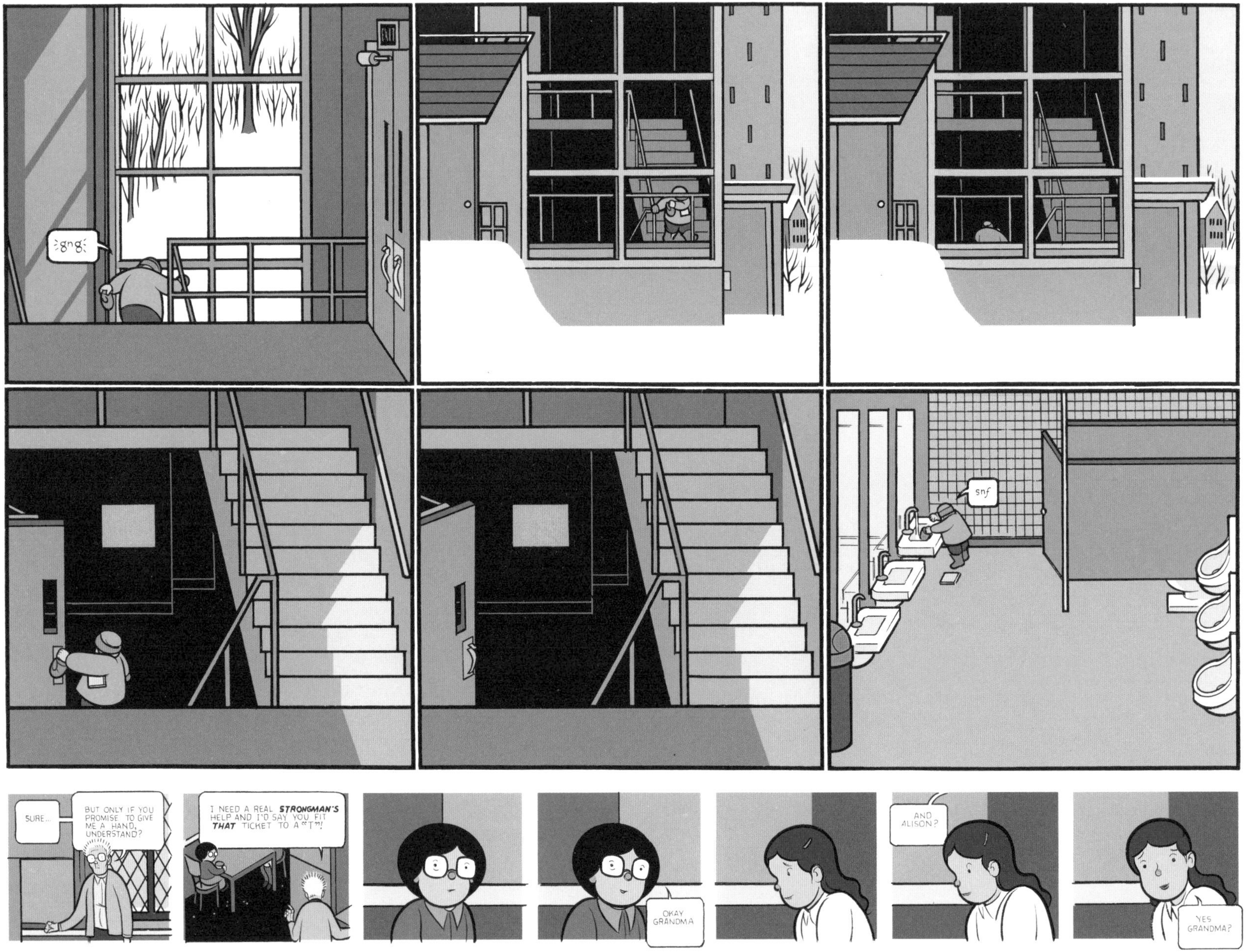
gng
snf
SURE...
BUT ONLY IF YOU PROMISE TO GIVE ME A HAND, UNDERSTAND?
I NEED A REAL **STRONGMAN'S** HELP AND I'D SAY YOU FIT ***THAT*** TICKET TO A "T"!
OKAY GRANDMA
AND ALISON?
YES GRANDMA?

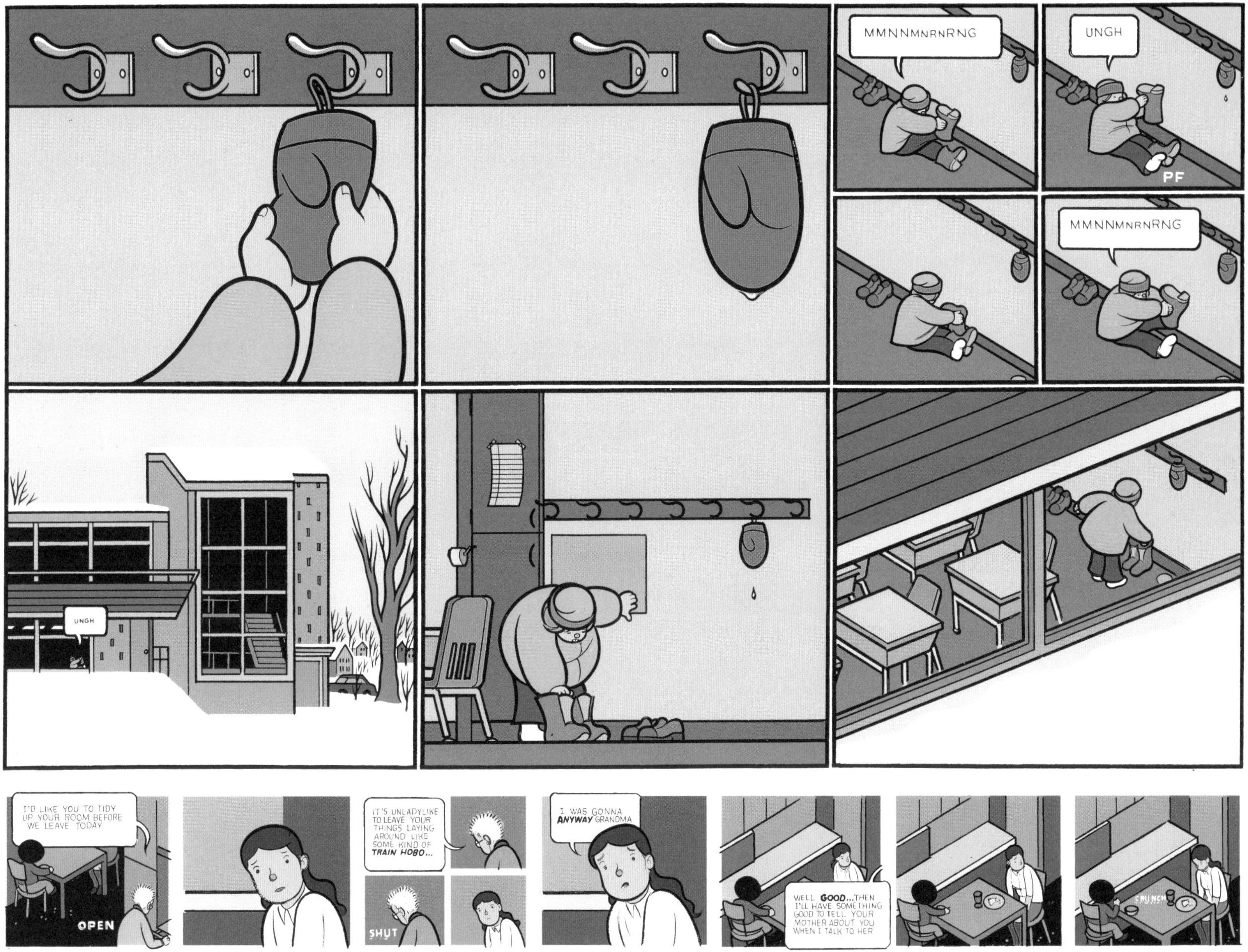
MMNNMNRNRNG
UNGH
PF
MMNNMNRNRNG
UNGH
I'D LIKE YOU TO TIDY UP YOUR ROOM BEFORE WE LEAVE TODAY
OPEN
IT'S UNLADYLIKE TO LEAVE YOUR THINGS LAYING AROUND LIKE SOME KIND OF **TRAIN HOBO...**
SHUT
I WAS GONNA **ANYWAY** GRANDMA
WELL **GOOD...** THEN I'LL HAVE SOMETHING GOOD TO TELL YOUR MOTHER ABOUT YOU WHEN I TALK TO HER
CRUNCH

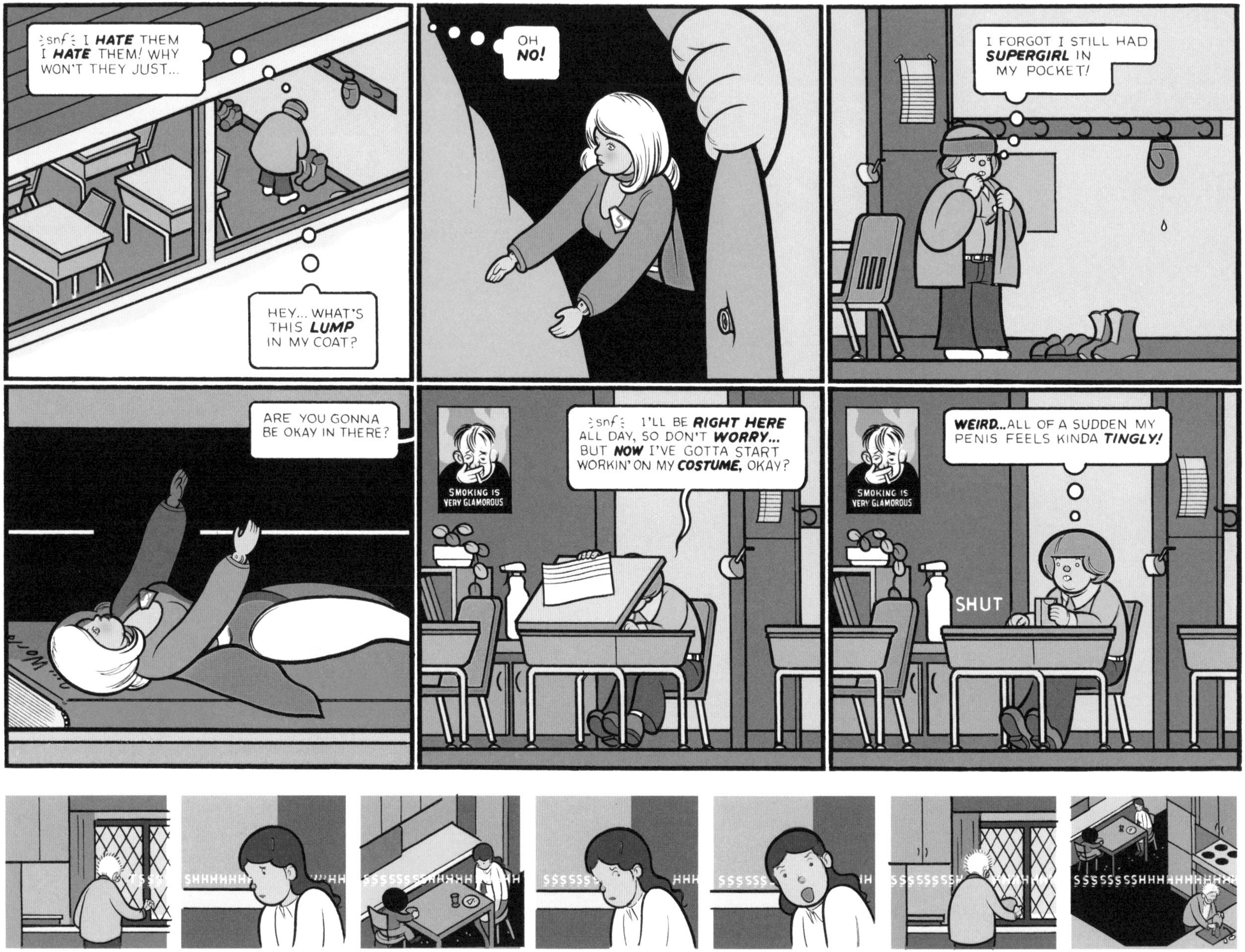

snf I HATE THEM I HATE THEM! WHY WON'T THEY JUST...
HEY... WHAT'S THIS LUMP IN MY COAT?
OH NO!
I FORGOT I STILL HAD SUPERGIRL IN MY POCKET!
ARE YOU GONNA BE OKAY IN THERE?
SMOKING IS VERY GLAMOROUS
snf I'LL BE RIGHT HERE ALL DAY, SO DON'T WORRY... BUT NOW I'VE GOTTA START WORKIN' ON MY COSTUME, OKAY?
SMOKING IS VERY GLAMOROUS
WEIRD... ALL OF A SUDDEN MY PENIS FEELS KINDA TINGLY!
SHUT
SHHHHHHH
SSSSSSSSHHHHHHHHHHHH

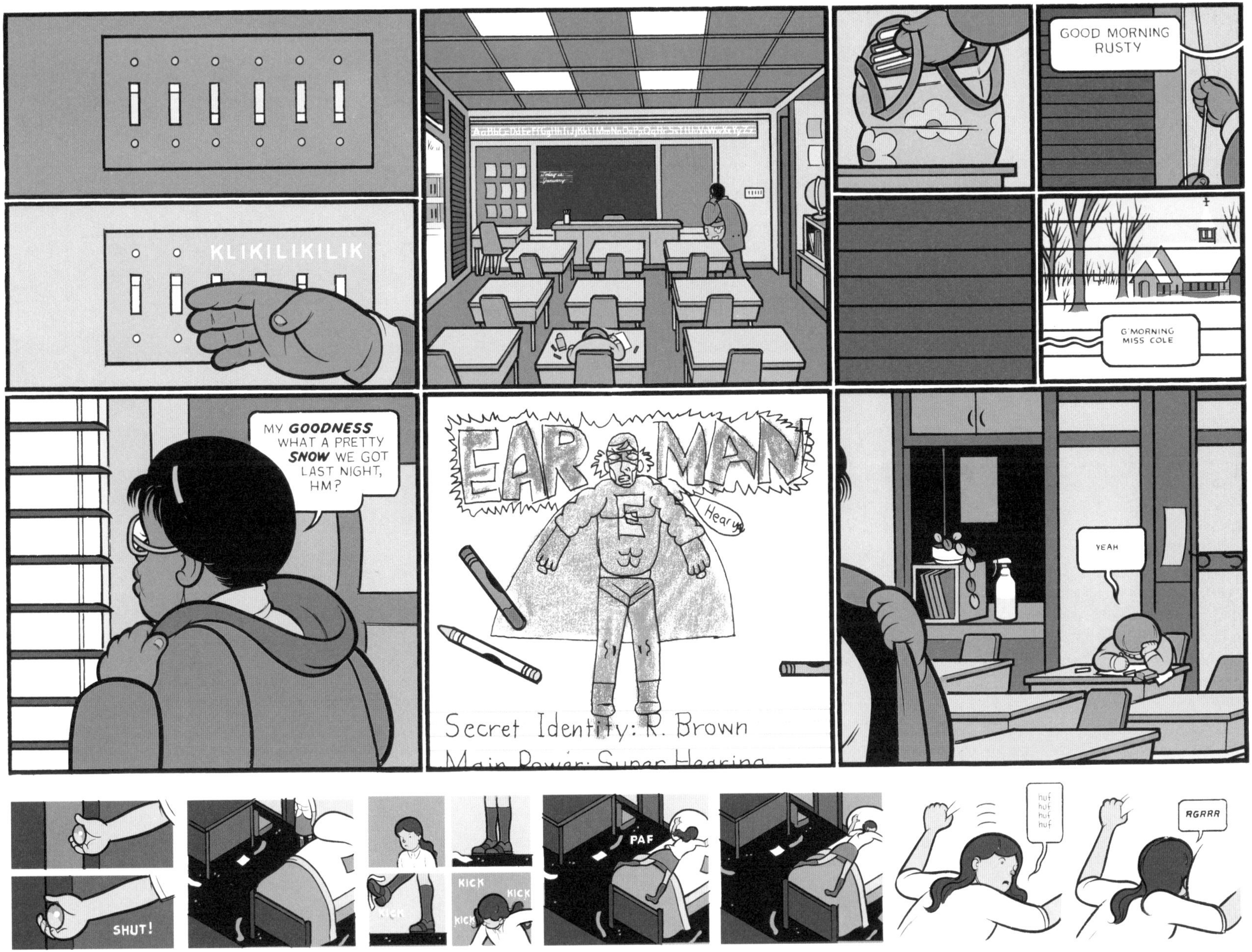

KLIKILIKILIK
GOOD MORNING RUSTY
G'MORNING MISS COLE
MY GOODNESS WHAT A PRETTY SNOW WE GOT LAST NIGHT, HM?
EAR MAN
Secret Identity: R. Brown
YEAH
SHUT!
KICK
KICK
KICK
KICK
PAF
huf huf huf huf
RGRRR

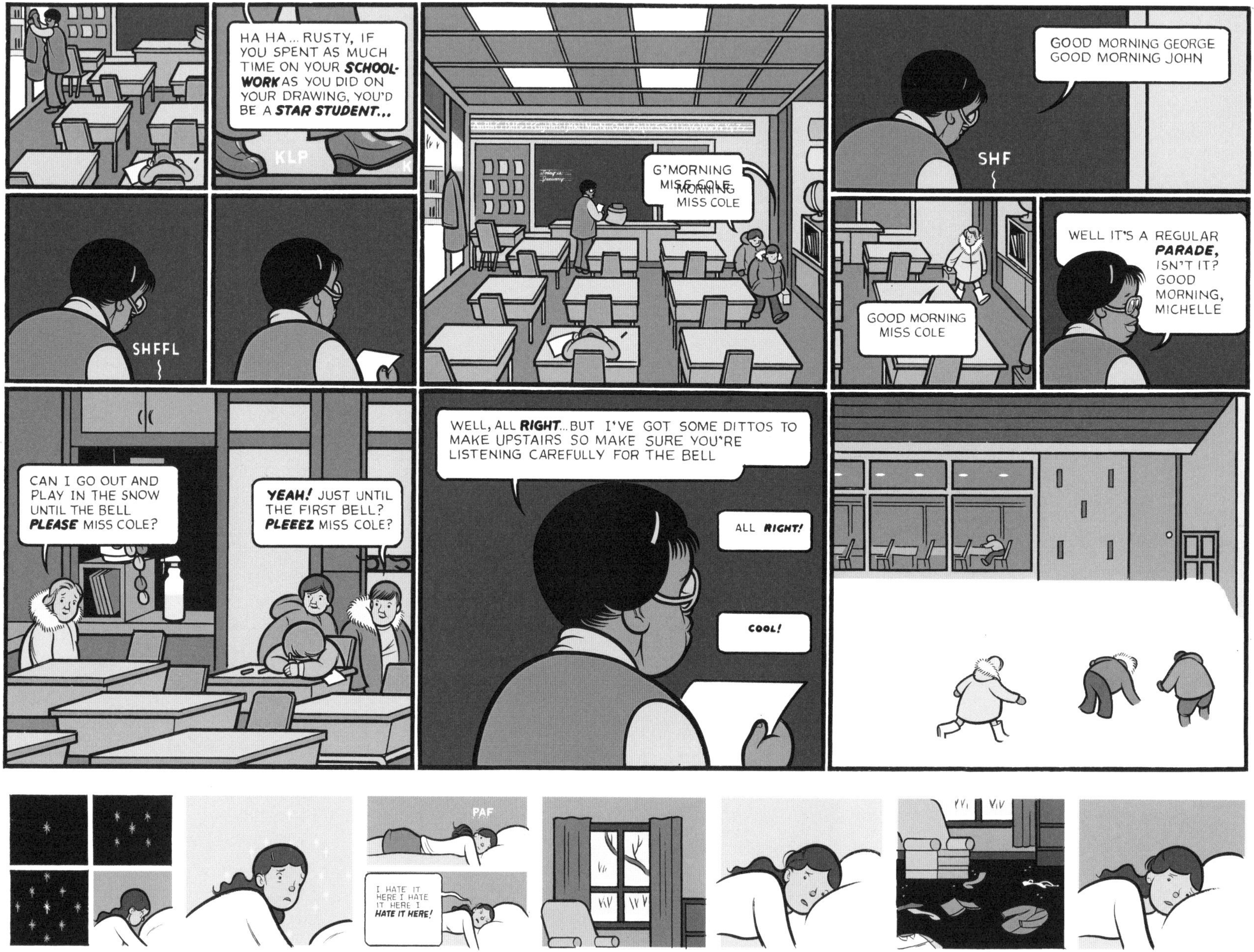
HA HA ... RUSTY, IF YOU SPENT AS MUCH TIME ON YOUR **SCHOOL-WORK** AS YOU DID ON YOUR DRAWING, YOU'D BE A **STAR STUDENT ...**
KLP
K
SHFFL
Today is January
G'MORNING MISS COLE
MORNING MISS COLE
GOOD MORNING GEORGE GOOD MORNING JOHN
SHF
GOOD MORNING MISS COLE
WELL IT'S A REGULAR **PARADE,** ISN'T IT? GOOD MORNING, MICHELLE
CAN I GO OUT AND PLAY IN THE SNOW UNTIL THE BELL **PLEASE** MISS COLE?
YEAH! JUST UNTIL THE FIRST BELL? **PLEEEZ** MISS COLE?
WELL, ALL **RIGHT**... BUT I'VE GOT SOME DITTOS TO MAKE UPSTAIRS SO MAKE SURE YOU'RE LISTENING CAREFULLY FOR THE BELL
ALL **RIGHT!**
COOL!
PAF
I HATE IT HERE I HATE IT HERE I **HATE IT HERE!**

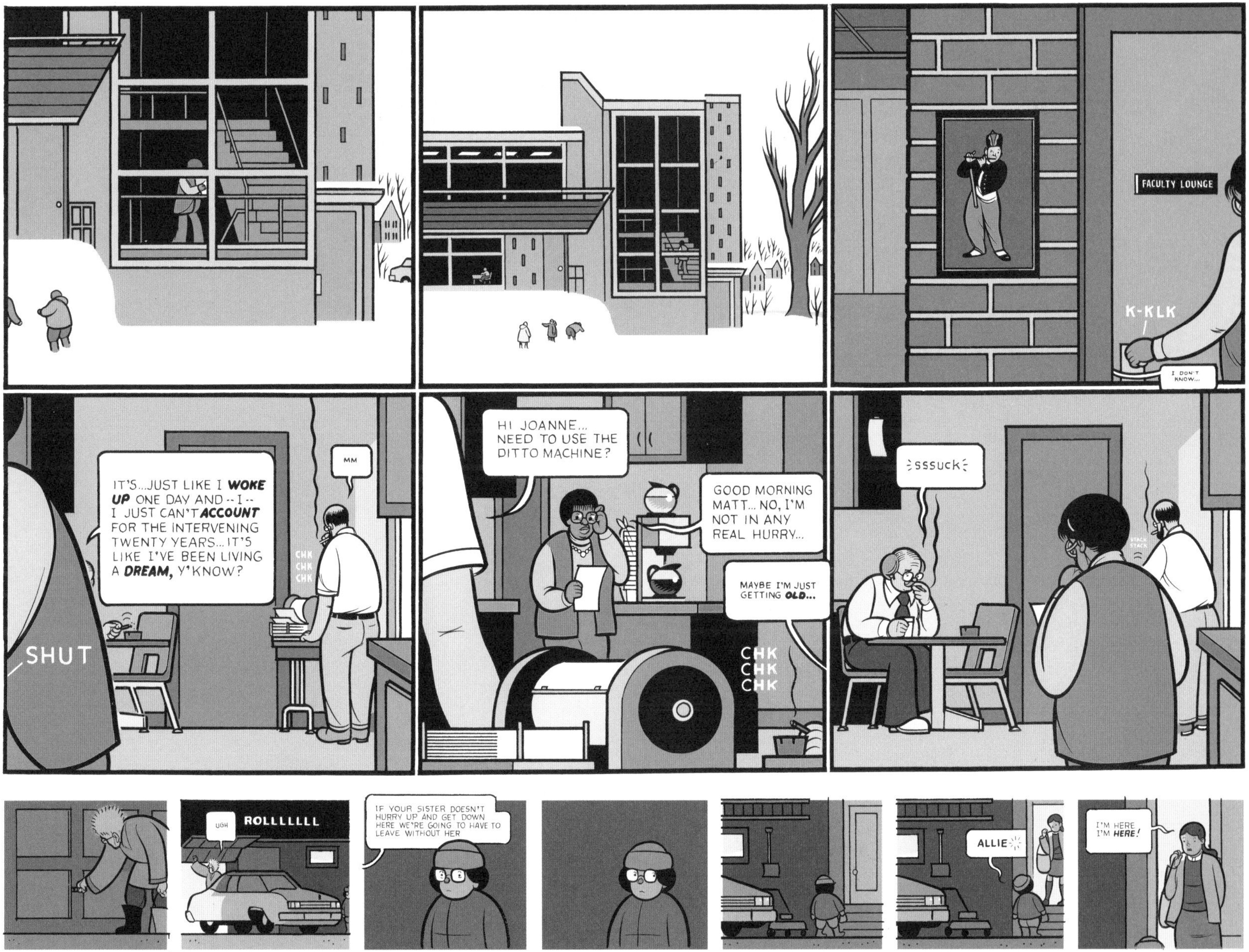
FACULTY LOUNGE
K-KLK
I DON'T KNOW...
SHUT
IT'S...JUST LIKE I **WOKE UP** ONE DAY AND -- I -- I JUST CAN'T **ACCOUNT** FOR THE INTERVENING TWENTY YEARS... IT'S LIKE I'VE BEEN LIVING A **DREAM,** Y'KNOW?
MM
CHK CHK CHK
HI JOANNE... NEED TO USE THE DITTO MACHINE?
GOOD MORNING MATT... NO, I'M NOT IN ANY REAL HURRY...
MAYBE I'M JUST GETTING **OLD...**
CHK CHK CHK
SSSUCK
STACK STACK
UGH
ROLLLLLLL
IF YOUR SISTER DOESN'T HURRY UP AND GET DOWN HERE WE'RE GOING TO HAVE TO LEAVE WITHOUT HER
ALLIE
I'M HERE I'M **HERE!**

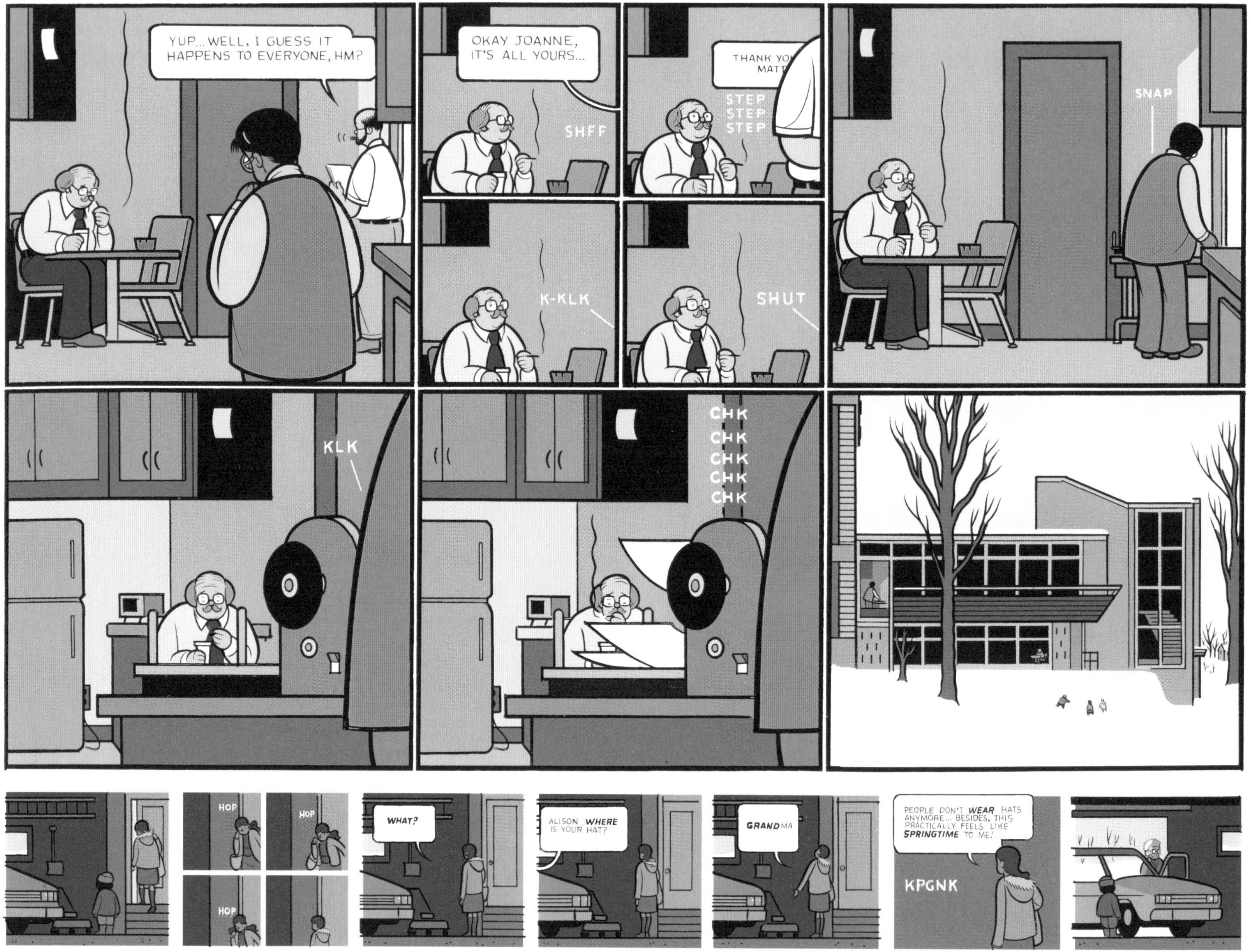

YUP... WELL, I GUESS IT HAPPENS TO EVERYONE, HM?
OKAY JOANNE, IT'S ALL YOURS...
SHFF
STEP STEP STEP
K-KLK
SHUT
SNAP
KLK
CHK CHK CHK CHK CHK
HOP
HOP
HOP
WHAT?
ALISON WHERE IS YOUR HAT?
GRANDMA
PEOPLE DON'T WEAR HATS ANYMORE... BESIDES, THIS PRACTICALLY FEELS LIKE SPRINGTIME TO ME!
KPGNK

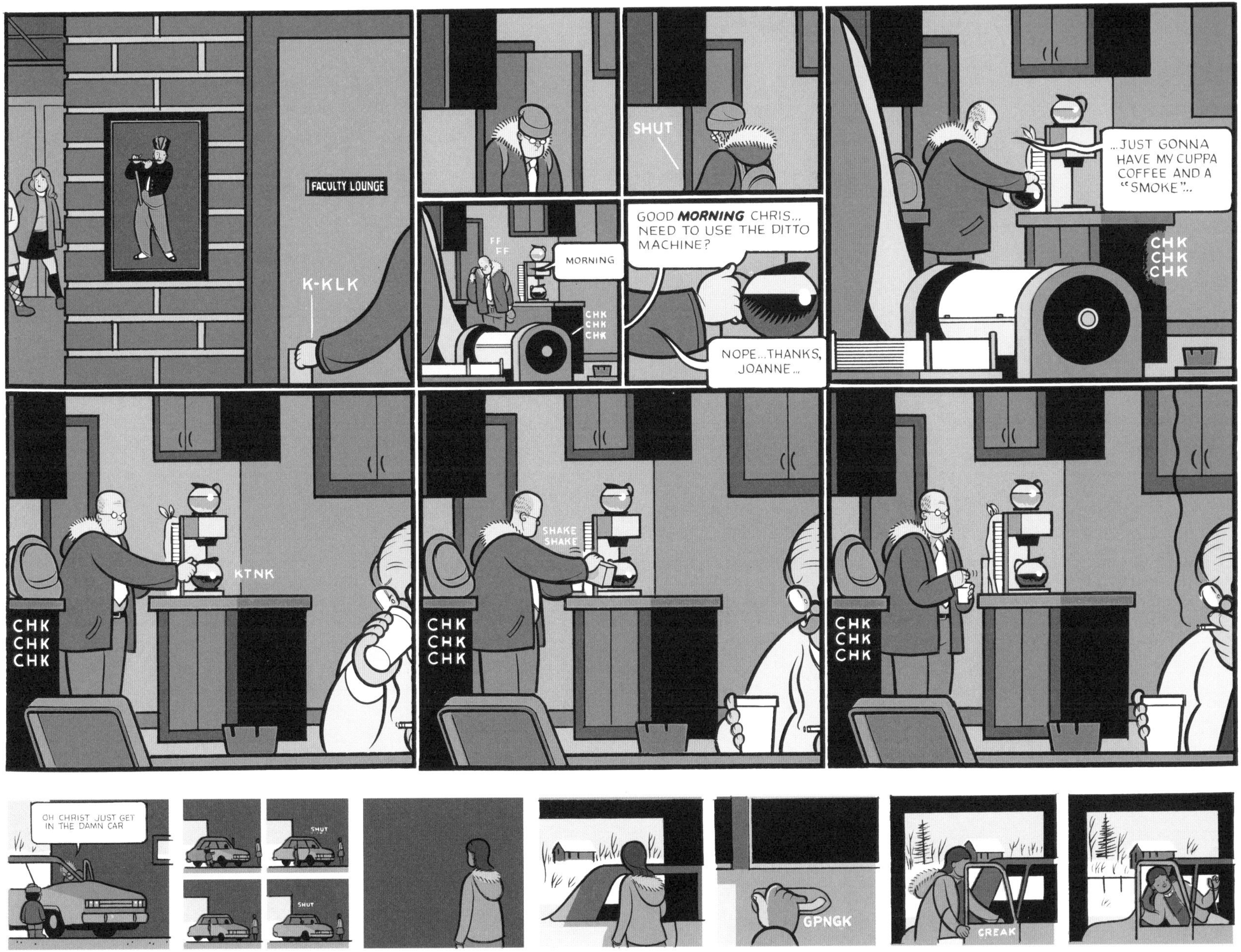
FACULTY LOUNGE
K-KLK
SHUT
FF
FF
MORNING
CHK
CHK
CHK
GOOD MORNING CHRIS... NEED TO USE THE DITTO MACHINE?
NOPE...THANKS, JOANNE...
...JUST GONNA HAVE MY CUPPA COFFEE AND A "SMOKE"...
CHK
CHK
CHK
CHK
CHK
CHK
KTNK
CHK
CHK
CHK
SHAKE
SHAKE
CHK
CHK
CHK
OH CHRIST JUST GET IN THE DAMN CAR
SHUT
SHUT
GPNGK
CREAK

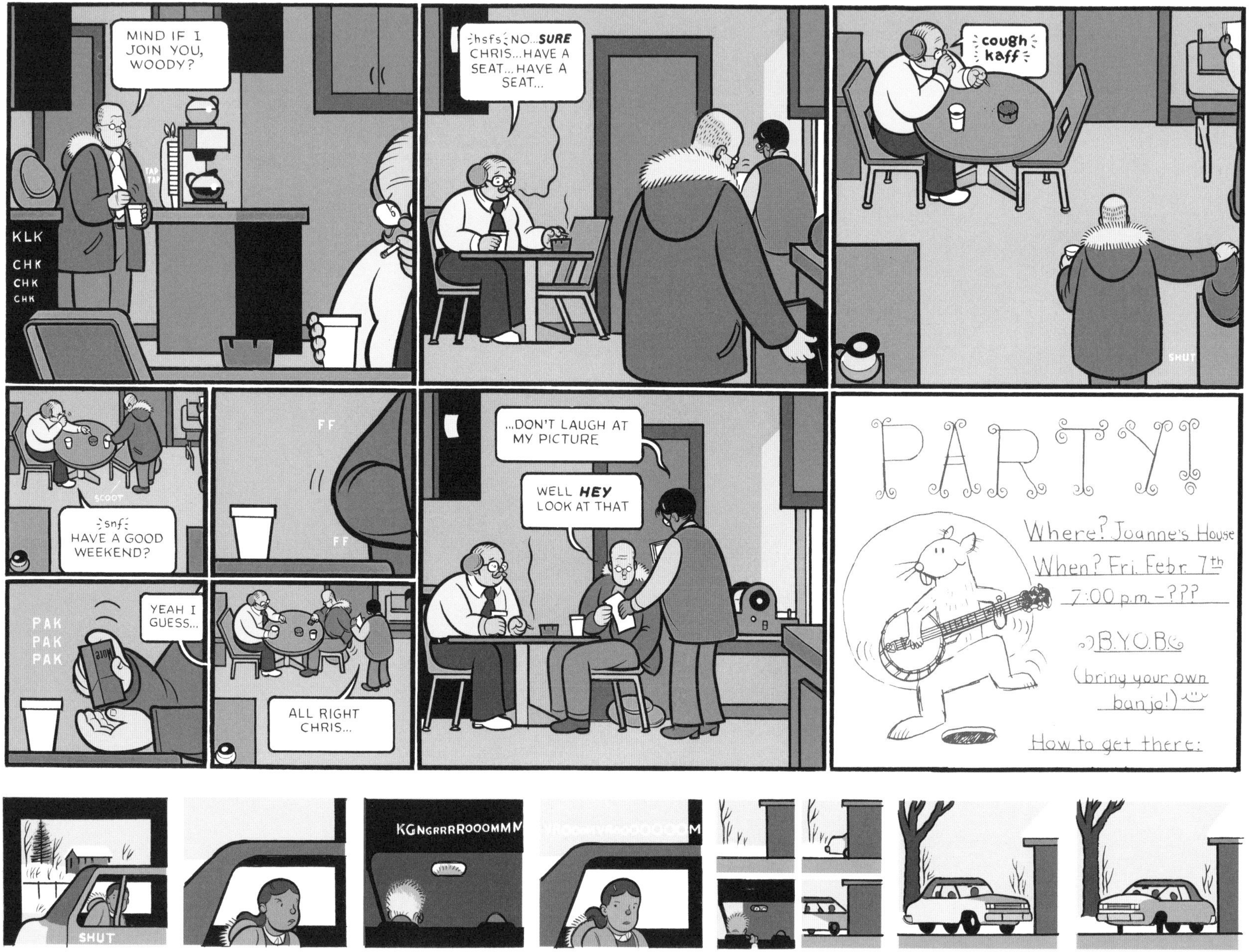
MIND IF I JOIN YOU, WOODY?
TAP TAP
KLK
CHK CHK CHK
hsfs NO... SURE CHRIS... HAVE A SEAT... HAVE A SEAT...
cough kaff
SHUT
SCOOT
snf HAVE A GOOD WEEKEND?
FF
FF
YEAH I GUESS...
PAK PAK PAK
ALL RIGHT CHRIS...
...DON'T LAUGH AT MY PICTURE
WELL HEY LOOK AT THAT
PARTY!
Where? Joanne's House
When? Fri. Febr. 7th
7:00 p.m. - ???
B.Y.O.B.
(bring your own banjo!)
How to get there:
SHUT
KGNGRRRROOOMMM

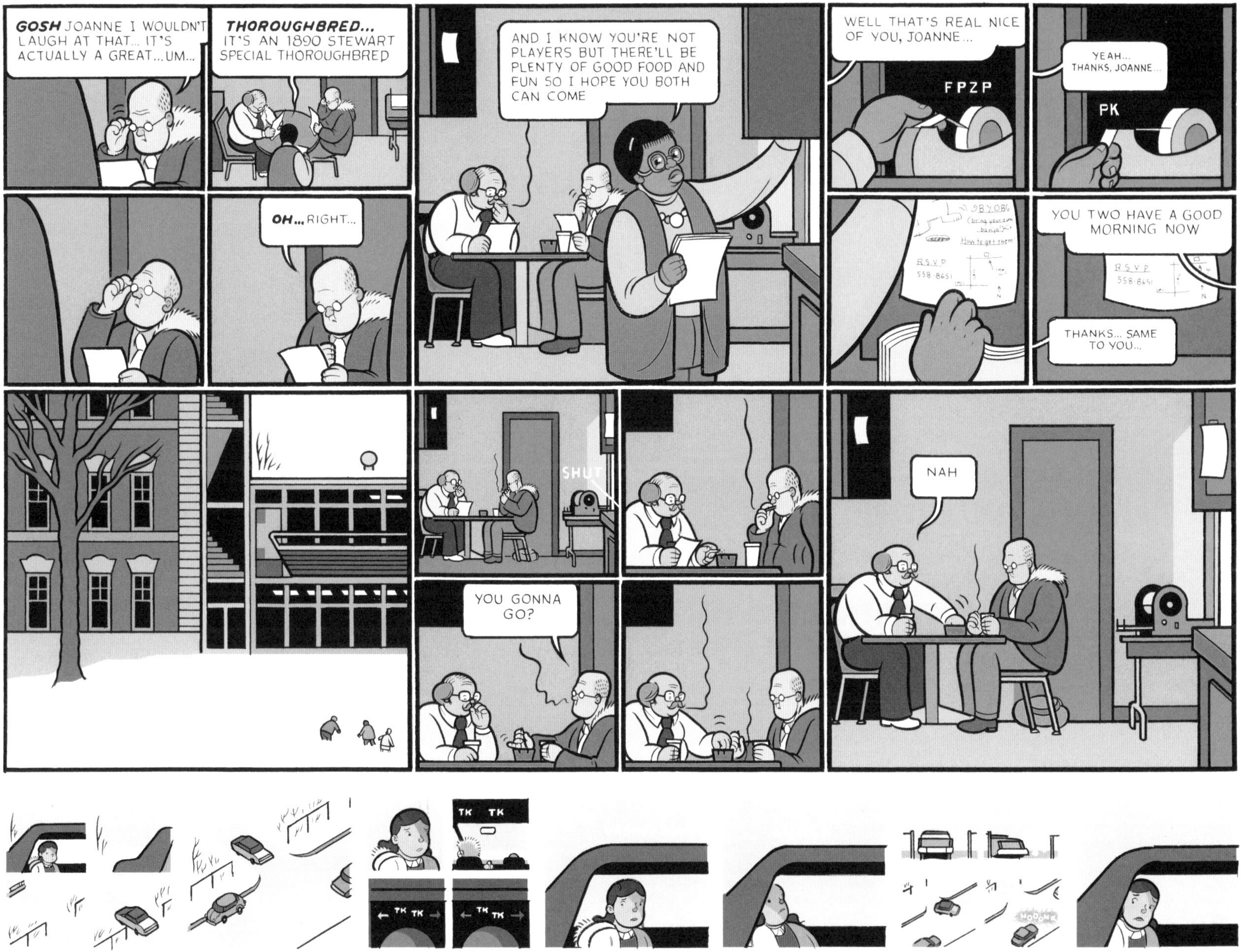
GOSH JOANNE I WOULDN'T LAUGH AT THAT... IT'S ACTUALLY A GREAT...UM...
THOROUGHBRED... IT'S AN 1890 STEWART SPECIAL THOROUGHBRED
OH... RIGHT...
AND I KNOW YOU'RE NOT PLAYERS BUT THERE'LL BE PLENTY OF GOOD FOOD AND FUN SO I HOPE YOU BOTH CAN COME
WELL THAT'S REAL NICE OF YOU, JOANNE...
FPZP
YEAH... THANKS, JOANNE...
PK
YOU TWO HAVE A GOOD MORNING NOW
THANKS... SAME TO YOU...
SHUT
YOU GONNA GO?
NAH
TK TK
TK TK
TK TK

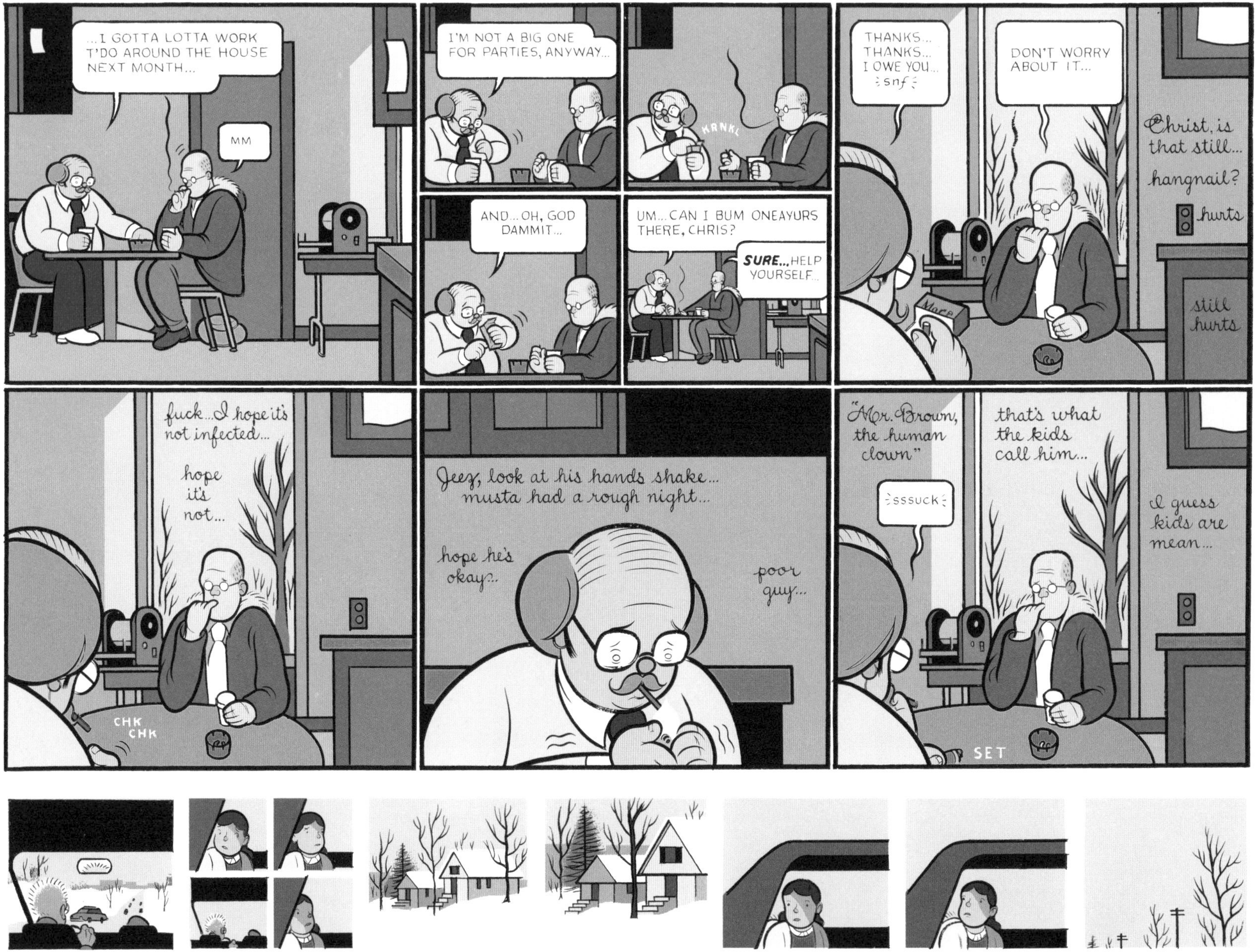

...I GOTTA LOTTA WORK T'DO AROUND THE HOUSE NEXT MONTH...
MM
I'M NOT A BIG ONE FOR PARTIES, ANYWAY...
KRNKL
AND... OH, GOD DAMMIT...
UM... CAN I BUM ONEAYURS THERE, CHRIS?
SURE... HELP YOURSELF...
THANKS... THANKS... I OWE YOU... snf
DON'T WORRY ABOUT IT...
Christ, is that still... hangnail?
hurts
still hurts
fuck... I hope it's not infected...
hope it's not...
CHK CHK
Jeez, look at his hands shake... musta had a rough night...
hope he's okay...
poor guy...
"Mr. Brown, the human clown"
that's what the kids call him...
sssuck
I guess kids are mean...
SET

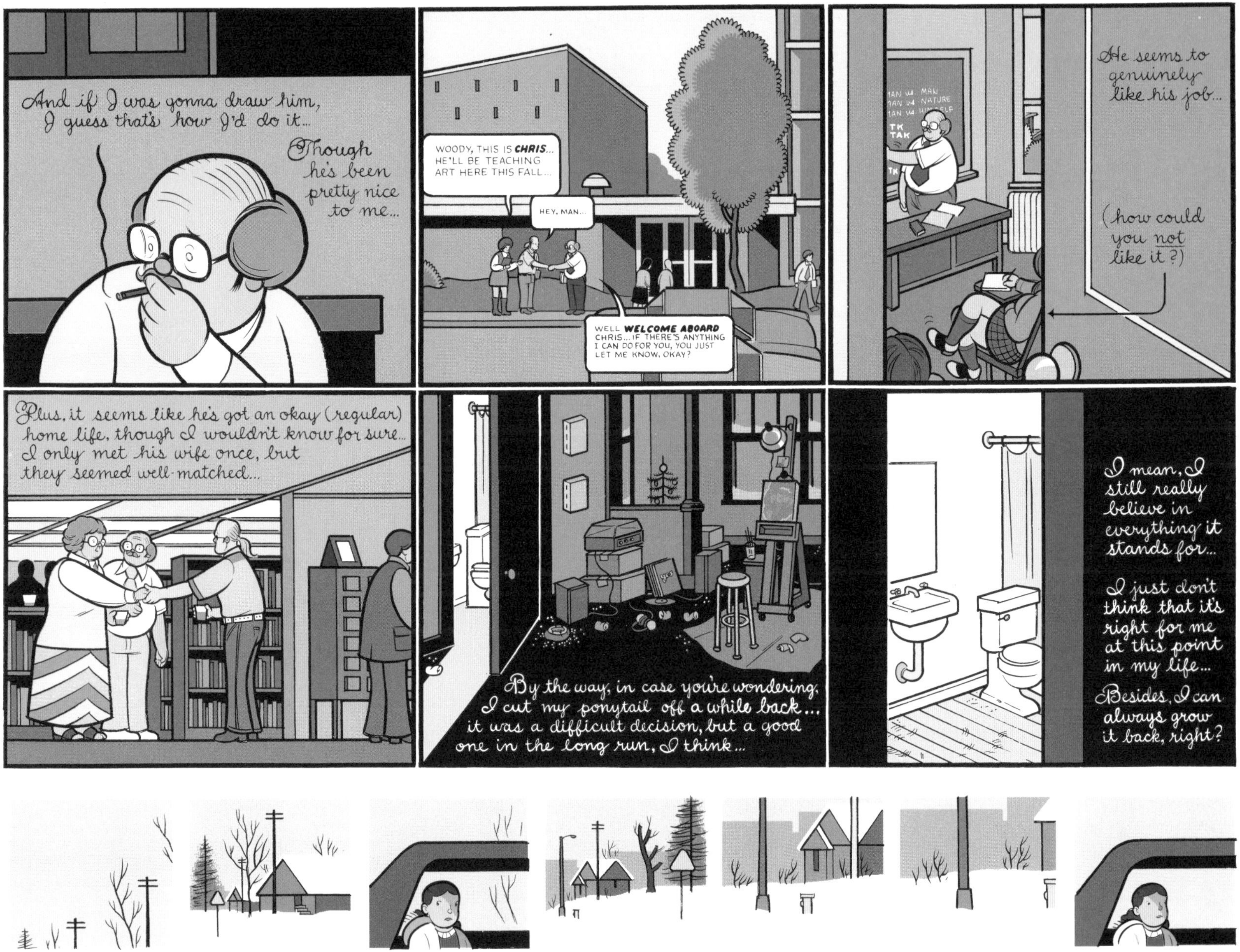
And if I was gonna draw him, I guess that's how I'd do it...
Though he's been pretty nice to me...
WOODY, THIS IS CHRIS... HE'LL BE TEACHING ART HERE THIS FALL...
HEY, MAN...
WELL WELCOME ABOARD CHRIS... IF THERE'S ANYTHING I CAN DO FOR YOU, YOU JUST LET ME KNOW, OKAY?
He seems to genuinely like his job...
TK TAK
TK
(how could you not like it?)
Plus, it seems like he's got an okay (regular) home life, though I wouldn't know for sure... I only met his wife once, but they seemed well-matched...
By the way, in case you're wondering, I cut my ponytail off a while back... it was a difficult decision, but a good one in the long run, I think...
I mean, I still really believe in everything it stands for...
I just don't think that it's right for me at this point in my life...
Besides, I can always grow it back, right?

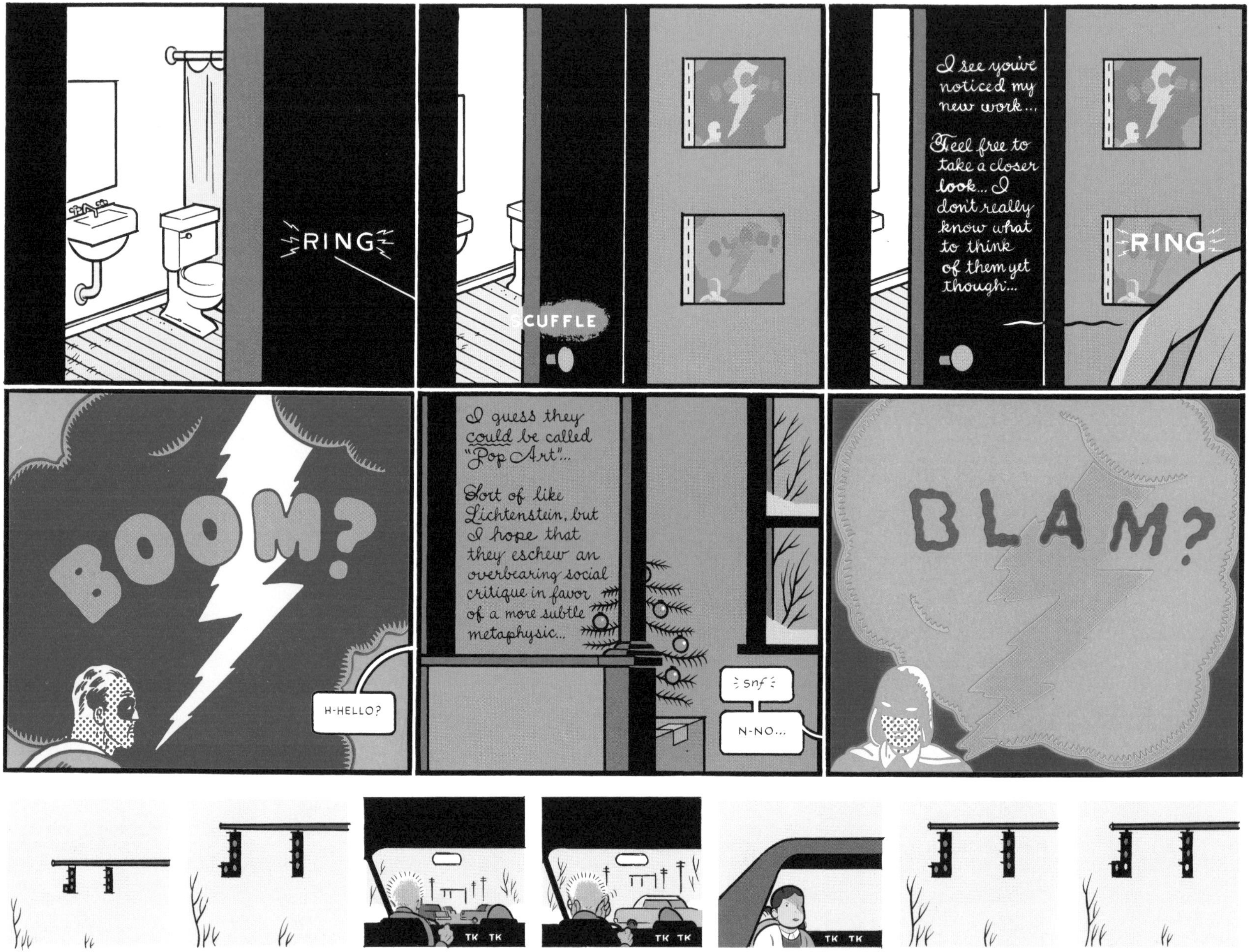
RING
SCUFFLE
I see you've noticed my new work... Feel free to take a closer look... I don't really know what to think of them yet though...
RING
BOOM?
H-HELLO?
I guess they could be called "Pop Art"... Sort of like Lichtenstein, but I hope that they eschew an overbearing social critique in favor of a more subtle metaphysic...
snf
N-NO...
BLAM?
TK TK
TK TK
TK TK

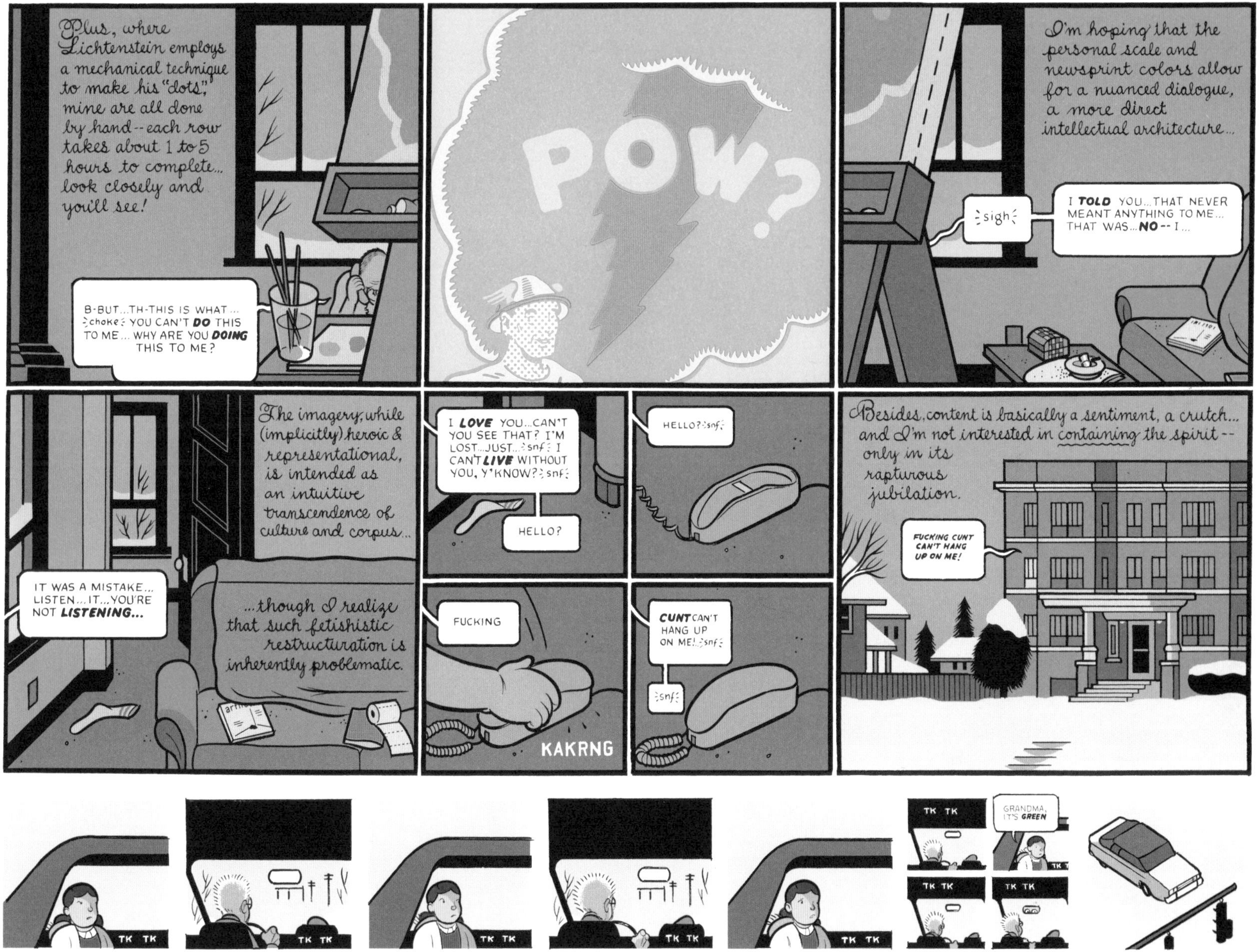
Plus, where Lichtenstein employs a mechanical technique to make his "dots," mine are all done by hand -- each row takes about 1 to 5 hours to complete... look closely and you'll see!
B-BUT...TH-THIS IS WHAT... choke YOU CAN'T **DO** THIS TO ME... WHY ARE YOU **DOING** THIS TO ME?
POW?
I'm hoping that the personal scale and newsprint colors allow for a nuanced dialogue, a more direct intellectual architecture...
sigh
I **TOLD** YOU...THAT NEVER MEANT ANYTHING TO ME... THAT WAS...**NO** -- I...
The imagery, while (implicitly) heroic & representational, is intended as an intuitive transcendence of culture and corpus...
IT WAS A MISTAKE... LISTEN...IT...YOU'RE NOT **LISTENING...**
...though I realize that such fetishistic restructuration is inherently problematic.
I **LOVE** YOU...CAN'T YOU SEE THAT? I'M LOST...JUST... snf I CAN'T **LIVE** WITHOUT YOU, Y'KNOW? snf
HELLO?
HELLO? snf
FUCKING
KAKRNG
CUNT CAN'T HANG UP ON ME! snf
snf
Besides, content is basically a sentiment, a crutch... and I'm not interested in containing the spirit -- only in its rapturous jubilation.
FUCKING CUNT CAN'T HANG UP ON ME!
TK TK
TK TK
TK TK
TK TK
TK TK
TK TK
GRANDMA, IT'S **GREEN**
TK TK
TK TK

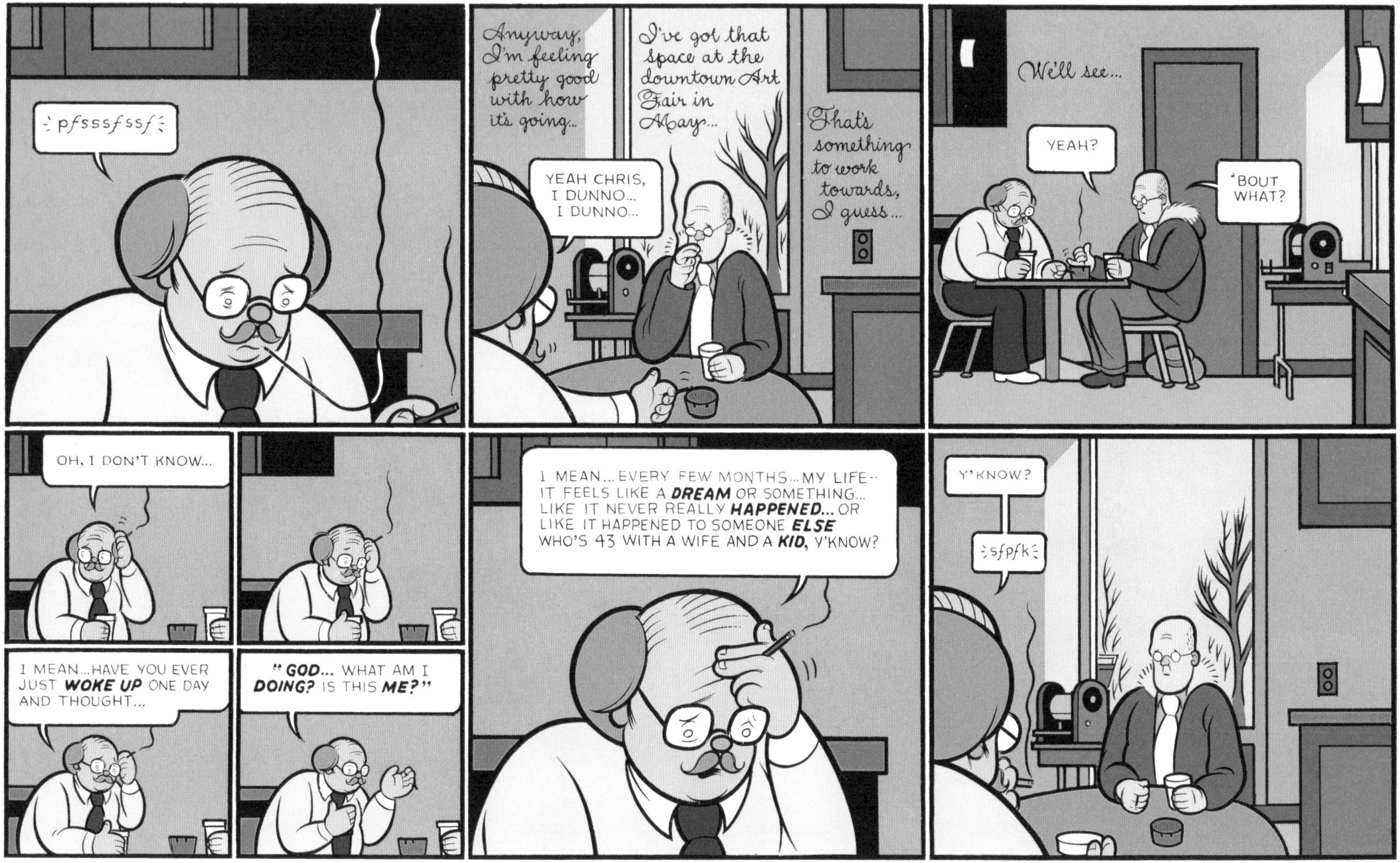
pfsssfssf
Anyway, I'm feeling pretty good with how it's going...
I've got that space at the downtown Art Fair in May...
YEAH CHRIS, I DUNNO... I DUNNO...
That's something to work towards, I guess...
We'll see...
YEAH?
'BOUT WHAT?
OH, I DON'T KNOW...
I MEAN...HAVE YOU EVER JUST WOKE UP ONE DAY AND THOUGHT...
"GOD... WHAT AM I DOING? IS THIS ME?"
I MEAN... EVERY FEW MONTHS... MY LIFE-- IT FEELS LIKE A DREAM OR SOMETHING... LIKE IT NEVER REALLY HAPPENED... OR LIKE IT HAPPENED TO SOMEONE ELSE WHO'S 43 WITH A WIFE AND A KID, Y'KNOW?
Y'KNOW?
sfpfk

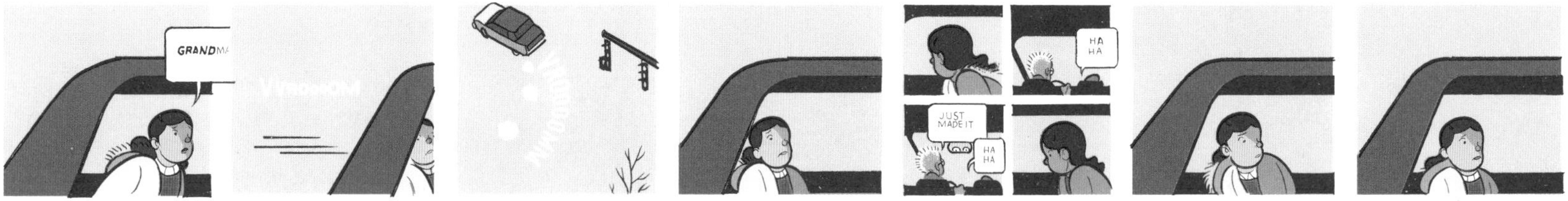
GRANDMA
HA HA
JUST MADE IT
HA HA

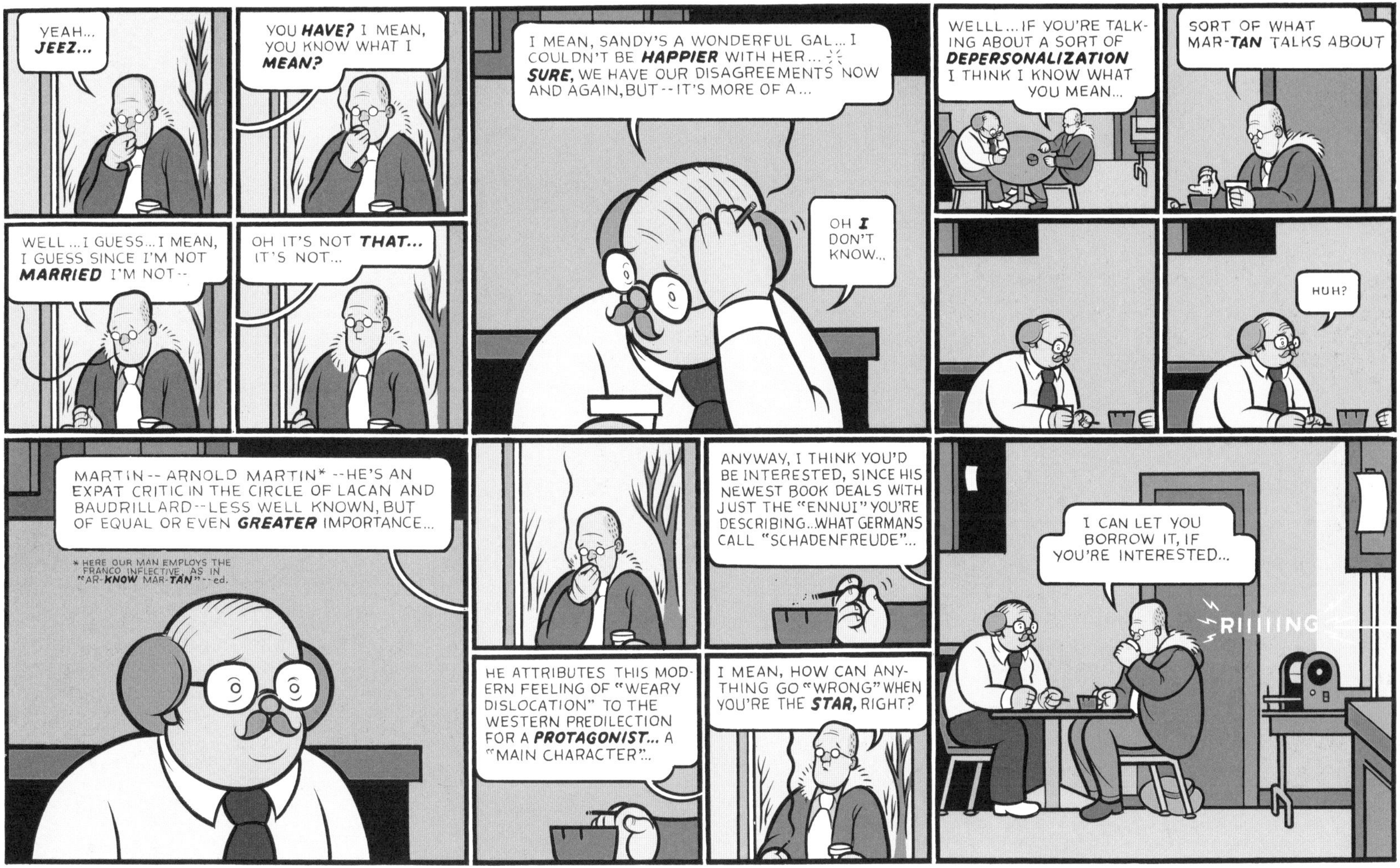
YEAH... **JEEZ...**
YOU **HAVE?** I MEAN, YOU KNOW WHAT I **MEAN?**
WELL ...I GUESS...I MEAN, I GUESS SINCE I'M NOT **MARRIED** I'M NOT--
OH IT'S NOT **THAT...** IT'S NOT...
I MEAN, SANDY'S A WONDERFUL GAL... I COULDN'T BE **HAPPIER** WITH HER... **SURE,** WE HAVE OUR DISAGREEMENTS NOW AND AGAIN, BUT--IT'S MORE OF A...
OH **I** DON'T KNOW...
WELLL... IF YOU'RE TALKING ABOUT A SORT OF **DEPERSONALIZATION** I THINK I KNOW WHAT YOU MEAN...
SORT OF WHAT MAR-**TAN** TALKS ABOUT
HUH?
MARTIN--ARNOLD MARTIN*--HE'S AN EXPAT CRITIC IN THE CIRCLE OF LACAN AND BAUDRILLARD--LESS WELL KNOWN, BUT OF EQUAL OR EVEN **GREATER** IMPORTANCE...
* HERE OUR MAN EMPLOYS THE FRANCO INFLECTIVE, AS IN "AR-**KNOW** MAR-**TAN**"--ed.
ANYWAY, I THINK YOU'D BE INTERESTED, SINCE HIS NEWEST BOOK DEALS WITH JUST THE "ENNUI" YOU'RE DESCRIBING...WHAT GERMANS CALL "SCHADENFREUDE"...
HE ATTRIBUTES THIS MODERN FEELING OF "WEARY DISLOCATION" TO THE WESTERN PREDILECTION FOR A **PROTAGONIST...** A "MAIN CHARACTER"...
I MEAN, HOW CAN ANYTHING GO "WRONG" WHEN YOU'RE THE **STAR,** RIGHT?
I CAN LET YOU BORROW IT, IF YOU'RE INTERESTED...
RIIIIING

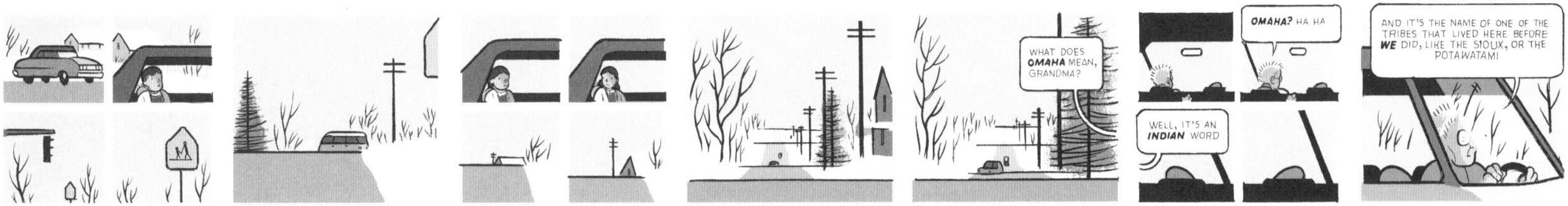
WHAT DOES **OMAHA** MEAN, GRANDMA?
OMAHA? HA HA
WELL, IT'S AN **INDIAN** WORD
AND IT'S THE NAME OF ONE OF THE TRIBES THAT LIVED HERE BEFORE **WE** DID, LIKE THE SIOUX, OR THE POTAWATAMI

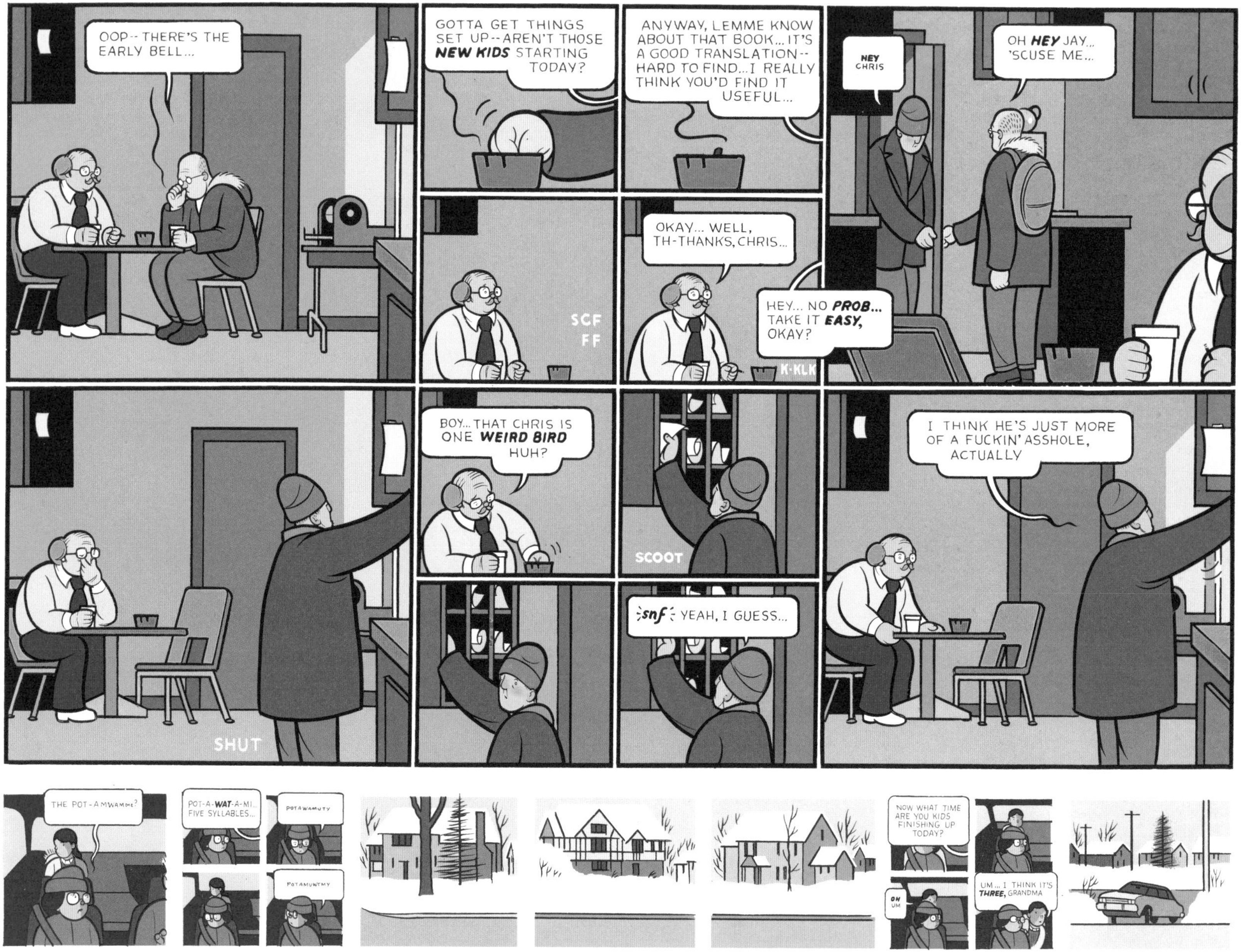

OOP-- THERE'S THE EARLY BELL...
GOTTA GET THINGS SET UP--AREN'T THOSE **NEW KIDS** STARTING TODAY?
ANYWAY, LEMME KNOW ABOUT THAT BOOK... IT'S A GOOD TRANSLATION--HARD TO FIND... I REALLY THINK YOU'D FIND IT USEFUL...
SCF FF
OKAY... WELL, TH-THANKS, CHRIS...
HEY... NO **PROB...** TAKE IT **EASY,** OKAY?
K-KLK
HEY CHRIS
OH **HEY** JAY... 'SCUSE ME...
SHUT
BOY... THAT CHRIS IS ONE **WEIRD BIRD** HUH?
SCOOT
snf YEAH, I GUESS...
I THINK HE'S JUST MORE OF A FUCKIN' ASSHOLE, ACTUALLY
THE POT-AMWAMME?
POT-A-**WAT**-A-MI... FIVE SYLLABLES...
POTAWAMUTY
POTAMUWTMY
NOW WHAT TIME ARE YOU KIDS FINISHING UP TODAY?
OH UM
UM... I THINK IT'S **THREE,** GRANDMA

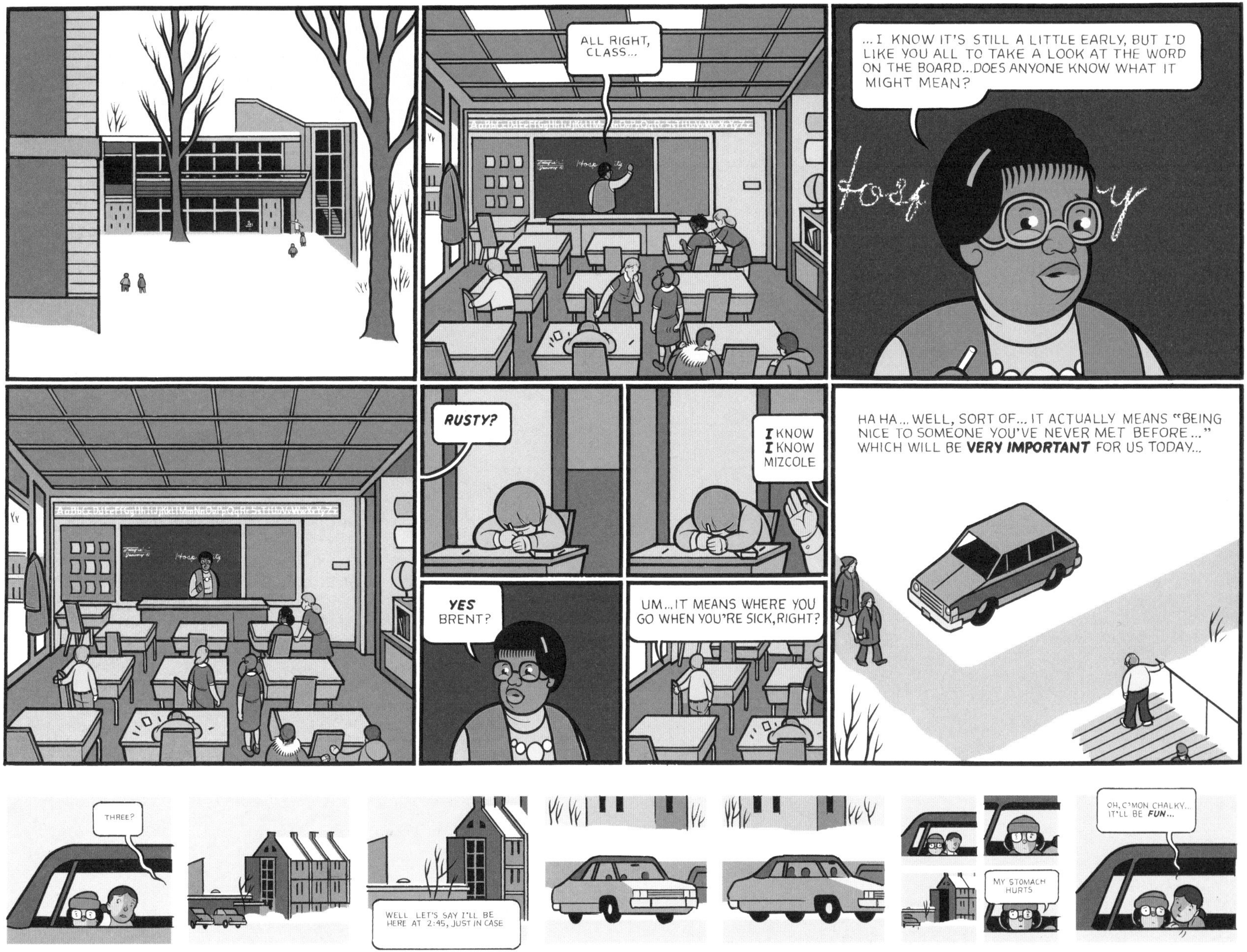
ALL RIGHT, CLASS...
...I KNOW IT'S STILL A LITTLE EARLY, BUT I'D LIKE YOU ALL TO TAKE A LOOK AT THE WORD ON THE BOARD...DOES ANYONE KNOW WHAT IT MIGHT MEAN?
RUSTY?
I KNOW I KNOW MIZCOLE
YES BRENT?
UM...IT MEANS WHERE YOU GO WHEN YOU'RE SICK, RIGHT?
HA HA... WELL, SORT OF... IT ACTUALLY MEANS "BEING NICE TO SOMEONE YOU'VE NEVER MET BEFORE..." WHICH WILL BE VERY IMPORTANT FOR US TODAY...
THREE?
WELL LET'S SAY I'LL BE HERE AT 2:45, JUST IN CASE
MY STOMACH HURTS
OH, C'MON CHALKY... IT'LL BE FUN...

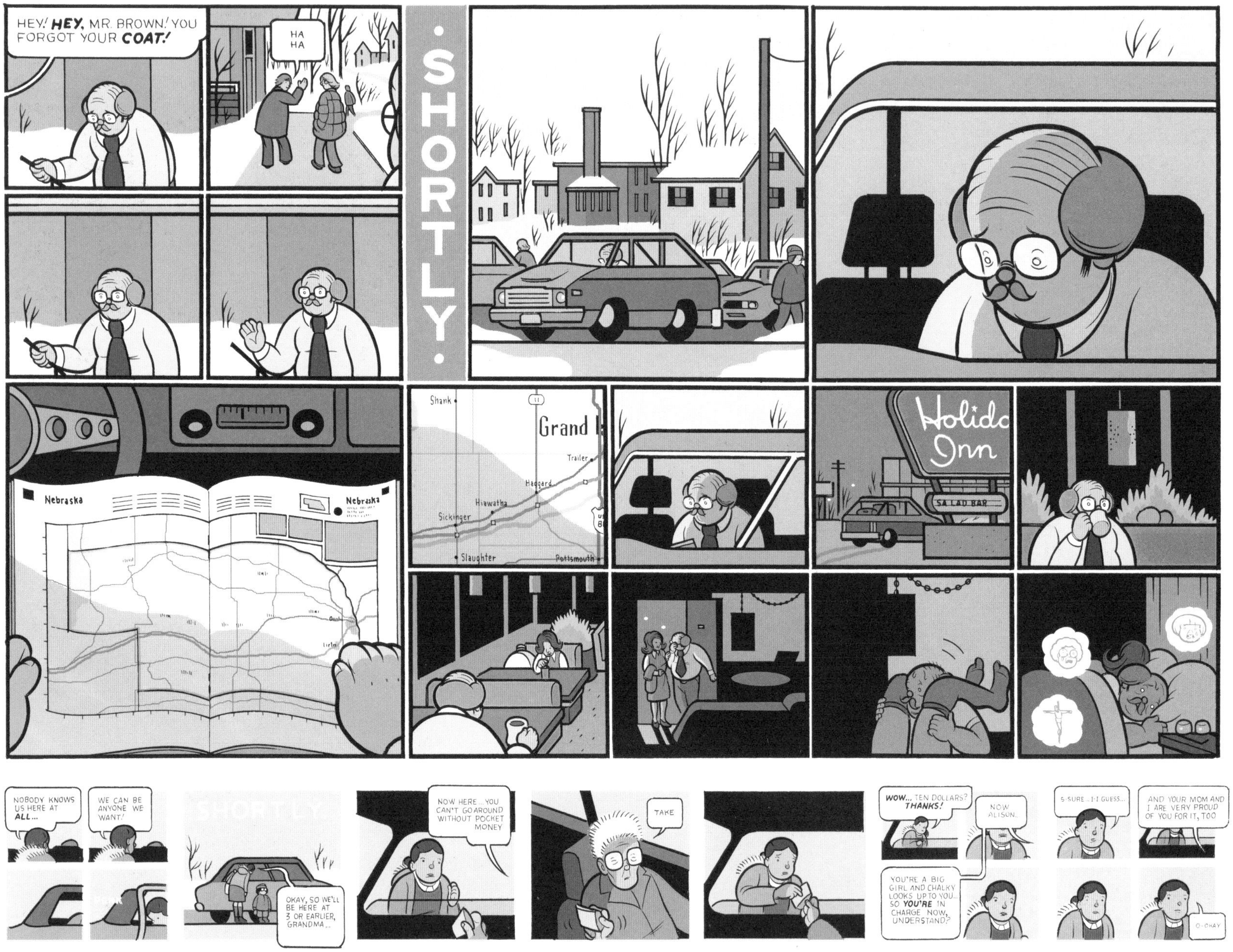
HEY! **HEY,** MR. BROWN! YOU FORGOT YOUR **COAT!**
HA HA
SHORTLY
Nebraska
Nebraska
Shank
Grand
Trailer
Haggard
Hiawatha
Sickinger
Slaughter
Pottsmouth
Holiday Inn
SALAD BAR
NOBODY KNOWS US HERE AT **ALL...**
WE CAN BE ANYONE WE WANT!
OKAY, SO WE'LL BE HERE AT 3 OR EARLIER, GRANDMA...
NOW HERE... YOU CAN'T GO AROUND WITHOUT POCKET MONEY
TAKE
WOW... TEN DOLLARS? **THANKS!**
NOW ALISON...
YOU'RE A BIG GIRL AND CHALKY LOOKS UP TO YOU... SO **YOU'RE** IN CHARGE NOW, UNDERSTAND?
S-SURE... I-I GUESS...
AND YOUR MOM AND I ARE VERY PROUD OF YOU FOR IT, TOO
O-OKAY

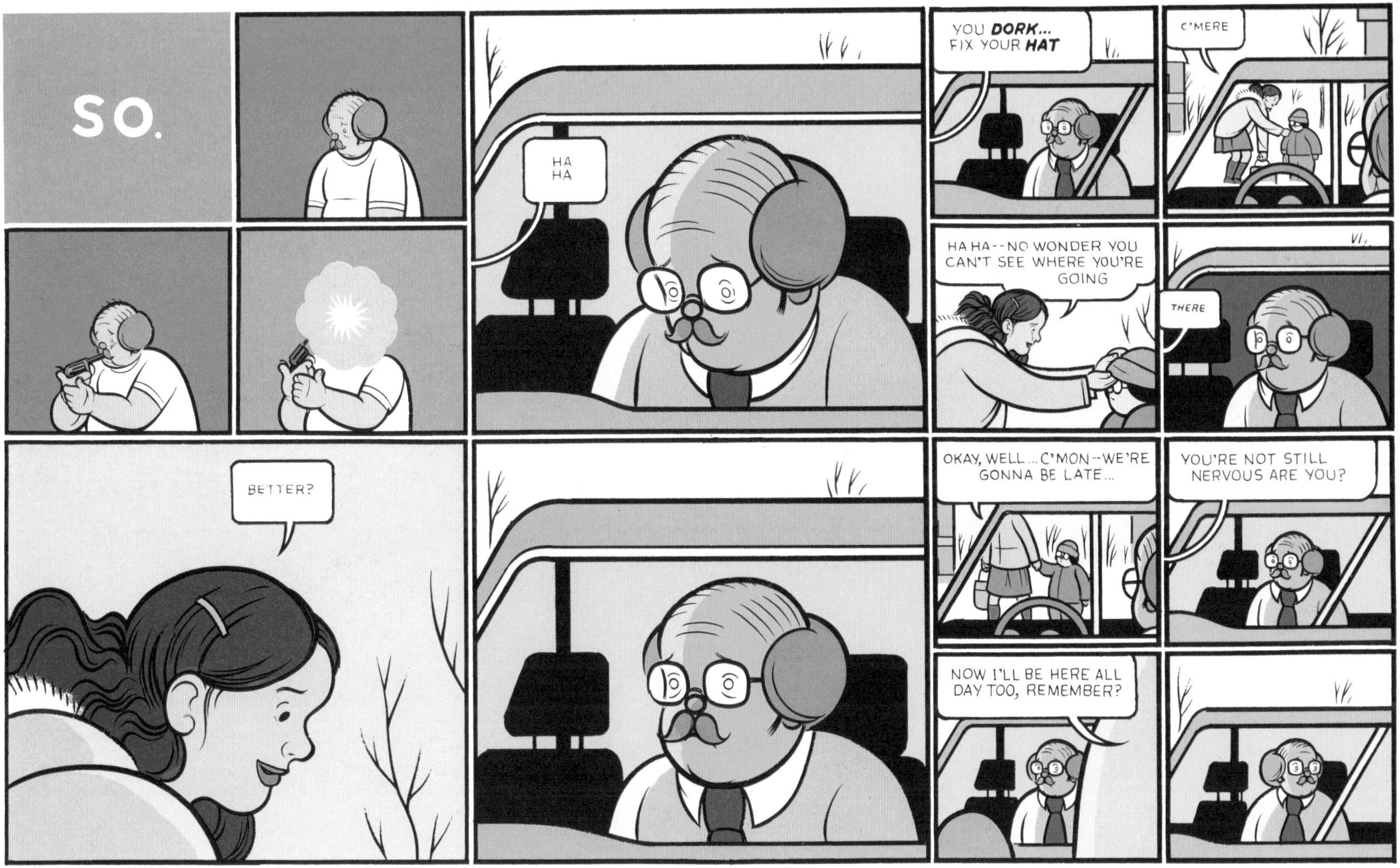
SO.
HA HA
YOU **DORK...** FIX YOUR **HAT**
C'MERE
HA HA--NO WONDER YOU CAN'T SEE WHERE YOU'RE GOING
THERE
BETTER?
OKAY, WELL... C'MON--WE'RE GONNA BE LATE...
YOU'RE NOT STILL NERVOUS ARE YOU?
NOW I'LL BE HERE ALL DAY TOO, REMEMBER?

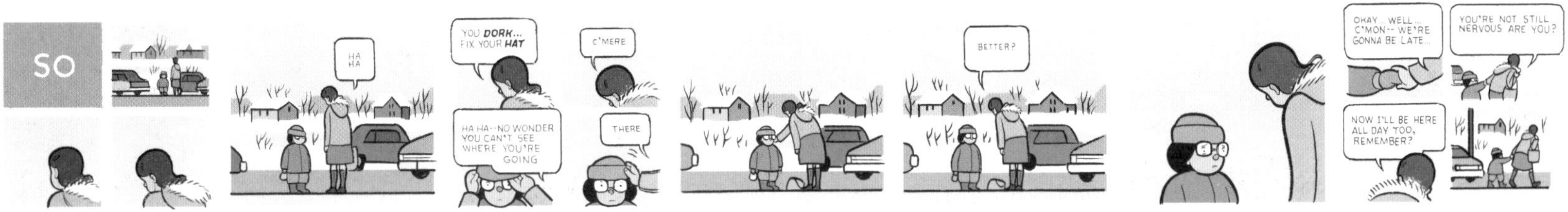
SO
HA HA
YOU **DORK...** FIX YOUR **HAT**
C'MERE
HA HA--NO WONDER YOU CAN'T SEE WHERE YOU'RE GOING
THERE
BETTER?
OKAY... WELL... C'MON-- WE'RE GONNA BE LATE...
YOU'RE NOT STILL NERVOUS ARE YOU?
NOW I'LL BE HERE ALL DAY TOO, REMEMBER?

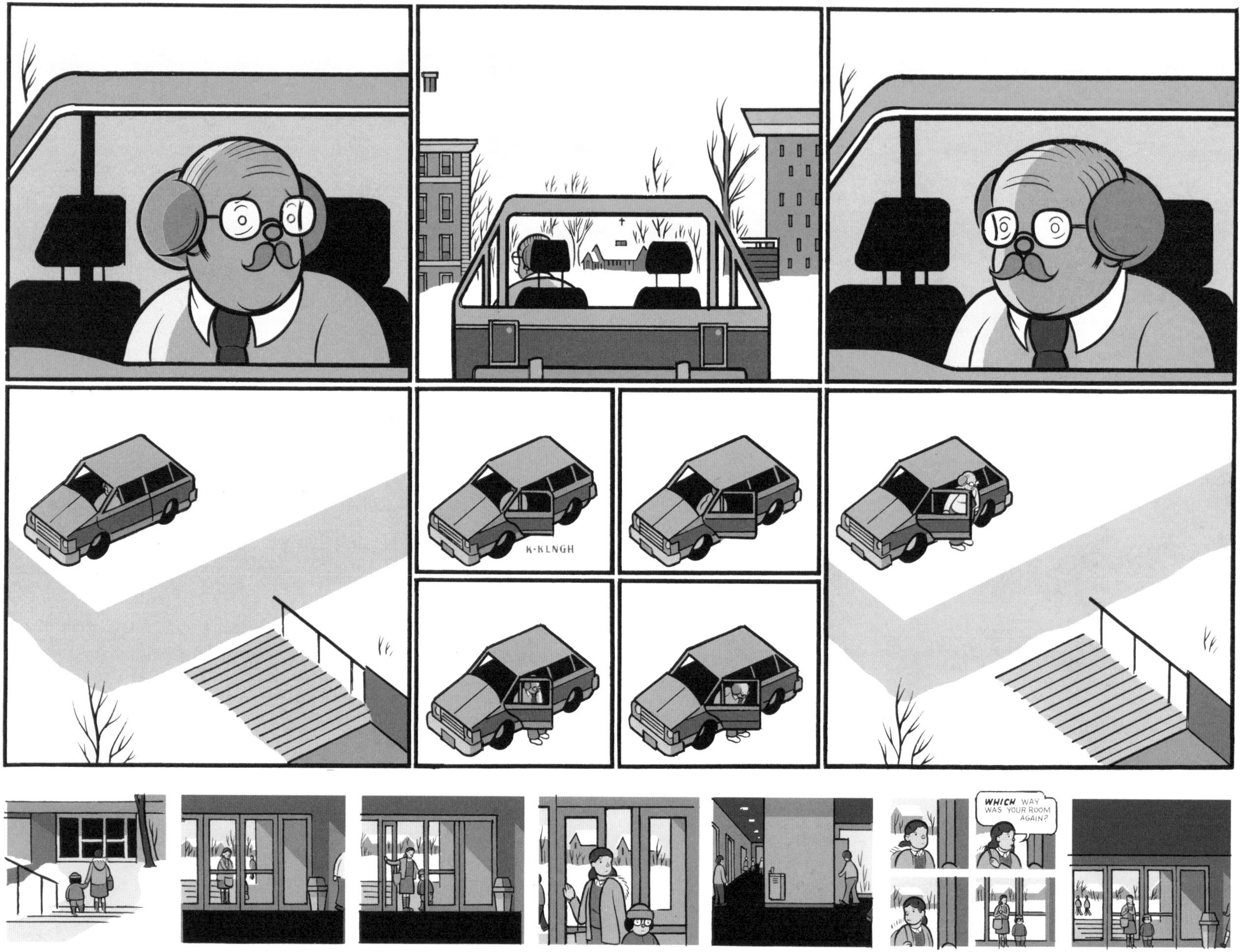
K-KLNGH
WHICH WAY WAS YOUR ROOM AGAIN?

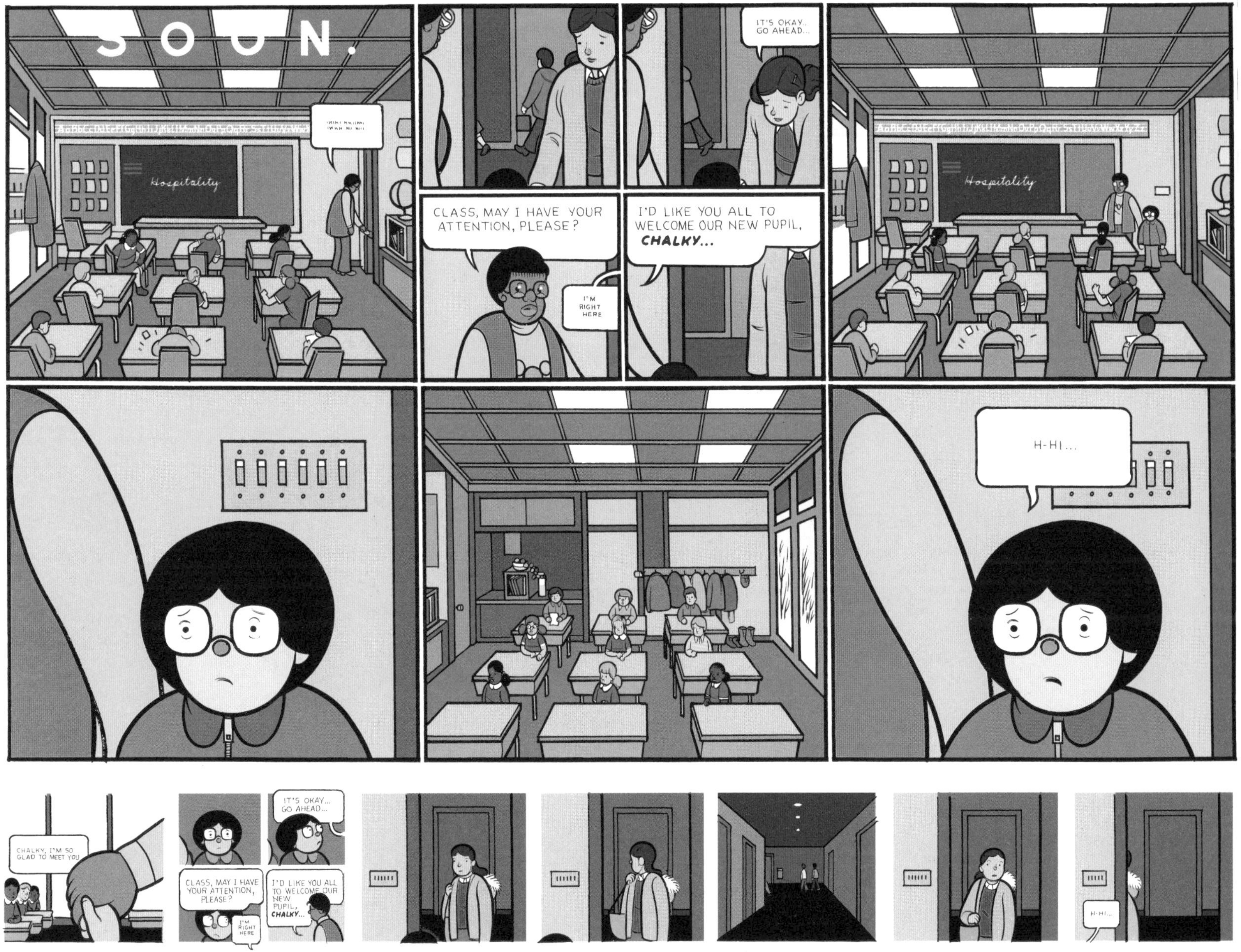
SOON.
Hospitality
IT'S OKAY.. GO AHEAD...
CLASS, MAY I HAVE YOUR ATTENTION, PLEASE?
I'M RIGHT HERE
I'D LIKE YOU ALL TO WELCOME OUR NEW PUPIL, CHALKY...
Hospitality
H-HI...
CHALKY, I'M SO GLAD TO MEET YOU
IT'S OKAY... GO AHEAD...
CLASS, MAY I HAVE YOUR ATTENTION, PLEASE?
I'M RIGHT HERE
I'D LIKE YOU ALL TO WELCOME OUR NEW PUPIL, CHALKY...
H-HI...

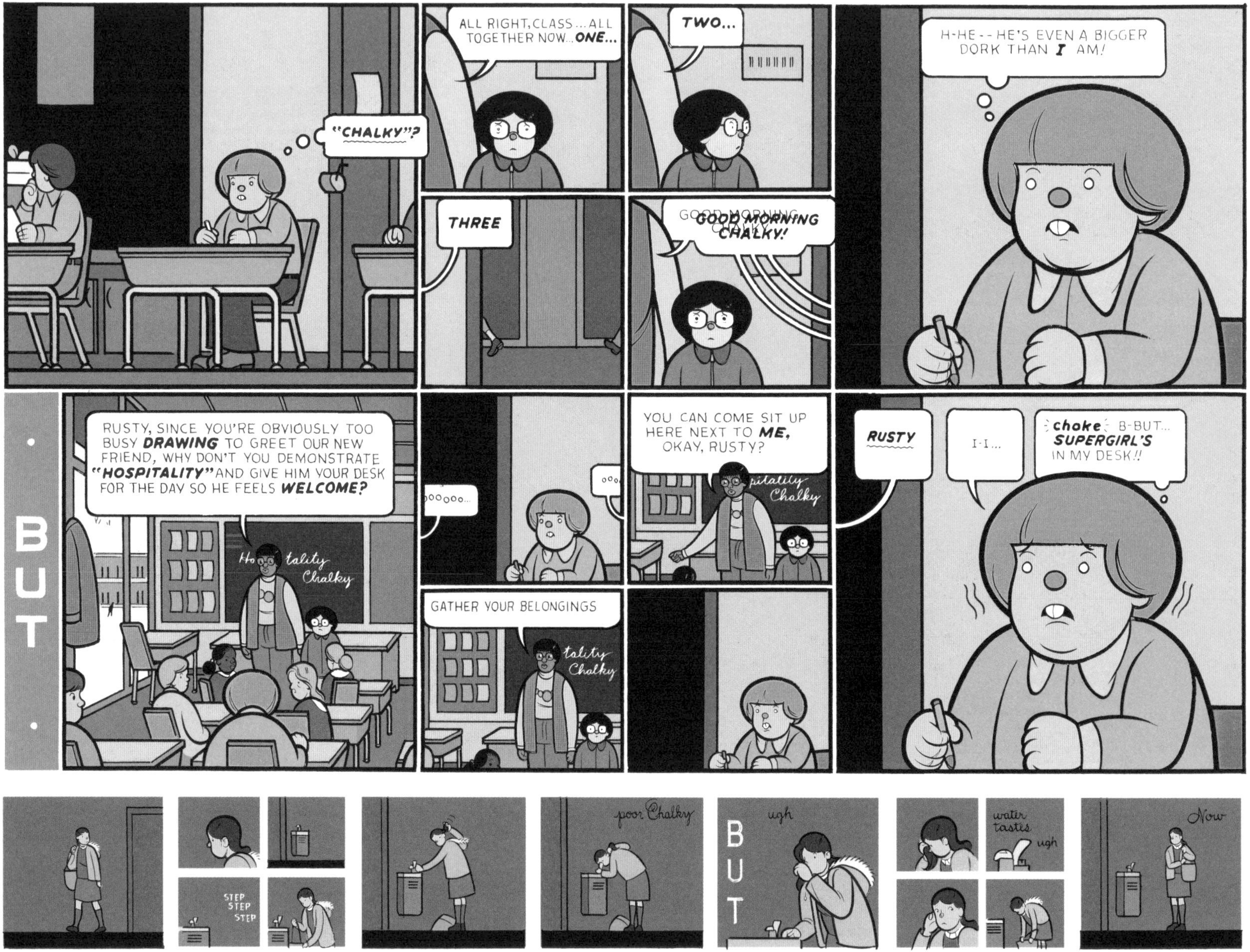
"CHALKY"?
ALL RIGHT, CLASS... ALL TOGETHER NOW... ONE...
TWO...
THREE
GOOD MORNING CHALKY!
H-HE--HE'S EVEN A BIGGER DORK THAN I AM!
BUT
RUSTY, SINCE YOU'RE OBVIOUSLY TOO BUSY DRAWING TO GREET OUR NEW FRIEND, WHY DON'T YOU DEMONSTRATE "HOSPITALITY" AND GIVE HIM YOUR DESK FOR THE DAY SO HE FEELS WELCOME?
Hospitality Chalky
GATHER YOUR BELONGINGS
YOU CAN COME SIT UP HERE NEXT TO ME, OKAY, RUSTY?
RUSTY
I-I...
choke B-BUT... SUPERGIRL'S IN MY DESK!!
STEP STEP STEP
poor Chalky
BUT
ugh
water tastes
ugh
Now

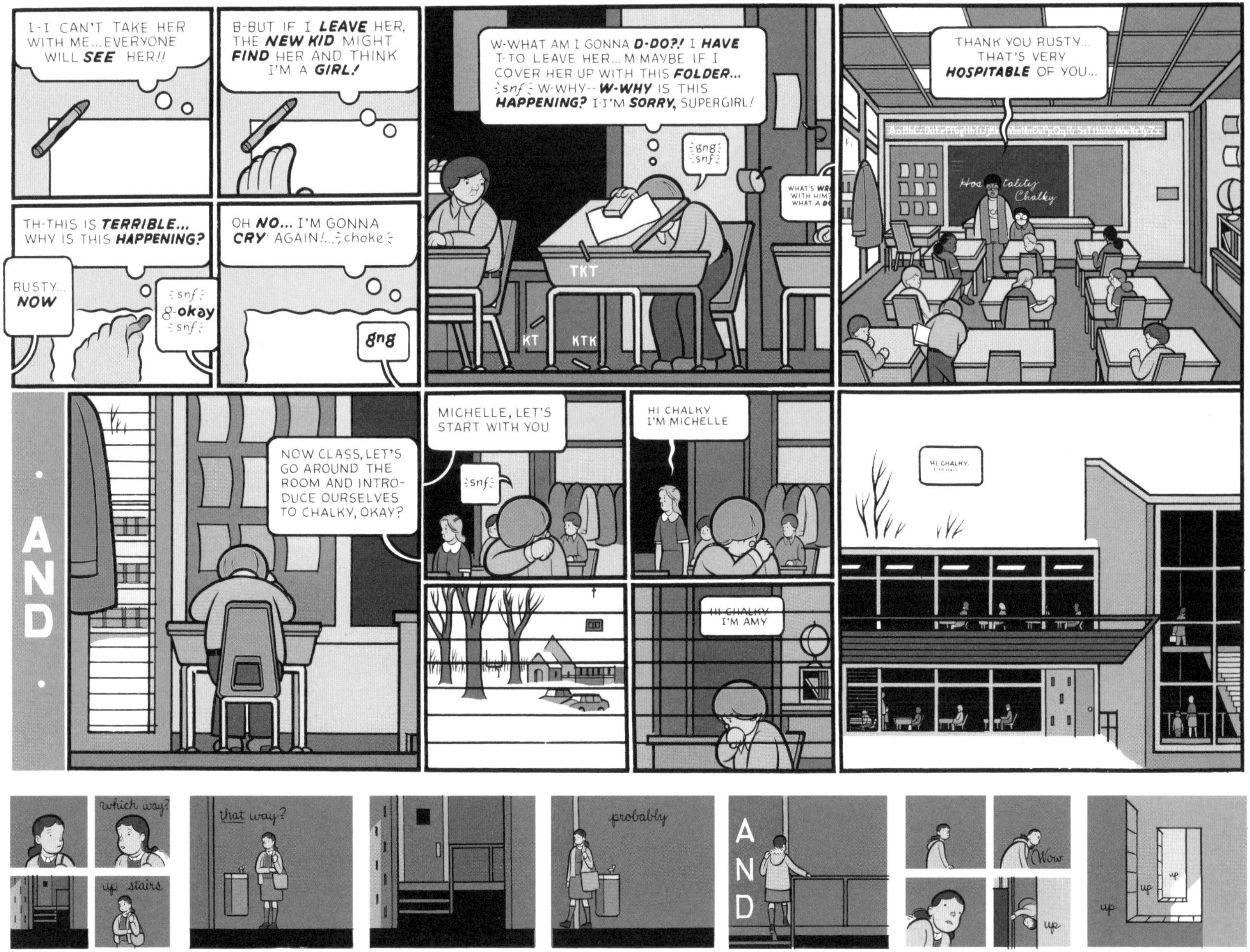
I-I CAN'T TAKE HER WITH ME... EVERYONE WILL **SEE** HER!!
B-BUT IF I **LEAVE** HER, THE **NEW KID** MIGHT **FIND** HER AND THINK I'M A **GIRL!**
TH-THIS IS **TERRIBLE...** WHY IS THIS **HAPPENING?**
RUSTY... **NOW**
snf g-**okay** snf
OH **NO...** I'M GONNA **CRY** AGAIN!... choke
gng
W-WHAT AM I GONNA **D-DO?!** I **HAVE** T-TO LEAVE HER... M-MAYBE IF I COVER HER UP WITH THIS **FOLDER...** snf W-WHY-- **W-WHY** IS THIS **HAPPENING?** I-I'M **SORRY,** SUPERGIRL!
gng snf
TKT
KT
KTK
THANK YOU RUSTY... THAT'S VERY **HOSPITABLE** OF YOU...
AND
NOW CLASS, LET'S GO AROUND THE ROOM AND INTRODUCE OURSELVES TO CHALKY, OKAY?
MICHELLE, LET'S START WITH YOU
snf
HI CHALKY I'M MICHELLE
~~HI CHALKY~~ I'M AMY
HI CHALKY...
which way?
up stairs
that way?
probably
AND
Wow
up
up
up
up
up

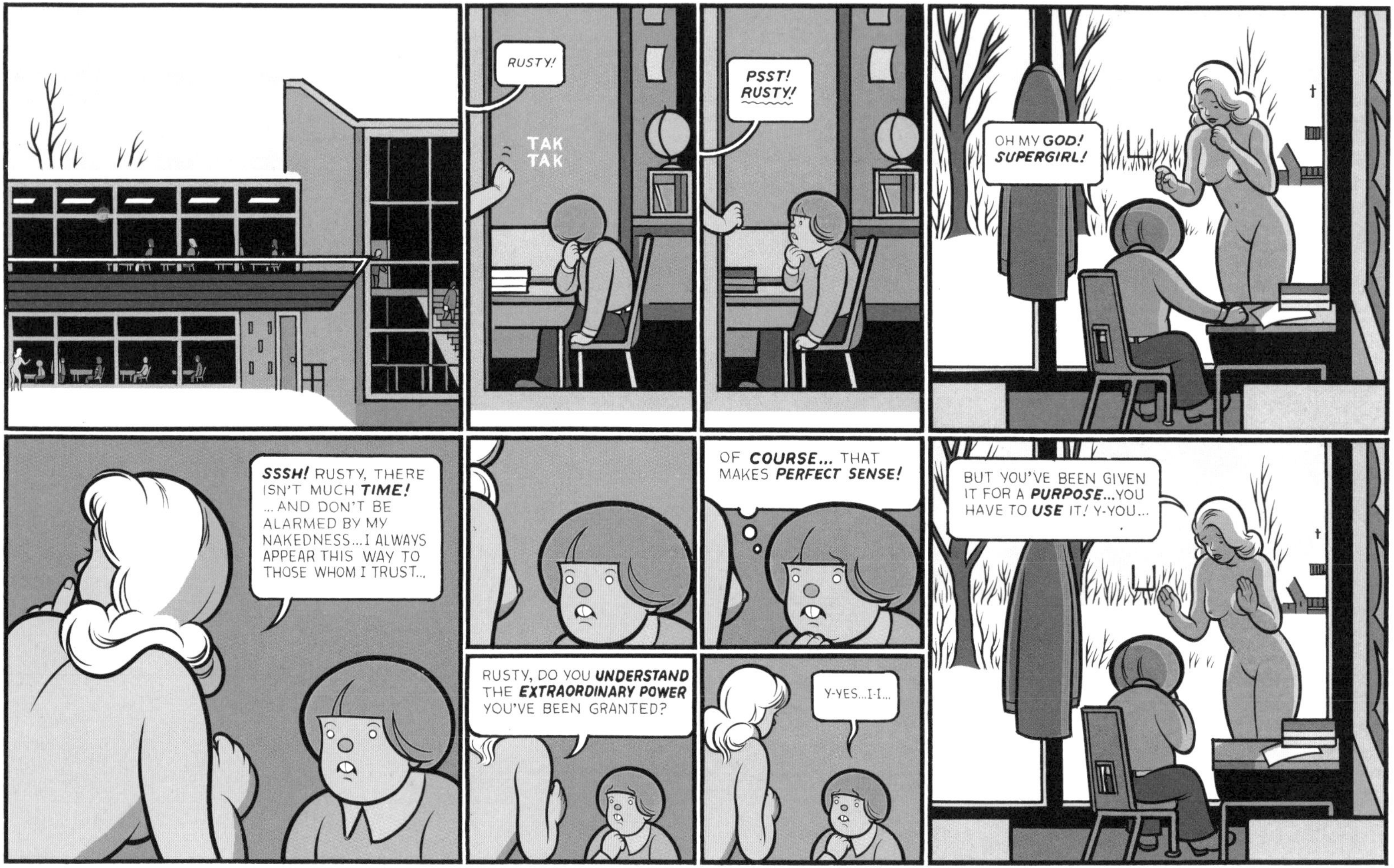
RUSTY!
TAK TAK
PSST! RUSTY!
OH MY GOD! SUPERGIRL!
SSSH! RUSTY, THERE ISN'T MUCH TIME! ...AND DON'T BE ALARMED BY MY NAKEDNESS...I ALWAYS APPEAR THIS WAY TO THOSE WHOM I TRUST...
OF COURSE... THAT MAKES PERFECT SENSE!
RUSTY, DO YOU UNDERSTAND THE EXTRAORDINARY POWER YOU'VE BEEN GRANTED?
Y-YES...I-I...
BUT YOU'VE BEEN GIVEN IT FOR A PURPOSE...YOU HAVE TO USE IT! Y-YOU...

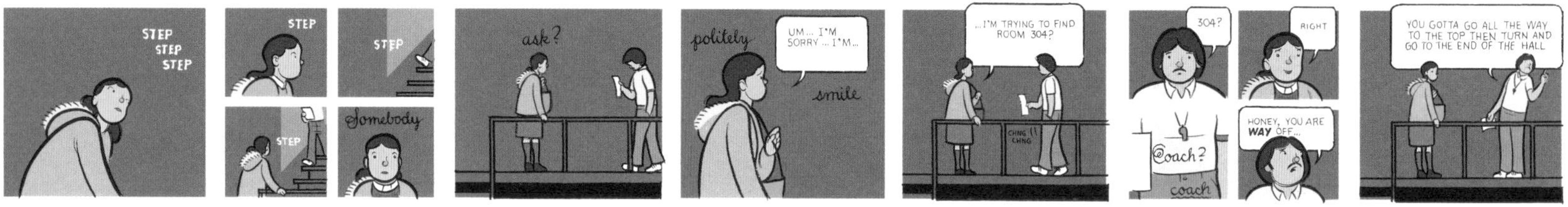
STEP STEP STEP
STEP
STEP
STEP
Somebody
ask?
politely
UM... I'M SORRY ... I'M...
smile
...I'M TRYING TO FIND ROOM 304?
CHNG CHNG
304?
Coach?
coach
RIGHT
HONEY, YOU ARE WAY OFF...
YOU GOTTA GO ALL THE WAY TO THE TOP THEN TURN AND GO TO THE END OF THE HALL

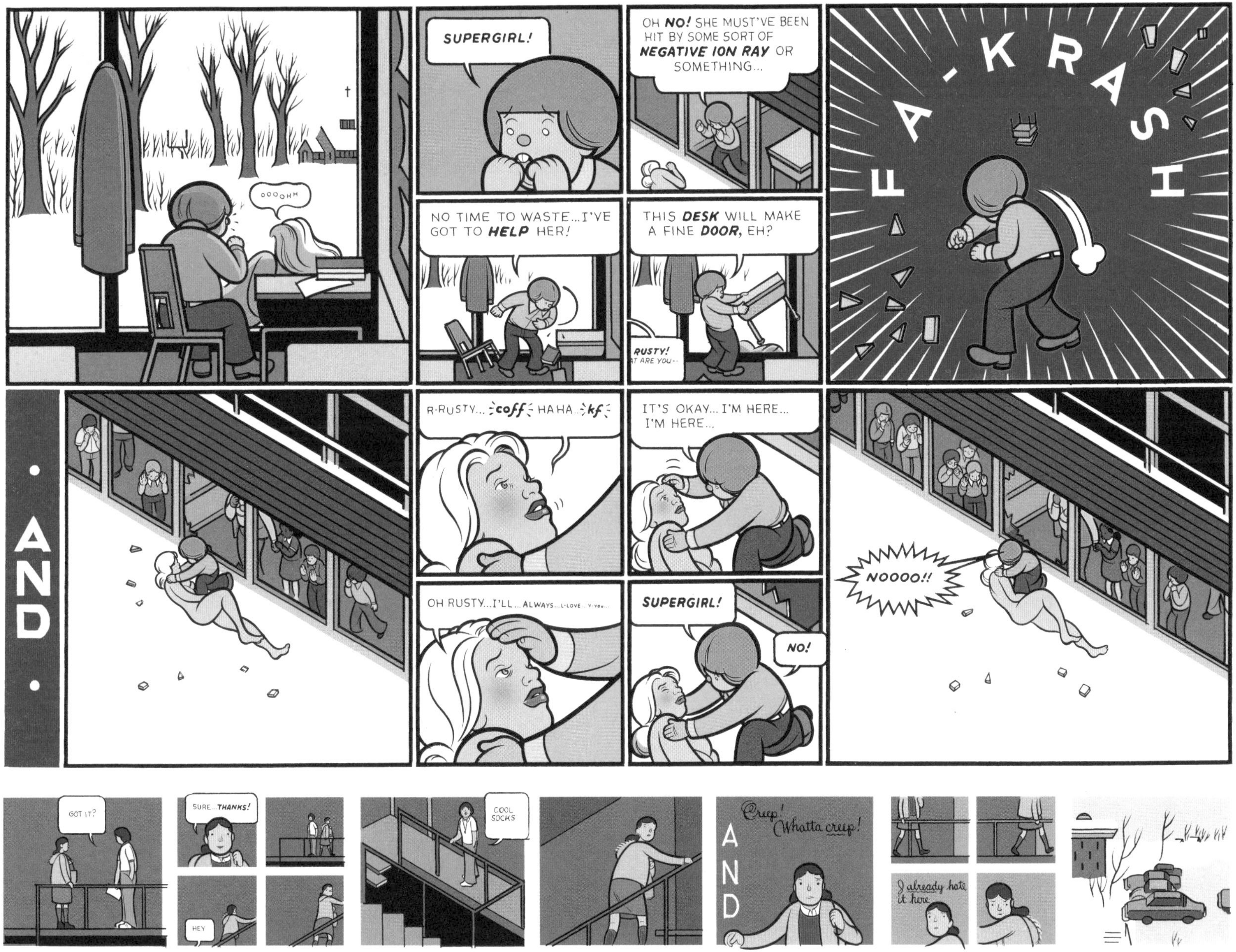

OOOOHH
SUPERGIRL!
OH NO! SHE MUST'VE BEEN HIT BY SOME SORT OF NEGATIVE ION RAY OR SOMETHING...
NO TIME TO WASTE...I'VE GOT TO HELP HER!
THIS DESK WILL MAKE A FINE DOOR, EH?
RUSTY!
AT ARE YOU--
FA-KRASH
AND
R-RUSTY... coff HA HA.. kf
IT'S OKAY... I'M HERE... I'M HERE...
OH RUSTY...I'LL...ALWAYS...L-LOVE...Y-YOU...
SUPERGIRL!
NO!
NOOOO!!
GOT IT?
SURE...THANKS!
HEY
COOL SOCKS
AND
Creep! Whatta creep!
I already hate it here

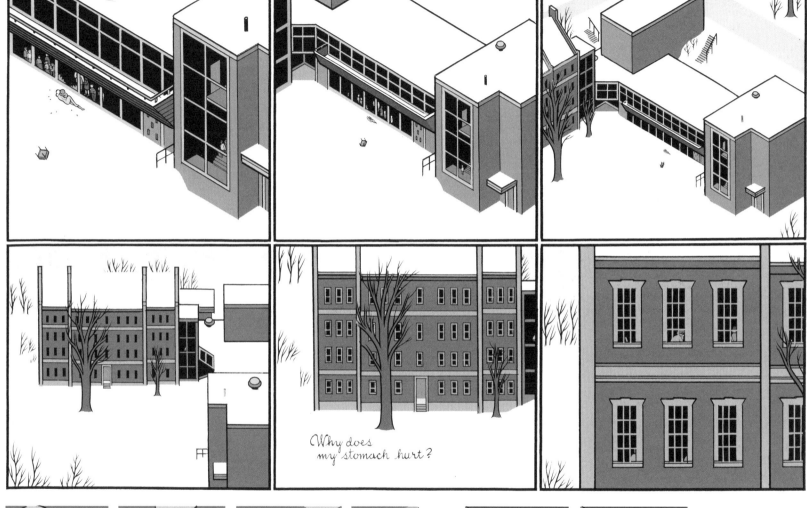

Why does
my stomach hurt?

my stomach
hurts

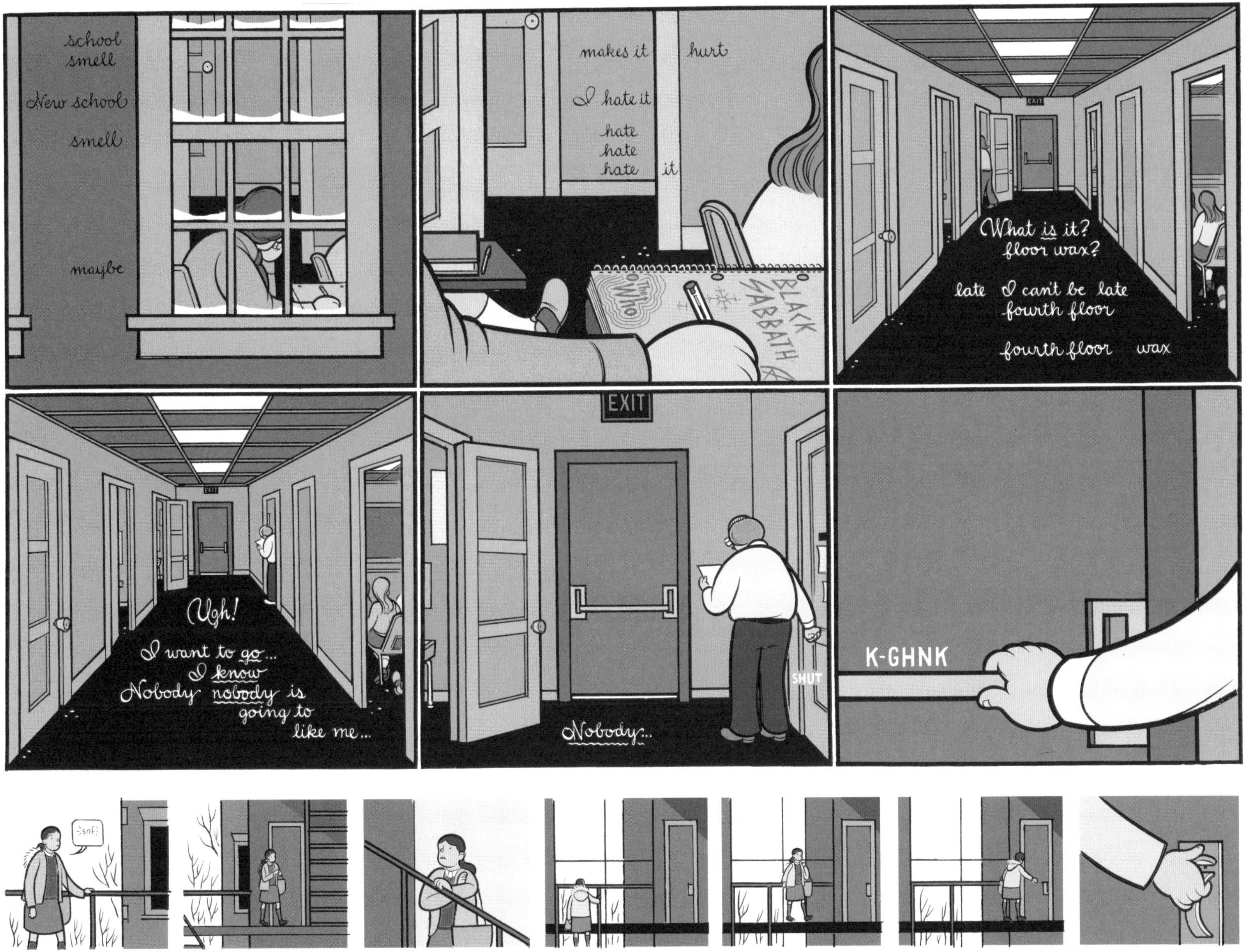
school smell
New school
smell
maybe
makes it hurt
I hate it
hate
hate
hate it
The Who
BLACK SABBATH
What is it?
floor wax?
late I can't be late
fourth floor
fourth floor wax
Ugh!
I want to go...
I know
Nobody nobody is
going to
like me...
EXIT
Nobody...
SHUT
K-GHNK
snf

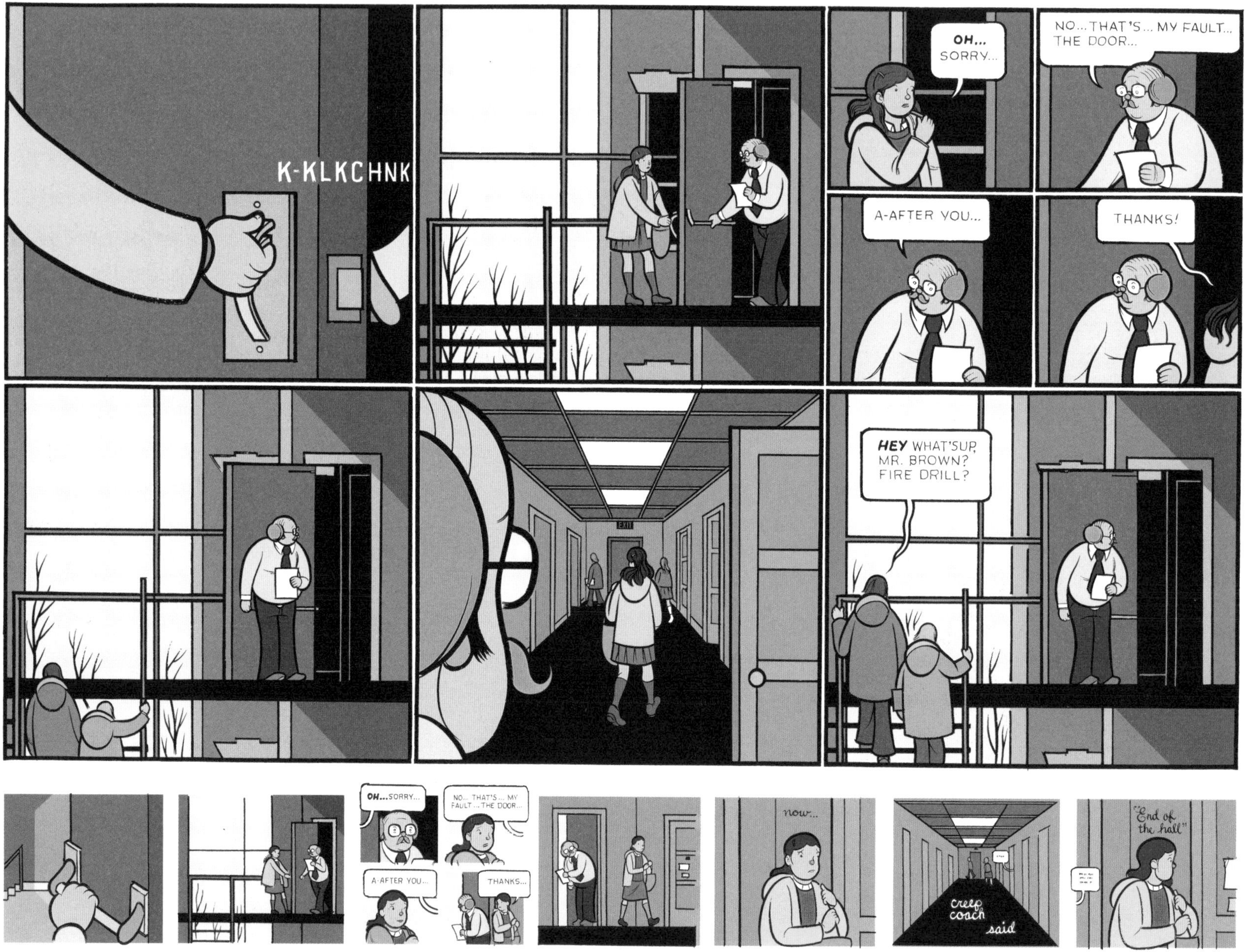
K-KLKCHNK
OH... SORRY...
NO... THAT'S... MY FAULT... THE DOOR...
A-AFTER YOU...
THANKS!
HEY WHAT'SUP, MR. BROWN? FIRE DRILL?
EXIT
OH...SORRY...
NO... THAT'S... MY FAULT ... THE DOOR...
A-AFTER YOU...
THANKS...
now...
creep coach said
"End of the hall"

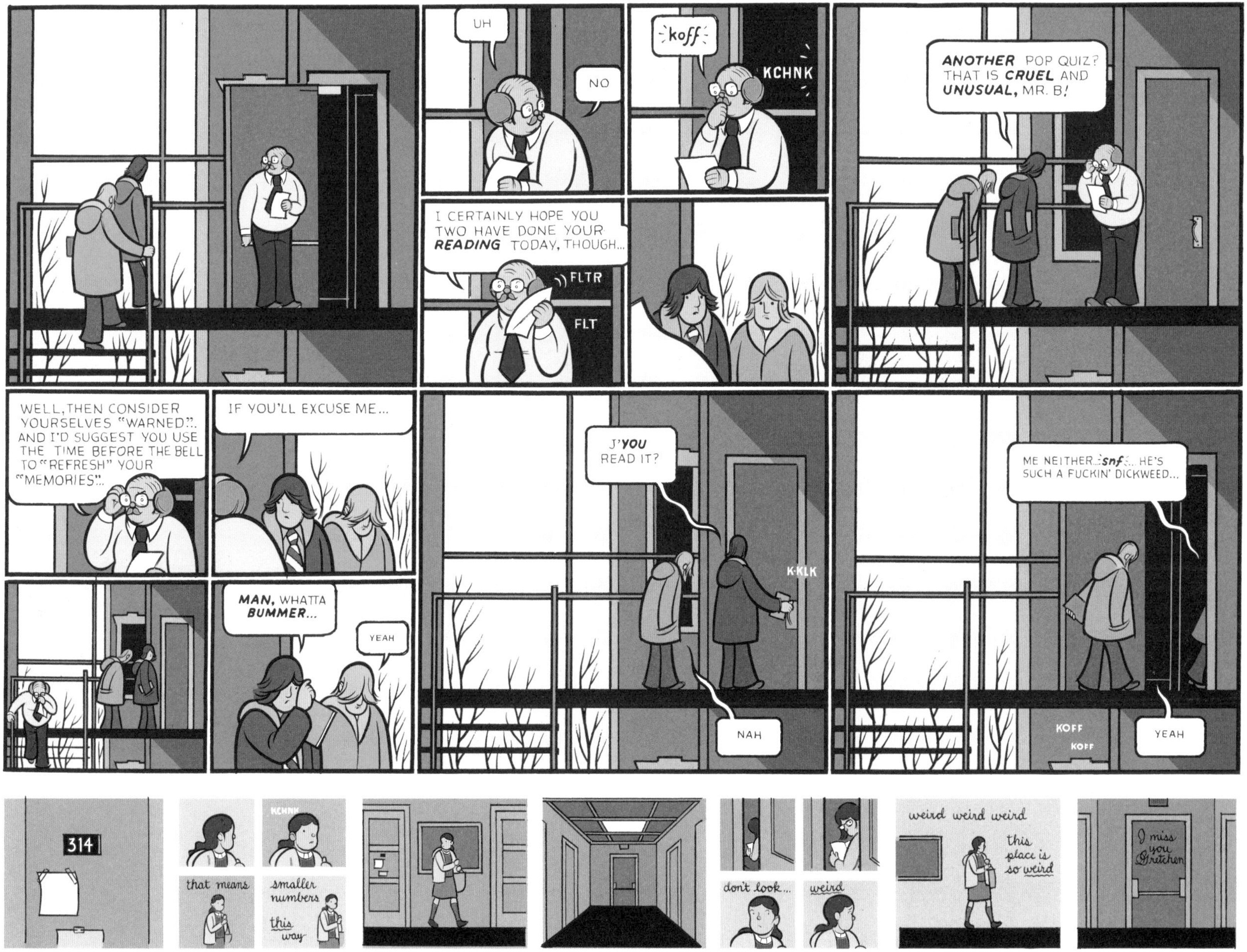
UH
NO
koff
KCHNK
I CERTAINLY HOPE YOU TWO HAVE DONE YOUR **READING** TODAY, THOUGH...
FLTR
FLT
ANOTHER POP QUIZ? THAT IS **CRUEL** AND **UNUSUAL,** MR. B!
WELL, THEN CONSIDER YOURSELVES "WARNED".. AND I'D SUGGEST YOU USE THE TIME BEFORE THE BELL TO "REFRESH" YOUR "MEMORIES"..
IF YOU'LL EXCUSE ME...
MAN, WHATTA **BUMMER...**
YEAH
J'**YOU** READ IT?
K-KLK
NAH
ME NEITHER...snf... HE'S SUCH A FUCKIN' DICKWEED...
KOFF
KOFF
YEAH
314
KCHNK
that means
smaller numbers this way
don't look...
weird
weird weird weird
this place is so weird
I miss you Gretchen

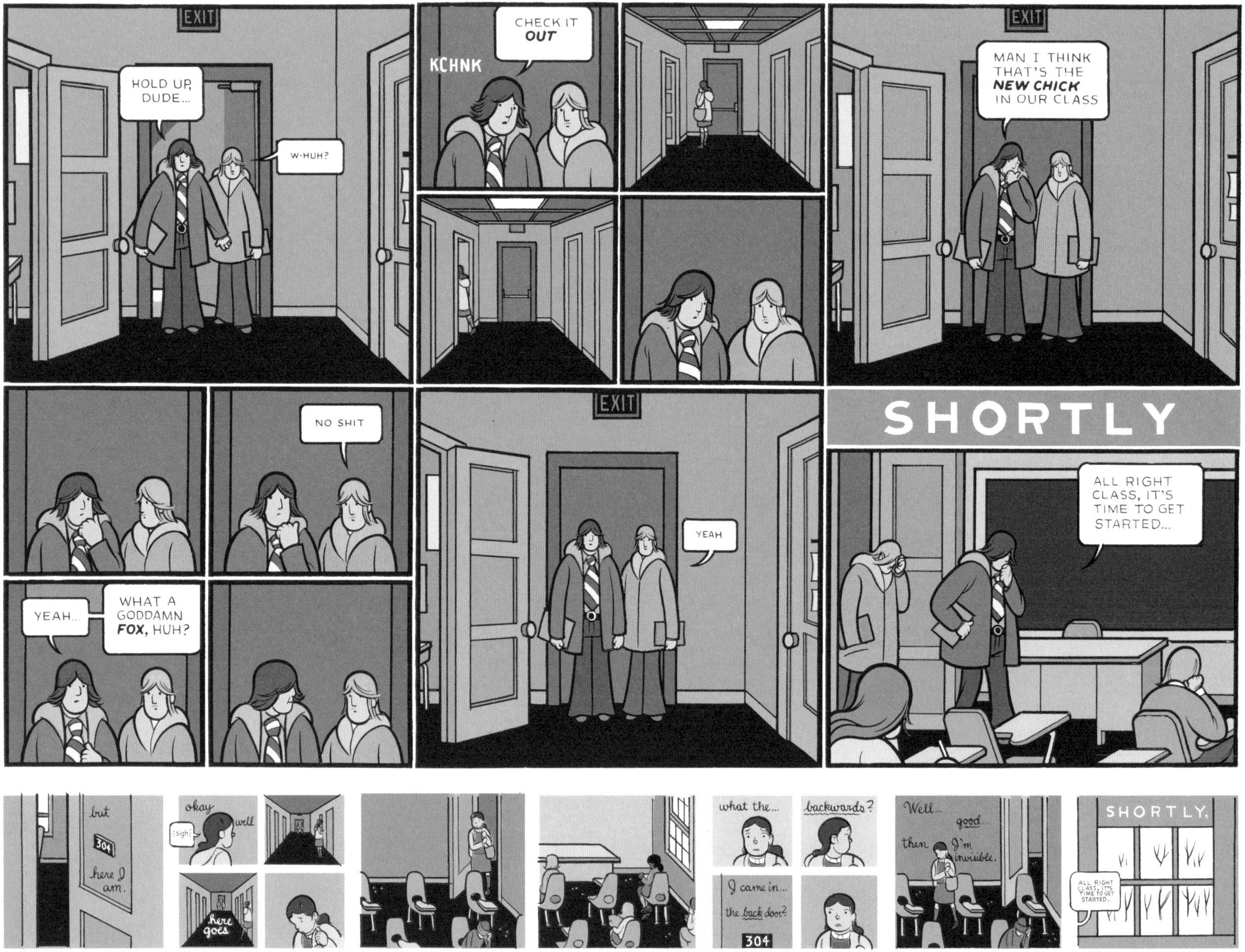
EXIT
HOLD UP, DUDE...
W-HUH?
KCHNK
CHECK IT OUT
EXIT
MAN I THINK THAT'S THE NEW CHICK IN OUR CLASS
NO SHIT
YEAH...
WHAT A GODDAMN FOX, HUH?
EXIT
YEAH
SHORTLY
ALL RIGHT CLASS, IT'S TIME TO GET STARTED...
but
304
here I am.
okay
sigh
well
here goes
what the...
backwards?
I came in...
the back door?
304
Well...
good...
then
I'm invisible.
SHORTLY,
ALL RIGHT CLASS, IT'S TIME TO GET STARTED...

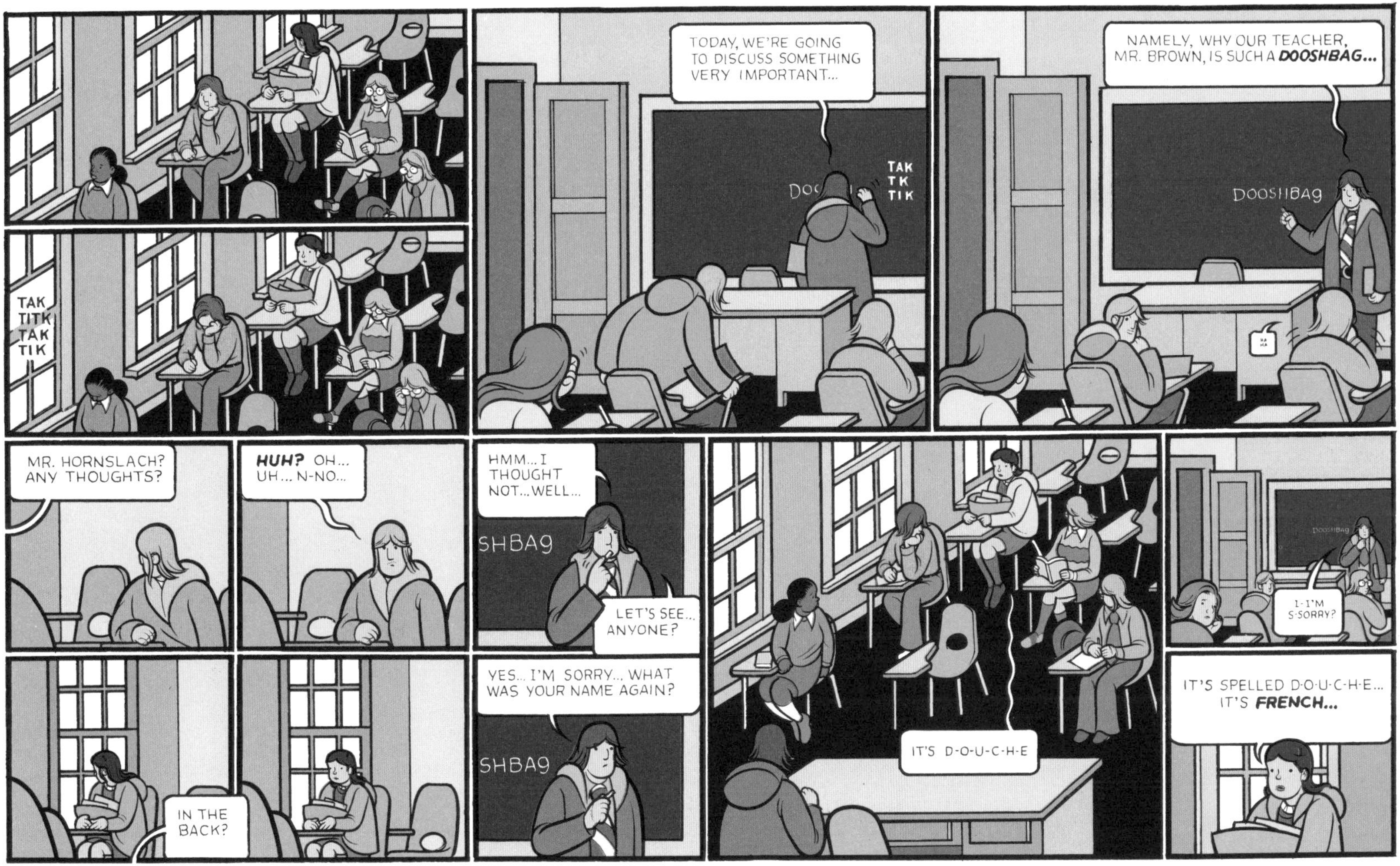
TAK TITK TAK TIK
TODAY, WE'RE GOING TO DISCUSS SOMETHING VERY IMPORTANT...
TAK TK TIK
NAMELY, WHY OUR TEACHER, MR. BROWN, IS SUCH A **DOOSHBAG...**
DOOSHBAG
MR. HORNSLACH? ANY THOUGHTS?
HUH? OH... UH... N-NO...
HMM... I THOUGHT NOT... WELL...
SHBAG
LET'S SEE... ANYONE?
IN THE BACK?
YES... I'M SORRY... WHAT WAS YOUR NAME AGAIN?
SHBAG
IT'S D-O-U-C-H-E
I-I'M S-SORRY?
IT'S SPELLED D-O-U-C-H-E... IT'S **FRENCH...**

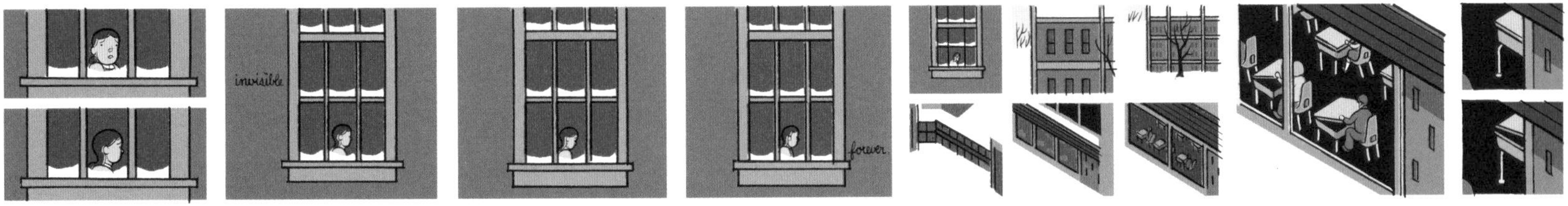
invisible
forever.

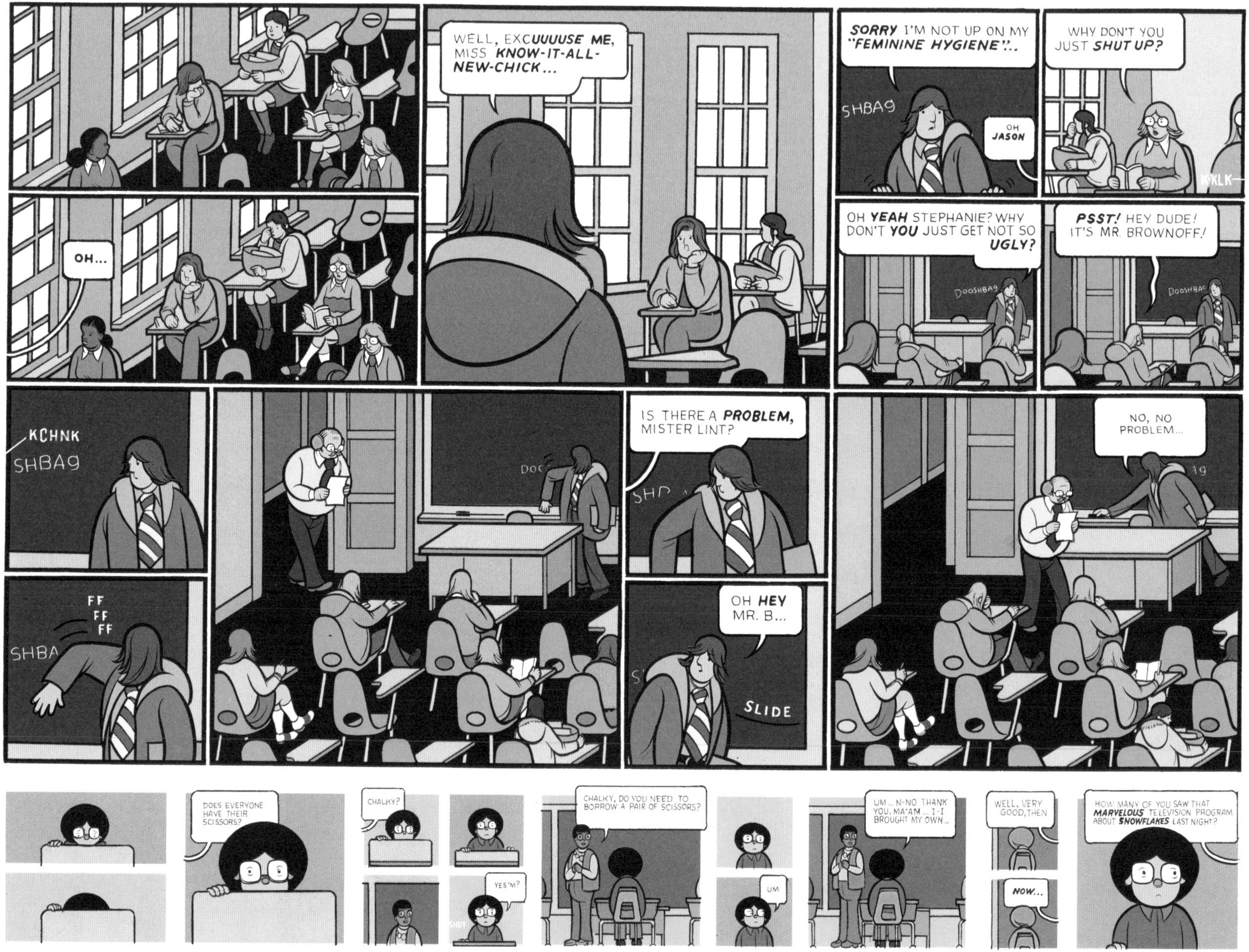
OH...
WELL, EXCUUUUSE ME, MISS KNOW-IT-ALL-NEW-CHICK...
SORRY I'M NOT UP ON MY "FEMININE HYGIENE"..
SHBAG
OH JASON
WHY DON'T YOU JUST SHUT UP?
OH YEAH STEPHANIE? WHY DON'T YOU JUST GET NOT SO UGLY?
DOOSHBAG
PSST! HEY DUDE! IT'S MR. BROWNOFF!
KCHNK
SHBAG
FF FF FF
SHBA
IS THERE A PROBLEM, MISTER LINT?
OH HEY MR. B...
SLIDE
NO, NO PROBLEM...
DOES EVERYONE HAVE THEIR SCISSORS?
CHALKY?
YES'M?
CHALKY, DO YOU NEED TO BORROW A PAIR OF SCISSORS?
UM
UM... N-NO THANK YOU, MA'AM... I-I BROUGHT MY OWN...
WELL, VERY GOOD, THEN
NOW...
HOW MANY OF YOU SAW THAT MARVELOUS TELEVISION PROGRAM ABOUT SNOWFLAKES LAST NIGHT?

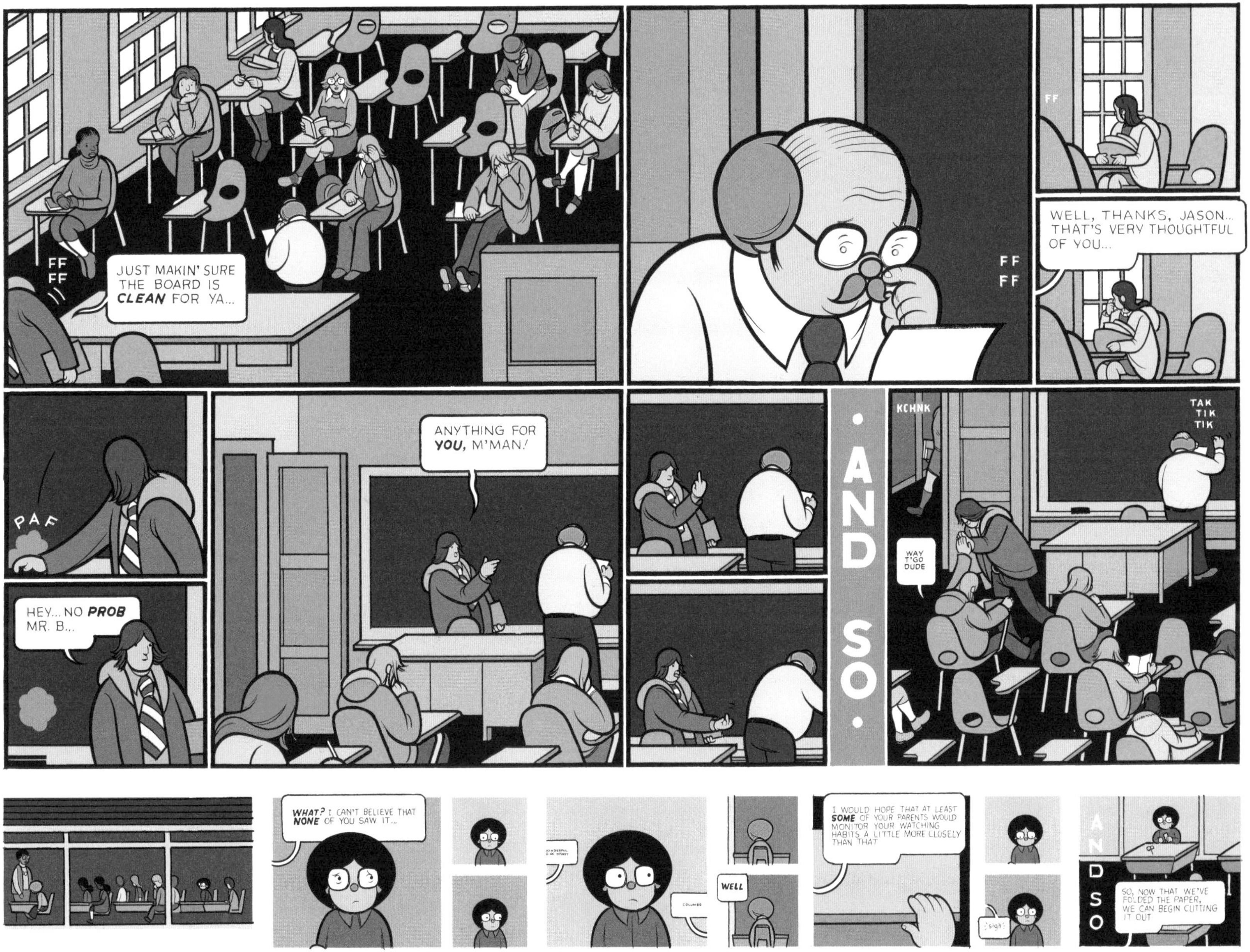

FF
FF
JUST MAKIN' SURE THE BOARD IS **CLEAN** FOR YA...
FF
FF
FF
WELL, THANKS, JASON... THAT'S VERY THOUGHTFUL OF YOU...
PAF
HEY... NO **PROB** MR. B...
ANYTHING FOR **YOU,** M'MAN!
• AND SO •
KCHNK
TAK
TIK
TIK
WAY T'GO DUDE
WHAT? I CAN'T BELIEVE THAT **NONE** OF YOU SAW IT...
COLUMBO
WELL
I WOULD HOPE THAT AT LEAST **SOME** OF YOUR PARENTS WOULD MONITOR YOUR WATCHING HABITS A LITTLE MORE CLOSELY THAN THAT
sigh
AND SO
SO, NOW THAT WE'VE FOLDED THE PAPER, WE CAN BEGIN CUTTING IT OUT

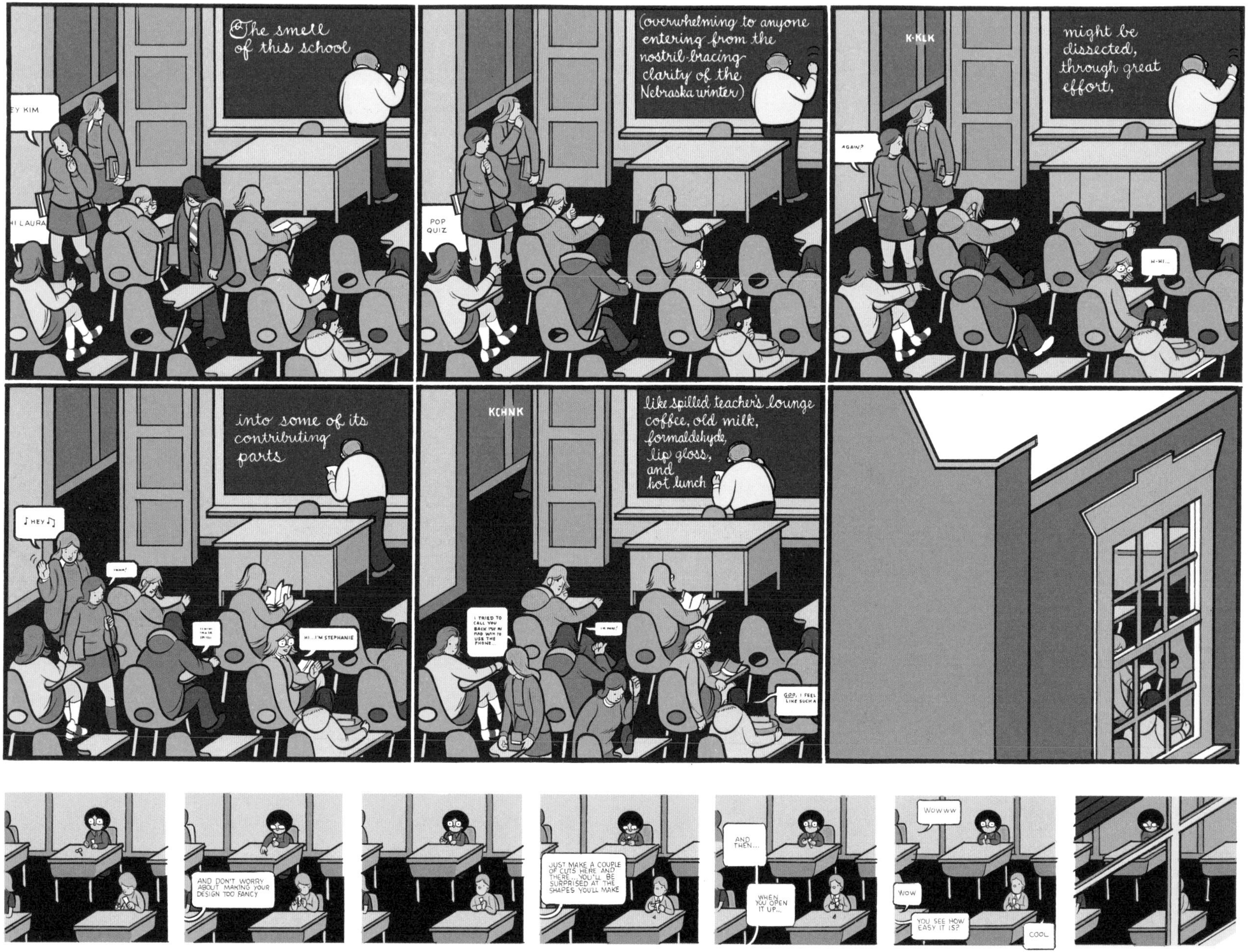
The smell of this school
EY KIM
HI LAURA
(overwhelming to anyone entering from the nostril-bracing clarity of the Nebraska winter)
POP QUIZ
K-KLK
might be dissected, through great effort,
AGAIN?
H-HI...
into some of its contributing parts
♪ HEY ♪
HI...I'M STEPHANIE
KCHNK
like spilled teacher's lounge coffee, old milk, formaldehyde, lip gloss, and hot lunch
I TRIED TO CALL YOU BACK
GOD, I FEEL LIKE SUCH A
AND DON'T WORRY ABOUT MAKING YOUR DESIGN TOO FANCY
JUST MAKE A COUPLE OF CUTS HERE AND THERE... YOU'LL BE SURPRISED AT THE SHAPES YOU'LL MAKE
AND THEN...
WHEN YOU OPEN IT UP...
WOWWW
WOW
YOU SEE HOW EASY IT IS?
COOL

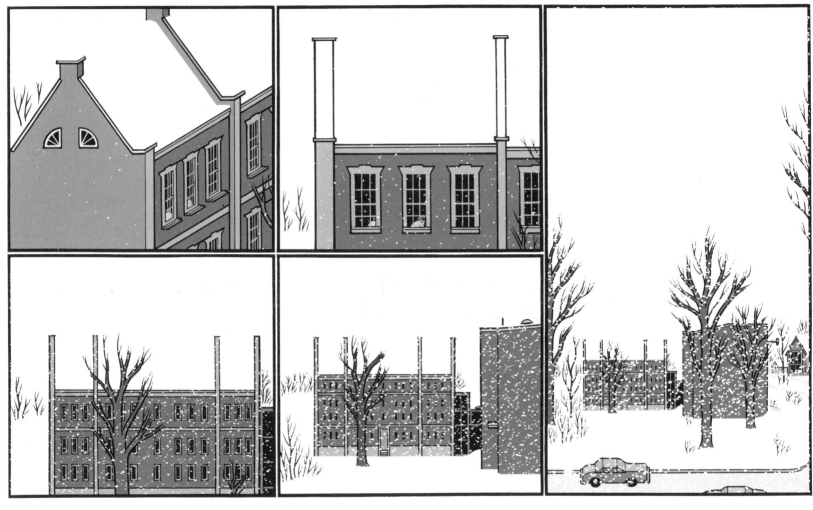

 But pinpointing the precise origin of any one of these components

 would eventually prove only about as useful

 as the successful extraction

 of the internal organs of a live frog, pinned into paraffin

 gasping

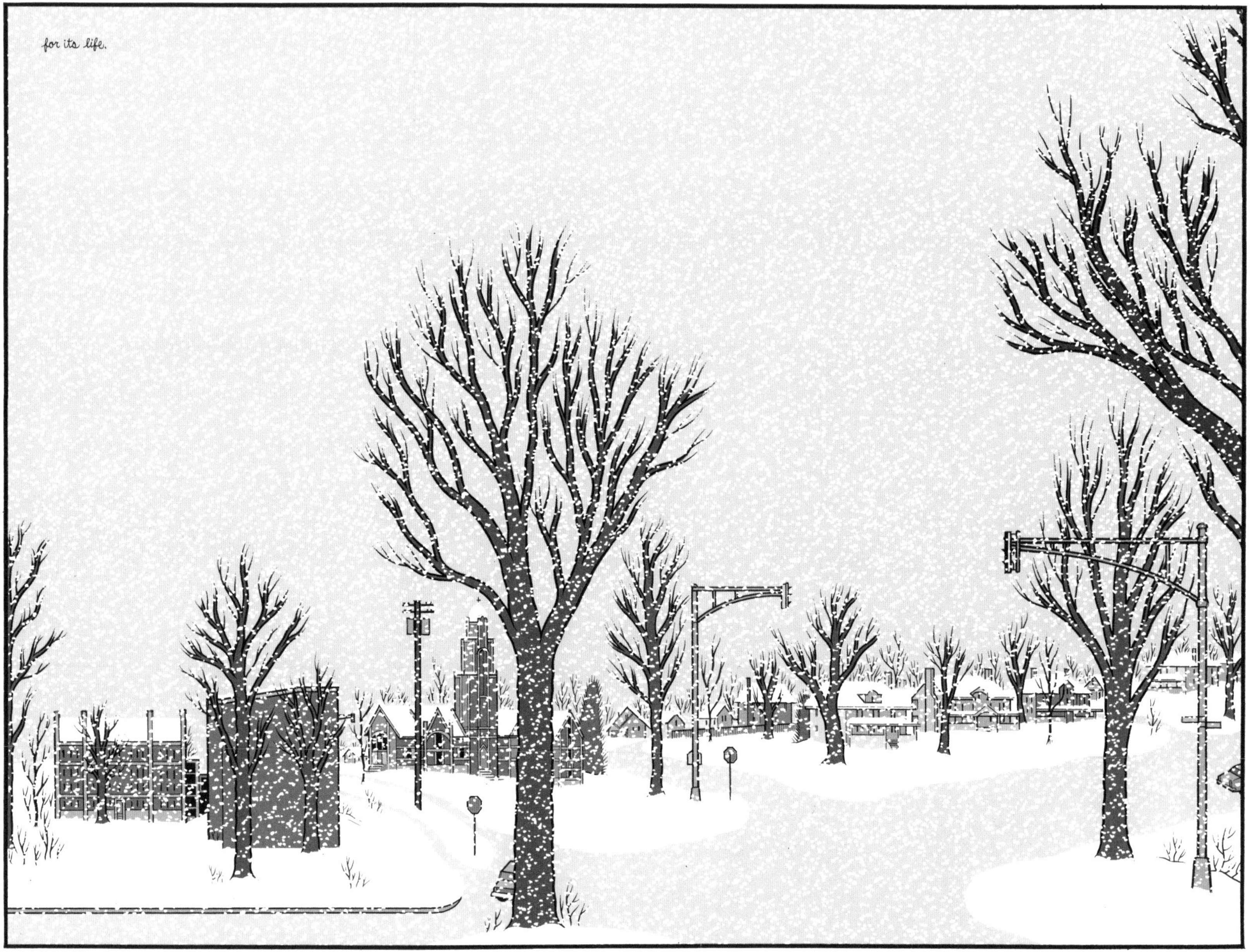
for its life.

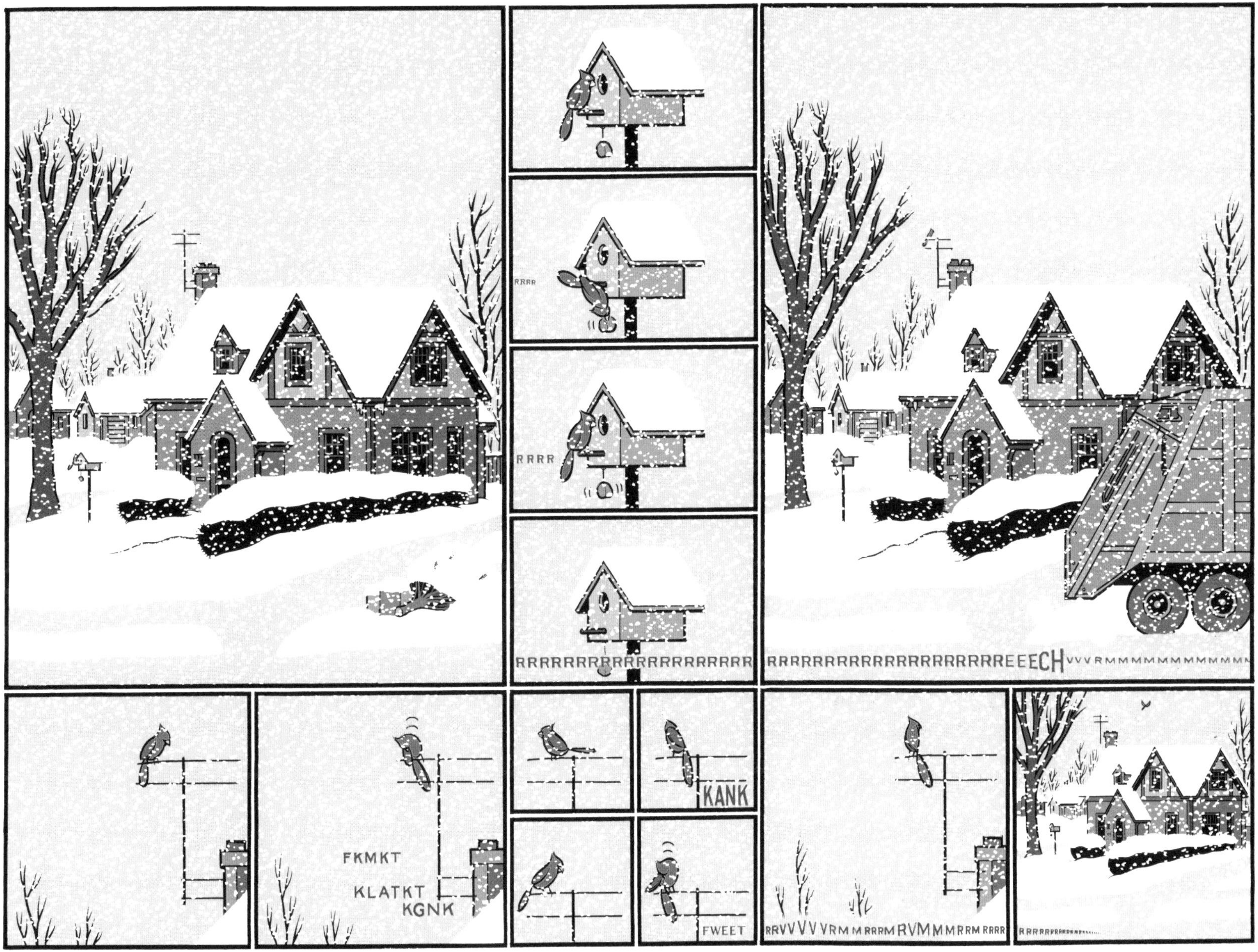

RRRR
RRRR
RRRRRRRRRRRRRRRRRRRRR
RRRRRRRRRRRRRRRRRRRRRRRRREEECH VVV RMMMMMMMMMMMMM
FKMKT
KLATKT
KGNK
KANK
FWEET
RRVVVVV VRM M RRRM RVMMMRRM RRRR
RRRRRRRRRRRRRRRR......

RUSTY BROWN

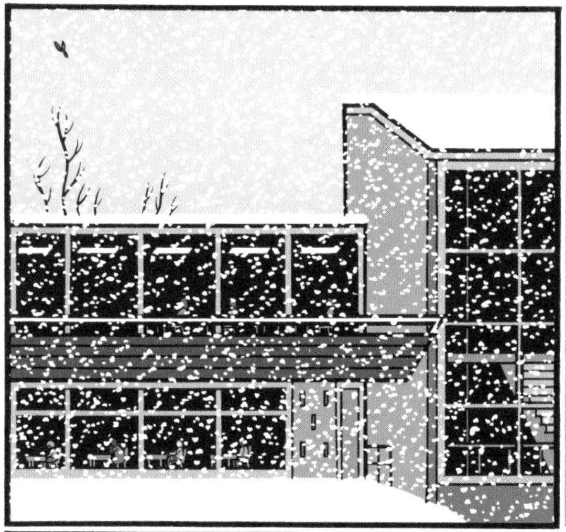

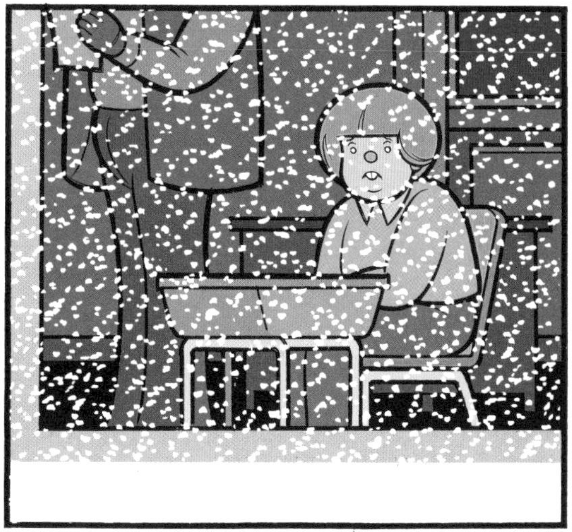

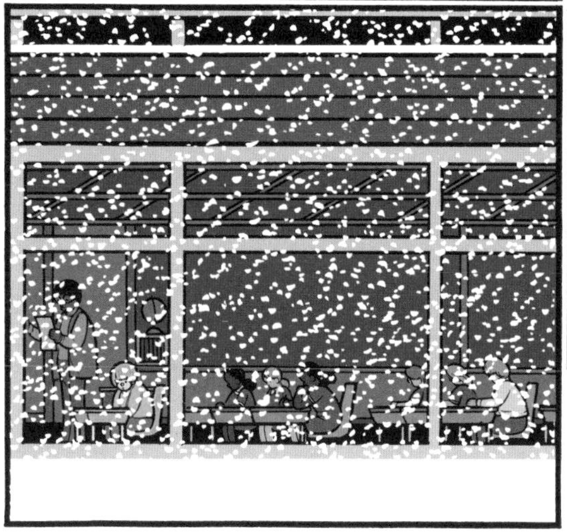

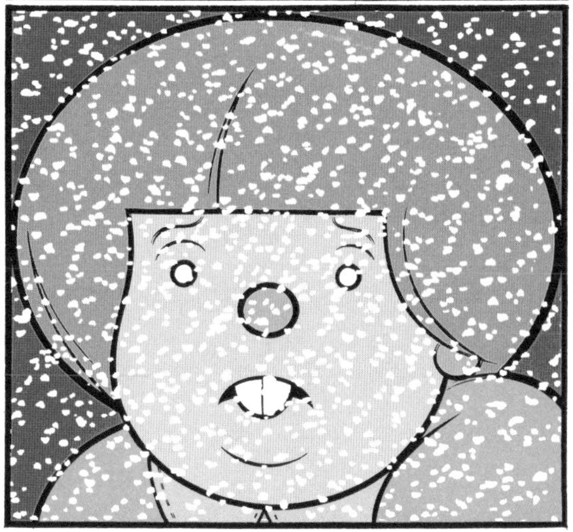

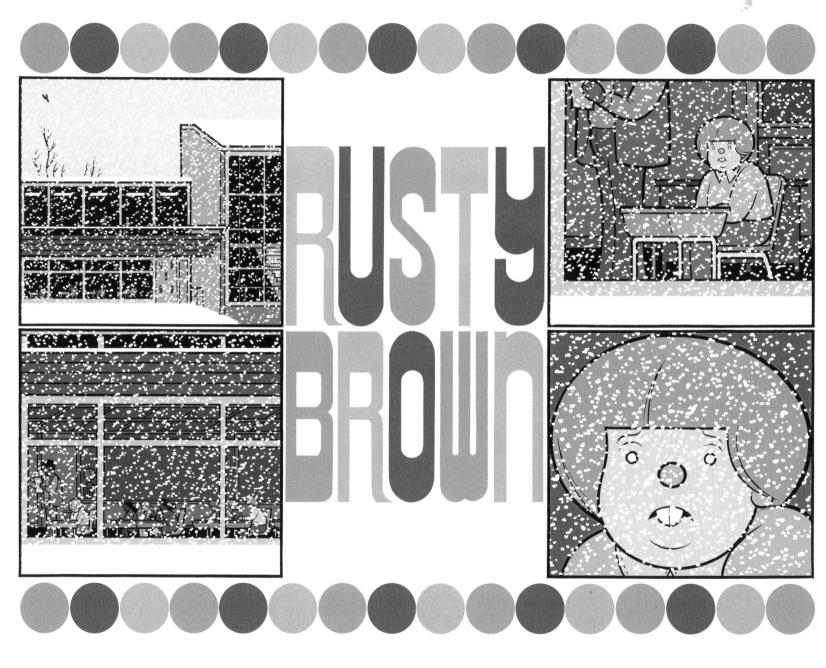

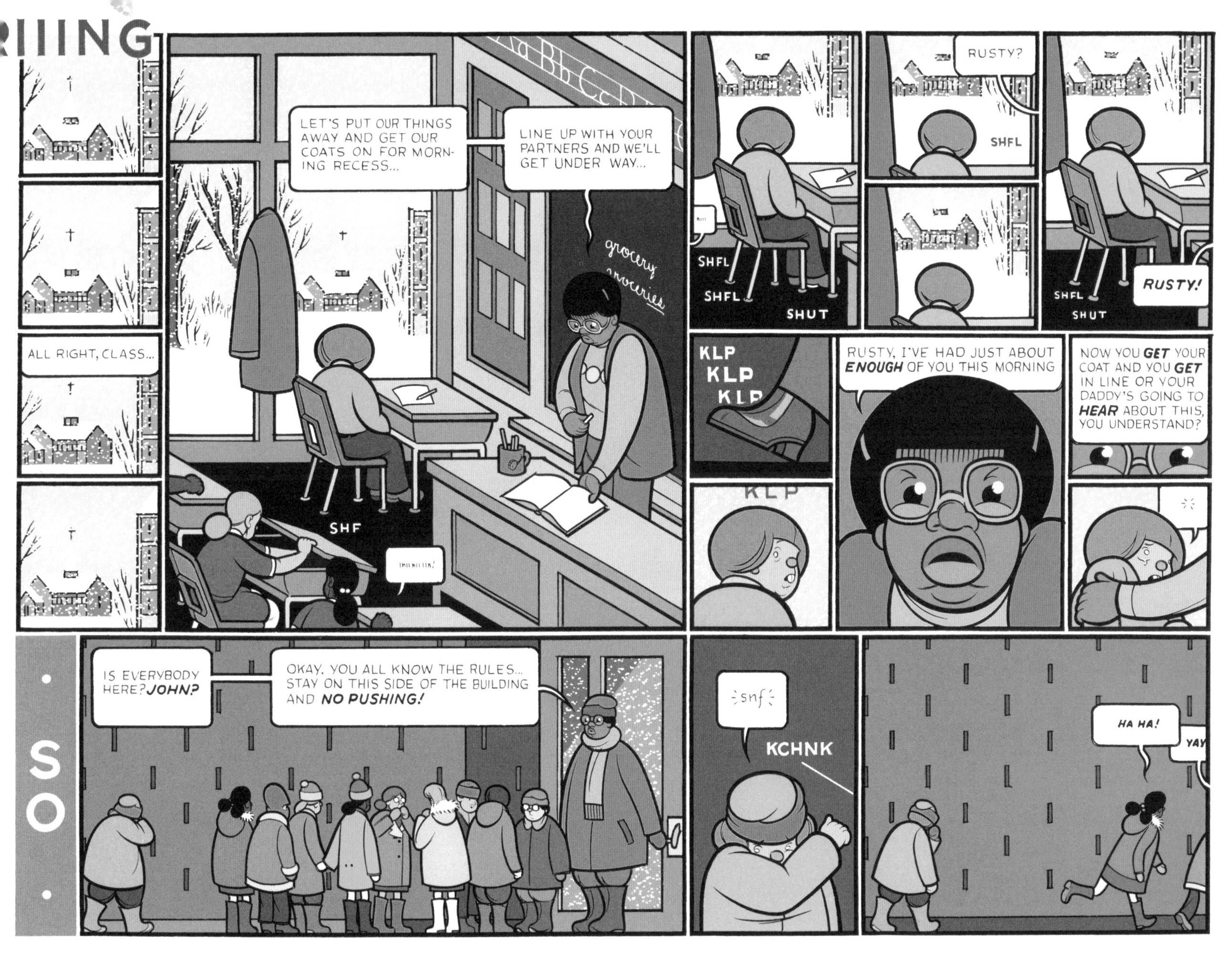

RIIING
ALL RIGHT, CLASS...
LET'S PUT OUR THINGS AWAY AND GET OUR COATS ON FOR MORNING RECESS...
LINE UP WITH YOUR PARTNERS AND WE'LL GET UNDER WAY...
grocery groceries
SHF
SHFL
SHFL
SHUT
RUSTY?
SHFL
SHFL
SHUT
RUSTY!
KLP
KLP
KLP
RUSTY, I'VE HAD JUST ABOUT ENOUGH OF YOU THIS MORNING
NOW YOU GET YOUR COAT AND YOU GET IN LINE OR YOUR DADDY'S GOING TO HEAR ABOUT THIS, YOU UNDERSTAND?
KLP
SO
IS EVERYBODY HERE? JOHN?
OKAY, YOU ALL KNOW THE RULES... STAY ON THIS SIDE OF THE BUILDING AND NO PUSHING!
snf
KCHNK
HA HA!
YAY

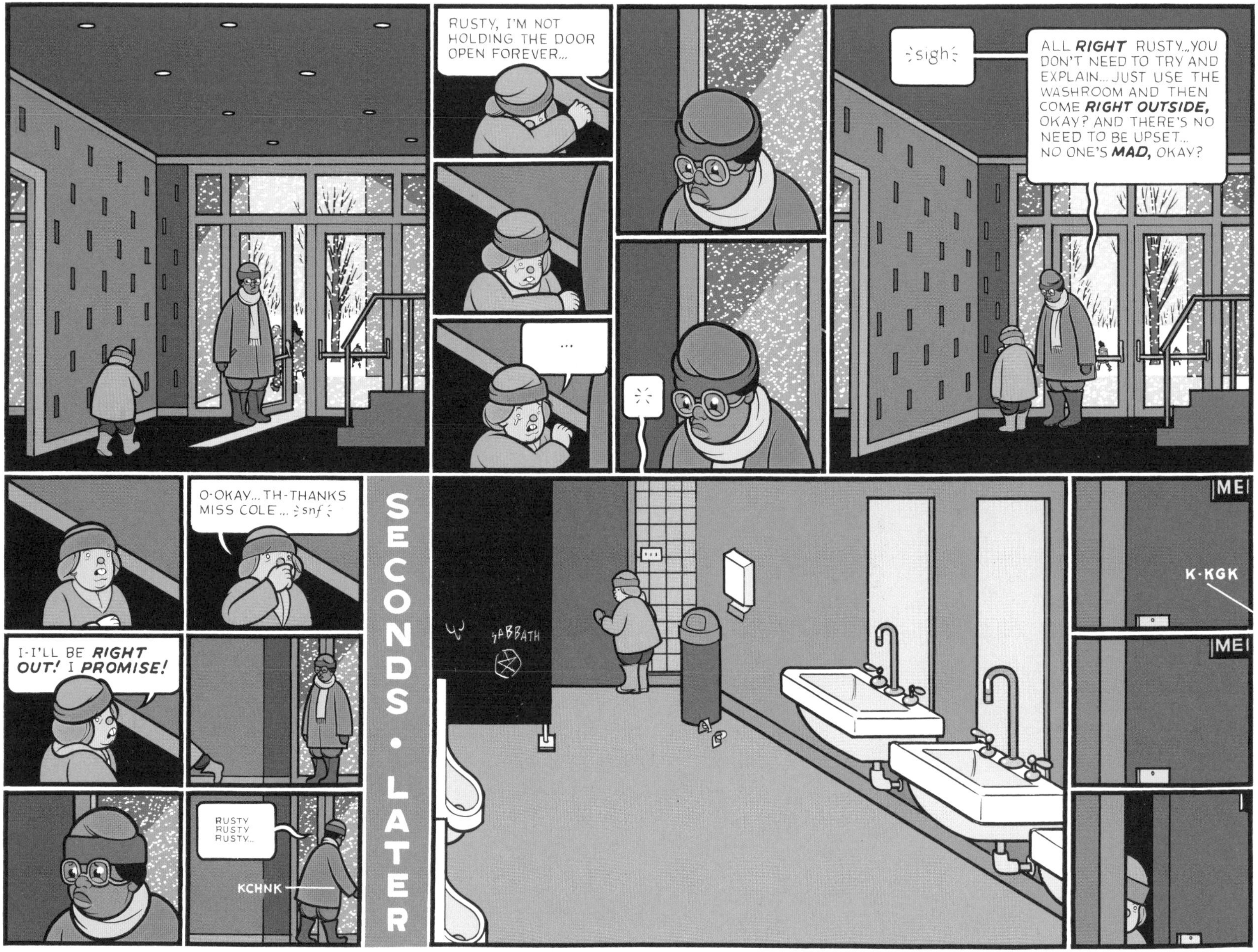
RUSTY, I'M NOT HOLDING THE DOOR OPEN FOREVER...
...
sigh
ALL RIGHT RUSTY... YOU DON'T NEED TO TRY AND EXPLAIN... JUST USE THE WASHROOM AND THEN COME RIGHT OUTSIDE, OKAY? AND THERE'S NO NEED TO BE UPSET... NO ONE'S MAD, OKAY?
O-OKAY... TH-THANKS MISS COLE... snf
I-I'LL BE RIGHT OUT! I PROMISE!
RUSTY RUSTY RUSTY...
KCHNK
SECONDS • LATER
SABBATH
K-KGK
MEI
MEI

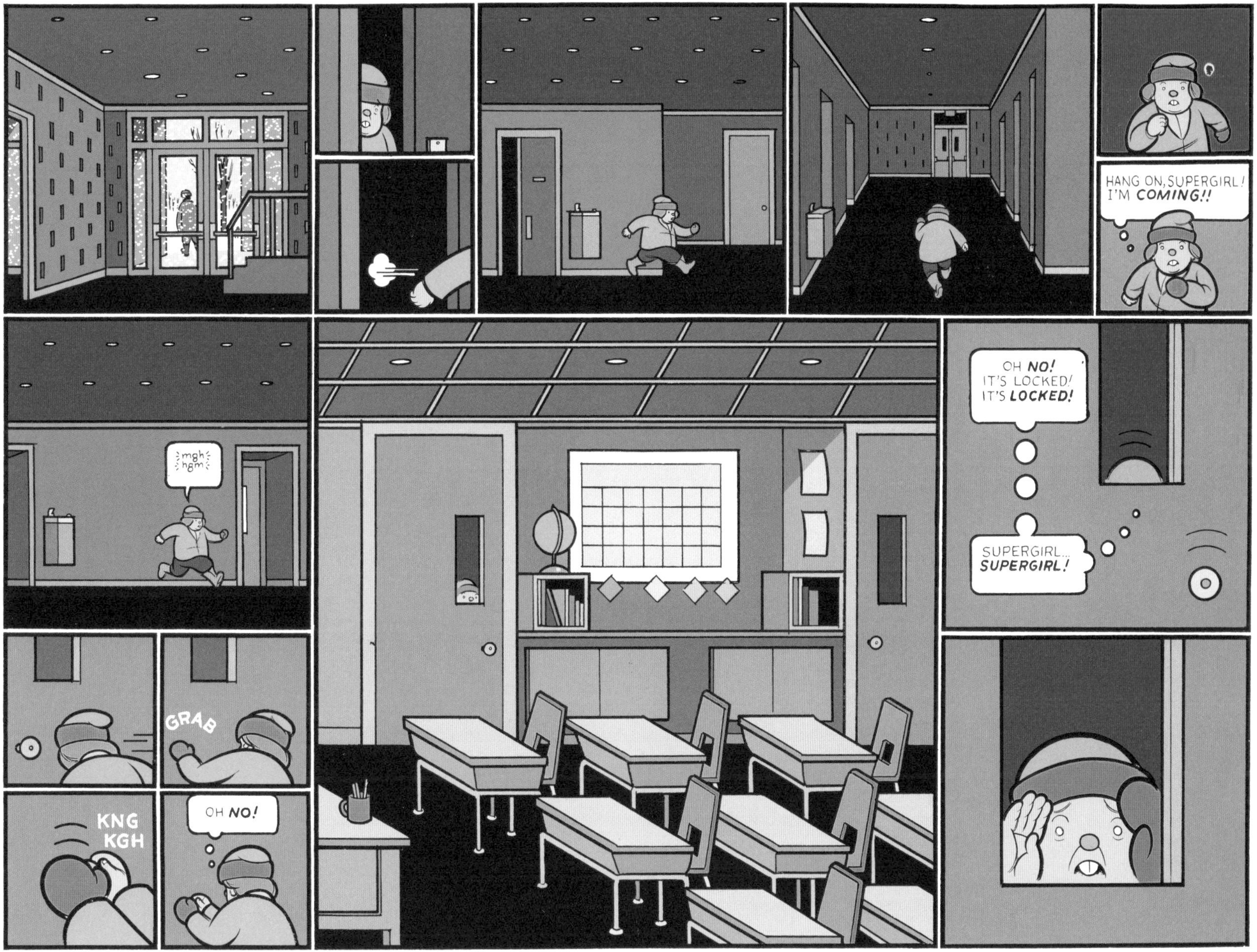
HANG ON, SUPERGIRL! I'M COMING!!
mgh hgm
GRAB
KNG KGH
OH NO!
OH NO! IT'S LOCKED! IT'S LOCKED!
SUPERGIRL... SUPERGIRL!

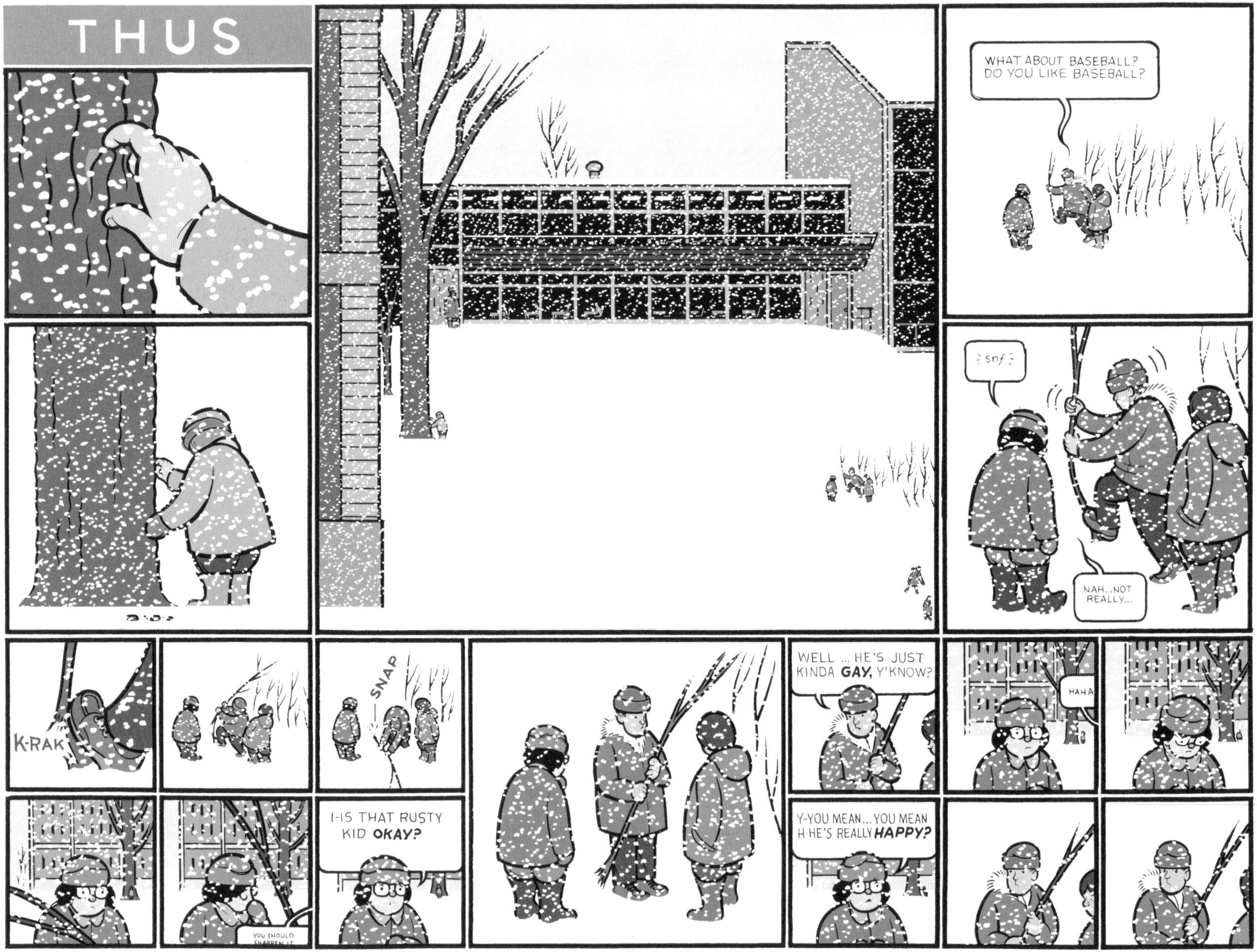
THUS
WHAT ABOUT BASEBALL? DO YOU LIKE BASEBALL?
snf
NAH...NOT REALLY...
K-RAK
SNAP
WELL ... HE'S JUST KINDA **GAY,** Y'KNOW?
HAHA
I-IS THAT RUSTY KID **OKAY?**
Y-YOU MEAN... YOU MEAN H-HE'S REALLY ***HAPPY?***
YOU SHOULD

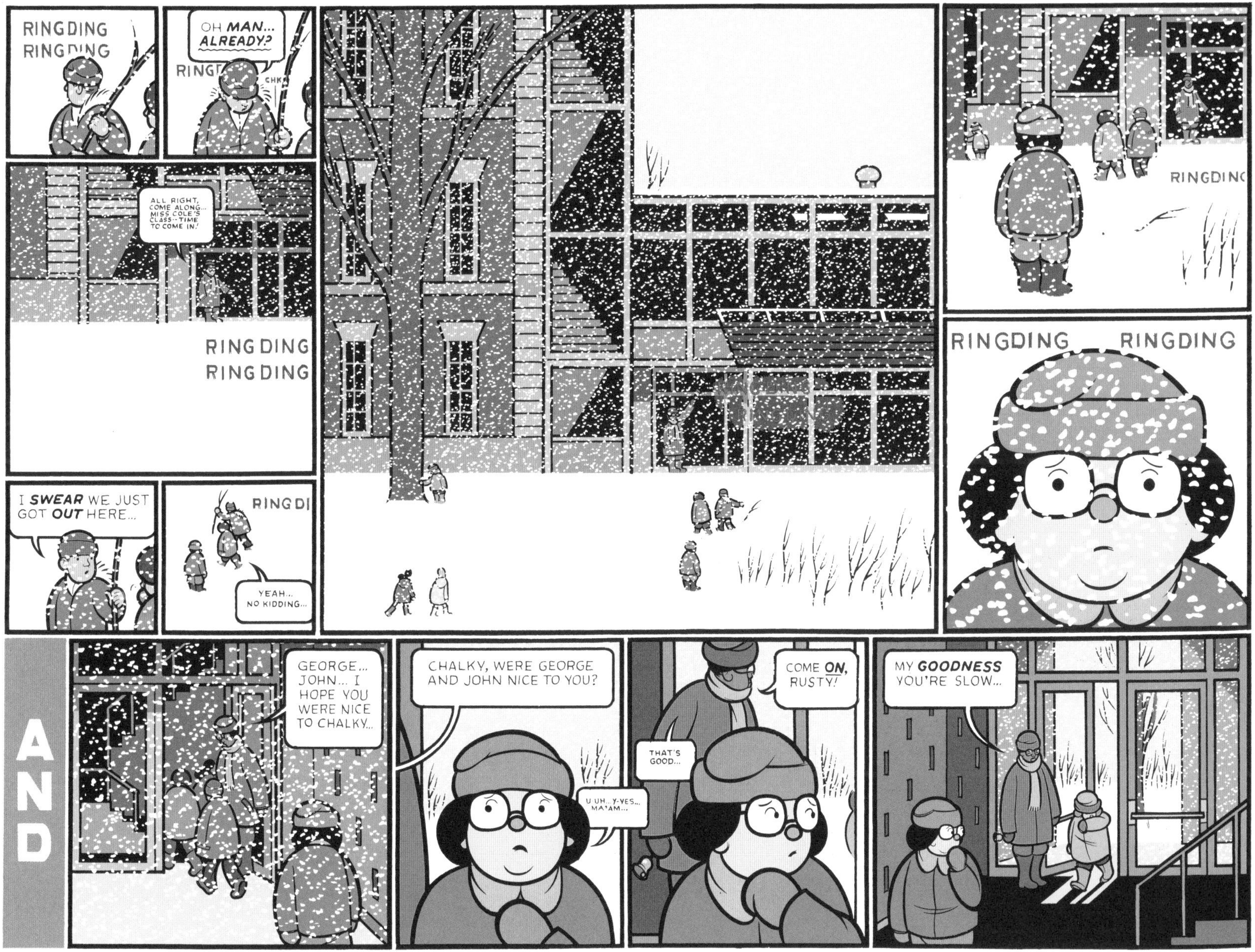

RINGDING
RINGDING
OH MAN... ALREADY?
RING
CHK
ALL RIGHT, COME ALONG... MISS COLE'S CLASS--TIME TO COME IN!
RINGDING
RINGDING
I SWEAR WE JUST GOT OUT HERE...
RINGDI
YEAH... NO KIDDING...
RINGDING
RINGDING
RINGDING
AND
GEORGE... JOHN... I HOPE YOU WERE NICE TO CHALKY...
CHALKY, WERE GEORGE AND JOHN NICE TO YOU?
U-UH...Y-YES... MA'AM...
THAT'S GOOD...
COME ON, RUSTY!
MY GOODNESS YOU'RE SLOW...

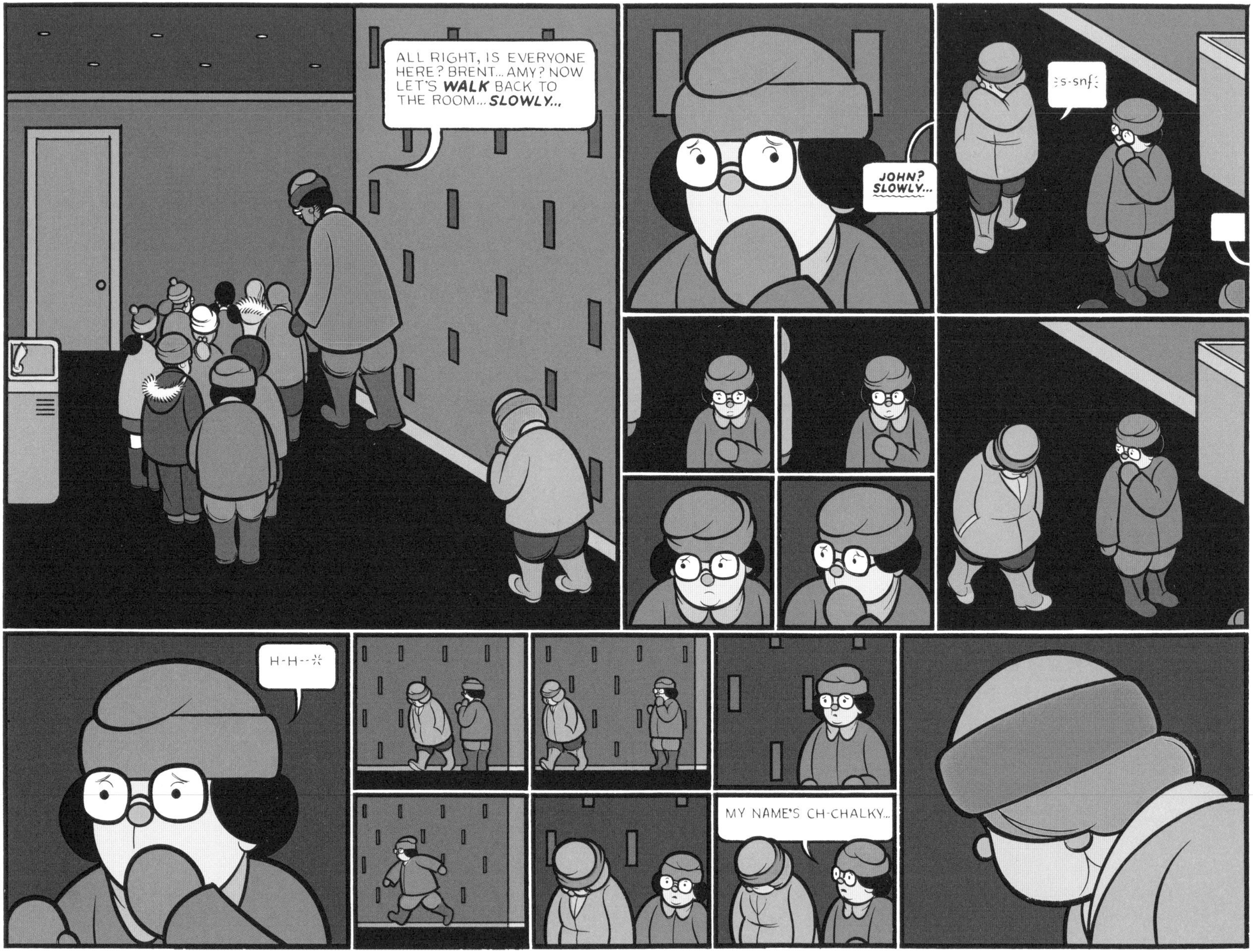
ALL RIGHT, IS EVERYONE HERE? BRENT... AMY? NOW LET'S **WALK** BACK TO THE ROOM... **SLOWLY...**
JOHN? SLOWLY...
s-snf
H-H--
MY NAME'S CH-CHALKY...

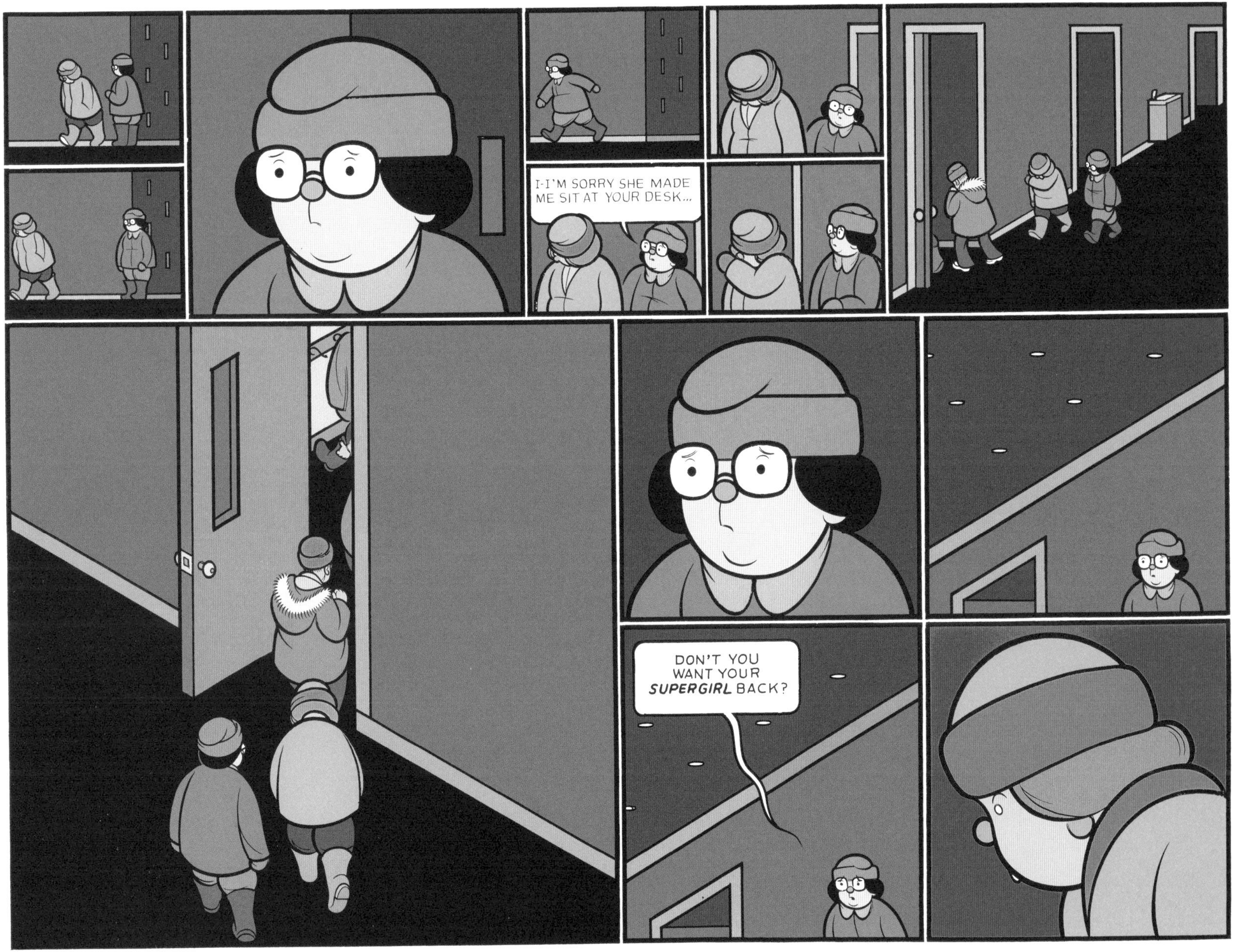
I-I'M SORRY SHE MADE ME SIT AT YOUR DESK...
DON'T YOU WANT YOUR *SUPERGIRL* BACK?

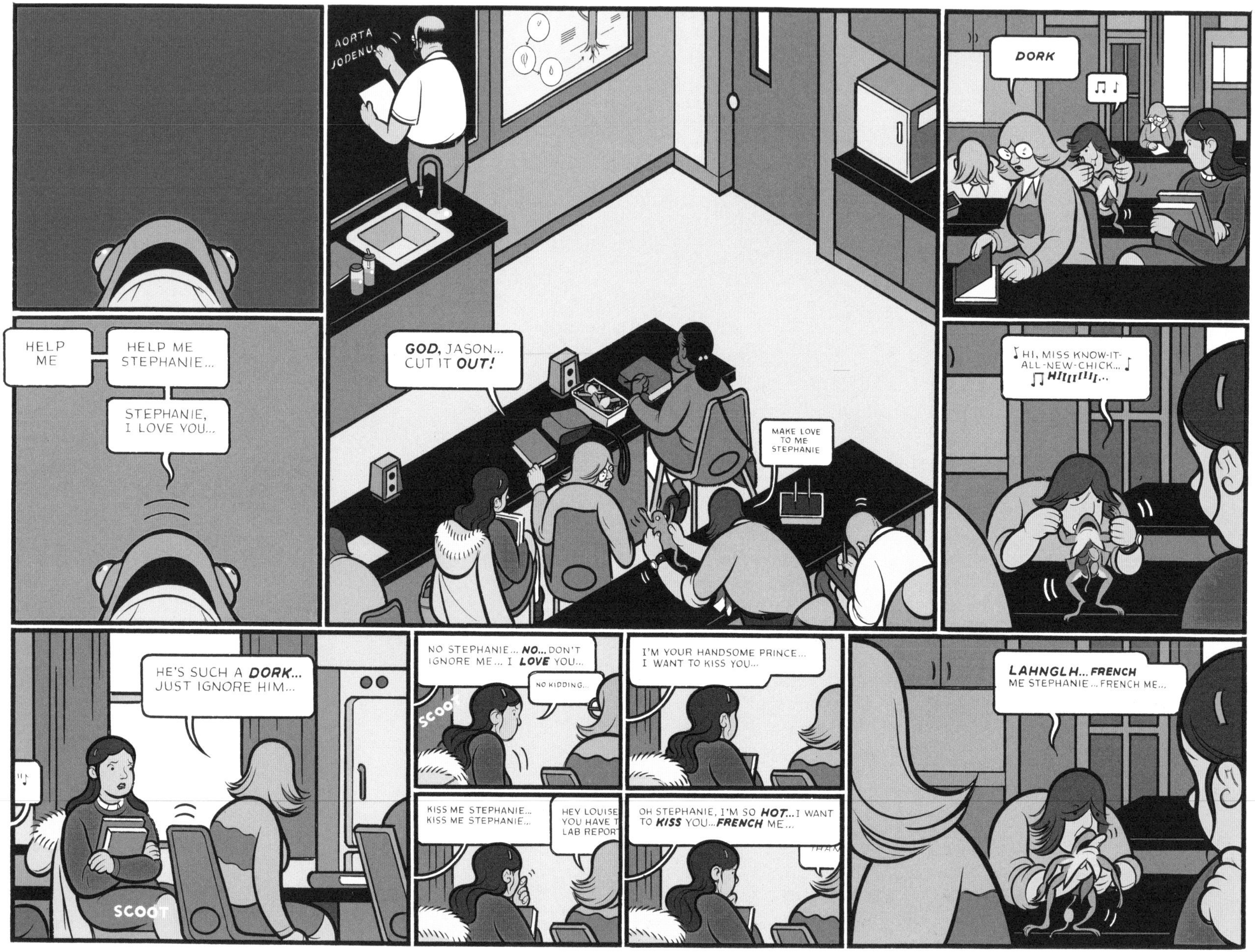

HELP ME
HELP ME STEPHANIE...
STEPHANIE, I LOVE YOU...
AORTA
JODENU
GOD, JASON... CUT IT OUT!
MAKE LOVE TO ME STEPHANIE
DORK
♪ HI, MISS KNOW-IT-ALL-NEW-CHICK... ♪ ♫ HIIIIIII...
HE'S SUCH A DORK... JUST IGNORE HIM...
SCOOT
NO STEPHANIE... NO... DON'T IGNORE ME... I LOVE YOU...
NO KIDDING...
SCOOT
I'M YOUR HANDSOME PRINCE... I WANT TO KISS YOU...
KISS ME STEPHANIE... KISS ME STEPHANIE...
HEY LOUISE YOU HAVE T LAB REPORT
OH STEPHANIE, I'M SO HOT... I WANT TO KISS YOU... FRENCH ME...
LAHNGLH... FRENCH ME STEPHANIE... FRENCH ME...

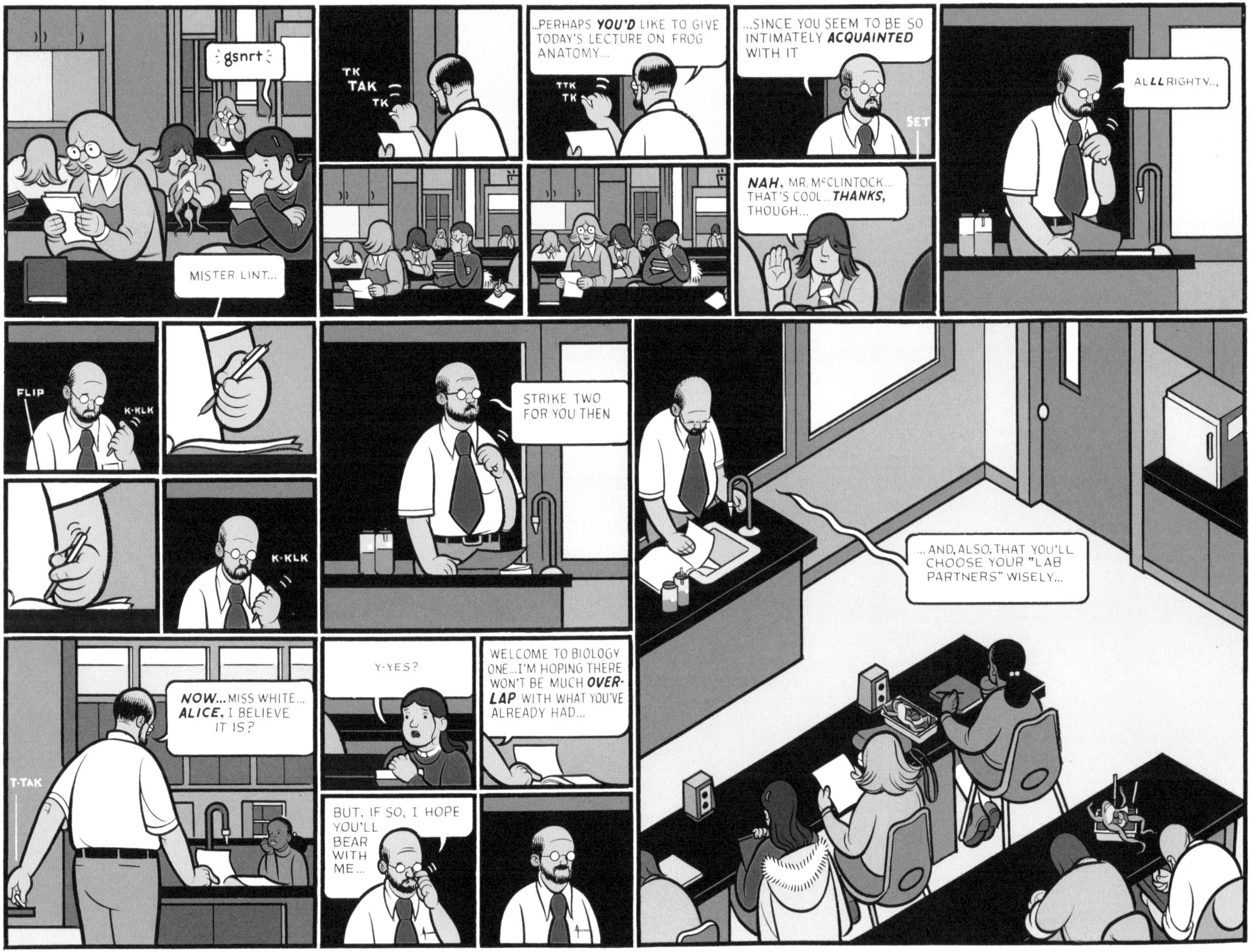
gsnrt
MISTER LINT...
TK
TAK
TK
...PERHAPS YOU'D LIKE TO GIVE TODAY'S LECTURE ON FROG ANATOMY...
TTK
TK
...SINCE YOU SEEM TO BE SO INTIMATELY ACQUAINTED WITH IT
SET
NAH, MR. McCLINTOCK... THAT'S COOL... THANKS, THOUGH...
ALLLRIGHTY...,
FLIP
K-KLK
K-KLK
STRIKE TWO FOR YOU THEN
...AND, ALSO, THAT YOU'LL CHOOSE YOUR "LAB PARTNERS" WISELY...
T-TAK
NOW... MISS WHITE... ALICE, I BELIEVE IT IS?
Y-YES?
WELCOME TO BIOLOGY ONE... I'M HOPING THERE WON'T BE MUCH OVER-LAP WITH WHAT YOU'VE ALREADY HAD...
BUT, IF SO, I HOPE YOU'LL BEAR WITH ME...

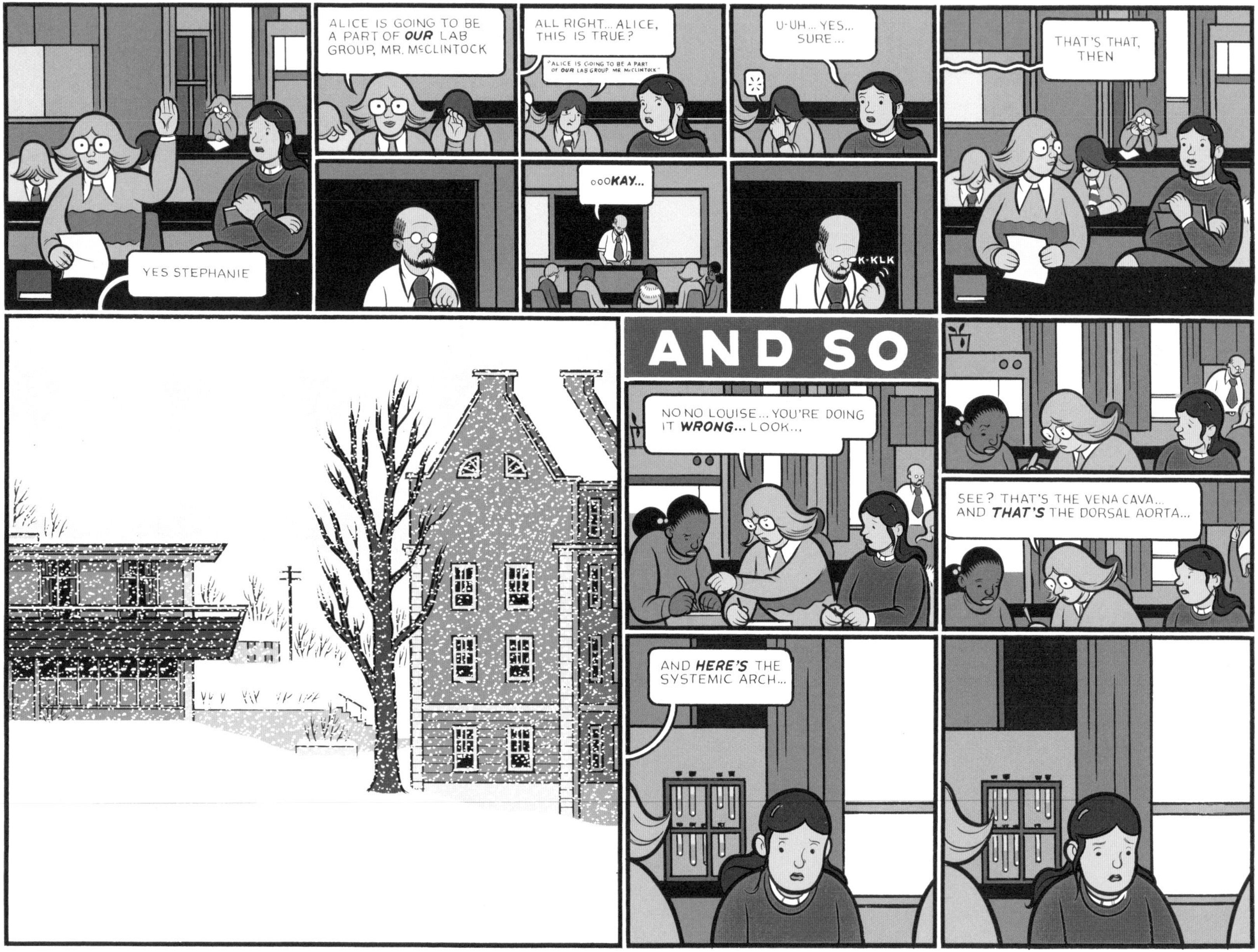

YES STEPHANIE
ALICE IS GOING TO BE A PART OF OUR LAB GROUP, MR. McCLINTOCK
ALL RIGHT... ALICE, THIS IS TRUE?
"ALICE IS GOING TO BE A PART OF OUR LAB GROUP, MR. McCLINTOCK"
U-UH... YES... SURE...
OOOKAY...
K-KLK
THAT'S THAT, THEN
AND SO
NO NO LOUISE... YOU'RE DOING IT WRONG... LOOK...
SEE? THAT'S THE VENA CAVA... AND THAT'S THE DORSAL AORTA...
AND HERE'S THE SYSTEMIC ARCH...

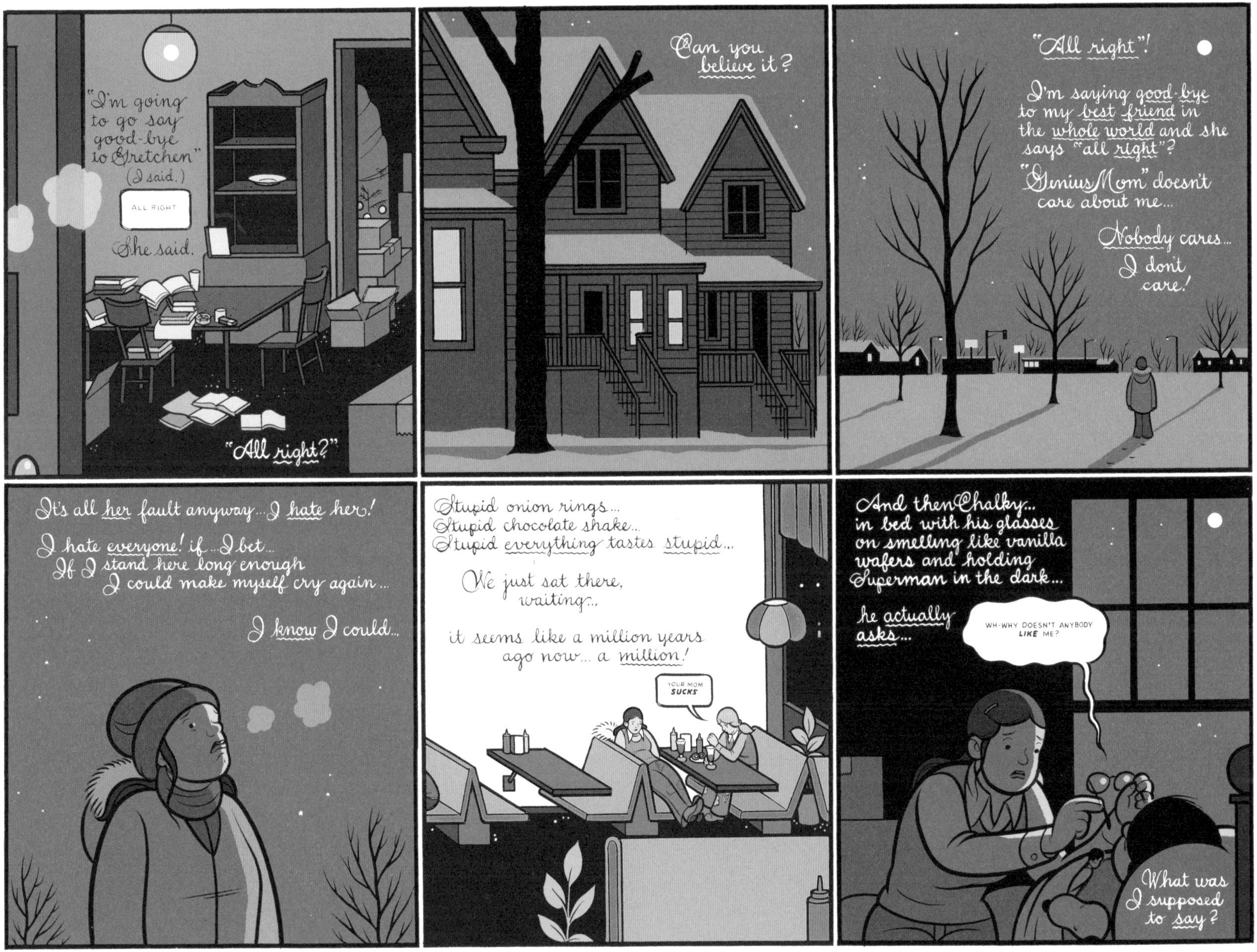
"I'm going to go say good-bye to Gretchen" (I said.)
ALL RIGHT
She said.
"All right?"
Can you believe it?
"All right"!
I'm saying good-bye to my best friend in the whole world and she says "all right"?
"Genius Mom" doesn't care about me...
Nobody cares...
I don't care!
It's all her fault anyway... I hate her!
I hate everyone! if... I bet... If I stand here long enough I could make myself cry again...
I know I could...
Stupid onion rings... Stupid chocolate shake... Stupid everything tastes stupid...
We just sat there, waiting...
it seems like a million years ago now... a million!
YOUR MOM SUCKS
And then Chalky... in bed with his glasses on smelling like vanilla wafers and holding Superman in the dark...
he actually asks...
WH-WHY DOESN'T ANYBODY LIKE ME?
What was I supposed to say?

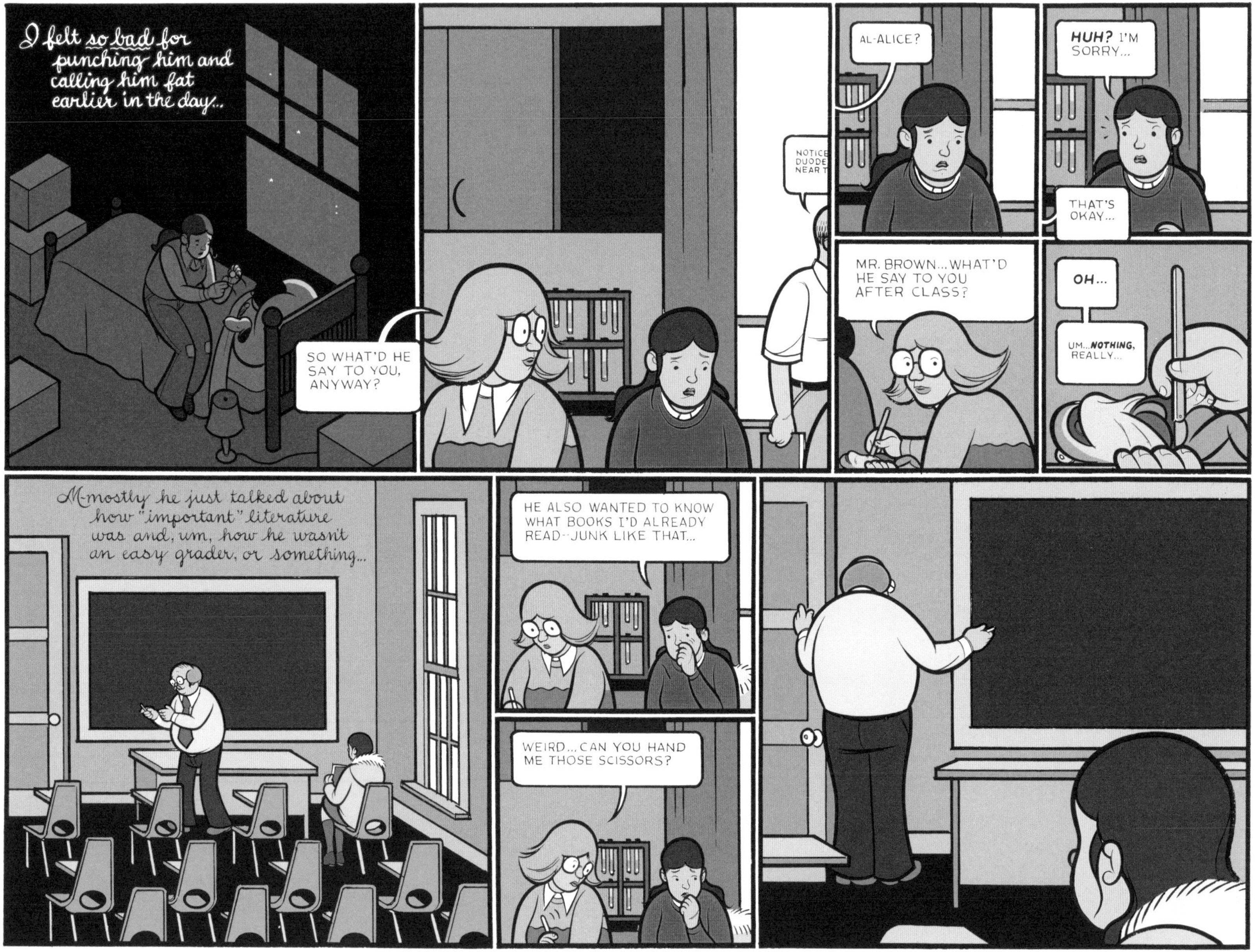

I felt so bad for punching him and calling him fat earlier in the day...
SO WHAT'D HE SAY TO YOU, ANYWAY?
NOTICE DUODE NEAR T
AL-ALICE?
HUH? I'M SORRY...
THAT'S OKAY...
MR. BROWN... WHAT'D HE SAY TO YOU AFTER CLASS?
OH...
UM... NOTHING, REALLY...
M-mostly he just talked about how "important" literature was and, um, how he wasn't an easy grader, or something...
HE ALSO WANTED TO KNOW WHAT BOOKS I'D ALREADY READ--JUNK LIKE THAT...
WEIRD... CAN YOU HAND ME THOSE SCISSORS?

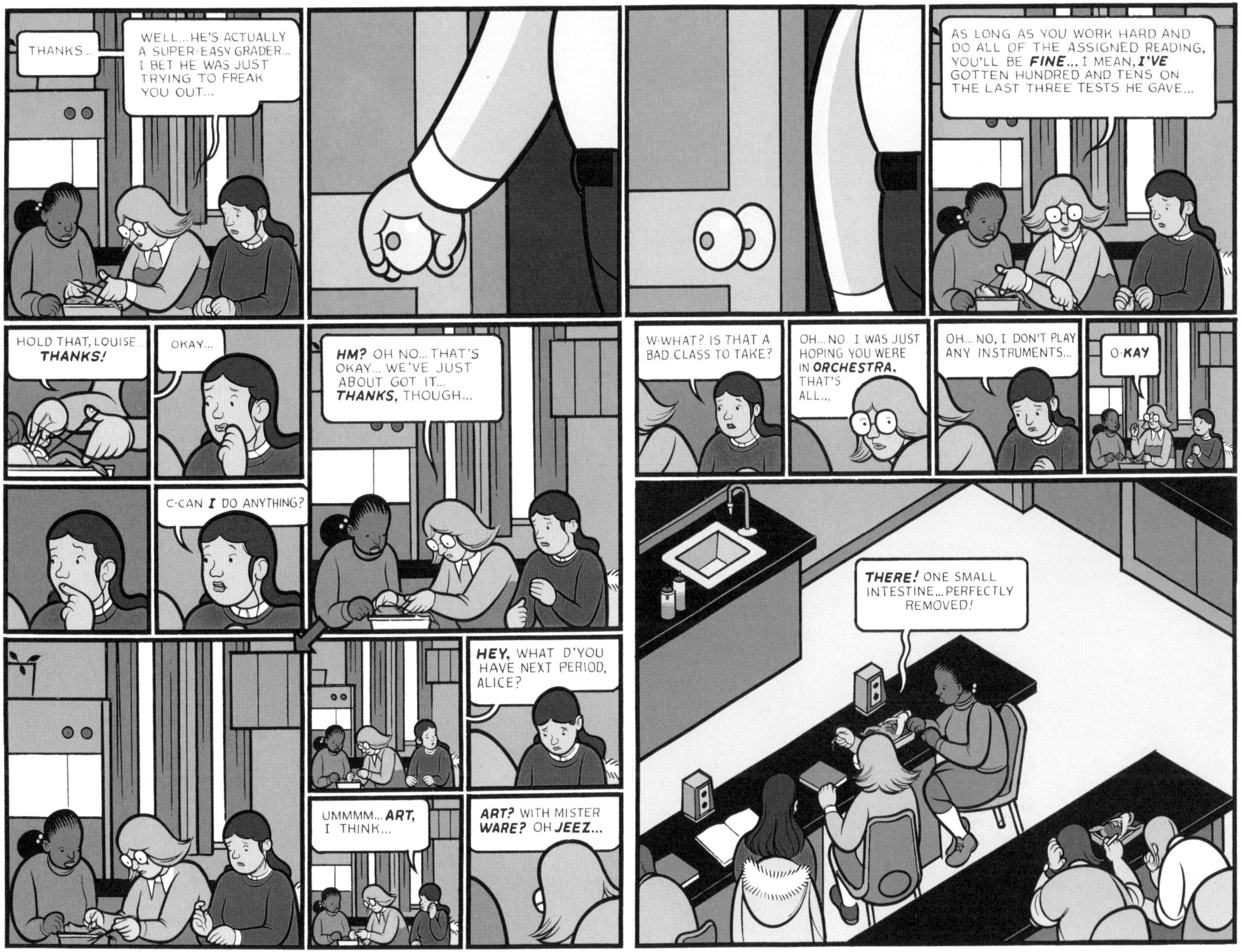
THANKS...
WELL... HE'S ACTUALLY A SUPER-EASY GRADER... I BET HE WAS JUST TRYING TO FREAK YOU OUT...
AS LONG AS YOU WORK HARD AND DO ALL OF THE ASSIGNED READING, YOU'LL BE **FINE...** I MEAN, ***I'VE*** GOTTEN HUNDRED AND TENS ON THE LAST THREE TESTS HE GAVE...
HOLD THAT, LOUISE... **THANKS!**
OKAY...
C-CAN ***I*** DO ANYTHING?
HM? OH NO... THAT'S OKAY... WE'VE JUST ABOUT GOT IT... **THANKS,** THOUGH...
HEY, WHAT D'YOU HAVE NEXT PERIOD, ALICE?
UMMMM... ***ART,*** I THINK...
ART? WITH MISTER ***WARE?*** OH ***JEEZ...***
W-WHAT? IS THAT A BAD CLASS TO TAKE?
OH... NO... I WAS JUST HOPING YOU WERE IN ***ORCHESTRA,*** THAT'S ALL...
OH... NO, I DON'T PLAY ANY INSTRUMENTS...
O-***KAY***
THERE! ONE SMALL INTESTINE... PERFECTLY REMOVED!

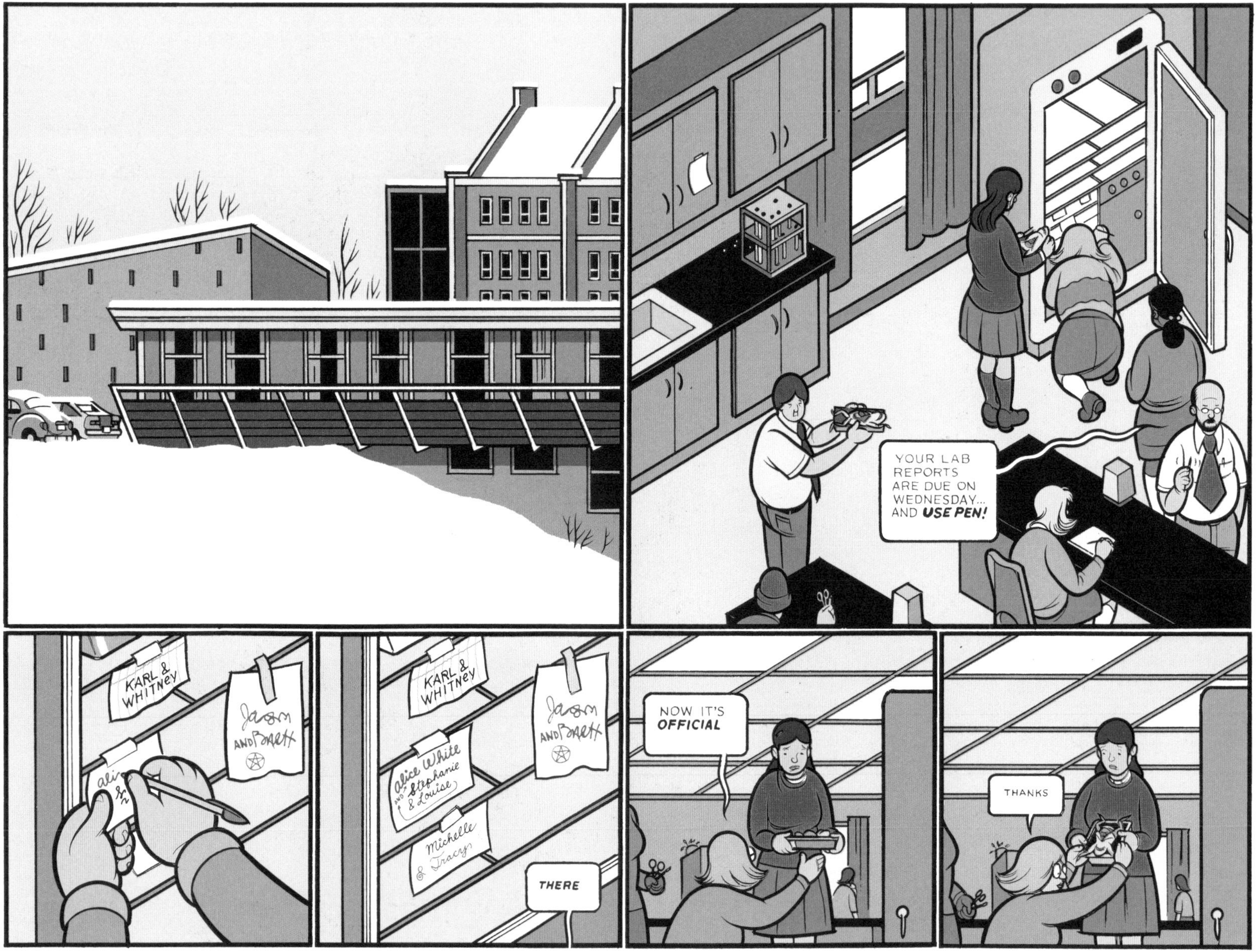

YOUR LAB REPORTS ARE DUE ON WEDNESDAY... AND **USE PEN!**
KARL & WHITNEY
Jason AND Brett
alice White and Stephanie & Louise
Michelle & Tracy
THERE
NOW IT'S **OFFICIAL**
THANKS

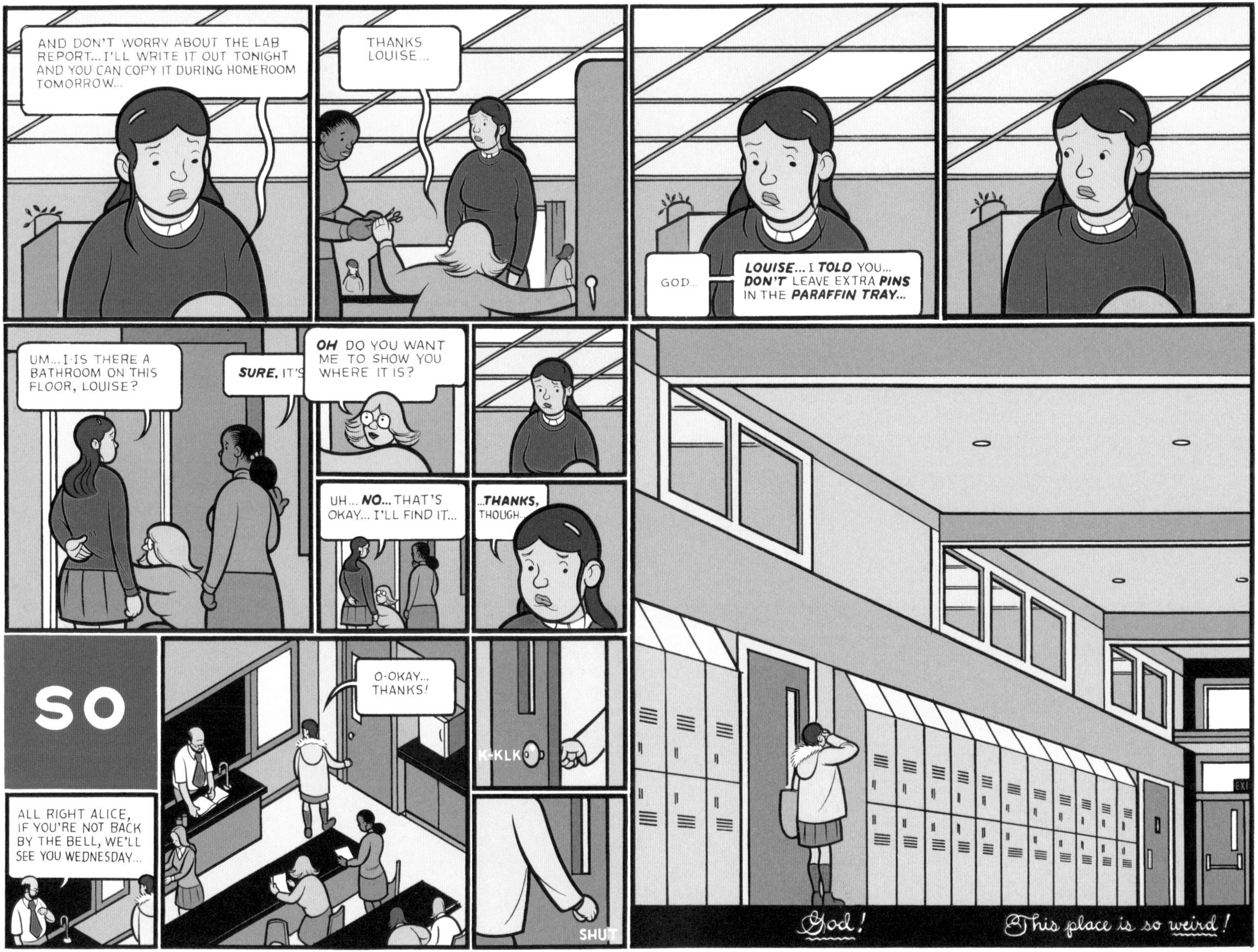
AND DON'T WORRY ABOUT THE LAB REPORT... I'LL WRITE IT OUT TONIGHT AND YOU CAN COPY IT DURING HOMEROOM TOMORROW...
THANKS LOUISE...
GOD...
LOUISE... I TOLD YOU... DON'T LEAVE EXTRA PINS IN THE PARAFFIN TRAY...
UM... I-IS THERE A BATHROOM ON THIS FLOOR, LOUISE?
SURE, IT'S
OH DO YOU WANT ME TO SHOW YOU WHERE IT IS?
UH... NO... THAT'S OKAY... I'LL FIND IT...
...THANKS, THOUGH...
SO
ALL RIGHT ALICE, IF YOU'RE NOT BACK BY THE BELL, WE'LL SEE YOU WEDNESDAY...
O-OKAY... THANKS!
K-KLK
SHUT
God!
This place is so weird!

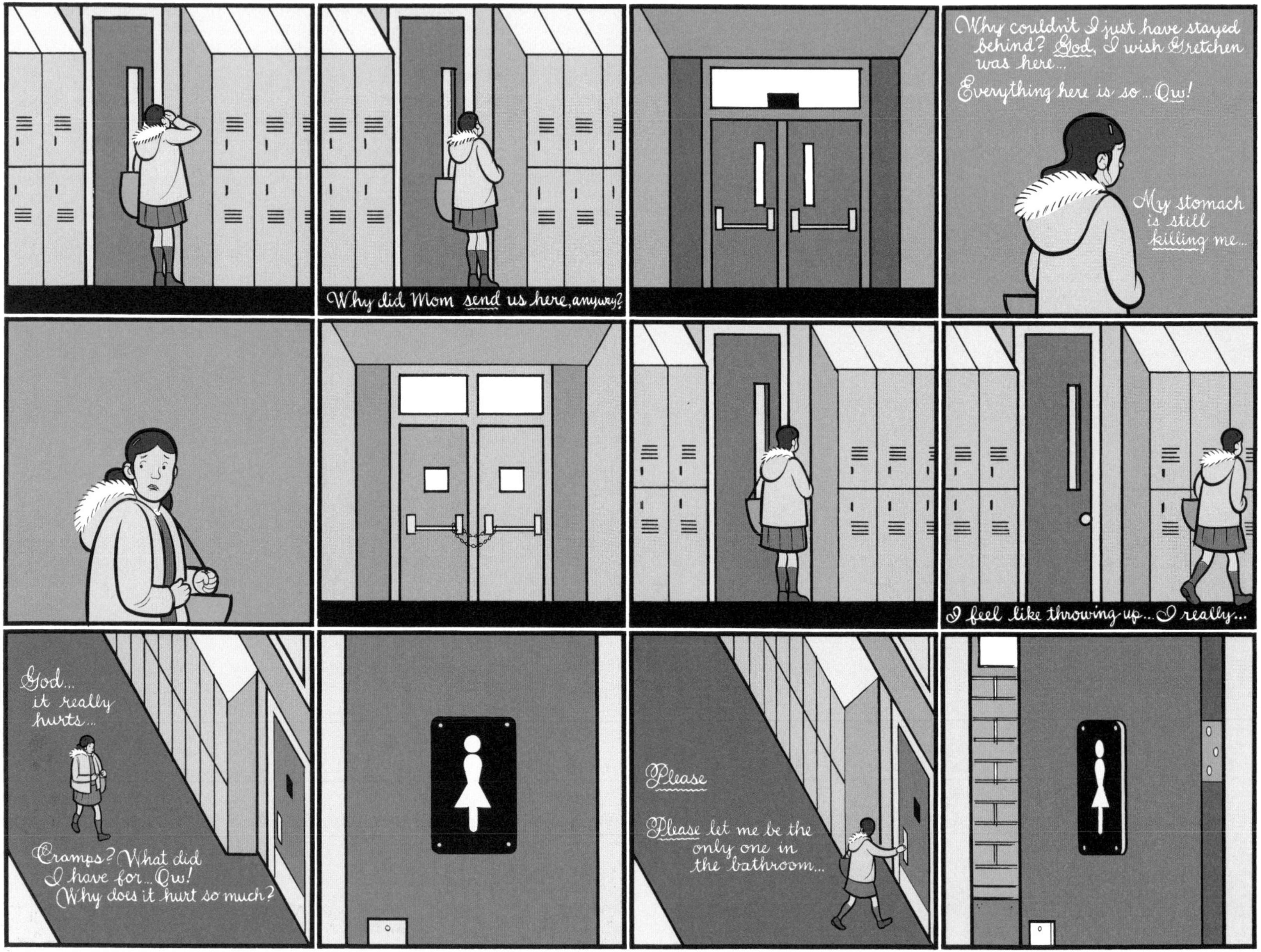
Why did Mom send us here, anyway?
Why couldn't I just have stayed behind? God, I wish Gretchen was here...
Everything here is so... Ow!
My stomach is still killing me...
I feel like throwing up... I really...
God... it really hurts...
Cramps? What did I have for... Ow! Why does it hurt so much?
Please
Please let me be the only one in the bathroom...

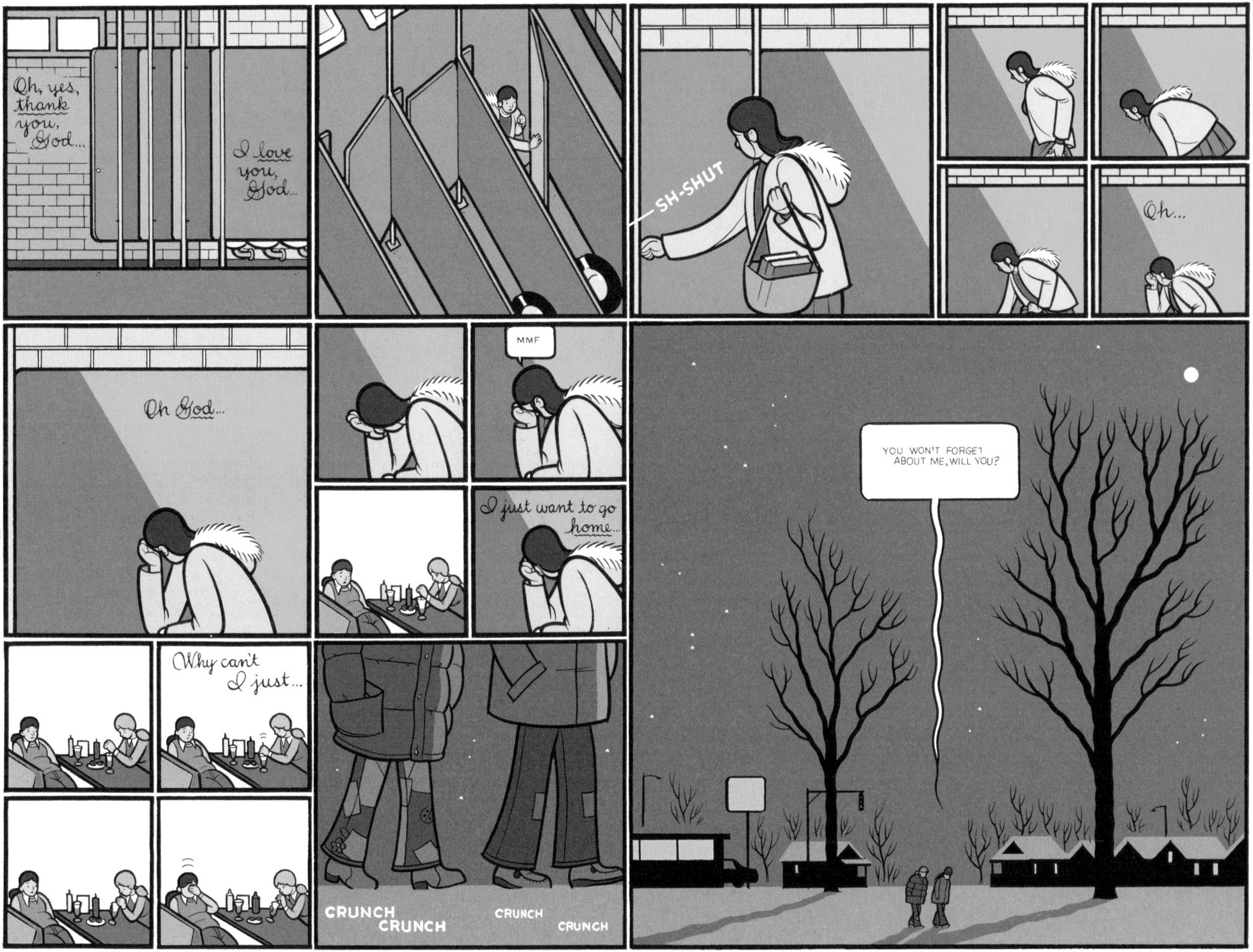
Oh, yes, thank you, God...
I love you, God...
SH-SHUT
Oh...
Oh God...
MMF
I just want to go home...
Why can't I just...
CRUNCH
CRUNCH
CRUNCH
CRUNCH
YOU WON'T FORGET ABOUT ME, WILL YOU?

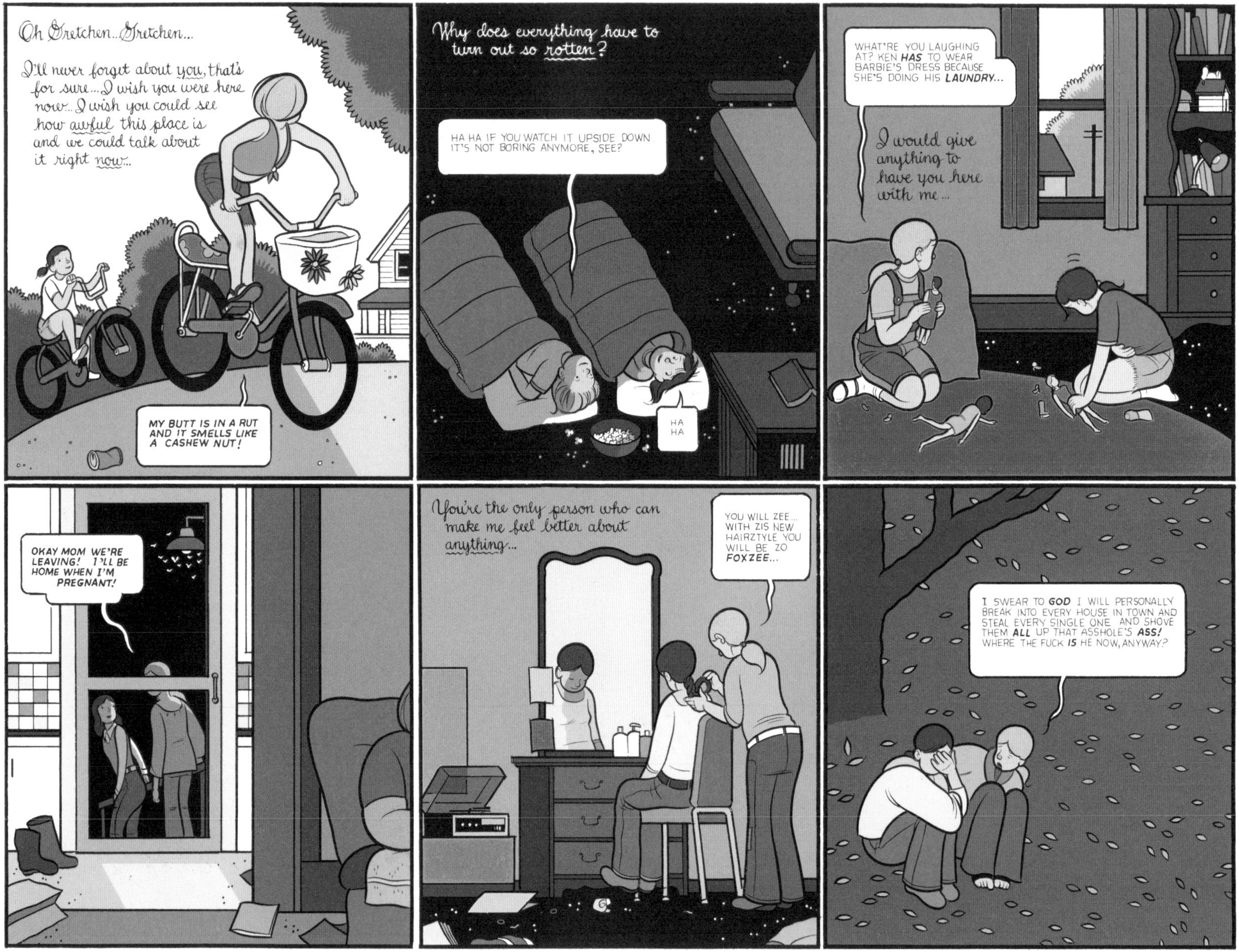
Oh Gretchen.. Gretchen...
I'll never forget about you, that's for sure... I wish you were here now.. I wish you could see how awful this place is and we could talk about it right now...
MY BUTT IS IN A RUT AND IT SMELLS LIKE A CASHEW NUT!
Why does everything have to turn out so rotten?
HA HA IF YOU WATCH IT UPSIDE DOWN IT'S NOT BORING ANYMORE, SEE?
HA HA
WHAT'RE YOU LAUGHING AT? KEN HAS TO WEAR BARBIE'S DRESS BECAUSE SHE'S DOING HIS LAUNDRY...
I would give anything to have you here with me...
OKAY MOM WE'RE LEAVING! I'LL BE HOME WHEN I'M PREGNANT!
You're the only person who can make me feel better about anything...
YOU WILL ZEE... WITH ZIS NEW HAIRZTYLE YOU WILL BE ZO FOXZEE...
I SWEAR TO GOD I WILL PERSONALLY BREAK INTO EVERY HOUSE IN TOWN AND STEAL EVERY SINGLE ONE AND SHOVE THEM ALL UP THAT ASSHOLE'S ASS! WHERE THE FUCK IS HE NOW, ANYWAY?

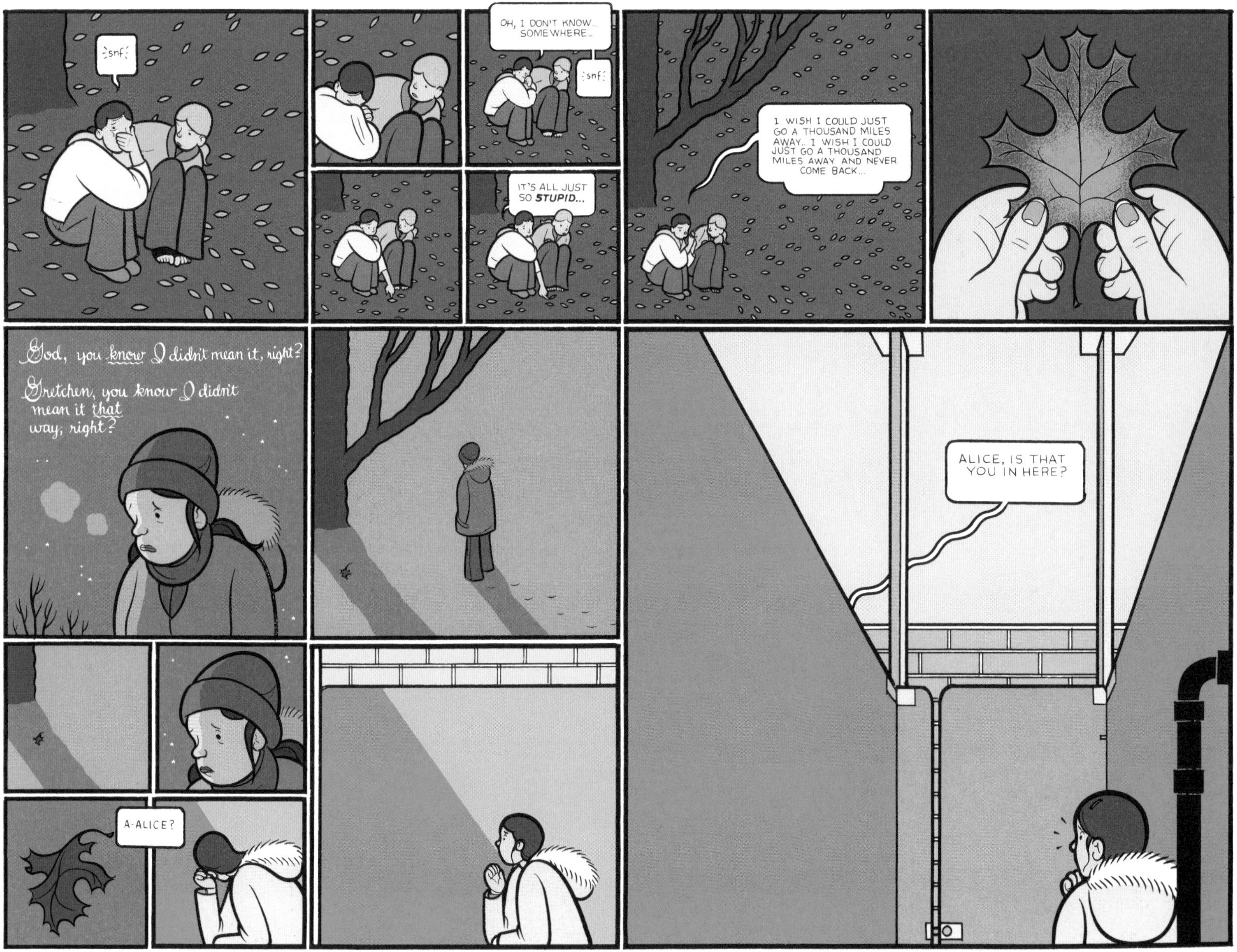
snf
OH, I DON'T KNOW... SOMEWHERE...
snf
IT'S ALL JUST SO STUPID...
I WISH I COULD JUST GO A THOUSAND MILES AWAY... I WISH I COULD JUST GO A THOUSAND MILES AWAY AND NEVER COME BACK...
God, you know I didn't mean it, right?
Gretchen, you know I didn't mean it that way, right?
A-ALICE?
ALICE, IS THAT YOU IN HERE?

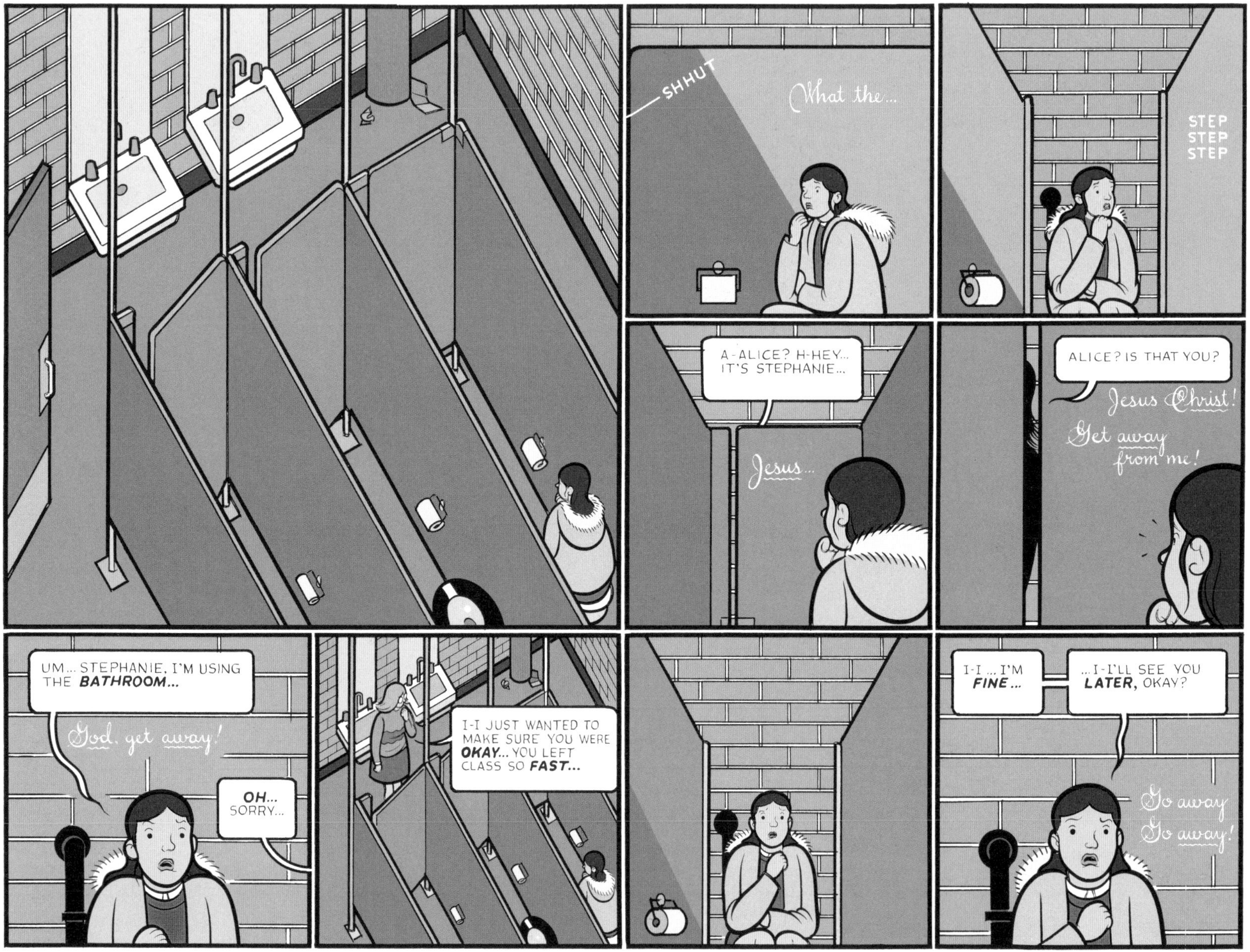
SHHUT
What the...
STEP
STEP
STEP
A-ALICE? H-HEY... IT'S STEPHANIE...
Jesus...
ALICE? IS THAT YOU?
Jesus Christ!
Get away from me!
UM... STEPHANIE, I'M USING THE BATHROOM...
God, get away!
OH... SORRY...
I-I JUST WANTED TO MAKE SURE YOU WERE OKAY... YOU LEFT CLASS SO FAST...
I-I ... I'M FINE...
...I-I'LL SEE YOU LATER, OKAY?
Go away
Go away!

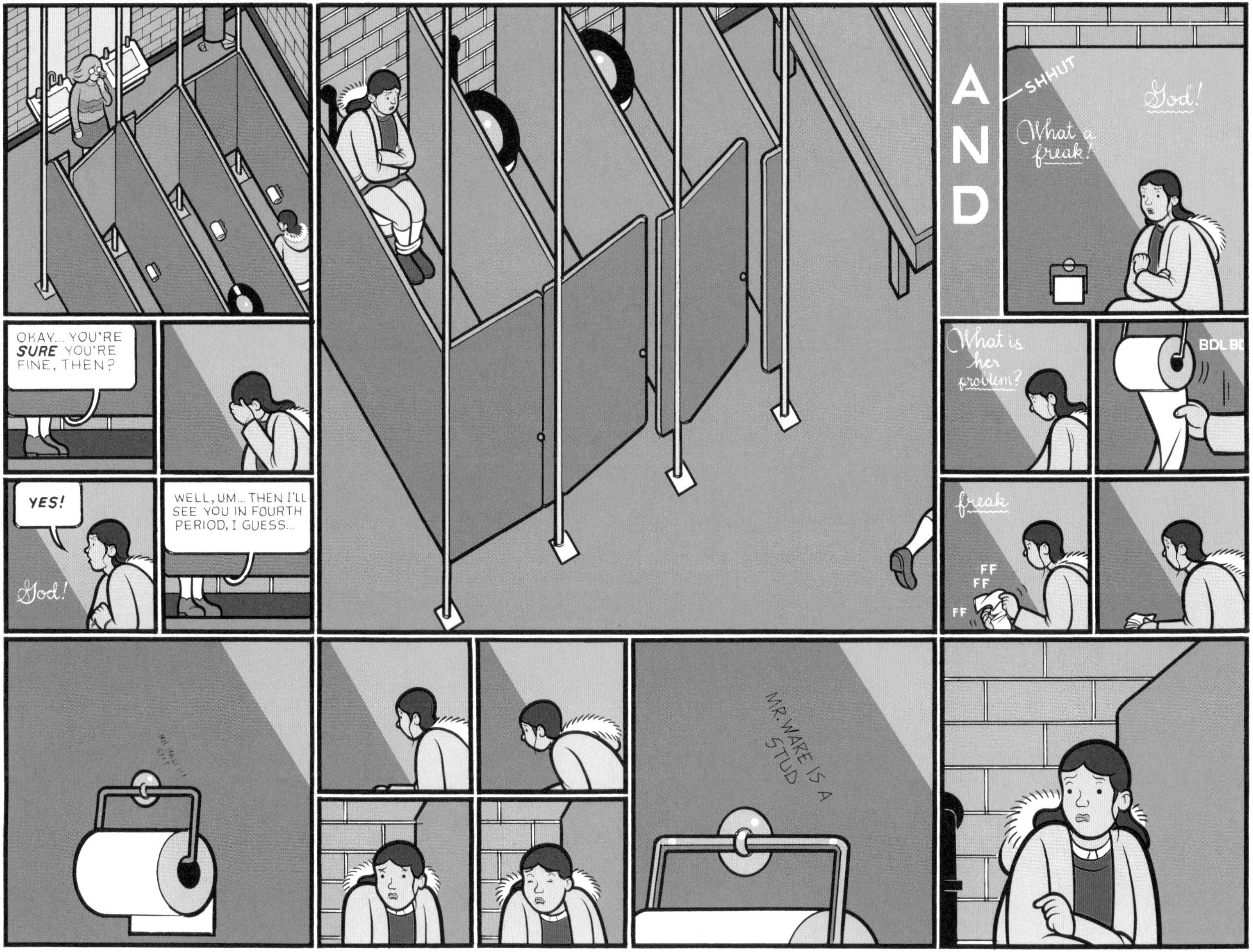

OKAY... YOU'RE SURE YOU'RE FINE, THEN?
YES!
God!
WELL, UM... THEN I'LL SEE YOU IN FOURTH PERIOD, I GUESS...
AND
SHHUT
What a freak!
God!
What is her problem?
BDLBD
freak
FF
FF
FF
MR. WARE IS A STUD

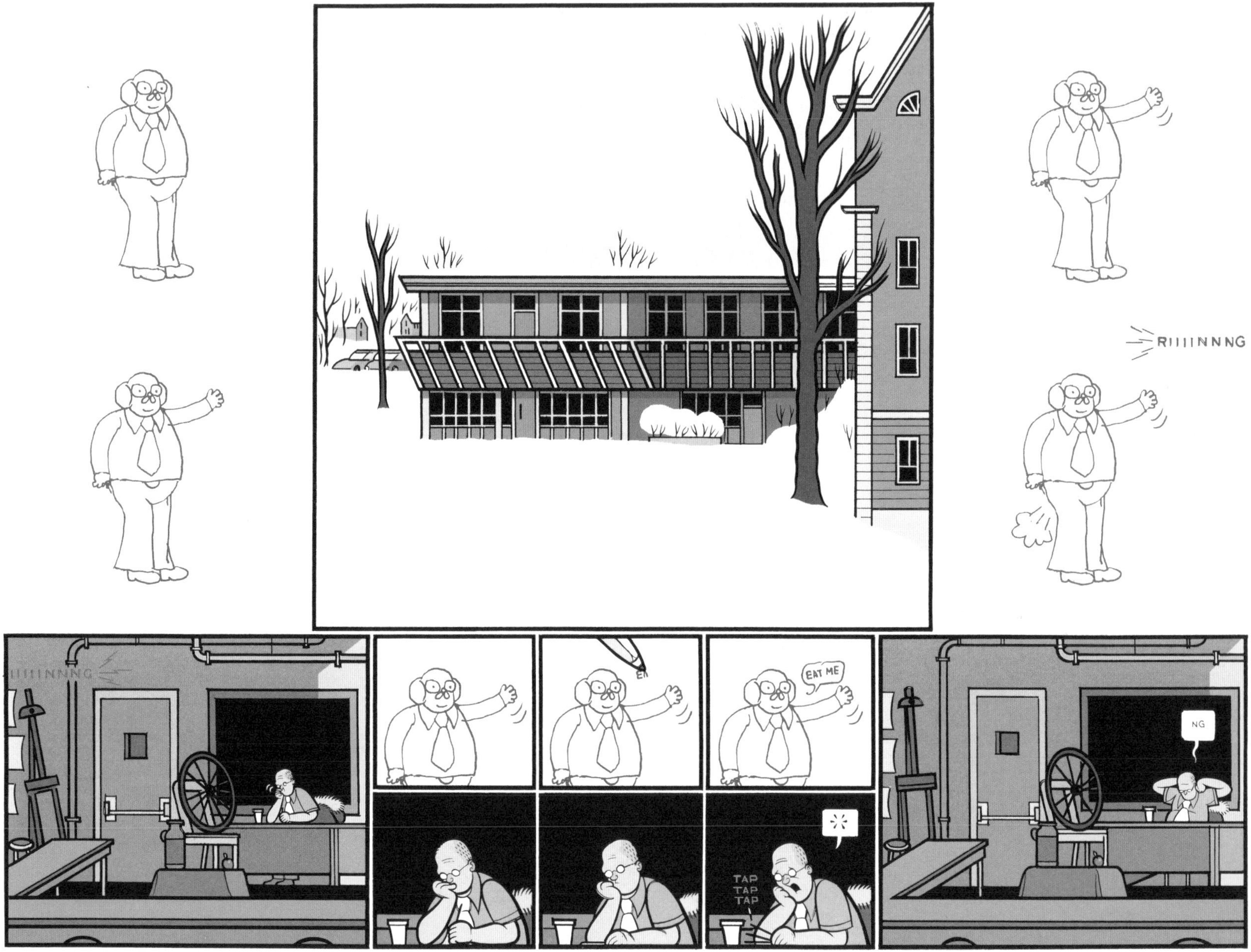
RIIIINNNG
IIIIINNNG
EA
EAT ME
TAP
TAP
TAP
NG

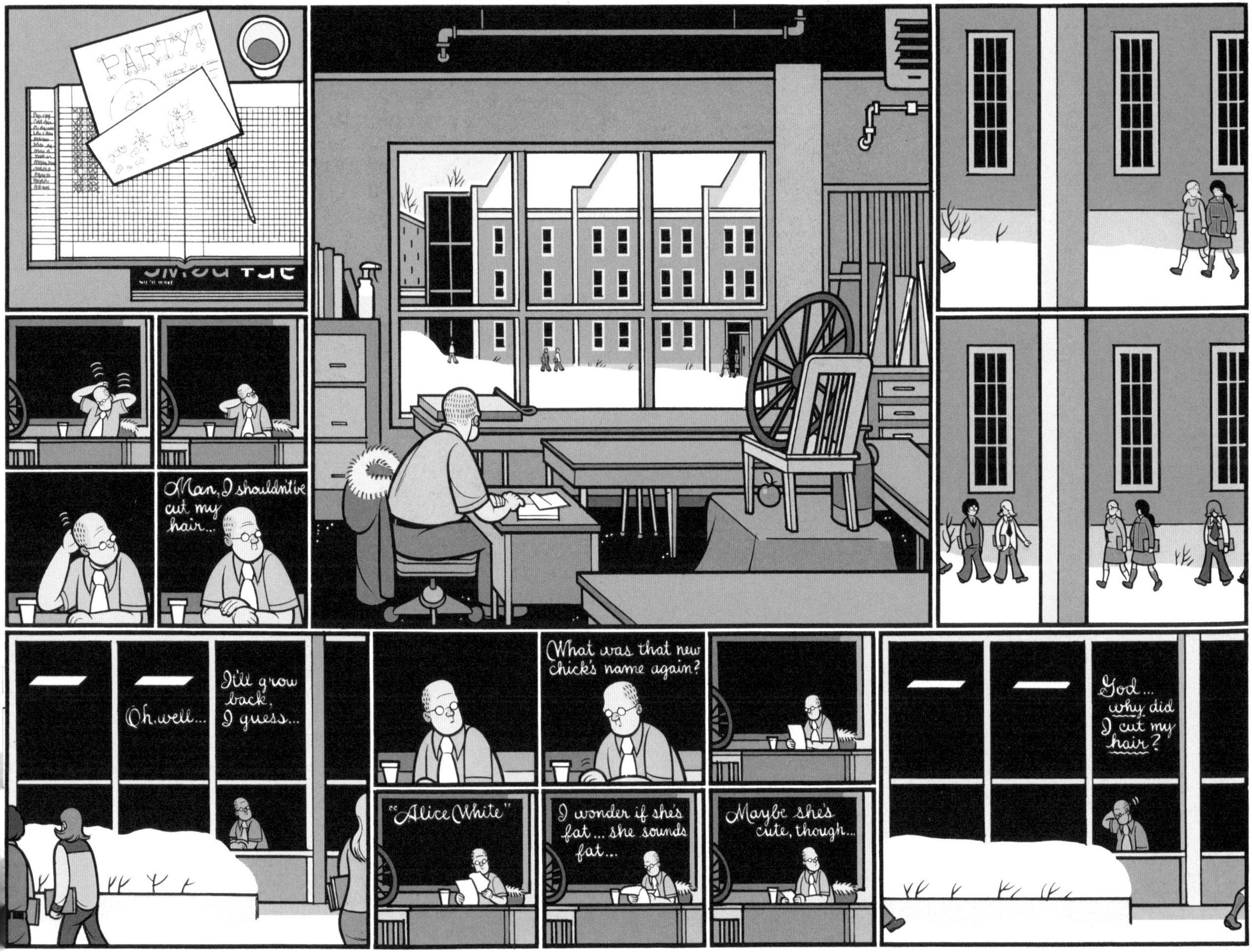
PARTY!
Man, I shouldn't've cut my hair...
Oh, well...
I'll grow back, I guess...
What was that new chick's name again?
"Alice White"
I wonder if she's fat... she sounds fat...
Maybe she's cute, though...
God... why did I cut my hair?

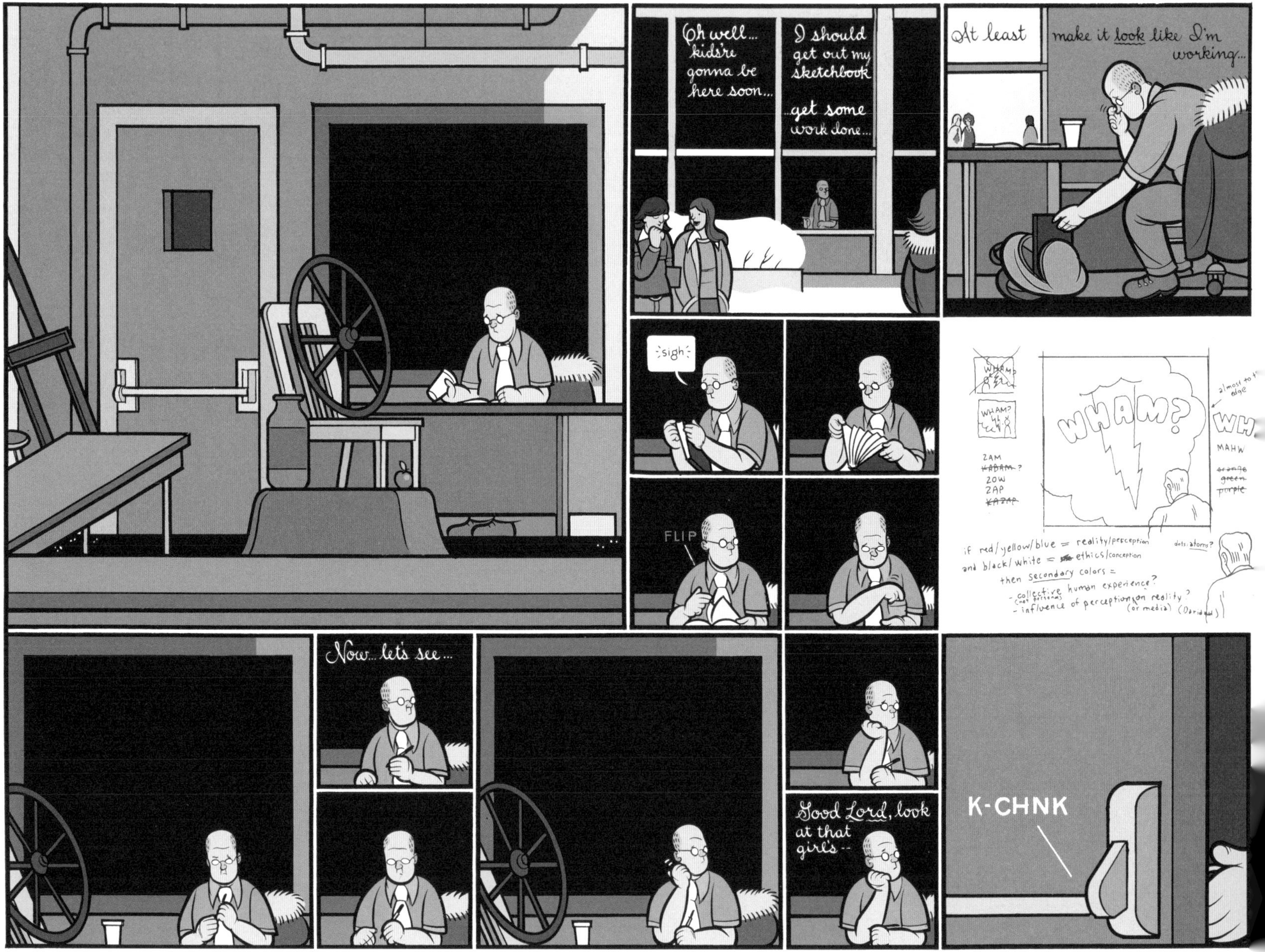
Oh well... kids're gonna be here soon...
I should get out my sketchbook
...get some work done...
At least
make it look like I'm working...
sigh
FLIP
WHAM?
ZAM
KABAM?
ZOW
ZAP
KAZAP
WHAM?
almost to the edge
MAHW
orange
green
purple
if red/yellow/blue = reality/perception
and black/white = ethics/conception
then secondary colors =
- collective human experience?
(not personal)
- influence of perception on reality?
(or media)
dots: atoms?
Now... let's see...
Good Lord, look at that girl's--
K-CHNK

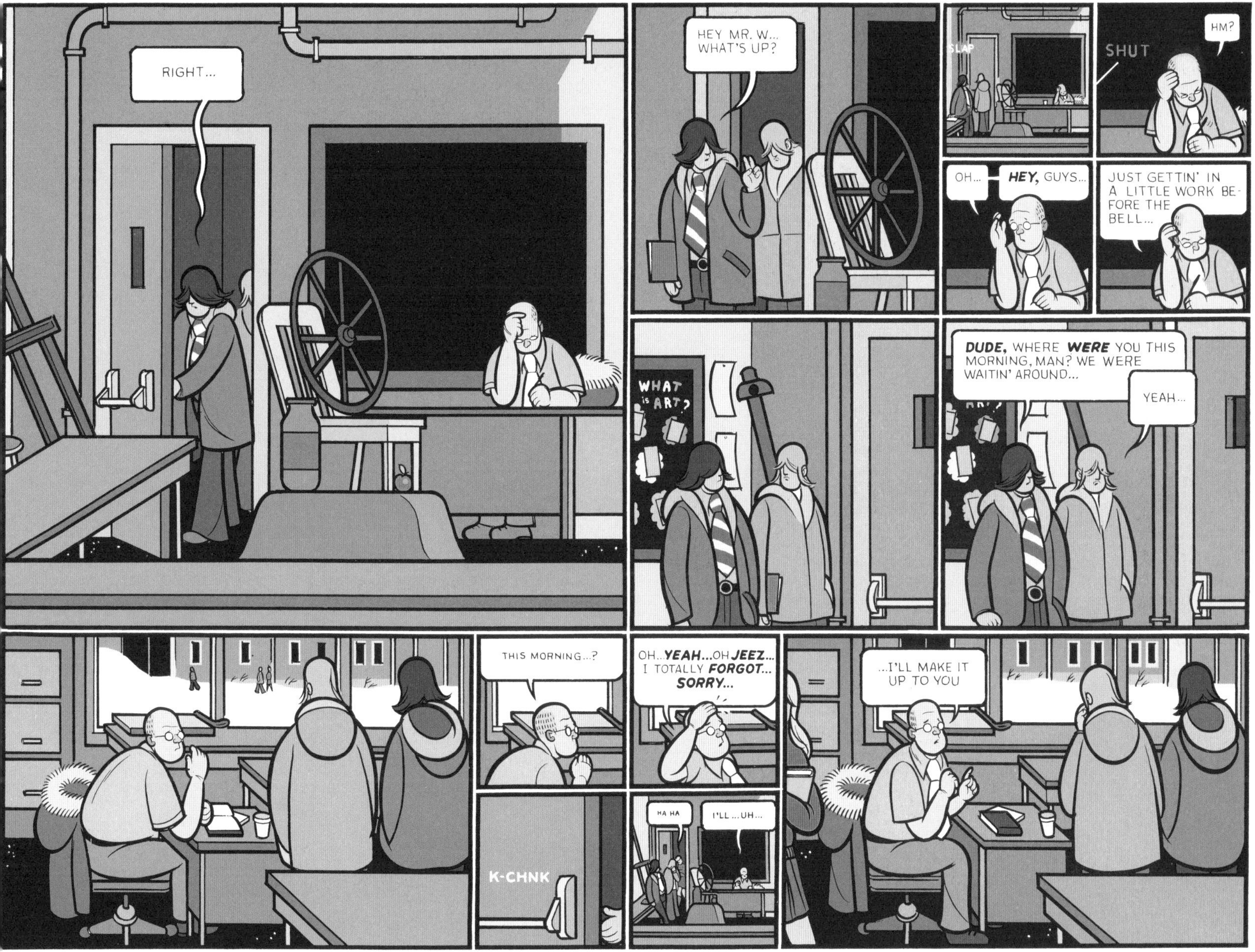
RIGHT...
HEY MR. W... WHAT'S UP?
SLAP
SHUT
HM?
OH...
HEY, GUYS...
JUST GETTIN' IN A LITTLE WORK BEFORE THE BELL...
WHAT is ART?
DUDE, WHERE WERE YOU THIS MORNING, MAN? WE WERE WAITIN' AROUND...
YEAH...
THIS MORNING...?
K-CHNK
OH...YEAH...OH JEEZ... I TOTALLY FORGOT... SORRY...
HA HA
I'LL ...UH...
...I'LL MAKE IT UP TO YOU

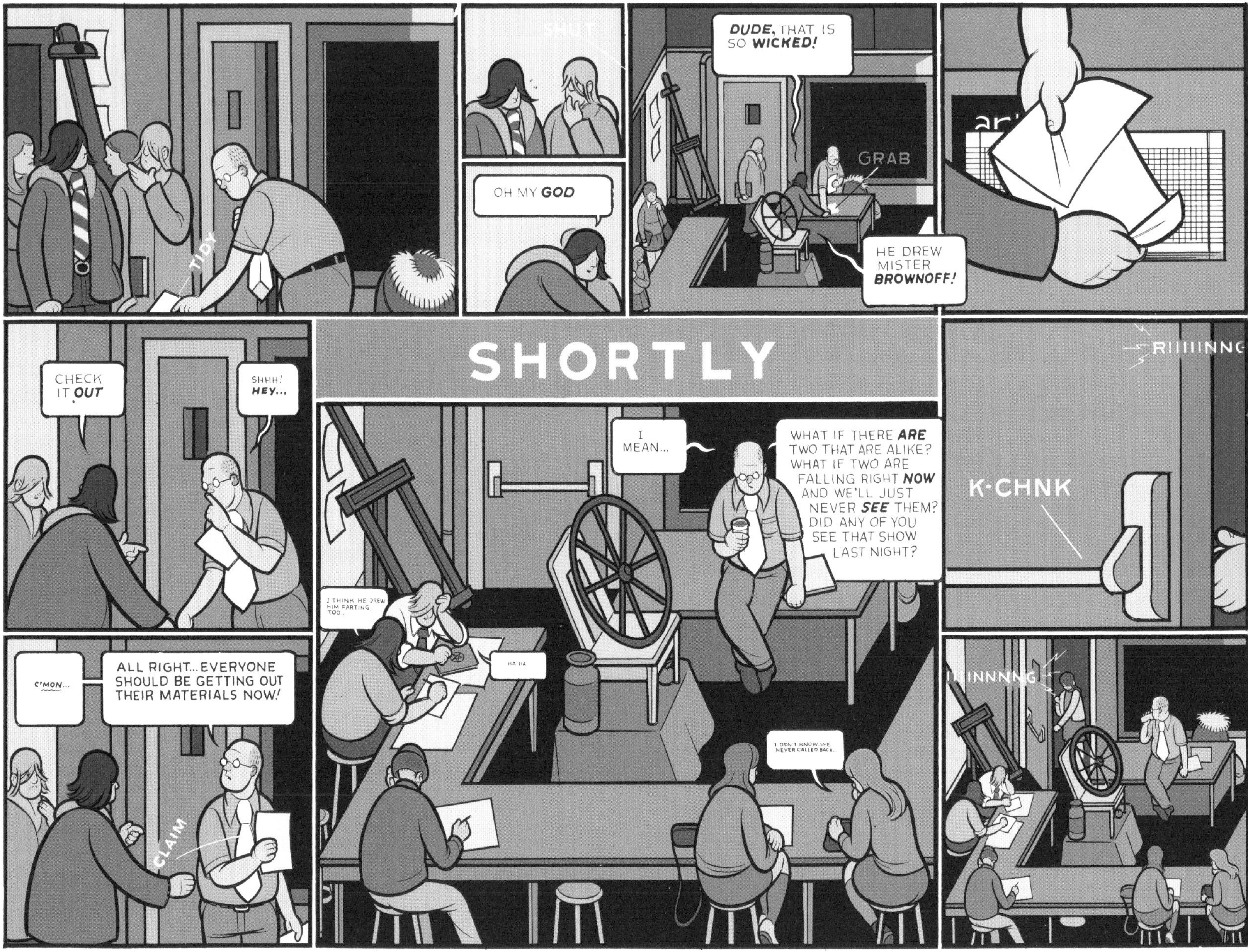
TIDY
SHUT
OH MY GOD
DUDE, THAT IS SO WICKED!
GRAB
HE DREW MISTER BROWNOFF!
CHECK IT OUT.
SHHH! HEY...
C'MON...
ALL RIGHT... EVERYONE SHOULD BE GETTING OUT THEIR MATERIALS NOW!
CLAIM
SHORTLY
I MEAN...
WHAT IF THERE ARE TWO THAT ARE ALIKE? WHAT IF TWO ARE FALLING RIGHT NOW AND WE'LL JUST NEVER SEE THEM? DID ANY OF YOU SEE THAT SHOW LAST NIGHT?
I THINK HE DREW HIM FARTING, TOO..
HA HA
I DON'T KNOW SHE NEVER CALLED BACK...
RIIIIINNG
K-CHNK
IIIINNNNG

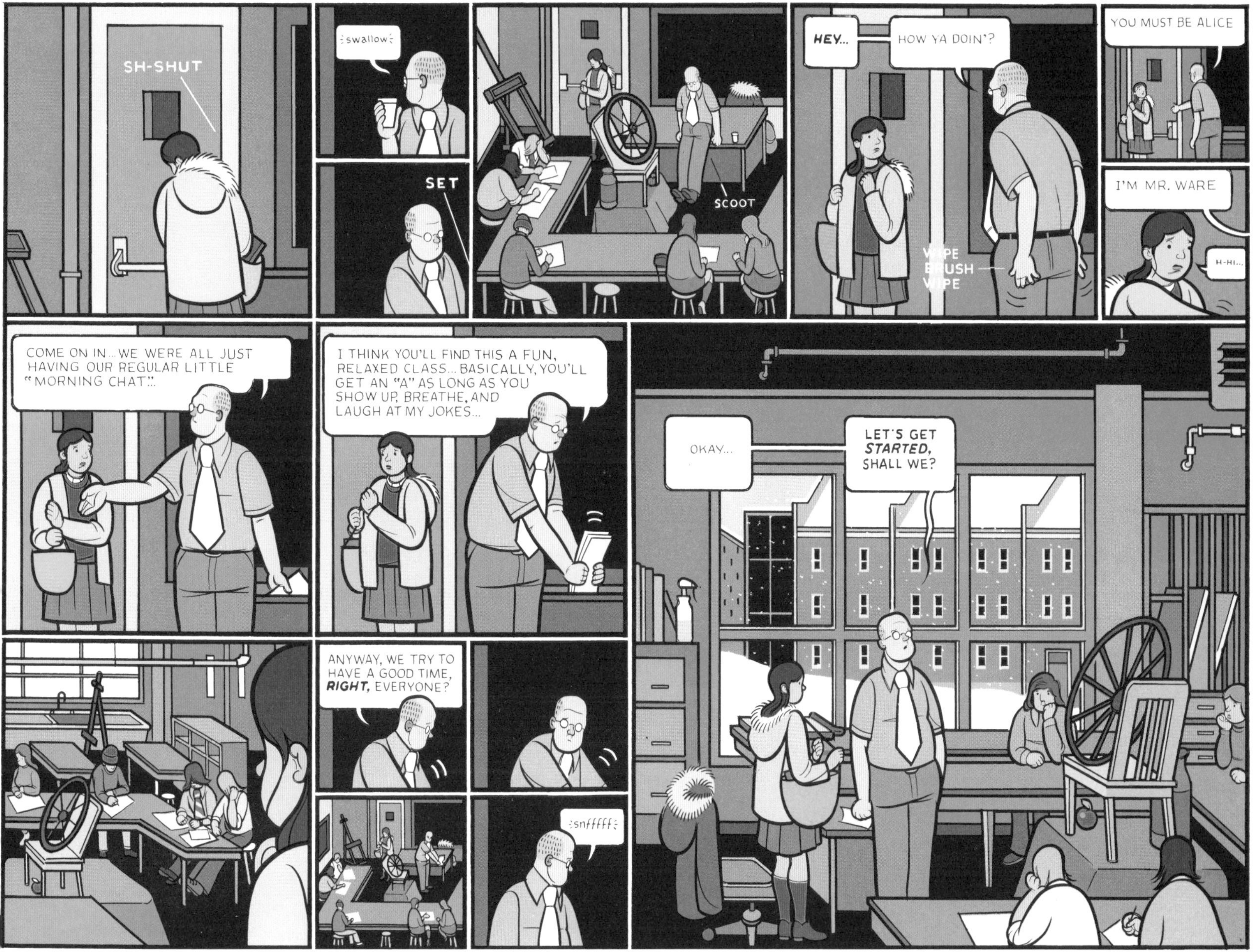
SH-SHUT
swallow
SET
SCOOT
HEY...
HOW YA DOIN'?
WIPE BRUSH WIPE
YOU MUST BE ALICE
I'M MR. WARE
H-HI...
COME ON IN... WE WERE ALL JUST HAVING OUR REGULAR LITTLE "MORNING CHAT."...
I THINK YOU'LL FIND THIS A FUN, RELAXED CLASS... BASICALLY, YOU'LL GET AN "A" AS LONG AS YOU SHOW UP, BREATHE, AND LAUGH AT MY JOKES...
ANYWAY, WE TRY TO HAVE A GOOD TIME, RIGHT, EVERYONE?
snfffff
OKAY...
LET'S GET STARTED, SHALL WE?

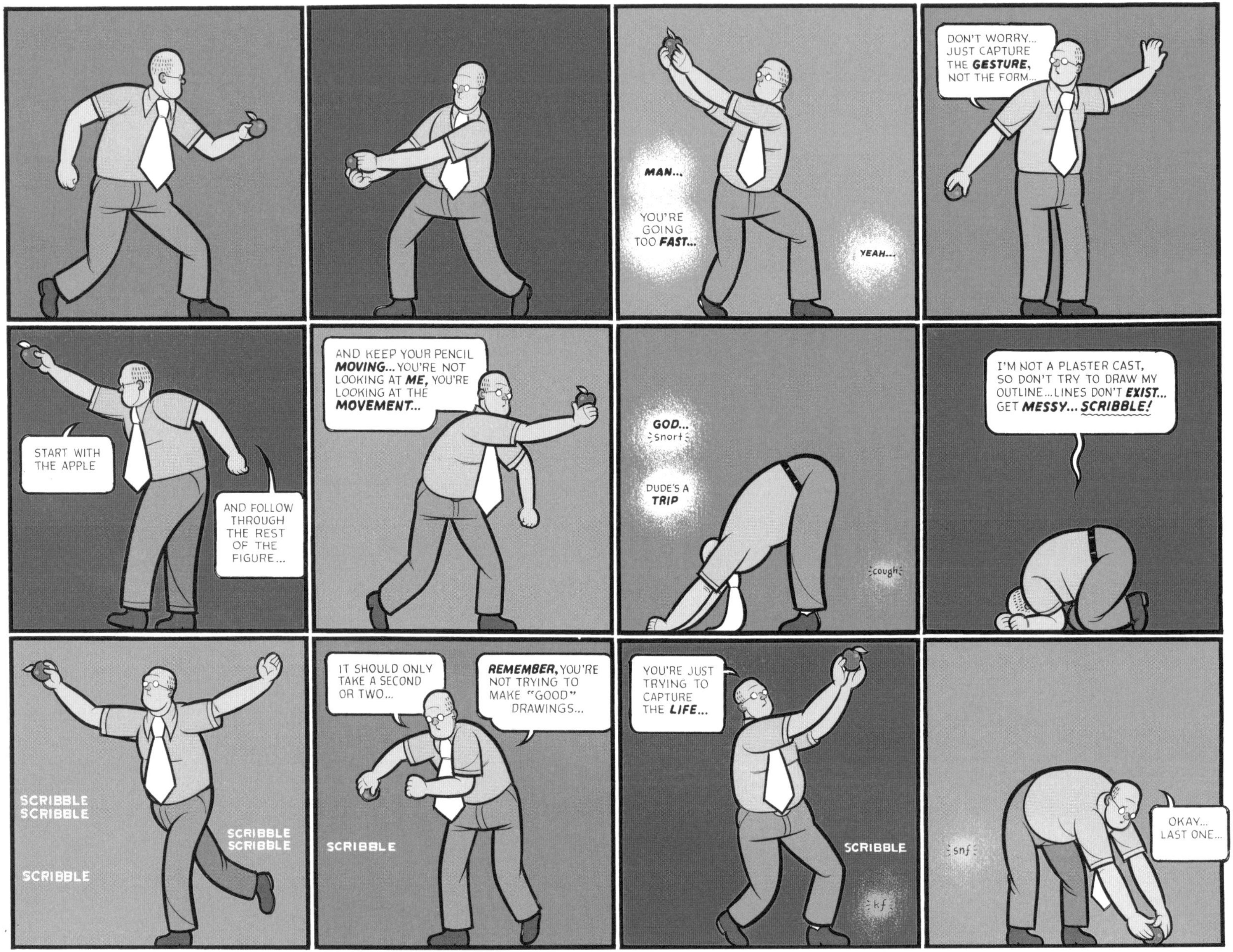
MAN...
YOU'RE GOING TOO FAST...
YEAH...
DON'T WORRY... JUST CAPTURE THE GESTURE, NOT THE FORM...
START WITH THE APPLE
AND FOLLOW THROUGH THE REST OF THE FIGURE...
AND KEEP YOUR PENCIL MOVING... YOU'RE NOT LOOKING AT ME, YOU'RE LOOKING AT THE MOVEMENT...
GOD... snort
DUDE'S A TRIP
cough
I'M NOT A PLASTER CAST, SO DON'T TRY TO DRAW MY OUTLINE... LINES DON'T EXIST... GET MESSY... SCRIBBLE!
SCRIBBLE SCRIBBLE
SCRIBBLE
SCRIBBLE SCRIBBLE
IT SHOULD ONLY TAKE A SECOND OR TWO...
REMEMBER, YOU'RE NOT TRYING TO MAKE "GOOD" DRAWINGS...
SCRIBBLE
YOU'RE JUST TRYING TO CAPTURE THE LIFE...
SCRIBBLE
kf
snf
OKAY... LAST ONE...

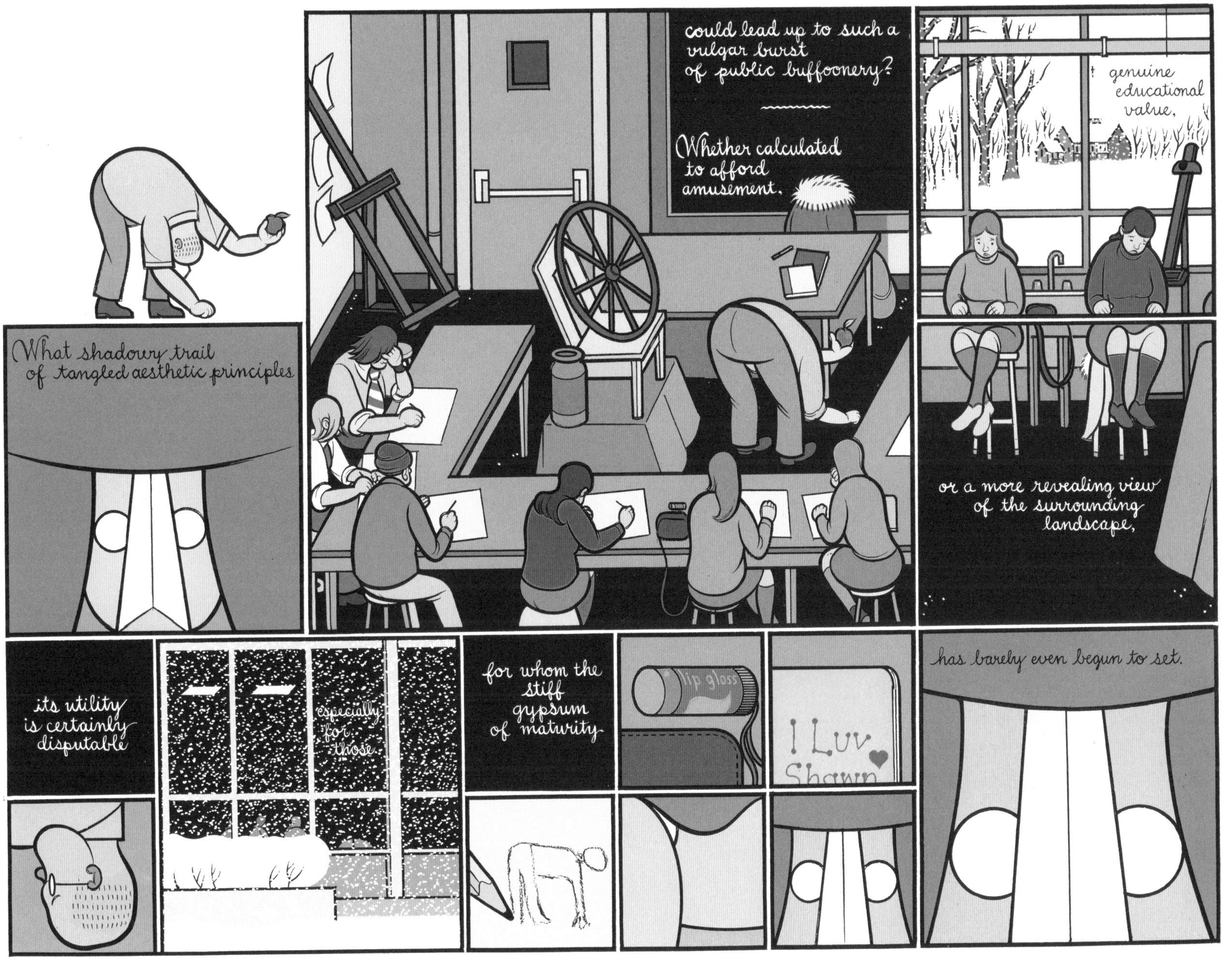

What shadowy trail of tangled aesthetic principles
could lead up to such a vulgar burst of public buffoonery?
Whether calculated to afford amusement,
genuine educational value,
or a more revealing view of the surrounding landscape,
its utility is certainly disputable
especially for those
for whom the stiff gypsum of maturity
lip gloss
I Luv Shawn
has barely even begun to set.

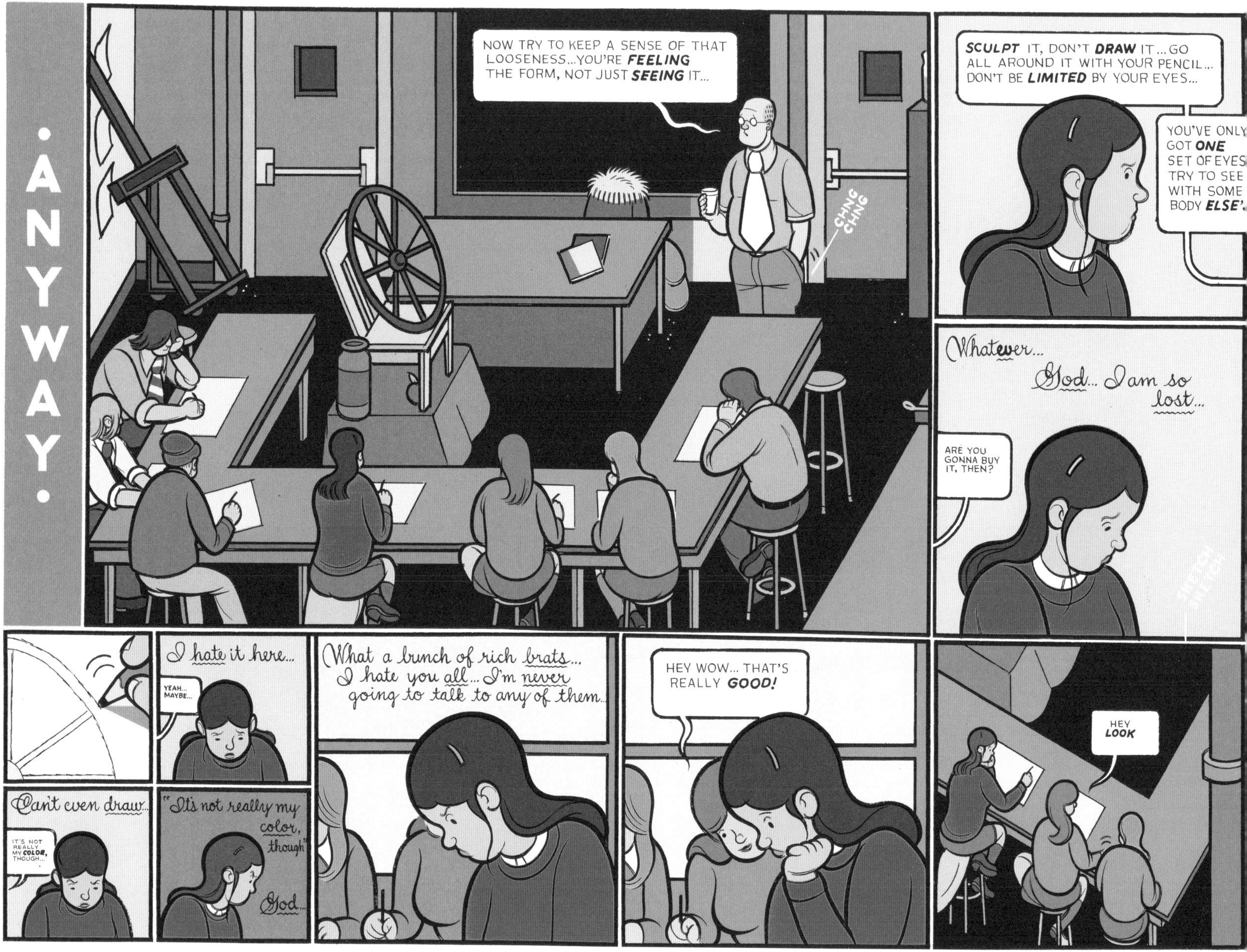

ANYWAY
NOW TRY TO KEEP A SENSE OF THAT LOOSENESS... YOU'RE FEELING THE FORM, NOT JUST SEEING IT...
CHNG CHNG
SCULPT IT, DON'T DRAW IT... GO ALL AROUND IT WITH YOUR PENCIL... DON'T BE LIMITED BY YOUR EYES...
YOU'VE ONLY GOT ONE SET OF EYES TRY TO SEE WITH SOME BODY ELSE'.
Whatever...
God... I am so lost...
ARE YOU GONNA BUY IT, THEN?
SKETCH SKETCH
I hate it here...
YEAH... MAYBE...
Can't even draw...
IT'S NOT REALLY MY COLOR, THOUGH...
"It's not really my color, though"
God...
What a bunch of rich brats... I hate you all... I'm never going to talk to any of them...
HEY WOW... THAT'S REALLY GOOD!
HEY LOOK

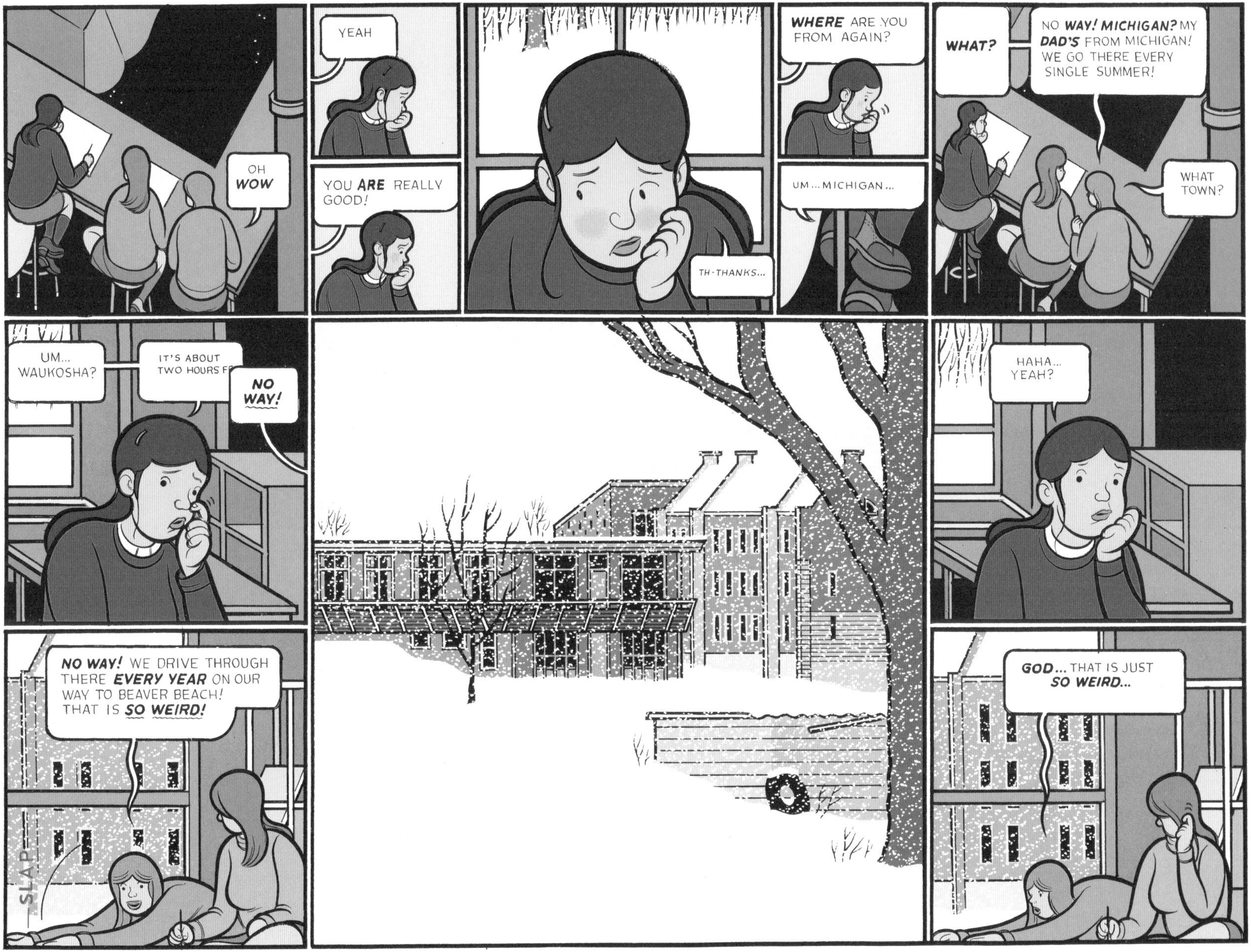

OH WOW
YEAH
YOU ARE REALLY GOOD!
TH-THANKS...
WHERE ARE YOU FROM AGAIN?
UM... MICHIGAN...
WHAT?
NO WAY! MICHIGAN? MY DAD'S FROM MICHIGAN! WE GO THERE EVERY SINGLE SUMMER!
WHAT TOWN?
UM... WAUKOSHA?
IT'S ABOUT TWO HOURS F
NO WAY!
NO WAY! WE DRIVE THROUGH THERE EVERY YEAR ON OUR WAY TO BEAVER BEACH! THAT IS SO WEIRD!
SLAP
HAHA... YEAH?
GOD... THAT IS JUST SO WEIRD...

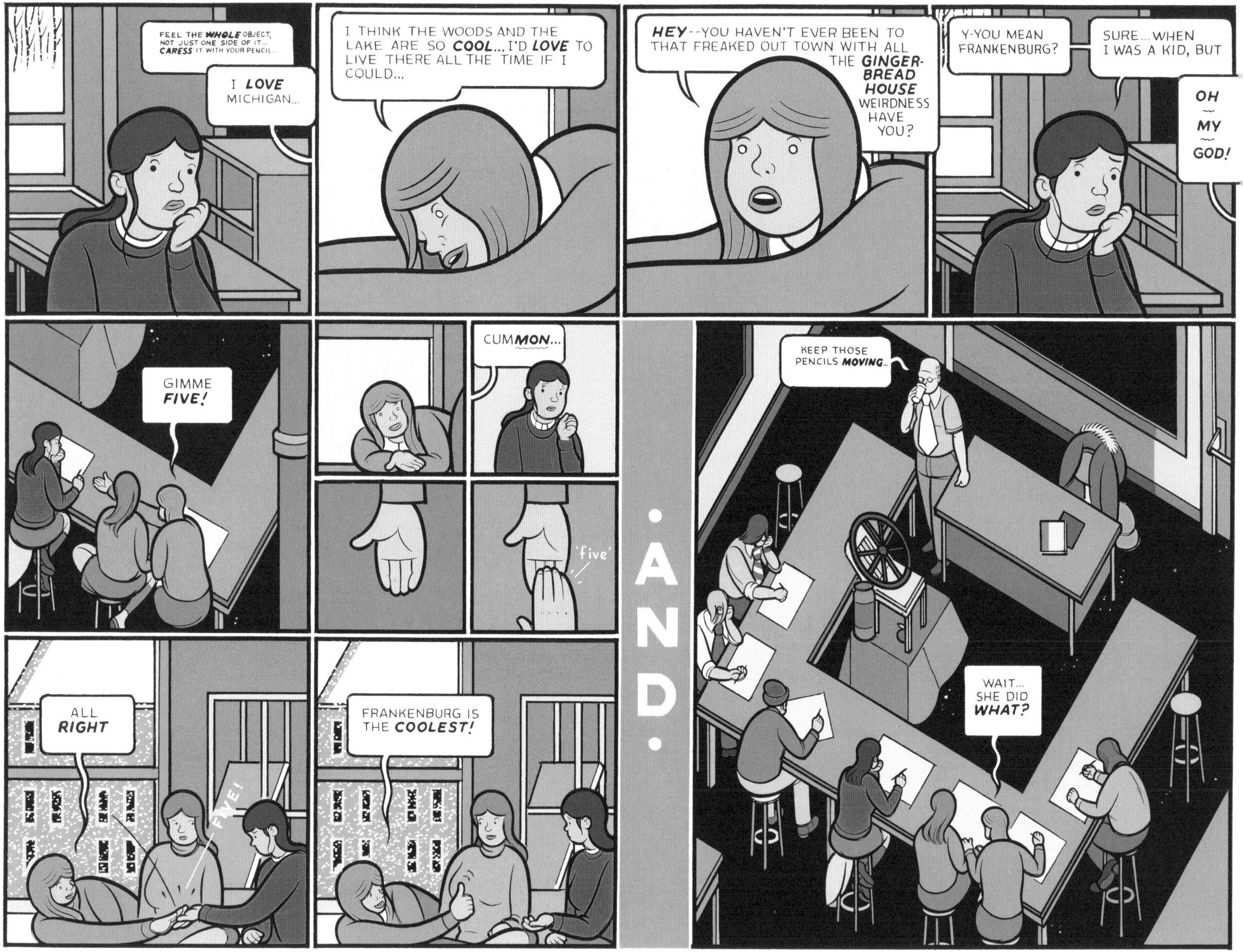
FEEL THE WHOLE OBJECT, NOT JUST ONE SIDE OF IT... CARESS IT WITH YOUR PENCIL...
I LOVE MICHIGAN...
I THINK THE WOODS AND THE LAKE ARE SO COOL... I'D LOVE TO LIVE THERE ALL THE TIME IF I COULD...
HEY--YOU HAVEN'T EVER BEEN TO THAT FREAKED OUT TOWN WITH ALL THE GINGER-BREAD HOUSE WEIRDNESS HAVE YOU?
Y-YOU MEAN FRANKENBURG?
SURE... WHEN I WAS A KID, BUT
OH ~ MY ~ GOD!
GIMME FIVE!
CUMMON...
'five'
ALL RIGHT
FIVE!
FRANKENBURG IS THE COOLEST!
AND
KEEP THOSE PENCILS MOVING...
WAIT... SHE DID WHAT?

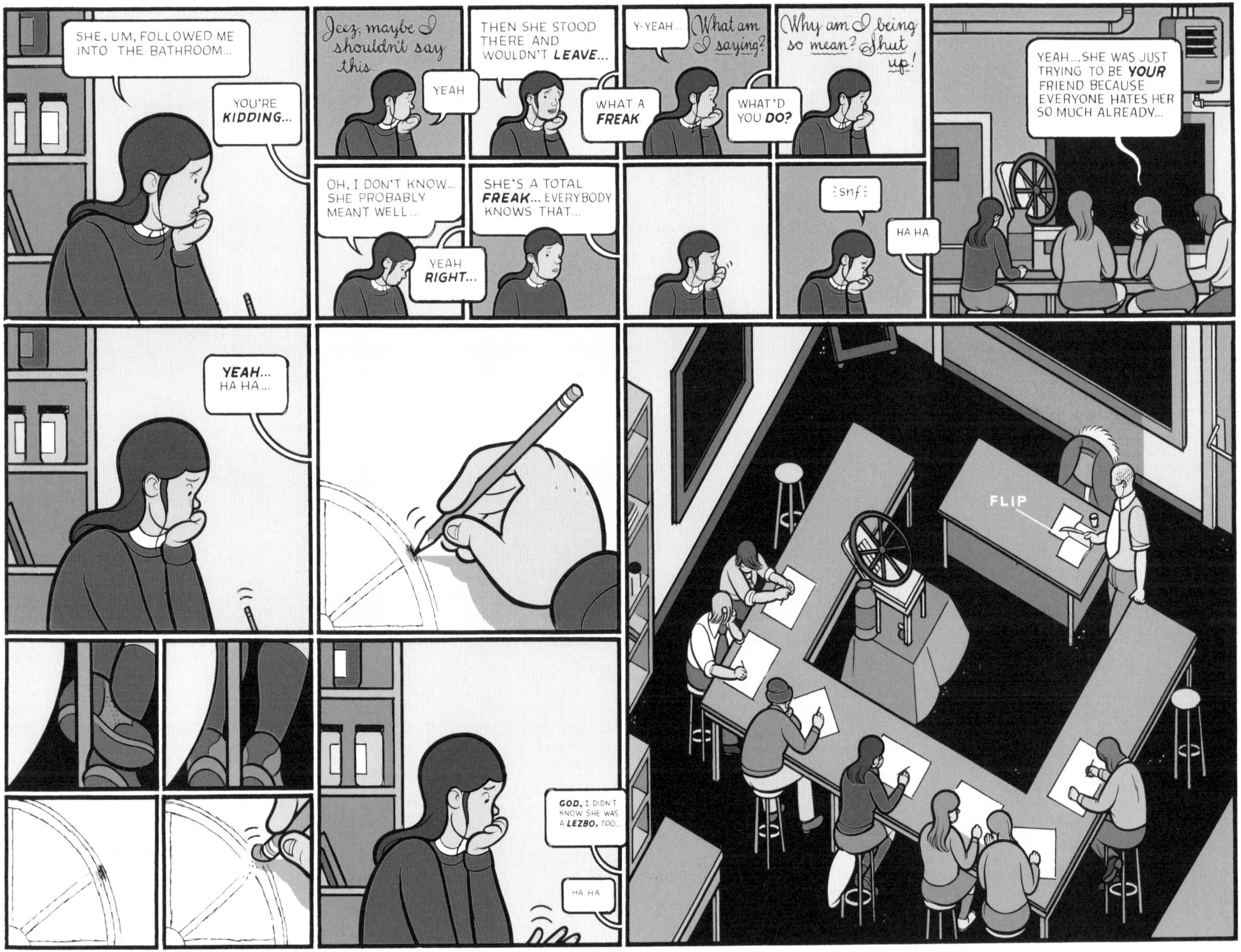

SHE, UM, FOLLOWED ME INTO THE BATHROOM...
YOU'RE **KIDDING...**
Jeez, maybe I shouldn't say this...
YEAH
THEN SHE STOOD THERE AND WOULDN'T **LEAVE...**
WHAT A **FREAK**
Y-YEAH...
What am I saying?
WHAT'D YOU **DO?**
Why am I being so mean? Shut up!
OH, I DON'T KNOW... SHE PROBABLY MEANT WELL...
YEAH **RIGHT...**
SHE'S A TOTAL **FREAK...** EVERYBODY KNOWS THAT...
snf
HA HA
YEAH... SHE WAS JUST TRYING TO BE **YOUR** FRIEND BECAUSE EVERYONE HATES HER SO MUCH ALREADY...
YEAH... HA HA...
FLIP
GOD, I DIDN'T KNOW SHE WAS A **LEZBO,** TOO...
HA HA

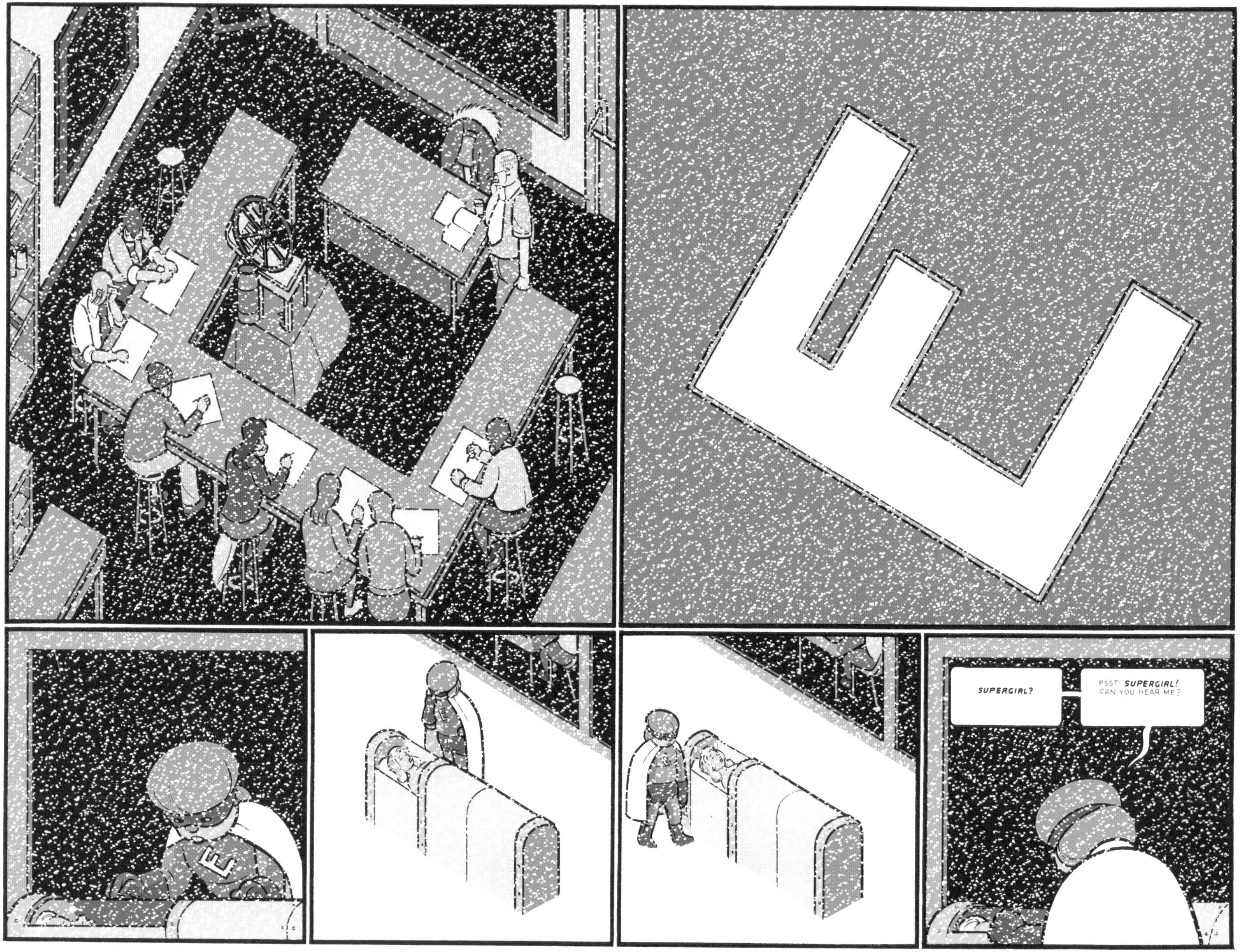
SUPERGIRL?
PSST! SUPERGIRL! CAN YOU HEAR ME?

EAR MAN

EAR MAN

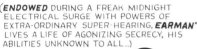

(*ENDOWED* DURING A FREAK MIDNIGHT ELECTRICAL SURGE WITH POWERS OF EXTRA-ORDINARY SUPER-HEARING, *EARMAN** LIVES A LIFE OF AGONIZING SECRECY, HIS ABILITIES UNKNOWN TO ALL...)

* FORMERLY "THE EAR-MAN" -- ed.

R-RUSTY? I-IS THAT YOU?

SSSHH... IT'S OKAY... I'M HERE... I'M HERE...

I'VE ENCASED YOU IN A CRYOGENIC SUPPORT CAPSULE...UNTIL I CAN FIND OUT WHO *DID* THIS TO YOU!

B-BUT H-HOW... WON'T *THEY* SEE?

DON'T WORRY... WE'RE SURROUNDED BY AN INVISIBILITY FIELD...

PLUS, I'VE CRAFTED A LIFELIKE REPLICA OF MYSELF SO THEY WON'T NOTICE I'M GONE FROM MY DESK...

¿sob¿ ¿choke¿ OH, RUSTY...

WHAT IS IT? DON'T CRY... EVERYTHING'S GOING TO BE ALL RIGHT...

I-I KNOW... I TRUST YOU, OF *ALL* PEOPLE... I-IT'S JUST THAT ¿snf¿ ALL THIS TIME, I'VE SO WANTED TO TELL YOU... H-HOW I'VE *FELT*...

OH, SUPERGIRL... I *KNOW*... AND I, TOO... BUT WE MUST BE *STRONG*... AND *ENDURE*...

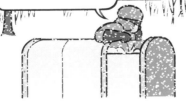

IF NOT FOR THIS FROZEN PRISON, I MIGHT TASTE THE NECTAR OF YOUR SWEET LIPS...

BUT, THE IMPLICIT EROS OF THE SCENE IS SO TANTALIZING TO OUR HERO, HE RE-PLAYS IT, WITH SLIGHT MODIFICATION...

LET ME TASTE THE NECTAR OF YOUR SWEET LIPS, IF ONLY FOR A MOMENT!

AND, AGAIN :

THE SWEET NECTAR OF YOUR SWEET LIPS... LET ME TASTE IT!

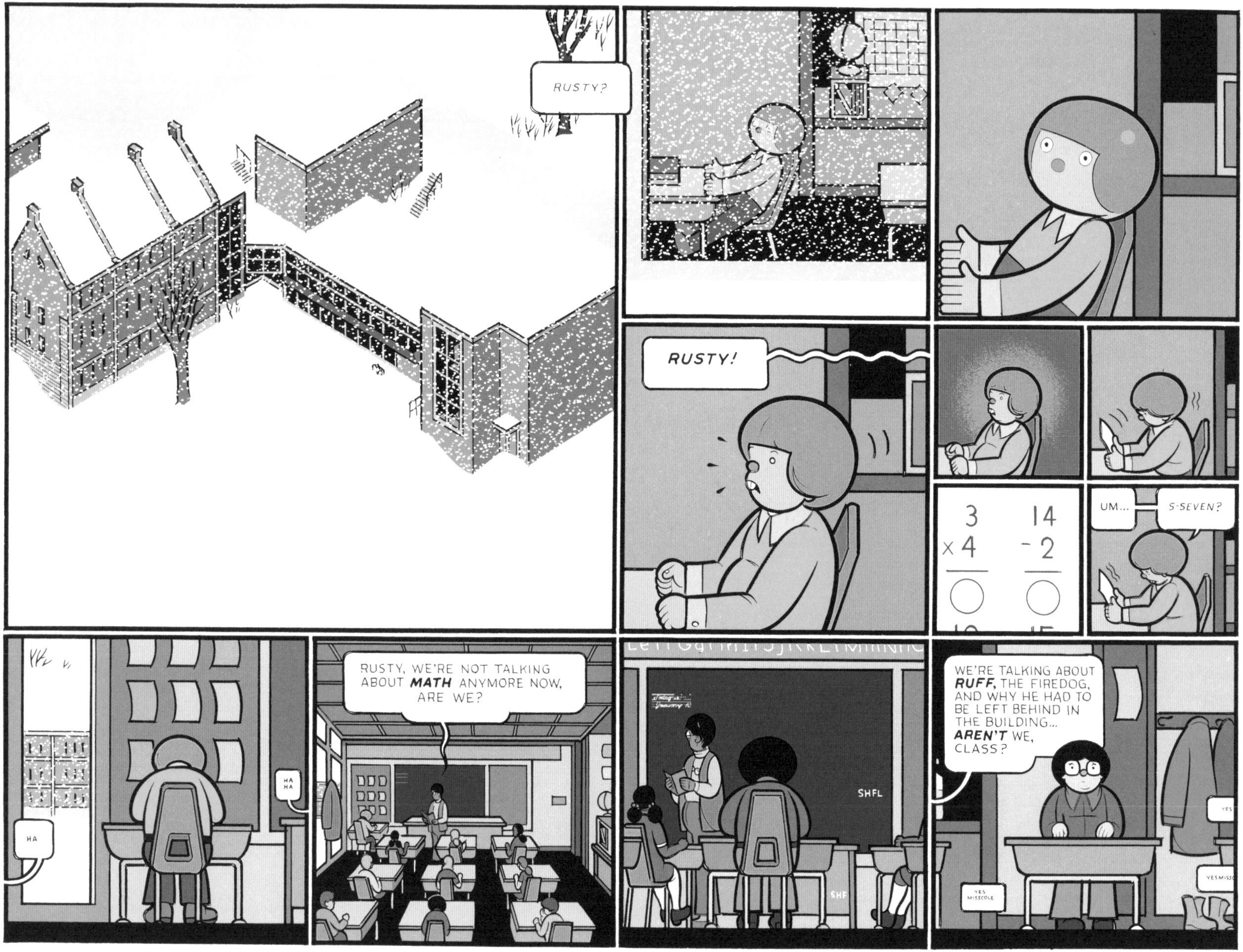
RUSTY?
RUSTY!
3
×4
14
-2
UM...
S-SEVEN?
HA
HA HA
RUSTY, WE'RE NOT TALKING ABOUT MATH ANYMORE NOW, ARE WE?
SHFL
SHF
WE'RE TALKING ABOUT RUFF, THE FIREDOG, AND WHY HE HAD TO BE LEFT BEHIND IN THE BUILDING... AREN'T WE, CLASS?
YES MISSCOLE
YES
YESMISS

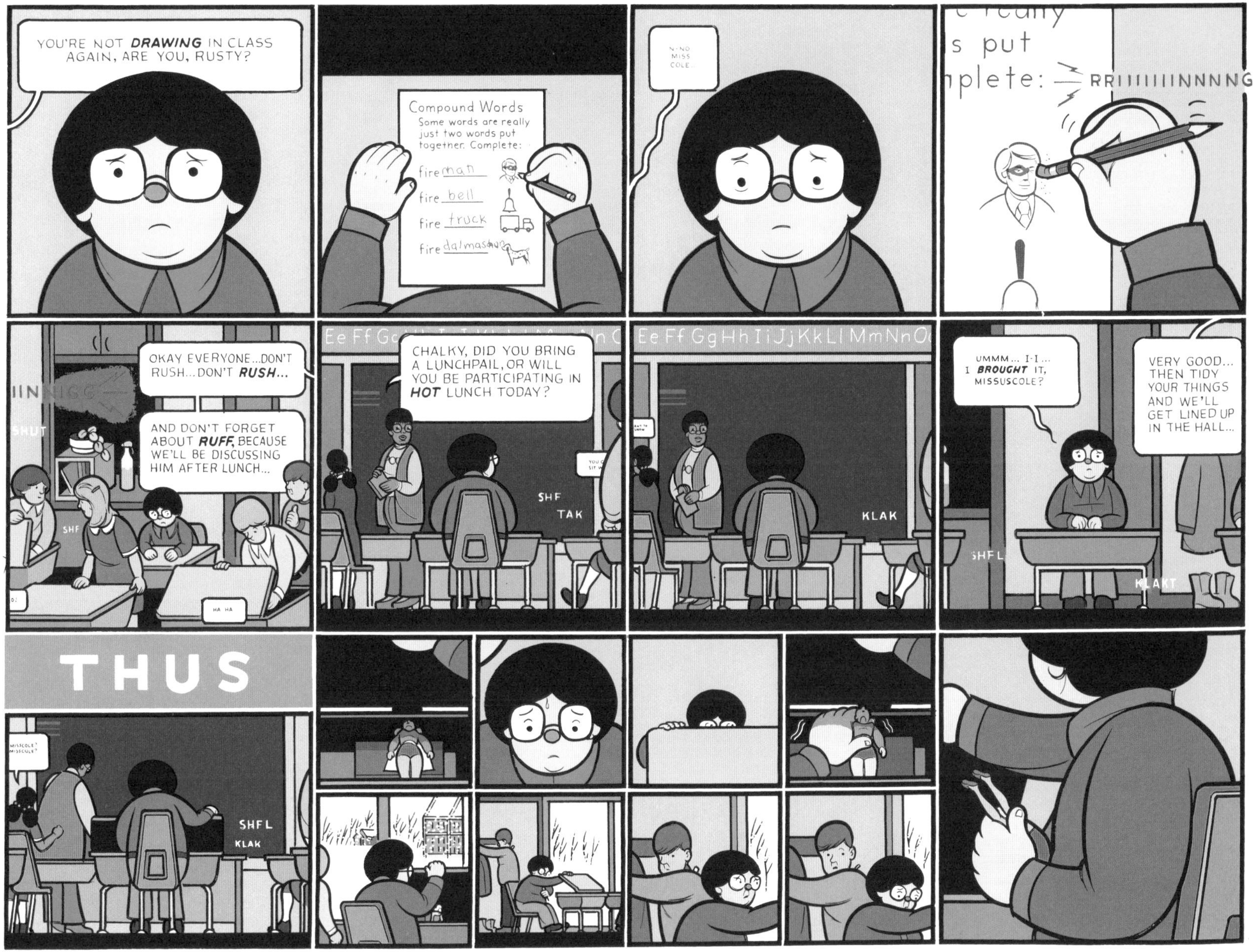
YOU'RE NOT **DRAWING** IN CLASS AGAIN, ARE YOU, RUSTY?
Compound Words
Some words are really just two words put together. Complete:
fire man
fire bell
fire truck
fire dalmashun
N-NO MISS COLE...
s put
nplete:
RRIIIIIIINNNNG
OKAY EVERYONE...DON'T RUSH...DON'T **RUSH**...
AND DON'T FORGET ABOUT **RUFF**, BECAUSE WE'LL BE DISCUSSING HIM AFTER LUNCH...
SHUT
SHF
HA HA
CHALKY, DID YOU BRING A LUNCHPAIL, OR WILL YOU BE PARTICIPATING IN **HOT** LUNCH TODAY?
SHF
TAK
KLAK
UMMM... I-I... I **BROUGHT** IT, MISSUSCOLE?
VERY GOOD... THEN TIDY YOUR THINGS AND WE'LL GET LINED UP IN THE HALL...
SHFL
KLAKT
THUS
MISSCOLE? MISSCOLE?
SHFL
KLAK

1. Born: seven years, ten months, and two days ago.

2. First tears of anguish.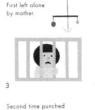

3. First left alone by mother.

4. First step.

5. First fall.

6. Last time to see father.

7. First time punched by sister.

8. First time hugged by sister.

9. Second time punched by sister.

10. First truly happy day.

11. First horrifying night.

12. First time to notice difference.

13. First day at preschool.

14. First time to sing songs to self.

15. First time to suck sugar off gumdrops and place them on a sunny windowsill.

16. First time to wad up Scotch tape, draw a face on it, and call it his only friend.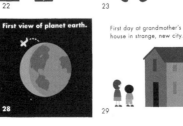

CHALKY WHITE.
A CONDENSED OVERVIEW of OUR HERO'S LIFE THUS FAR.

17. First real friend.

18. First time real friend finds a better friend.

19. Second time to wad up Scotch tape, draw a face on it, and call it his only friend.

20. First time Scotch tape wad is stomped flat by former first friend.

21. First comic book.

22. First science fiction book.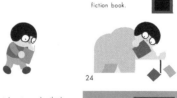

23. Fiftieth comic book.

24. Fiftieth science fiction book.

25. First name called for reading comic books.

26. Six hundred and forty third name called for reading science fiction books.

27. First move away from home.

28. First view of planet earth.

29. First day at grandmother's house in strange, new city.

30.

31. First day (today) at brand-new school.

32. ANY WAY

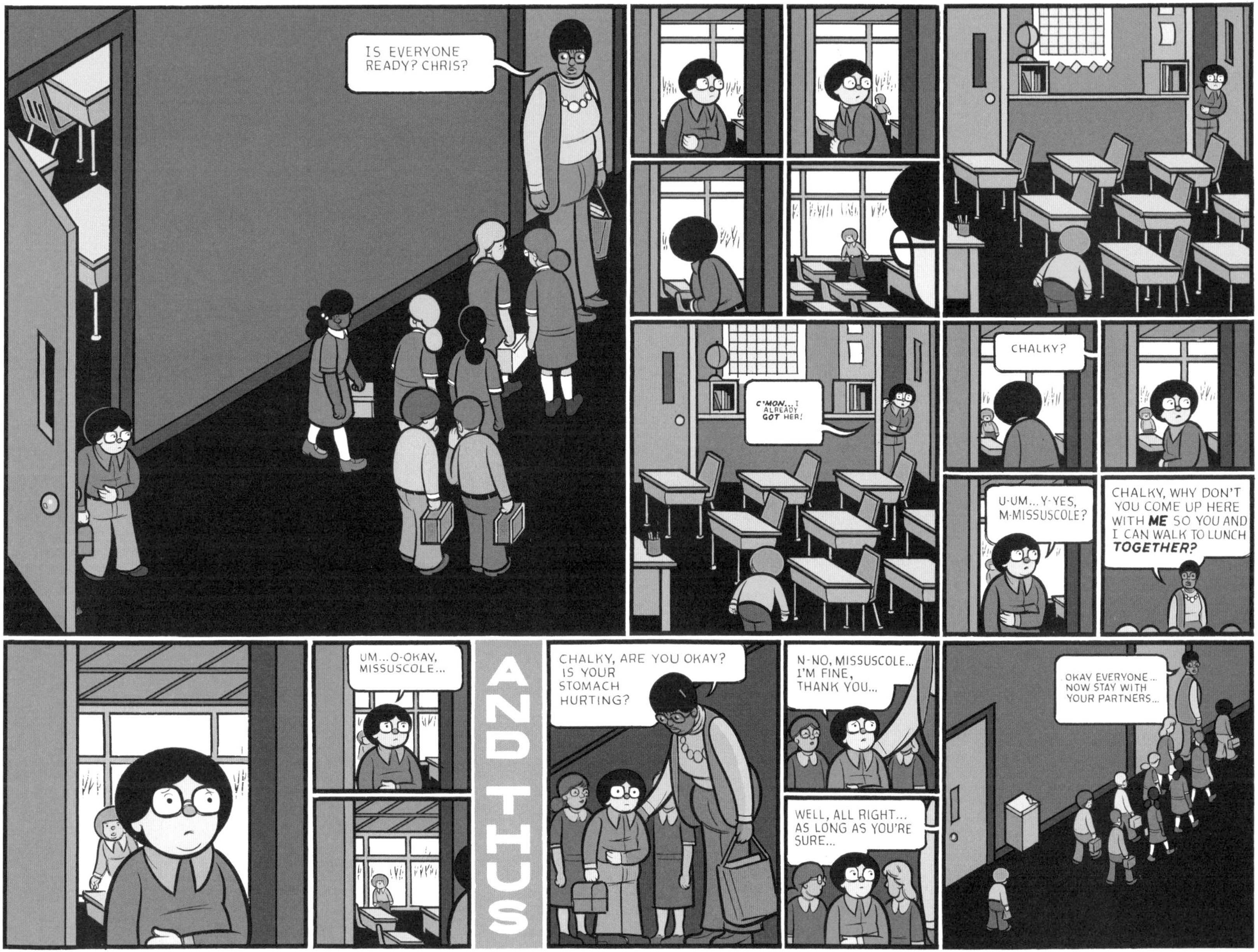
IS EVERYONE READY? CHRIS?
C'MON... I ALREADY GOT HER!
CHALKY?
U-UM... Y-YES, M-MISSUSCOLE?
CHALKY, WHY DON'T YOU COME UP HERE WITH ME SO YOU AND I CAN WALK TO LUNCH TOGETHER?
UM... O-OKAY, MISSUSCOLE...
AND THUS
CHALKY, ARE YOU OKAY? IS YOUR STOMACH HURTING?
N-NO, MISSUSCOLE... I'M FINE, THANK YOU...
WELL, ALL RIGHT... AS LONG AS YOU'RE SURE...
OKAY EVERYONE... NOW STAY WITH YOUR PARTNERS...

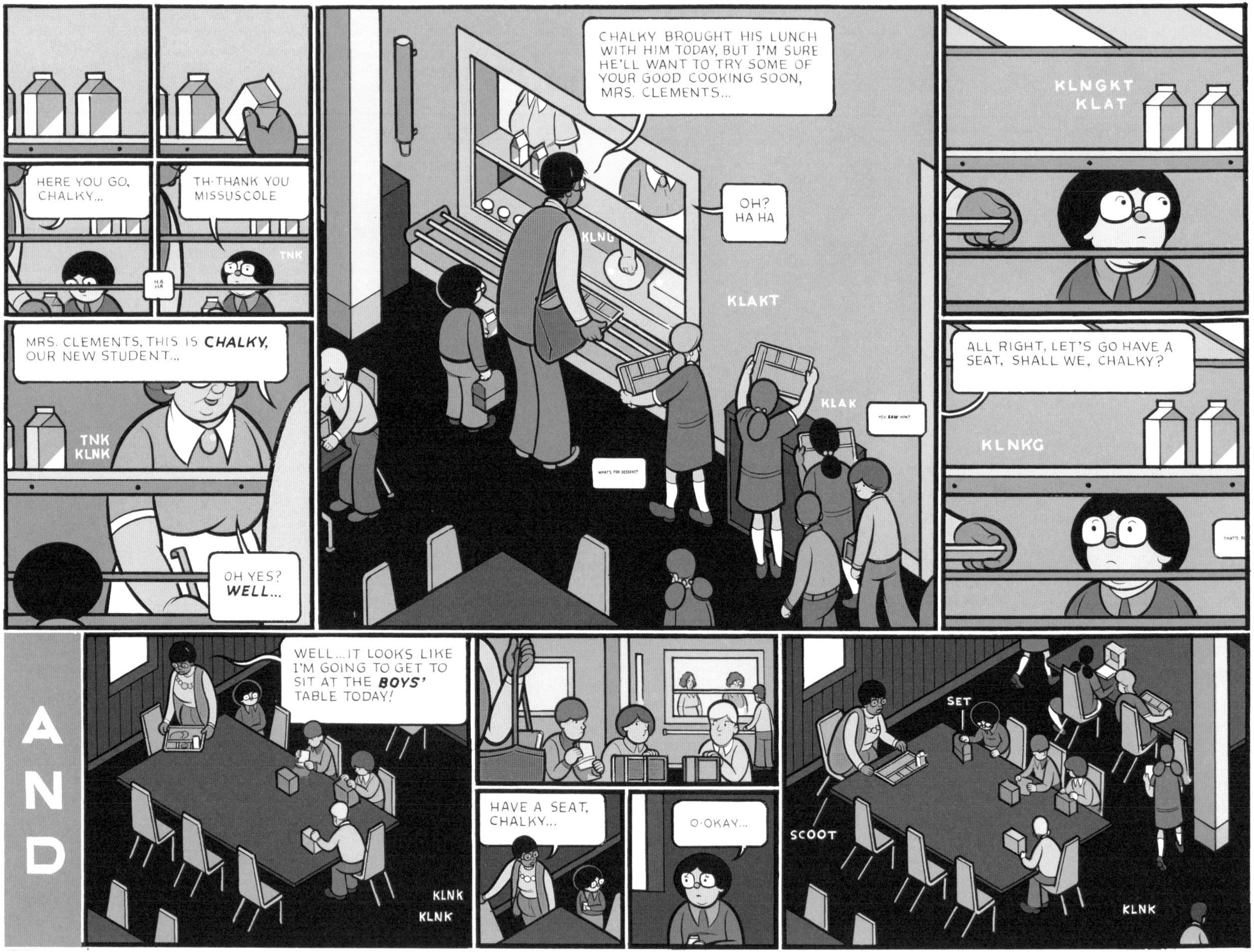
HERE YOU GO, CHALKY...
HA HA
TH-THANK YOU MISSUSCOLE
TNK
MRS. CLEMENTS, THIS IS **CHALKY,** OUR NEW STUDENT...
TNK KLNK
OH YES? **WELL...**
CHALKY BROUGHT HIS LUNCH WITH HIM TODAY, BUT I'M SURE HE'LL WANT TO TRY SOME OF YOUR GOOD COOKING SOON, MRS. CLEMENTS...
OH? HA HA
KLNG
KLAKT
KLAK
YOU **SAW** HIM?
WHAT'S FOR DESSERT?
KLNGKT KLAT
ALL RIGHT, LET'S GO HAVE A SEAT, SHALL WE, CHALKY?
KLNKG
AND
WELL... IT LOOKS LIKE I'M GOING TO GET TO SIT AT THE **BOYS'** TABLE TODAY!
KLNK
KLNK
HAVE A SEAT, CHALKY...
O-OKAY...
SET
SCOOT
KLNK

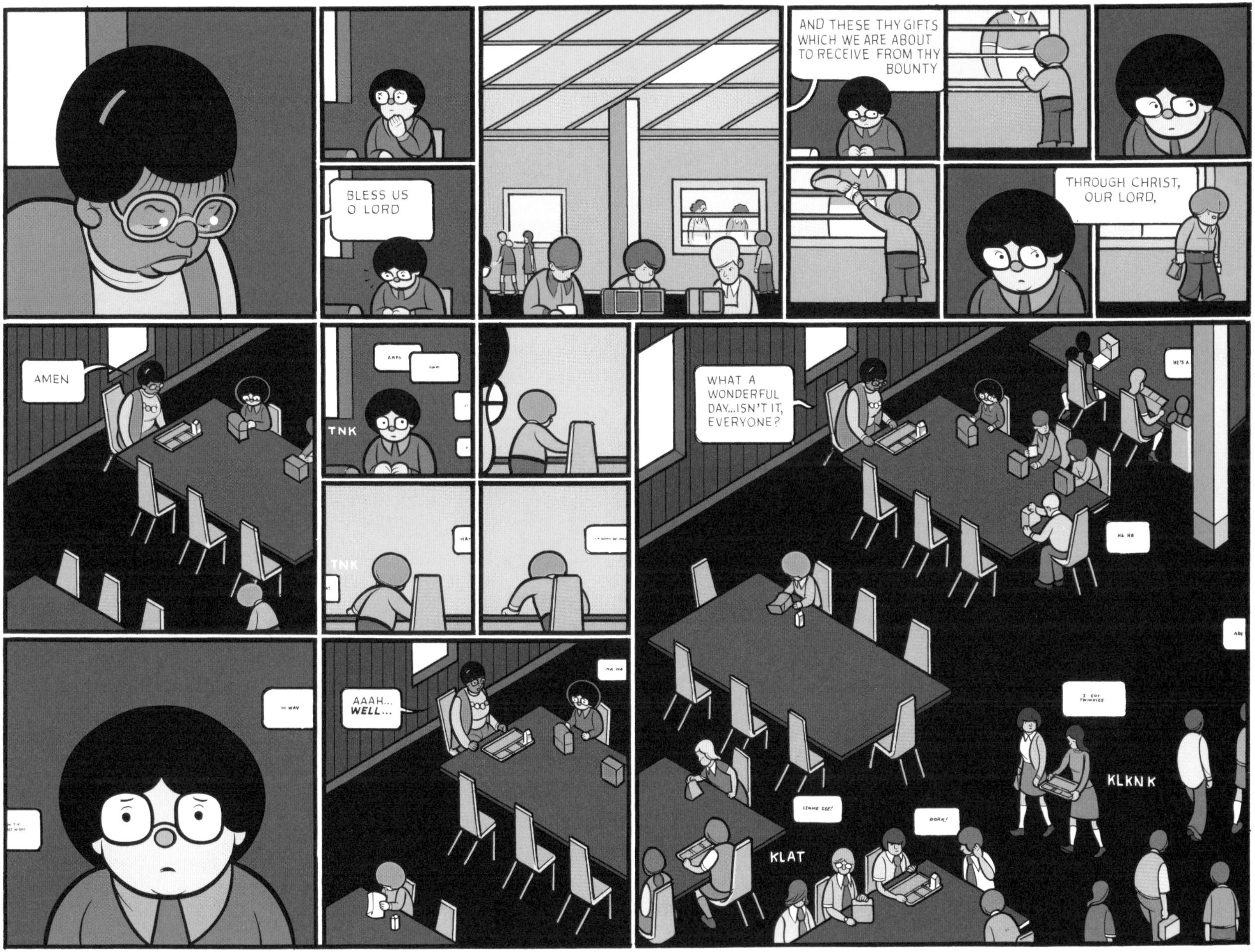
BLESS US O LORD
AND THESE THY GIFTS WHICH WE ARE ABOUT TO RECEIVE FROM THY BOUNTY
THROUGH CHRIST, OUR LORD,
AMEN
TNK
TNK
WHAT A WONDERFUL DAY...ISN'T IT, EVERYONE?
HA HA
NO WAY
AAAH... **WELL...**
HA HA
I GOT TWINKIES
KLKNK
LEMME SEE!
DORK!
KLAT

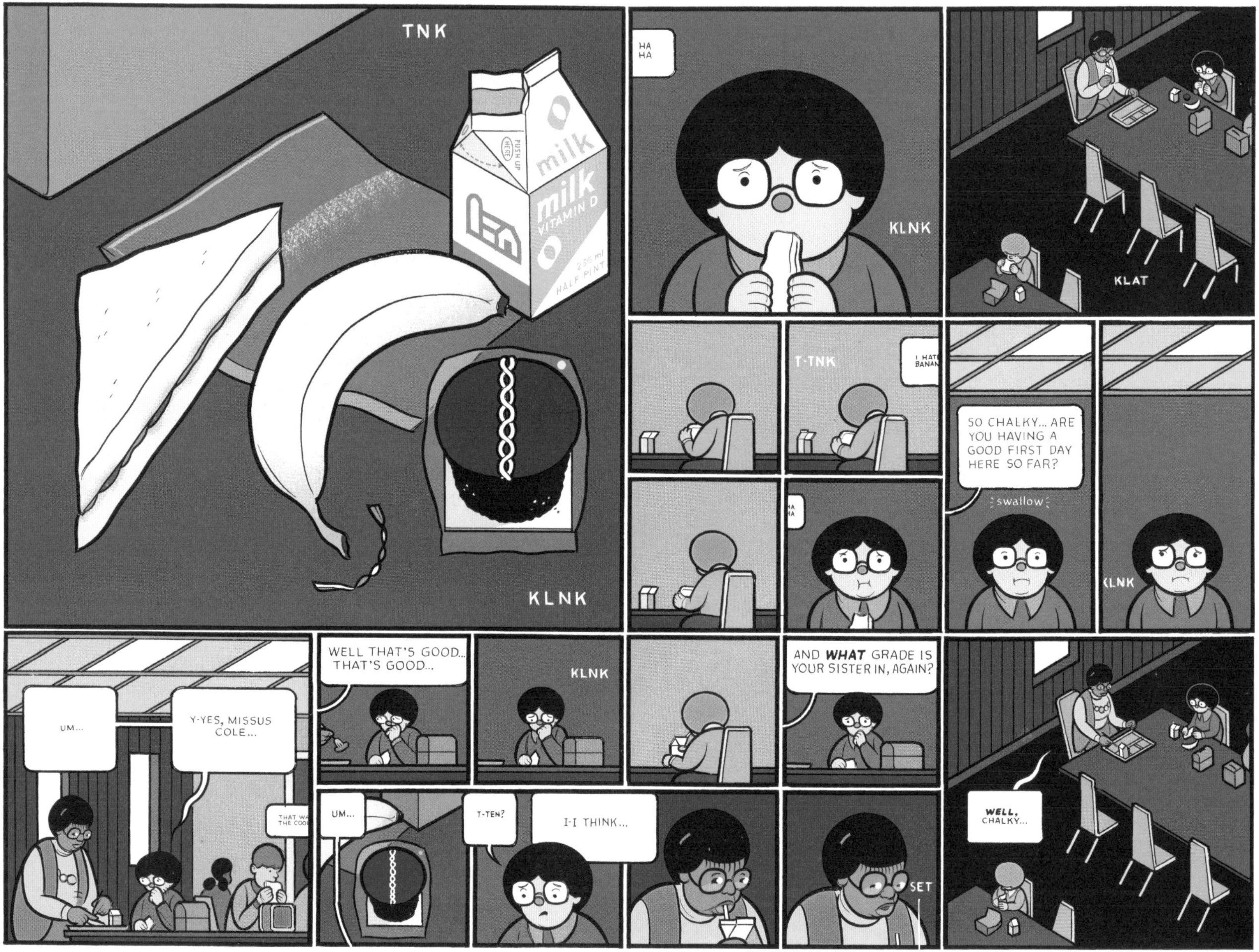
TNK
PUSH UP HERE
milk
milk VITAMIN D
236 ml HALF PINT
KLNK
HA HA
KLNK
KLAT
T-TNK
SO CHALKY... ARE YOU HAVING A GOOD FIRST DAY HERE SO FAR?
swallow
KLNK
UM...
Y-YES, MISSUS COLE...
WELL THAT'S GOOD... THAT'S GOOD...
KLNK
AND **WHAT** GRADE IS YOUR SISTER IN, AGAIN?
UM...
T-TEN?
I-I THINK...
SET
WELL, CHALKY...

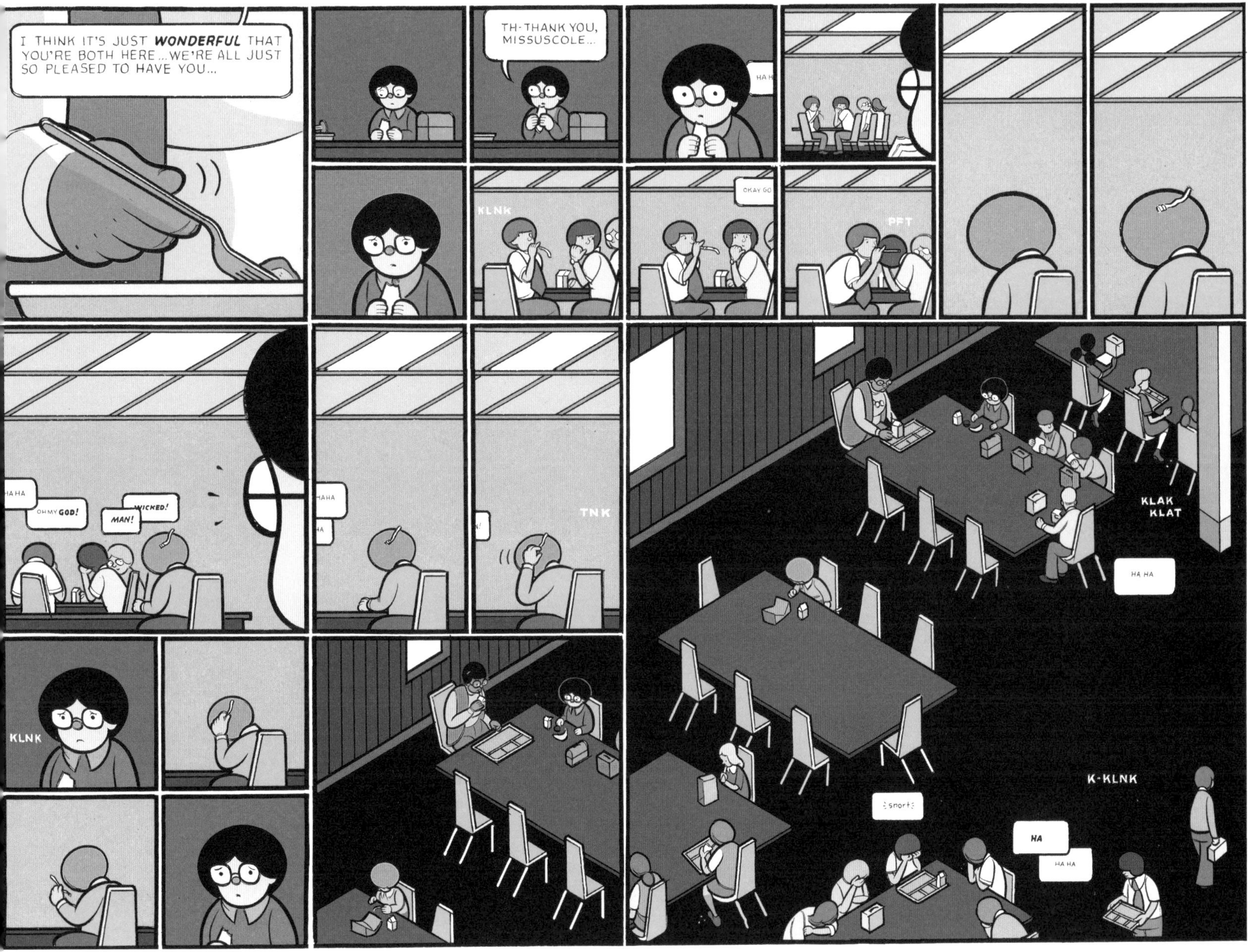
I THINK IT'S JUST **WONDERFUL** THAT YOU'RE BOTH HERE... WE'RE ALL JUST SO PLEASED TO HAVE YOU...
TH-THANK YOU, MISSUSCOLE...
KLNK
OKAY GO
PFT
OH MY GOD!
MAN!
WICKED!
TNK
KLNK
KLAK KLAT
HA HA
K-KLNK
snort
HA
HA HA

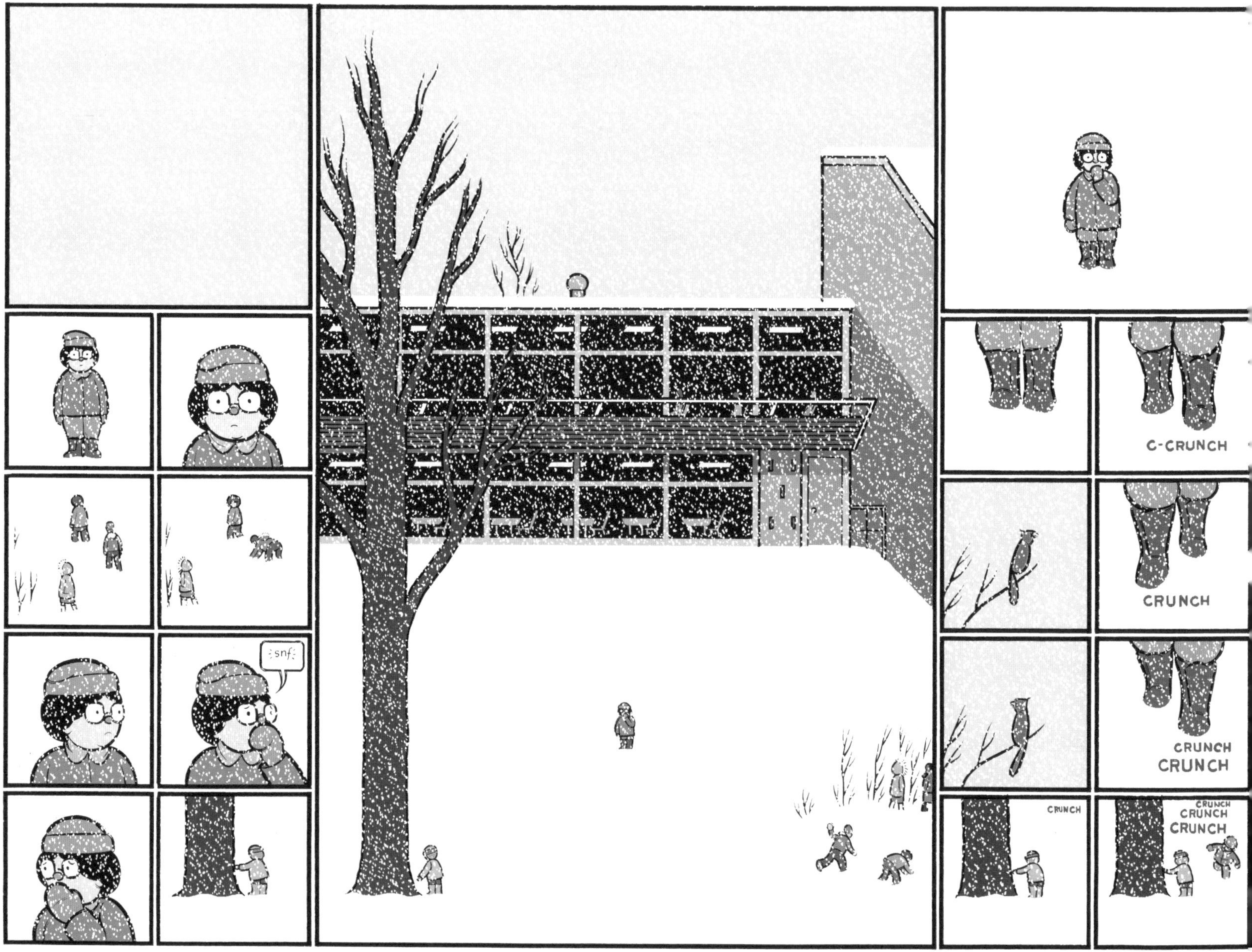
snf
C-CRUNCH
CRUNCH
CRUNCH
CRUNCH
CRUNCH
CRUNCH
CRUNCH
CRUNCH

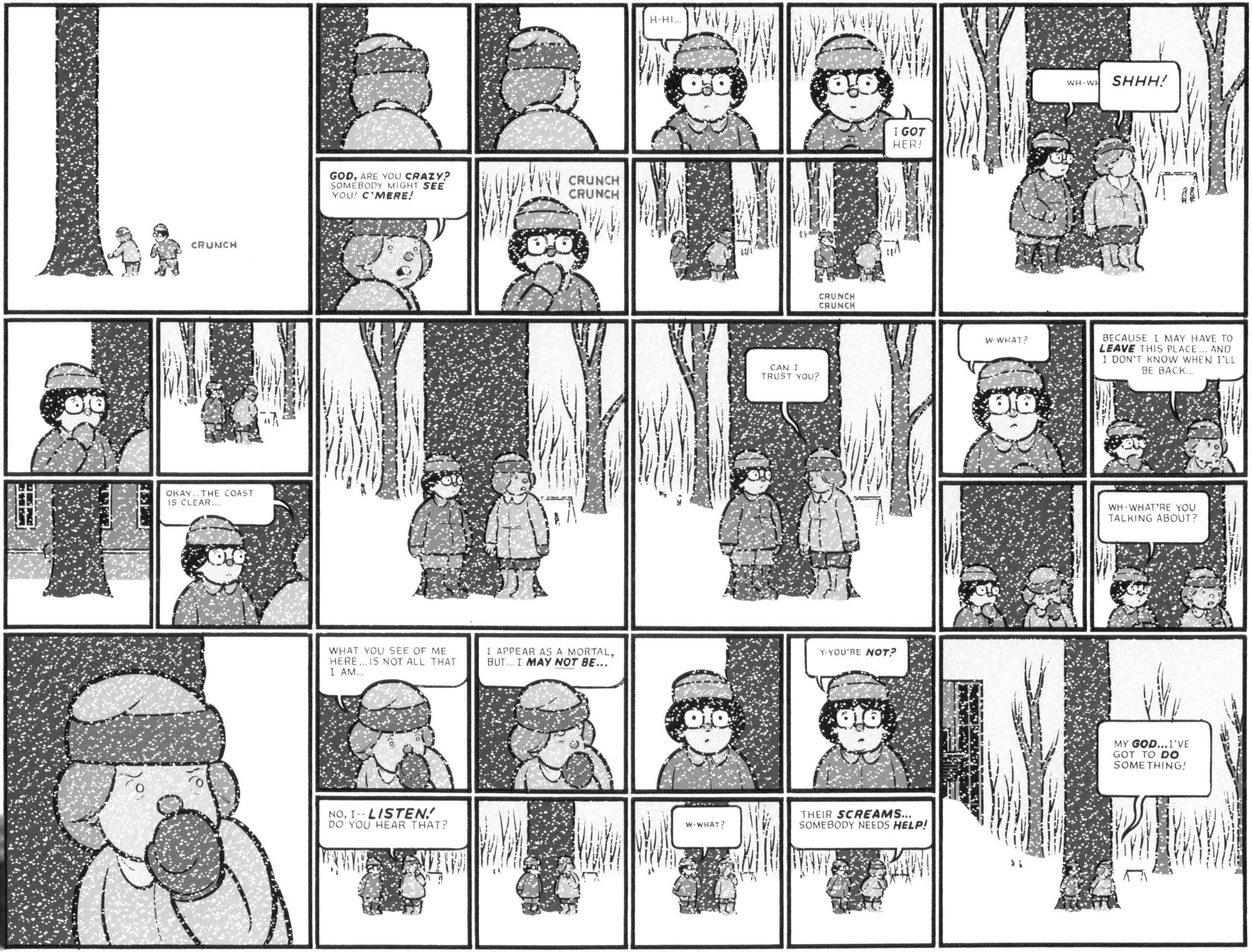

CRUNCH
H-HI...
I GOT HER!
GOD, ARE YOU CRAZY? SOMEBODY MIGHT SEE YOU! C'MERE!
CRUNCH CRUNCH
CRUNCH CRUNCH
WH-WH
SHHH!
OKAY... THE COAST IS CLEAR...
CAN I TRUST YOU?
W-WHAT?
BECAUSE I MAY HAVE TO LEAVE THIS PLACE... AND I DON'T KNOW WHEN I'LL BE BACK...
WH-WHAT'RE YOU TALKING ABOUT?
WHAT YOU SEE OF ME HERE... IS NOT ALL THAT I AM...
I APPEAR AS A MORTAL, BUT... I MAY NOT BE...
Y-YOU'RE NOT?
NO, I-- LISTEN! DO YOU HEAR THAT?
W-WHAT?
THEIR SCREAMS... SOMEBODY NEEDS HELP!
MY GOD... I'VE GOT TO DO SOMETHING!

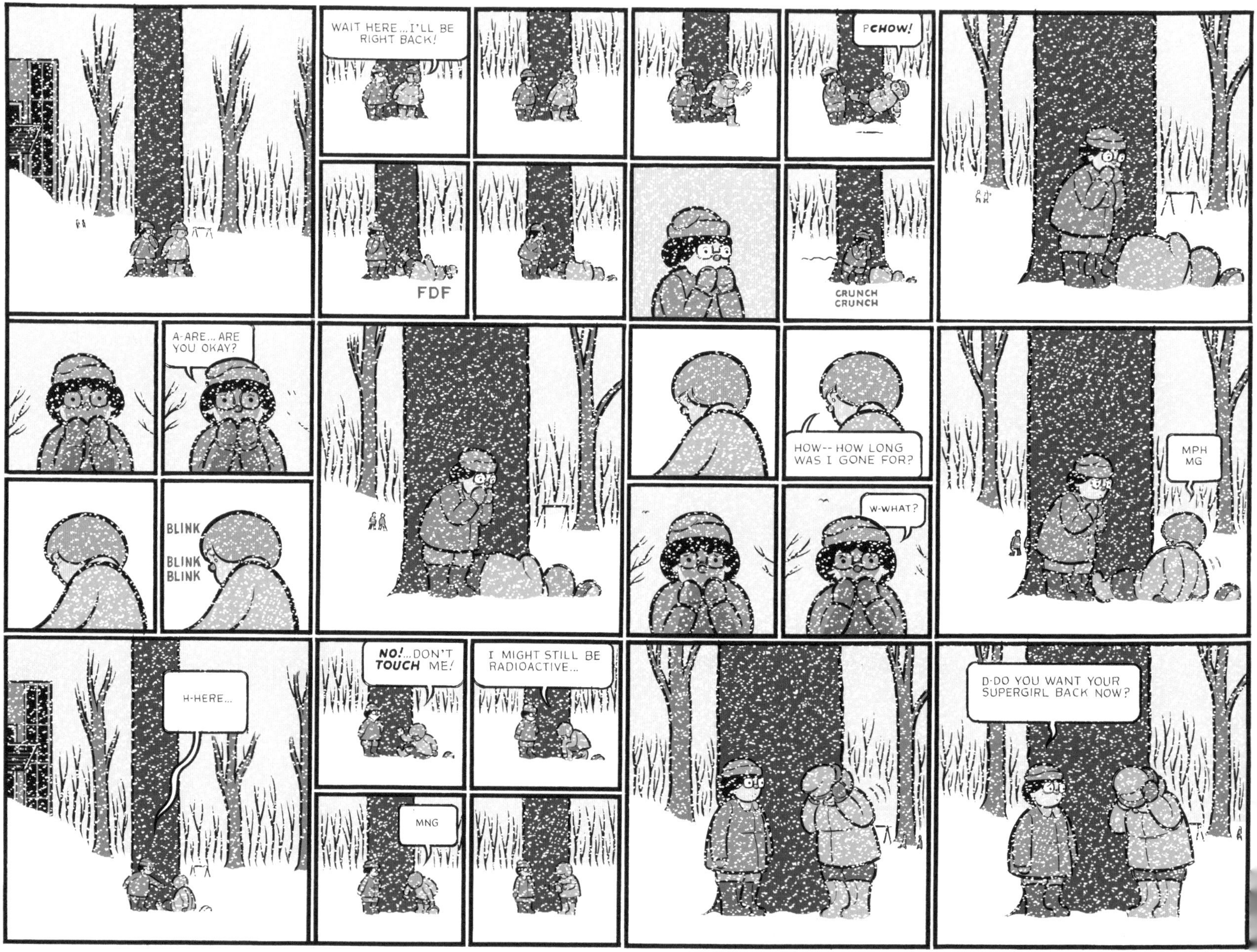
WAIT HERE...I'LL BE RIGHT BACK!
PCHOW!
FDF
CRUNCH CRUNCH
A-ARE... ARE YOU OKAY?
BLINK
BLINK BLINK
HOW-- HOW LONG WAS I GONE FOR?
W-WHAT?
MPH MG
H-HERE...
NO!...DON'T TOUCH ME!
I MIGHT STILL BE RADIOACTIVE...
MNG
D-DO YOU WANT YOUR SUPERGIRL BACK NOW?

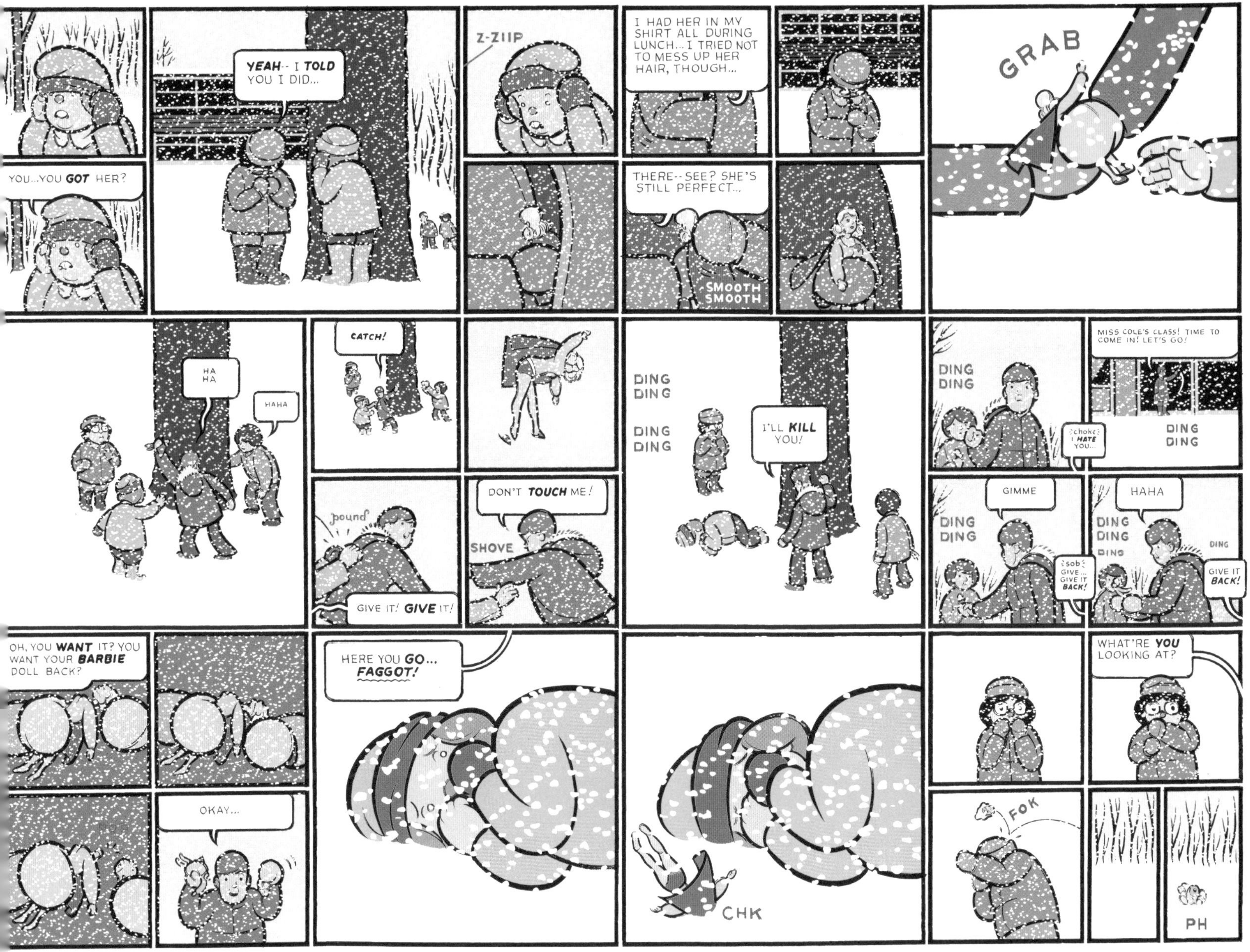
YOU...YOU **GOT** HER?
YEAH-- I **TOLD** YOU I DID...
Z-ZIIP
I HAD HER IN MY SHIRT ALL DURING LUNCH... I TRIED NOT TO MESS UP HER HAIR, THOUGH...
THERE--SEE? SHE'S STILL PERFECT...
SMOOTH SMOOTH
GRAB
HA HA
HAHA
CATCH!
pound
GIVE IT! **GIVE** IT!
DON'T **TOUCH** ME!
SHOVE
DING DING
DING DING
I'LL **KILL** YOU!
DING DING
choke I **HATE** YOU...
MISS COLE'S CLASS! TIME TO COME IN! LET'S GO!
DING DING
GIMME
DING DING
sob GIVE... GIVE IT **BACK!**
HAHA
DING DING DING
DING
GIVE IT **BACK!**
OH, YOU **WANT** IT? YOU WANT YOUR **BARBIE** DOLL BACK?
OKAY...
HERE YOU **GO**... **FAGGOT!**
CHK
WHAT'RE **YOU** LOOKING AT?
FOK
PH

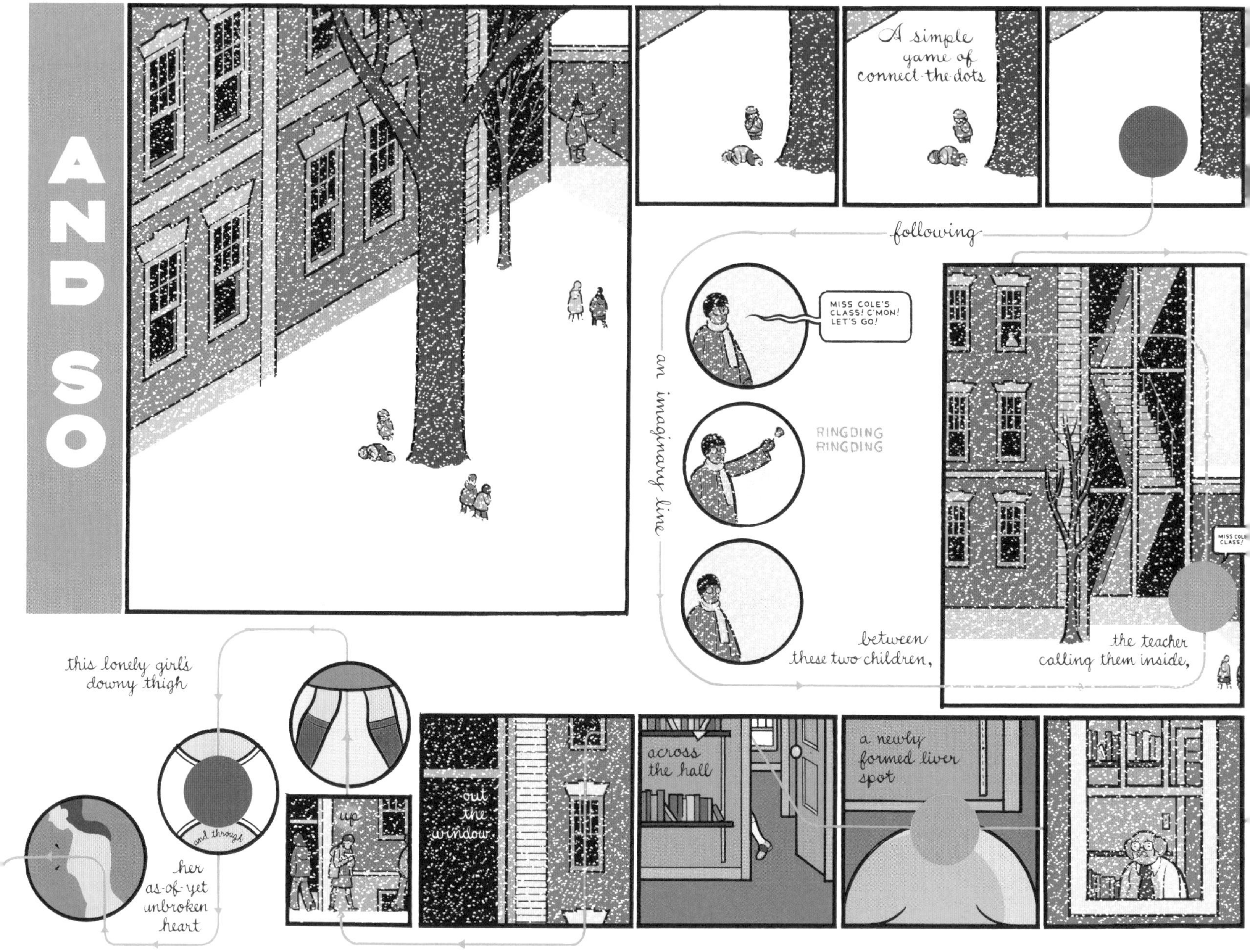
AND SO
A simple game of connect-the-dots
following
an imaginary line
MISS COLE'S CLASS! C'MON! LET'S GO!
RINGDING RINGDING
between these two children,
the teacher calling them inside,
out the window,
across the hall
a newly formed liver spot
up
and through
this lonely girl's downy thigh
her as-of-yet unbroken heart

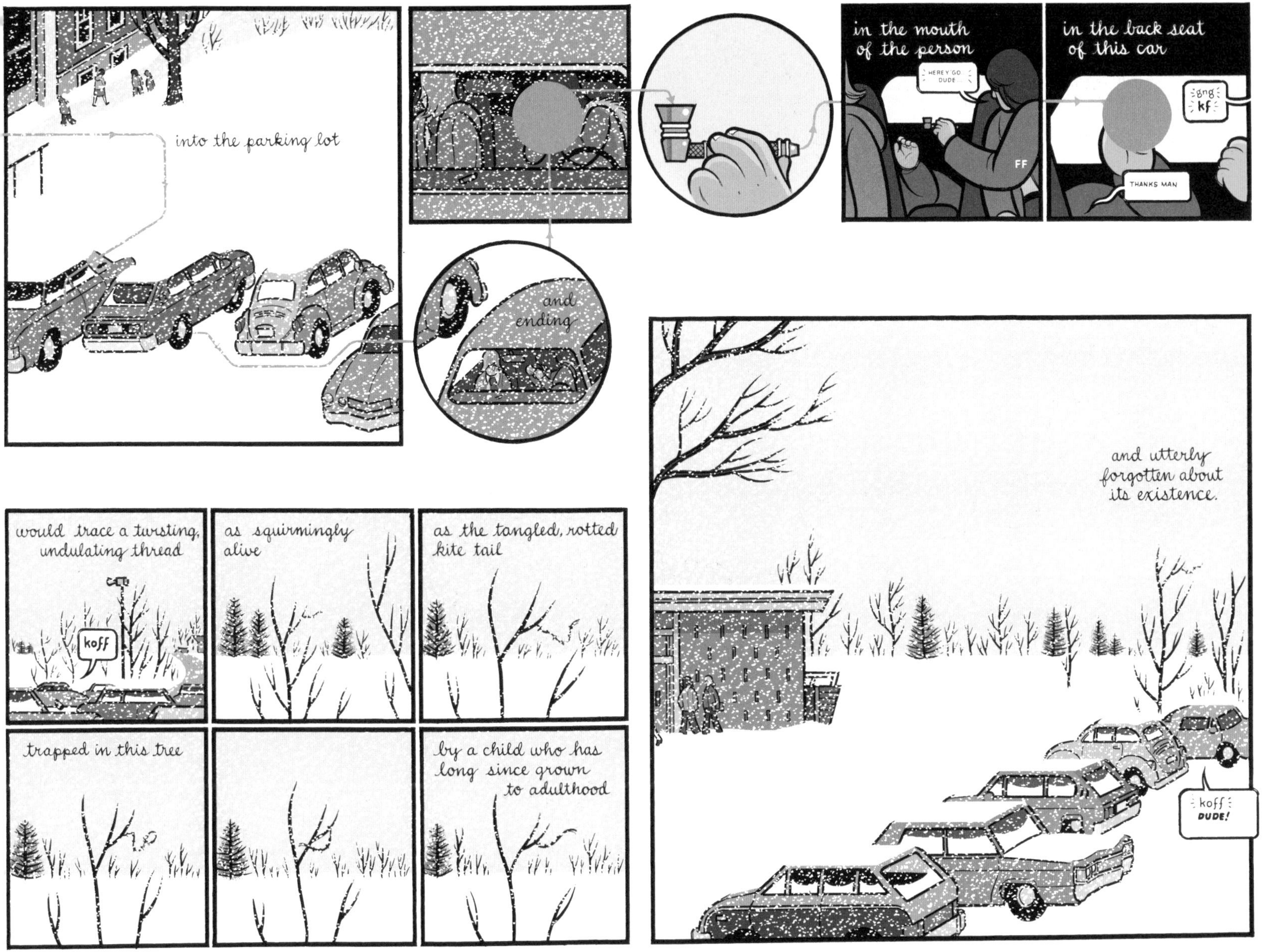

into the parking lot
and ending
in the mouth of the person
HERE Y'GO DUDE
FF
in the back seat of this car
gng kf
THANKS MAN
would trace a twisting, undulating thread
koff
as squirmingly alive
as the tangled, rotted kite tail
trapped in this tree
by a child who has long since grown to adulthood
and utterly forgotten about its existence.
koff DUDE!

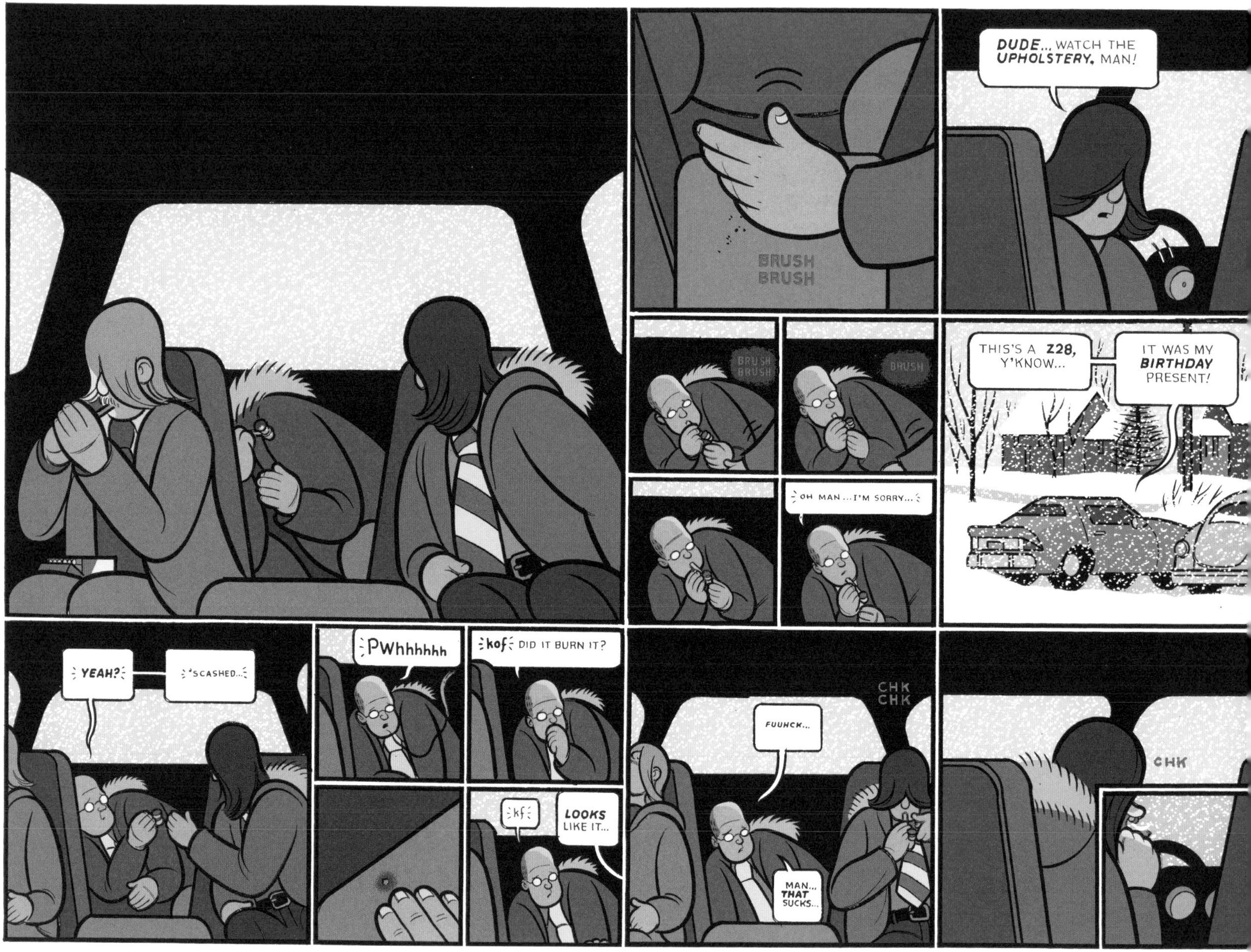
BRUSH
BRUSH
DUDE... WATCH THE UPHOLSTERY, MAN!
BRUSH
BRUSH
BRUSH
OH MAN... I'M SORRY...
THIS'S A Z28, Y'KNOW...
IT WAS MY BIRTHDAY PRESENT!
YEAH?
'SCASHED...
PWhhhhhh
kof DID IT BURN IT?
kf
LOOKS LIKE IT...
CHK
CHK
FUUHCK...
MAN... THAT SUCKS...
CHK

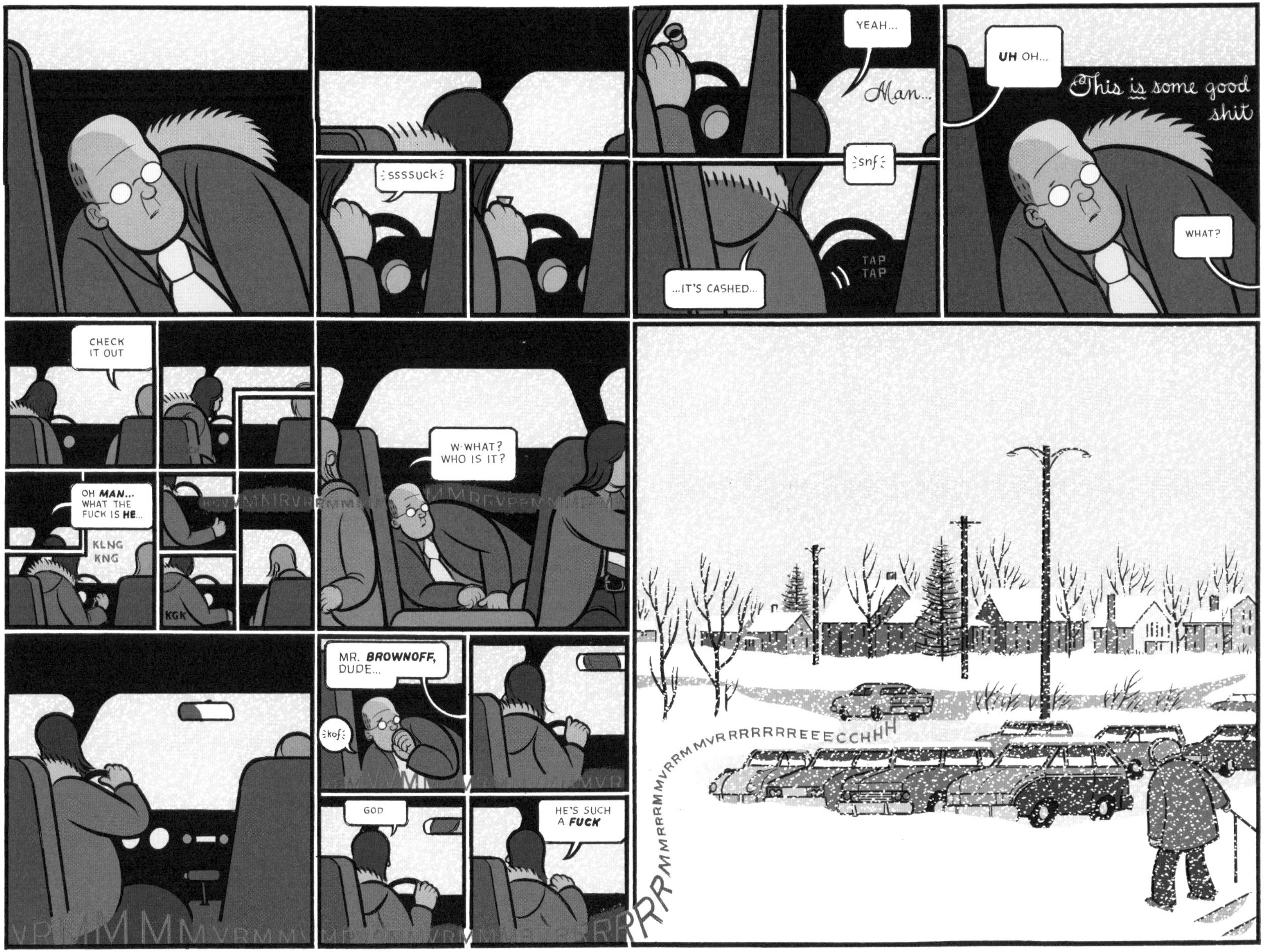

YEAH...
Man...
UH OH...
This is some good shit
ssssuck
snf
...IT'S CASHED...
TAP TAP
WHAT?
CHECK IT OUT
OH MAN... WHAT THE FUCK IS HE...
KLNG KNG
KGK
W-WHAT? WHO IS IT?
MR. BROWNOFF, DUDE...
kof
GOD
HE'S SUCH A FUCK
MMRRRMMVRRMMVRRRRRRRRREEECCHHH

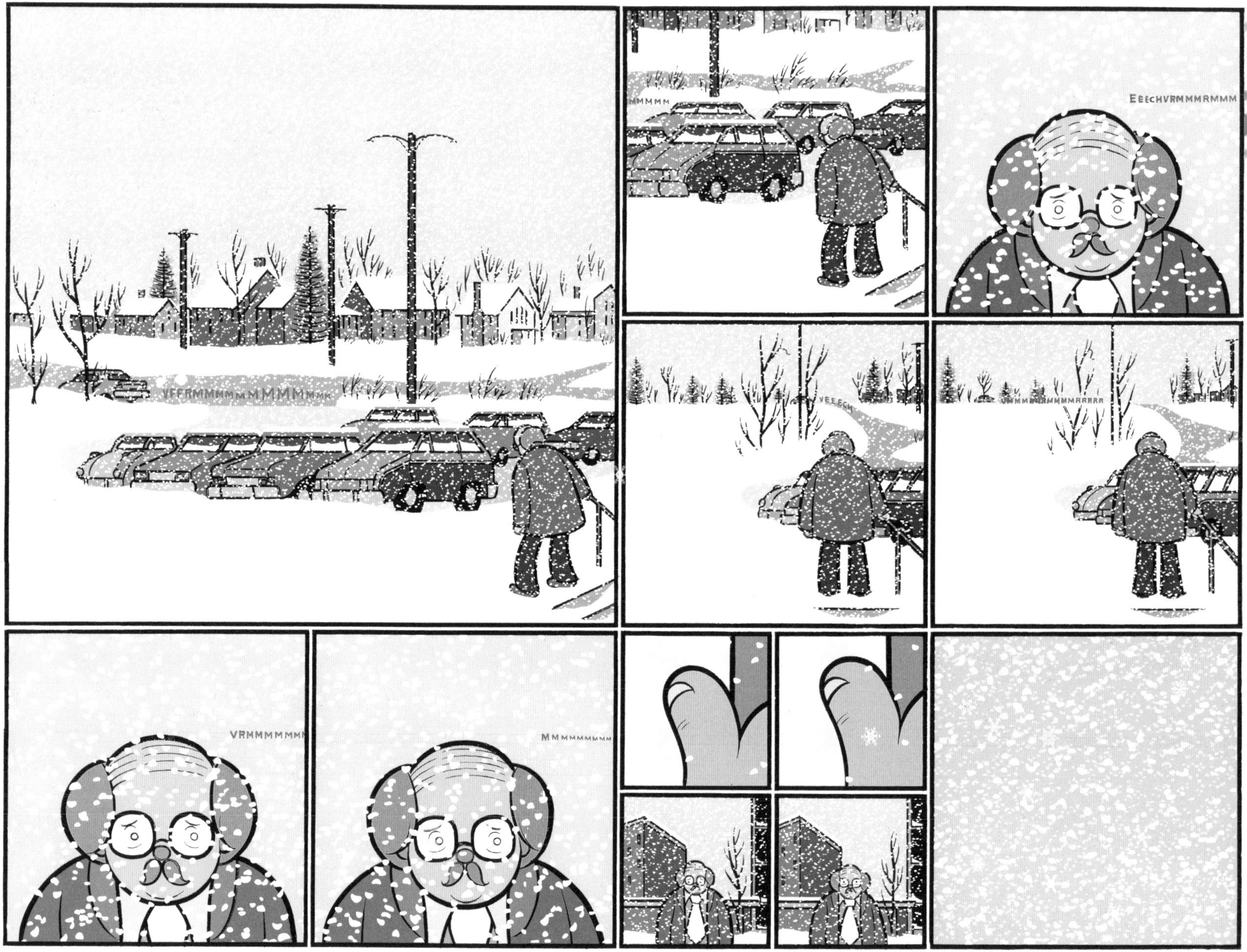
VFFRMMMMMMMMMMMMMK
MMMMM
EEECHVRMMMMRMMM
VEEECH
VRMMMMMMM
MMMMMMMM

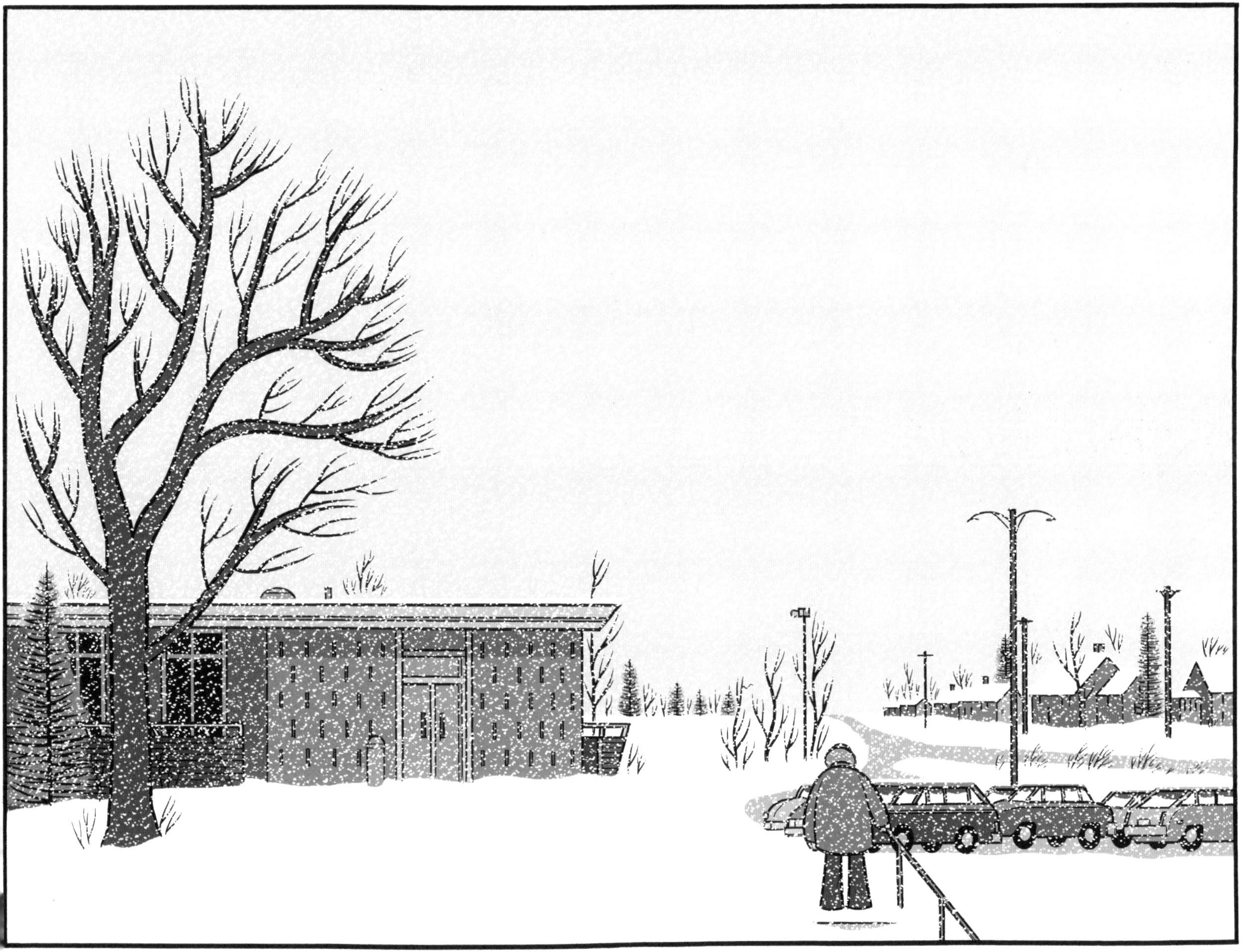

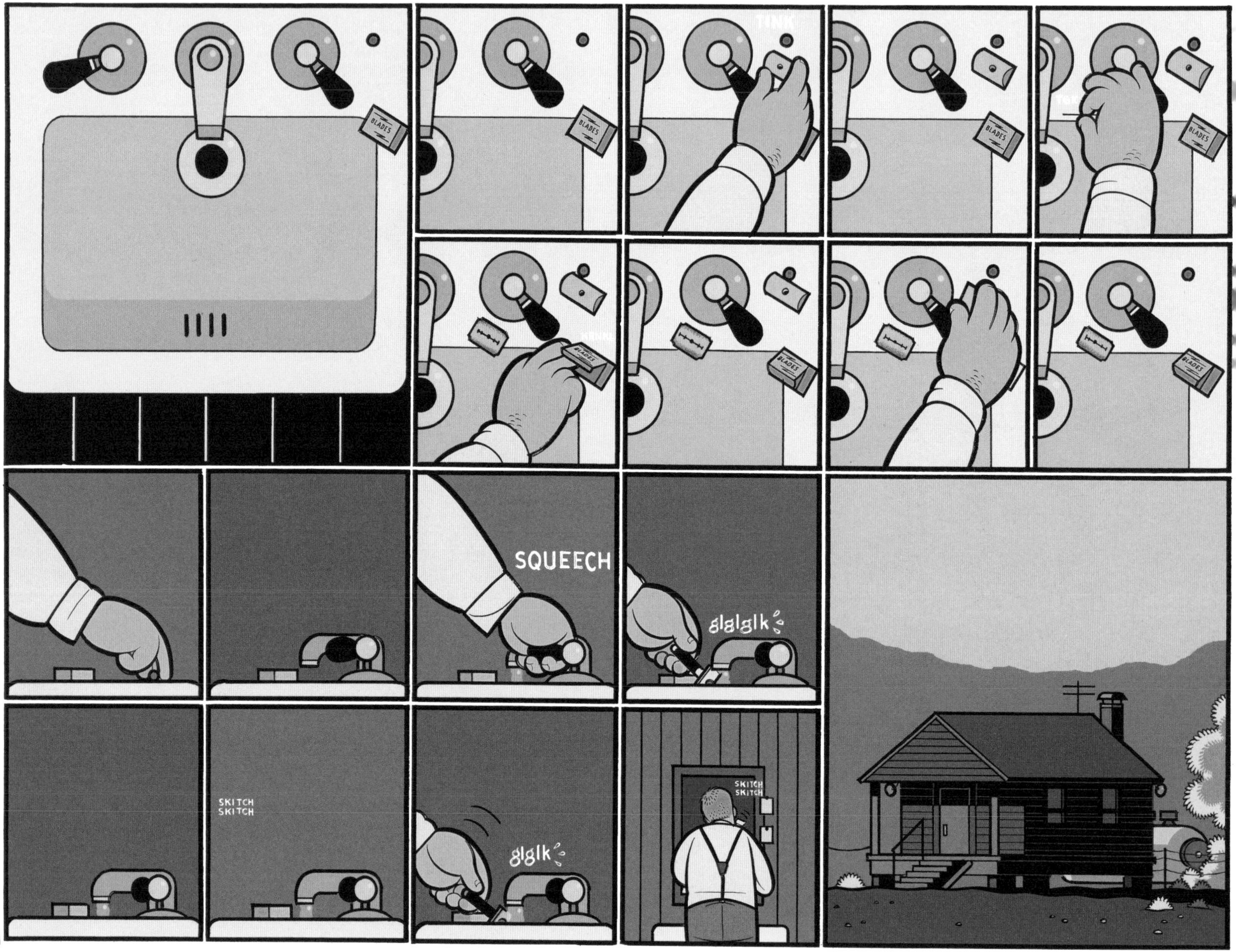
BLADES
TINK
BLADES
SQUEECH
glglglk
SKITCH
SKITCH
glglk
SKITCH
SKITCH

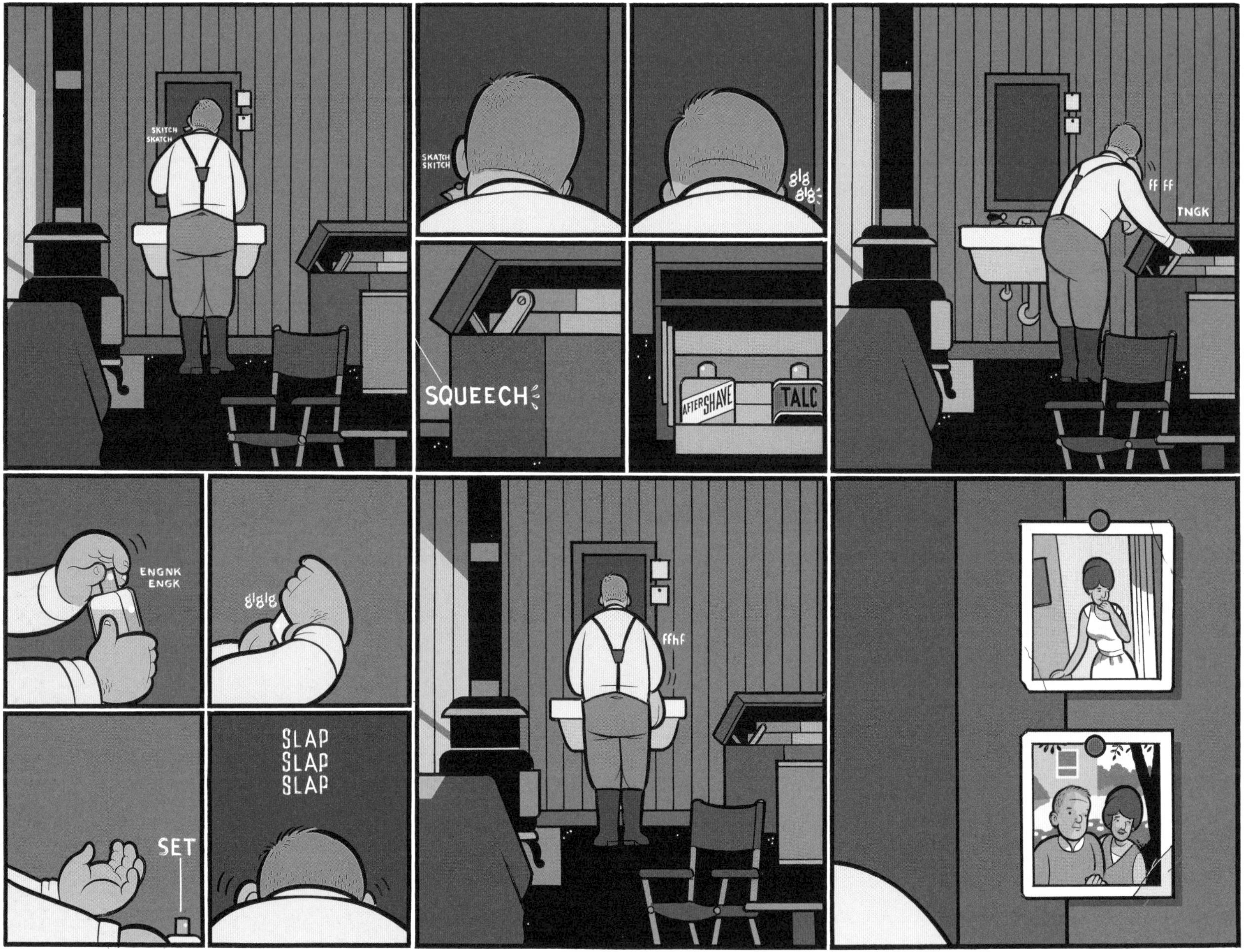
SKITCH
SKATCH
SKATCH
SKITCH
glg
glg
SQUEECH
AFTERSHAVE
TALC
ff ff
TNGK
ENGNK
ENGK
glglg
ffhf
SET
SLAP
SLAP
SLAP

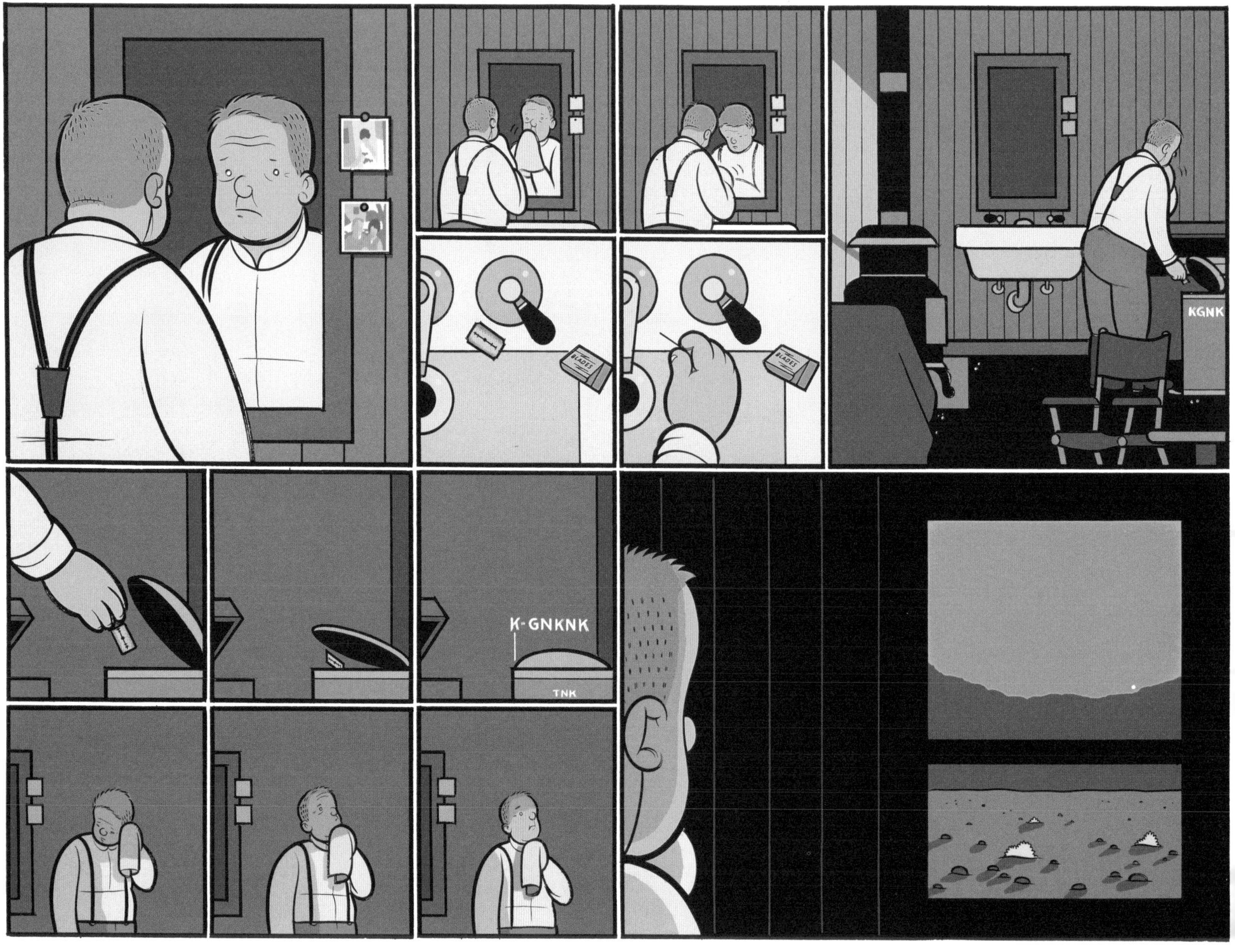
BLADES
BLADES
KGNK
K-GNKNK
TNK

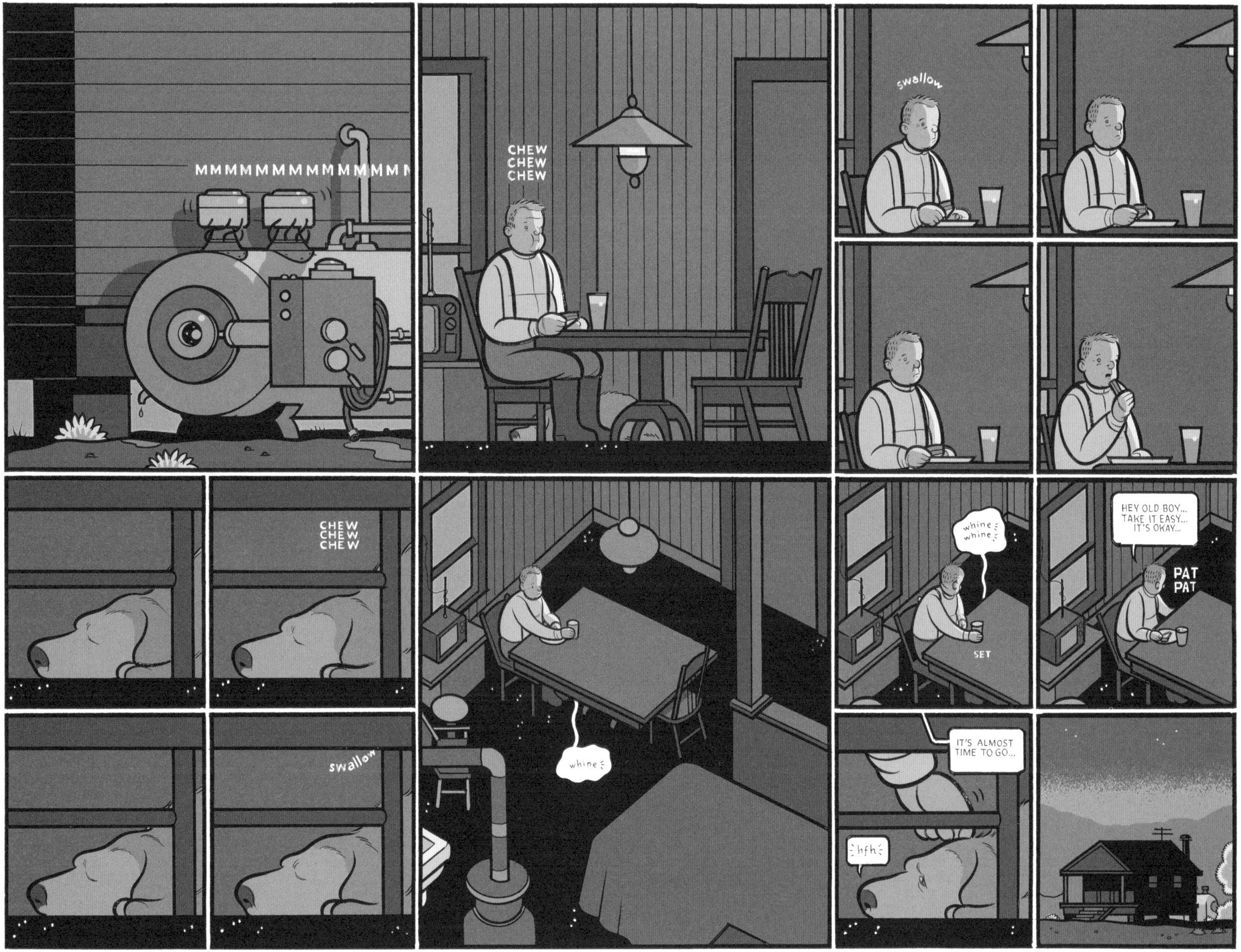

MMMMMMMMMMMMMMMM
CHEW CHEW CHEW
swallow
CHEW CHEW CHEW
swallow
whine
whine whine
SET
HEY OLD BOY... TAKE IT EASY... IT'S OKAY...
PAT PAT
IT'S ALMOST TIME TO GO...
hfh

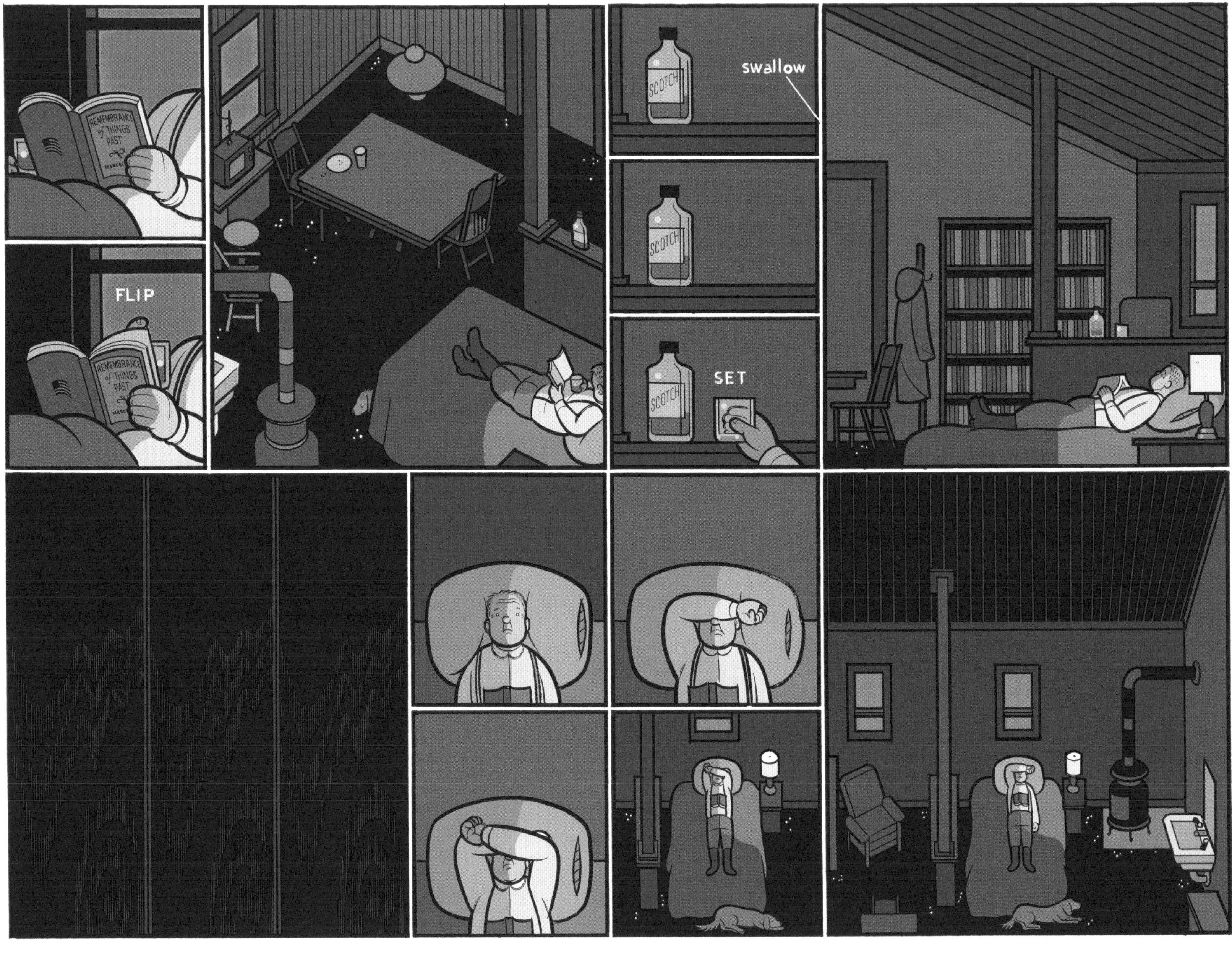
REMEMBRANCE of THINGS PAST
FLIP
REMEMBRANCE of THINGS PAST
SCOTCH
swallow
SCOTCH
SCOTCH
SET

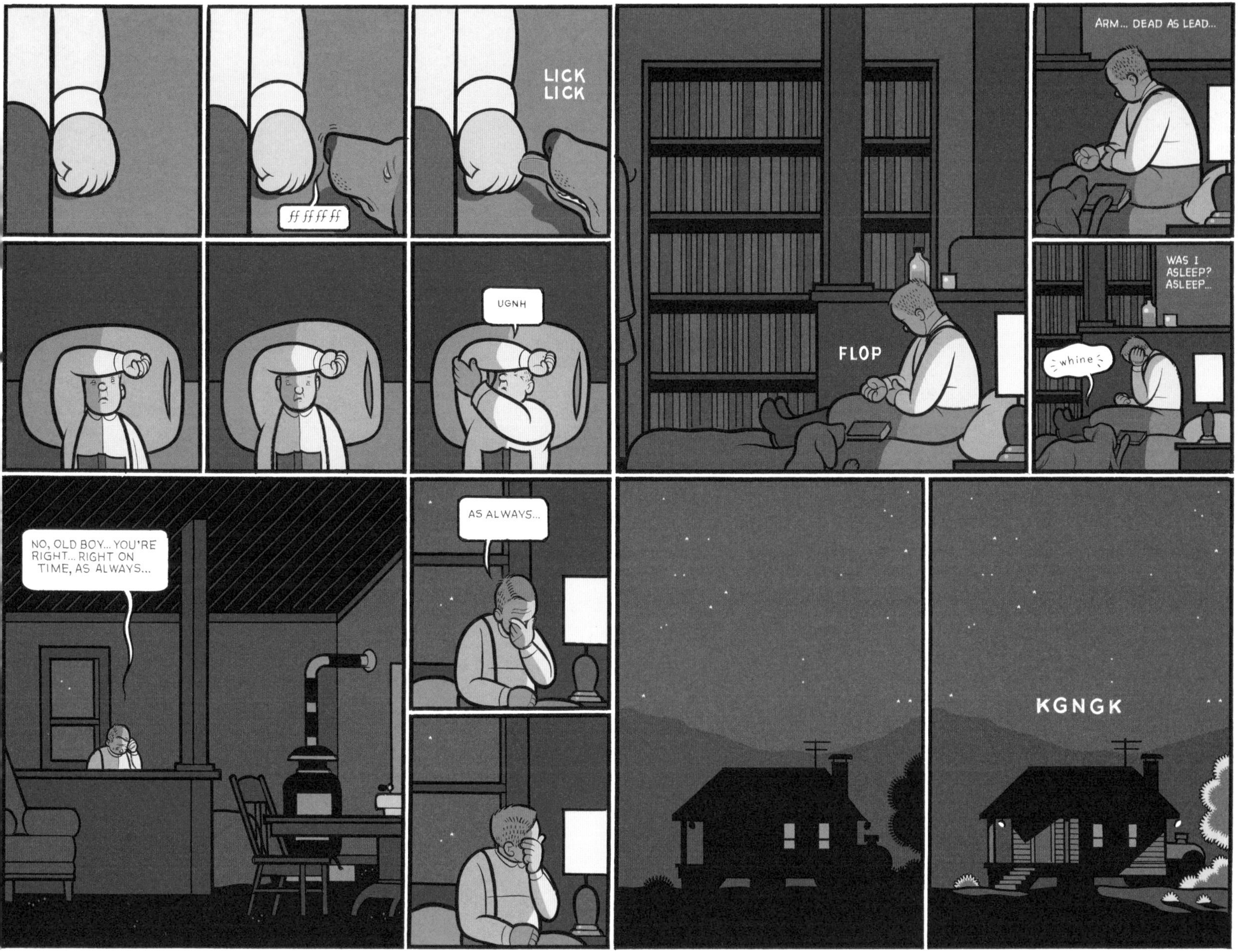

ff ff ff ff
LICK LICK
ARM... DEAD AS LEAD...
UGNH
FLOP
WAS I ASLEEP? ASLEEP...
whine
NO, OLD BOY... YOU'RE RIGHT... RIGHT ON TIME, AS ALWAYS...
AS ALWAYS...
KGNGK

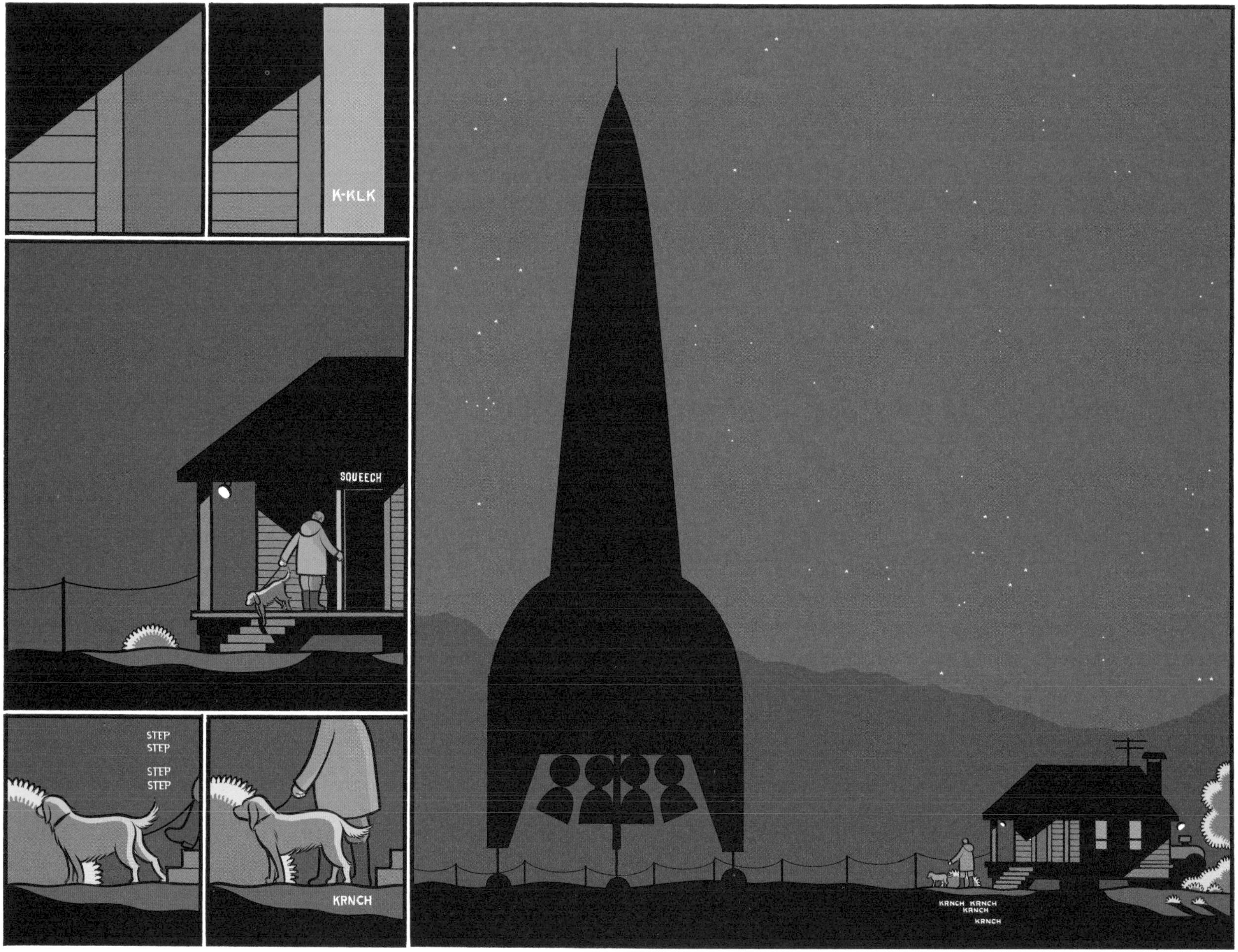
K-KLK
SQUEECH
STEP
STEP
STEP
STEP
KRNCH
KRNCH KRNCH
KRNCH
KRNCH

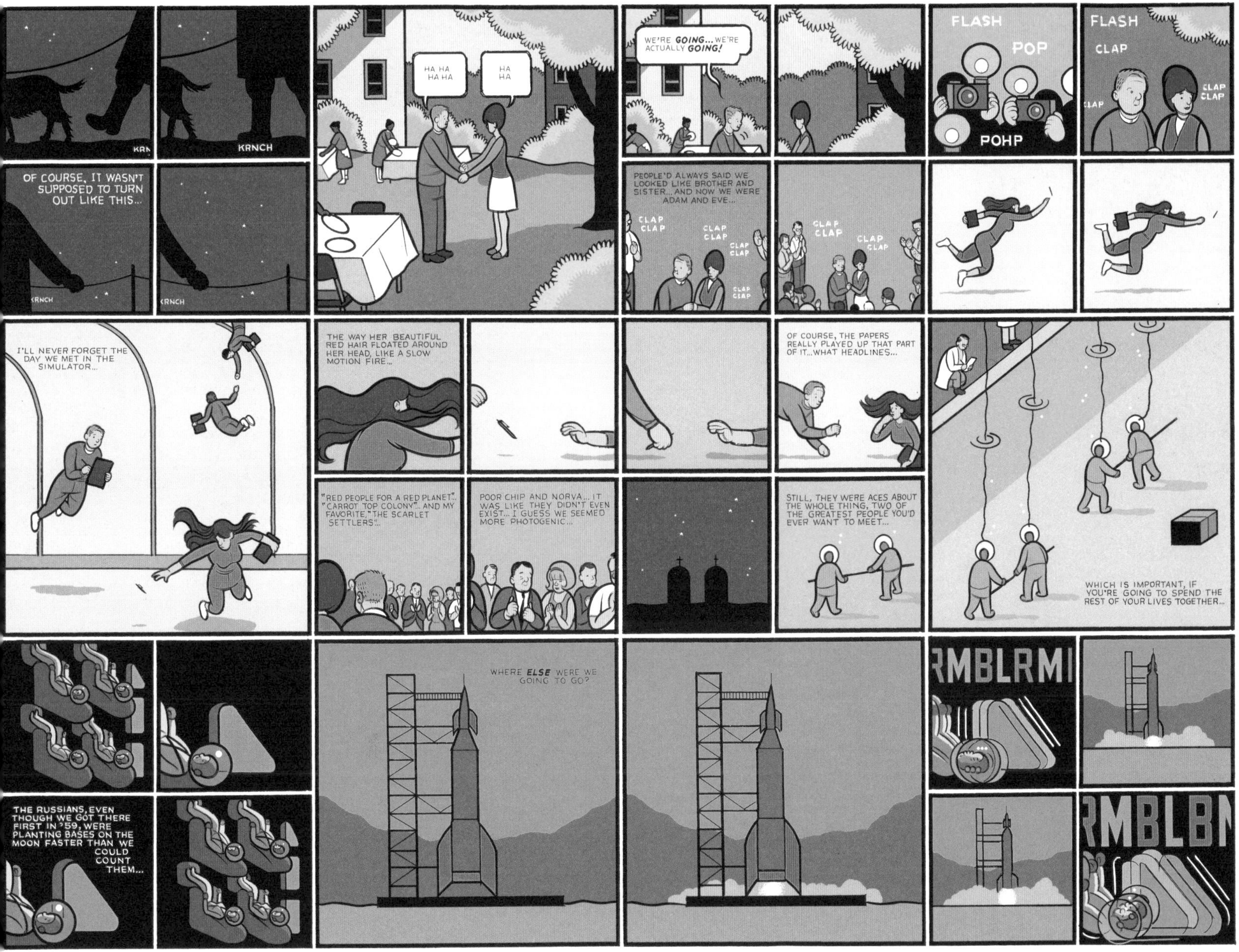
KRN
KRNCH
OF COURSE, IT WASN'T SUPPOSED TO TURN OUT LIKE THIS...
KRNCH
KRNCH
HA HA HA HA
HA HA
WE'RE GOING... WE'RE ACTUALLY GOING!
FLASH
POP
POHP
FLASH
CLAP
CLAP
CLAP CLAP
PEOPLE'D ALWAYS SAID WE LOOKED LIKE BROTHER AND SISTER... AND NOW WE WERE ADAM AND EVE...
CLAP CLAP
CLAP CLAP
CLAP CLAP
CLAP CLAP
CLAP CLAP
CLAP CLAP
I'LL NEVER FORGET THE DAY WE MET IN THE SIMULATOR...
THE WAY HER BEAUTIFUL RED HAIR FLOATED AROUND HER HEAD, LIKE A SLOW MOTION FIRE...
OF COURSE, THE PAPERS REALLY PLAYED UP THAT PART OF IT... WHAT HEADLINES...
"RED PEOPLE FOR A RED PLANET". "CARROT TOP COLONY"... AND MY FAVORITE, "THE SCARLET SETTLERS"...
POOR CHIP AND NORVA... IT WAS LIKE THEY DIDN'T EVEN EXIST... I GUESS WE SEEMED MORE PHOTOGENIC...
STILL, THEY WERE ACES ABOUT THE WHOLE THING, TWO OF THE GREATEST PEOPLE YOU'D EVER WANT TO MEET...
WHICH IS IMPORTANT, IF YOU'RE GOING TO SPEND THE REST OF YOUR LIVES TOGETHER...
THE RUSSIANS, EVEN THOUGH WE GOT THERE FIRST IN '59, WERE PLANTING BASES ON THE MOON FASTER THAN WE COULD COUNT THEM...
WHERE ELSE WERE WE GOING TO GO?
RMBLRMI
RMBLBN

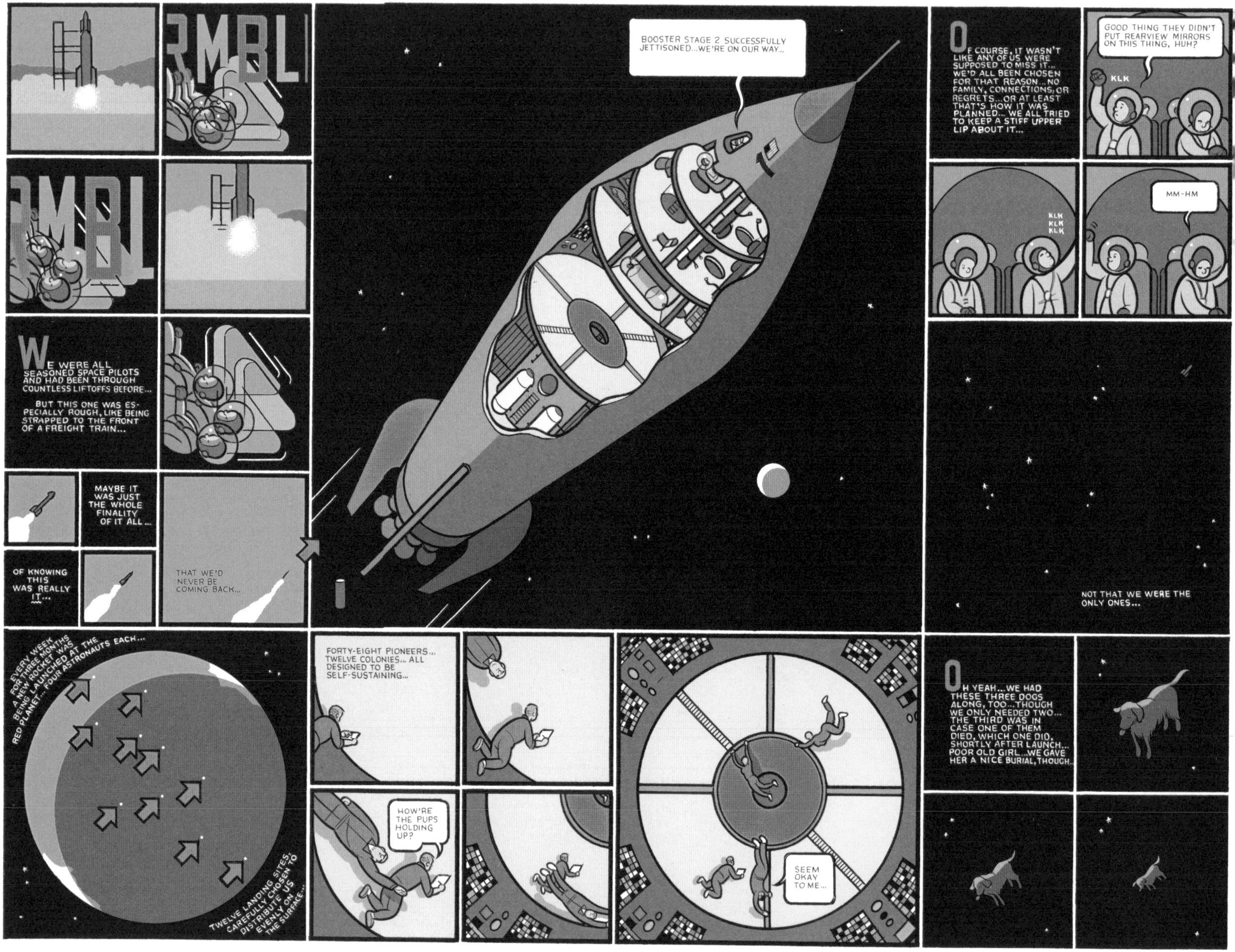

RMBL
RMBL
WE WERE ALL SEASONED SPACE PILOTS AND HAD BEEN THROUGH COUNTLESS LIFTOFFS BEFORE...
BUT THIS ONE WAS ESPECIALLY ROUGH, LIKE BEING STRAPPED TO THE FRONT OF A FREIGHT TRAIN...
MAYBE IT WAS JUST THE WHOLE FINALITY OF IT ALL...
OF KNOWING THIS WAS REALLY IT...
THAT WE'D NEVER BE COMING BACK...
BOOSTER STAGE 2 SUCCESSFULLY JETTISONED... WE'RE ON OUR WAY...
OF COURSE, IT WASN'T LIKE ANY OF US WERE SUPPOSED TO MISS IT... WE'D ALL BEEN CHOSEN FOR THAT REASON... NO FAMILY, CONNECTIONS, OR REGRETS... OR AT LEAST THAT'S HOW IT WAS PLANNED... WE ALL TRIED TO KEEP A STIFF UPPER LIP ABOUT IT...
GOOD THING THEY DIDN'T PUT REARVIEW MIRRORS ON THIS THING, HUH?
KLK
KLK KLK KLK
MM-HM
NOT THAT WE WERE THE ONLY ONES...
EVERY WEEK FOR THREE MONTHS A NEW ROCKET WAS BEING LAUNCHED AT THE RED PLANET... FOUR ASTRONAUTS EACH...
TWELVE LANDING SITES, CAREFULLY CHOSEN TO DISTRIBUTE US EVENLY ON THE SURFACE...
FORTY-EIGHT PIONEERS... TWELVE COLONIES... ALL DESIGNED TO BE SELF-SUSTAINING...
HOW'RE THE PUPS HOLDING UP?
SEEM OKAY TO ME...
OH YEAH... WE HAD THESE THREE DOGS ALONG, TOO... THOUGH WE ONLY NEEDED TWO... THE THIRD WAS IN CASE ONE OF THEM DIED, WHICH ONE DID, SHORTLY AFTER LAUNCH... POOR OLD GIRL... WE GAVE HER A NICE BURIAL, THOUGH...

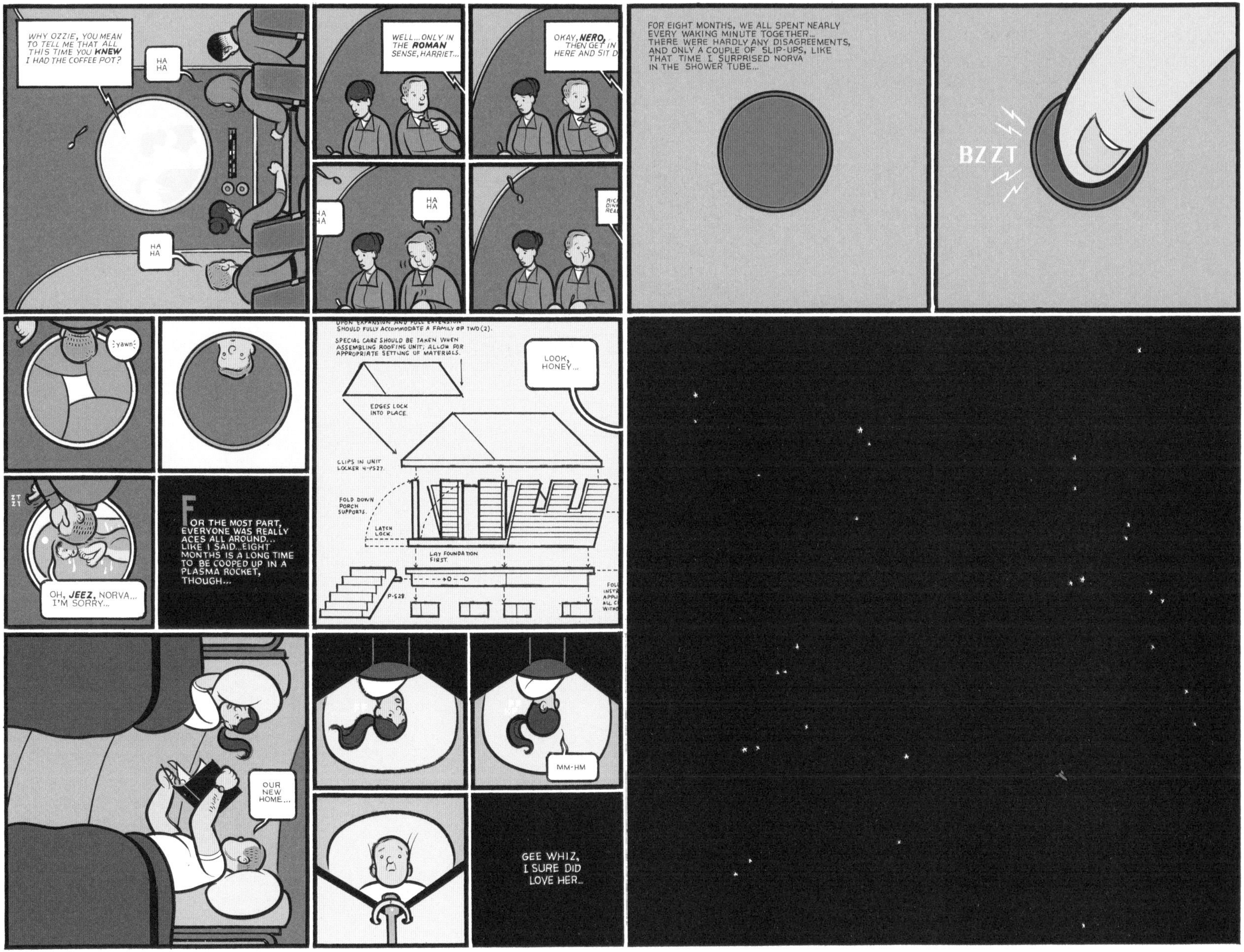
WHY OZZIE, YOU MEAN TO TELL ME THAT ALL THIS TIME YOU **KNEW** I HAD THE COFFEE POT?
HA HA
HA HA
WELL... ONLY IN THE **ROMAN** SENSE, HARRIET...
OKAY, **NERO**, THEN GET IN HERE AND SIT D
HA HA
HA HA
FOR EIGHT MONTHS, WE ALL SPENT NEARLY EVERY WAKING MINUTE TOGETHER... THERE WERE HARDLY ANY DISAGREEMENTS, AND ONLY A COUPLE OF SLIP-UPS, LIKE THAT TIME I SURPRISED NORVA IN THE SHOWER TUBE...
BZZT
yawn
ZT ZT
OH, **JEEZ**, NORVA... I'M SORRY...
FOR THE MOST PART, EVERYONE WAS REALLY ACES ALL AROUND... LIKE I SAID... EIGHT MONTHS IS A LONG TIME TO BE COOPED UP IN A PLASMA ROCKET, THOUGH...
SHOULD FULLY ACCOMMODATE A FAMILY OF TWO (2).
SPECIAL CARE SHOULD BE TAKEN WHEN ASSEMBLING ROOFING UNIT; ALLOW FOR APPROPRIATE SETTLING OF MATERIALS.
EDGES LOCK INTO PLACE.
CLIPS IN UNIT LOCKER 4-P527.
FOLD DOWN PORCH SUPPORTS.
LATCH LOCK
LAY FOUNDATION FIRST.
P-528
LOOK, HONEY...
OUR NEW HOME...
MM-HM
GEE WHIZ, I SURE DID LOVE HER...

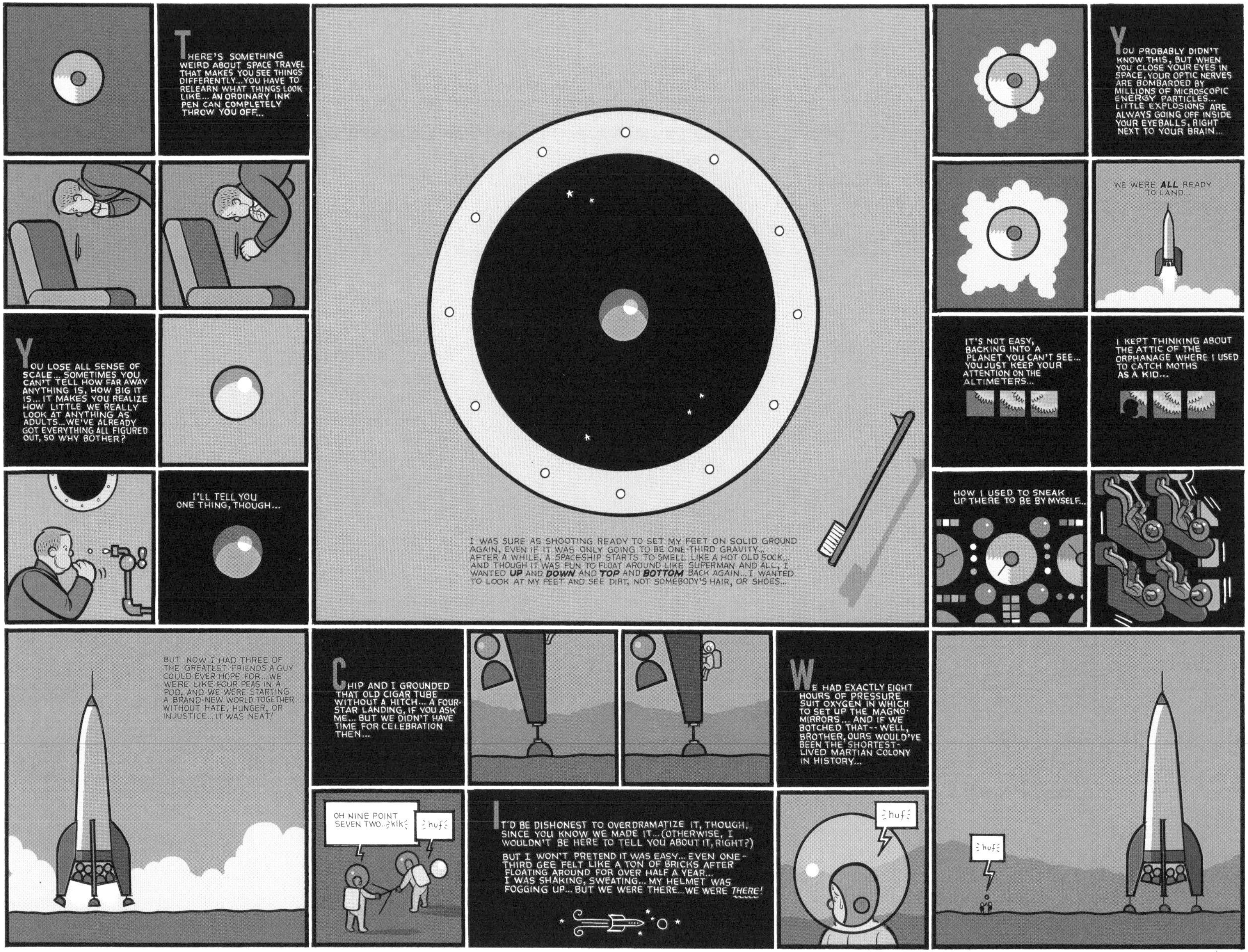
THERE'S SOMETHING WEIRD ABOUT SPACE TRAVEL THAT MAKES YOU SEE THINGS DIFFERENTLY... YOU HAVE TO RELEARN WHAT THINGS LOOK LIKE... AN ORDINARY INK PEN CAN COMPLETELY THROW YOU OFF...
YOU LOSE ALL SENSE OF SCALE... SOMETIMES YOU CAN'T TELL HOW FAR AWAY ANYTHING IS, HOW BIG IT IS... IT MAKES YOU REALIZE HOW LITTLE WE REALLY LOOK AT ANYTHING AS ADULTS... WE'VE ALREADY GOT EVERYTHING ALL FIGURED OUT, SO WHY BOTHER?
I'LL TELL YOU ONE THING, THOUGH...
I WAS SURE AS SHOOTING READY TO SET MY FEET ON SOLID GROUND AGAIN, EVEN IF IT WAS ONLY GOING TO BE ONE-THIRD GRAVITY... AFTER A WHILE, A SPACESHIP STARTS TO SMELL LIKE A HOT OLD SOCK... AND THOUGH IT WAS FUN TO FLOAT AROUND LIKE SUPERMAN AND ALL, I WANTED UP AND DOWN AND TOP AND BOTTOM BACK AGAIN... I WANTED TO LOOK AT MY FEET AND SEE DIRT, NOT SOMEBODY'S HAIR, OR SHOES...
YOU PROBABLY DIDN'T KNOW THIS, BUT WHEN YOU CLOSE YOUR EYES IN SPACE, YOUR OPTIC NERVES ARE BOMBARDED BY MILLIONS OF MICROSCOPIC ENERGY PARTICLES... LITTLE EXPLOSIONS ARE ALWAYS GOING OFF INSIDE YOUR EYEBALLS, RIGHT NEXT TO YOUR BRAIN...
WE WERE ALL READY TO LAND...
IT'S NOT EASY, BACKING INTO A PLANET YOU CAN'T SEE... YOU JUST KEEP YOUR ATTENTION ON THE ALTIMETERS...
I KEPT THINKING ABOUT THE ATTIC OF THE ORPHANAGE WHERE I USED TO CATCH MOTHS AS A KID...
HOW I USED TO SNEAK UP THERE TO BE BY MYSELF...
BUT NOW I HAD THREE OF THE GREATEST FRIENDS A GUY COULD EVER HOPE FOR... WE WERE LIKE FOUR PEAS IN A POD, AND WE WERE STARTING A BRAND-NEW WORLD TOGETHER... WITHOUT HATE, HUNGER, OR INJUSTICE... IT WAS NEAT!
CHIP AND I GROUNDED THAT OLD CIGAR TUBE WITHOUT A HITCH... A FOUR-STAR LANDING, IF YOU ASK ME... BUT WE DIDN'T HAVE TIME FOR CELEBRATION THEN...
WE HAD EXACTLY EIGHT HOURS OF PRESSURE SUIT OXYGEN IN WHICH TO SET UP THE MAGNO-MIRRORS... AND IF WE BOTCHED THAT-- WELL, BROTHER, OURS WOULD'VE BEEN THE SHORTEST-LIVED MARTIAN COLONY IN HISTORY...
OH NINE POINT SEVEN TWO... klk
huf
IT'D BE DISHONEST TO OVERDRAMATIZE IT, THOUGH, SINCE YOU KNOW WE MADE IT... (OTHERWISE, I WOULDN'T BE HERE TO TELL YOU ABOUT IT, RIGHT?)
BUT I WON'T PRETEND IT WAS EASY... EVEN ONE-THIRD GEE FELT LIKE A TON OF BRICKS AFTER FLOATING AROUND FOR OVER HALF A YEAR... I WAS SHAKING, SWEATING... MY HELMET WAS FOGGING UP... BUT WE WERE THERE... WE WERE THERE!
huf
huf

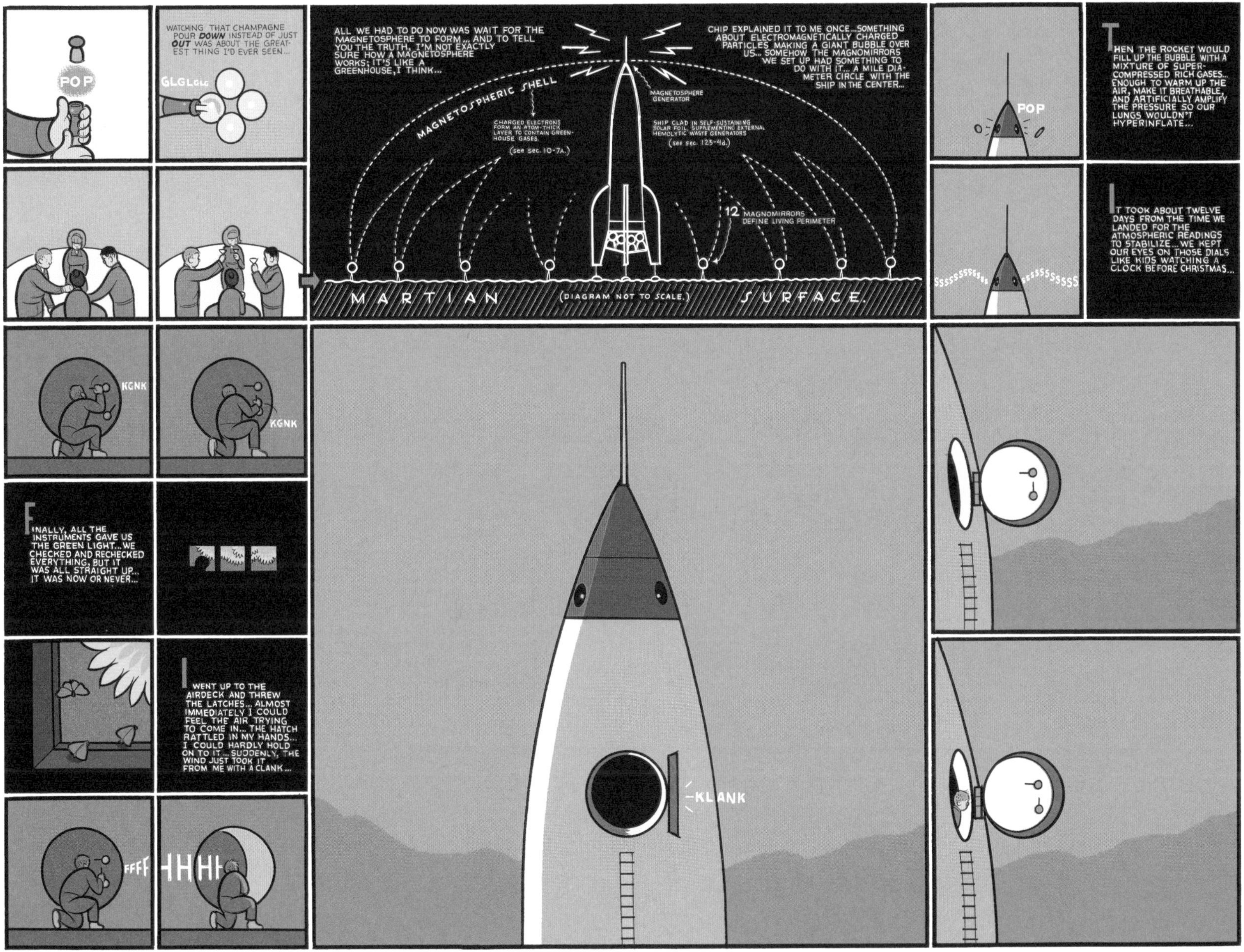
POP
WATCHING THAT CHAMPAGNE POUR DOWN INSTEAD OF JUST OUT WAS ABOUT THE GREATEST THING I'D EVER SEEN...
GLGLGLG
ALL WE HAD TO DO NOW WAS WAIT FOR THE MAGNETOSPHERE TO FORM... AND TO TELL YOU THE TRUTH, I'M NOT EXACTLY SURE HOW A MAGNETOSPHERE WORKS; IT'S LIKE A GREENHOUSE, I THINK...
MAGNETOSPHERIC SHELL
CHARGED ELECTRONS FORM AN ATOM-THICK LAYER TO CONTAIN GREENHOUSE GASES.
(see sec. 10-7A.)
MAGNETOSPHERE GENERATOR
SHIP CLAD IN SELF-SUSTAINING SOLAR FOIL, SUPPLEMENTING EXTERNAL HEMOLYTIC WASTE GENERATORS
(see sec. 123-4d.)
CHIP EXPLAINED IT TO ME ONCE...SOMETHING ABOUT ELECTROMAGNETICALLY CHARGED PARTICLES MAKING A GIANT BUBBLE OVER US... SOMEHOW THE MAGNOMIRRORS WE SET UP HAD SOMETHING TO DO WITH IT... A MILE DIAMETER CIRCLE WITH THE SHIP IN THE CENTER...
12 MAGNOMIRRORS DEFINE LIVING PERIMETER
MARTIAN (DIAGRAM NOT TO SCALE.) SURFACE.
POP
SSSSSSSSSS
THEN THE ROCKET WOULD FILL UP THE BUBBLE WITH A MIXTURE OF SUPER-COMPRESSED RICH GASES... ENOUGH TO WARM UP THE AIR, MAKE IT BREATHABLE, AND ARTIFICIALLY AMPLIFY THE PRESSURE SO OUR LUNGS WOULDN'T HYPERINFLATE...
IT TOOK ABOUT TWELVE DAYS FROM THE TIME WE LANDED FOR THE ATMOSPHERIC READINGS TO STABILIZE... WE KEPT OUR EYES ON THOSE DIALS LIKE KIDS WATCHING A CLOCK BEFORE CHRISTMAS...
KGNK
KGNK
FINALLY, ALL THE INSTRUMENTS GAVE US THE GREEN LIGHT... WE CHECKED AND RECHECKED EVERYTHING, BUT IT WAS ALL STRAIGHT UP... IT WAS NOW OR NEVER...
I WENT UP TO THE AIRDECK AND THREW THE LATCHES... ALMOST IMMEDIATELY I COULD FEEL THE AIR TRYING TO COME IN... THE HATCH RATTLED IN MY HANDS... I COULD HARDLY HOLD ON TO IT... SUDDENLY, THE WIND JUST TOOK IT FROM ME WITH A CLANK...
FFFFHHHH
KLANK

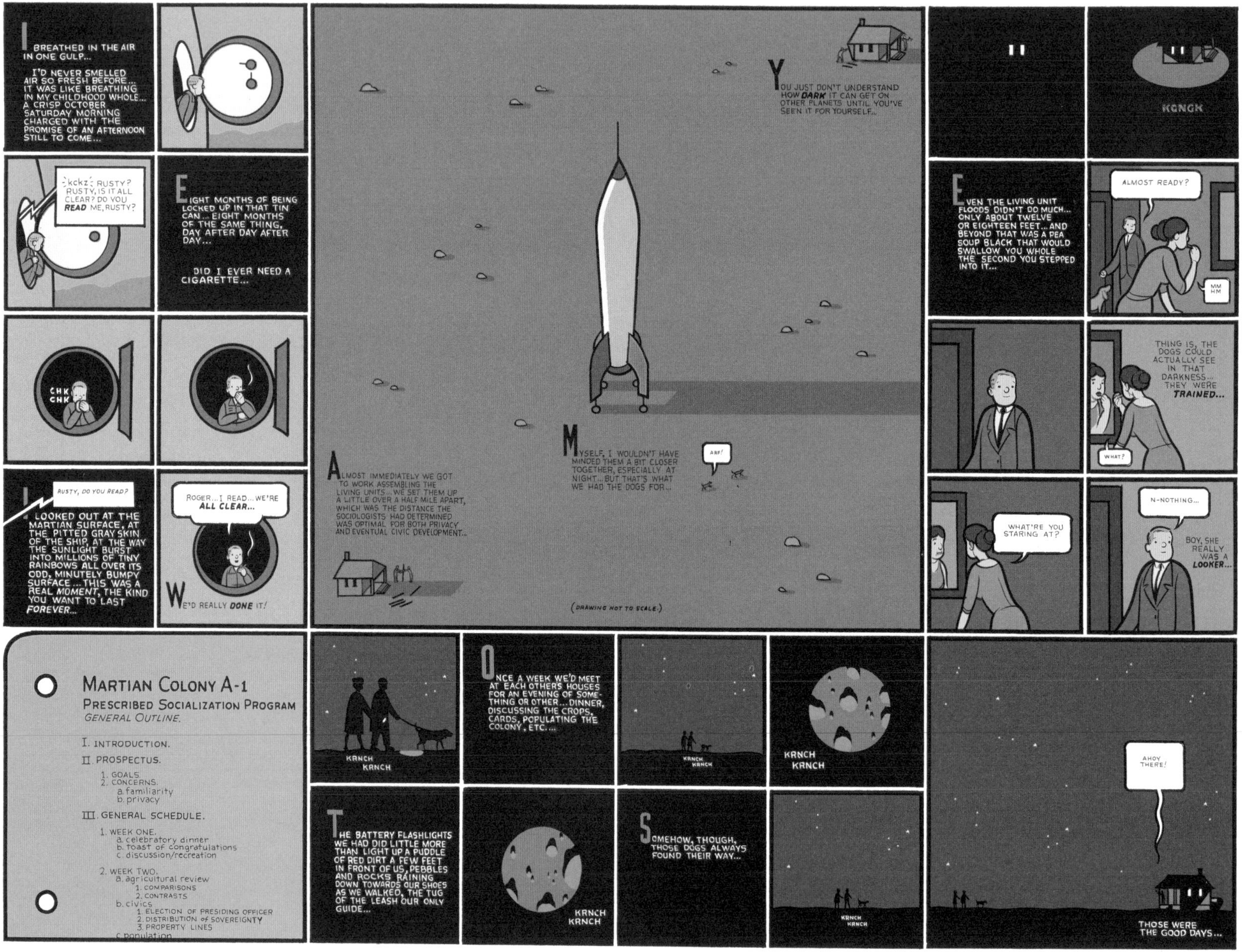

I BREATHED IN THE AIR IN ONE GULP...
I'D NEVER SMELLED AIR SO FRESH BEFORE... IT WAS LIKE BREATHING IN MY CHILDHOOD WHOLE... A CRISP OCTOBER SATURDAY MORNING CHARGED WITH THE PROMISE OF AN AFTERNOON STILL TO COME...
kckz RUSTY? RUSTY, IS IT ALL CLEAR? DO YOU READ ME, RUSTY?
EIGHT MONTHS OF BEING LOCKED UP IN THAT TIN CAN... EIGHT MONTHS OF THE SAME THING, DAY AFTER DAY AFTER DAY...
DID I EVER NEED A CIGARETTE...
CHK CHK
RUSTY, DO YOU READ?
I LOOKED OUT AT THE MARTIAN SURFACE, AT THE PITTED GRAY SKIN OF THE SHIP, AT THE WAY THE SUNLIGHT BURST INTO MILLIONS OF TINY RAINBOWS ALL OVER ITS ODD, MINUTELY BUMPY SURFACE... THIS WAS A REAL MOMENT, THE KIND YOU WANT TO LAST FOREVER...
ROGER... I READ... WE'RE ALL CLEAR...
WE'D REALLY DONE IT!
YOU JUST DON'T UNDERSTAND HOW DARK IT CAN GET ON OTHER PLANETS UNTIL YOU'VE SEEN IT FOR YOURSELF...
ALMOST IMMEDIATELY WE GOT TO WORK ASSEMBLING THE LIVING UNITS... WE SET THEM UP A LITTLE OVER A HALF MILE APART, WHICH WAS THE DISTANCE THE SOCIOLOGISTS HAD DETERMINED WAS OPTIMAL FOR BOTH PRIVACY AND EVENTUAL CIVIC DEVELOPMENT...
MYSELF, I WOULDN'T HAVE MINDED THEM A BIT CLOSER TOGETHER, ESPECIALLY AT NIGHT... BUT THAT'S WHAT WE HAD THE DOGS FOR...
ARF!
(DRAWING NOT TO SCALE.)
KGNGK
EVEN THE LIVING UNIT FLOODS DIDN'T DO MUCH... ONLY ABOUT TWELVE OR EIGHTEEN FEET... AND BEYOND THAT WAS A PEA SOUP BLACK THAT WOULD SWALLOW YOU WHOLE THE SECOND YOU STEPPED INTO IT...
ALMOST READY?
MM HM
THING IS, THE DOGS COULD ACTUALLY SEE IN THAT DARKNESS... THEY WERE TRAINED...
WHAT?
WHAT'RE YOU STARING AT?
N-NOTHING...
BOY, SHE REALLY WAS A LOOKER...
MARTIAN COLONY A-1
PRESCRIBED SOCIALIZATION PROGRAM
GENERAL OUTLINE.
I. INTRODUCTION.
II. PROSPECTUS.
1. GOALS.
2. CONCERNS.
a. familiarity
b. privacy
III. GENERAL SCHEDULE.
1. WEEK ONE.
a. celebratory dinner
b. toast of congratulations
c. discussion/recreation
2. WEEK TWO.
a. agricultural review
1. COMPARISONS
2. CONTRASTS
b. civics
1. ELECTION OF PRESIDING OFFICER
2. DISTRIBUTION of SOVEREIGNTY
3. PROPERTY LINES
c. population
KRNCH KRNCH
ONCE A WEEK WE'D MEET AT EACH OTHERS HOUSES FOR AN EVENING OF SOMETHING OR OTHER... DINNER, DISCUSSING THE CROPS, CARDS, POPULATING THE COLONY, ETC...
KRNCH KRNCH
KRNCH KRNCH
THE BATTERY FLASHLIGHTS WE HAD DID LITTLE MORE THAN LIGHT UP A PUDDLE OF RED DIRT A FEW FEET IN FRONT OF US, PEBBLES AND ROCKS RAINING DOWN TOWARDS OUR SHOES AS WE WALKED, THE TUG OF THE LEASH OUR ONLY GUIDE...
KRNCH KRNCH
SOMEHOW, THOUGH, THOSE DOGS ALWAYS FOUND THEIR WAY...
KRNCH KRNCH
AHOY THERE!
THOSE WERE THE GOOD DAYS...

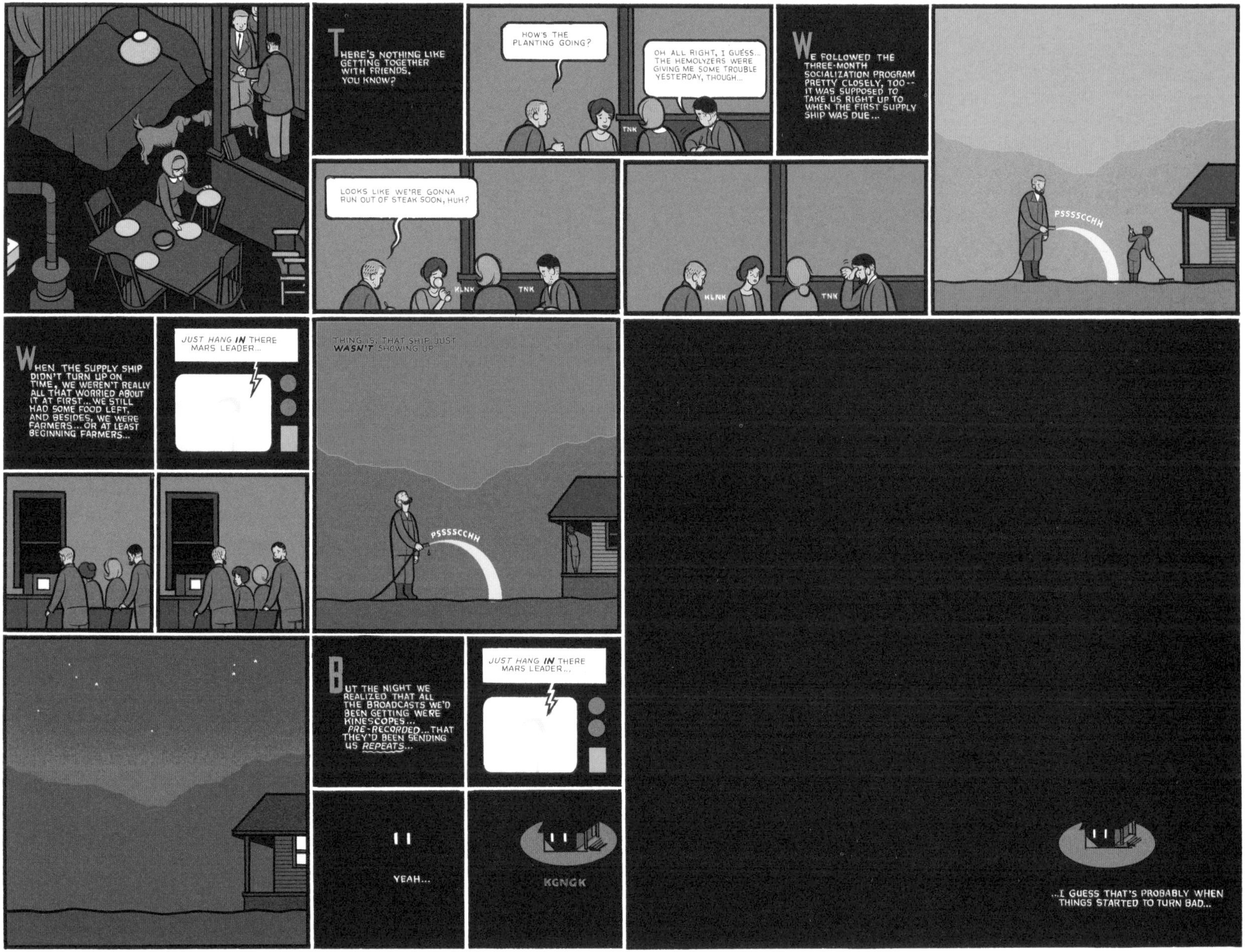

THERE'S NOTHING LIKE GETTING TOGETHER WITH FRIENDS, YOU KNOW?
HOW'S THE PLANTING GOING?
OH ALL RIGHT, I GUESS... THE HEMOLYZERS WERE GIVING ME SOME TROUBLE YESTERDAY, THOUGH...
TNK
WE FOLLOWED THE THREE-MONTH SOCIALIZATION PROGRAM PRETTY CLOSELY, TOO -- IT WAS SUPPOSED TO TAKE US RIGHT UP TO WHEN THE FIRST SUPPLY SHIP WAS DUE...
LOOKS LIKE WE'RE GONNA RUN OUT OF STEAK SOON, HUH?
KLNK
TNK
KLNK
TNK
PSSSSCCHH
WHEN THE SUPPLY SHIP DIDN'T TURN UP ON TIME, WE WEREN'T REALLY ALL THAT WORRIED ABOUT IT AT FIRST... WE STILL HAD SOME FOOD LEFT, AND BESIDES, WE WERE FARMERS... OR AT LEAST BEGINNING FARMERS...
JUST HANG IN THERE MARS LEADER...
THING IS, THAT SHIP JUST WASN'T SHOWING UP...
PSSSSCCHH
BUT THE NIGHT WE REALIZED THAT ALL THE BROADCASTS WE'D BEEN GETTING WERE KINESCOPES... PRE-RECORDED... THAT THEY'D BEEN SENDING US REPEATS...
JUST HANG IN THERE MARS LEADER...
YEAH...
KGNGK
...I GUESS THAT'S PROBABLY WHEN THINGS STARTED TO TURN BAD...

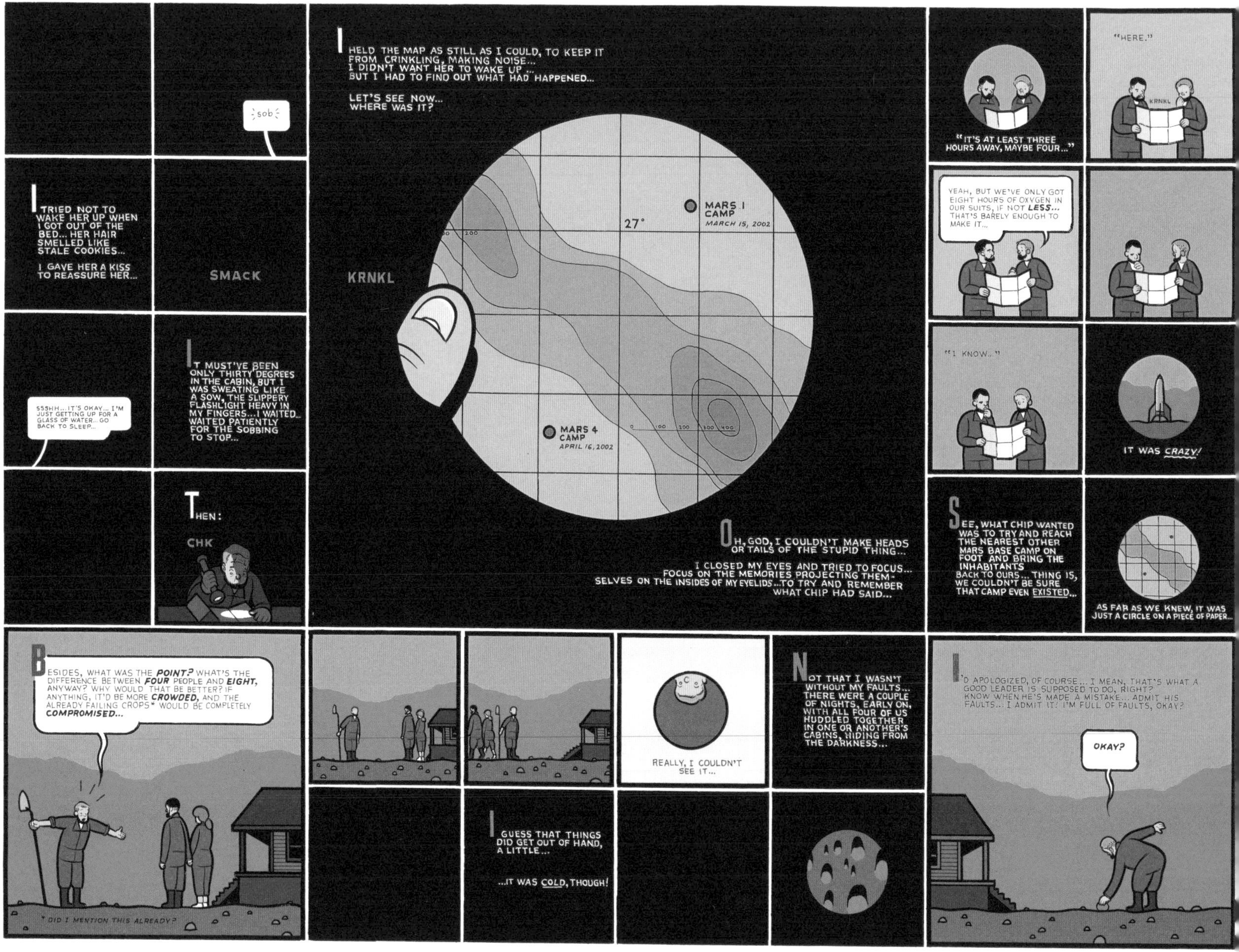

sob
I TRIED NOT TO WAKE HER UP WHEN I GOT OUT OF THE BED... HER HAIR SMELLED LIKE STALE COOKIES...
I GAVE HER A KISS TO REASSURE HER...
SMACK
SSSHH... IT'S OKAY... I'M JUST GETTING UP FOR A GLASS OF WATER... GO BACK TO SLEEP...
IT MUST'VE BEEN ONLY THIRTY DEGREES IN THE CABIN, BUT I WAS SWEATING LIKE A SOW, THE SLIPPERY FLASHLIGHT HEAVY IN MY FINGERS... I WAITED... WAITED PATIENTLY FOR THE SOBBING TO STOP...
THEN:
CHK
I HELD THE MAP AS STILL AS I COULD, TO KEEP IT FROM CRINKLING, MAKING NOISE... I DIDN'T WANT HER TO WAKE UP... BUT I HAD TO FIND OUT WHAT HAD HAPPENED...
LET'S SEE NOW... WHERE WAS IT?
KRNKL
MARS 1 CAMP
MARCH 15, 2002
27°
MARS 4 CAMP
APRIL 16, 2002
0 100 200 300 400
OH, GOD, I COULDN'T MAKE HEADS OR TAILS OF THE STUPID THING...
I CLOSED MY EYES AND TRIED TO FOCUS... FOCUS ON THE MEMORIES PROJECTING THEMSELVES ON THE INSIDES OF MY EYELIDS... TO TRY AND REMEMBER WHAT CHIP HAD SAID...
"IT'S AT LEAST THREE HOURS AWAY, MAYBE FOUR..."
"HERE."
KRNKL
YEAH, BUT WE'VE ONLY GOT EIGHT HOURS OF OXYGEN IN OUR SUITS, IF NOT LESS... THAT'S BARELY ENOUGH TO MAKE IT...
"I KNOW..."
IT WAS CRAZY!
SEE, WHAT CHIP WANTED WAS TO TRY AND REACH THE NEAREST OTHER MARS BASE CAMP ON FOOT AND BRING THE INHABITANTS BACK TO OURS... THING IS, WE COULDN'T BE SURE THAT CAMP EVEN EXISTED...
AS FAR AS WE KNEW, IT WAS JUST A CIRCLE ON A PIECE OF PAPER...
BESIDES, WHAT WAS THE POINT? WHAT'S THE DIFFERENCE BETWEEN FOUR PEOPLE AND EIGHT, ANYWAY? WHY WOULD THAT BE BETTER? IF ANYTHING, IT'D BE MORE CROWDED, AND THE ALREADY FAILING CROPS* WOULD BE COMPLETELY COMPROMISED...
* DID I MENTION THIS ALREADY?
REALLY, I COULDN'T SEE IT...
I GUESS THAT THINGS DID GET OUT OF HAND, A LITTLE...
...IT WAS COLD, THOUGH!
NOT THAT I WASN'T WITHOUT MY FAULTS... THERE WERE A COUPLE OF NIGHTS, EARLY ON, WITH ALL FOUR OF US HUDDLED TOGETHER IN ONE OR ANOTHER'S CABINS, HIDING FROM THE DARKNESS...
I'D APOLOGIZED, OF COURSE... I MEAN, THAT'S WHAT A GOOD LEADER IS SUPPOSED TO DO, RIGHT? KNOW WHEN HE'S MADE A MISTAKE... ADMIT HIS FAULTS... I ADMIT IT! I'M FULL OF FAULTS, OKAY?
OKAY?

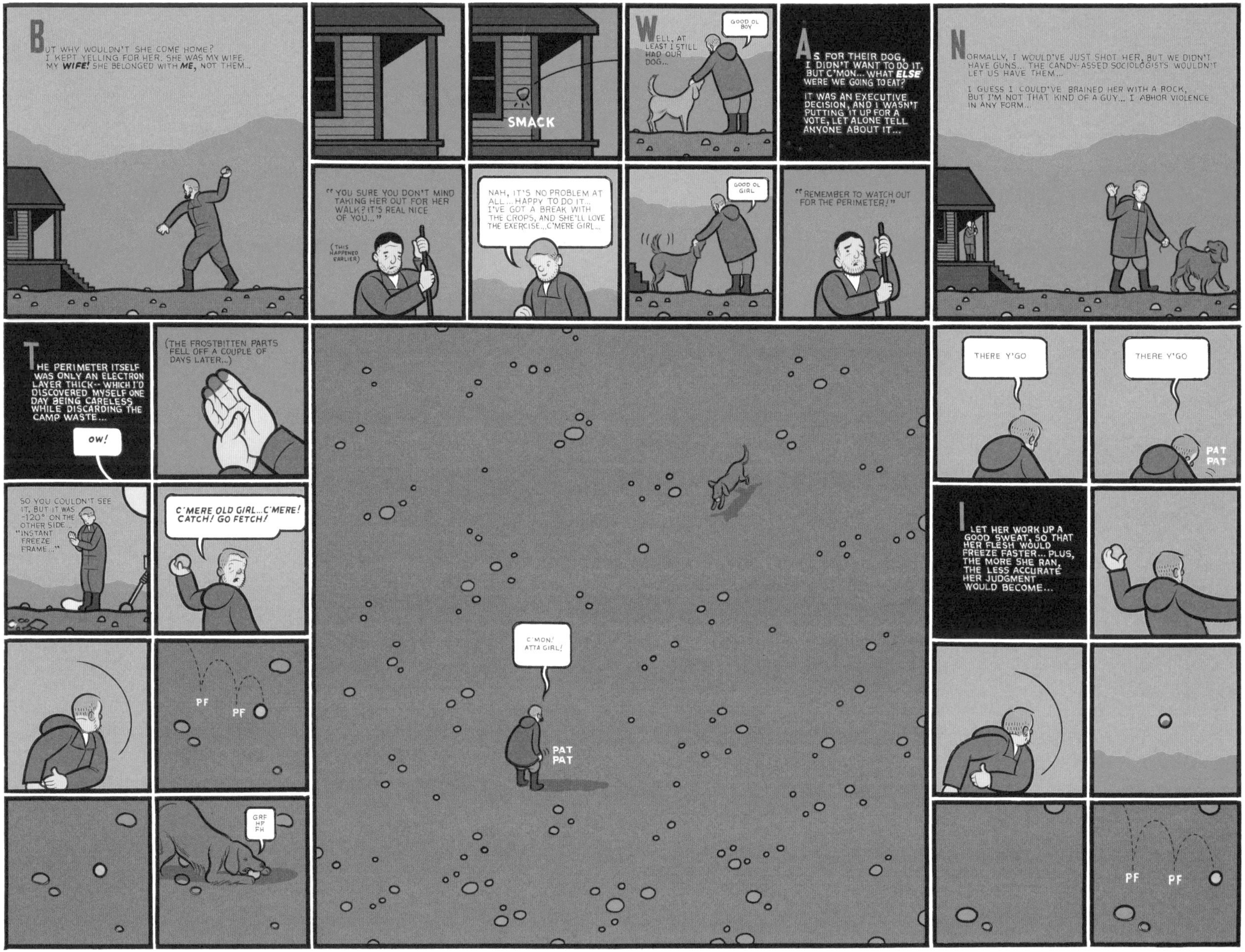
BUT WHY WOULDN'T SHE COME HOME? I KEPT YELLING FOR HER. SHE WAS MY WIFE. MY **WIFE!** SHE BELONGED WITH **ME**, NOT THEM...
SMACK
WELL, AT LEAST I STILL HAD OUR DOG...
GOOD OL BOY
AS FOR THEIR DOG, I DIDN'T WANT TO DO IT, BUT C'MON... WHAT **ELSE** WERE WE GOING TO EAT?
IT WAS AN EXECUTIVE DECISION, AND I WASN'T PUTTING IT UP FOR A VOTE, LET ALONE TELL ANYONE ABOUT IT...
"YOU SURE YOU DON'T MIND TAKING HER OUT FOR HER WALK? IT'S REAL NICE OF YOU..."
(THIS HAPPENED EARLIER)
NAH, IT'S NO PROBLEM AT ALL... HAPPY TO DO IT... I'VE GOT A BREAK WITH THE CROPS, AND SHE'LL LOVE THE EXERCISE... C'MERE GIRL...
GOOD OL GIRL
"REMEMBER TO WATCH OUT FOR THE PERIMETER!"
NORMALLY, I WOULD'VE JUST SHOT HER, BUT WE DIDN'T HAVE GUNS... THE CANDY-ASSED SOCIOLOGISTS WOULDN'T LET US HAVE THEM...
I GUESS I COULD'VE BRAINED HER WITH A ROCK, BUT I'M NOT THAT KIND OF A GUY... I ABHOR VIOLENCE IN ANY FORM...
THE PERIMETER ITSELF WAS ONLY AN ELECTRON LAYER THICK-- WHICH I'D DISCOVERED MYSELF ONE DAY BEING CARELESS WHILE DISCARDING THE CAMP WASTE...
OW!
(THE FROSTBITTEN PARTS FELL OFF A COUPLE OF DAYS LATER...)
SO YOU COULDN'T SEE IT, BUT IT WAS -120° ON THE OTHER SIDE... "INSTANT FREEZE FRAME..."
C'MERE OLD GIRL... C'MERE! CATCH! GO FETCH!
PF
PF
GRF HF FH
C'MON! ATTA GIRL!
PAT PAT
THERE Y'GO
THERE Y'GO
PAT PAT
I LET HER WORK UP A GOOD SWEAT, SO THAT HER FLESH WOULD FREEZE FASTER... PLUS, THE MORE SHE RAN, THE LESS ACCURATE HER JUDGMENT WOULD BECOME...
PF
PF

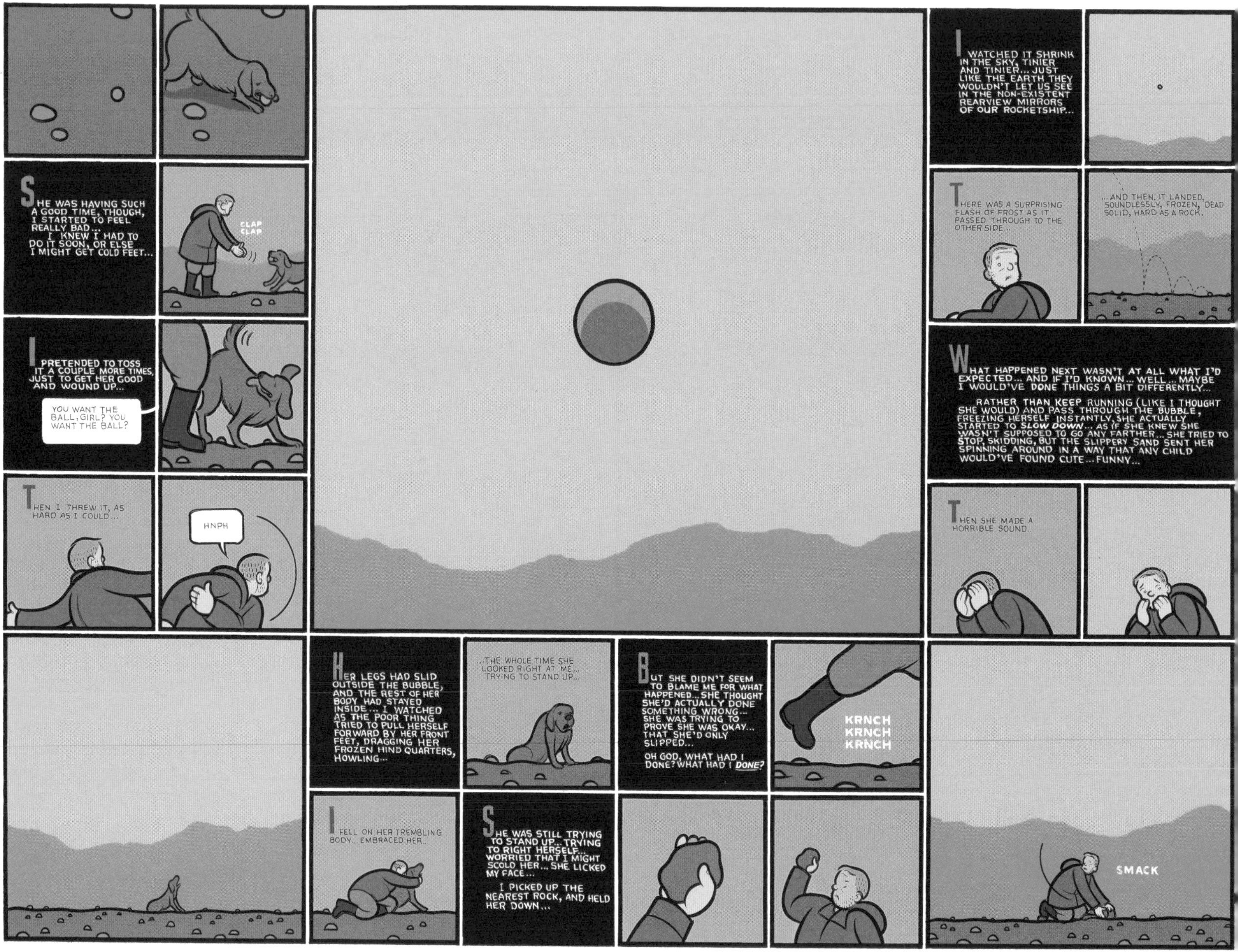

SHE WAS HAVING SUCH A GOOD TIME, THOUGH, I STARTED TO FEEL REALLY BAD... I KNEW I HAD TO DO IT SOON, OR ELSE I MIGHT GET COLD FEET...
CLAP CLAP
I PRETENDED TO TOSS IT A COUPLE MORE TIMES, JUST TO GET HER GOOD AND WOUND UP...
YOU WANT THE BALL, GIRL? YOU WANT THE BALL?
THEN I THREW IT, AS HARD AS I COULD...
HNPH
I WATCHED IT SHRINK IN THE SKY, TINIER AND TINIER... JUST LIKE THE EARTH THEY WOULDN'T LET US SEE IN THE NON-EXISTENT REARVIEW MIRRORS OF OUR ROCKETSHIP...
THERE WAS A SURPRISING FLASH OF FROST AS IT PASSED THROUGH TO THE OTHER SIDE...
...AND THEN, IT LANDED, SOUNDLESSLY, FROZEN, DEAD SOLID, HARD AS A ROCK.
WHAT HAPPENED NEXT WASN'T AT ALL WHAT I'D EXPECTED... AND IF I'D KNOWN... WELL... MAYBE I WOULD'VE DONE THINGS A BIT DIFFERENTLY...
RATHER THAN KEEP RUNNING (LIKE I THOUGHT SHE WOULD) AND PASS THROUGH THE BUBBLE, FREEZING HERSELF INSTANTLY, SHE ACTUALLY STARTED TO SLOW DOWN... AS IF SHE KNEW SHE WASN'T SUPPOSED TO GO ANY FARTHER... SHE TRIED TO STOP, SKIDDING, BUT THE SLIPPERY SAND SENT HER SPINNING AROUND IN A WAY THAT ANY CHILD WOULD'VE FOUND CUTE... FUNNY...
THEN SHE MADE A HORRIBLE SOUND..
HER LEGS HAD SLID OUTSIDE THE BUBBLE, AND THE REST OF HER BODY HAD STAYED INSIDE... I WATCHED AS THE POOR THING TRIED TO PULL HERSELF FORWARD BY HER FRONT FEET, DRAGGING HER FROZEN HIND QUARTERS, HOWLING...
...THE WHOLE TIME SHE LOOKED RIGHT AT ME... TRYING TO STAND UP...
BUT SHE DIDN'T SEEM TO BLAME ME FOR WHAT HAPPENED... SHE THOUGHT SHE'D ACTUALLY DONE SOMETHING WRONG... SHE WAS TRYING TO PROVE SHE WAS OKAY... THAT SHE'D ONLY SLIPPED...
OH GOD, WHAT HAD I DONE? WHAT HAD I DONE?
KRNCH KRNCH KRNCH
I FELL ON HER TREMBLING BODY... EMBRACED HER...
SHE WAS STILL TRYING TO STAND UP... TRYING TO RIGHT HERSELF... WORRIED THAT I MIGHT SCOLD HER... SHE LICKED MY FACE...
I PICKED UP THE NEAREST ROCK, AND HELD HER DOWN...
SMACK

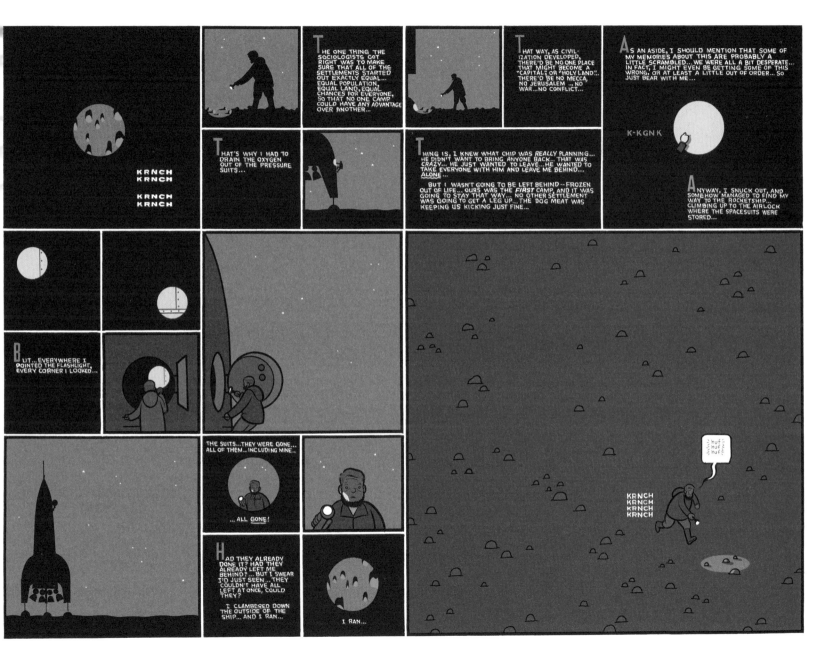

KRNCH
KRNCH

KRNCH
KRNCH

THE ONE THING THE SOCIOLOGISTS GOT RIGHT WAS TO MAKE SURE THAT ALL OF THE SETTLEMENTS STARTED OUT EXACTLY EQUAL... EQUAL POPULATION, EQUAL LAND, EQUAL CHANCES FOR EVERYONE, SO THAT NO ONE CAMP COULD HAVE ANY ADVANTAGE OVER ANOTHER...

THAT WAY, AS CIVIL-IZATION DEVELOPED, THERE'D BE NO ONE PLACE THAT MIGHT BECOME A "CAPITAL" OR "HOLY LAND"... THERE'D BE NO MECCA, NO JERUSALEM ... NO WAR...NO CONFLICT...

AS AN ASIDE, I SHOULD MENTION THAT SOME OF MY MEMORIES ABOUT THIS ARE PROBABLY A LITTLE SCRAMBLED... WE WERE ALL A BIT DESPERATE... IN FACT, I MIGHT EVEN BE GETTING SOME OF THIS WRONG, OR AT LEAST A LITTLE OUT OF ORDER... SO JUST BEAR WITH ME...

THAT'S WHY I HAD TO DRAIN THE OXYGEN OUT OF THE PRESSURE SUITS...

THING IS, I KNEW WHAT CHIP WAS *REALLY* PLANNING... HE DIDN'T WANT TO BRING ANYONE BACK... THAT WAS *CRAZY*... HE JUST WANTED TO LEAVE...HE WANTED TO TAKE EVERYONE WITH HIM AND LEAVE ME BEHIND... _ALONE_...

BUT I WASN'T GOING TO BE LEFT BEHIND -- FROZEN OUT OF LIFE... OURS WAS THE *FIRST* CAMP, AND IT WAS GOING TO STAY THAT WAY... NO OTHER SETTLEMENT WAS GOING TO GET A LEG UP... THE DOG MEAT WAS KEEPING US KICKING JUST FINE...

K-KGNK

ANYWAY, I SNUCK OUT, AND SOMEHOW MANAGED TO FIND MY WAY TO THE ROCKETSHIP... CLIMBING UP TO THE AIRLOCK WHERE THE SPACESUITS WERE STORED...

BUT... EVERYWHERE I POINTED THE FLASHLIGHT, EVERY CORNER I LOOKED...

THE SUITS...THEY WERE GONE... ALL OF THEM... INCLUDING MINE...

... ALL GONE!

HAD THEY ALREADY DONE IT? HAD THEY ALREADY LEFT ME BEHIND?... BUT I SWEAR I'D JUST SEEN... THEY COULDN'T HAVE ALL LEFT AT ONCE, COULD THEY?

I CLAMBERED DOWN THE OUTSIDE OF THE SHIP... AND I RAN...

I RAN...

huf
huf
huf

KRNCH
KRNCH
KRNCH
KRNCH

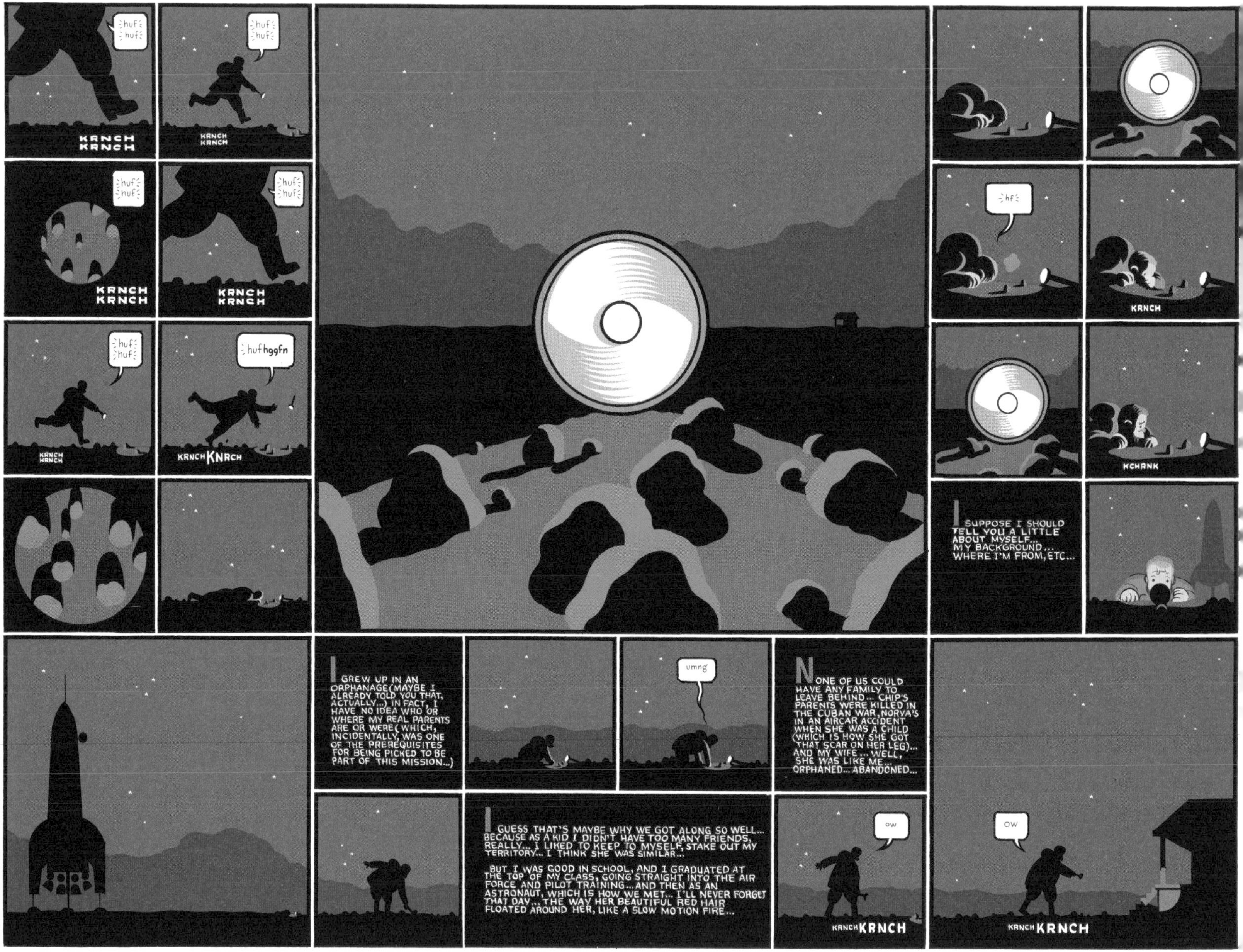
huf huf
KRNCH KRNCH
huf huf
KRNCH KRNCH
huf huf
KRNCH KRNCH
huf huf
KRNCH KRNCH
huf huf
KRNCH KRNCH
hufhggfn
KRNCH KNRCH
hf
KRNCH
KCHANK
I SUPPOSE I SHOULD TELL YOU A LITTLE ABOUT MYSELF... MY BACKGROUND... WHERE I'M FROM, ETC...
I GREW UP IN AN ORPHANAGE (MAYBE I ALREADY TOLD YOU THAT, ACTUALLY...) IN FACT, I HAVE NO IDEA WHO OR WHERE MY REAL PARENTS ARE OR WERE (WHICH, INCIDENTALLY, WAS ONE OF THE PREREQUISITES FOR BEING PICKED TO BE PART OF THIS MISSION...)
umng
NONE OF US COULD HAVE ANY FAMILY TO LEAVE BEHIND... CHIP'S PARENTS WERE KILLED IN THE CUBAN WAR, NORVA'S IN AN AIRCAR ACCIDENT WHEN SHE WAS A CHILD (WHICH IS HOW SHE GOT THAT SCAR ON HER LEG)... AND MY WIFE... WELL, SHE WAS LIKE ME... ORPHANED... ABANDONED...
I GUESS THAT'S MAYBE WHY WE GOT ALONG SO WELL... BECAUSE AS A KID I DIDN'T HAVE TOO MANY FRIENDS, REALLY... I LIKED TO KEEP TO MYSELF, STAKE OUT MY TERRITORY... I THINK SHE WAS SIMILAR...
BUT I WAS GOOD IN SCHOOL, AND I GRADUATED AT THE TOP OF MY CLASS, GOING STRAIGHT INTO THE AIR FORCE AND PILOT TRAINING... AND THEN AS AN ASTRONAUT, WHICH IS HOW WE MET... I'LL NEVER FORGET THAT DAY... THE WAY HER BEAUTIFUL RED HAIR FLOATED AROUND HER, LIKE A SLOW MOTION FIRE...
ow
KRNCH KRNCH
ow
KRNCH KRNCH

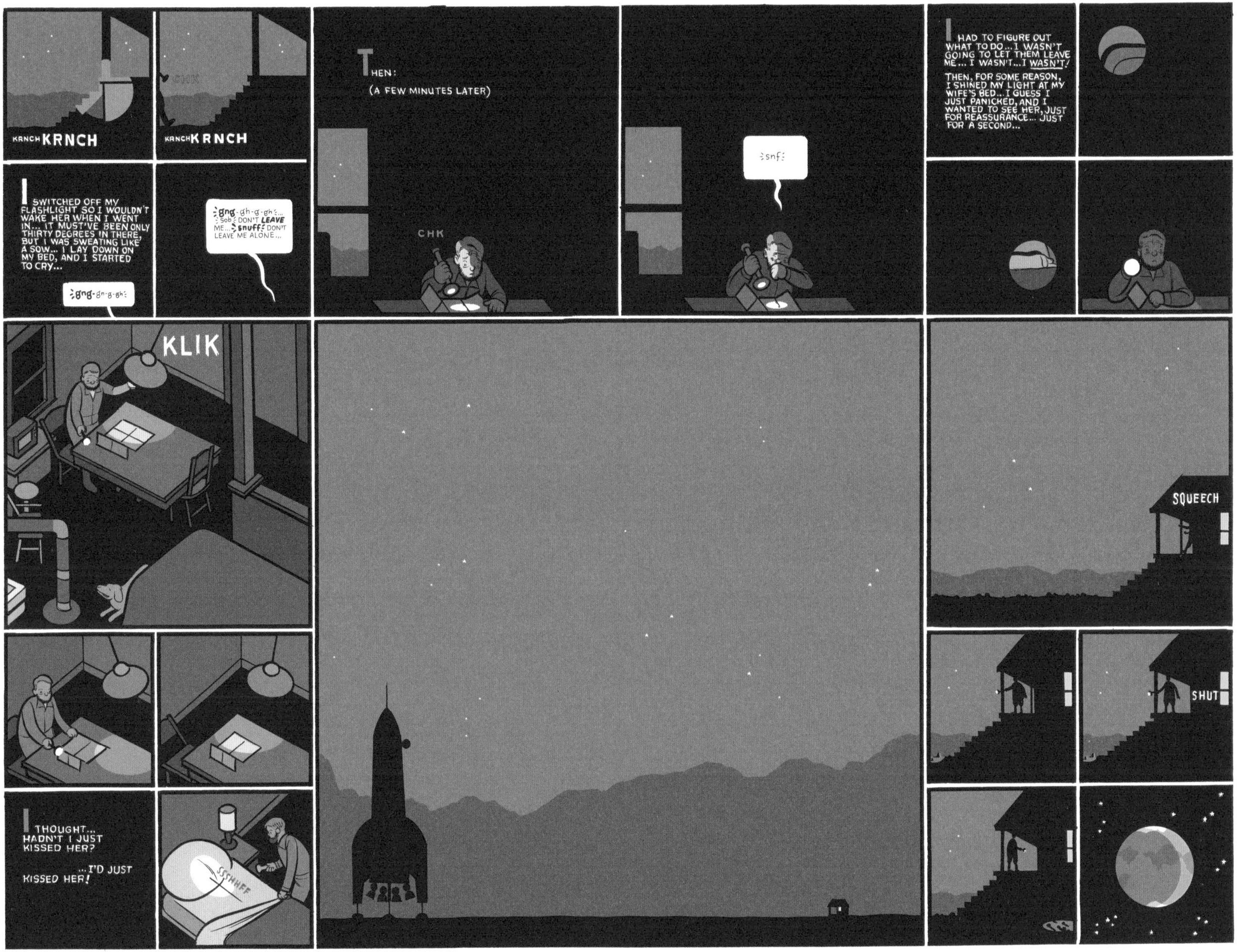
KRNCH KRNCH
CHK
KRNCH KRNCH
I SWITCHED OFF MY FLASHLIGHT SO I WOULDN'T WAKE HER WHEN I WENT IN... IT MUST'VE BEEN ONLY THIRTY DEGREES IN THERE, BUT I WAS SWEATING LIKE A SOW... I LAY DOWN ON MY BED, AND I STARTED TO CRY...
gng-gh-g-gh
gng-gh-g-gh... sob DON'T LEAVE ME... snuff DON'T LEAVE ME ALONE...
THEN:
(A FEW MINUTES LATER)
CHK
snf
I HAD TO FIGURE OUT WHAT TO DO... I WASN'T GOING TO LET THEM LEAVE ME... I WASN'T... I WASN'T!
THEN, FOR SOME REASON, I SHINED MY LIGHT AT MY WIFE'S BED... I GUESS I JUST PANICKED, AND I WANTED TO SEE HER, JUST FOR REASSURANCE... JUST FOR A SECOND...
KLIK
I THOUGHT... HADN'T I JUST KISSED HER?
...I'D JUST KISSED HER!
SSSHHFF
SQUEECH
SHUT

KRNCH KRNCH
KRNCH KRNCH
KRNCH KRNCH
I REMEMBERED THE EXTRA SPACESUIT IN THE ESCAPE POD... IF THEY HADN'T GOTTEN TO THAT, MAYBE I STILL HAD A CHANCE -- BUT HOW WAS I GOING TO FIND WHICH WAY THEY'D GONE? THERE WERE THOUSANDS OF ROUTES OVER THOSE HILLS...
...I RAN BACK TO THE SHIP, RETRACING MY STEPS...
KRNCH
KRNCH KRNCH
KRNCH
IT WAS INDISPUTABLE... CLEAR AS DAY...
FRESH SPACESUIT FOOTPRINTS, GOING AWAY FROM THE SHIP... TWO SETS OF THEM...
huf
huf
huf
huf
hngh
KGLUNK
I HADN'T BEEN INSIDE THE SHIP FOR... MONTHS, I GUESS... THOUGH IT SEEMED LIKE YEARS... I FUMBLED MY WAY DOWN ITS LENGTH... DOWN... DOWN THROUGH TUBES THAT WERE REALLY ONLY MEANT FOR ZERO GEE... THE INSTRUMENT PANELS WERE FROSTED OVER WITH PINK GRIT... COULD IT ALL HAVE CORRODED THAT QUICKLY?
huf
STEP STEP
STEP STEP
I FOUND MY WAY TO THE ESCAPE POD... TREMBLING, I SHINED MY LIGHT DOWN...
(IF THEY'D REMEMBERED THAT EXTRA SUIT, ALL HOPE WAS LOST... THERE WAS NO OTHER WAY TO FOLLOW THEM...)
I HELD MY BREATH, AND LOOKED IN...
IT WAS THERE!
IT WAS THERE... THE STUPID IDIOTS HAD LEFT IT!
THEY HAD NO CHANCE NOW... I'D CATCH UP WITH THEM... I'D BRING THEM BACK!
I QUICKLY SUITED UP... THERE WAS NO TIME TO WASTE... NO TIME TO WASTE...
KRNCH

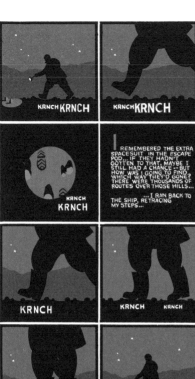

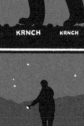

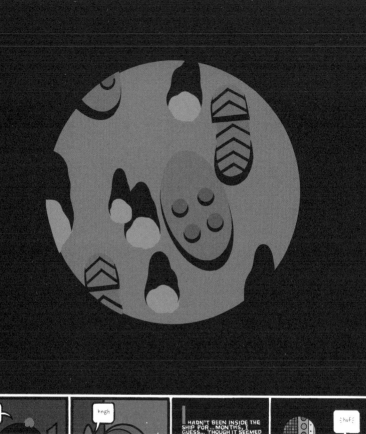

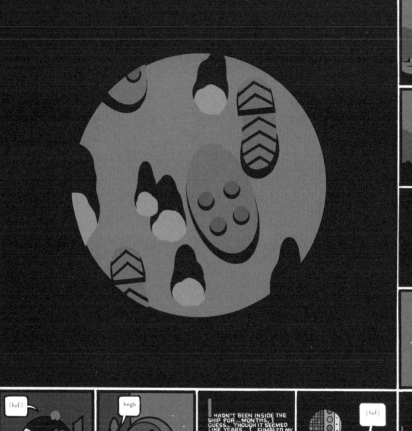

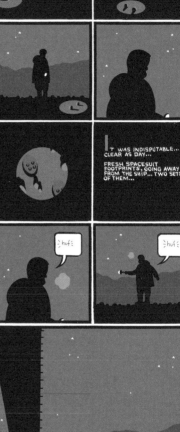

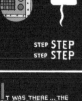

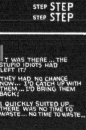

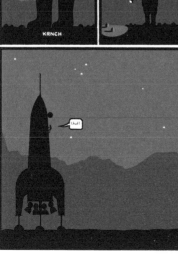

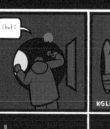

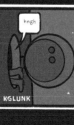

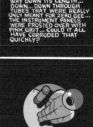

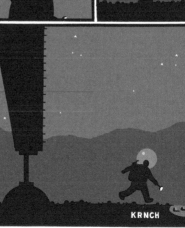

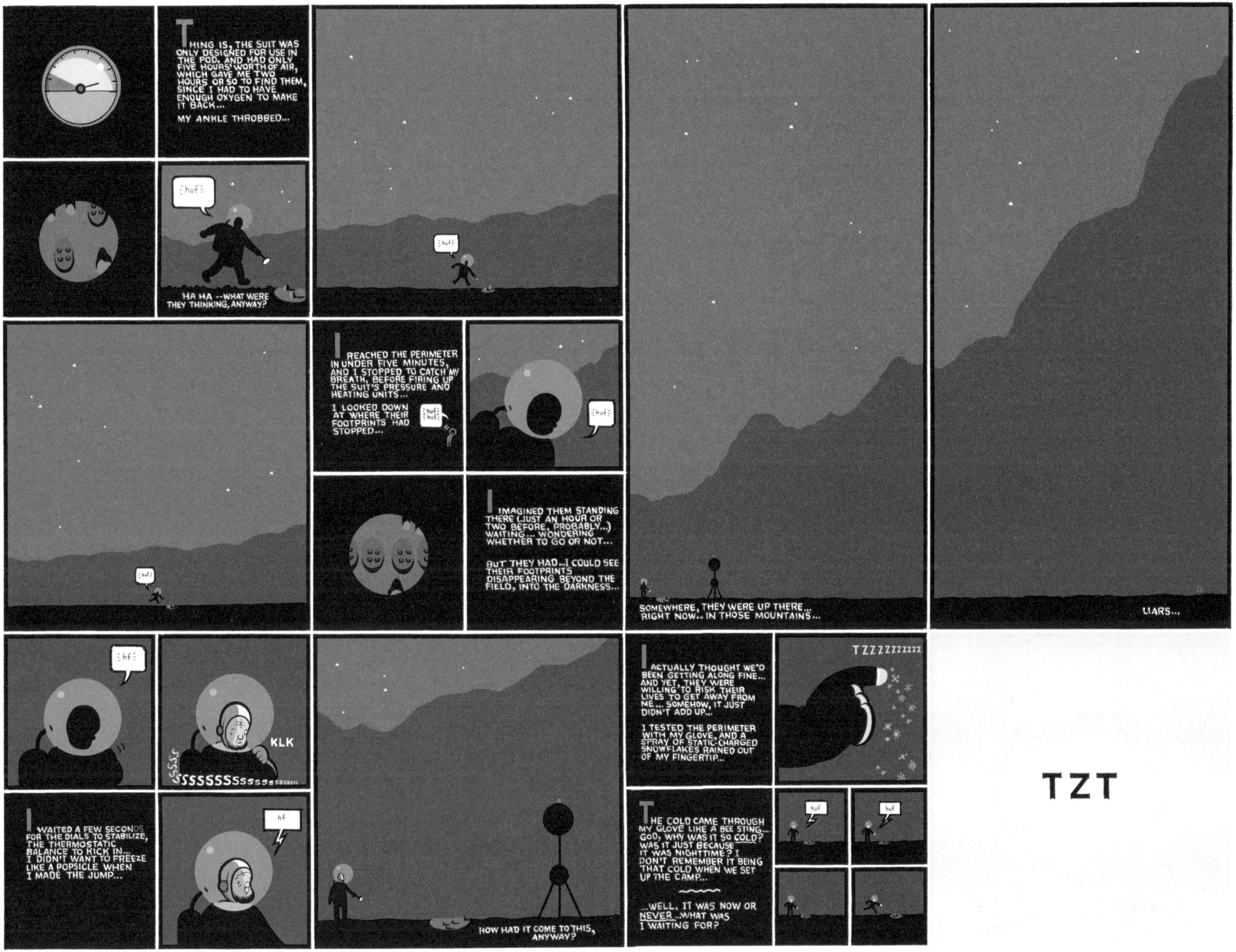
THING IS, THE SUIT WAS ONLY DESIGNED FOR USE IN THE POD, AND HAD ONLY FIVE HOURS' WORTH OF AIR, WHICH GAVE ME TWO HOURS OR SO TO FIND THEM, SINCE I HAD TO HAVE ENOUGH OXYGEN TO MAKE IT BACK...
MY ANKLE THROBBED...
huf
HA HA --WHAT WERE THEY THINKING, ANYWAY?
huf
huf
I REACHED THE PERIMETER IN UNDER FIVE MINUTES, AND I STOPPED TO CATCH MY BREATH, BEFORE FIRING UP THE SUIT'S PRESSURE AND HEATING UNITS...
I LOOKED DOWN AT WHERE THEIR FOOTPRINTS HAD STOPPED...
huf huf
huf
I IMAGINED THEM STANDING THERE (JUST AN HOUR OR TWO BEFORE, PROBABLY...) WAITING... WONDERING WHETHER TO GO OR NOT...
BUT THEY HAD... I COULD SEE THEIR FOOTPRINTS DISAPPEARING BEYOND THE FIELD, INTO THE DARKNESS...
SOMEWHERE, THEY WERE UP THERE... RIGHT NOW... IN THOSE MOUNTAINS...
LIARS...
hf
KLK
SSSSSSSSSSSSSSSSSSSSSS
I WAITED A FEW SECONDS FOR THE DIALS TO STABILIZE, THE THERMOSTATIC BALANCE TO KICK IN... I DIDN'T WANT TO FREEZE LIKE A POPSICLE WHEN I MADE THE JUMP...
hf
HOW HAD IT COME TO THIS, ANYWAY?
I ACTUALLY THOUGHT WE'D BEEN GETTING ALONG FINE... AND YET, THEY WERE WILLING TO RISK THEIR LIVES TO GET AWAY FROM ME... SOMEHOW, IT JUST DIDN'T ADD UP...
I TESTED THE PERIMETER WITH MY GLOVE, AND A SPRAY OF STATIC-CHARGED SNOWFLAKES RAINED OUT OF MY FINGERTIP...
TZZZZZZZZZZ
TZT
THE COLD CAME THROUGH MY GLOVE LIKE A BEE STING... GOD, WHY WAS IT SO COLD? WAS IT JUST BECAUSE IT WAS NIGHTTIME? I DON'T REMEMBER IT BEING THAT COLD WHEN WE SET UP THE CAMP...
...WELL, IT WAS NOW OR NEVER... WHAT WAS I WAITING FOR?
huf
huf

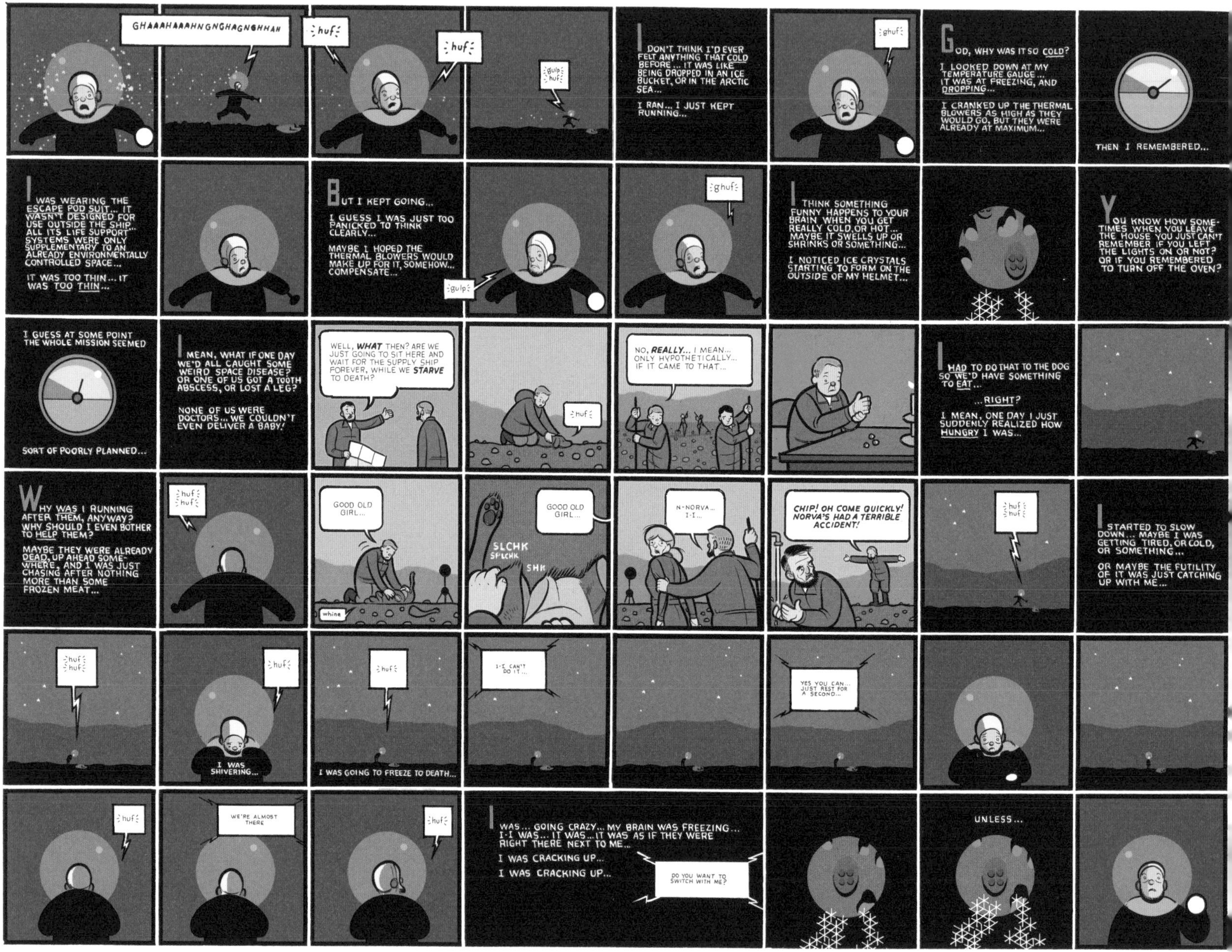

GHAAAHAAAHNGNGHAGNGHHAH
huf
huf
gulp huf
I DON'T THINK I'D EVER FELT ANYTHING THAT COLD BEFORE... IT WAS LIKE BEING DROPPED IN AN ICE BUCKET, OR IN THE ARCTIC SEA...
I RAN... I JUST KEPT RUNNING...
ghuf
GOD, WHY WAS IT SO COLD?
I LOOKED DOWN AT MY TEMPERATURE GAUGE... IT WAS AT FREEZING, AND DROPPING...
I CRANKED UP THE THERMAL BLOWERS AS HIGH AS THEY WOULD GO, BUT THEY WERE ALREADY AT MAXIMUM...
THEN I REMEMBERED...
I WAS WEARING THE ESCAPE POD SUIT... IT WASN'T DESIGNED FOR USE OUTSIDE THE SHIP... ALL ITS LIFE SUPPORT SYSTEMS WERE ONLY SUPPLEMENTARY TO AN ALREADY ENVIRONMENTALLY CONTROLLED SPACE...
IT WAS TOO THIN... IT WAS TOO THIN...
BUT I KEPT GOING...
I GUESS I WAS JUST TOO PANICKED TO THINK CLEARLY...
MAYBE I HOPED THE THERMAL BLOWERS WOULD MAKE UP FOR IT, SOMEHOW... COMPENSATE...
gulp
ghuf
I THINK SOMETHING FUNNY HAPPENS TO YOUR BRAIN WHEN YOU GET REALLY COLD, OR HOT... MAYBE IT SWELLS UP OR SHRINKS OR SOMETHING...
I NOTICED ICE CRYSTALS STARTING TO FORM ON THE OUTSIDE OF MY HELMET...
YOU KNOW HOW SOMETIMES WHEN YOU LEAVE THE HOUSE YOU JUST CAN'T REMEMBER IF YOU LEFT THE LIGHTS ON OR NOT? OR IF YOU REMEMBERED TO TURN OFF THE OVEN?
I GUESS AT SOME POINT THE WHOLE MISSION SEEMED
SORT OF POORLY PLANNED...
I MEAN, WHAT IF ONE DAY WE'D ALL CAUGHT SOME WEIRD SPACE DISEASE? OR ONE OF US GOT A TOOTH ABSCESS, OR LOST A LEG?
NONE OF US WERE DOCTORS... WE COULDN'T EVEN DELIVER A BABY!
WELL, WHAT THEN? ARE WE JUST GOING TO SIT HERE AND WAIT FOR THE SUPPLY SHIP FOREVER, WHILE WE STARVE TO DEATH?
huf
NO, REALLY... I MEAN... ONLY HYPOTHETICALLY... IF IT CAME TO THAT...
I HAD TO DO THAT TO THE DOG SO WE'D HAVE SOMETHING TO EAT...
...RIGHT?
I MEAN, ONE DAY I JUST SUDDENLY REALIZED HOW HUNGRY I WAS...
WHY WAS I RUNNING AFTER THEM, ANYWAY? WHY SHOULD I EVEN BOTHER TO HELP THEM?
MAYBE THEY WERE ALREADY DEAD, UP AHEAD SOMEWHERE, AND I WAS JUST CHASING AFTER NOTHING MORE THAN SOME FROZEN MEAT...
huf huf
GOOD OLD GIRL...
whine
GOOD OLD GIRL...
SLCHK
SPLCHK
SHK
N-NORVA... I-I...
CHIP! OH COME QUICKLY! NORVA'S HAD A TERRIBLE ACCIDENT!
huf huf
I STARTED TO SLOW DOWN... MAYBE I WAS GETTING TIRED, OR COLD, OR SOMETHING...
OR MAYBE THE FUTILITY OF IT WAS JUST CATCHING UP WITH ME...
huf huf
huf
I WAS SHIVERING...
huf
I WAS GOING TO FREEZE TO DEATH...
I-I CAN'T DO IT...
YES YOU CAN... JUST REST FOR A SECOND...
huf
WE'RE ALMOST THERE
huf
I WAS... GOING CRAZY... MY BRAIN WAS FREEZING... I-I WAS... IT WAS... IT WAS AS IF THEY WERE RIGHT THERE NEXT TO ME...
I WAS CRACKING UP...
I WAS CRACKING UP...
DO YOU WANT TO SWITCH WITH ME?
UNLESS...

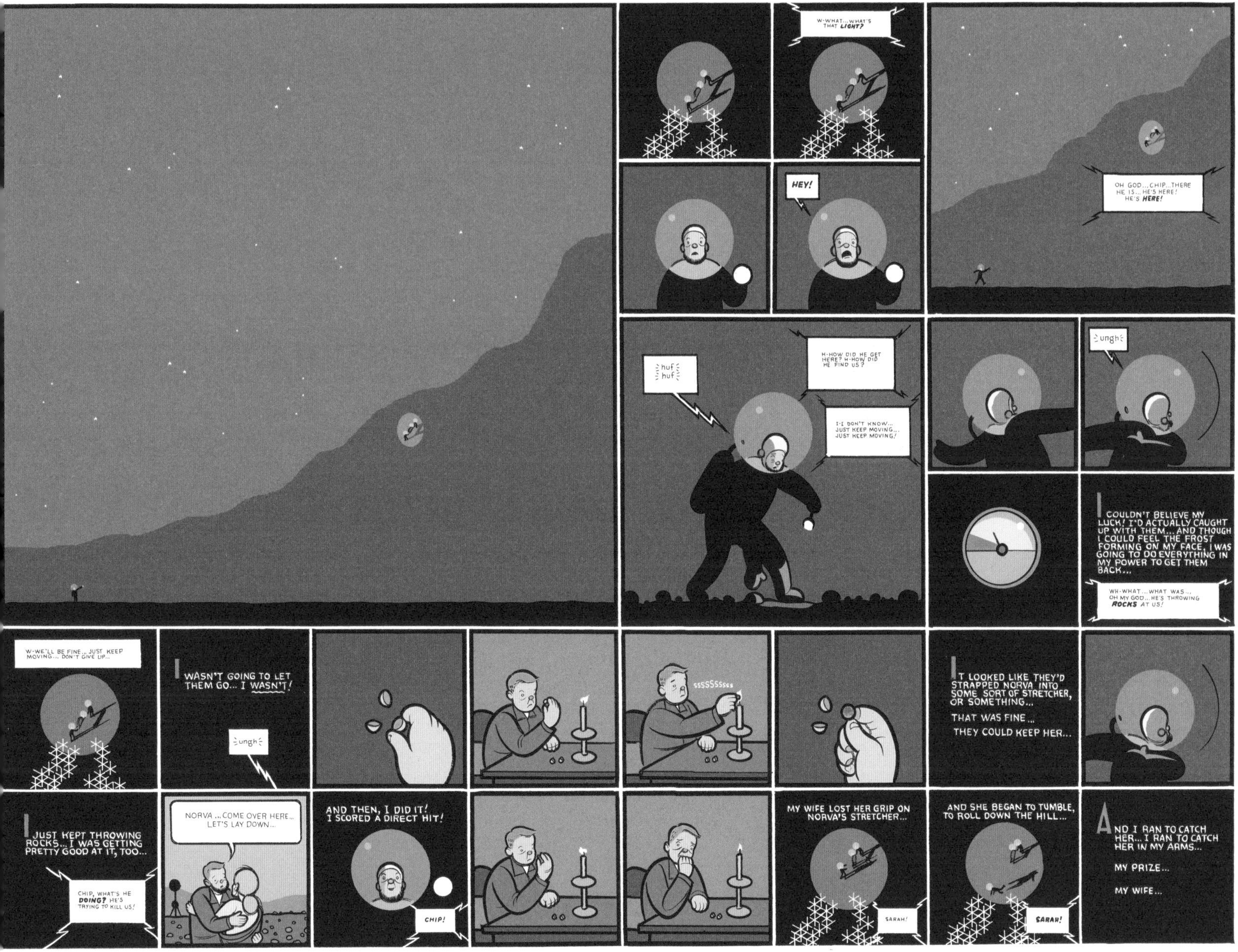
W-WHAT... WHAT'S THAT LIGHT?
HEY!
OH GOD... CHIP... THERE HE IS... HE'S HERE! HE'S HERE!
huf huf
H-HOW DID HE GET HERE? H-HOW DID HE FIND US?
I-I DON'T KNOW... JUST KEEP MOVING... JUST KEEP MOVING!
ungh
I COULDN'T BELIEVE MY LUCK! I'D ACTUALLY CAUGHT UP WITH THEM... AND THOUGH I COULD FEEL THE FROST FORMING ON MY FACE, I WAS GOING TO DO EVERYTHING IN MY POWER TO GET THEM BACK...
WH-WHAT... WHAT WAS... OH MY GOD... HE'S THROWING ROCKS AT US!
W-WE'LL BE FINE... JUST KEEP MOVING... DON'T GIVE UP...
I WASN'T GOING TO LET THEM GO... I WASN'T!
ungh
IT LOOKED LIKE THEY'D STRAPPED NORVA INTO SOME SORT OF STRETCHER, OR SOMETHING...
THAT WAS FINE...
THEY COULD KEEP HER...
I JUST KEPT THROWING ROCKS... I WAS GETTING PRETTY GOOD AT IT, TOO...
CHIP, WHAT'S HE DOING? HE'S TRYING TO KILL US!
NORVA... COME OVER HERE... LET'S LAY DOWN...
AND THEN, I DID IT! I SCORED A DIRECT HIT!
CHIP!
MY WIFE LOST HER GRIP ON NORVA'S STRETCHER...
SARAH!
AND SHE BEGAN TO TUMBLE, TO ROLL DOWN THE HILL...
SARAH!
AND I RAN TO CATCH HER... I RAN TO CATCH HER IN MY ARMS...
MY PRIZE...
MY WIFE...

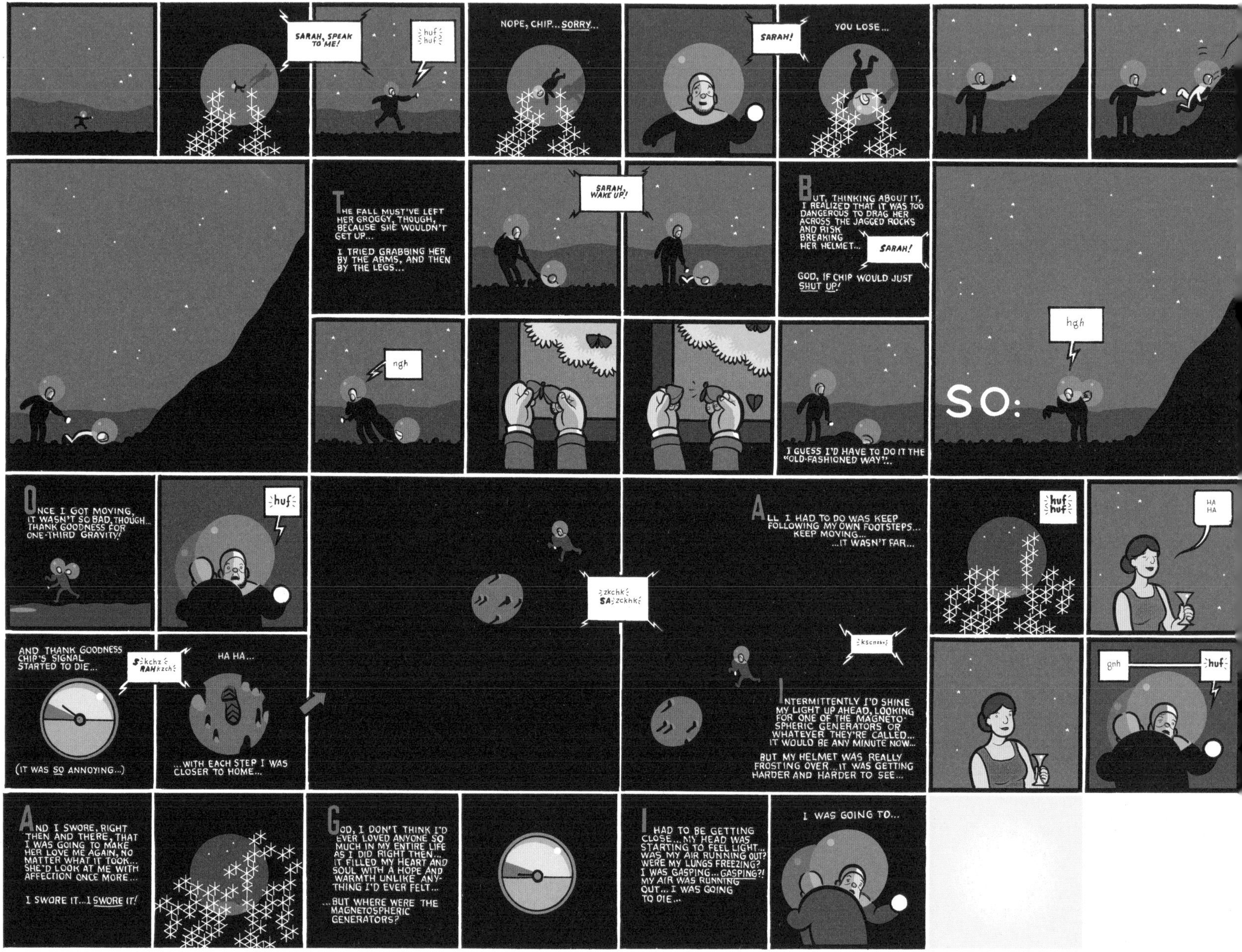
SARAH, SPEAK TO ME!
huf huf
NOPE, CHIP... SORRY...
SARAH!
YOU LOSE...
THE FALL MUST'VE LEFT HER GROGGY, THOUGH, BECAUSE SHE WOULDN'T GET UP...
I TRIED GRABBING HER BY THE ARMS, AND THEN BY THE LEGS...
SARAH, WAKE UP!
BUT, THINKING ABOUT IT, I REALIZED THAT IT WAS TOO DANGEROUS TO DRAG HER ACROSS THE JAGGED ROCKS AND RISK BREAKING HER HELMET...
SARAH!
GOD, IF CHIP WOULD JUST SHUT UP!
ngh
I GUESS I'D HAVE TO DO IT THE "OLD-FASHIONED WAY"...
hgh
SO:
ONCE I GOT MOVING, IT WASN'T SO BAD, THOUGH... THANK GOODNESS FOR ONE-THIRD GRAVITY!
huf
AND THANK GOODNESS CHIP'S SIGNAL STARTED TO DIE...
S kchz RAH kzch
(IT WAS SO ANNOYING...)
HA HA...
...WITH EACH STEP I WAS CLOSER TO HOME...
zkchk SA zckhk
ALL I HAD TO DO WAS KEEP FOLLOWING MY OWN FOOTSTEPS... KEEP MOVING... ...IT WASN'T FAR...
INTERMITTENTLY I'D SHINE MY LIGHT UP AHEAD, LOOKING FOR ONE OF THE MAGNETO-SPHERIC GENERATORS OR WHATEVER THEY'RE CALLED... IT WOULD BE ANY MINUTE NOW...
BUT MY HELMET WAS REALLY FROSTING OVER... IT WAS GETTING HARDER AND HARDER TO SEE...
huf huf
HA HA
gnh
huf
AND I SWORE, RIGHT THEN AND THERE, THAT I WAS GOING TO MAKE HER LOVE ME AGAIN, NO MATTER WHAT IT TOOK... SHE'D LOOK AT ME WITH AFFECTION ONCE MORE...
I SWORE IT... I SWORE IT!
GOD, I DON'T THINK I'D EVER LOVED ANYONE SO MUCH IN MY ENTIRE LIFE AS I DID RIGHT THEN... IT FILLED MY HEART AND SOUL WITH A HOPE AND WARMTH UNLIKE ANYTHING I'D EVER FELT...
...BUT WHERE WERE THE MAGNETOSPHERIC GENERATORS?
I HAD TO BE GETTING CLOSE... MY HEAD WAS STARTING TO FEEL LIGHT... WAS MY AIR RUNNING OUT? WERE MY LUNGS FREEZING? I WAS GASPING... GASPING?! MY AIR WAS RUNNING OUT... I WAS GOING TO DIE...
I WAS GOING TO...

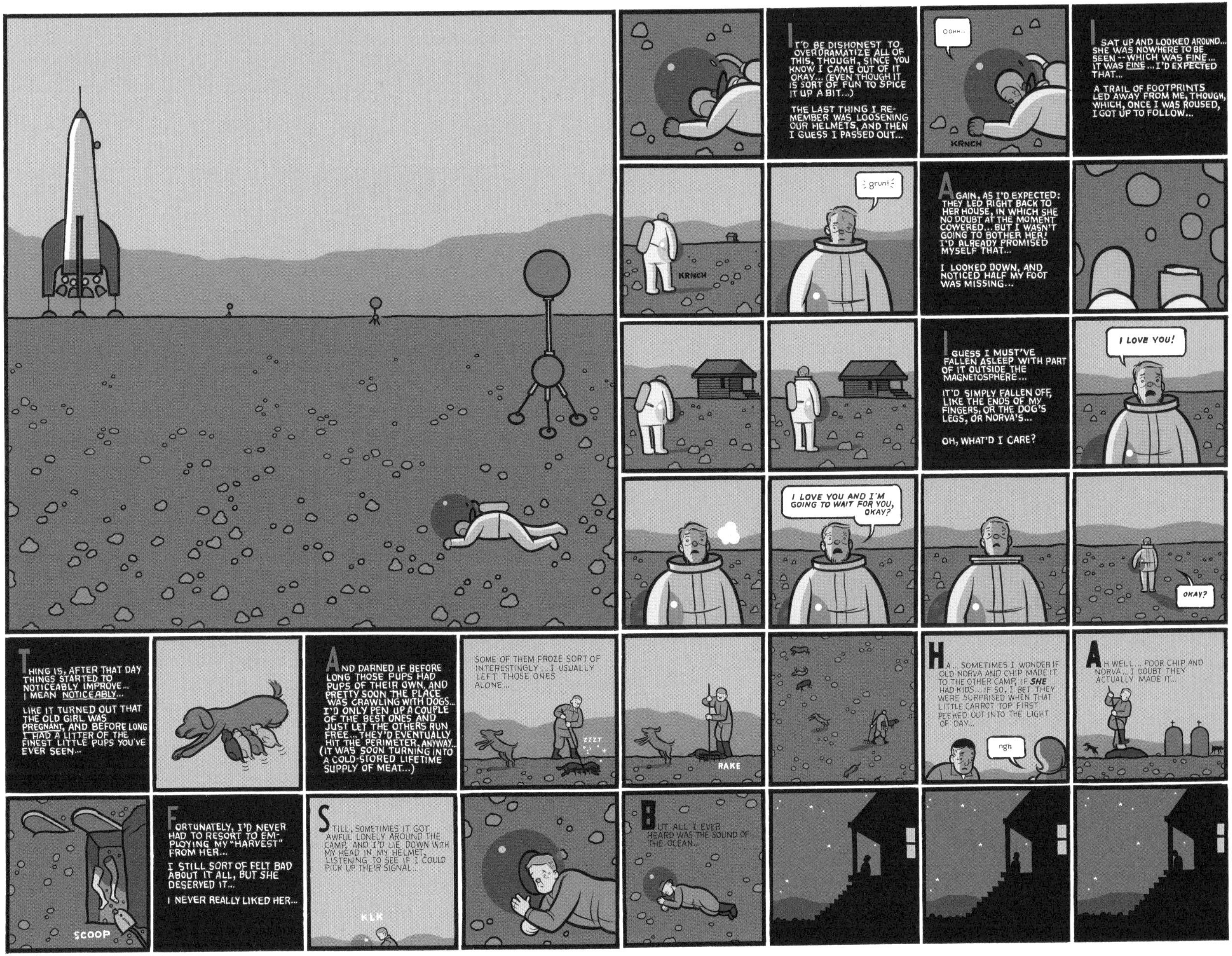
OOHH...
KRNCH
I'D BE DISHONEST TO OVERDRAMATIZE ALL OF THIS, THOUGH, SINCE YOU KNOW I CAME OUT OF IT OKAY... (EVEN THOUGH IT IS SORT OF FUN TO SPICE IT UP A BIT...)
THE LAST THING I REMEMBER WAS LOOSENING OUR HELMETS, AND THEN I GUESS I PASSED OUT...
OOHH...
KRNCH
I SAT UP AND LOOKED AROUND... SHE WAS NOWHERE TO BE SEEN -- WHICH WAS FINE... IT WAS FINE... I'D EXPECTED THAT...
A TRAIL OF FOOTPRINTS LED AWAY FROM ME, THOUGH, WHICH, ONCE I WAS ROUSED, I GOT UP TO FOLLOW...
KRNCH
grunt
AGAIN, AS I'D EXPECTED: THEY LED RIGHT BACK TO HER HOUSE, IN WHICH SHE NO DOUBT AT THE MOMENT COWERED... BUT I WASN'T GOING TO BOTHER HER! I'D ALREADY PROMISED MYSELF THAT...
I LOOKED DOWN, AND NOTICED HALF MY FOOT WAS MISSING...
I GUESS I MUST'VE FALLEN ASLEEP WITH PART OF IT OUTSIDE THE MAGNETOSPHERE...
IT'D SIMPLY FALLEN OFF, LIKE THE ENDS OF MY FINGERS, OR THE DOG'S LEGS, OR NORVA'S...
OH, WHAT'D I CARE?
I LOVE YOU!
I LOVE YOU AND I'M GOING TO WAIT FOR YOU, OKAY?
OKAY?
THING IS, AFTER THAT DAY THINGS STARTED TO NOTICEABLY IMPROVE... I MEAN NOTICEABLY...
LIKE IT TURNED OUT THAT THE OLD GIRL WAS PREGNANT, AND BEFORE LONG I HAD A LITTER OF THE FINEST LITTLE PUPS YOU'VE EVER SEEN...
AND DARNED IF BEFORE LONG THOSE PUPS HAD PUPS OF THEIR OWN, AND PRETTY SOON THE PLACE WAS CRAWLING WITH DOGS... I'D ONLY PEN UP A COUPLE OF THE BEST ONES AND JUST LET THE OTHERS RUN FREE... THEY'D EVENTUALLY HIT THE PERIMETER, ANYWAY... (IT WAS SOON TURNING INTO A COLD-STORED LIFETIME SUPPLY OF MEAT...)
SOME OF THEM FROZE SORT OF INTERESTINGLY ... I USUALLY LEFT THOSE ONES ALONE...
ZZZT
RAKE
HA... SOMETIMES I WONDER IF OLD NORVA AND CHIP MADE IT TO THE OTHER CAMP, IF SHE HAD KIDS... IF SO, I BET THEY WERE SURPRISED WHEN THAT LITTLE CARROT TOP FIRST PEEKED OUT INTO THE LIGHT OF DAY...
ngh
AH WELL... POOR CHIP AND NORVA... I DOUBT THEY ACTUALLY MADE IT...
SCOOP
FORTUNATELY, I'D NEVER HAD TO RESORT TO EMPLOYING MY "HARVEST" FROM HER...
I STILL SORT OF FELT BAD ABOUT IT ALL, BUT SHE DESERVED IT...
I NEVER REALLY LIKED HER...
STILL, SOMETIMES IT GOT AWFUL LONELY AROUND THE CAMP, AND I'D LIE DOWN WITH MY HEAD IN MY HELMET, LISTENING TO SEE IF I COULD PICK UP THEIR SIGNAL...
KLK
BUT ALL I EVER HEARD WAS THE SOUND OF THE OCEAN...

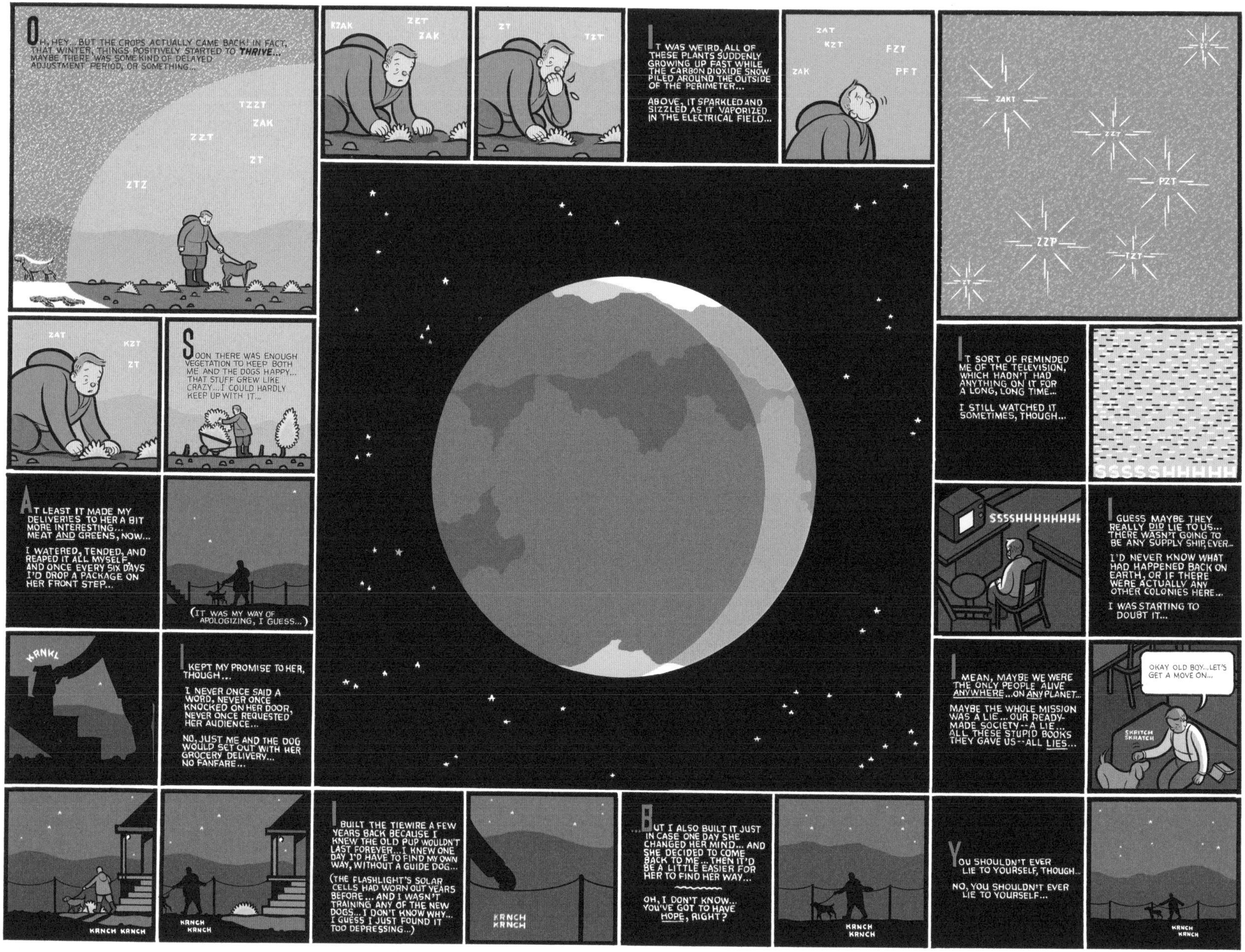

OH, HEY... BUT THE CROPS ACTUALLY CAME BACK! IN FACT, THAT WINTER, THINGS POSITIVELY STARTED TO **THRIVE**... MAYBE THERE WAS SOME KIND OF DELAYED ADJUSTMENT PERIOD, OR SOMETHING...
TZZT
ZAK
ZZT
ZT
ZTZ
KZAK
ZZT
ZAK
ZT
TZT
IT WAS WEIRD, ALL OF THESE PLANTS SUDDENLY GROWING UP FAST WHILE THE CARBON DIOXIDE SNOW PILED AROUND THE OUTSIDE OF THE PERIMETER...
ABOVE, IT SPARKLED AND SIZZLED AS IT VAPORIZED IN THE ELECTRICAL FIELD...
ZAT
KZT
FZT
ZAK
PFT
ZAKT
ZT
ZZT
PZT
ZZP
TZT
ZT
ZAT
KZT
ZT
SOON THERE WAS ENOUGH VEGETATION TO KEEP BOTH ME AND THE DOGS HAPPY... THAT STUFF GREW LIKE CRAZY... I COULD HARDLY KEEP UP WITH IT...
AT LEAST IT MADE MY DELIVERIES TO HER A BIT MORE INTERESTING... MEAT AND GREENS, NOW...
I WATERED, TENDED, AND REAPED IT ALL MYSELF, AND ONCE EVERY SIX DAYS I'D DROP A PACKAGE ON HER FRONT STEP...
(IT WAS MY WAY OF APOLOGIZING, I GUESS...)
KRNKL
I KEPT MY PROMISE TO HER, THOUGH...
I NEVER ONCE SAID A WORD, NEVER ONCE KNOCKED ON HER DOOR, NEVER ONCE REQUESTED HER AUDIENCE...
NO, JUST ME AND THE DOG WOULD SET OUT WITH HER GROCERY DELIVERY... NO FANFARE...
IT SORT OF REMINDED ME OF THE TELEVISION, WHICH HADN'T HAD ANYTHING ON IT FOR A LONG, LONG TIME...
I STILL WATCHED IT SOMETIMES, THOUGH...
SSSSSHHHHH
SSSSHHHHHHHH
I GUESS MAYBE THEY REALLY DID LIE TO US... THERE WASN'T GOING TO BE ANY SUPPLY SHIP, EVER...
I'D NEVER KNOW WHAT HAD HAPPENED BACK ON EARTH, OR IF THERE WERE ACTUALLY ANY OTHER COLONIES HERE...
I WAS STARTING TO DOUBT IT...
I MEAN, MAYBE WE WERE THE ONLY PEOPLE ALIVE ANYWHERE... ON ANY PLANET...
MAYBE THE WHOLE MISSION WAS A LIE... OUR READY-MADE SOCIETY--A LIE... ALL THESE STUPID BOOKS THEY GAVE US--ALL LIES...
OKAY OLD BOY... LET'S GET A MOVE ON...
SKRITCH SKRATCH
KRNCH KRNCH
KRNCH KRNCH
I BUILT THE TIEWIRE A FEW YEARS BACK BECAUSE I KNEW THE OLD PUP WOULDN'T LAST FOREVER... I KNEW ONE DAY I'D HAVE TO FIND MY OWN WAY, WITHOUT A GUIDE DOG...
(THE FLASHLIGHT'S SOLAR CELLS HAD WORN OUT YEARS BEFORE... AND I WASN'T TRAINING ANY OF THE NEW DOGS... I DON'T KNOW WHY... I GUESS I JUST FOUND IT TOO DEPRESSING...)
KRNCH KRNCH
...BUT I ALSO BUILT IT JUST IN CASE ONE DAY SHE CHANGED HER MIND... AND SHE DECIDED TO COME BACK TO ME... THEN IT'D BE A LITTLE EASIER FOR HER TO FIND HER WAY...
OH, I DON'T KNOW... YOU'VE GOT TO HAVE HOPE, RIGHT?
KRNCH KRNCH
YOU SHOULDN'T EVER LIE TO YOURSELF, THOUGH...
NO, YOU SHOULDN'T EVER LIE TO YOURSELF...
KRNCH KRNCH

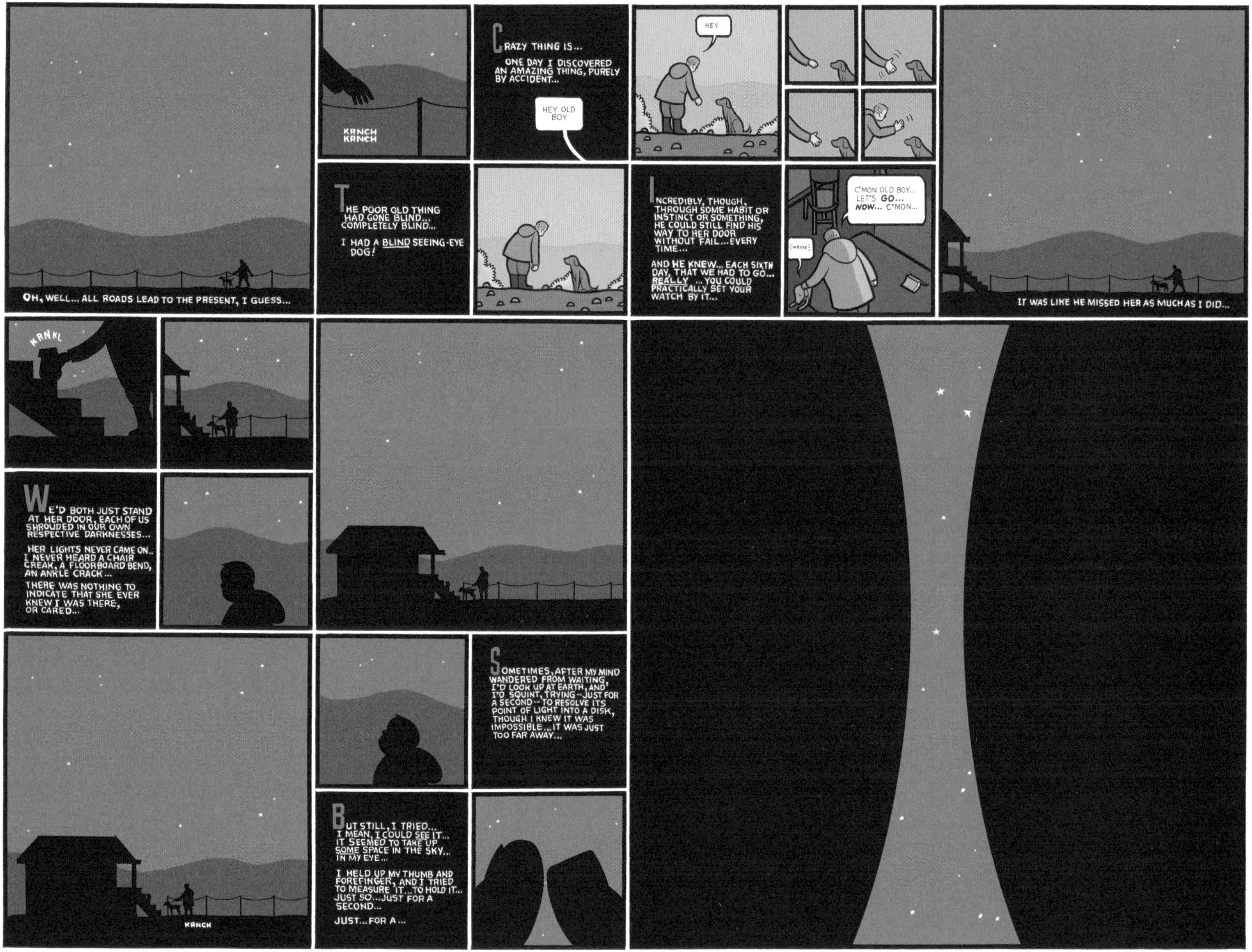
OH, WELL... ALL ROADS LEAD TO THE PRESENT, I GUESS...
KRNCH KRNCH
CRAZY THING IS...
ONE DAY I DISCOVERED AN AMAZING THING, PURELY BY ACCIDENT...
HEY OLD BOY
THE POOR OLD THING HAD GONE BLIND... COMPLETELY BLIND...
I HAD A BLIND SEEING-EYE DOG!
HEY
INCREDIBLY, THOUGH, THROUGH SOME HABIT OR INSTINCT OR SOMETHING, HE COULD STILL FIND HIS WAY TO HER DOOR WITHOUT FAIL... EVERY TIME...
AND HE KNEW... EACH SIXTH DAY, THAT WE HAD TO GO... REALLY ...YOU COULD PRACTICALLY SET YOUR WATCH BY IT...
C'MON OLD BOY... LET'S GO... NOW... C'MON...
whine
IT WAS LIKE HE MISSED HER AS MUCH AS I DID...
KRNKL
WE'D BOTH JUST STAND AT HER DOOR, EACH OF US SHROUDED IN OUR OWN RESPECTIVE DARKNESSES...
HER LIGHTS NEVER CAME ON... I NEVER HEARD A CHAIR CREAK, A FLOORBOARD BEND, AN ANKLE CRACK...
THERE WAS NOTHING TO INDICATE THAT SHE EVER KNEW I WAS THERE, OR CARED...
KRNCH
SOMETIMES, AFTER MY MIND WANDERED FROM WAITING, I'D LOOK UP AT EARTH, AND I'D SQUINT, TRYING -- JUST FOR A SECOND -- TO RESOLVE ITS POINT OF LIGHT INTO A DISK, THOUGH I KNEW IT WAS IMPOSSIBLE... IT WAS JUST TOO FAR AWAY...
BUT STILL, I TRIED... I MEAN, I COULD SEE IT... IT SEEMED TO TAKE UP SOME SPACE IN THE SKY... IN MY EYE...
I HELD UP MY THUMB AND FOREFINGER, AND I TRIED TO MEASURE IT... TO HOLD IT... JUST SO... JUST FOR A SECOND...
JUST... FOR A...

Sometimes, after my mind wandered from waiting, I'd look up at the Earth, and I'd squint, trying, just for a second, to resolve its point of light into a disk, though I knew it was impossible ... it was just too far away ...

The dark figure stood, silhouetted against the bejewelled Martian sky. A puff of breath rose, floated, dissipated. A bootcrunch in black gravel. A silent dog, standing, blindly staring straight ahead, its nose bouncing on the scent of the breeze.

But still, I tried ... I mean, I could see it ... it seemed to take up some space in the sky ... in my eye ...

The parka lisped as he raised his arm and squinted up into the bottom of the celestial bowl. A six-minute-old sixty-million-mile-long needle of starlight pierced his cornea, threaded through the vitreous gel of his eyeball, and scratched a spark on the slippery back moviescreen of his retina.

A silverpoint sliver of thought shot quick to his cortex, gave a little shrug, and still radioed back "Planet Earth."

I held up my thumb and forefinger, and I tried to measure it ... to hold it ... just so ... just for a second ... just ... for a ...

The blurry black mountains of his fingers closed in, erasing the stars, one by one, crushing down with a weight of time and knowledge and horror afforded only by a million years of human evolution.

A fraction of an inch apart, the mountains stopped moving. And they paused there, shivering.

THE END

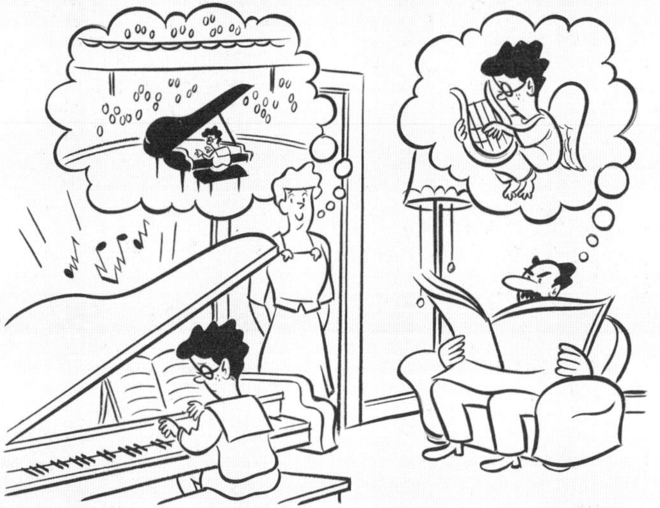

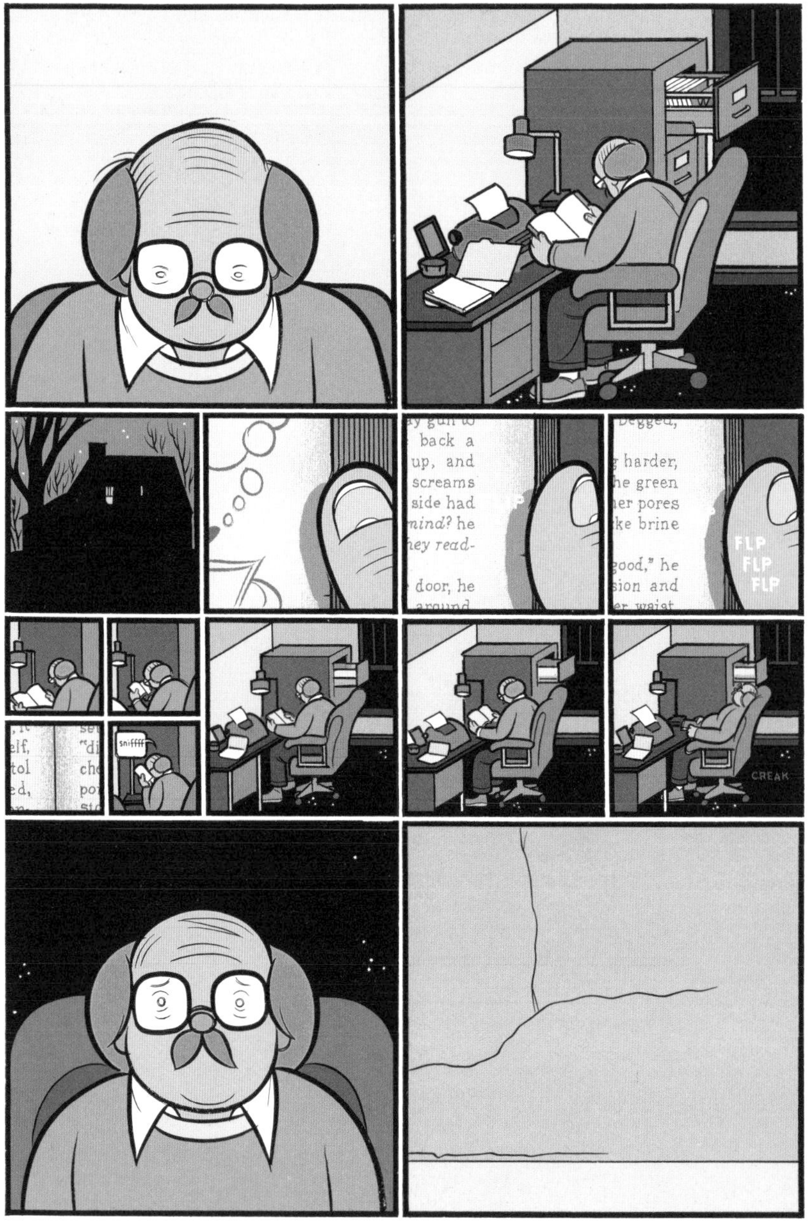
FLP
FLP
FLP
sniffff
CREAK

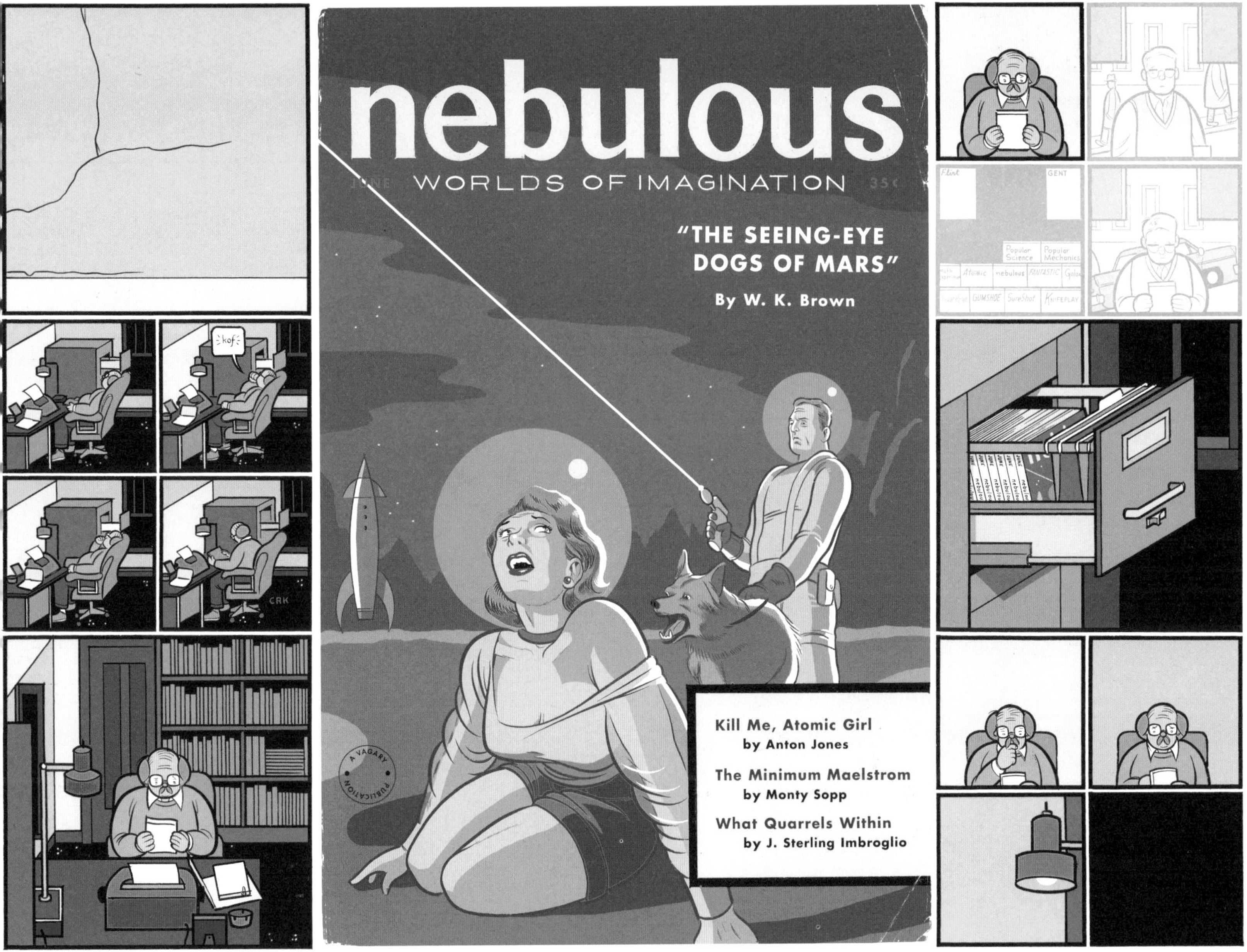
kof
CRK
nebulous
JUNE WORLDS OF IMAGINATION 35¢
"THE SEEING-EYE DOGS OF MARS"
By W. K. Brown
A VAGARY PUBLICATION
Kill Me, Atomic Girl
by Anton Jones
The Minimum Maelstrom
by Monty Sopp
What Quarrels Within
by J. Sterling Imbroglio
Flint
GENT
Popular Science
Popular Mechanics
Atomic
nebulous
FANTASTIC
GUMSHOE
SureShot
KNIFEPLAY

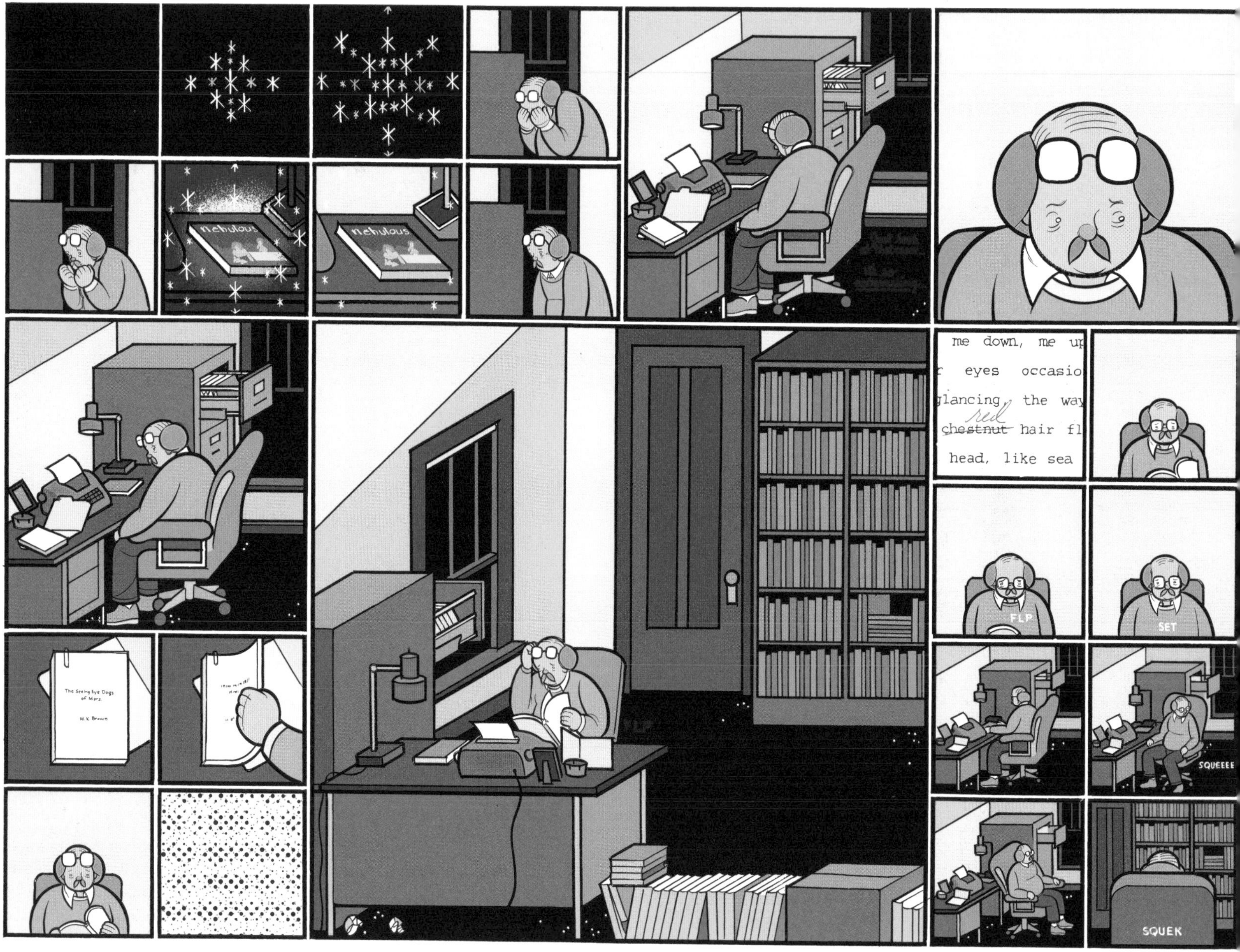
nebulous
nebulous
The Seeing Eye Dogs of Mars.
W. K. Brown
me down, me up
eyes occasio
glancing, the way
red
chestnut hair fl
head, like sea
FLP
SET
SQUEEEE
SQUEK

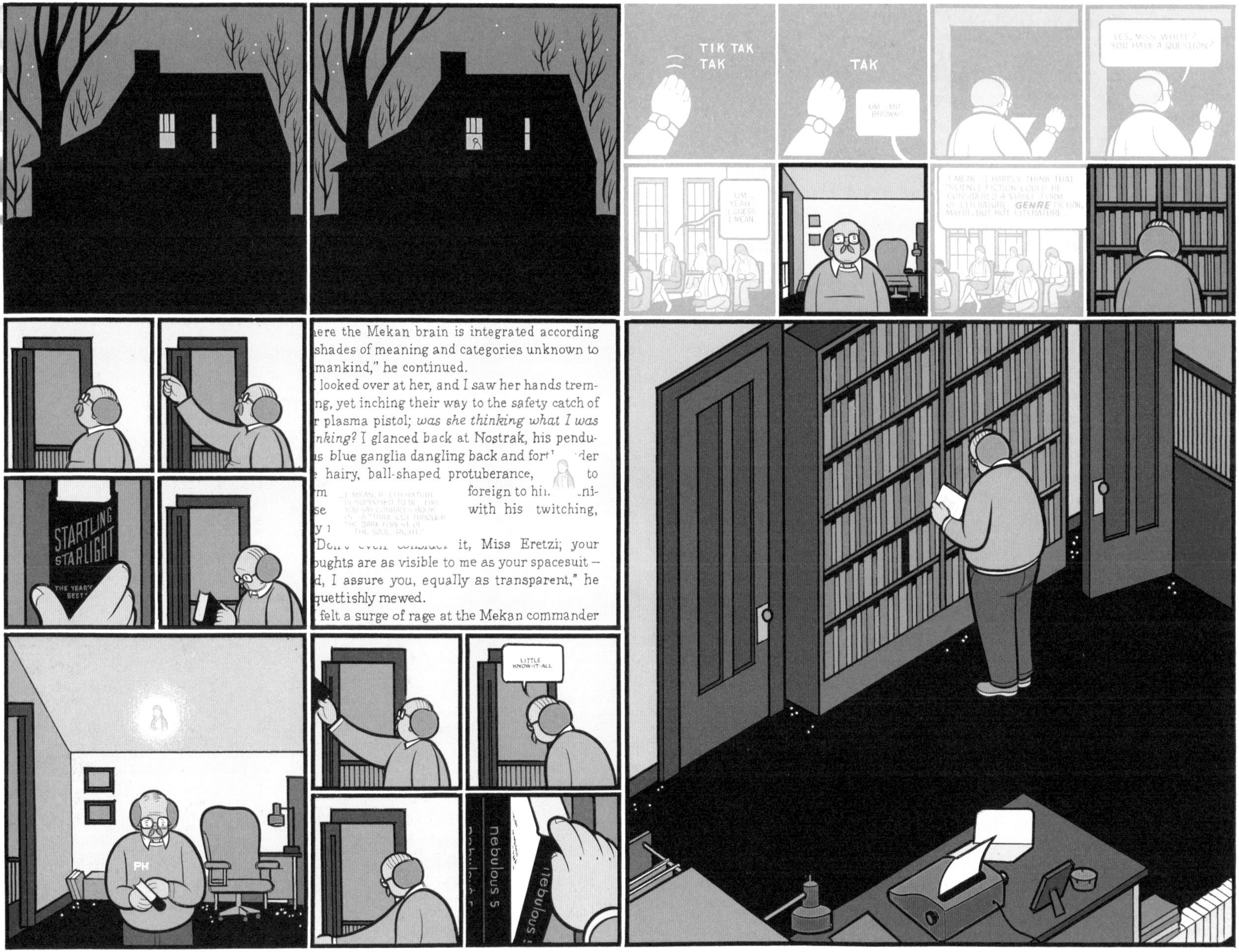
TIK TAK
TAK
TAK
UM... MR. BROWN?
YES, MISS WHITE? YOU HAVE A QUESTION?
UM... YEAH... I GUESS... I MEAN...
I MEAN... I HARDLY THINK THAT "SCIENCE FICTION" COULD BE CONSIDERED A VIABLE FORM OF LITERATURE... GENRE FICTION, MAYBE, BUT NOT LITERATURE...
STARTLING STARLIGHT
THE YEAR'S BEST
ıere the Mekan brain is integrated according
shades of meaning and categories unknown to
mankind," he continued.
I looked over at her, and I saw her hands trem-
ng, yet inching their way to the safety catch of
r plasma pistol; *was she thinking what I was*
nking? I glanced back at Nostrak, his pendu-
s blue ganglia dangling back and fort' der
hairy, ball-shaped protuberance, to
m foreign to hi ni-
se with his twitching,
y
"Don't even consider it, Miss Eretzi; your
oughts are as visible to me as your spacesuit –
d, I assure you, equally as transparent," he
quettishly mewed.
I felt a surge of rage at the Mekan commander
...I MEAN, IF LITERATURE IS SUPPOSED TO BE... YOU SAY CONRAD'S BOOK IS... A "TRAIL CUT THROUGH THE DARK FOREST OF THE SOUL," RIGHT?
PH
LITTLE KNOW-IT-ALL
nebulous 5
nebulous 5

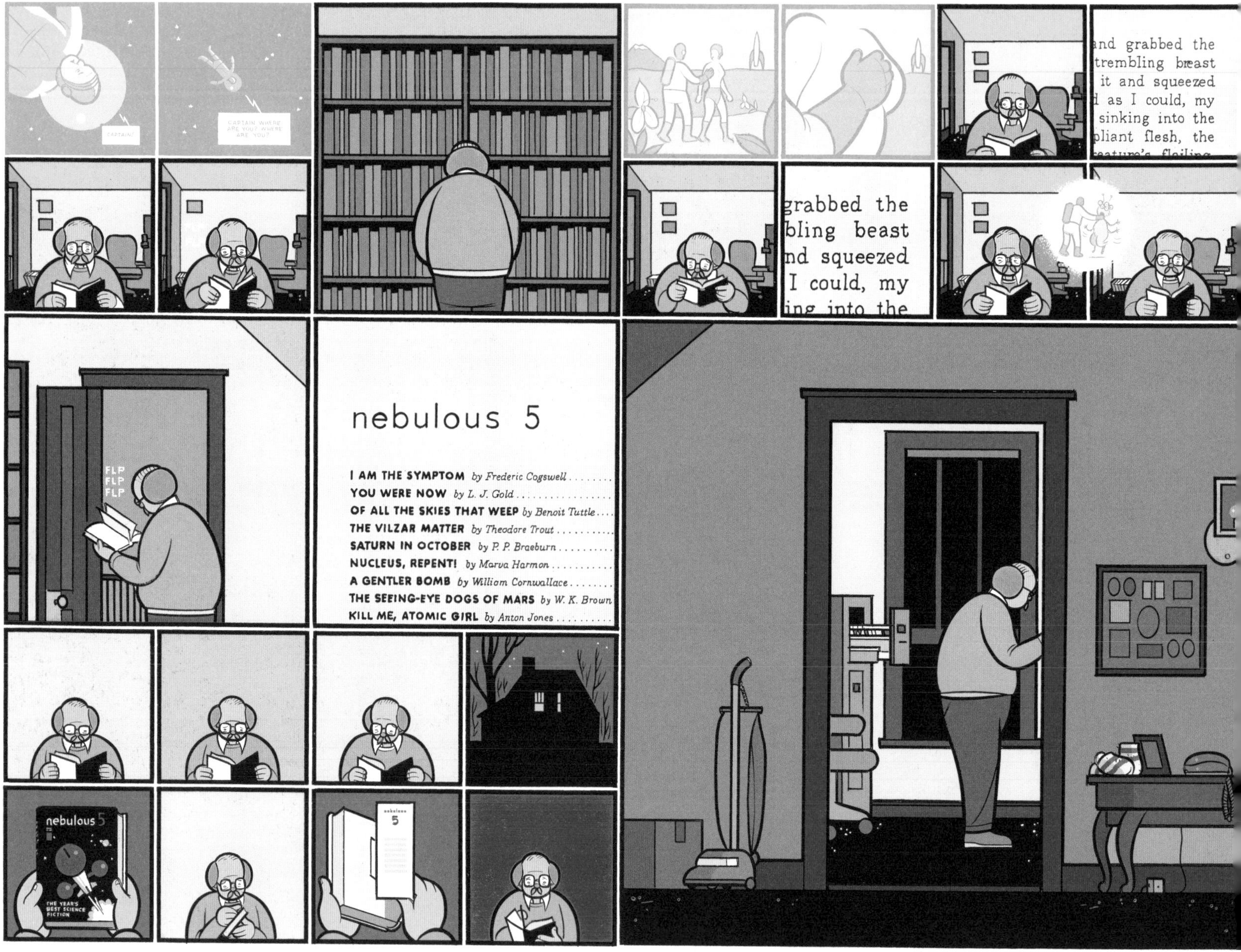
CAPTAIN!
CAPTAIN WHERE ARE YOU? WHERE ARE YOU?
and grabbed the
trembling beast
it and squeezed
as I could, my
sinking into the
pliant flesh, the
grabbed the
bling beast
nd squeezed
I could, my
FLP
FLP
FLP
nebulous 5
I AM THE SYMPTOM by Frederic Cogswell........
YOU WERE NOW by L. J. Gold................
OF ALL THE SKIES THAT WEEP by Benoit Tuttle....
THE VILZAR MATTER by Theodore Trout..........
SATURN IN OCTOBER by P. P. Braeburn.........
NUCLEUS, REPENT! by Marva Harmon..........
A GENTLER BOMB by William Cornwallace........
THE SEEING-EYE DOGS OF MARS by W. K. Brown
KILL ME, ATOMIC GIRL by Anton Jones..........
nebulous 5
THE YEAR'S BEST SCIENCE FICTION
5

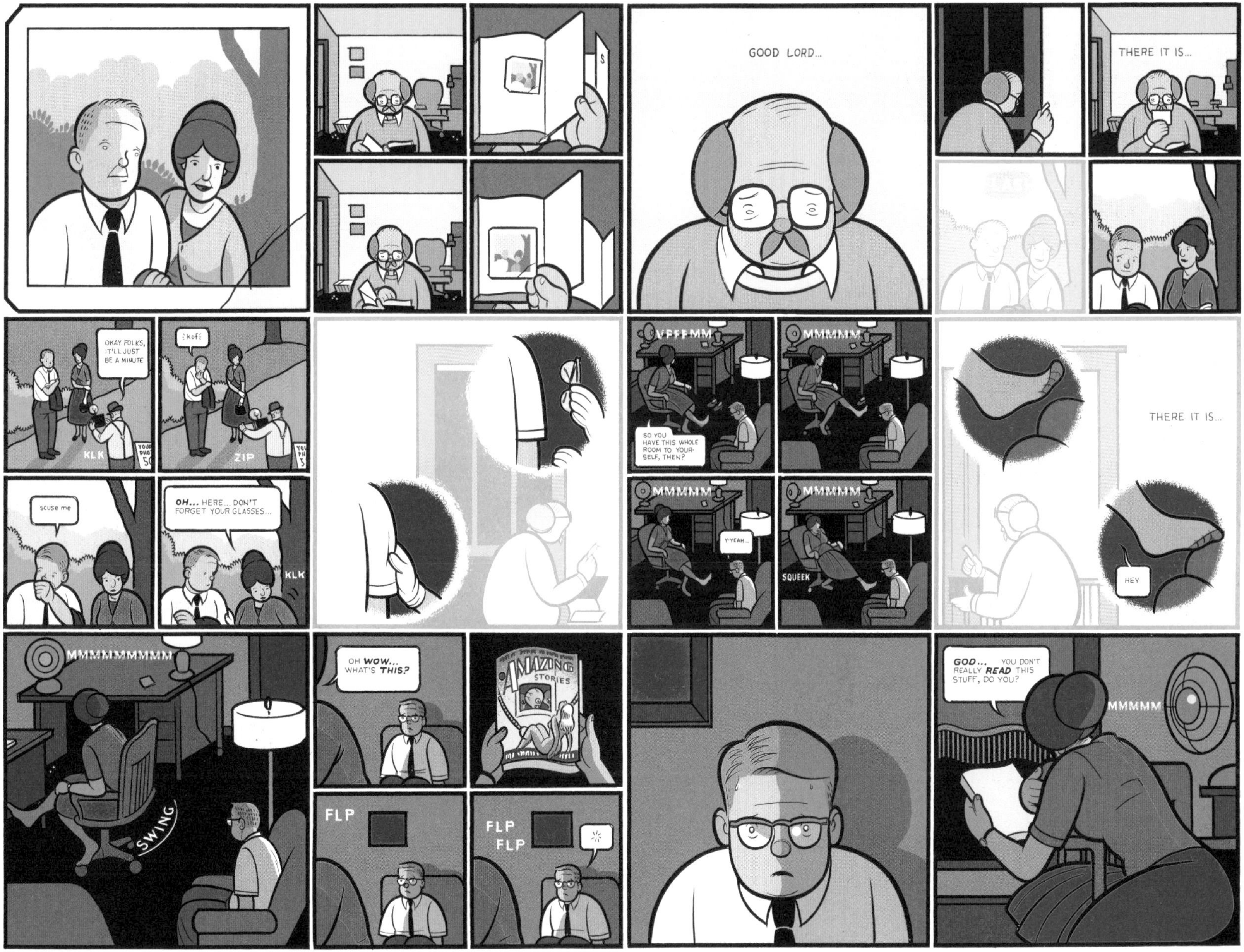
GOOD LORD...
THERE IT IS...
OKAY FOLKS, IT'LL JUST BE A MINUTE
KLK
kof
ZIP
scuse me
OH... HERE... DON'T FORGET YOUR GLASSES...
KLK
VFFFMM
SO YOU HAVE THIS WHOLE ROOM TO YOURSELF, THEN?
MMMMM
MMMMM
Y-YEAH...
MMMMM
SQUEEK
THERE IT IS...
HEY
MMMMMMMMMM
SWING
OH WOW... WHAT'S THIS?
AMAZING STORIES
FLP
FLP FLP
GOD... YOU DON'T REALLY READ THIS STUFF, DO YOU?
MMMMM

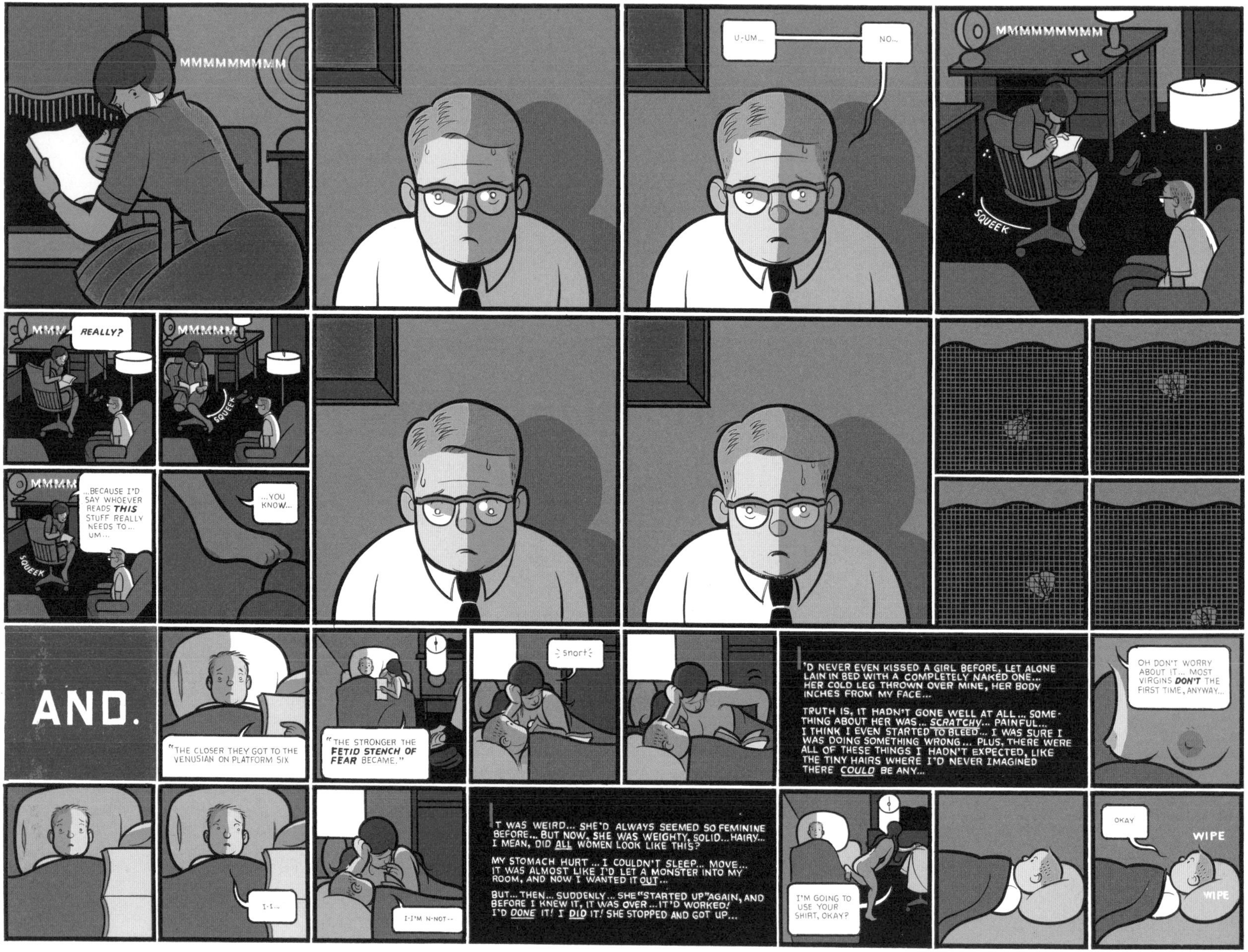
MMMMMMMMM
U-UM...
NO...
MMMMMMMMM
SQUEEK
MMM
REALLY?
MMMMM
SQUEEK
MMMM
...BECAUSE I'D SAY WHOEVER READS THIS STUFF REALLY NEEDS TO... UM...
SQUEEK
...YOU KNOW...
AND.
"THE CLOSER THEY GOT TO THE VENUSIAN ON PLATFORM SIX
"THE STRONGER THE FETID STENCH OF FEAR BECAME."
snort
I'D NEVER EVEN KISSED A GIRL BEFORE, LET ALONE LAIN IN BED WITH A COMPLETELY NAKED ONE... HER COLD LEG THROWN OVER MINE, HER BODY INCHES FROM MY FACE...
TRUTH IS, IT HADN'T GONE WELL AT ALL... SOMETHING ABOUT HER WAS... SCRATCHY... PAINFUL... I THINK I EVEN STARTED TO BLEED... I WAS SURE I WAS DOING SOMETHING WRONG... PLUS, THERE WERE ALL OF THESE THINGS I HADN'T EXPECTED, LIKE THE TINY HAIRS WHERE I'D NEVER IMAGINED THERE COULD BE ANY...
OH DON'T WORRY ABOUT IT... MOST VIRGINS DON'T THE FIRST TIME, ANYWAY...
I-I...
I-I'M N-NOT--
IT WAS WEIRD... SHE'D ALWAYS SEEMED SO FEMININE BEFORE... BUT NOW, SHE WAS WEIGHTY, SOLID... HAIRY... I MEAN, DID ALL WOMEN LOOK LIKE THIS?
MY STOMACH HURT... I COULDN'T SLEEP... MOVE... IT WAS ALMOST LIKE I'D LET A MONSTER INTO MY ROOM, AND NOW I WANTED IT OUT...
BUT... THEN... SUDDENLY... SHE "STARTED UP" AGAIN, AND BEFORE I KNEW IT, IT WAS OVER... IT'D WORKED! I'D DONE IT! I DID IT! SHE STOPPED AND GOT UP...
I'M GOING TO USE YOUR SHIRT, OKAY?
OKAY
WIPE
WIPE

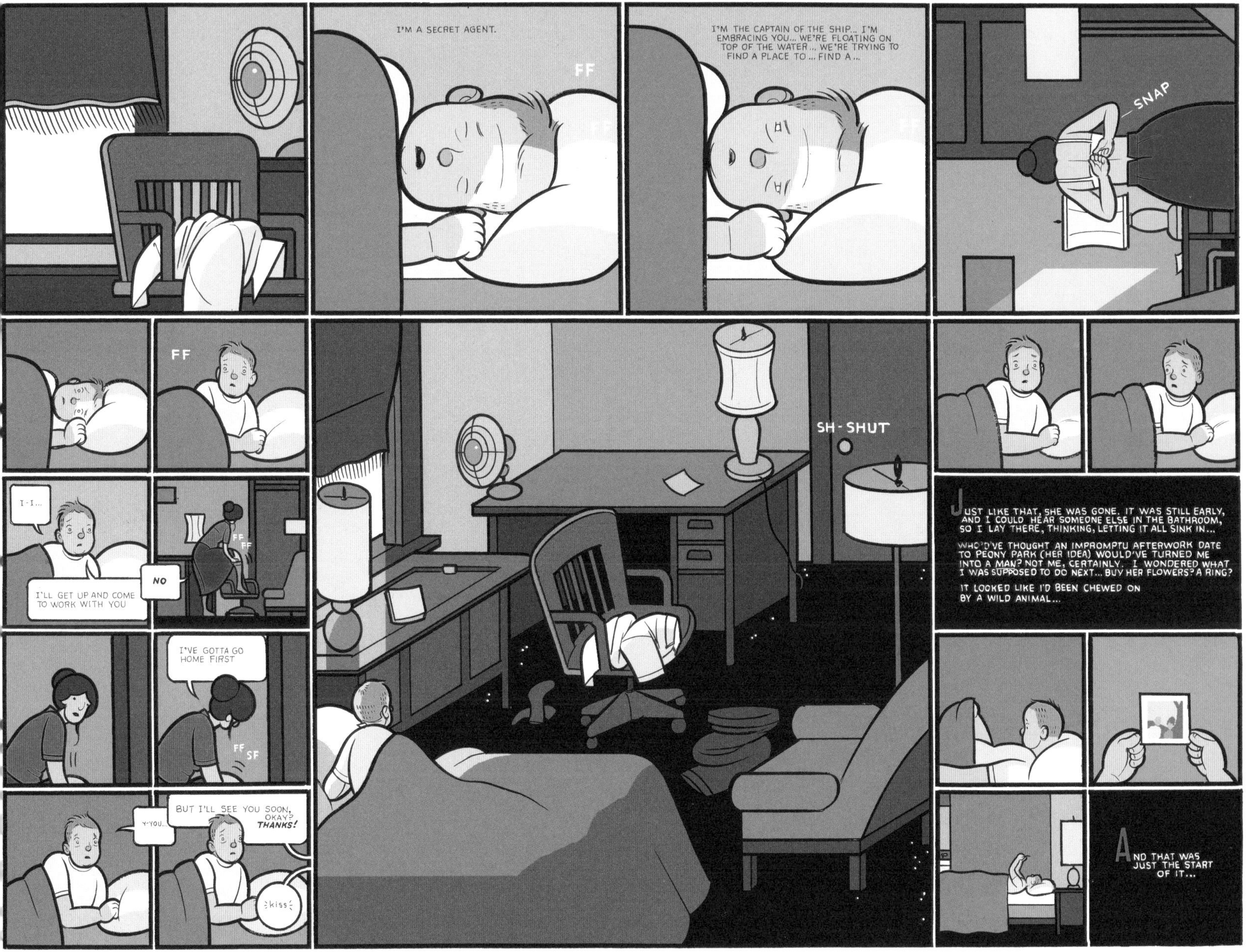
I'M A SECRET AGENT.
FF
FF
I'M THE CAPTAIN OF THE SHIP... I'M EMBRACING YOU... WE'RE FLOATING ON TOP OF THE WATER... WE'RE TRYING TO FIND A PLACE TO... FIND A...
FF
SNAP
FF
I-I...
I'LL GET UP AND COME TO WORK WITH YOU
NO
FF
FF
I'VE GOTTA GO HOME FIRST
FF SF
Y-YOU...
BUT I'LL SEE YOU SOON, OKAY? THANKS!
kiss
SH-SHUT
JUST LIKE THAT, SHE WAS GONE. IT WAS STILL EARLY, AND I COULD HEAR SOMEONE ELSE IN THE BATHROOM, SO I LAY THERE, THINKING, LETTING IT ALL SINK IN...
WHO'D'VE THOUGHT AN IMPROMPTU AFTERWORK DATE TO PEONY PARK (HER IDEA) WOULD'VE TURNED ME INTO A MAN? NOT ME, CERTAINLY. I WONDERED WHAT I WAS SUPPOSED TO DO NEXT... BUY HER FLOWERS? A RING?
IT LOOKED LIKE I'D BEEN CHEWED ON BY A WILD ANIMAL...
AND THAT WAS JUST THE START OF IT...

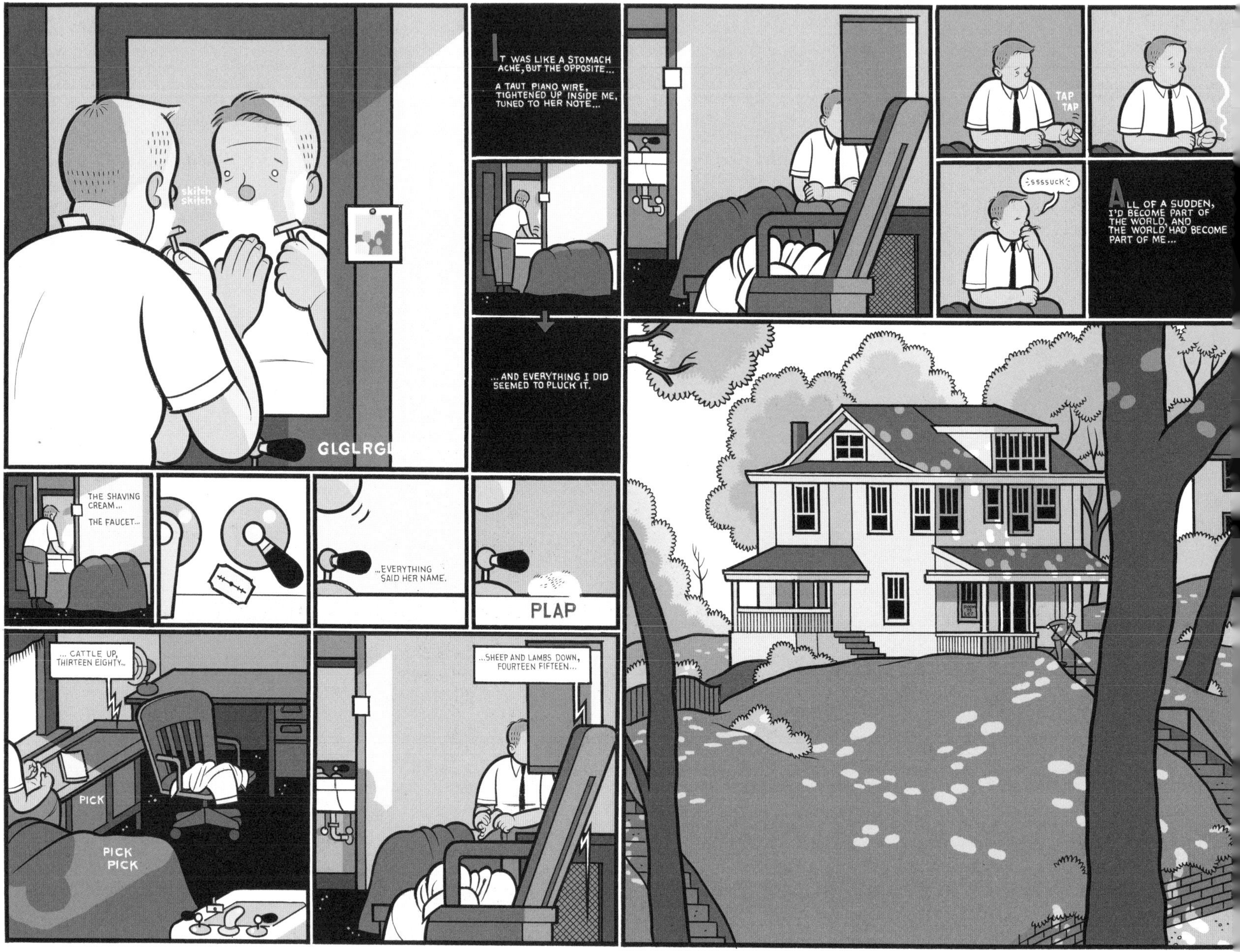
skitch
skitch
GLGLRG
IT WAS LIKE A STOMACH ACHE, BUT THE OPPOSITE...
A TAUT PIANO WIRE, TIGHTENED UP INSIDE ME, TUNED TO HER NOTE...
...AND EVERYTHING I DID SEEMED TO PLUCK IT.
THE SHAVING CREAM...
THE FAUCET...
...EVERYTHING SAID HER NAME.
PLAP
...CATTLE UP, THIRTEEN EIGHTY...
PICK
PICK
PICK
...SHEEP AND LAMBS DOWN, FOURTEEN FIFTEEN...
TAP
TAP
SSSSUCK
ALL OF A SUDDEN, I'D BECOME PART OF THE WORLD, AND THE WORLD HAD BECOME PART OF ME...

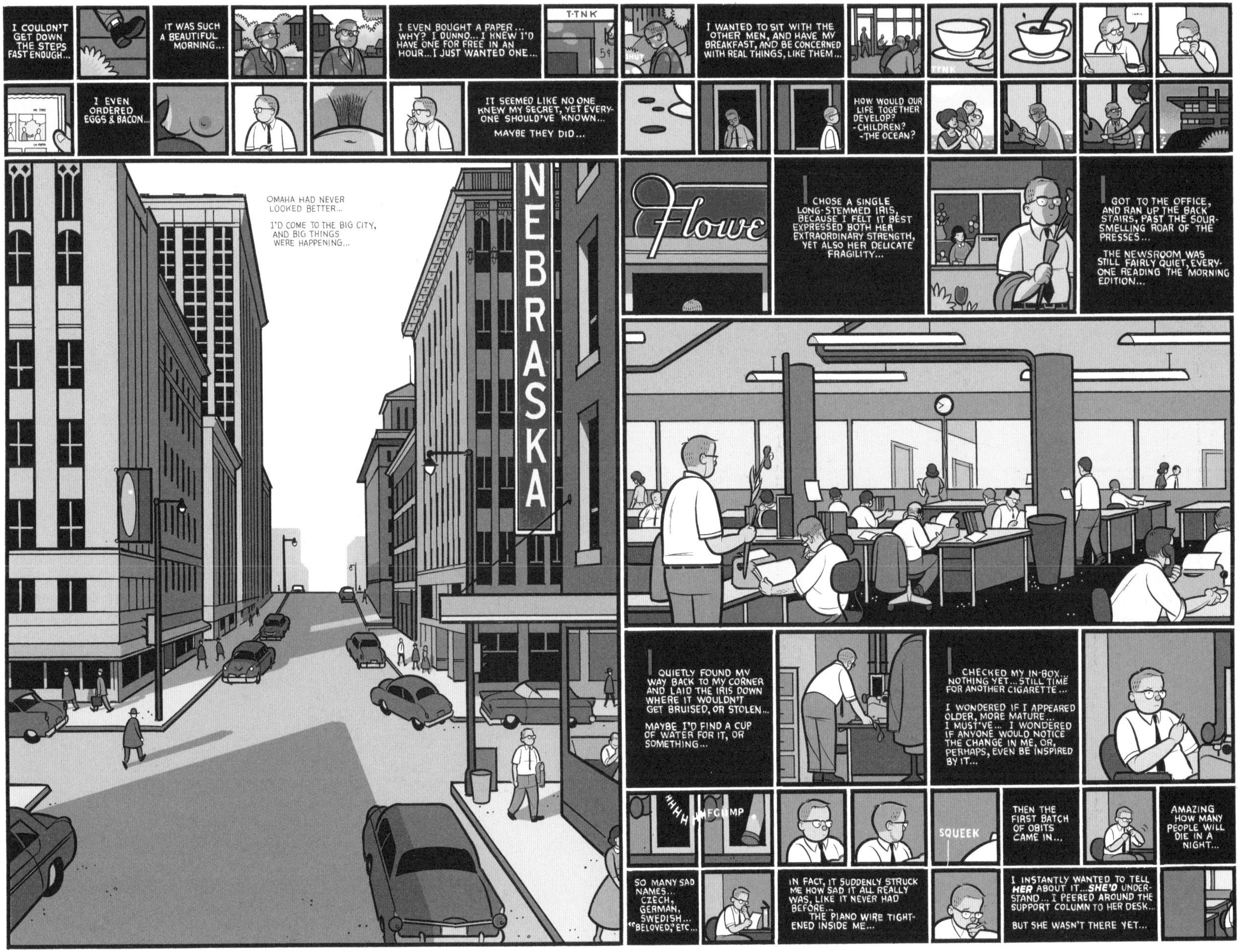

I COULDN'T GET DOWN THE STEPS FAST ENOUGH...
IT WAS SUCH A BEAUTIFUL MORNING...
I EVEN BOUGHT A PAPER... WHY? I DUNNO... I KNEW I'D HAVE ONE FOR FREE IN AN HOUR... I JUST WANTED ONE...
T-TNK
5¢
SHUT
I WANTED TO SIT WITH THE OTHER MEN, AND HAVE MY BREAKFAST, AND BE CONCERNED WITH REAL THINGS, LIKE THEM...
TTNK
I EVEN ORDERED EGGS & BACON...
IT SEEMED LIKE NO ONE KNEW MY SECRET, YET EVERYONE SHOULD'VE KNOWN...
MAYBE THEY DID...
HOW WOULD OUR LIFE TOGETHER DEVELOP? -CHILDREN? -THE OCEAN?
OMAHA HAD NEVER LOOKED BETTER...
I'D COME TO THE BIG CITY, AND BIG THINGS WERE HAPPENING...
NEBRASKA
Flowe
I CHOSE A SINGLE LONG-STEMMED IRIS, BECAUSE I FELT IT BEST EXPRESSED BOTH HER EXTRAORDINARY STRENGTH, YET ALSO HER DELICATE FRAGILITY...
I GOT TO THE OFFICE, AND RAN UP THE BACK STAIRS, PAST THE SOUR-SMELLING ROAR OF THE PRESSES...
THE NEWSROOM WAS STILL FAIRLY QUIET, EVERYONE READING THE MORNING EDITION...
I QUIETLY FOUND MY WAY BACK TO MY CORNER AND LAID THE IRIS DOWN WHERE IT WOULDN'T GET BRUISED, OR STOLEN...
MAYBE I'D FIND A CUP OF WATER FOR IT, OR SOMETHING...
I CHECKED MY IN-BOX... NOTHING YET... STILL TIME FOR ANOTHER CIGARETTE...
I WONDERED IF I APPEARED OLDER, MORE MATURE... I MUST'VE... I WONDERED IF ANYONE WOULD NOTICE THE CHANGE IN ME, OR, PERHAPS, EVEN BE INSPIRED BY IT...
HHHHHMFGUMP
SQUEEK
THEN THE FIRST BATCH OF OBITS CAME IN...
AMAZING HOW MANY PEOPLE WILL DIE IN A NIGHT...
SO MANY SAD NAMES... CZECH, GERMAN, SWEDISH... "BELOVED," ETC...
IN FACT, IT SUDDENLY STRUCK ME HOW SAD IT ALL REALLY WAS, LIKE IT NEVER HAD BEFORE...
THE PIANO WIRE TIGHTENED INSIDE ME...
I INSTANTLY WANTED TO TELL **HER** ABOUT IT... **SHE'D** UNDERSTAND... I PEERED AROUND THE SUPPORT COLUMN TO HER DESK...
BUT SHE WASN'T THERE YET...

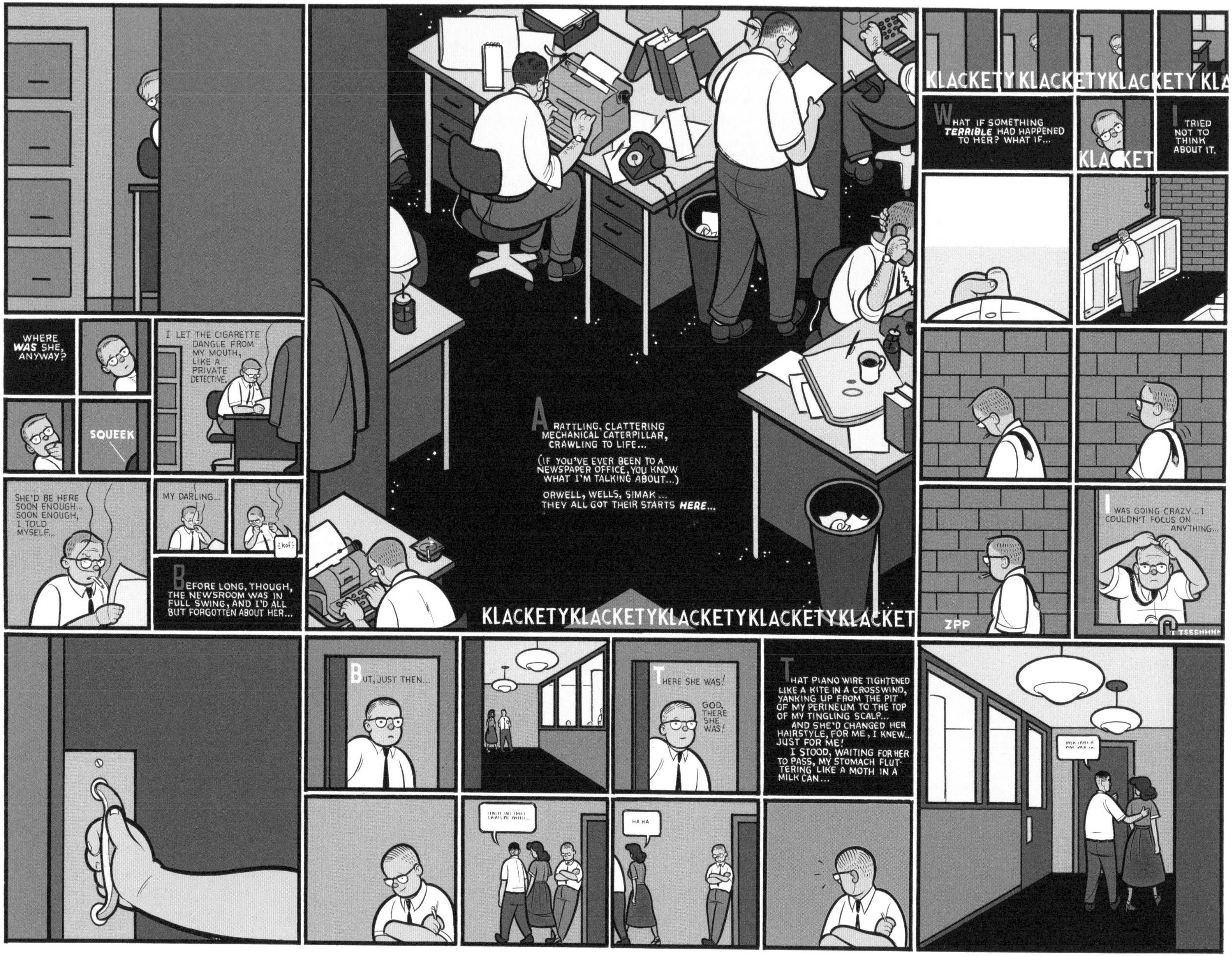

WHERE WAS SHE, ANYWAY?
I LET THE CIGARETTE DANGLE FROM MY MOUTH, LIKE A PRIVATE DETECTIVE.
SQUEEK
SHE'D BE HERE SOON ENOUGH... SOON ENOUGH, I TOLD MYSELF...
MY DARLING...
kof
BEFORE LONG, THOUGH, THE NEWSROOM WAS IN FULL SWING, AND I'D ALL BUT FORGOTTEN ABOUT HER...
A RATTLING, CLATTERING MECHANICAL CATERPILLAR, CRAWLING TO LIFE...
(IF YOU'VE EVER BEEN TO A NEWSPAPER OFFICE, YOU KNOW WHAT I'M TALKING ABOUT...)
ORWELL, WELLS, SIMAK... THEY ALL GOT THEIR STARTS HERE...
KLACKETYKLACKETYKLACKETYKLACKETYKLACKET
KLACKETY KLACKETYKLACKETY KLA
WHAT IF SOMETHING TERRIBLE HAD HAPPENED TO HER? WHAT IF...
KLACKET
I TRIED NOT TO THINK ABOUT IT.
ZPP
I WAS GOING CRAZY... I COULDN'T FOCUS ON ANYTHING...
TSSSHHHH
BUT, JUST THEN...
THERE SHE WAS!
GOD, THERE SHE WAS!
THAT PIANO WIRE TIGHTENED LIKE A KITE IN A CROSSWIND, YANKING UP FROM THE PIT OF MY PERINEUM TO THE TOP OF MY TINGLING SCALP...
AND SHE'D CHANGED HER HAIRSTYLE, FOR ME, I KNEW... JUST FOR ME!
I STOOD, WAITING FOR HER TO PASS, MY STOMACH FLUTTERING LIKE A MOTH IN A MILK CAN...
HA HA

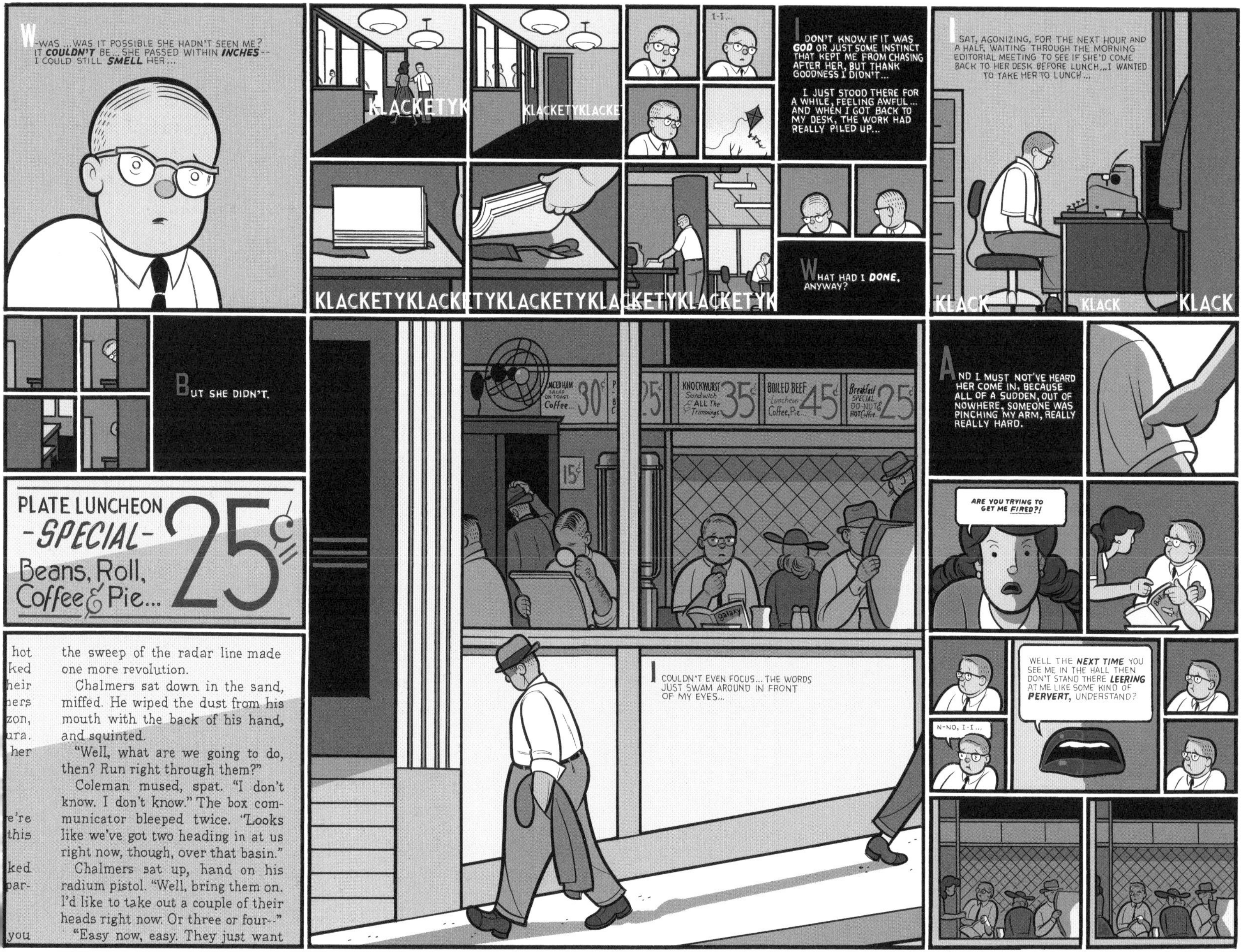

W-WAS ...WAS IT POSSIBLE SHE HADN'T SEEN ME? IT COULDN'T BE... SHE PASSED WITHIN INCHES-- I COULD STILL SMELL HER...
KLACKETYK
KLACKETYKLACKE
I-I...
I DON'T KNOW IF IT WAS GOD OR JUST SOME INSTINCT THAT KEPT ME FROM CHASING AFTER HER, BUT THANK GOODNESS I DIDN'T...
I JUST STOOD THERE FOR A WHILE, FEELING AWFUL... AND WHEN I GOT BACK TO MY DESK, THE WORK HAD REALLY PILED UP...
I SAT, AGONIZING, FOR THE NEXT HOUR AND A HALF, WAITING THROUGH THE MORNING EDITORIAL MEETING TO SEE IF SHE'D COME BACK TO HER DESK BEFORE LUNCH...I WANTED TO TAKE HER TO LUNCH...
KLACKETYKLACKETYKLACKETYKLACKETYKLACKETYK
WHAT HAD I DONE, ANYWAY?
KLACK
KLACK
KLACK
BUT SHE DIDN'T.
PLATE LUNCHEON -SPECIAL- Beans, Roll, Coffee & Pie... 25¢
the sweep of the radar line made one more revolution.
Chalmers sat down in the sand, miffed. He wiped the dust from his mouth with the back of his hand, and squinted.
"Well, what are we going to do, then? Run right through them?"
Coleman mused, spat. "I don't know. I don't know." The box communicator bleeped twice. "Looks like we've got two heading in at us right now, though, over that basin."
Chalmers sat up, hand on his radium pistol. "Well, bring them on. I'd like to take out a couple of their heads right now. Or three or four--"
"Easy now, easy. They just want
KNOCKWURST Sandwich & ALL The Trimmings 35¢
BOILED BEEF -Luncheon- Coffee, Pie... 45¢
Breakfast SPECIAL DO-NUT & HOT Coffee... 25¢
15¢
I COULDN'T EVEN FOCUS... THE WORDS JUST SWAM AROUND IN FRONT OF MY EYES...
AND I MUST NOT'VE HEARD HER COME IN, BECAUSE ALL OF A SUDDEN, OUT OF NOWHERE, SOMEONE WAS PINCHING MY ARM, REALLY REALLY HARD.
ARE YOU TRYING TO GET ME FIRED?!
WELL THE NEXT TIME YOU SEE ME IN THE HALL THEN DON'T STAND THERE LEERING AT ME LIKE SOME KIND OF PERVERT, UNDERSTAND?
N-NO, I-I...

gng· gn·gn·g...

snffff

THE REST OF THAT AFTERNOON WAS ONE OF THE WORST OF MY ENTIRE LIFE...

:gnng:

HOW I MADE IT BACK TO THE OFFICE AND GOT THOSE OBITS DONE I DON'T KNOW... IT WAS *AWFUL*... I KNEW I'D NEVER SEE HER AGAIN, EVER...

I STOLE A ROLL OF TOILET PAPER FROM DOWN THE HALL BECAUSE I'D USED UP ALL MY HANKIES...

gng·
gn·

I COULD STILL SMELL HER ON MY PILLOW...

THIRTY MINUTES LATER

C-CAPTAIN... I-I...
I-I CAN HARDLY SEE YOU NOW...

IT'S THE MOMENTUM, SMITH... WHEN THE SHIP EXPLODED, IT THREW US ALL IN DIFFERENT DIRECTIONS...

WE'LL... FALL... UNTIL WE GET CAUGHT IN THE GRAVITATIONAL FIELD OF A PLANET...

AND THEN WE'LL FALL... FALL TOWARD THE SURFACE... BURN... IN THE ATMOSPHERE...

KNOCK
KNOCK

:kzzk: CAPTAIN...
NO!... *NO!*...

FF

WHO'D BE KNOCKING ON MY DOOR AT THAT TIME OF NIGHT?

I MUST'VE BEEN PLAYING THE RADIO TOO LOUDLY...

I TURNED IT DOWN AND PADDED TO THE DOOR TO APOLOGIZE...

K·KLK

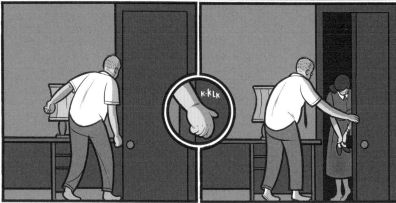

♪ HI ♪

KISS

I SNUCK PAST YOUR LANDLADY... SHE'S ASLEEP IN THE PARLOR...

OH *BOY* WHAT A *DAY!*

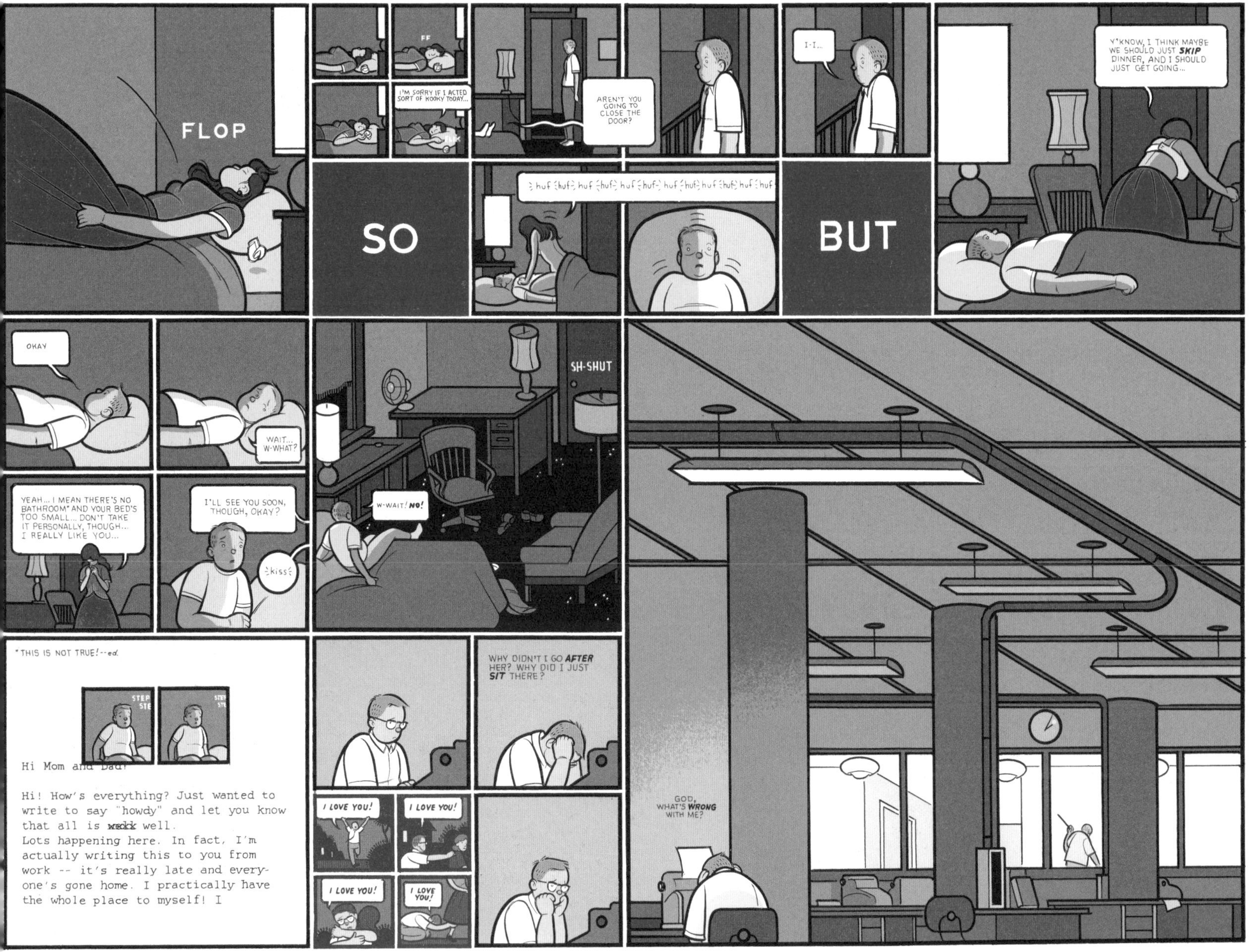

FLOP
FF
I'M SORRY IF I ACTED SORT OF KOOKY TODAY...
AREN'T YOU GOING TO CLOSE THE DOOR?
I-I...
Y'KNOW, I THINK MAYBE WE SHOULD JUST SKIP DINNER, AND I SHOULD JUST GET GOING...
SO
huf huf huf huf huf huf huf huf huf huf huf huf
BUT
OKAY
WAIT... W-WHAT?
YEAH... I MEAN THERE'S NO BATHROOM* AND YOUR BED'S TOO SMALL... DON'T TAKE IT PERSONALLY, THOUGH... I REALLY LIKE YOU...
I'LL SEE YOU SOON, THOUGH, OKAY?
kiss
SH-SHUT
W-WAIT! NO!
*THIS IS NOT TRUE! --ed.
Hi Mom and Dad!
Hi! How's everything? Just wanted to write to say "howdy" and let you know that all is well.
Lots happening here. In fact, I'm actually writing this to you from work -- it's really late and everyone's gone home. I practically have the whole place to myself! I
WHY DIDN'T I GO AFTER HER? WHY DID I JUST SIT THERE?
I LOVE YOU!
I LOVE YOU!
I LOVE YOU!
I LOVE YOU!
GOD, WHAT'S WRONG WITH ME?

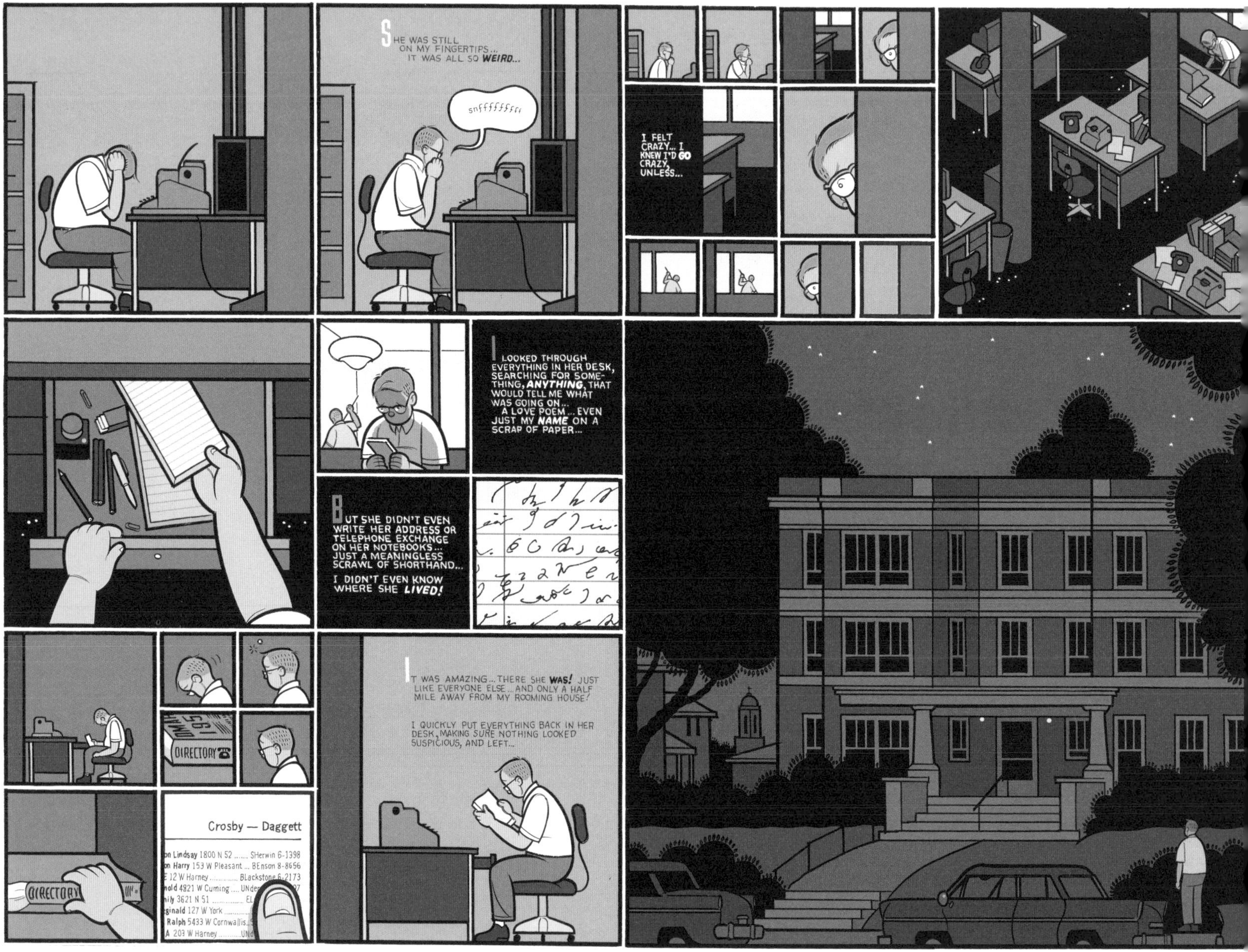
SHE WAS STILL ON MY FINGERTIPS... IT WAS ALL SO WEIRD...
snffffffff
I FELT CRAZY... I KNEW I'D GO CRAZY, UNLESS...
I LOOKED THROUGH EVERYTHING IN HER DESK, SEARCHING FOR SOMETHING, ANYTHING, THAT WOULD TELL ME WHAT WAS GOING ON... A LOVE POEM... EVEN JUST MY NAME ON A SCRAP OF PAPER...
BUT SHE DIDN'T EVEN WRITE HER ADDRESS OR TELEPHONE EXCHANGE ON HER NOTEBOOKS... JUST A MEANINGLESS SCRAWL OF SHORTHAND...
I DIDN'T EVEN KNOW WHERE SHE LIVED!
DIRECTORY
Crosby — Daggett
on Lindsay 1800 N 52 ...... SHerwin 6-1398
on Harry 153 W Pleasant ... BEnson 8-8656
E 12 W Harney .... BLackstone 6-2173
hold 4821 W Cuming .... UNde
nily 3621 N 51 .... EL
ginald 127 W York ....
Ralph 5433 W Cornwallis..
A 203 W Harney ....UNd
IT WAS AMAZING... THERE SHE WAS! JUST LIKE EVERYONE ELSE... AND ONLY A HALF MILE AWAY FROM MY ROOMING HOUSE!
I QUICKLY PUT EVERYTHING BACK IN HER DESK, MAKING SURE NOTHING LOOKED SUSPICIOUS, AND LEFT...

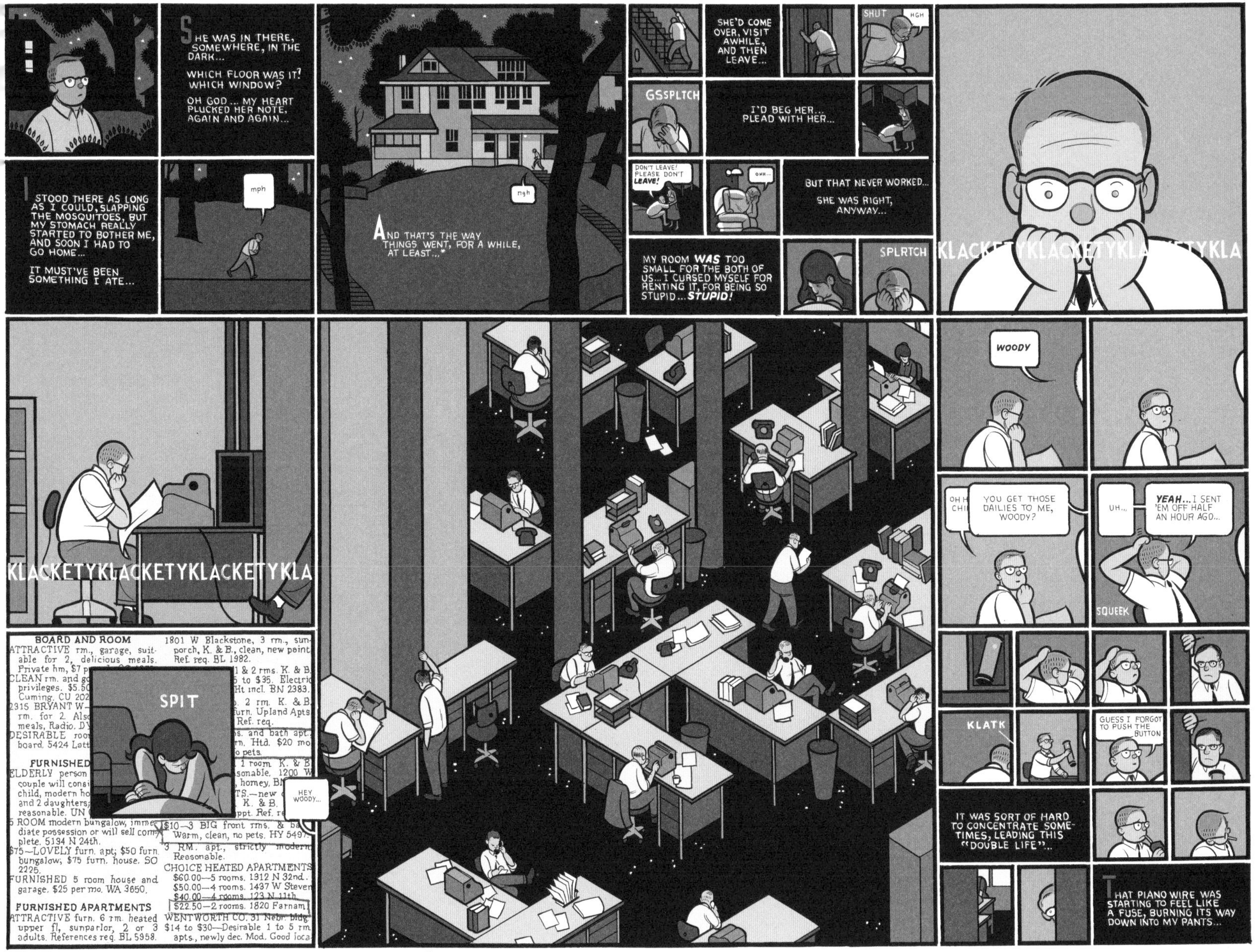
SHE WAS IN THERE, SOMEWHERE, IN THE DARK...
WHICH FLOOR WAS IT? WHICH WINDOW?
OH GOD... MY HEART PLUCKED HER NOTE, AGAIN AND AGAIN...
I STOOD THERE AS LONG AS I COULD, SLAPPING THE MOSQUITOES, BUT MY STOMACH REALLY STARTED TO BOTHER ME, AND SOON I HAD TO GO HOME...
IT MUST'VE BEEN SOMETHING I ATE...
mph
ngh
AND THAT'S THE WAY THINGS WENT, FOR A WHILE, AT LEAST...*
SHE'D COME OVER, VISIT AWHILE, AND THEN LEAVE...
SHUT
HGH
GSSPLTCH
I'D BEG HER... PLEAD WITH HER...
DON'T LEAVE! PLEASE DON'T LEAVE!
OHH...
BUT THAT NEVER WORKED...
SHE WAS RIGHT, ANYWAY...
MY ROOM WAS TOO SMALL FOR THE BOTH OF US... I CURSED MYSELF FOR RENTING IT, FOR BEING SO STUPID... STUPID!
SPLRTCH
KLACKETYKLACKETYKLACKETYKLA
KLACKETYKLACKETYKLACKETYKLA
BOARD AND ROOM
ATTRACTIVE rm., garage, suitable for 2, delicious meals. Private hm, $7 p
CLEAN rm. and go privileges. $5.50 Cuming. CU 202
2315 BRYANT W— rm. for 2. Also meals, Radio. DY
DESIRABLE roo board. 5424 Latt
FURNISHED
ELDERLY person couple will consi child, modern ho and 2 daughters; reasonable. UN
5 ROOM modern bungalow, immediate possession or will sell complete. 5134 N 24th.
$75—LOVELY furn. apt; $50 furn. bungalow; $75 furn. house. SO 2225.
FURNISHED 5 room house and garage. $25 per mo. WA 3650.
FURNISHED APARTMENTS
ATTRACTIVE furn. 6 rm. heated upper fl, sunparlor, 2 or 3 adults. References req. BL 5958.
1801 W Blackstone, 3 rm., sunporch, K. & B., clean, new paint Ref. req. BL 1982.
1 & 2 rms. K. & B. 5 to $35. Electric Ht incl. BN 2383.
2 rm. K. & B. furn. Upland Apts Ref. req.
s. and bath apt. rn. Htd. $20 mo o pets.
1 room K. & B sonable. 1200 W , homey, BN TS.—new K. & B. ppt. Ref. re
$10—3 BIG front rms. & ba Warm, clean, no pets. HY 5497.
3 RM. apt., strictly modern Reasonable.
CHOICE HEATED APARTMENTS
$60.00—5 rooms. 1312 N 32nd.
$50.00—4 rooms. 1437 W Steven
$40.00—4 rooms. 123 N 11th
$22.50—2 rooms. 1820 Farnam
WENTWORTH CO. 31 Nebr. bldg.
$14 to $30—Desirable 1 to 5 rm. apts., newly dec. Mod. Good loca-
SPIT
HEY WOODY...
WOODY
OH H CHI
YOU GET THOSE DAILIES TO ME, WOODY?
UH...
YEAH... I SENT 'EM OFF HALF AN HOUR AGO...
SQUEEK
KLATK
GUESS I FORGOT TO PUSH THE BUTTON
IT WAS SORT OF HARD TO CONCENTRATE SOMETIMES, LEADING THIS "DOUBLE LIFE"...
THAT PIANO WIRE WAS STARTING TO FEEL LIKE A FUSE, BURNING ITS WAY DOWN INTO MY PANTS...

* TWO DAYS & TWO NIGHTS--ed.

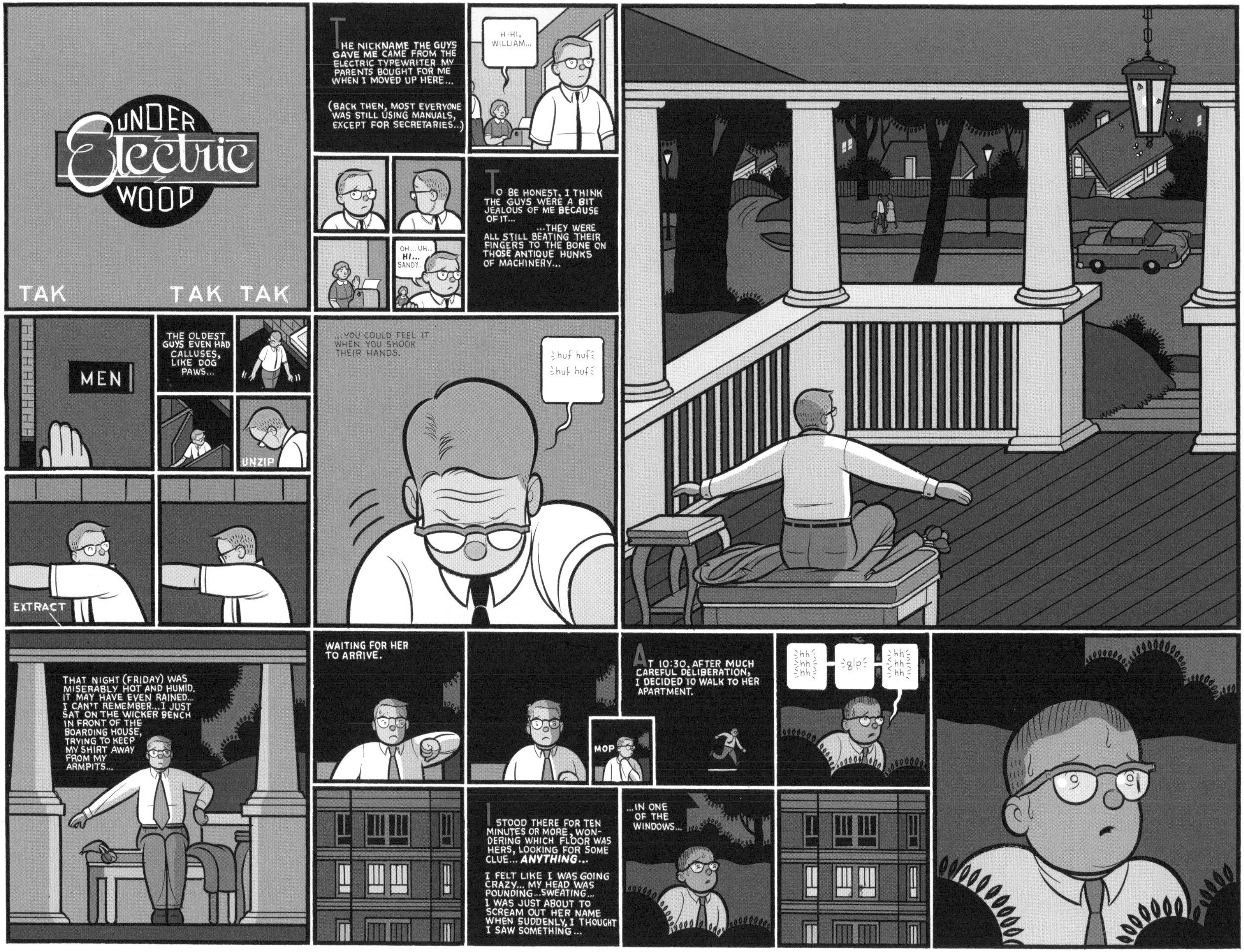

UNDER Electric WOOD
TAK
TAK TAK
THE NICKNAME THE GUYS GAVE ME CAME FROM THE ELECTRIC TYPEWRITER MY PARENTS BOUGHT FOR ME WHEN I MOVED UP HERE...
(BACK THEN, MOST EVERYONE WAS STILL USING MANUALS, EXCEPT FOR SECRETARIES...)
H-HI, WILLIAM...
OH... UH... HI... SANDY...
TO BE HONEST, I THINK THE GUYS WERE A BIT JEALOUS OF ME BECAUSE OF IT...
...THEY WERE ALL STILL BEATING THEIR FINGERS TO THE BONE ON THOSE ANTIQUE HUNKS OF MACHINERY...
MEN
THE OLDEST GUYS EVEN HAD CALLUSES, LIKE DOG PAWS...
UNZIP
EXTRACT
...YOU COULD FEEL IT WHEN YOU SHOOK THEIR HANDS.
huf huf
huf huf
THAT NIGHT (FRIDAY) WAS MISERABLY HOT AND HUMID. IT MAY HAVE EVEN RAINED... I CAN'T REMEMBER... I JUST SAT ON THE WICKER BENCH IN FRONT OF THE BOARDING HOUSE, TRYING TO KEEP MY SHIRT AWAY FROM MY ARMPITS...
WAITING FOR HER TO ARRIVE.
MOP
AT 10:30, AFTER MUCH CAREFUL DELIBERATION, I DECIDED TO WALK TO HER APARTMENT.
hh hh hh
glp
hh hh hh
I STOOD THERE FOR TEN MINUTES OR MORE, WONDERING WHICH FLOOR WAS HERS, LOOKING FOR SOME CLUE... ANYTHING...
I FELT LIKE I WAS GOING CRAZY... MY HEAD WAS POUNDING... SWEATING... I WAS JUST ABOUT TO SCREAM OUT HER NAME WHEN SUDDENLY, I THOUGHT I SAW SOMETHING...
...IN ONE OF THE WINDOWS...

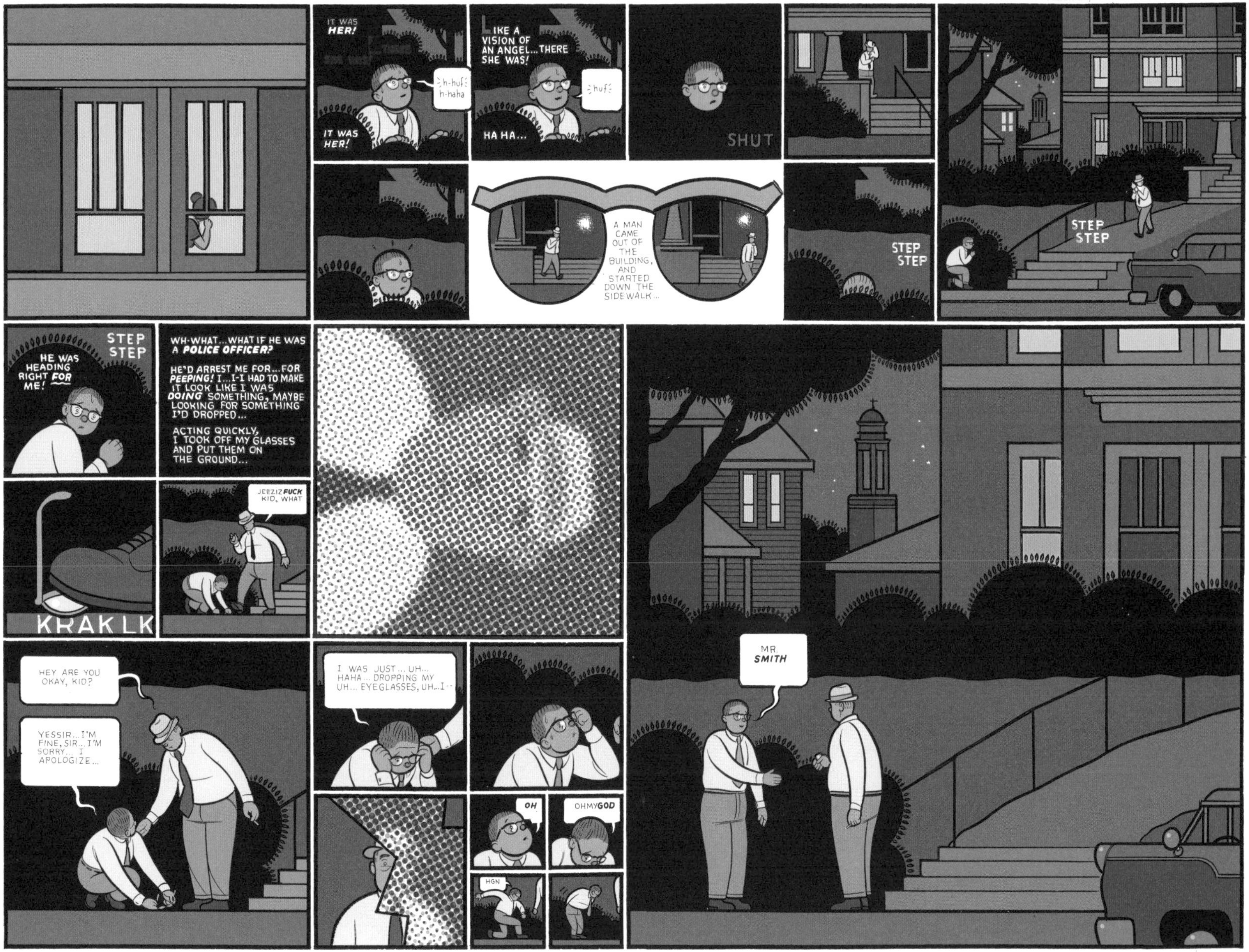
IT WAS HER!
IT WAS HER!
h-huf h-haha
LIKE A VISION OF AN ANGEL... THERE SHE WAS!
huf
HA HA...
SHUT
A MAN CAME OUT OF THE BUILDING, AND STARTED DOWN THE SIDEWALK...
STEP STEP
STEP STEP
STEP STEP
HE WAS HEADING RIGHT FOR ME!
WH-WHAT... WHAT IF HE WAS A POLICE OFFICER?
HE'D ARREST ME FOR... FOR PEEPING! I... I-I HAD TO MAKE IT LOOK LIKE I WAS DOING SOMETHING, MAYBE LOOKING FOR SOMETHING I'D DROPPED...
ACTING QUICKLY, I TOOK OFF MY GLASSES AND PUT THEM ON THE GROUND...
KRAKLK
JEEZIZ FUCK KID, WHAT
HEY ARE YOU OKAY, KID?
YESSIR... I'M FINE, SIR... I'M SORRY... I APOLOGIZE...
I WAS JUST... UH... HAHA... DROPPING MY UH... EYEGLASSES, UH... I--
OH
OHMYGOD
HGN
MR. SMITH

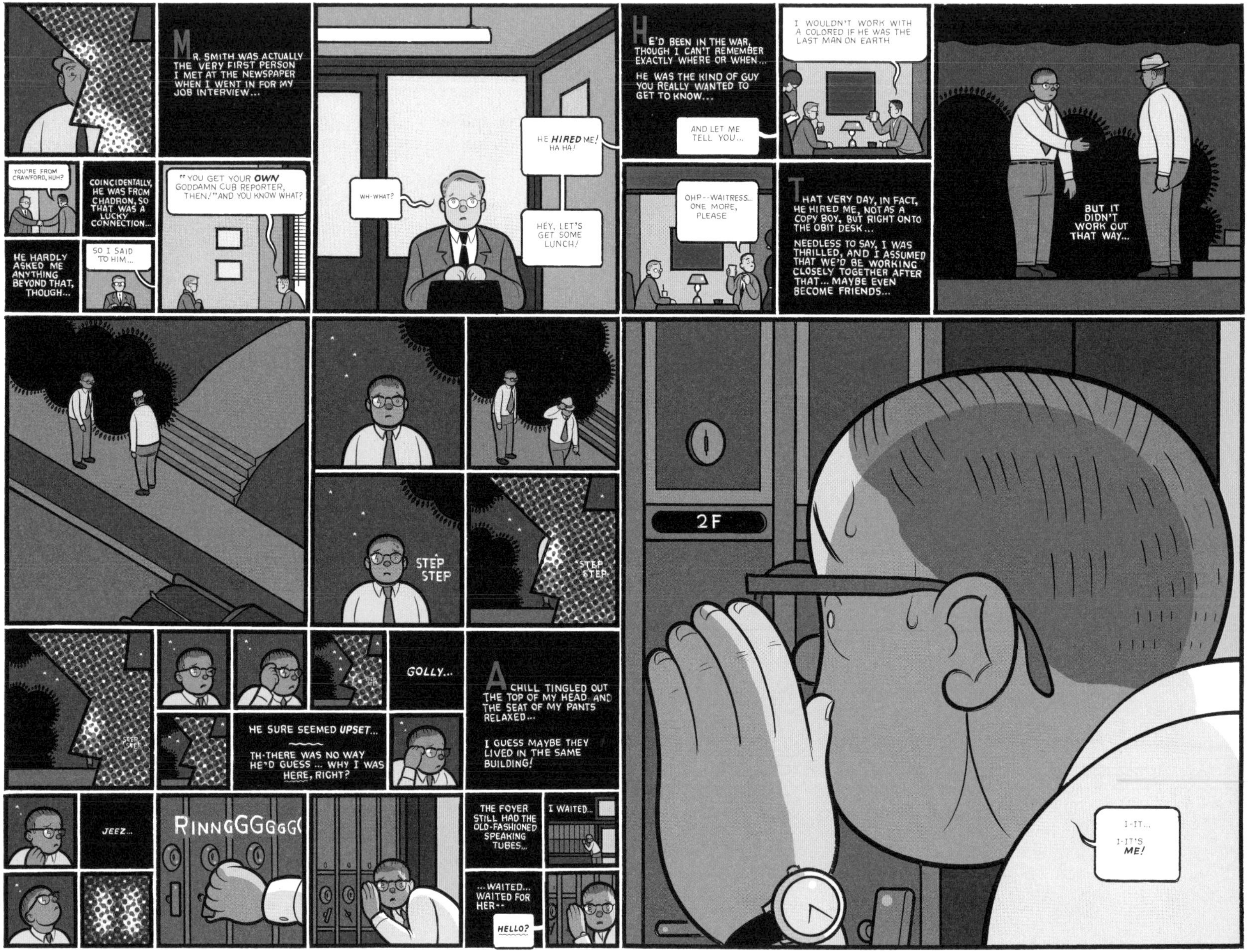

MR. SMITH WAS ACTUALLY THE VERY FIRST PERSON I MET AT THE NEWSPAPER WHEN I WENT IN FOR MY JOB INTERVIEW...
YOU'RE FROM CRAWFORD, HUH?
COINCIDENTALLY, HE WAS FROM CHADRON, SO THAT WAS A LUCKY CONNECTION...
HE HARDLY ASKED ME ANYTHING BEYOND THAT, THOUGH...
SO I SAID TO HIM...
"YOU GET YOUR OWN GODDAMN CUB REPORTER, THEN!" AND YOU KNOW WHAT?
HE HIRED ME! HA HA!
WH-WHAT?
HEY, LET'S GET SOME LUNCH!
HE'D BEEN IN THE WAR, THOUGH I CAN'T REMEMBER EXACTLY WHERE OR WHEN...
HE WAS THE KIND OF GUY YOU REALLY WANTED TO GET TO KNOW...
AND LET ME TELL YOU...
I WOULDN'T WORK WITH A COLORED IF HE WAS THE LAST MAN ON EARTH
OHP--WAITRESS... ONE MORE, PLEASE
THAT VERY DAY, IN FACT, HE HIRED ME, NOT AS A COPY BOY, BUT RIGHT ONTO THE OBIT DESK...
NEEDLESS TO SAY, I WAS THRILLED, AND I ASSUMED THAT WE'D BE WORKING CLOSELY TOGETHER AFTER THAT... MAYBE EVEN BECOME FRIENDS...
BUT IT DIDN'T WORK OUT THAT WAY...
STEP STEP
STEP STEP
GOLLY...
A CHILL TINGLED OUT THE TOP OF MY HEAD AND THE SEAT OF MY PANTS RELAXED...
I GUESS MAYBE THEY LIVED IN THE SAME BUILDING!
HE SURE SEEMED UPSET...
TH-THERE WAS NO WAY HE'D GUESS ... WHY I WAS HERE, RIGHT?
JEEZ...
RINNGGGggg
THE FOYER STILL HAD THE OLD-FASHIONED SPEAKING TUBES...
I WAITED...
...WAITED... WAITED FOR HER--
HELLO?
2F
I-IT...
I-IT'S ME!

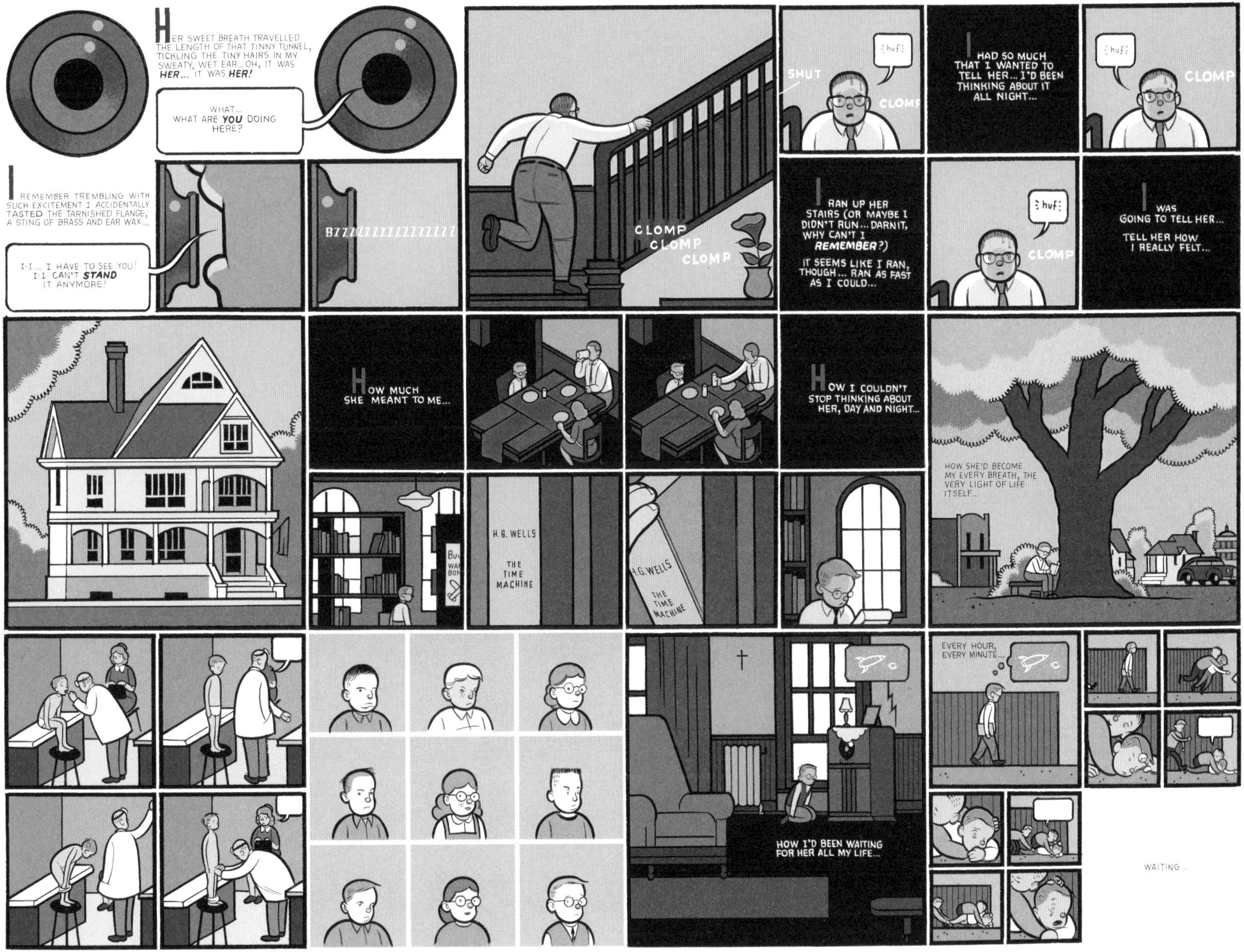
HER SWEET BREATH TRAVELLED THE LENGTH OF THAT TINNY TUNNEL, TICKLING THE TINY HAIRS IN MY SWEATY, WET EAR... OH, IT WAS HER... IT WAS HER!
WHAT... WHAT ARE YOU DOING HERE?
I REMEMBER TREMBLING WITH SUCH EXCITEMENT I ACCIDENTALLY TASTED THE TARNISHED FLANGE, A STING OF BRASS AND EAR WAX...
I-I... I HAVE TO SEE YOU! I-I CAN'T STAND IT ANYMORE!
BZZZZZZZZZZZZZZZZZ
CLOMP
CLOMP
CLOMP
SHUT
huf
CLOMP
I HAD SO MUCH THAT I WANTED TO TELL HER... I'D BEEN THINKING ABOUT IT ALL NIGHT...
huf
CLOMP
I RAN UP HER STAIRS (OR MAYBE I DIDN'T RUN... DARNIT, WHY CAN'T I REMEMBER?)
IT SEEMS LIKE I RAN, THOUGH... RAN AS FAST AS I COULD...
huf
CLOMP
I WAS GOING TO TELL HER...
TELL HER HOW I REALLY FELT...
HOW MUCH SHE MEANT TO ME...
HOW I COULDN'T STOP THINKING ABOUT HER, DAY AND NIGHT...
HOW SHE'D BECOME MY EVERY BREATH, THE VERY LIGHT OF LIFE ITSELF...
H.G. WELLS
THE TIME MACHINE
H.G. WELLS
THE TIME MACHINE
HOW I'D BEEN WAITING FOR HER ALL MY LIFE...
EVERY HOUR, EVERY MINUTE...
WAITING...

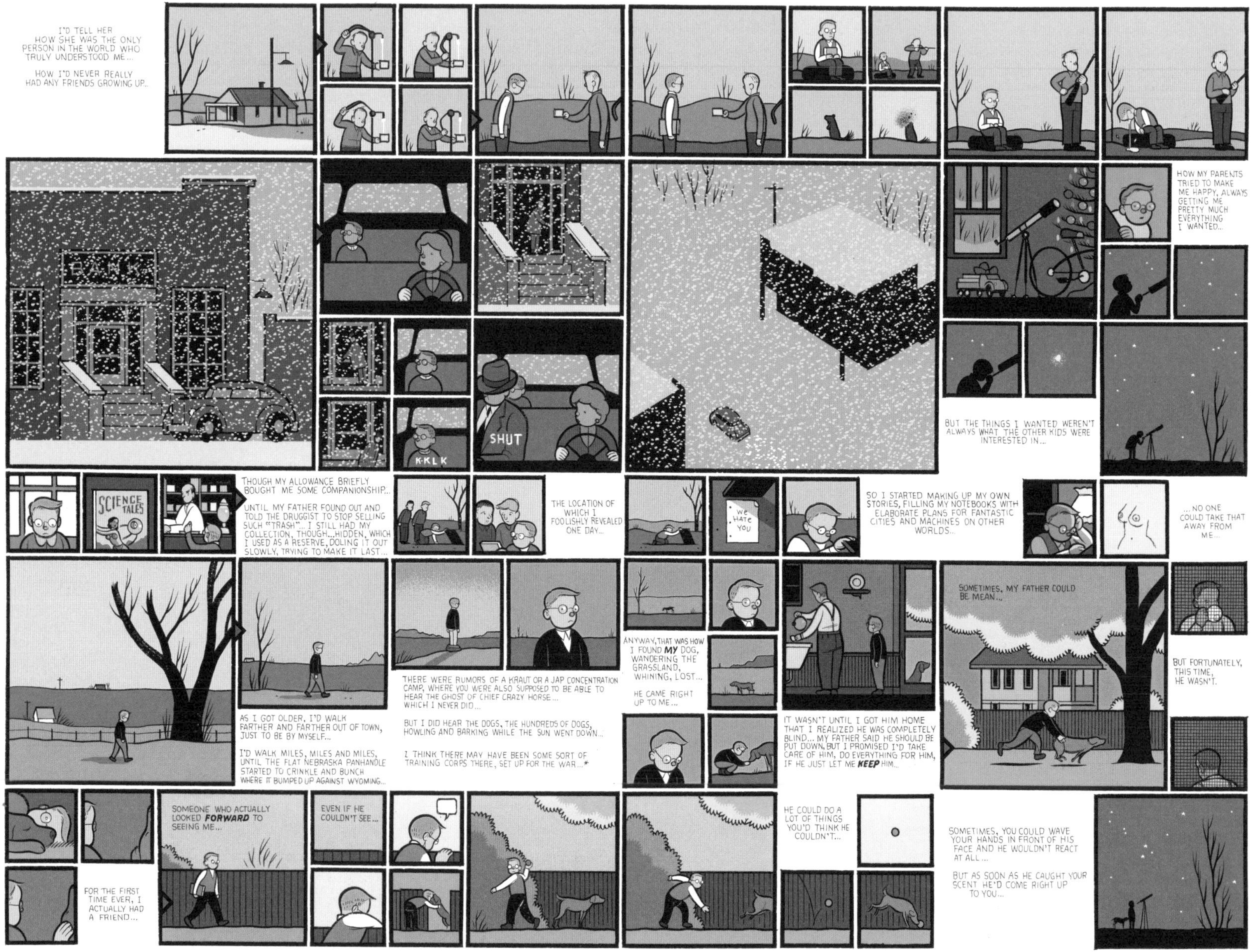
I'D TELL HER
HOW SHE WAS THE ONLY PERSON IN THE WORLD WHO TRULY UNDERSTOOD ME...
HOW I'D NEVER REALLY HAD ANY FRIENDS GROWING UP...
BANK
K-KLK
SHUT
HOW MY PARENTS TRIED TO MAKE ME HAPPY, ALWAYS GETTING ME PRETTY MUCH EVERYTHING I WANTED...
BUT THE THINGS I WANTED WEREN'T ALWAYS WHAT THE OTHER KIDS WERE INTERESTED IN...
SCIENCE TALES
THOUGH MY ALLOWANCE BRIEFLY BOUGHT ME SOME COMPANIONSHIP...
UNTIL MY FATHER FOUND OUT AND TOLD THE DRUGGIST TO STOP SELLING SUCH "TRASH"... I STILL HAD MY COLLECTION, THOUGH...HIDDEN, WHICH I USED AS A RESERVE, DOLING IT OUT SLOWLY, TRYING TO MAKE IT LAST...
THE LOCATION OF WHICH I FOOLISHLY REVEALED ONE DAY...
WE HATE YOU
SO I STARTED MAKING UP MY OWN STORIES, FILLING MY NOTEBOOKS WITH ELABORATE PLANS FOR FANTASTIC CITIES AND MACHINES ON OTHER WORLDS...
...NO ONE COULD TAKE THAT AWAY FROM ME...
AS I GOT OLDER, I'D WALK FARTHER AND FARTHER OUT OF TOWN, JUST TO BE BY MYSELF...
I'D WALK MILES, MILES AND MILES, UNTIL THE FLAT NEBRASKA PANHANDLE STARTED TO CRINKLE AND BUNCH WHERE IT BUMPED UP AGAINST WYOMING...
THERE WERE RUMORS OF A KRAUT OR A JAP CONCENTRATION CAMP, WHERE YOU WERE ALSO SUPPOSED TO BE ABLE TO HEAR THE GHOST OF CHIEF CRAZY HORSE... WHICH I NEVER DID...
BUT I DID HEAR THE DOGS, THE HUNDREDS OF DOGS, HOWLING AND BARKING WHILE THE SUN WENT DOWN...
I THINK THERE MAY HAVE BEEN SOME SORT OF TRAINING CORPS THERE, SET UP FOR THE WAR...*
ANYWAY, THAT WAS HOW I FOUND **MY** DOG, WANDERING THE GRASSLAND, WHINING, LOST...
HE CAME RIGHT UP TO ME...
IT WASN'T UNTIL I GOT HIM HOME THAT I REALIZED HE WAS COMPLETELY BLIND... MY FATHER SAID HE SHOULD BE PUT DOWN, BUT I PROMISED I'D TAKE CARE OF HIM, DO EVERYTHING FOR HIM, IF HE JUST LET ME **KEEP** HIM...
SOMETIMES, MY FATHER COULD BE MEAN...
BUT FORTUNATELY, THIS TIME, HE WASN'T.
FOR THE FIRST TIME EVER, I ACTUALLY HAD A FRIEND...
SOMEONE WHO ACTUALLY LOOKED **FORWARD** TO SEEING ME...
EVEN IF HE COULDN'T SEE...
HE COULD DO A LOT OF THINGS YOU'D THINK HE COULDN'T...
SOMETIMES, YOU COULD WAVE YOUR HANDS IN FRONT OF HIS FACE AND HE WOULDN'T REACT AT ALL...
BUT AS SOON AS HE CAUGHT YOUR SCENT HE'D COME RIGHT UP TO YOU...

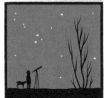

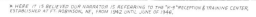

* HERE IT IS BELIEVED OUR NARRATOR IS REFERRING TO THE "K-9" RECEPTION & TRAINING CENTER, ESTABLISHED AT FT. ROBINSON, NE, FROM 1942 UNTIL JUNE OF 1946.

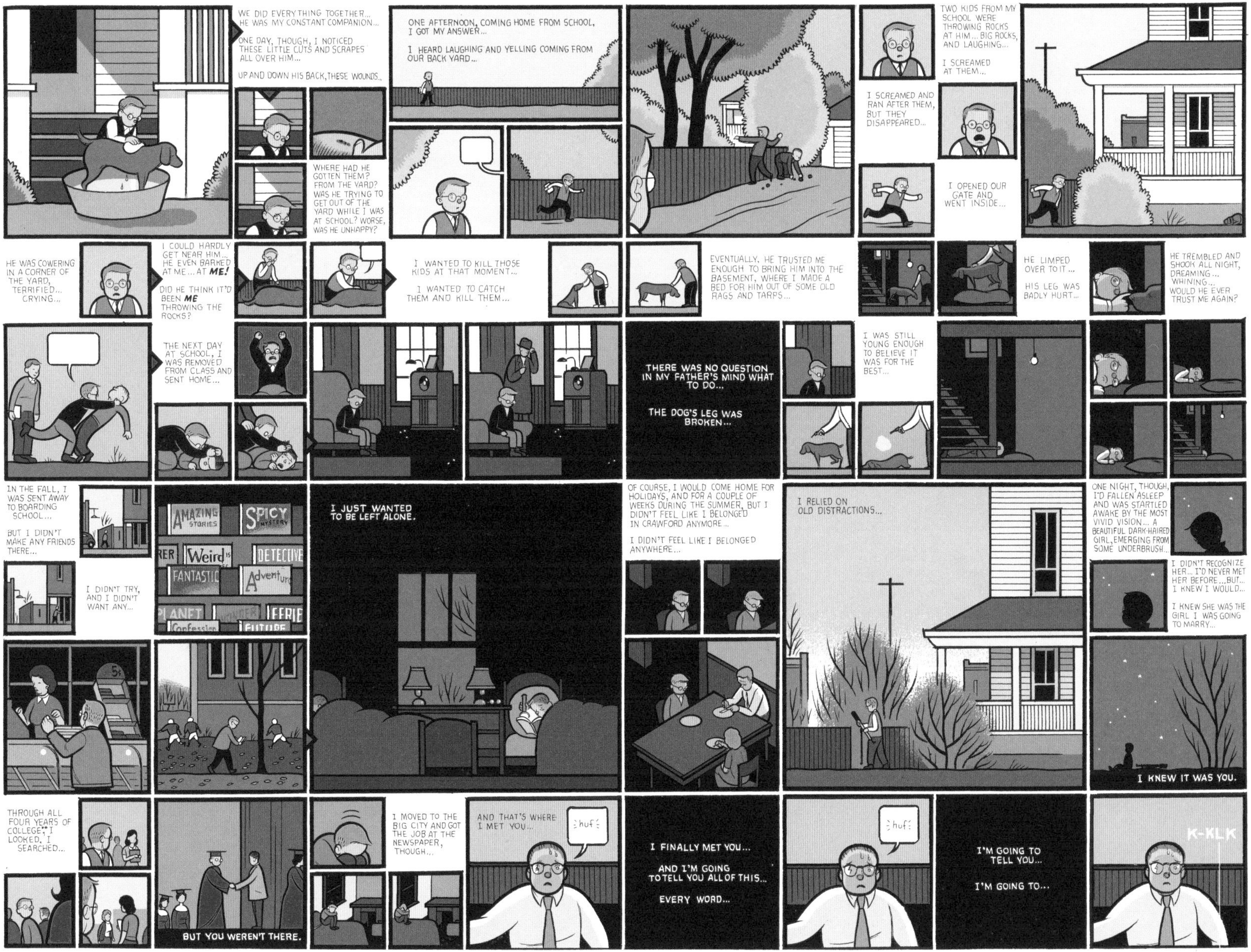
WE DID EVERYTHING TOGETHER... HE WAS MY CONSTANT COMPANION...
ONE DAY, THOUGH, I NOTICED THESE LITTLE CUTS AND SCRAPES ALL OVER HIM...
UP AND DOWN HIS BACK, THESE WOUNDS...
WHERE HAD HE GOTTEN THEM? FROM THE YARD? WAS HE TRYING TO GET OUT OF THE YARD WHILE I WAS AT SCHOOL? WORSE, WAS HE UNHAPPY?
ONE AFTERNOON, COMING HOME FROM SCHOOL, I GOT MY ANSWER...
I HEARD LAUGHING AND YELLING COMING FROM OUR BACK YARD...
TWO KIDS FROM MY SCHOOL WERE THROWING ROCKS AT HIM... BIG ROCKS, AND LAUGHING...
I SCREAMED AT THEM...
I SCREAMED AND RAN AFTER THEM, BUT THEY DISAPPEARED...
I OPENED OUR GATE AND WENT INSIDE...
HE WAS COWERING IN A CORNER OF THE YARD, TERRIFIED... CRYING...
I COULD HARDLY GET NEAR HIM... HE EVEN BARKED AT ME... AT ME!
DID HE THINK IT'D BEEN ME THROWING THE ROCKS?
I WANTED TO KILL THOSE KIDS AT THAT MOMENT...
I WANTED TO CATCH THEM AND KILL THEM...
EVENTUALLY, HE TRUSTED ME ENOUGH TO BRING HIM INTO THE BASEMENT, WHERE I MADE A BED FOR HIM OUT OF SOME OLD RAGS AND TARPS...
HE LIMPED OVER TO IT...
HIS LEG WAS BADLY HURT...
HE TREMBLED AND SHOOK ALL NIGHT, DREAMING... WHINING... WOULD HE EVER TRUST ME AGAIN?
THE NEXT DAY AT SCHOOL, I WAS REMOVED FROM CLASS AND SENT HOME...
THERE WAS NO QUESTION IN MY FATHER'S MIND WHAT TO DO...
THE DOG'S LEG WAS BROKEN...
I WAS STILL YOUNG ENOUGH TO BELIEVE IT WAS FOR THE BEST...
IN THE FALL, I WAS SENT AWAY TO BOARDING SCHOOL...
BUT I DIDN'T MAKE ANY FRIENDS THERE...
I DIDN'T TRY, AND I DIDN'T WANT ANY...
AMAZING STORIES
SPICY MYSTERY
Weird
DETECTIVE
FANTASTIC
Adventure
PLANET
EERIE
Confession
FUTURE
I JUST WANTED TO BE LEFT ALONE.
OF COURSE, I WOULD COME HOME FOR HOLIDAYS, AND FOR A COUPLE OF WEEKS DURING THE SUMMER, BUT I DIDN'T FEEL LIKE I BELONGED IN CRAWFORD ANYMORE...
I DIDN'T FEEL LIKE I BELONGED ANYWHERE...
I RELIED ON OLD DISTRACTIONS...
ONE NIGHT, THOUGH, I'D FALLEN ASLEEP AND WAS STARTLED AWAKE BY THE MOST VIVID VISION... A BEAUTIFUL DARK-HAIRED GIRL, EMERGING FROM SOME UNDERBRUSH...
I DIDN'T RECOGNIZE HER... I'D NEVER MET HER BEFORE... BUT... I KNEW I WOULD...
I KNEW SHE WAS THE GIRL I WAS GOING TO MARRY...
I KNEW IT WAS YOU.
THROUGH ALL FOUR YEARS OF COLLEGE,** I LOOKED. I SEARCHED...
BUT YOU WEREN'T THERE.
I MOVED TO THE BIG CITY AND GOT THE JOB AT THE NEWSPAPER, THOUGH...
AND THAT'S WHERE I MET YOU...
huf
I FINALLY MET YOU...
AND I'M GOING TO TELL YOU ALL OF THIS...
EVERY WORD...
huf
I'M GOING TO TELL YOU...
I'M GOING TO...
K-KLK

** *UNIVERSITY OF NEBRASKA AT LINCOLN, 1951-1955.*

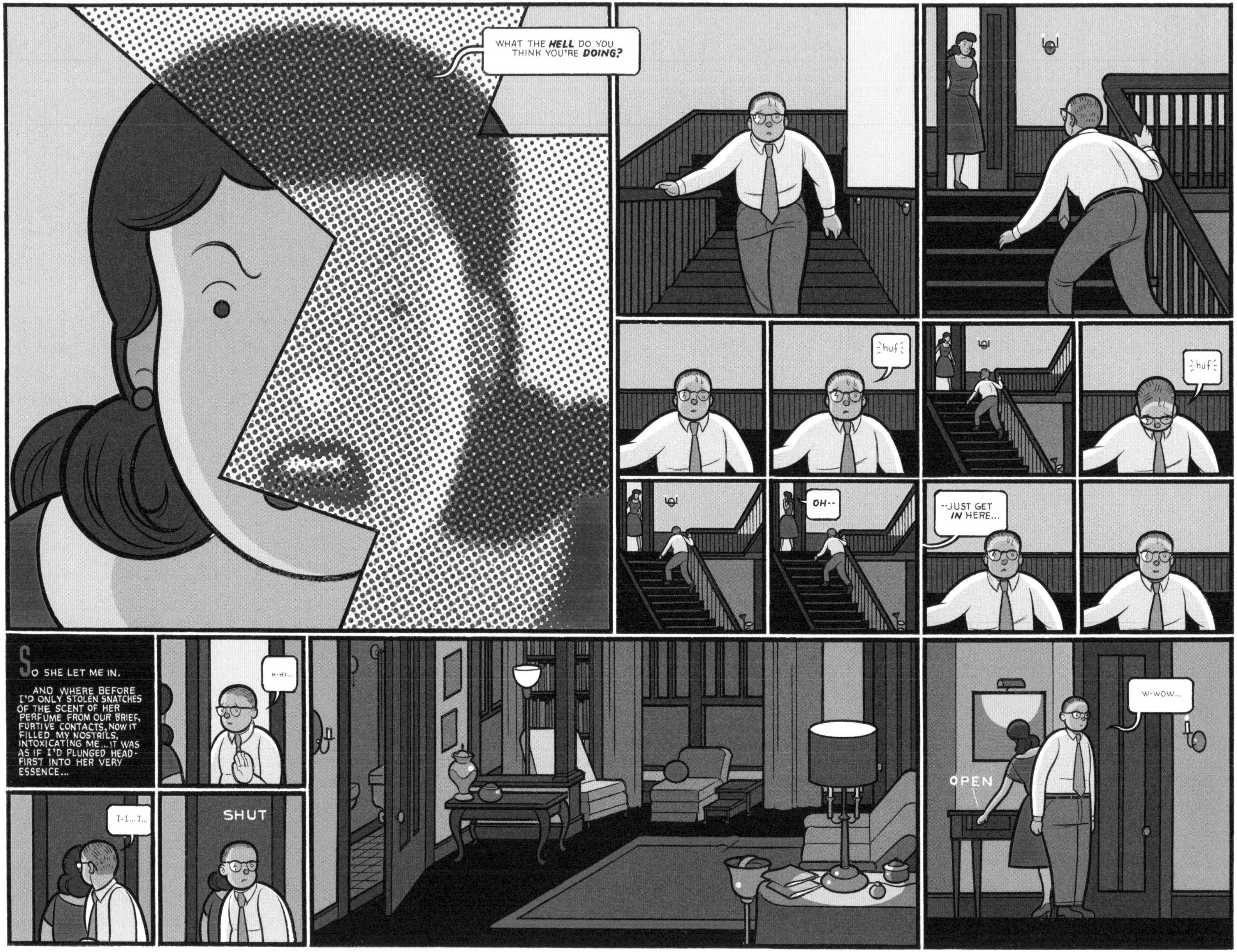
WHAT THE **HELL** DO YOU THINK YOU'RE **DOING?**
huf
huf
OH--
--JUST GET **IN** HERE...
SO SHE LET ME IN.
AND WHERE BEFORE I'D ONLY STOLEN SNATCHES OF THE SCENT OF HER PERFUME FROM OUR BRIEF, FURTIVE CONTACTS, NOW IT FILLED MY NOSTRILS, INTOXICATING ME... IT WAS AS IF I'D PLUNGED HEAD-FIRST INTO HER VERY ESSENCE...
H-HI...
I-I... I...
SHUT
W-WOW...
OPEN

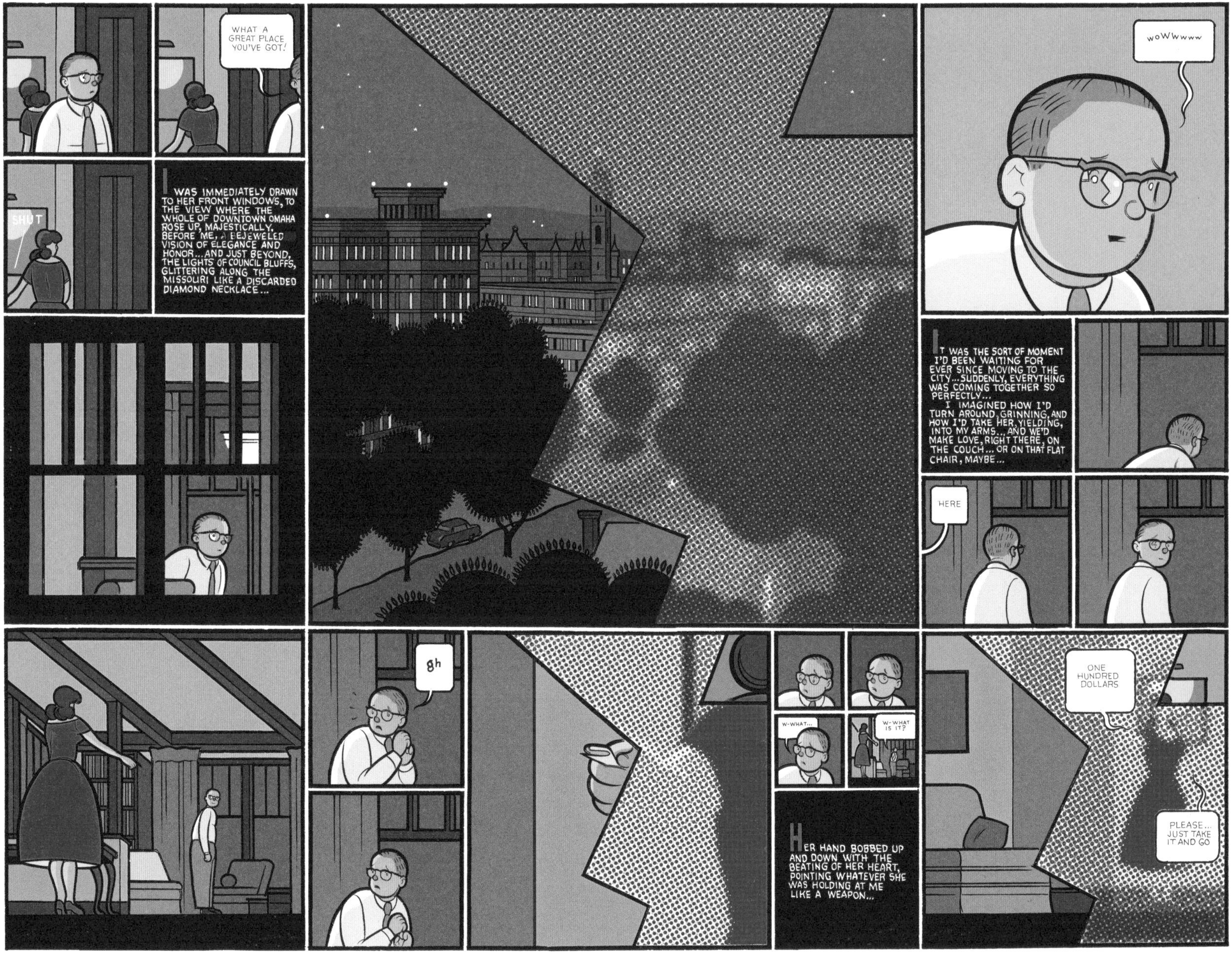
WHAT A GREAT PLACE YOU'VE GOT!
SHUT
I WAS IMMEDIATELY DRAWN TO HER FRONT WINDOWS, TO THE VIEW WHERE THE WHOLE OF DOWNTOWN OMAHA ROSE UP, MAJESTICALLY, BEFORE ME, A BEJEWELED VISION OF ELEGANCE AND HONOR... AND JUST BEYOND, THE LIGHTS OF COUNCIL BLUFFS, GLITTERING ALONG THE MISSOURI LIKE A DISCARDED DIAMOND NECKLACE...
woWWwww
IT WAS THE SORT OF MOMENT I'D BEEN WAITING FOR EVER SINCE MOVING TO THE CITY... SUDDENLY, EVERYTHING WAS COMING TOGETHER SO PERFECTLY...
I IMAGINED HOW I'D TURN AROUND, GRINNING, AND HOW I'D TAKE HER, YIELDING, INTO MY ARMS... AND WE'D MAKE LOVE, RIGHT THERE, ON THE COUCH... OR ON THAT FLAT CHAIR, MAYBE...
HERE
gh
W-WHAT...
W-WHAT IS IT?
HER HAND BOBBED UP AND DOWN WITH THE BEATING OF HER HEART, POINTING WHATEVER SHE WAS HOLDING AT ME LIKE A WEAPON...
ONE HUNDRED DOLLARS
PLEASE... JUST TAKE IT AND GO

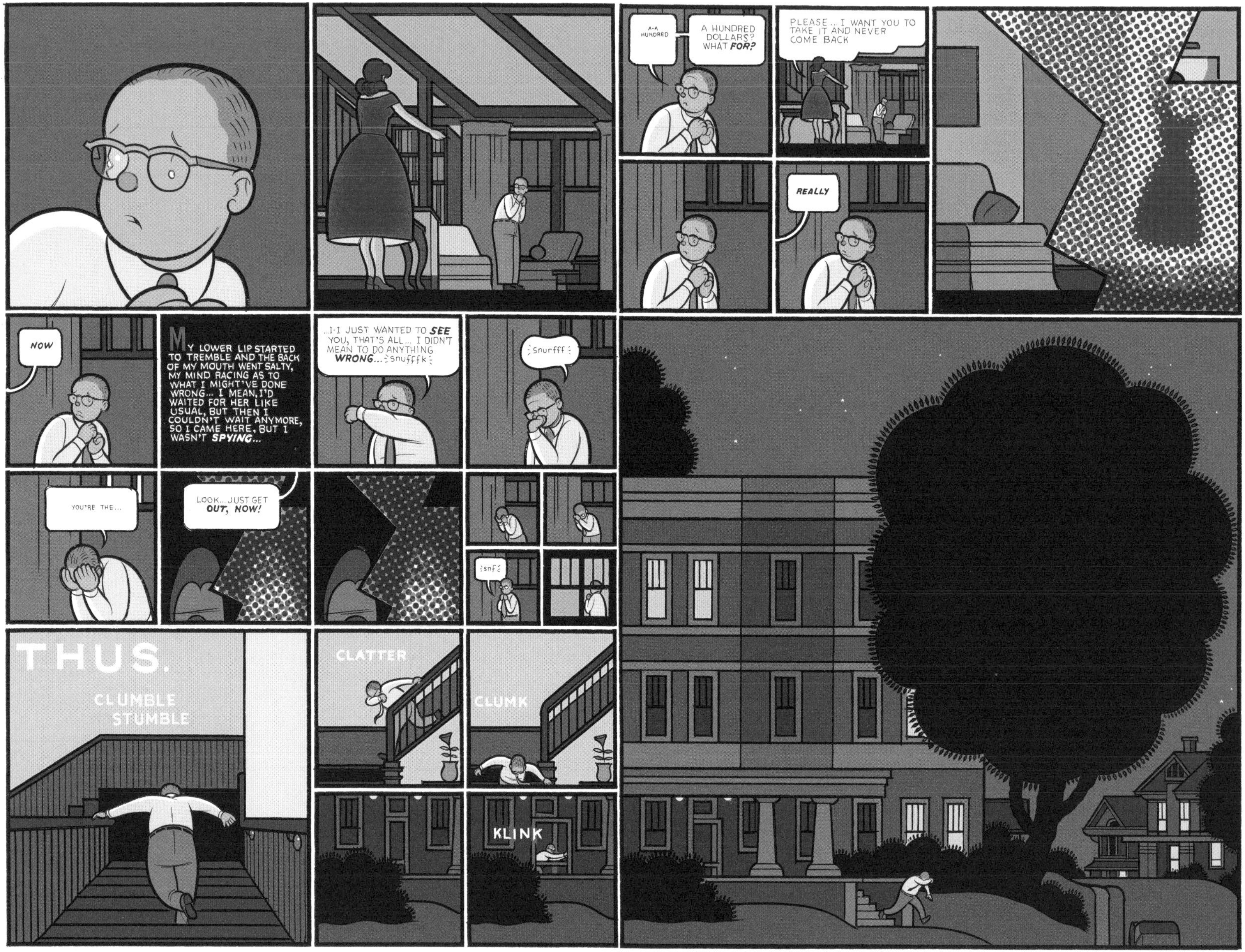
A-A HUNDRED
A HUNDRED DOLLARS? WHAT FOR?
PLEASE ... I WANT YOU TO TAKE IT AND NEVER COME BACK
REALLY
NOW
MY LOWER LIP STARTED TO TREMBLE AND THE BACK OF MY MOUTH WENT SALTY, MY MIND RACING AS TO WHAT I MIGHT'VE DONE WRONG... I MEAN, I'D WAITED FOR HER LIKE USUAL, BUT THEN I COULDN'T WAIT ANYMORE, SO I CAME HERE, BUT I WASN'T SPYING...
...I-I JUST WANTED TO SEE YOU, THAT'S ALL... I DIDN'T MEAN TO DO ANYTHING WRONG... snufffk
snurfff
YOU'RE THE...
LOOK... JUST GET OUT, NOW!
snf
THUS.
CLUMBLE STUMBLE
CLATTER
CLUMK
KLINK

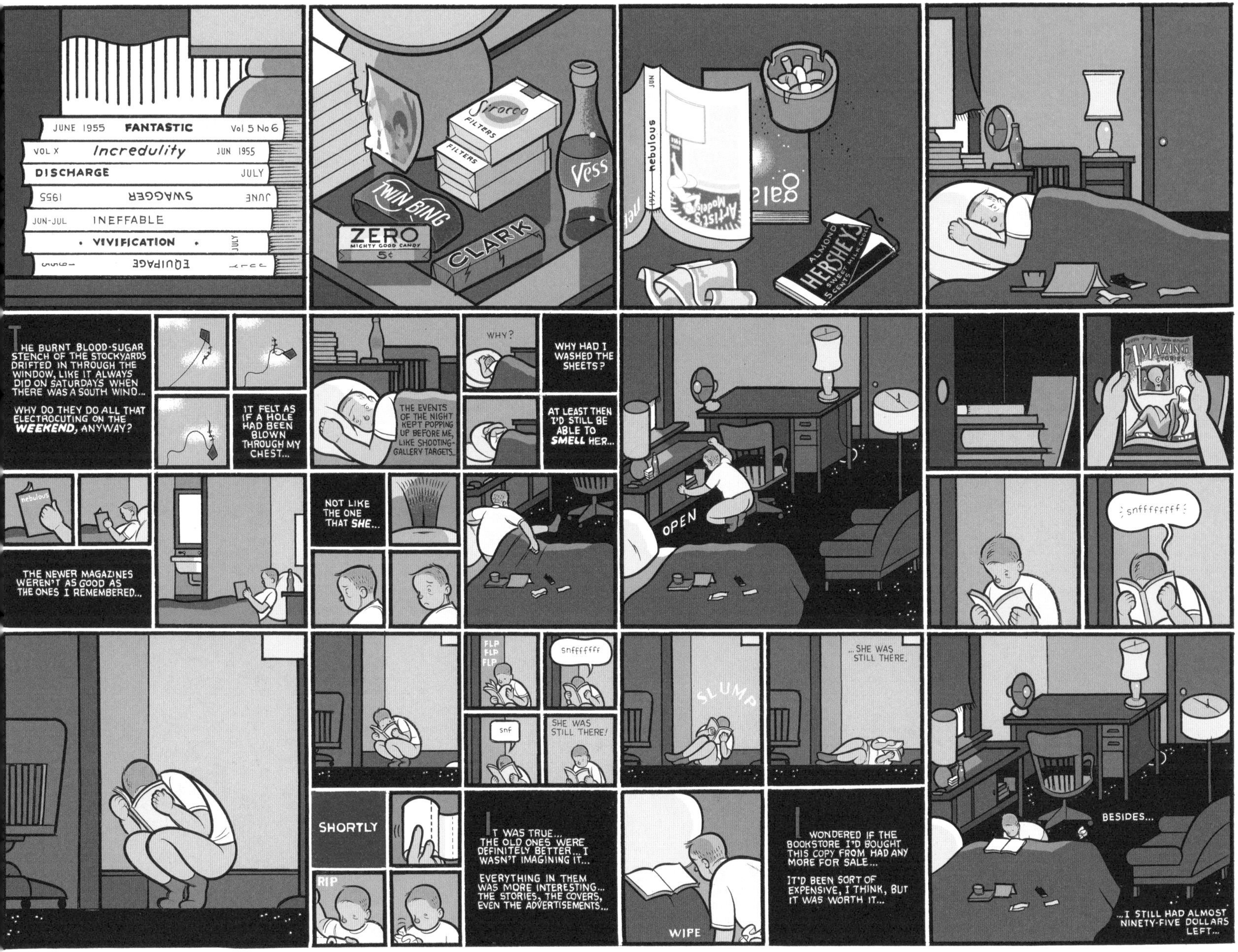

JUNE 1955 FANTASTIC Vol 5 No 6
VOL X Incredulity JUN 1955
DISCHARGE JULY
1955 SWAGGER JUNE
JUN-JUL INEFFABLE
VIVIFICATION JULY
EQUIPAGE
Sirocco FILTERS
FILTERS
TWIN BING
ZERO MIGHTY GOOD CANDY 5¢
CLARK
Vess
JUN
nebulous
1955
Artist's Models
ALMOND HERSHEY'S SWEET MILK CHOC 5 CENTS
THE BURNT BLOOD-SUGAR STENCH OF THE STOCKYARDS DRIFTED IN THROUGH THE WINDOW, LIKE IT ALWAYS DID ON SATURDAYS WHEN THERE WAS A SOUTH WIND...
WHY DO THEY DO ALL THAT ELECTROCUTING ON THE **WEEKEND,** ANYWAY?
IT FELT AS IF A HOLE HAD BEEN BLOWN THROUGH MY CHEST...
THE EVENTS OF THE NIGHT KEPT POPPING UP BEFORE ME, LIKE SHOOTING-GALLERY TARGETS...
WHY?
WHY HAD I WASHED THE SHEETS?
AT LEAST THEN I'D STILL BE ABLE TO **SMELL** HER...
OPEN
AMAZING STORIES
nebulous
THE NEWER MAGAZINES WEREN'T AS GOOD AS THE ONES I REMEMBERED...
NOT LIKE THE ONE THAT **SHE**...
snfffffffff
FLP FLP FLP
snffffffff
snf
SHE WAS STILL THERE!
SLUMP
...SHE WAS STILL THERE.
SHORTLY
RIP
IT WAS TRUE... THE OLD ONES WERE DEFINITELY BETTER... I WASN'T IMAGINING IT...
EVERYTHING IN THEM WAS MORE INTERESTING... THE STORIES, THE COVERS, EVEN THE ADVERTISEMENTS...
WIPE
I WONDERED IF THE BOOKSTORE I'D BOUGHT THIS COPY FROM HAD ANY MORE FOR SALE...
IT'D BEEN SORT OF EXPENSIVE, I THINK, BUT IT WAS WORTH IT...
BESIDES...
...I STILL HAD ALMOST NINETY-FIVE DOLLARS LEFT...

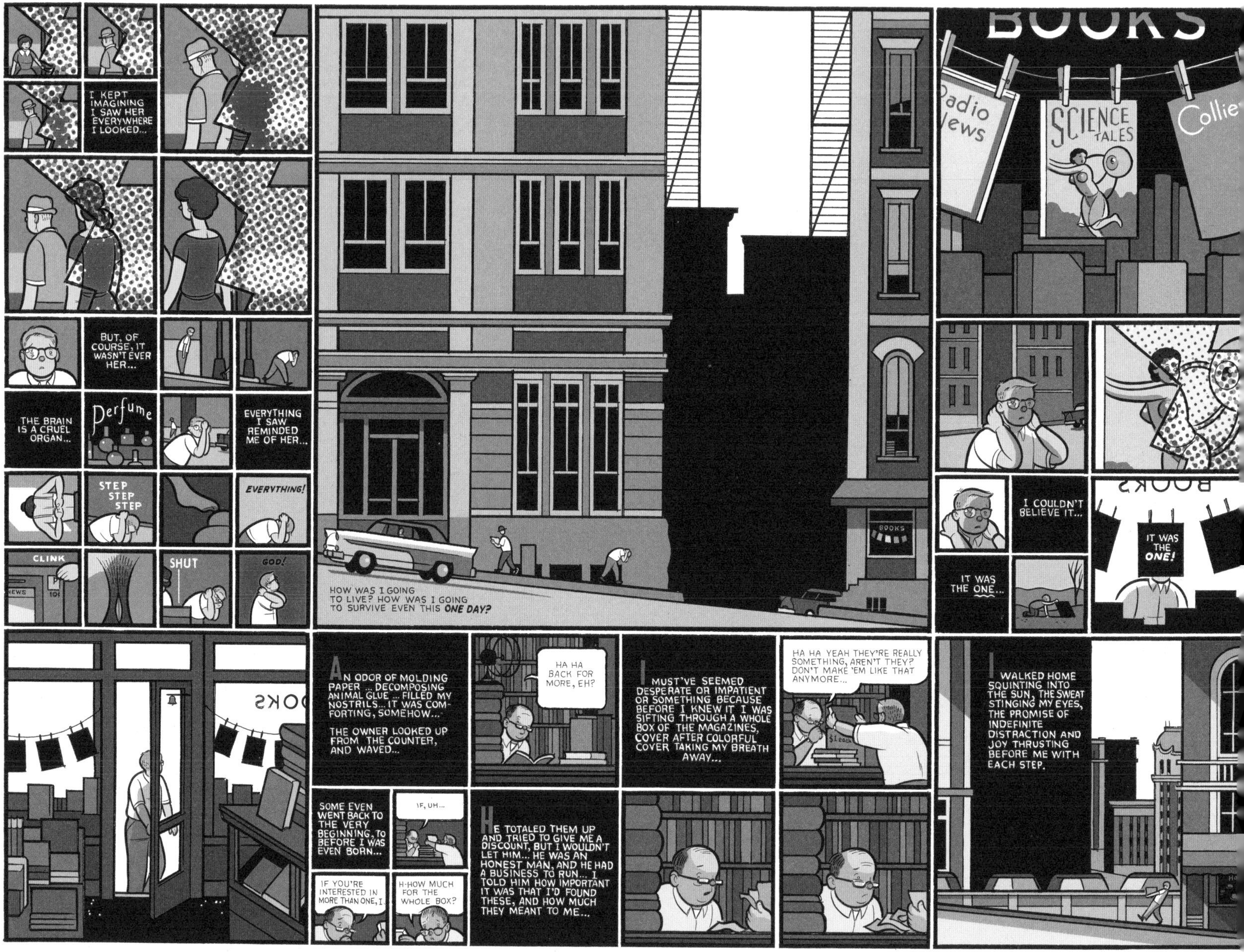

I KEPT IMAGINING I SAW HER EVERYWHERE I LOOKED...
BUT, OF COURSE, IT WASN'T EVER HER...
THE BRAIN IS A CRUEL ORGAN...
Perfume
EVERYTHING I SAW REMINDED ME OF HER...
STEP STEP STEP
EVERYTHING!
CLINK
NEWS
SHUT
GOD!
HOW WAS I GOING TO LIVE? HOW WAS I GOING TO SURVIVE EVEN THIS ONE DAY?
BOOKS
BOOKS
Radio News
SCIENCE TALES
Collie
I COULDN'T BELIEVE IT...
IT WAS THE ONE...
IT WAS THE ONE!
AN ODOR OF MOLDING PAPER ... DECOMPOSING ANIMAL GLUE ... FILLED MY NOSTRILS... IT WAS COMFORTING, SOMEHOW...
THE OWNER LOOKED UP FROM THE COUNTER, AND WAVED...
HA HA BACK FOR MORE, EH?
I MUST'VE SEEMED DESPERATE OR IMPATIENT OR SOMETHING BECAUSE BEFORE I KNEW IT I WAS SIFTING THROUGH A WHOLE BOX OF THE MAGAZINES, COVER AFTER COLORFUL COVER TAKING MY BREATH AWAY...
HA HA YEAH THEY'RE REALLY SOMETHING, AREN'T THEY? DON'T MAKE 'EM LIKE THAT ANYMORE...
$1 each
I WALKED HOME SQUINTING INTO THE SUN, THE SWEAT STINGING MY EYES, THE PROMISE OF INDEFINITE DISTRACTION AND JOY THRUSTING BEFORE ME WITH EACH STEP.
SOME EVEN WENT BACK TO THE VERY BEGINNING, TO BEFORE I WAS EVEN BORN...
IF, UH...
IF YOU'RE INTERESTED IN MORE THAN ONE, I...
H-HOW MUCH FOR THE WHOLE BOX?
HE TOTALED THEM UP AND TRIED TO GIVE ME A DISCOUNT, BUT I WOULDN'T LET HIM... HE WAS AN HONEST MAN, AND HE HAD A BUSINESS TO RUN... I TOLD HIM HOW IMPORTANT IT WAS THAT I'D FOUND THESE, AND HOW MUCH THEY MEANT TO ME...

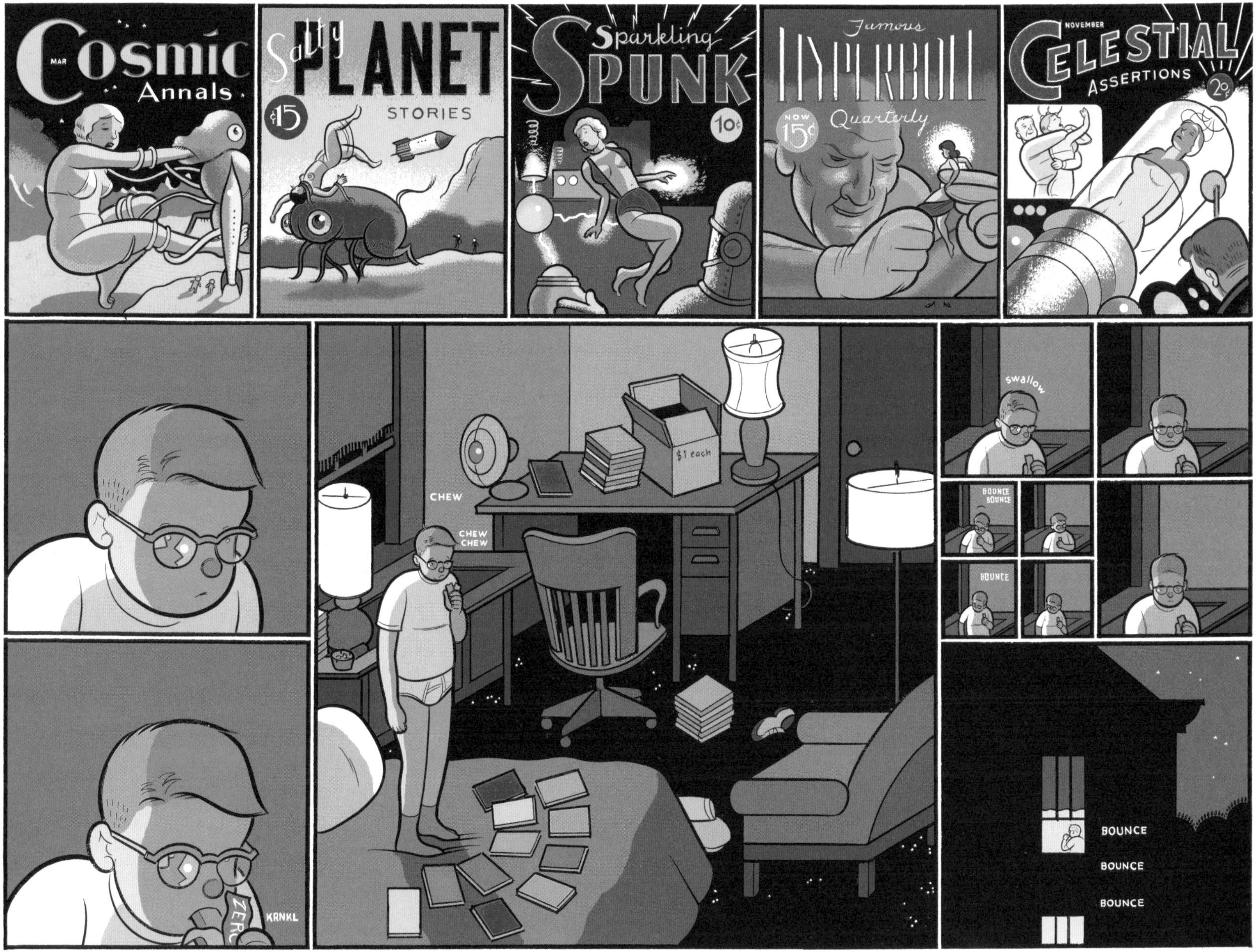

MAR
Cosmic
Annals
Salty
PLANET
¢15
STORIES
Sparkling
SPUNK
10¢
Famous
HYPERBOLE
NOW 15¢
Quarterly
NOVEMBER
CELESTIAL
ASSERTIONS
2¢
ZERO
KRNKL
CHEW
CHEW
CHEW
$1 each
swallow
BOUNCE
BOUNCE
BOUNCE
BOUNCE
BOUNCE
BOUNCE

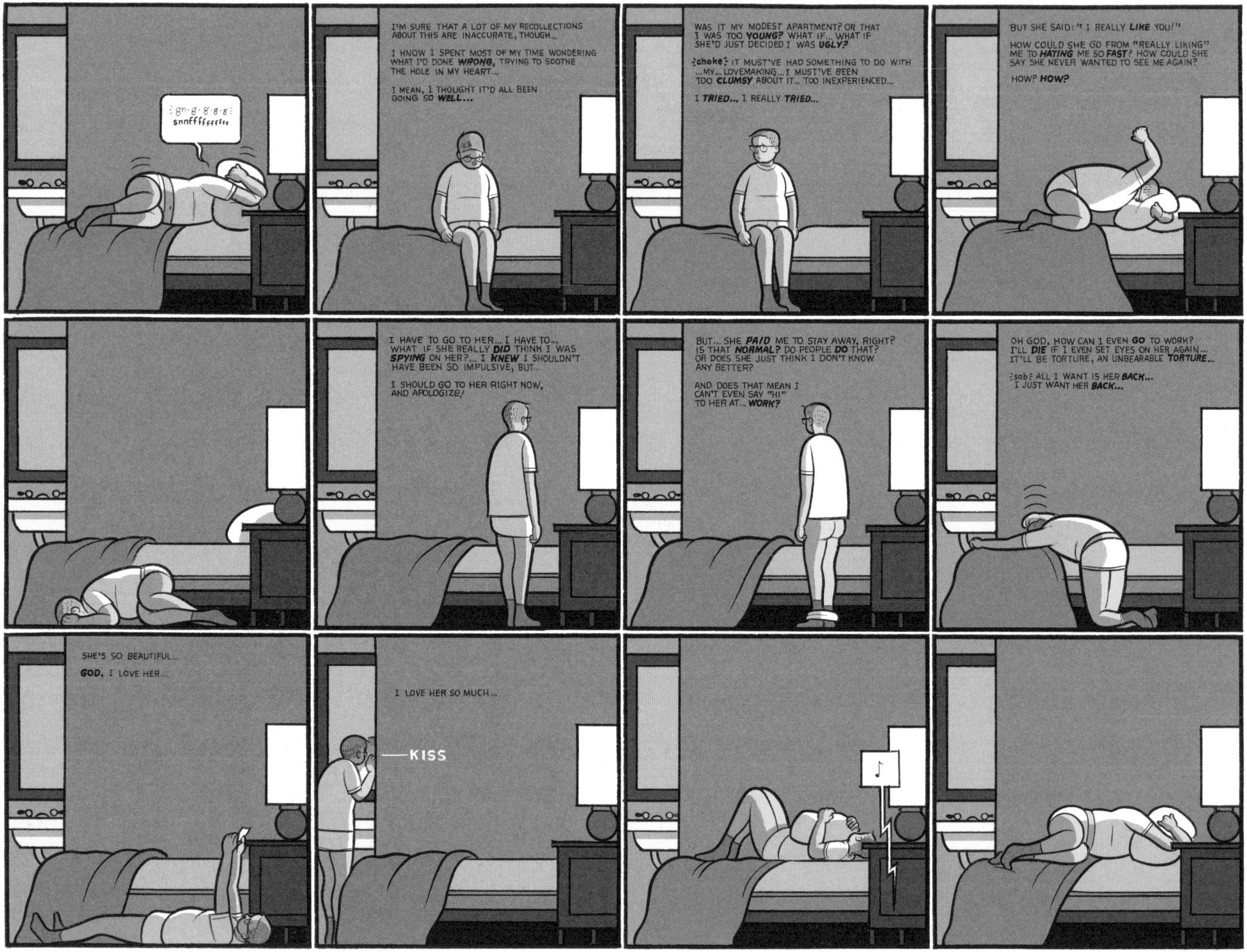
gn-g-g-g-g snnffffffffff
I'M SURE THAT A LOT OF MY RECOLLECTIONS ABOUT THIS ARE INACCURATE, THOUGH...
I KNOW I SPENT MOST OF MY TIME WONDERING WHAT I'D DONE **WRONG**, TRYING TO SOOTHE THE HOLE IN MY HEART...
I MEAN, I THOUGHT IT'D ALL BEEN GOING SO **WELL...**
WAS IT MY MODEST APARTMENT? OR THAT I WAS TOO **YOUNG?** WHAT IF... WHAT IF SHE'D JUST DECIDED I WAS **UGLY?**
choke IT MUST'VE HAD SOMETHING TO DO WITH ...MY... LOVEMAKING... I MUST'VE BEEN TOO **CLUMSY** ABOUT IT... TOO INEXPERIENCED...
I **TRIED...** I REALLY **TRIED...**
BUT SHE SAID: "I REALLY **LIKE** YOU!"
HOW COULD SHE GO FROM "REALLY LIKING" ME TO **HATING** ME SO **FAST**? HOW COULD SHE SAY SHE NEVER WANTED TO SEE ME AGAIN?
HOW? **HOW?**
I HAVE TO GO TO HER... I HAVE TO... WHAT IF SHE REALLY **DID** THINK I WAS **SPYING** ON HER?... I **KNEW** I SHOULDN'T HAVE BEEN SO IMPULSIVE, BUT...
I SHOULD GO TO HER RIGHT NOW, AND APOLOGIZE!
BUT... SHE **PAID** ME TO STAY AWAY, RIGHT? IS THAT **NORMAL?** DO PEOPLE **DO** THAT? OR DOES SHE JUST THINK I DON'T KNOW ANY BETTER?
AND DOES THAT MEAN I CAN'T EVEN SAY "HI" TO HER AT... **WORK?**
OH GOD, HOW CAN I EVEN **GO** TO WORK? I'LL **DIE** IF I EVEN SET EYES ON HER AGAIN... IT'LL BE TORTURE, AN UNBEARABLE **TORTURE...**
sob ALL I WANT IS HER **BACK...** I JUST WANT HER **BACK...**
SHE'S SO BEAUTIFUL...
GOD, I LOVE HER...
I LOVE HER SO MUCH...
KISS

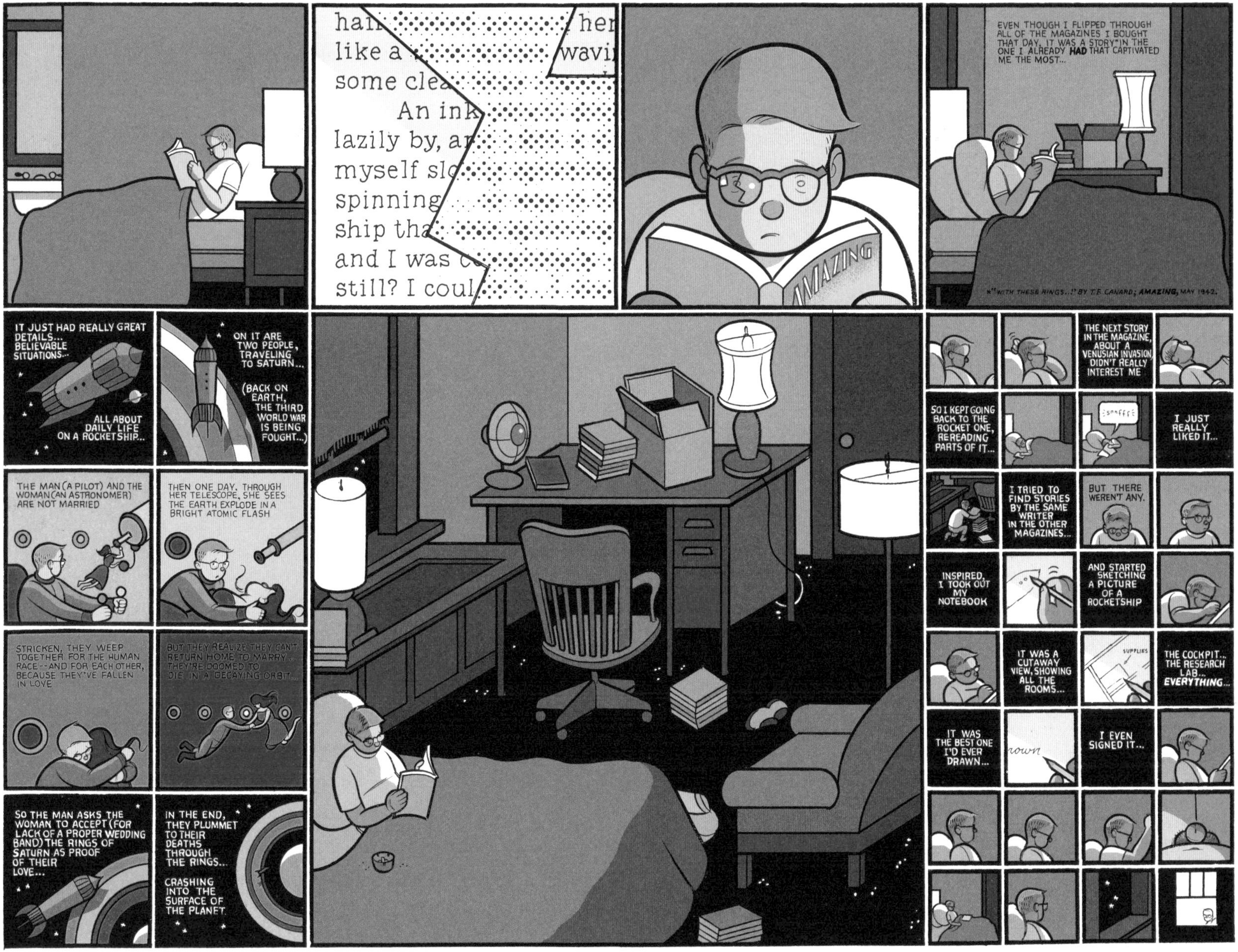

ham
her
like a
wavi
some clea
An ink
lazily by, a
myself sl
spinning
ship tha
and I was c
still? I coul
AMAZING
EVEN THOUGH I FLIPPED THROUGH ALL OF THE MAGAZINES I BOUGHT THAT DAY, IT WAS A STORY* IN THE ONE I ALREADY **HAD** THAT CAPTIVATED ME THE MOST...
*"WITH THESE RINGS...!" BY T.F. CANARD; **AMAZING**, MAY 1942.
IT JUST HAD REALLY GREAT DETAILS... BELIEVABLE SITUATIONS...
ALL ABOUT DAILY LIFE ON A ROCKETSHIP...
ON IT ARE TWO PEOPLE, TRAVELING TO SATURN...
(BACK ON EARTH, THE THIRD WORLD WAR IS BEING FOUGHT...)
THE MAN (A PILOT) AND THE WOMAN (AN ASTRONOMER) ARE NOT MARRIED
THEN ONE DAY, THROUGH HER TELESCOPE, SHE SEES THE EARTH EXPLODE IN A BRIGHT ATOMIC FLASH
STRICKEN, THEY WEEP TOGETHER FOR THE HUMAN RACE--AND FOR EACH OTHER, BECAUSE THEY'VE FALLEN IN LOVE
BUT THEY REALIZE THEY CAN'T RETURN HOME TO MARRY... THEY'RE DOOMED TO DIE IN A DECAYING ORBIT...
SO THE MAN ASKS THE WOMAN TO ACCEPT (FOR LACK OF A PROPER WEDDING BAND) THE RINGS OF SATURN AS PROOF OF THEIR LOVE...
IN THE END, THEY PLUMMET TO THEIR DEATHS THROUGH THE RINGS...
CRASHING INTO THE SURFACE OF THE PLANET.
THE NEXT STORY IN THE MAGAZINE, ABOUT A VENUSIAN INVASION, DIDN'T REALLY INTEREST ME
SO I KEPT GOING BACK TO THE ROCKET ONE, REREADING PARTS OF IT...
snnfff
I JUST REALLY LIKED IT...
I TRIED TO FIND STORIES BY THE SAME WRITER IN THE OTHER MAGAZINES...
BUT THERE WEREN'T ANY.
INSPIRED, I TOOK OUT MY NOTEBOOK
AND STARTED SKETCHING A PICTURE OF A ROCKETSHIP
IT WAS A CUTAWAY VIEW, SHOWING ALL THE ROOMS...
SUPPLIES
THE COCKPIT... THE RESEARCH LAB... *EVERYTHING*...
IT WAS THE BEST ONE I'D EVER DRAWN...
rown
I EVEN SIGNED IT...

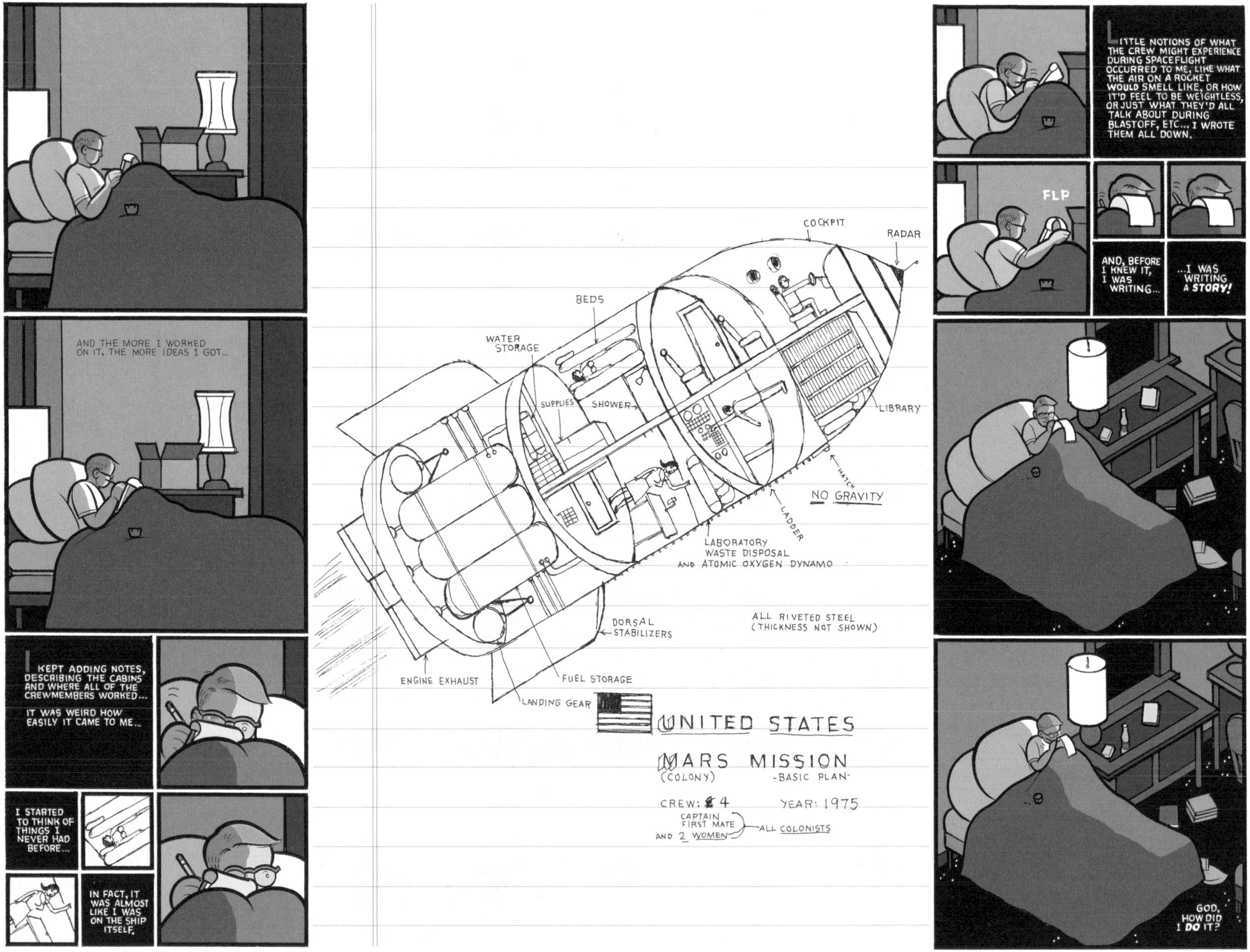
AND THE MORE I WORKED ON IT, THE MORE IDEAS I GOT...
I KEPT ADDING NOTES, DESCRIBING THE CABINS AND WHERE ALL OF THE CREWMEMBERS WORKED...
IT WAS WEIRD HOW EASILY IT CAME TO ME...
I STARTED TO THINK OF THINGS I NEVER HAD BEFORE...
IN FACT, IT WAS ALMOST LIKE I WAS ON THE SHIP ITSELF.
COCKPIT
RADAR
BEDS
WATER STORAGE
SUPPLIES
SHOWER
LIBRARY
HATCH
NO GRAVITY
LADDER
LABORATORY
WASTE DISPOSAL
AND ATOMIC OXYGEN DYNAMO
DORSAL STABILIZERS
ALL RIVETED STEEL
(THICKNESS NOT SHOWN)
ENGINE EXHAUST
FUEL STORAGE
LANDING GEAR
UNITED STATES
MARS MISSION
(COLONY)
-BASIC PLAN-
CREW: 4
YEAR: 1975
CAPTAIN
FIRST MATE
AND 2 WOMEN
ALL COLONISTS
LITTLE NOTIONS OF WHAT THE CREW MIGHT EXPERIENCE DURING SPACEFLIGHT OCCURRED TO ME, LIKE WHAT THE AIR ON A ROCKET WOULD SMELL LIKE, OR HOW IT'D FEEL TO BE WEIGHTLESS, OR JUST WHAT THEY'D ALL TALK ABOUT DURING BLASTOFF, ETC... I WROTE THEM ALL DOWN.
FLP
AND, BEFORE I KNEW IT, I WAS WRITING...
...I WAS WRITING A STORY!
GOD, HOW DID I DO IT?

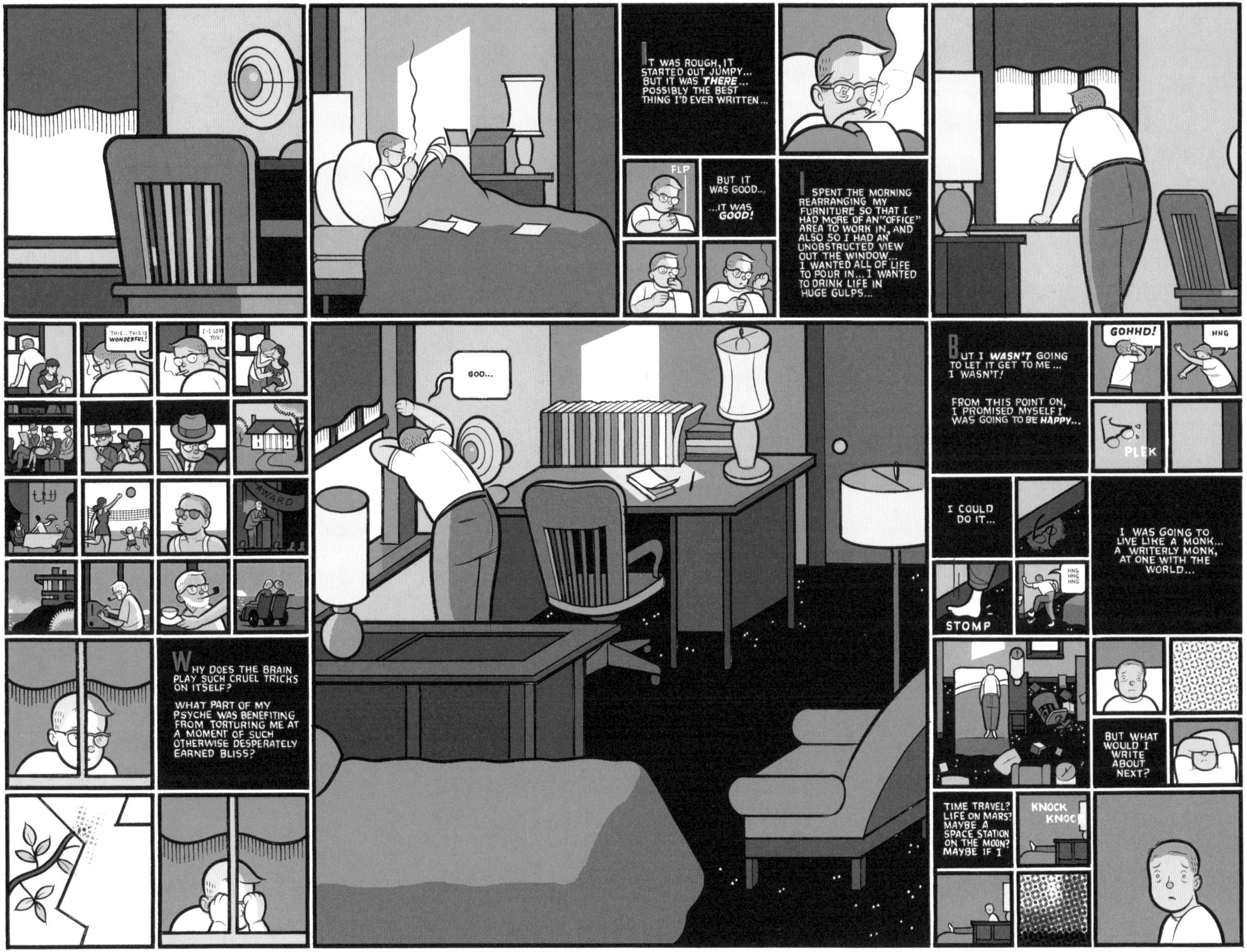

IT WAS ROUGH, IT STARTED OUT JUMPY... BUT IT WAS **THERE**... POSSIBLY THE BEST THING I'D EVER WRITTEN...
FLP
BUT IT WAS GOOD...
...IT WAS **GOOD!**
I SPENT THE MORNING REARRANGING MY FURNITURE SO THAT I HAD MORE OF AN "OFFICE" AREA TO WORK IN, AND ALSO SO I HAD AN UNOBSTRUCTED VIEW OUT THE WINDOW... I WANTED ALL OF LIFE TO POUR IN... I WANTED TO DRINK LIFE IN HUGE GULPS...
THIS... THIS IS **WONDERFUL!**
I-I LOVE YOU!
AWARD
WHY DOES THE BRAIN PLAY SUCH CRUEL TRICKS ON ITSELF?
WHAT PART OF MY PSYCHE WAS BENEFITING FROM TORTURING ME AT A MOMENT OF SUCH OTHERWISE DESPERATELY EARNED BLISS?
GOD...
BUT I **WASN'T** GOING TO LET IT GET TO ME... I WASN'T!
FROM THIS POINT ON, I PROMISED MYSELF I WAS GOING TO BE **HAPPY**...
GOHHD!
HNG
PLEK
I COULD DO IT...
I WAS GOING TO LIVE LIKE A MONK... A WRITERLY MONK, AT ONE WITH THE WORLD...
STOMP
HNG HNG HNG
BUT WHAT WOULD I WRITE ABOUT NEXT?
TIME TRAVEL? LIFE ON MARS? MAYBE A SPACE STATION ON THE MOON? MAYBE IF I
KNOCK KNOC

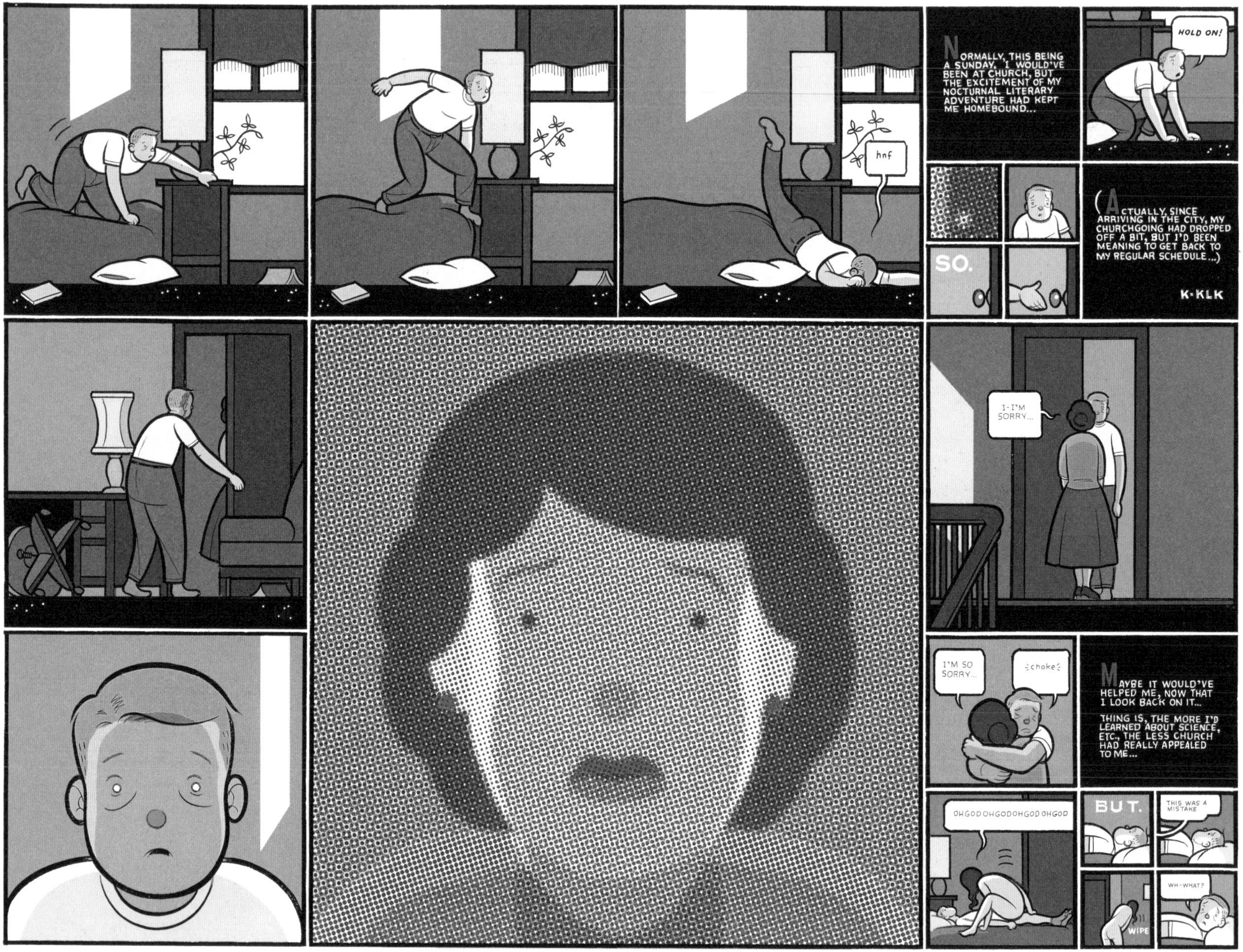

hnf
NORMALLY, THIS BEING A SUNDAY, I WOULD'VE BEEN AT CHURCH, BUT THE EXCITEMENT OF MY NOCTURNAL LITERARY ADVENTURE HAD KEPT ME HOMEBOUND...
HOLD ON!
SO.
(ACTUALLY, SINCE ARRIVING IN THE CITY, MY CHURCHGOING HAD DROPPED OFF A BIT, BUT I'D BEEN MEANING TO GET BACK TO MY REGULAR SCHEDULE...)
K-KLK
I-I'M SORRY...
I'M SO SORRY...
choke
MAYBE IT WOULD'VE HELPED ME, NOW THAT I LOOK BACK ON IT...
THING IS, THE MORE I'D LEARNED ABOUT SCIENCE, ETC., THE LESS CHURCH HAD REALLY APPEALED TO ME...
OHGODOHGODOHGODOHGOD
BUT.
THIS WAS A MISTAKE
WIPE
WH-WHAT?

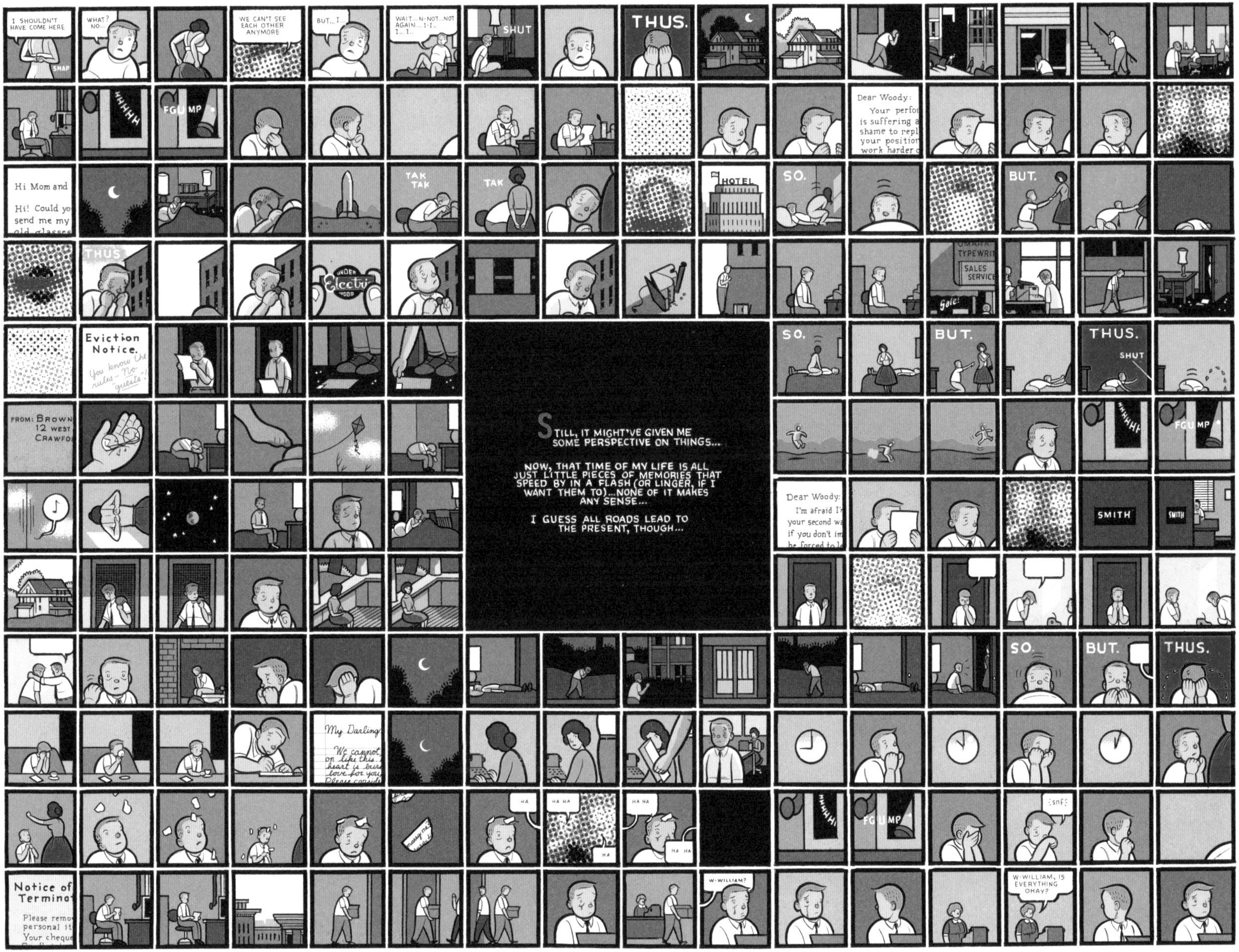
I SHOULDN'T HAVE COME HERE
SNAP
WHAT? NO...
WE CAN'T SEE EACH OTHER ANYMORE
BUT... I...
WAIT... N-NOT...NOT AGAIN... I-I.. I... I..
SHUT
THUS.
FGUMP
Dear Woody:
Your perfor
is suffering a
shame to repl
your position
work harder
Hi Mom and
Hi! Could yo
send me my
TAK TAK
TAK
HOTEL
SO.
BUT.
THUS
OMAHA
TYPEWRIT
SALES
SERVICE
Sale!
Eviction Notice.
You know the rules — No guests!
SO.
BUT.
THUS.
SHUT
FROM: BROWN
12 WEST
CRAWFO
STILL, IT MIGHT'VE GIVEN ME SOME PERSPECTIVE ON THINGS...
NOW, THAT TIME OF MY LIFE IS ALL JUST LITTLE PIECES OF MEMORIES THAT SPEED BY IN A FLASH (OR LINGER, IF I WANT THEM TO)...NONE OF IT MAKES ANY SENSE...
I GUESS ALL ROADS LEAD TO THE PRESENT, THOUGH...
FGUMP
Dear Woody:
I'm afraid I'
your second wa
if you don't im
SMITH
SMITH
SO.
BUT.
THUS.
My Darling
We cannot
on like this.
heart is bur
love for you
HA
HA HA
HA
HA HA
HA HA
FGUMP
snff
Notice of
Terminat
Please remo
personal it
Your cheque
W-WILLIAM?
W-WILLIAM, IS EVERYTHING OKAY?

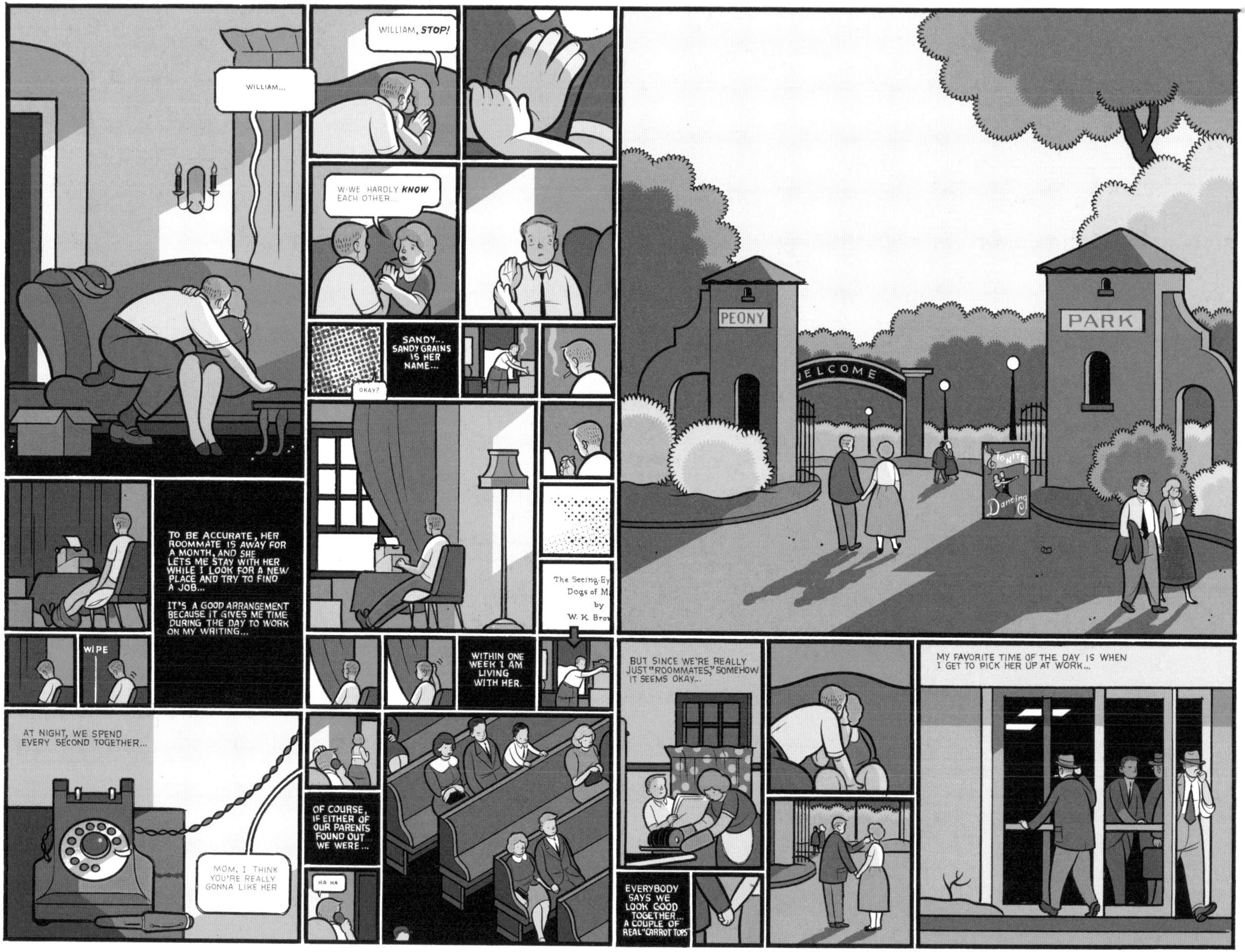
WILLIAM...
WILLIAM, STOP!
W-WE HARDLY KNOW EACH OTHER...
OKAY?
SANDY... SANDY GRAINS IS HER NAME...
TO BE ACCURATE, HER ROOMMATE IS AWAY FOR A MONTH, AND SHE LETS ME STAY WITH HER WHILE I LOOK FOR A NEW PLACE AND TRY TO FIND A JOB...
IT'S A GOOD ARRANGEMENT BECAUSE IT GIVES ME TIME DURING THE DAY TO WORK ON MY WRITING...
WIPE
WITHIN ONE WEEK I AM LIVING WITH HER.
AT NIGHT, WE SPEND EVERY SECOND TOGETHER...
MOM, I THINK YOU'RE REALLY GONNA LIKE HER
OF COURSE, IF EITHER OF OUR PARENTS FOUND OUT WE WERE...
HA HA
PEONY
PARK
WELCOME
TONITE
Dancing
BUT SINCE WE'RE REALLY JUST "ROOMMATES," SOMEHOW IT SEEMS OKAY...
EVERYBODY SAYS WE LOOK GOOD TOGETHER... A COUPLE OF REAL "CARROT TOPS"
MY FAVORITE TIME OF THE DAY IS WHEN I GET TO PICK HER UP AT WORK...

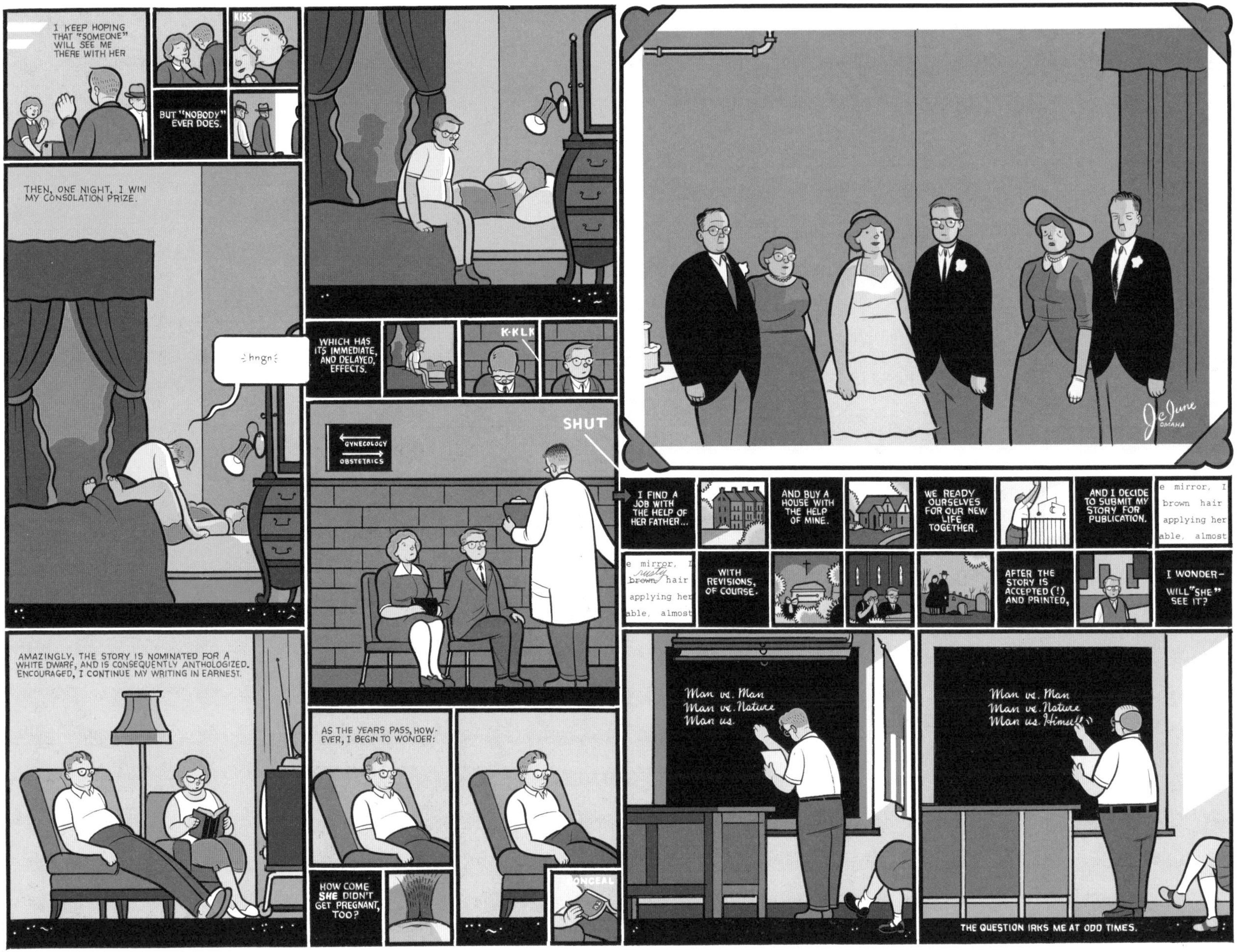

I KEEP HOPING THAT "SOMEONE" WILL SEE ME THERE WITH HER
KISS
BUT "NOBODY" EVER DOES.
THEN, ONE NIGHT, I WIN MY CONSOLATION PRIZE.
hngn
WHICH HAS ITS IMMEDIATE, AND DELAYED, EFFECTS.
K-KLK
GYNECOLOGY
OBSTETRICS
SHUT
AMAZINGLY, THE STORY IS NOMINATED FOR A WHITE DWARF, AND IS CONSEQUENTLY ANTHOLOGIZED. ENCOURAGED, I CONTINUE MY WRITING IN EARNEST.
AS THE YEARS PASS, HOWEVER, I BEGIN TO WONDER:
HOW COME SHE DIDN'T GET PREGNANT, TOO?
JeJune OMAHA
I FIND A JOB WITH THE HELP OF HER FATHER...
AND BUY A HOUSE WITH THE HELP OF MINE.
WE READY OURSELVES FOR OUR NEW LIFE TOGETHER.
AND I DECIDE TO SUBMIT MY STORY FOR PUBLICATION.
e mirror, I brown hair applying her able, almost
e mirror, I rusty ~~brown~~ hair applying her able, almost
WITH REVISIONS, OF COURSE.
AFTER THE STORY IS ACCEPTED (!) AND PRINTED,
I WONDER– WILL "SHE" SEE IT?
Man vs. Man
Man vs. Nature
Man vs.
Man vs. Man
Man vs. Nature
Man vs. Himself
THE QUESTION IRKS ME AT ODD TIMES.

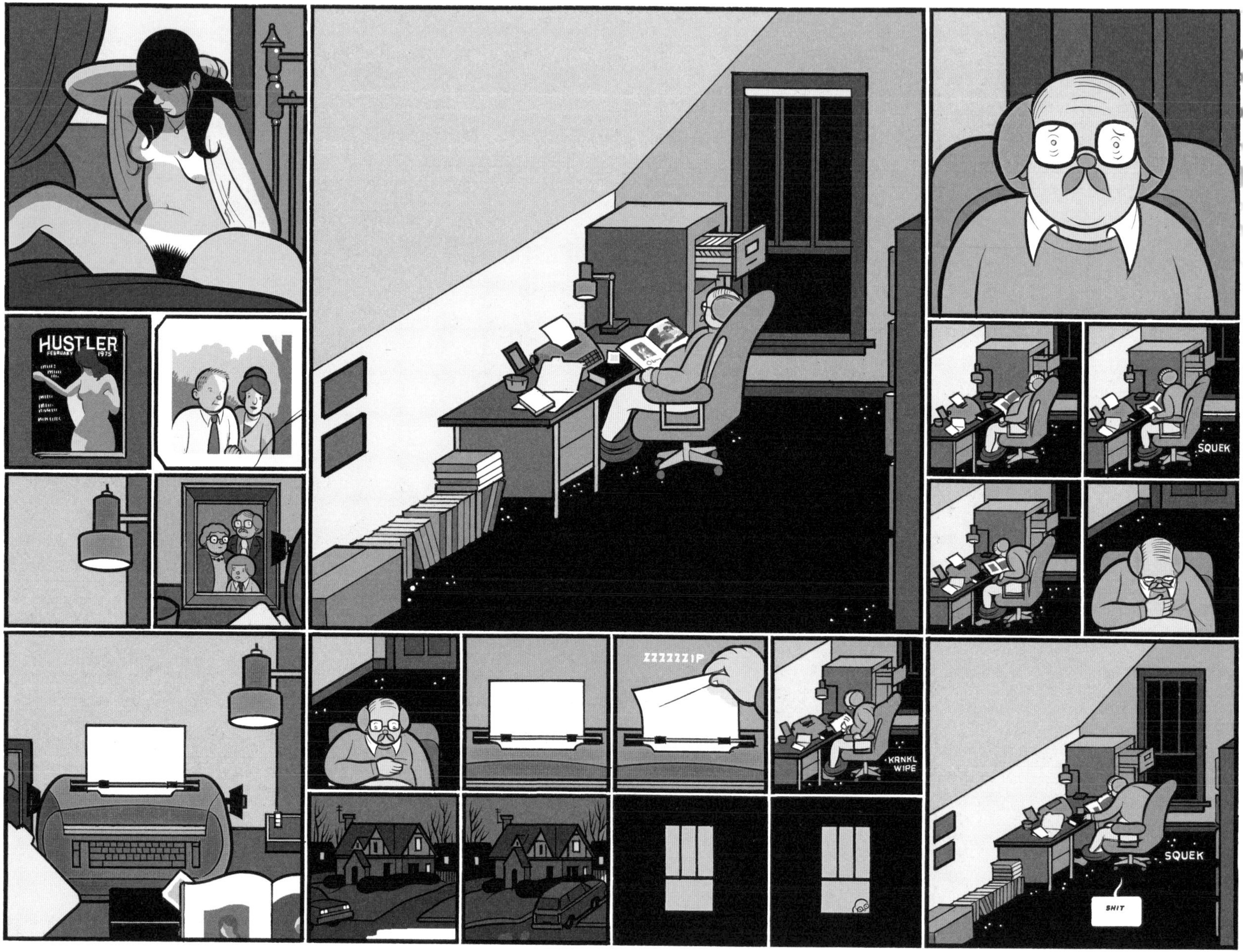

HUSTLER
FEBRUARY 1975
SQUEK
ZZZZZZIP
KRNKL
WIPE
SQUEK
SHIT

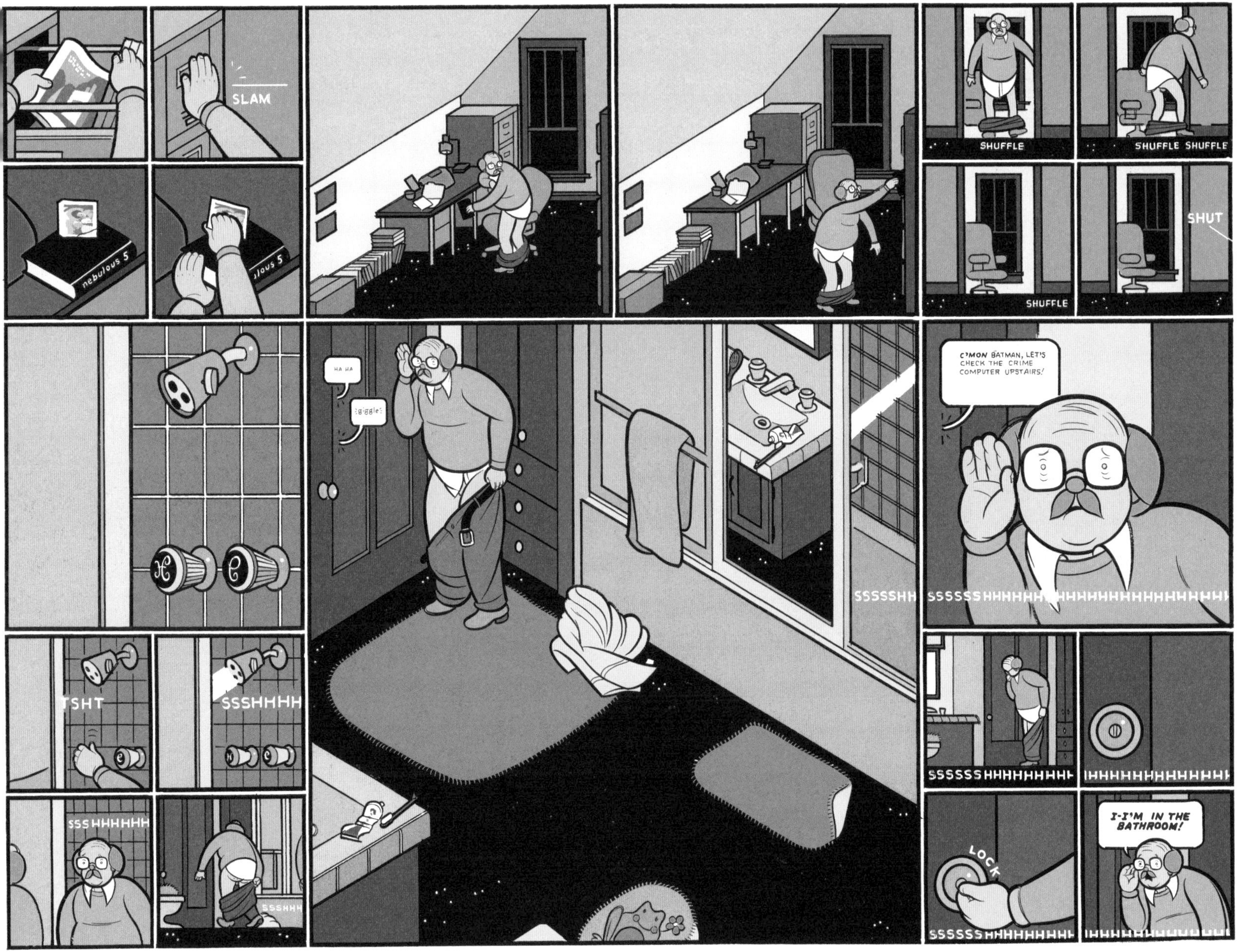

SLAM
nebulous 5
ulous 5
SHUFFLE
SHUFFLE SHUFFLE
SHUFFLE
SHUT
TSHT
SSSHHHH
SSSHHHHHH
SSSHHH
HA HA
giggle
SSSSSHH
C'MON BATMAN, LET'S CHECK THE CRIME COMPUTER UPSTAIRS!
SSSSSSHHHHHHHHHHHHHHHHHHHHHHHHH
SSSSSSHHHHHHHHHHHHHHHHHHHHHHH
LOCK
SSSSSSHHHHHHHHHHHHHHHHHHHHHHH
I-I'M IN THE BATHROOM!

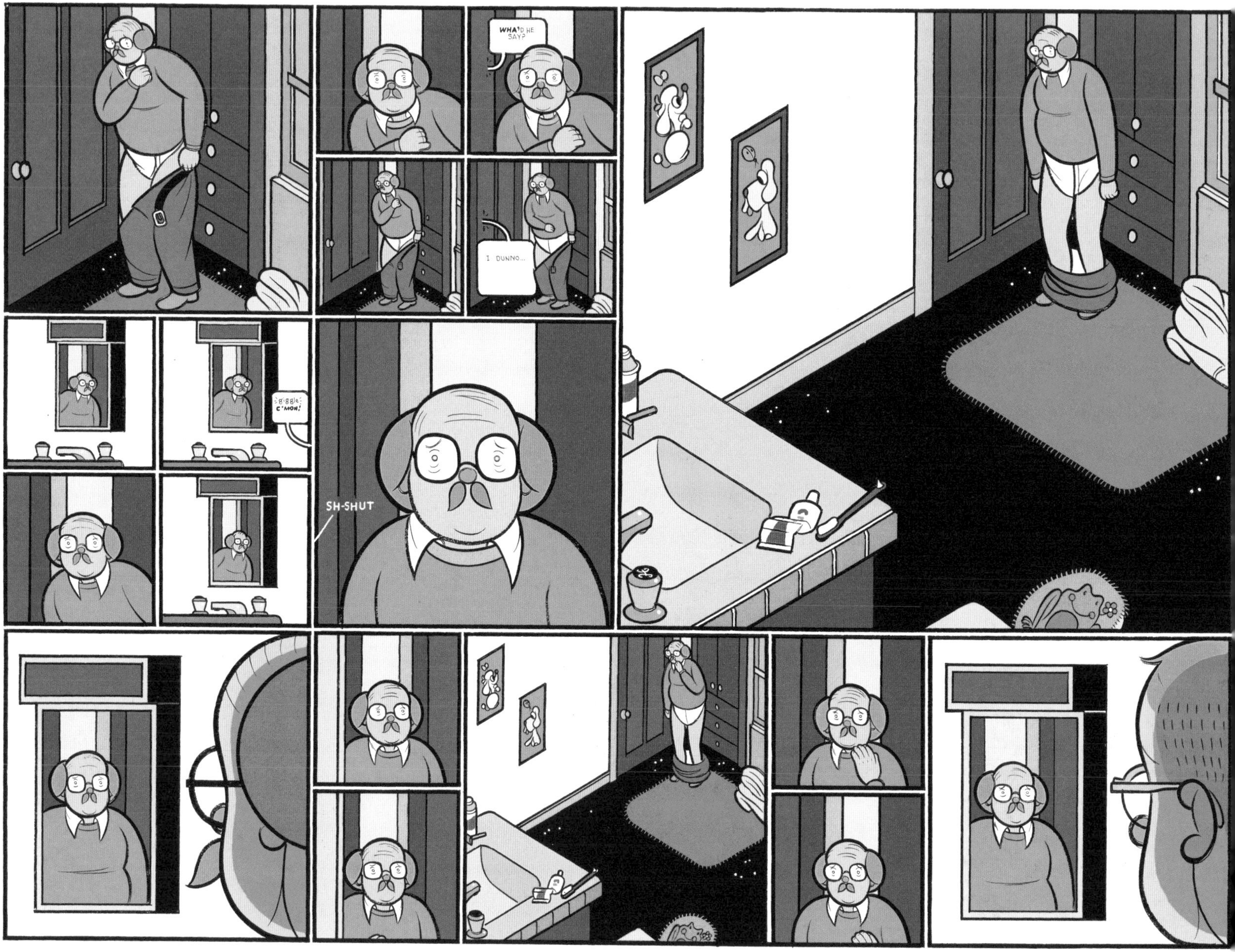
WHA'D HE SAY?
I DUNNO...
giggle C'MON!
SH-SHUT

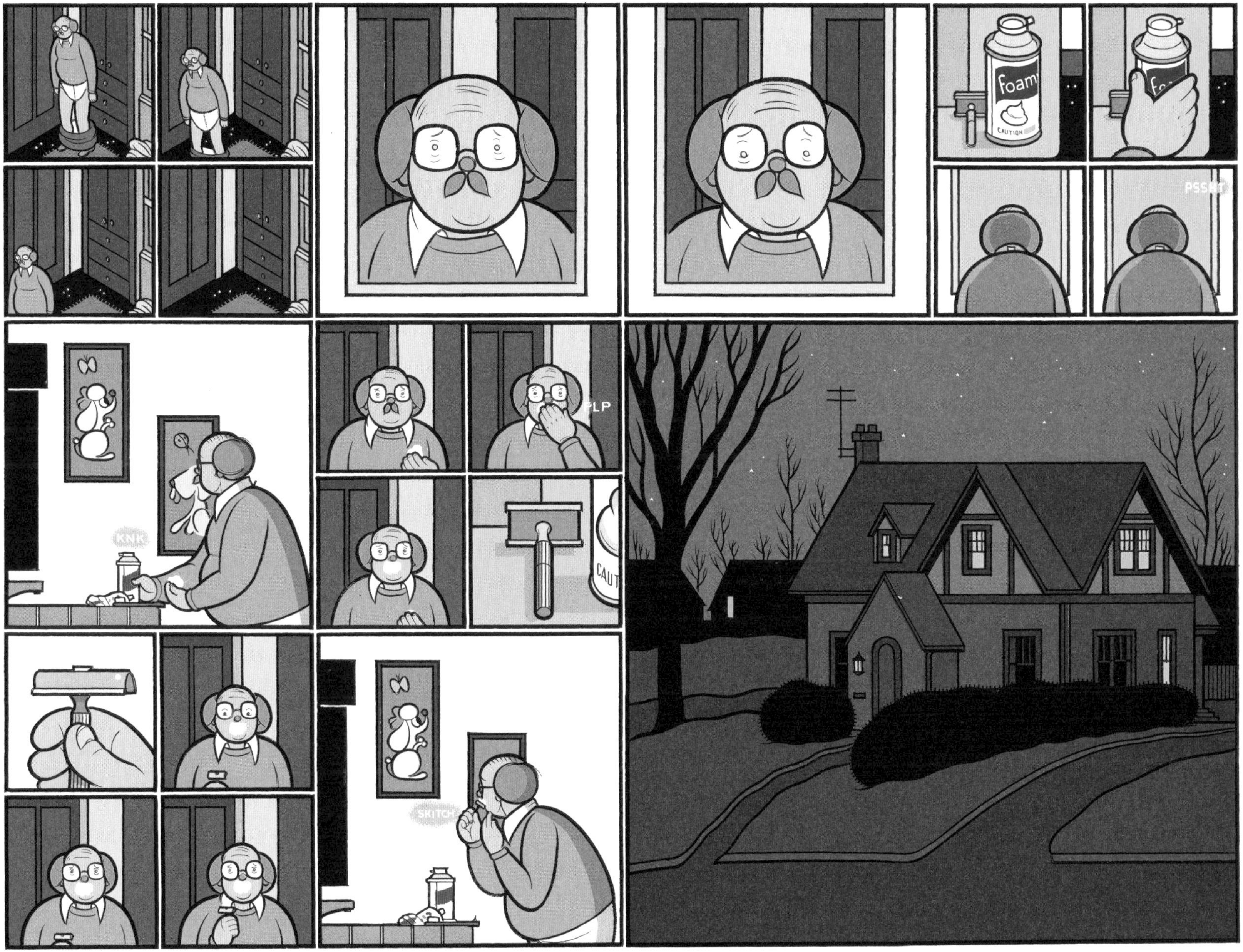
foamy
CAUTION
PSSHT
KNK
PLP
SKITCH

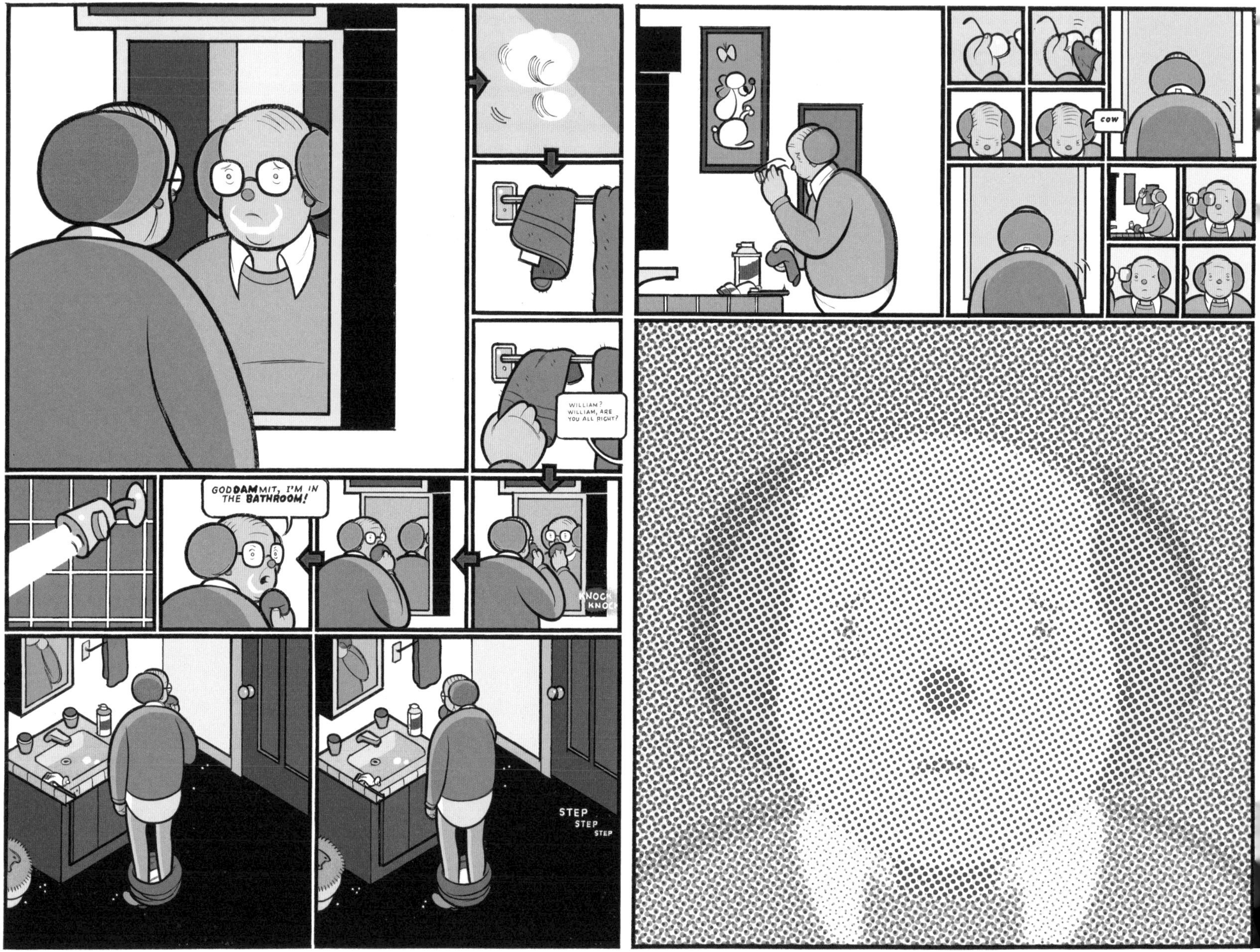
WILLIAM? WILLIAM, ARE YOU ALL RIGHT?
KNOCK
GODDAMMIT, I'M IN THE BATHROOM!
STEP
STEP
STEP
COW

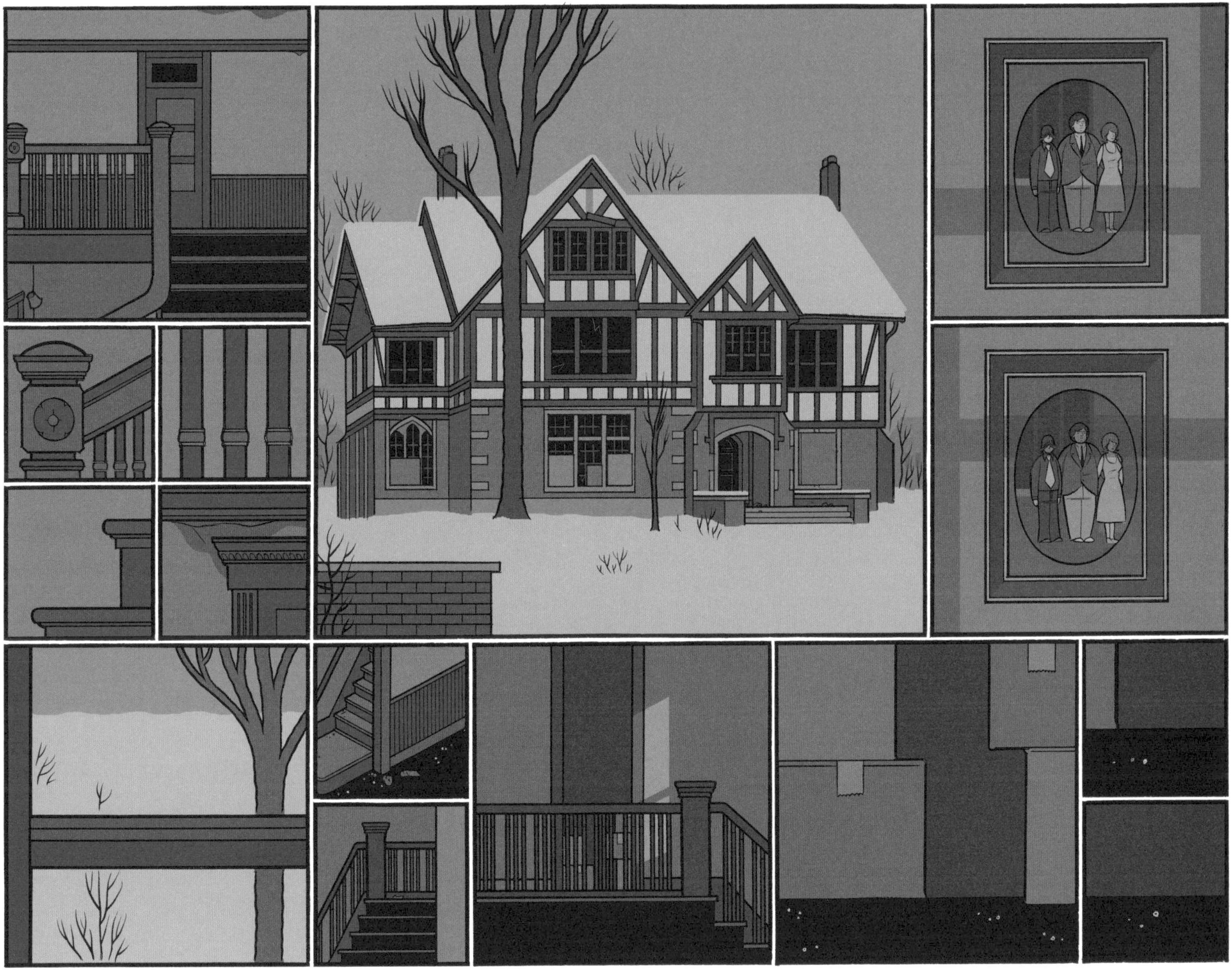

.

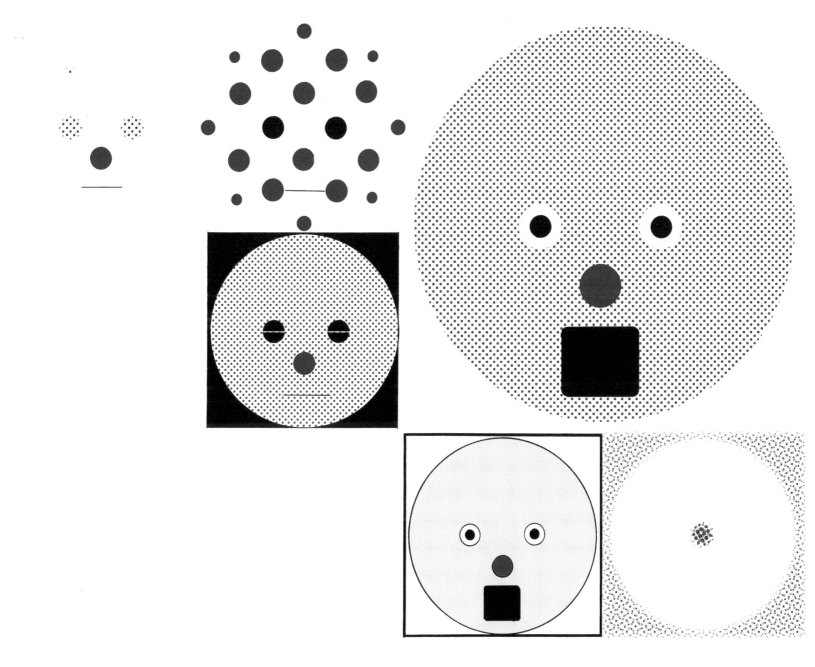

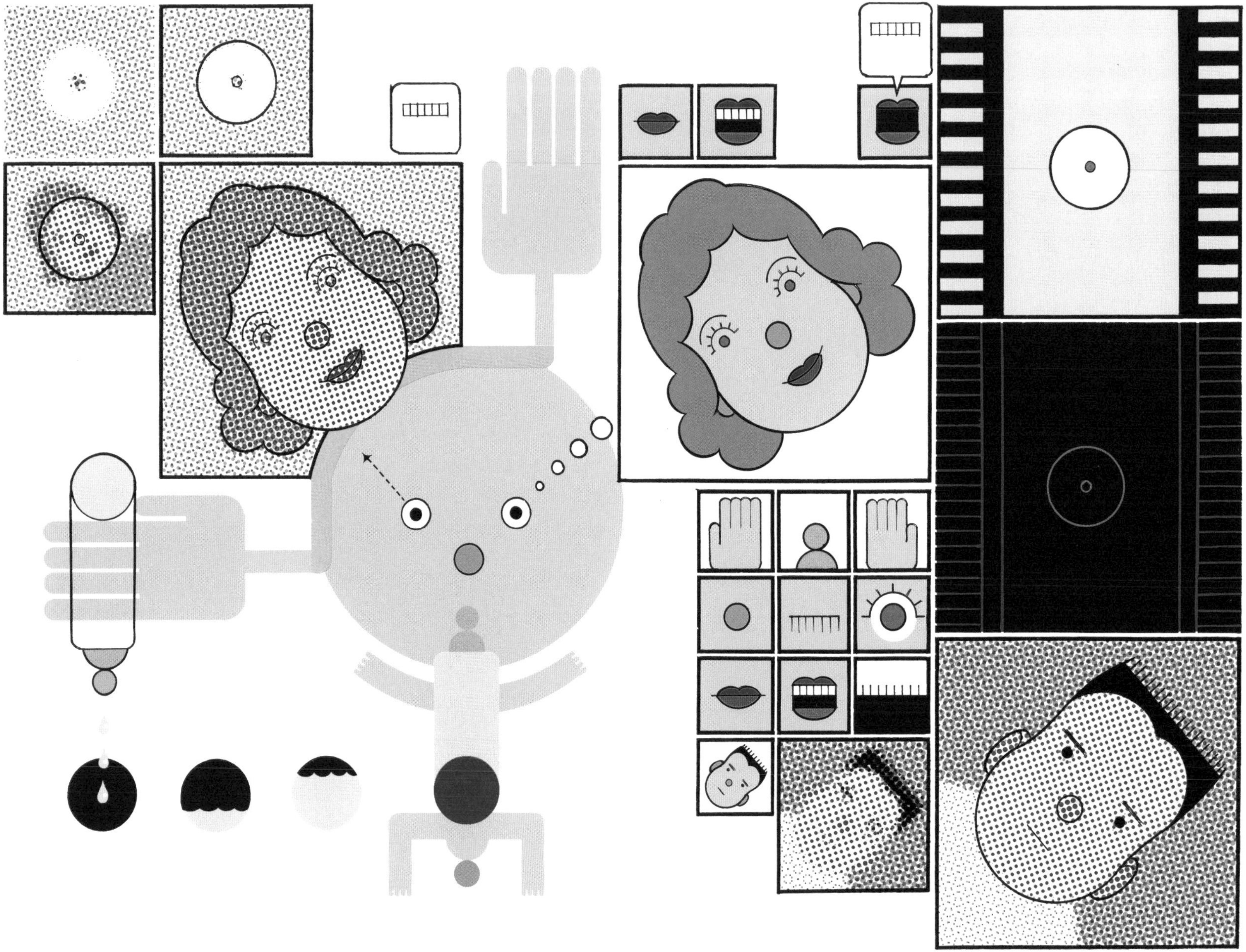

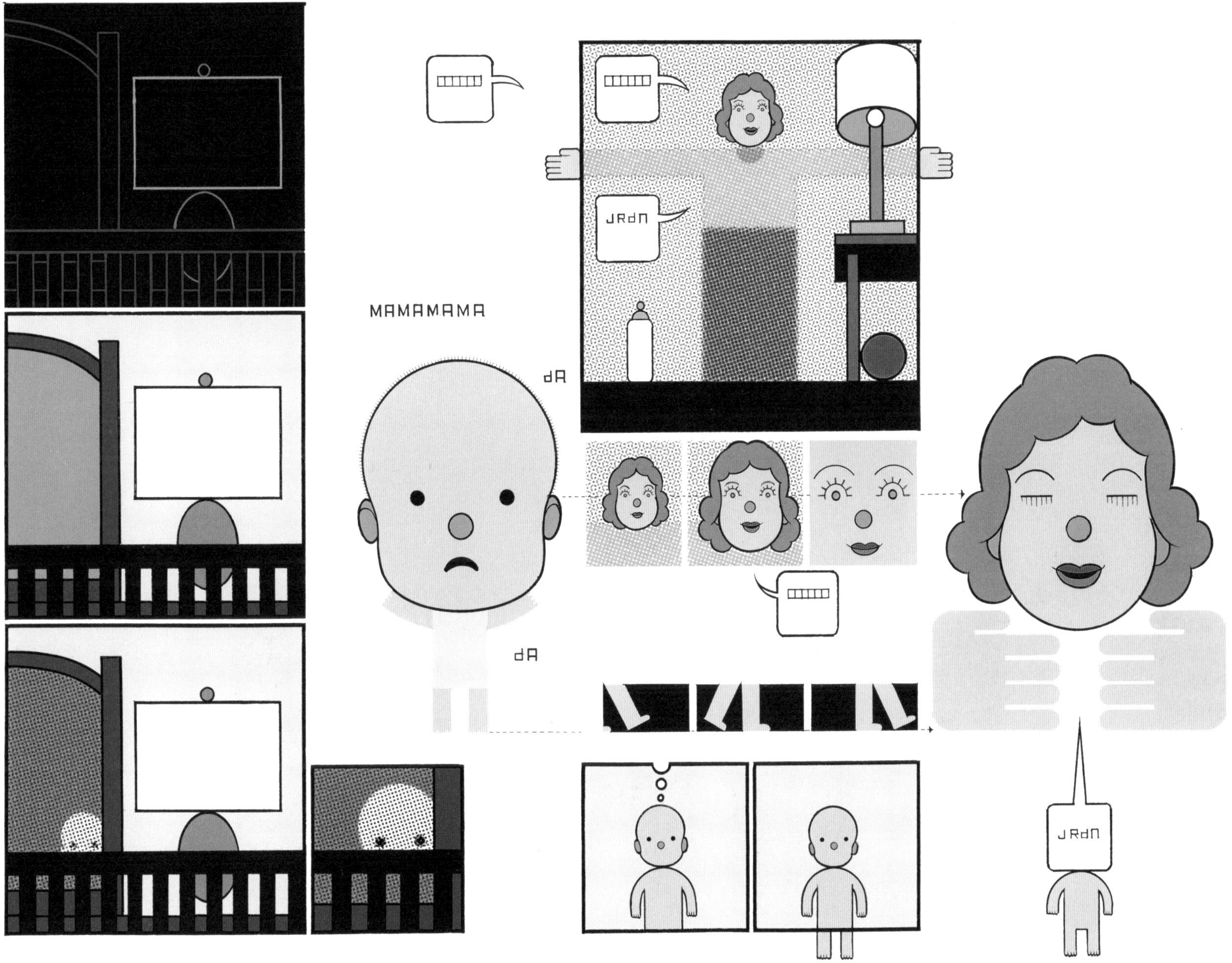
JRdn
MAMAMAMA
dA
dA
JRdn

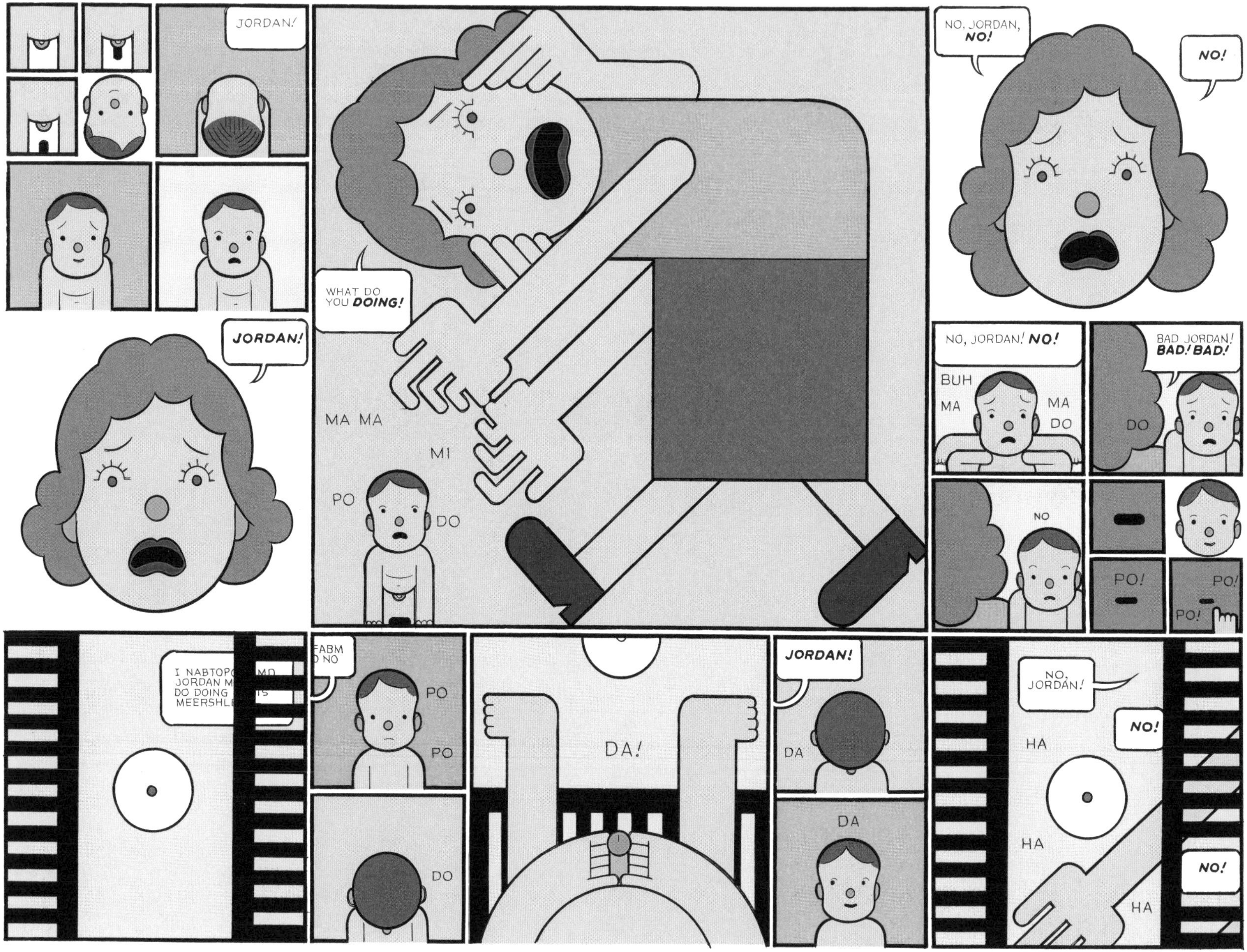
JORDAN!
WHAT DO YOU DOING!
MA MA
MI
PO
DO
NO, JORDAN, NO!
NO!
JORDAN!
NO, JORDAN! NO!
BUH
MA
MA
DO
BAD JORDAN! BAD! BAD!
DO
NO
PO!
PO!
PO!
I NABTOPO MD
JORDAN M
DO DOING TS
MEERSHLE
FABM
NO
PO
PO
DO
DA!
JORDAN!
DA
DA
NO, JORDAN!
NO!
HA
HA
NO!
HA

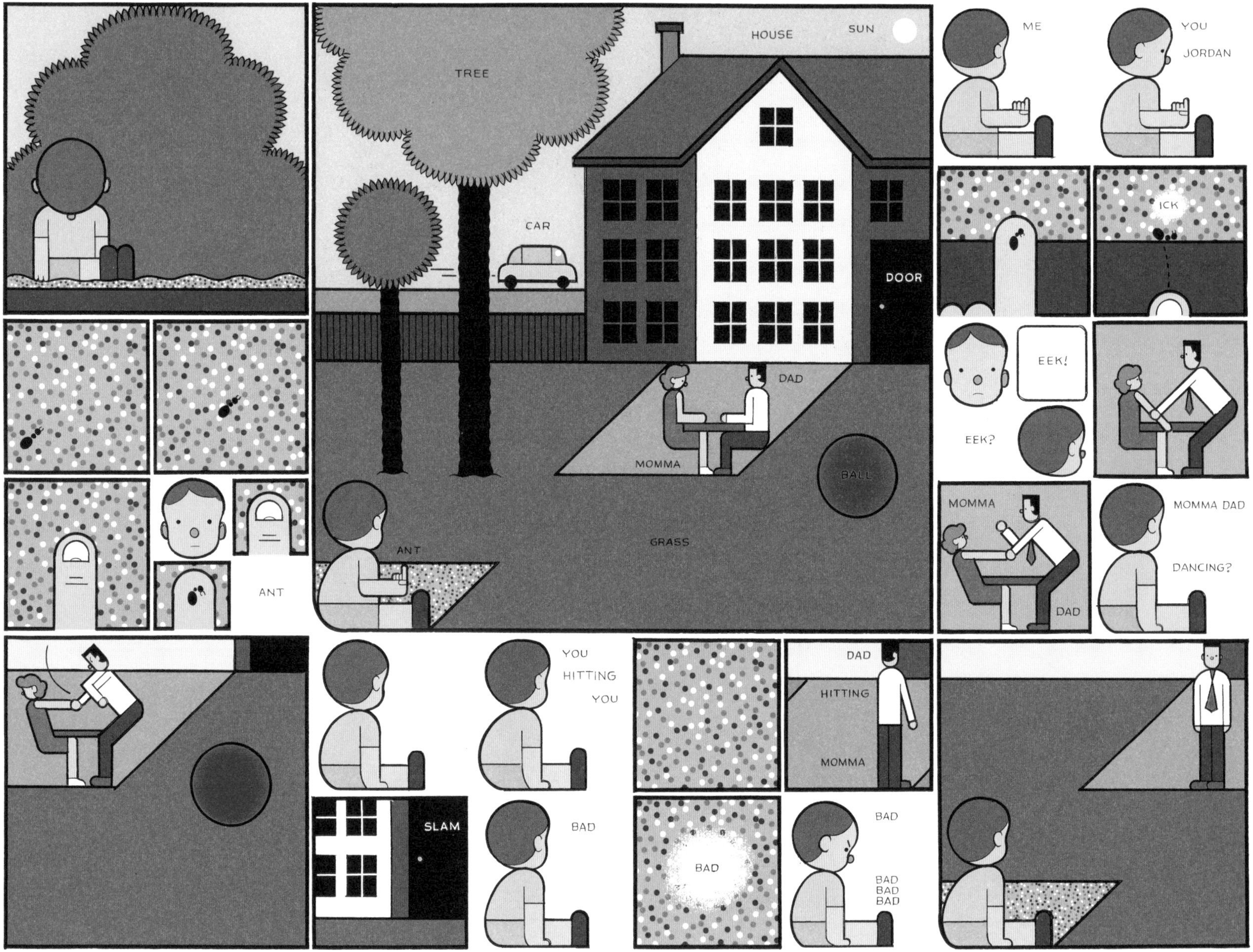
ANT
TREE
HOUSE
SUN
CAR
DOOR
DAD
MOMMA
BALL
ANT
GRASS
ME
YOU
JORDAN
ICK
EEK!
EEK?
MOMMA
DAD
MOMMA DAD
DANCING?
YOU
HITTING
YOU
SLAM
BAD
DAD
HITTING
MOMMA
BAD
BAD
BAD
BAD
BAD

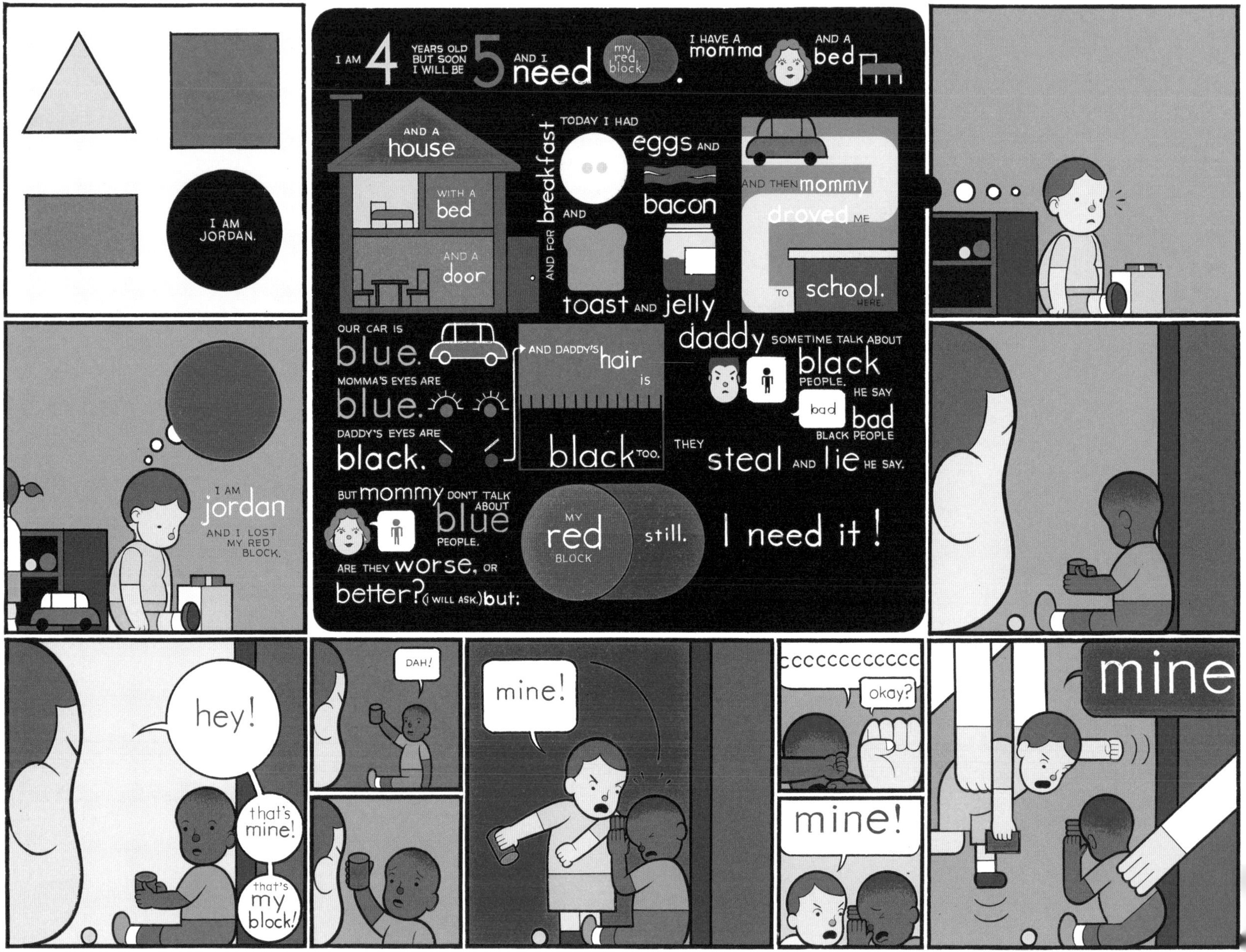

I AM JORDAN.
I AM 4 YEARS OLD BUT SOON I WILL BE 5 AND I need
my red block.
I HAVE A momma
AND A bed
AND A house
WITH A bed
AND A door
AND FOR breakfast
TODAY I HAD eggs AND bacon
AND toast AND jelly
AND THEN mommy droved ME
TO school.
HERE.
OUR CAR IS blue.
MOMMA'S EYES ARE blue.
DADDY'S EYES ARE black.
AND DADDY'S hair is black TOO.
daddy SOMETIME TALK ABOUT black PEOPLE.
HE SAY
bad
bad BLACK PEOPLE
THEY steal AND lie HE SAY.
BUT mommy DON'T TALK ABOUT blue PEOPLE.
ARE THEY worse, OR better? (I WILL ASK.) but:
MY red BLOCK
still.
I need it!
I AM jordan
AND I LOST MY RED BLOCK.
hey!
that's mine!
that's my block!
DAH!
mine!
cccccccccccc
okay?
mine!
mine

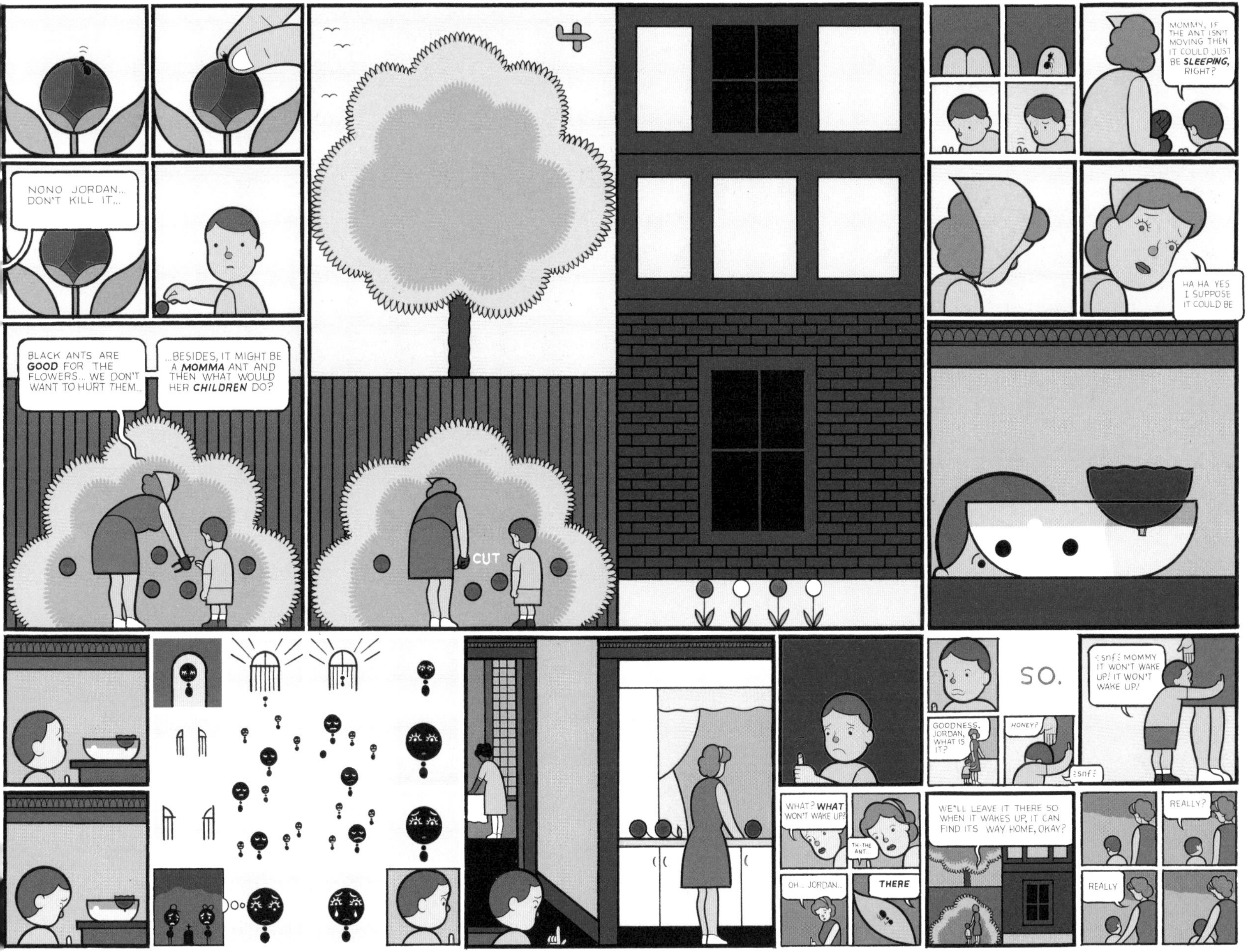

NONO JORDAN... DON'T KILL IT...
BLACK ANTS ARE **GOOD** FOR THE FLOWERS... WE DON'T WANT TO HURT THEM...
...BESIDES, IT MIGHT BE A **MOMMA** ANT AND THEN WHAT WOULD HER **CHILDREN** DO?
CUT
MOMMY, IF THE ANT ISN'T MOVING THEN IT COULD JUST BE ***SLEEPING,*** RIGHT?
HA HA YES I SUPPOSE IT COULD BE
SO.
GOODNESS, JORDAN, WHAT IS IT?
HONEY?
snf
snf MOMMY IT WON'T WAKE UP! IT WON'T WAKE UP!
WHAT? **WHAT** WON'T WAKE UP?
TH-THE ANT...
OH... JORDAN...
THERE
WE'LL LEAVE IT THERE SO WHEN IT WAKES UP, IT CAN FIND ITS WAY HOME, OKAY?
REALLY?
REALLY

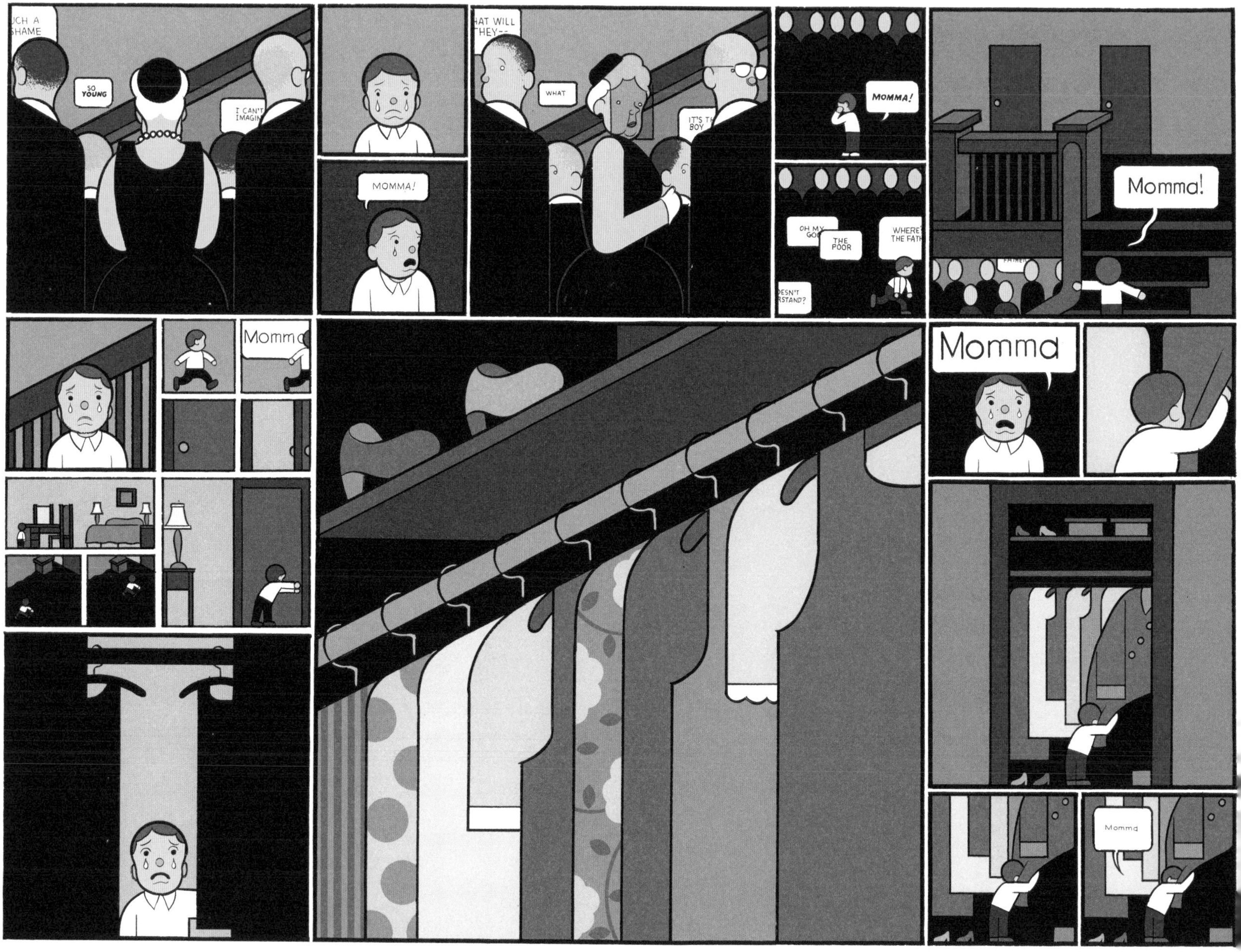

UCH A SHAME
SO YOUNG
I CAN'T IMAGIN
MOMMA!
HAT WILL THEY--
WHAT
IT'S TH BOY
MOMMA!
OH MY GO
THE POOR
WHERE'S THE FATH
ESN'T RSTAND?
Momma!
Momm
Momma
Momma

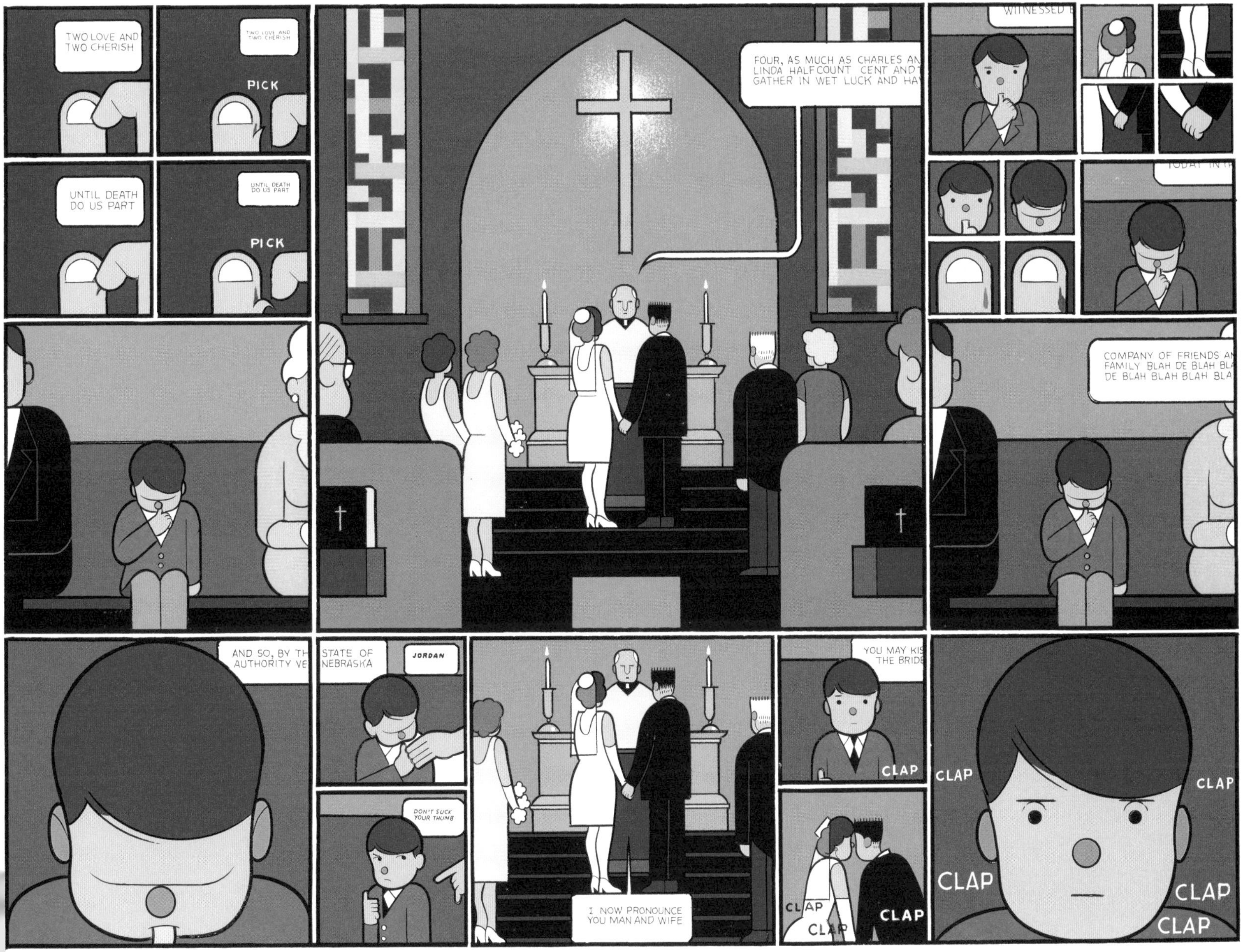

TWO LOVE AND TWO CHERISH
TWO LOVE AND TWO CHERISH
PICK
UNTIL DEATH DO US PART
UNTIL DEATH DO US PART
PICK
FOUR, AS MUCH AS CHARLES AN
LINDA HALFCOUNT CENT AND T
GATHER IN WET LUCK AND HA
WITNESSED B
TODAY IN TH
COMPANY OF FRIENDS AN
FAMILY BLAH DE BLAH BLA
DE BLAH BLAH BLAH BLA
AND SO, BY TH
AUTHORITY VE
STATE OF
NEBRASKA
JORDAN
DON'T SUCK YOUR THUMB
I NOW PRONOUNCE YOU MAN AND WIFE
YOU MAY KIS
THE BRIDE
CLAP
CLAP
CLAP
CLAP
CLAP
CLAP
CLAP
CLAP
CLAP
CLAP

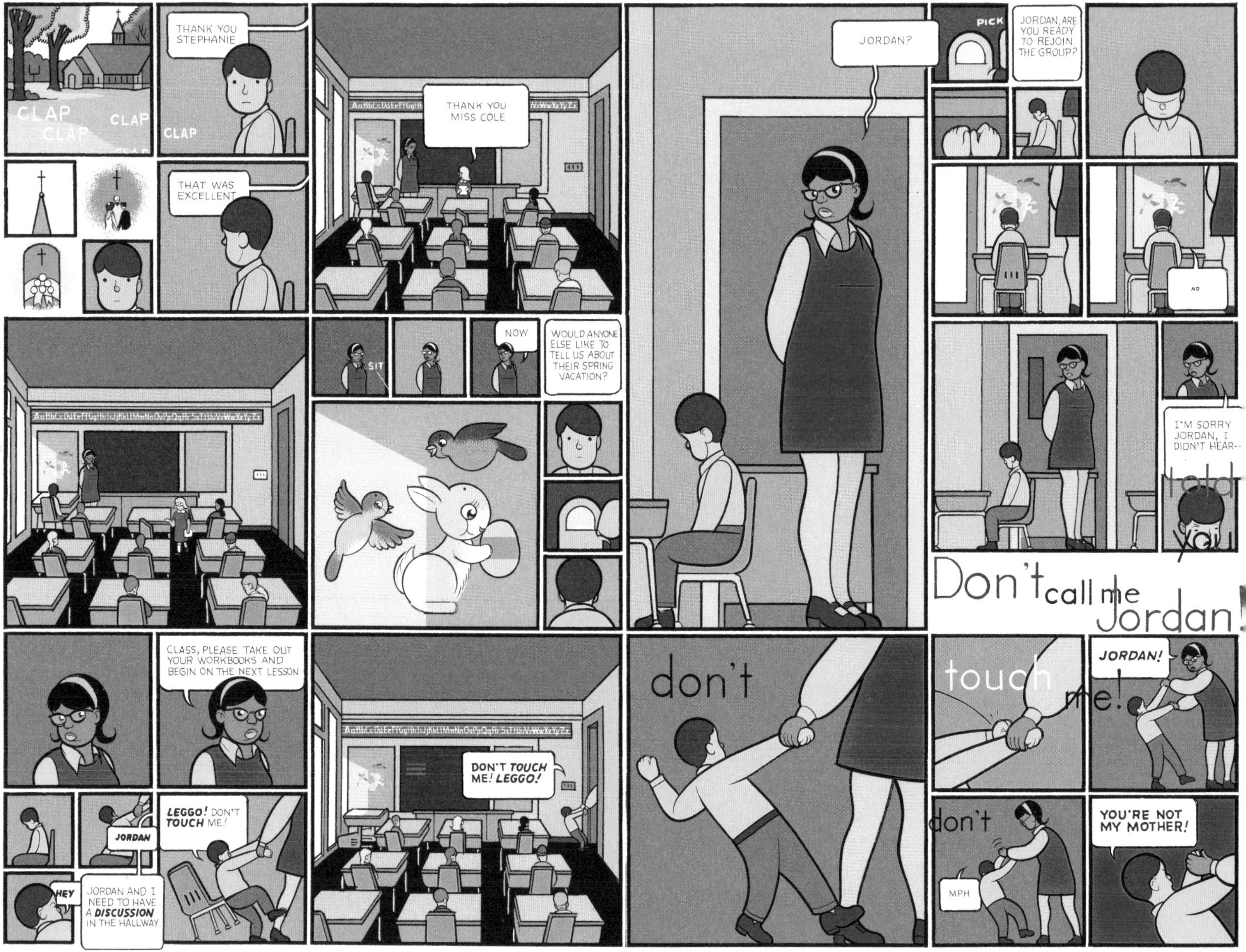

CLAP CLAP CLAP
CLAP
THANK YOU STEPHANIE
THAT WAS EXCELLENT
THANK YOU MISS COLE
SIT
NOW
WOULD ANYONE ELSE LIKE TO TELL US ABOUT THEIR SPRING VACATION?
CLASS, PLEASE TAKE OUT YOUR WORKBOOKS AND BEGIN ON THE NEXT LESSON
JORDAN
HEY
JORDAN AND I NEED TO HAVE A DISCUSSION IN THE HALLWAY
LEGGO! DON'T TOUCH ME!
DON'T TOUCH ME! LEGGO!
JORDAN?
PICK
JORDAN, ARE YOU READY TO REJOIN THE GROUP?
NO
I'M SORRY JORDAN, I DIDN'T HEAR--
told you
Don't call me Jordan!
don't
touch
me!
JORDAN!
don't
MPH
YOU'RE NOT MY MOTHER!

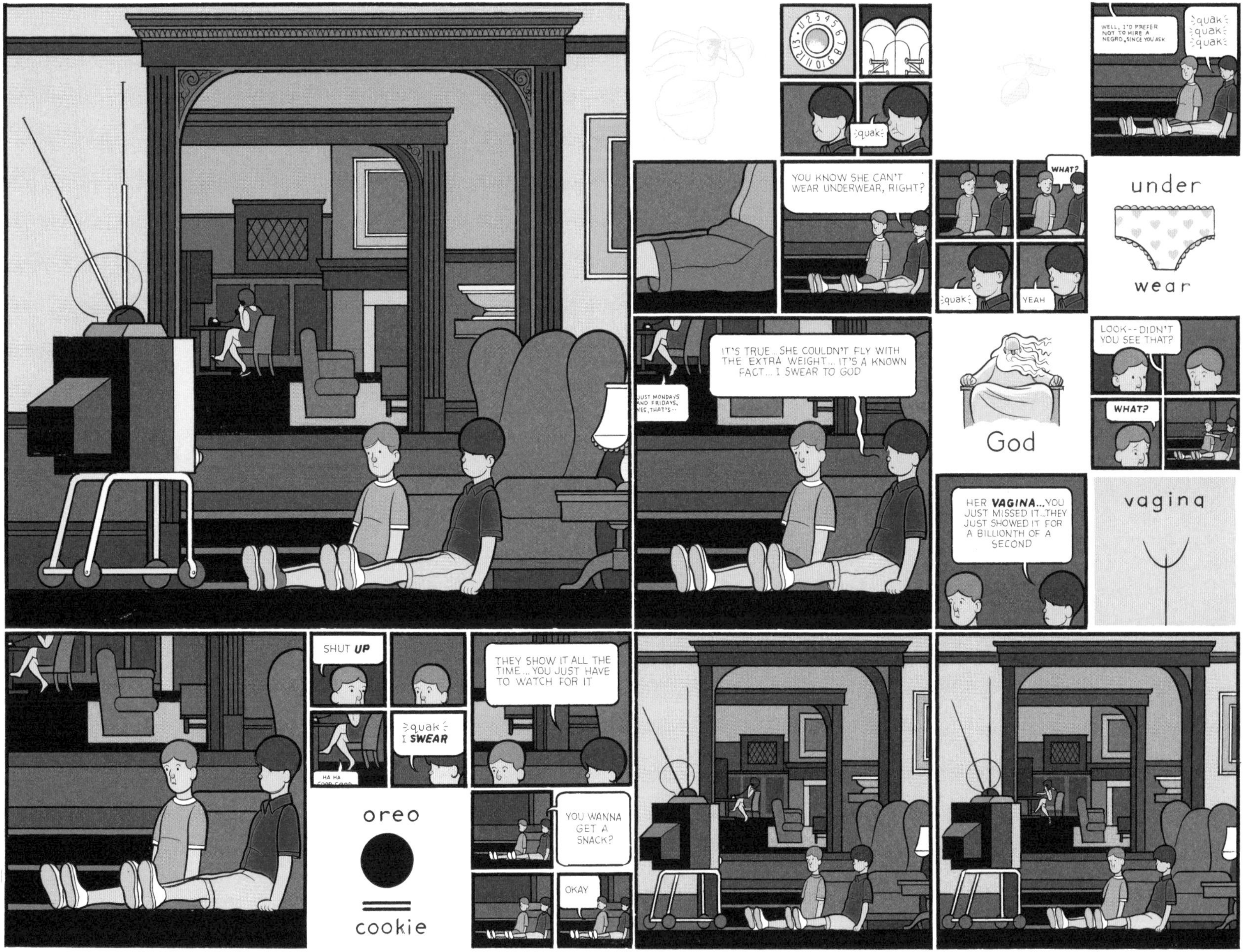
quak
WELL, I'D PREFER NOT TO HIRE A NEGRO, SINCE YOU ASK
quak quak quak
YOU KNOW SHE CAN'T WEAR UNDERWEAR, RIGHT?
quak
WHAT?
YEAH
under
wear
JUST MONDAYS AND FRIDAYS, YES, THAT'S--
IT'S TRUE... SHE COULDN'T FLY WITH THE EXTRA WEIGHT... IT'S A KNOWN FACT... I SWEAR TO GOD
God
LOOK--DIDN'T YOU SEE THAT?
WHAT?
HER VAGINA...YOU JUST MISSED IT...THEY JUST SHOWED IT FOR A BILLIONTH OF A SECOND
vagina
SHUT UP
HA HA
quak I SWEAR
THEY SHOW IT ALL THE TIME... YOU JUST HAVE TO WATCH FOR IT
oreo
cookie
YOU WANNA GET A SNACK?
OKAY

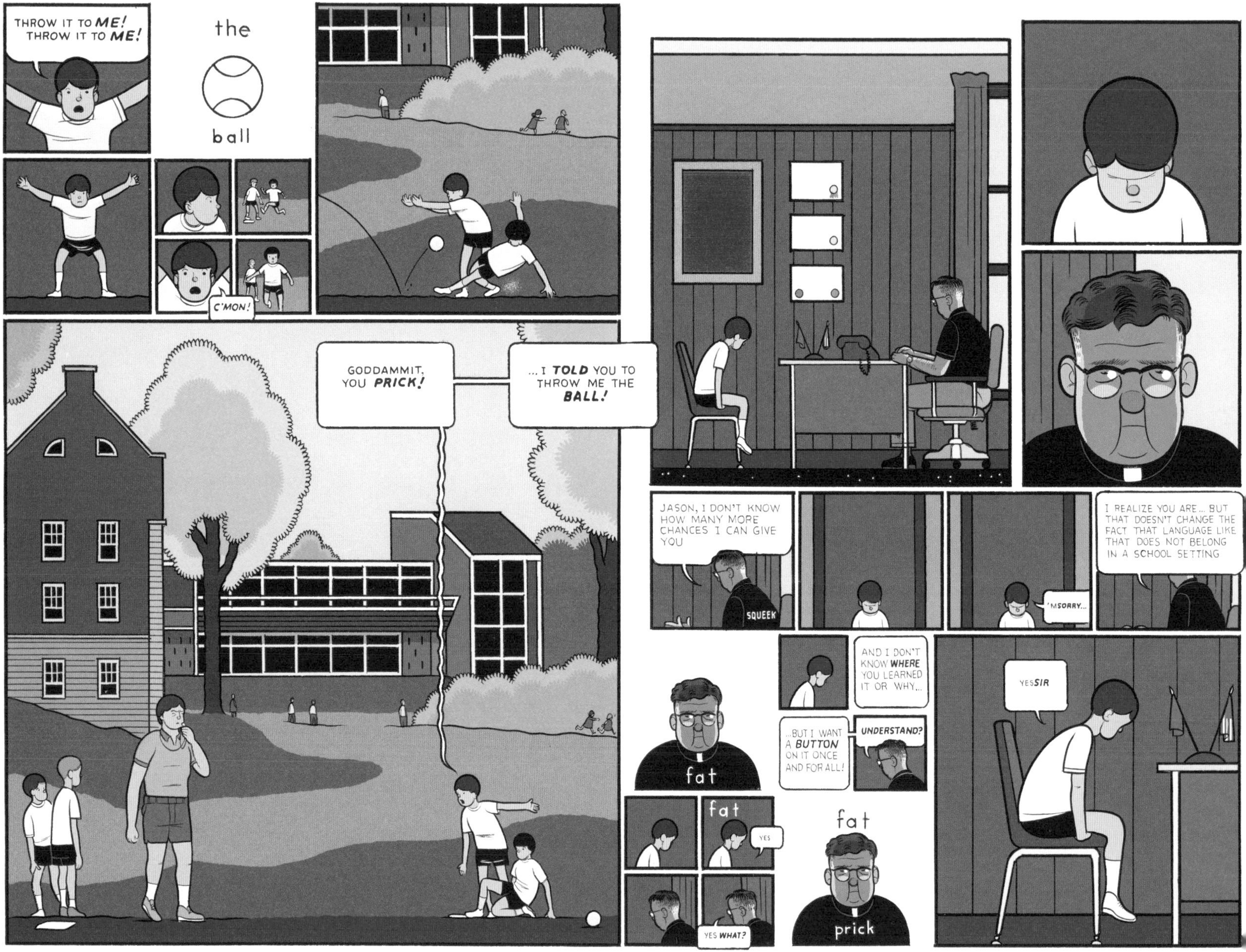
THROW IT TO ME! THROW IT TO ME!
the
ball
C'MON!
GODDAMMIT, YOU PRICK!
...I TOLD YOU TO THROW ME THE BALL!
JASON, I DON'T KNOW HOW MANY MORE CHANCES I CAN GIVE YOU
SQUEEK
'MSORRY...
I REALIZE YOU ARE... BUT THAT DOESN'T CHANGE THE FACT THAT LANGUAGE LIKE THAT DOES NOT BELONG IN A SCHOOL SETTING
AND I DON'T KNOW WHERE YOU LEARNED IT OR WHY...
...BUT I WANT A BUTTON ON IT ONCE AND FOR ALL!
UNDERSTAND?
fat
fat
YES
YES WHAT?
fat
prick
YES SIR

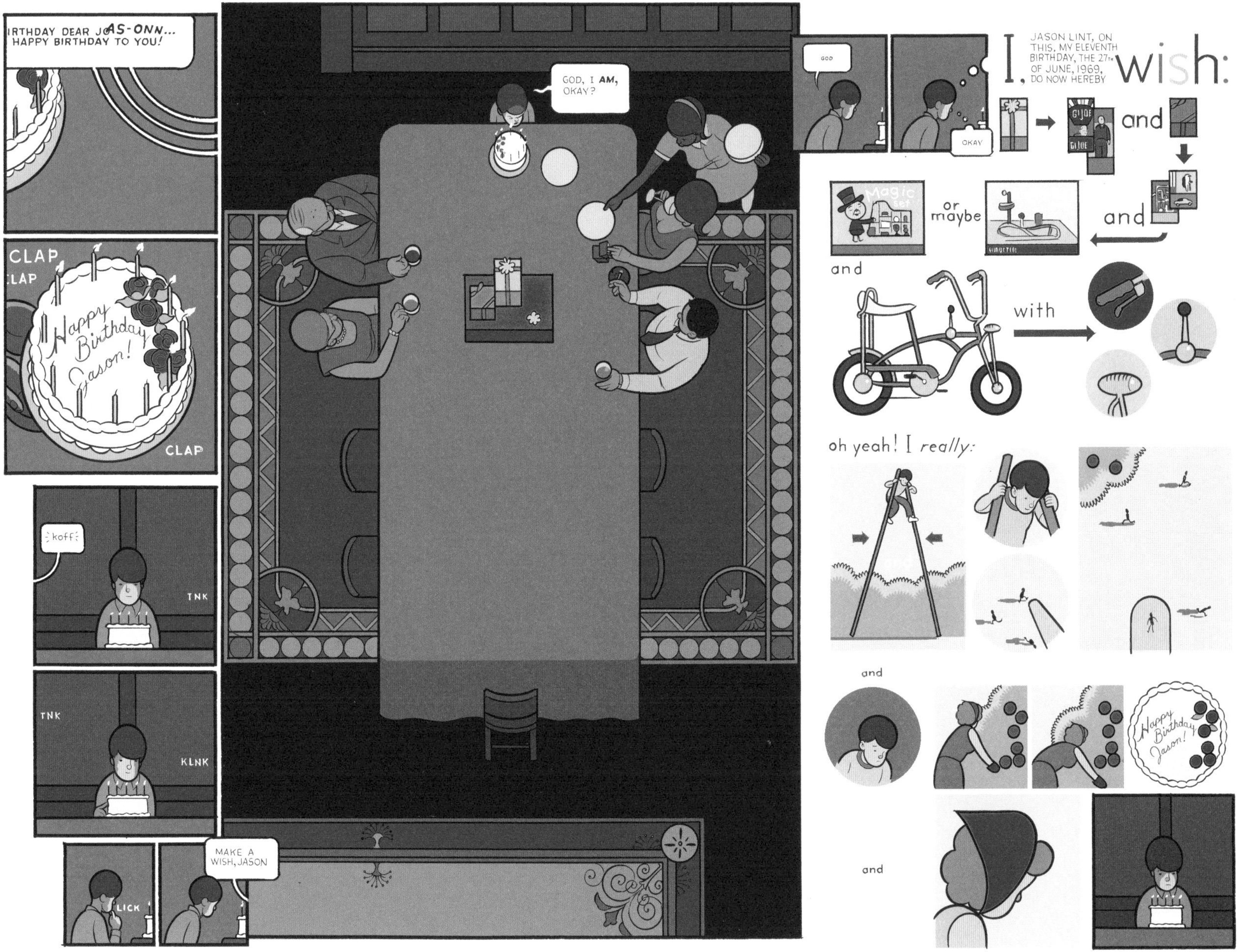

IRTHDAY DEAR JAS-ONN...
HAPPY BIRTHDAY TO YOU!
CLAP
CLAP
LAP
Happy Birthday Jason!
CLAP
koff
TNK
TNK
KLNK
LICK
MAKE A WISH, JASON
GOD, I AM, OKAY?
GOD
OKAY
I, JASON LINT, ON THIS, MY ELEVENTH BIRTHDAY, THE 27TH OF JUNE, 1969, DO NOW HEREBY wish:
and
Magic set
or maybe
and
and
with
oh yeah! I really:
and
Happy Birthday Jason!
and

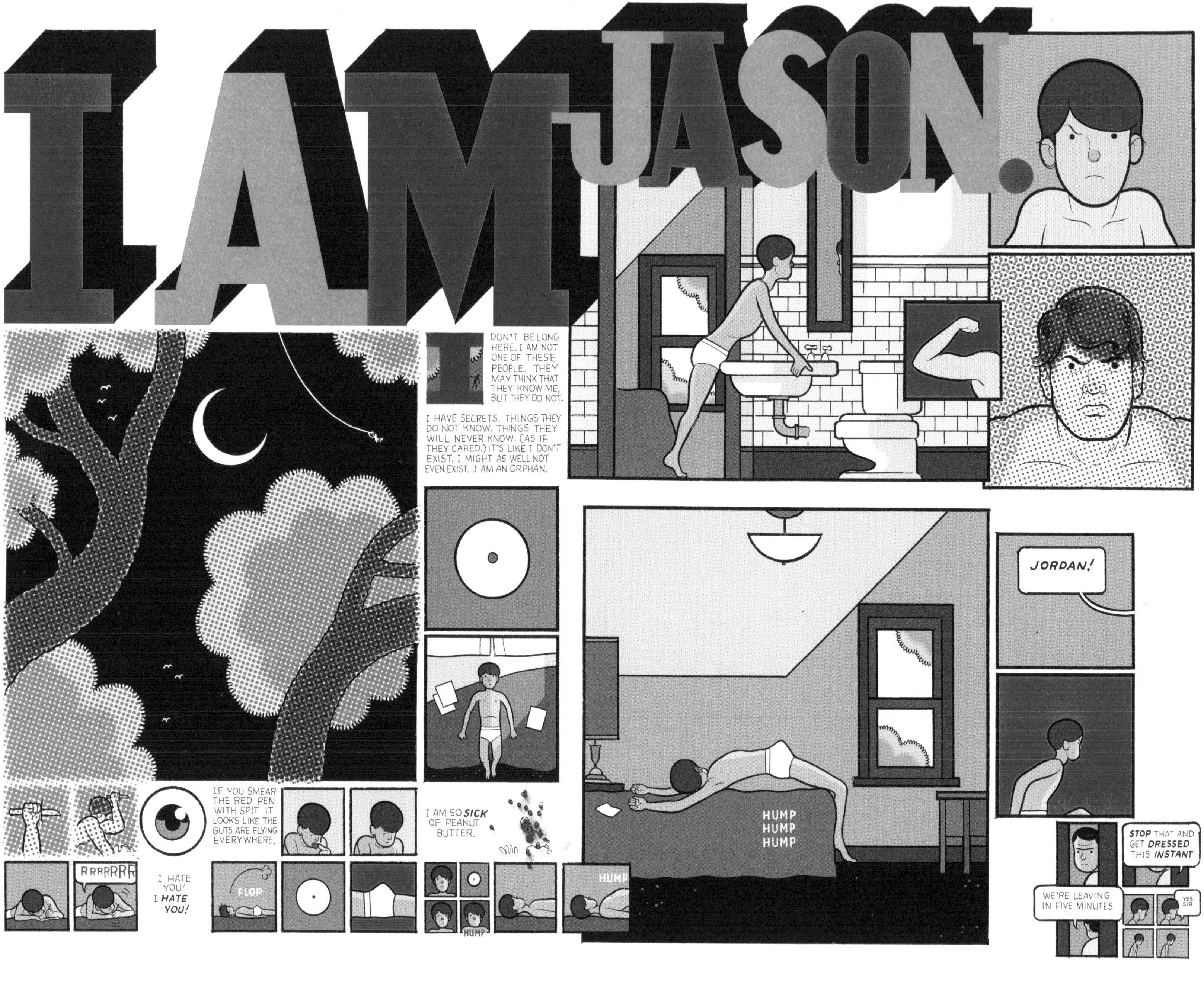
I AM JASON.
I DON'T BELONG HERE. I AM NOT ONE OF THESE PEOPLE. THEY MAY THINK THAT THEY KNOW ME, BUT THEY DO NOT.
I HAVE SECRETS. THINGS THEY DO NOT KNOW. THINGS THEY WILL NEVER KNOW. (AS IF THEY CARED.) IT'S LIKE I DON'T EXIST. I MIGHT AS WELL NOT EVEN EXIST. I AM AN ORPHAN.
IF YOU SMEAR THE RED PEN WITH SPIT IT LOOKS LIKE THE GUTS ARE FLYING EVERYWHERE.
I AM SO SICK OF PEANUT BUTTER.
RRRRRRR
I HATE YOU! I HATE YOU!
FLOP
HUMP
HUMP HUMP HUMP
HUMP
JORDAN!
STOP THAT AND GET DRESSED THIS INSTANT
WE'RE LEAVING IN FIVE MINUTES
YES SIR

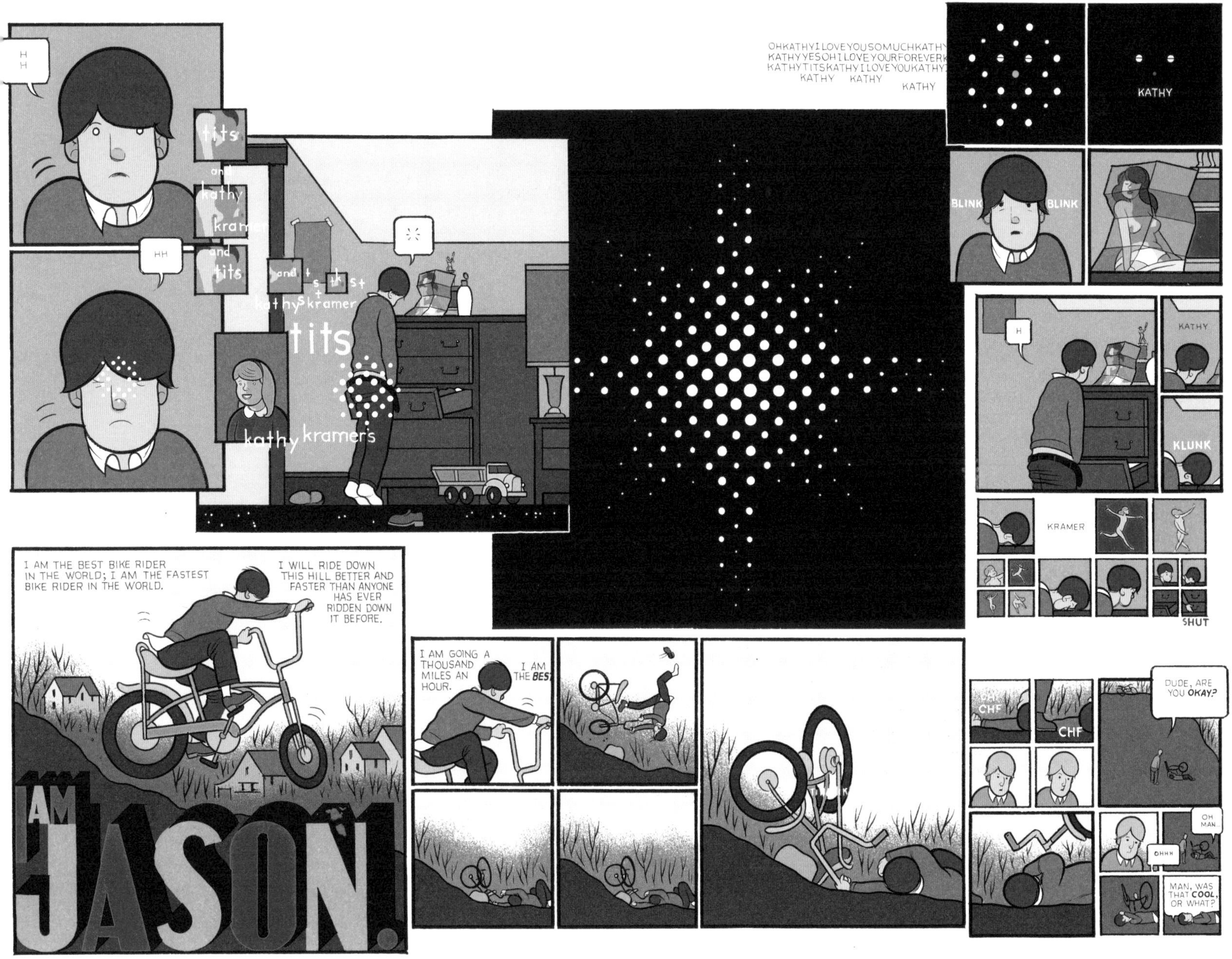
H H
tits
and
kathy
kramer
and
tits
HH
and
kathy kramer
tits
kathy kramer's
OHKATHYI LOVEYOUSOMUCHKATHY
KATHYYESOHI LOVEYOURFOREVERK
KATHYTITSKATHYI LOVEYOUKATHYI
KATHY KATHY KATHY
KATHY
BLINK
BLINK
H
KATHY
KLUNK
KRAMER
SHUT
I AM THE BEST BIKE RIDER IN THE WORLD; I AM THE FASTEST BIKE RIDER IN THE WORLD.
I WILL RIDE DOWN THIS HILL BETTER AND FASTER THAN ANYONE HAS EVER RIDDEN DOWN IT BEFORE.
I AM JASON.
I AM GOING A THOUSAND MILES AN HOUR.
I AM THE BEST
CHF
CHF
DUDE, ARE YOU OKAY?
OH MAN...
OHHH
MAN, WAS THAT COOL, OR WHAT?

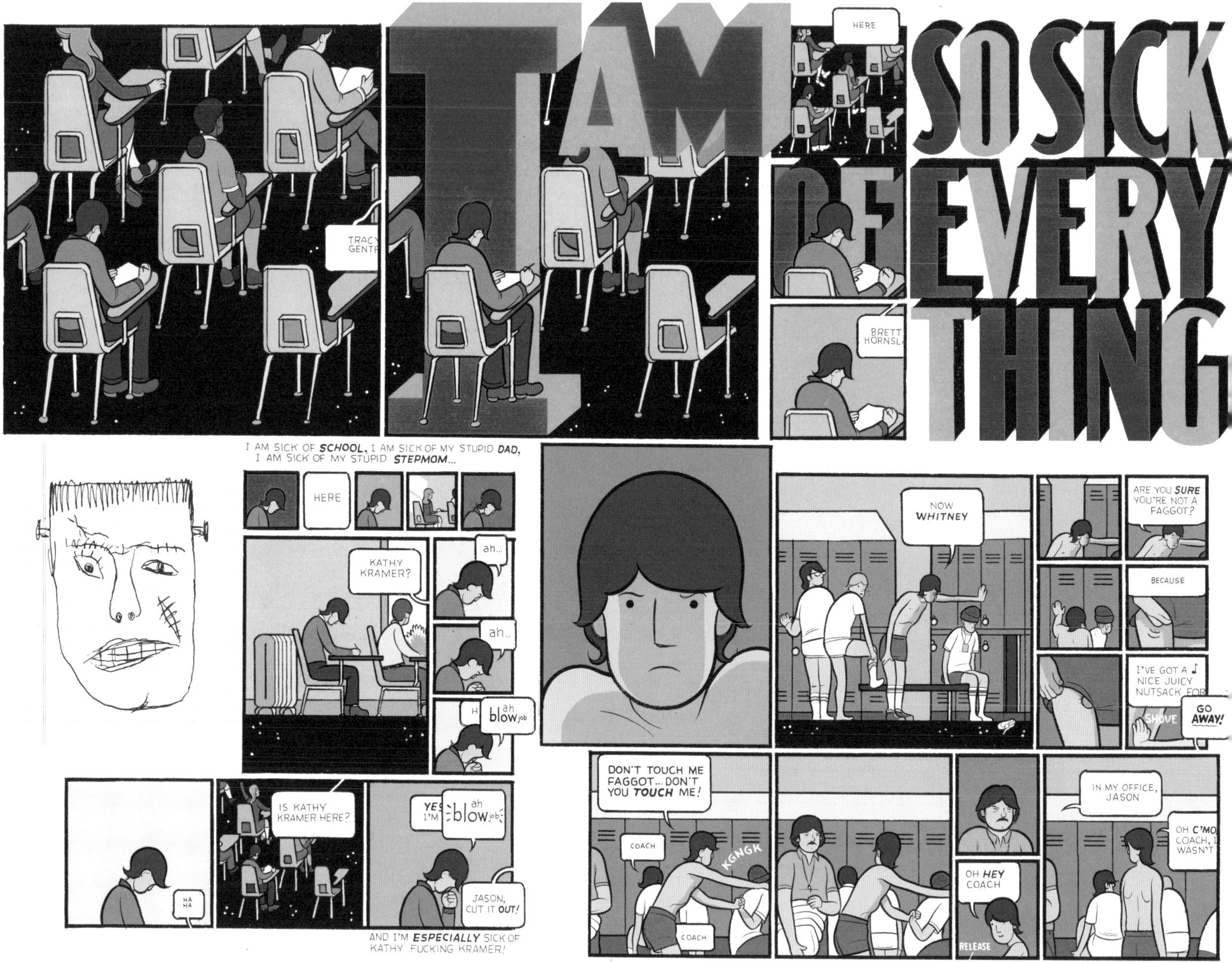
TRACY GENTR
I AM SO SICK OF EVERYTHING
HERE
BRETT HORNSL
I AM SICK OF SCHOOL, I AM SICK OF MY STUPID DAD, I AM SICK OF MY STUPID STEPMOM...
HERE
KATHY KRAMER?
ah...
ah...
ah blowjob
HA HA
IS KATHY KRAMER HERE?
YES I'M
ah blowjob
JASON, CUT IT OUT!
AND I'M ESPECIALLY SICK OF KATHY FUCKING KRAMER!
NOW WHITNEY
ARE YOU SURE YOU'RE NOT A FAGGOT?
BECAUSE
I'VE GOT A ♪ NICE JUICY NUTSACK FOR
SHOVE
GO AWAY!
DON'T TOUCH ME FAGGOT... DON'T YOU TOUCH ME!
COACH
KGNGK
COACH
OH HEY COACH
RELEASE
IN MY OFFICE, JASON
OH C'MO COACH, I WASN'T

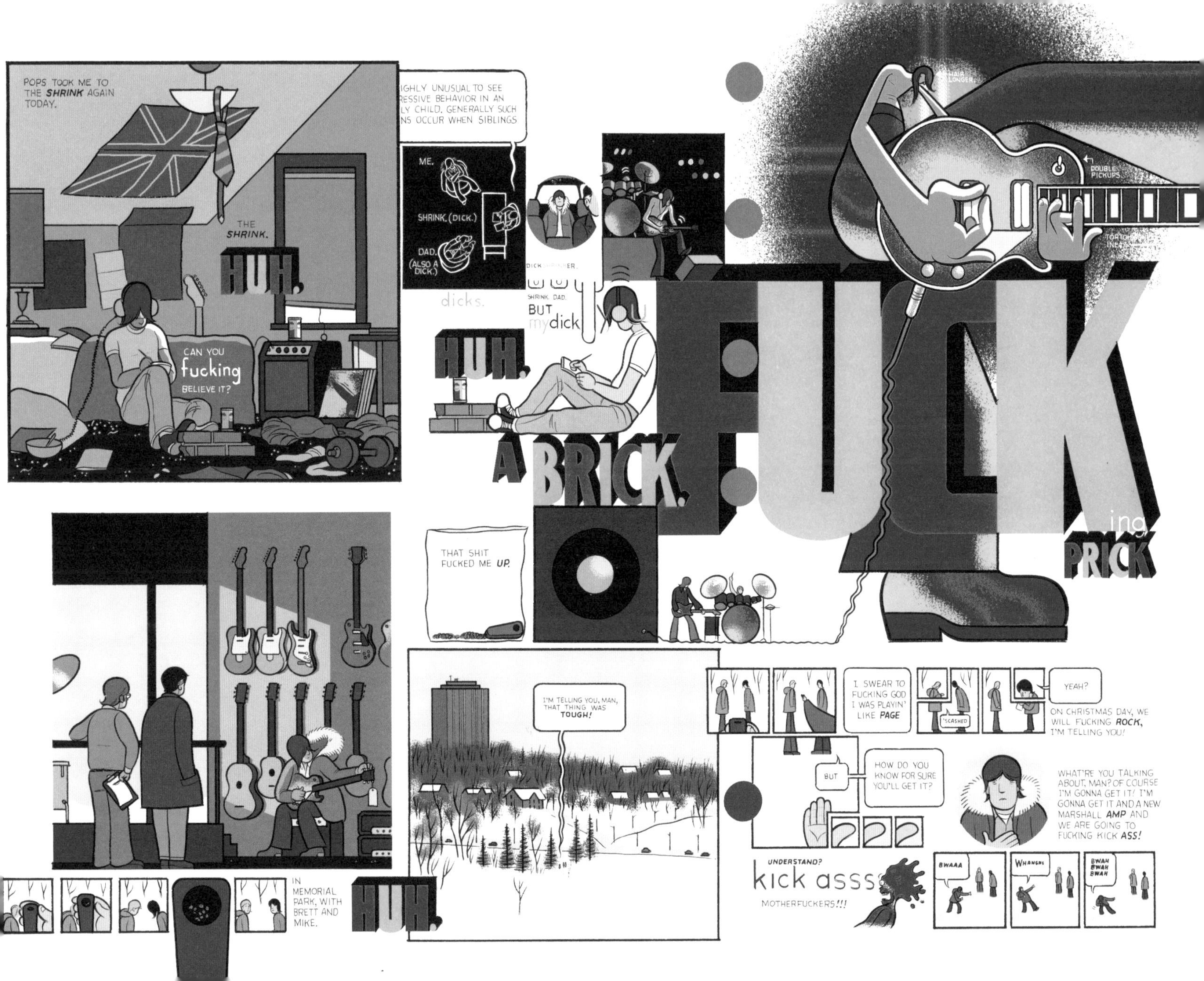

POPS TOOK ME TO THE SHRINK AGAIN TODAY.
THE SHRINK.
HUH.
CAN YOU fucking BELIEVE IT?
IGHLY UNUSUAL TO SEE RESSIVE BEHAVIOR IN AN LY CHILD. GENERALLY SUCH NS OCCUR WHEN SIBLINGS
ME.
SHRINK. (DICK.)
DAD. (ALSO A DICK.)
dicks.
SHRINK. DAD.
BUT mydick YOU
HUH.
A BRICK.
HAIR LONGER.
DOUBLE PICKUPS.
FUCK ing
PRICK
THAT SHIT FUCKED ME UP.
I'M TELLING YOU, MAN, THAT THING WAS TOUGH!
I SWEAR TO FUCKING GOD I WAS PLAYIN' LIKE PAGE
'SCASHED
YEAH?
ON CHRISTMAS DAY, WE WILL FUCKING ROCK, I'M TELLING YOU!
BUT
HOW DO YOU KNOW FOR SURE YOU'LL GET IT?
WHAT'RE YOU TALKING ABOUT, MAN? OF COURSE I'M GONNA GET IT! I'M GONNA GET IT AND A NEW MARSHALL AMP AND WE ARE GOING TO FUCKING KICK ASS!
UNDERSTAND?
kick asss
MOTHERFUCKERS!!!
BWAAA
BWAH BWAH BWAH
IN MEMORIAL PARK, WITH BRETT AND MIKE.
HUH.

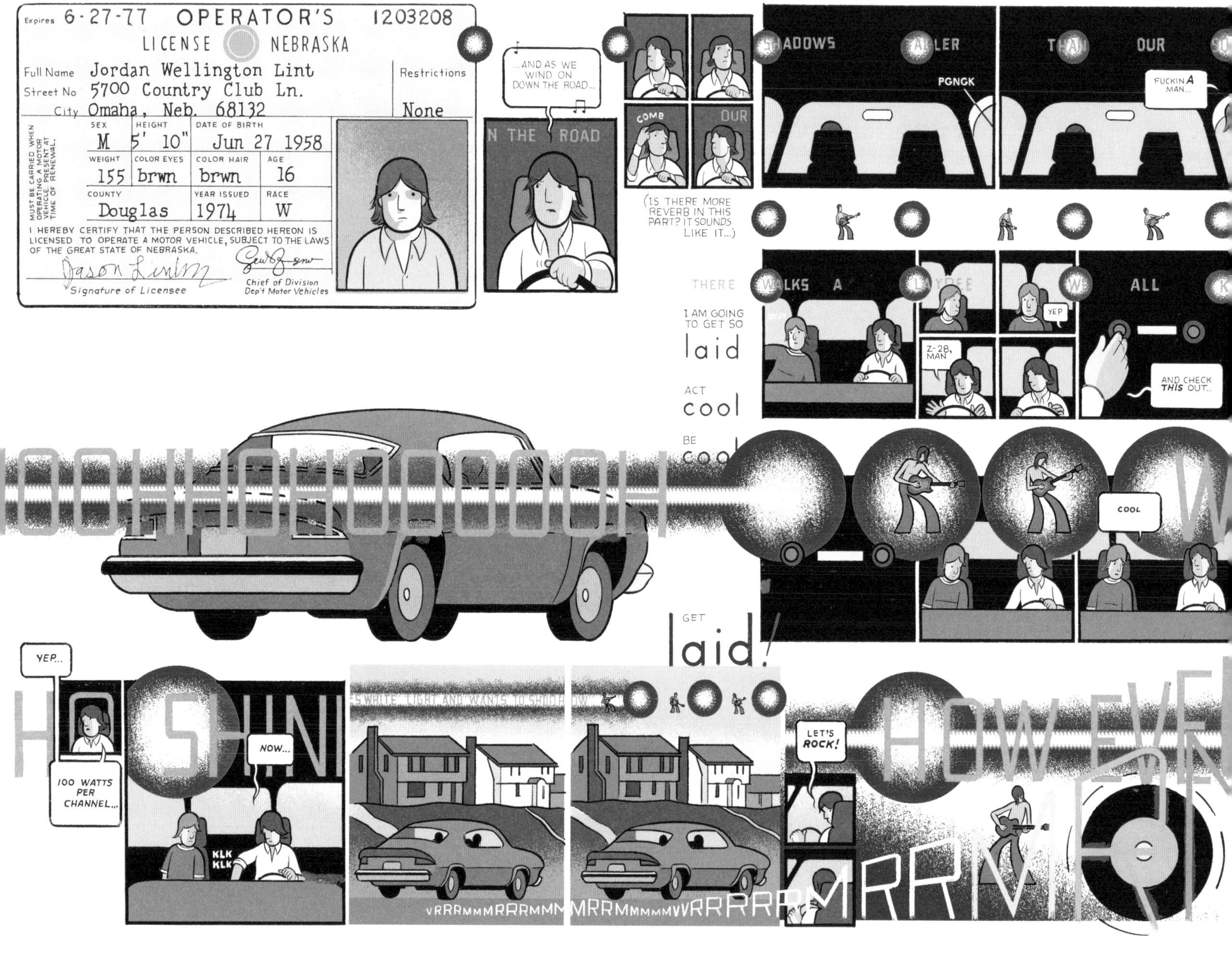
Expires 6-27-77 OPERATOR'S 1203208
LICENSE NEBRASKA
Full Name Jordan Wellington Lint
Street No 5700 Country Club Ln.
City Omaha, Neb. 68132
Restrictions None
SEX M HEIGHT 5' 10" DATE OF BIRTH Jun 27 1958
WEIGHT 155 COLOR EYES brwn COLOR HAIR brwn AGE 16
COUNTY Douglas YEAR ISSUED 1974 RACE W
MUST BE CARRIED WHEN OPERATING A MOTOR VEHICLE. PRESENT AT TIME OF RENEWAL.
I HEREBY CERTIFY THAT THE PERSON DESCRIBED HEREON IS LICENSED TO OPERATE A MOTOR VEHICLE, SUBJECT TO THE LAWS OF THE GREAT STATE OF NEBRASKA.
Signature of Licensee
Chief of Division Dep't Motor Vehicles
...AND AS WE WIND ON DOWN THE ROAD...
N THE ROAD
COMB
OUR
(IS THERE MORE REVERB IN THIS PART? IT SOUNDS LIKE IT...)
HADOWS
LLER
THAN
OUR
PGNGK
FUCKIN A MAN...
THERE
WALKS A
YEP
Z-28, MAN
ALL
AND CHECK THIS OUT...
I AM GOING TO GET SO laid
ACT cool
BE cool
COOL
GET laid!
YEP...
100 WATTS PER CHANNEL...
NOW...
KLK KLK
LET'S ROCK!
VRRRMMMRRRMMMRRRMMMMMVVRRRRR

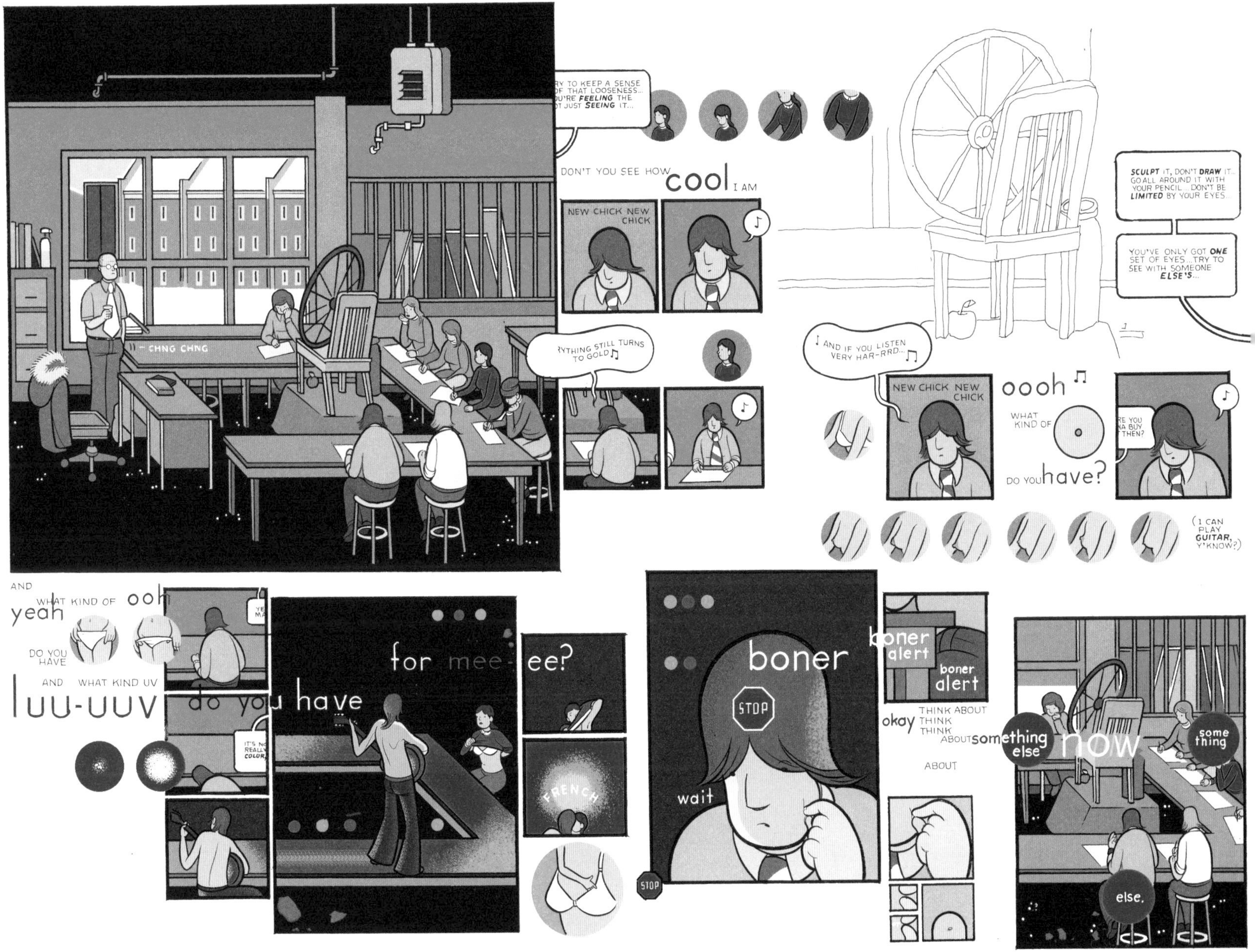
CHNG CHNG
RY TO KEEP A SENSE OF THAT LOOSENESS... OU'RE **FEELING** THE OT JUST **SEEING** IT...
DON'T YOU SEE HOW cool I AM
NEW CHICK NEW CHICK
♪
RYTHING STILL TURNS TO GOLD♫
♪
SCULPT IT, DON'T **DRAW** IT... GO ALL AROUND IT WITH YOUR PENCIL... DON'T BE **LIMITED** BY YOUR EYES...
YOU'VE ONLY GOT **ONE** SET OF EYES... TRY TO SEE WITH SOMEONE **ELSE'S**...
♩ AND IF YOU LISTEN VERY HAR-RRD...♫
NEW CHICK NEW CHICK
oooh ♫
WHAT KIND OF
DO YOU have?
♪
(I CAN PLAY **GUITAR**, Y'KNOW?)
AND
yeah WHAT KIND OF ooh
DO YOU HAVE
AND WHAT KIND UV
luu-uuv
do you have
for mee-ee?
FRENCH
boner
STOP
wait
STOP
boner alert
boner alert
okay THINK ABOUT
THINK
THINK
ABOUT something else
ABOUT
now
some thing
else.

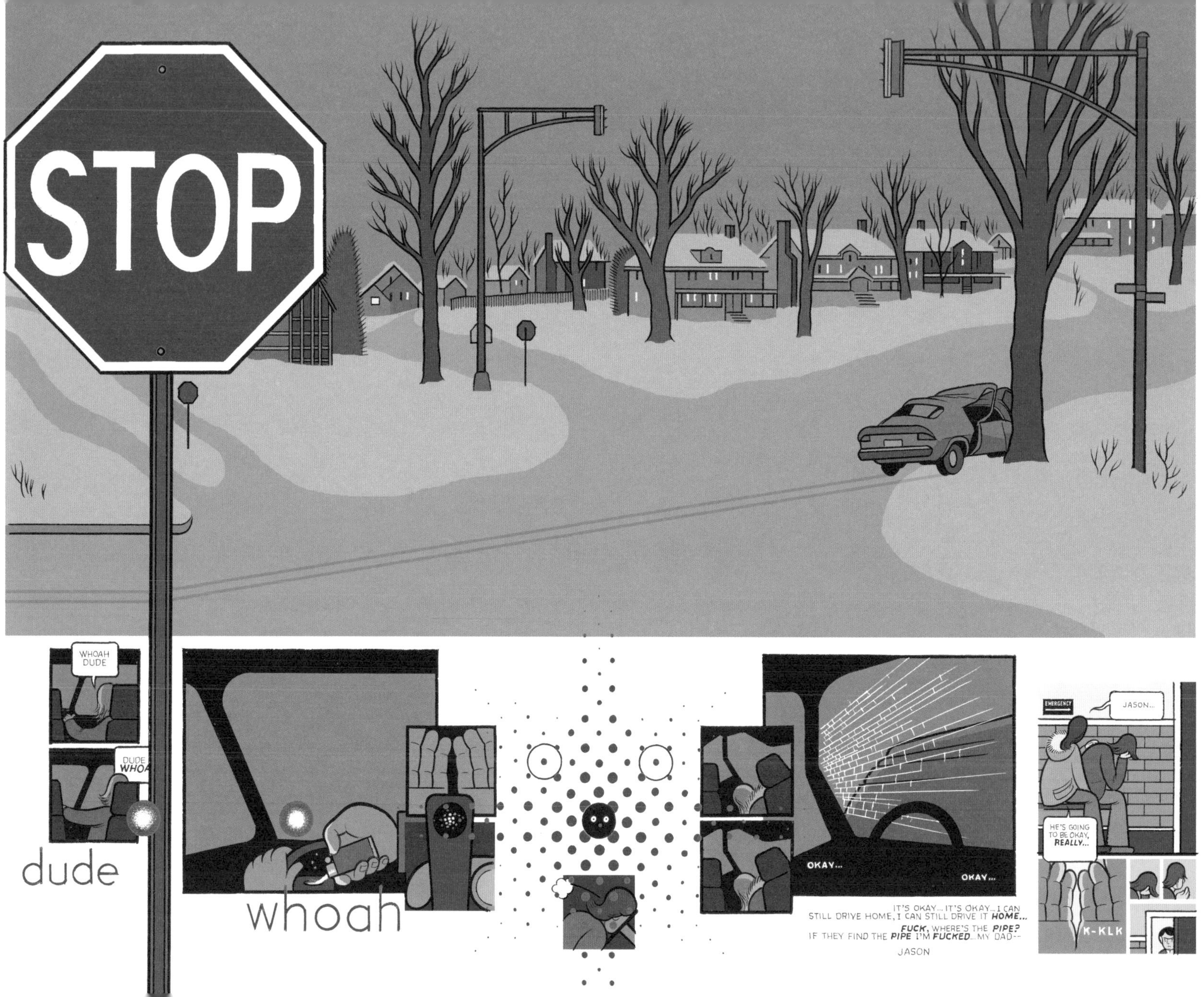

STOP
WHOAH DUDE
DUDE WHOA
dude
whoah
OKAY...
OKAY...
IT'S OKAY... IT'S OKAY... I CAN STILL DRIYE HOME, I CAN STILL DRIVE IT **HOME...**
FUCK, WHERE'S THE ***PIPE?*** IF THEY FIND THE ***PIPE*** I'M ***FUCKED***... MY DAD--
JASON
EMERGENCY
JASON...
HE'S GOING TO BE OKAY, **REALLY...**
K-KLK

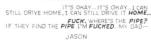

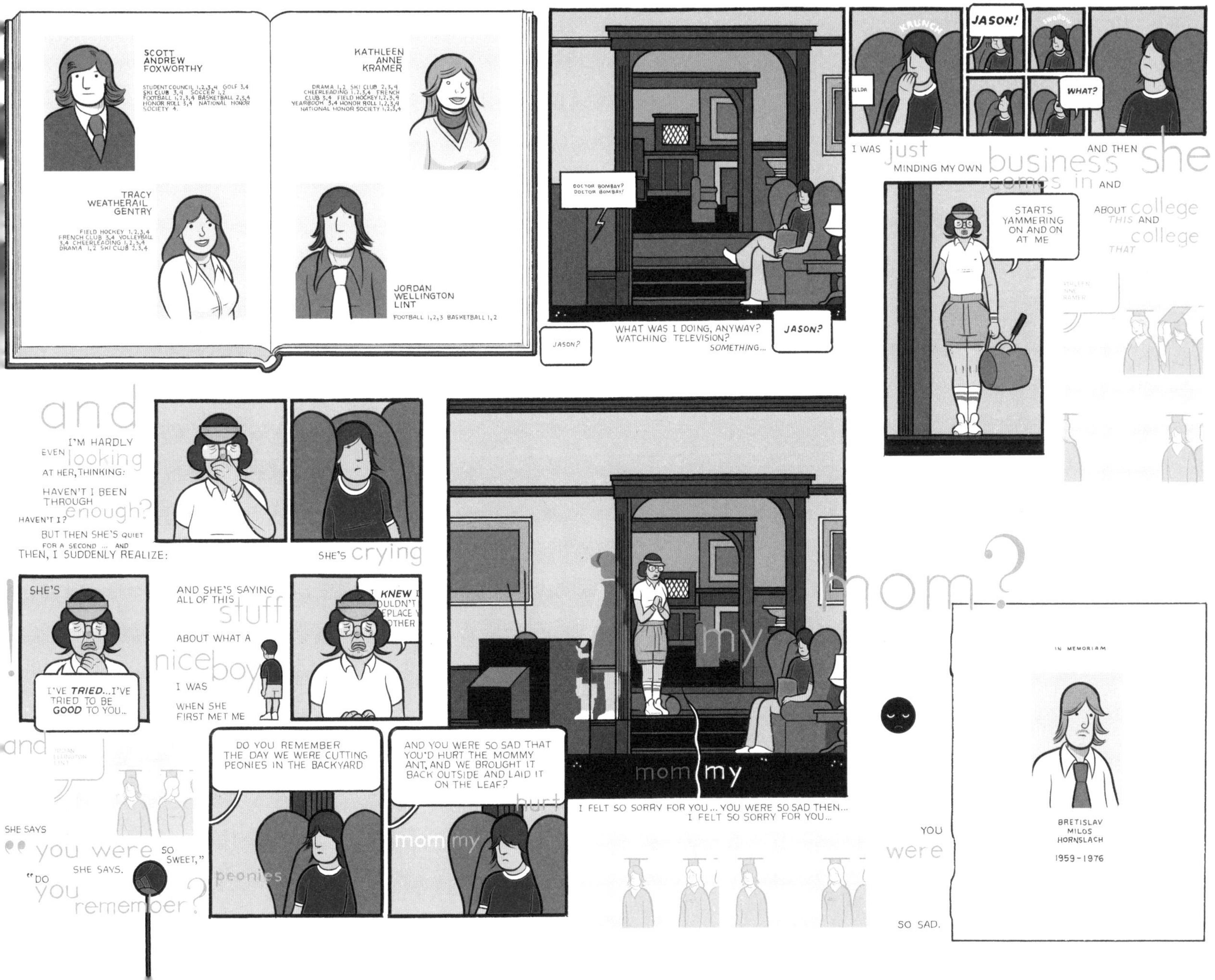

SCOTT ANDREW FOXWORTHY
STUDENT COUNCIL 1,2,3,4 GOLF 3,4 SKI CLUB 3,4 SOCCER 1,2 FOOTBALL 1,2,3,4 BASKETBALL 2,3,4 HONOR ROLL 3,4 NATIONAL HONOR SOCIETY 4
KATHLEEN ANNE KRAMER
DRAMA 1,2 SKI CLUB 2,3,4 CHEERLEADING 1,2,3,4 FRENCH CLUB 3,4 FIELD HOCKEY 1,2,3,4 YEARBOOK 3,4 HONOR ROLL 1,2,3,4 NATIONAL HONOR SOCIETY 1,2,3,4
TRACY WEATHERAIL GENTRY
FIELD HOCKEY 1,2,3,4 FRENCH CLUB 3,4 VOLLEYBALL 3,4 CHEERLEADING 1,2,3,4 DRAMA 1,2 SKI CLUB 2,3,4
JORDAN WELLINGTON LINT
FOOTBALL 1,2,3 BASKETBALL 1,2
DOCTOR BOMBAY? DOCTOR BOMBAY!
JASON?
WHAT WAS I DOING, ANYWAY? WATCHING TELEVISION? SOMETHING...
JASON?
KRUNCH
JASON!
swallow
WHAT?
I WAS just MINDING MY OWN business AND THEN she comes in AND
STARTS YAMMERING ON AND ON AT ME
ABOUT college THIS AND college THAT
and EVEN I'M HARDLY looking AT HER, THINKING:
HAVEN'T I BEEN THROUGH enough? HAVEN'T I?
BUT THEN SHE'S QUIET FOR A SECOND ... AND THEN, I SUDDENLY REALIZE:
SHE'S crying
SHE'S
I'VE TRIED...I'VE TRIED TO BE GOOD TO YOU...
AND SHE'S SAYING ALL OF THIS stuff ABOUT WHAT A nice boy I WAS WHEN SHE FIRST MET ME
I KNEW I ...OULDN'T ...EPLACE Y... ...OTHER
mom?
my
mom my
I FELT SO SORRY FOR YOU... YOU WERE SO SAD THEN... I FELT SO SORRY FOR YOU...
and
SHE SAYS "you were SO SWEET," SHE SAYS. "DO you remember?
DO YOU REMEMBER THE DAY WE WERE CUTTING PEONIES IN THE BACKYARD
peonies
AND YOU WERE SO SAD THAT YOU'D HURT THE MOMMY ANT, AND WE BROUGHT IT BACK OUTSIDE AND LAID IT ON THE LEAF?
hurt
mom my
YOU were SO SAD.
IN MEMORIAM
BRETISLAV MILOS HORNSLACH
1959-1976

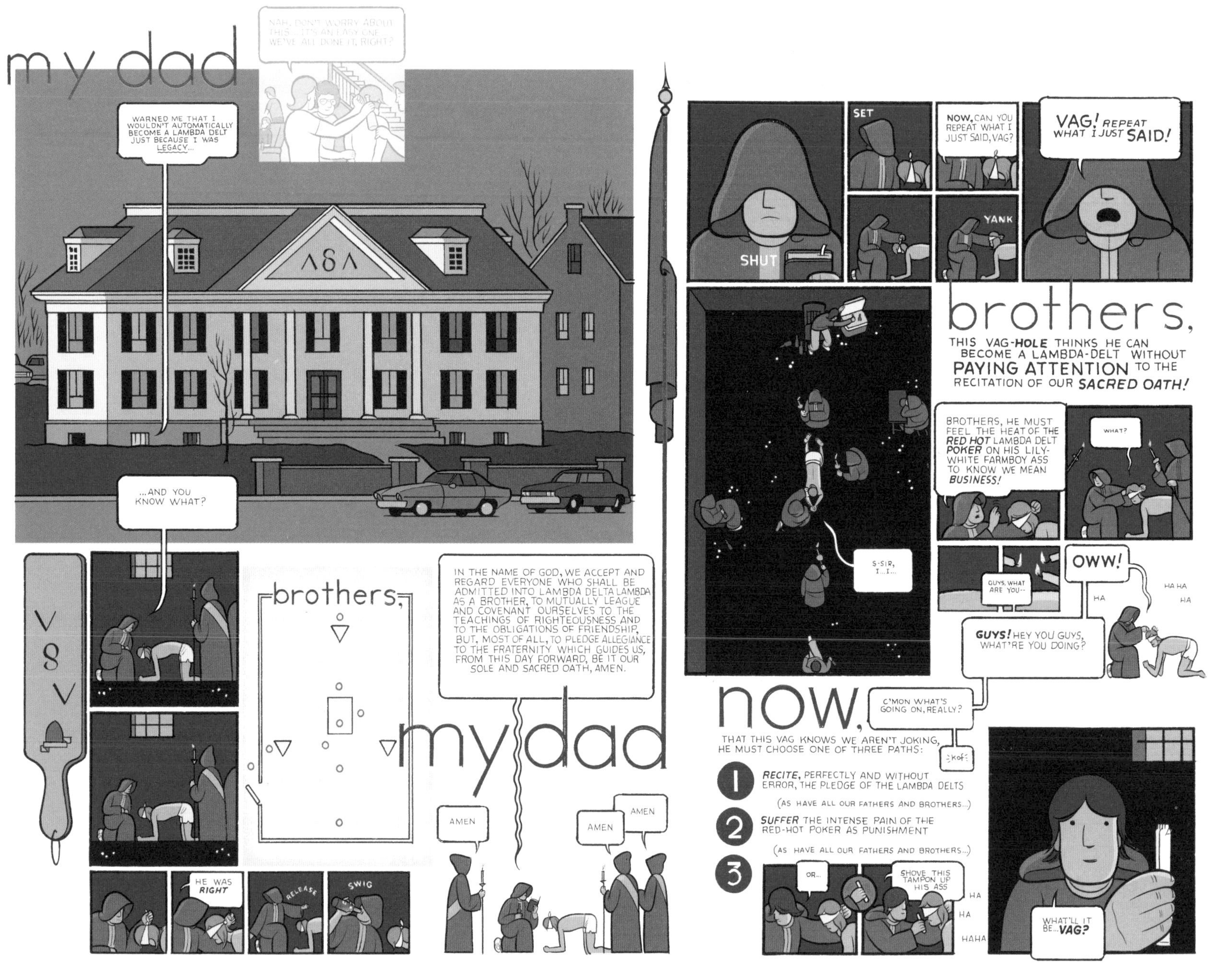

my dad
NAH, DON'T WORRY ABOUT THIS... IT'S AN EASY ONE... WE'VE ALL DONE IT, RIGHT?
WARNED ME THAT I WOULDN'T AUTOMATICALLY BECOME A LAMBDA DELT JUST BECAUSE I WAS LEGACY...
ΛδΛ
...AND YOU KNOW WHAT?
ΛδΛ
HE WAS RIGHT
RELEASE
SWIG
brothers,
IN THE NAME OF GOD, WE ACCEPT AND REGARD EVERYONE WHO SHALL BE ADMITTED INTO LAMBDA DELTA LAMBDA AS A BROTHER, TO MUTUALLY LEAGUE AND COVENANT OURSELVES TO THE TEACHINGS OF RIGHTEOUSNESS AND TO THE OBLIGATIONS OF FRIENDSHIP, BUT, MOST OF ALL, TO PLEDGE ALLEGIANCE TO THE FRATERNITY WHICH GUIDES US, FROM THIS DAY FORWARD, BE IT OUR SOLE AND SACRED OATH, AMEN.
my dad
AMEN
AMEN
AMEN
SHUT
SET
NOW, CAN YOU REPEAT WHAT I JUST SAID, VAG?
YANK
VAG! REPEAT WHAT I JUST SAID!
S-SIR, I...I...
brothers,
THIS VAG-HOLE THINKS HE CAN BECOME A LAMBDA-DELT WITHOUT PAYING ATTENTION TO THE RECITATION OF OUR SACRED OATH!
BROTHERS, HE MUST FEEL THE HEAT OF THE RED HOT LAMBDA DELT POKER ON HIS LILY-WHITE FARMBOY ASS TO KNOW WE MEAN BUSINESS!
WHAT?
GUYS, WHAT ARE YOU--
OWW!
HA
HA HA
HA
GUYS! HEY YOU GUYS, WHAT'RE YOU DOING?
now,
C'MON WHAT'S GOING ON, REALLY?
THAT THIS VAG KNOWS WE AREN'T JOKING, HE MUST CHOOSE ONE OF THREE PATHS:
KOF
1 RECITE, PERFECTLY AND WITHOUT ERROR, THE PLEDGE OF THE LAMBDA DELTS
(AS HAVE ALL OUR FATHERS AND BROTHERS...)
2 SUFFER THE INTENSE PAIN OF THE RED-HOT POKER AS PUNISHMENT
(AS HAVE ALL OUR FATHERS AND BROTHERS...)
3
OR...
SHOVE THIS TAMPON UP HIS ASS
HA
HA
HAHA
WHAT'LL IT BE...VAG?

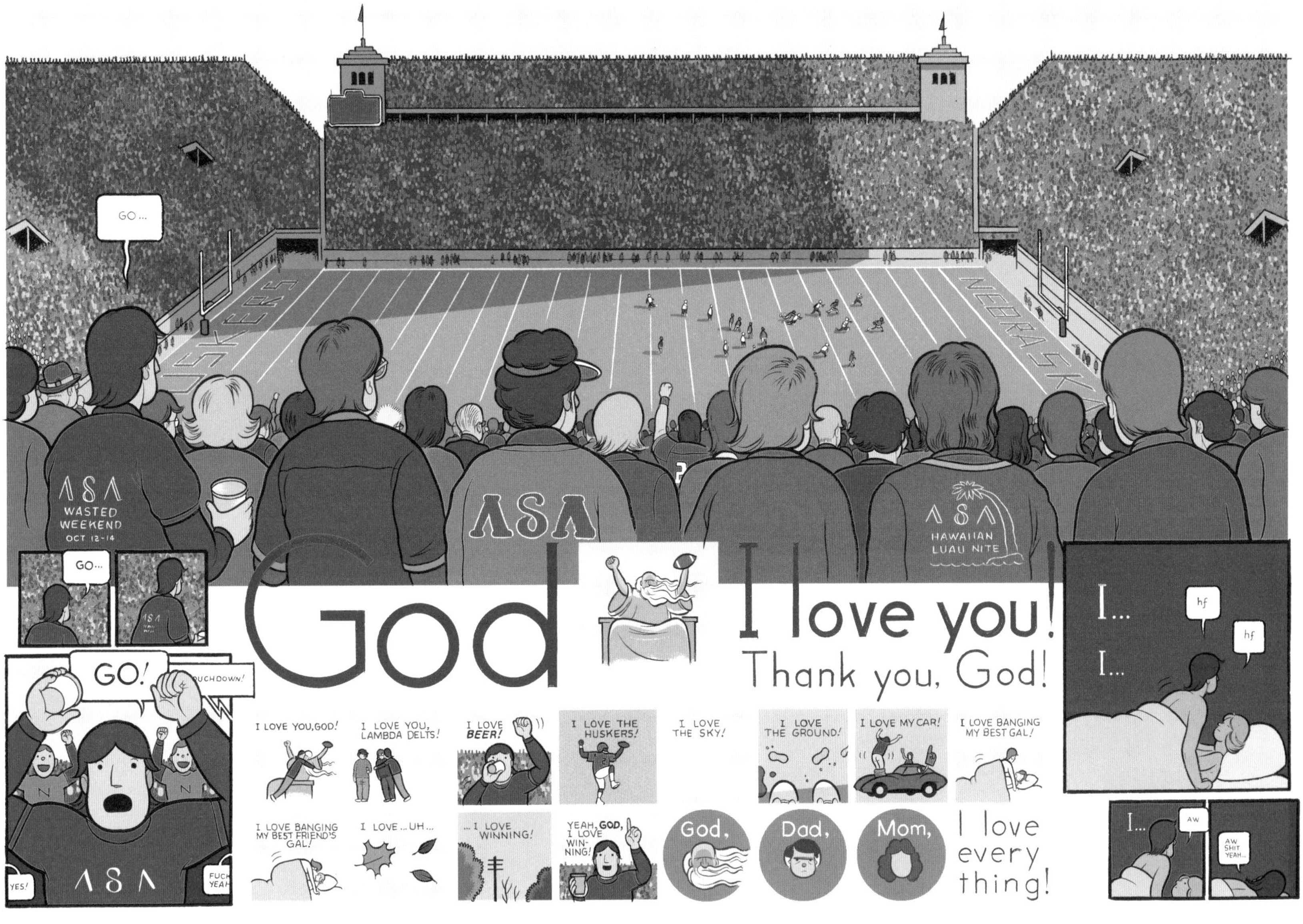
GO...
ΛΔΛ
WASTED
WEEKEND
OCT 12-14
ΛΔΛ
ΛΔΛ
HAWAIIAN
LUAU NITE
GO...
GO!
OUCHDOWN!
YES!
ΛΔΛ
FUCK
YEAH
God
I love you!
Thank you, God!
I...
hf
I...
hf
I LOVE YOU, GOD!
I LOVE YOU, LAMBDA DELTS!
I LOVE BEER!
I LOVE THE HUSKERS!
I LOVE THE SKY!
I LOVE THE GROUND!
I LOVE MY CAR!
I LOVE BANGING MY BEST GAL!
I LOVE BANGING MY BEST FRIEND'S GAL!
I LOVE... UH...
...I LOVE WINNING!
YEAH, GOD, I LOVE WIN-NING!
God,
Dad,
Mom,
I love every thing!
I...
AW
AW SHIT YEAH...

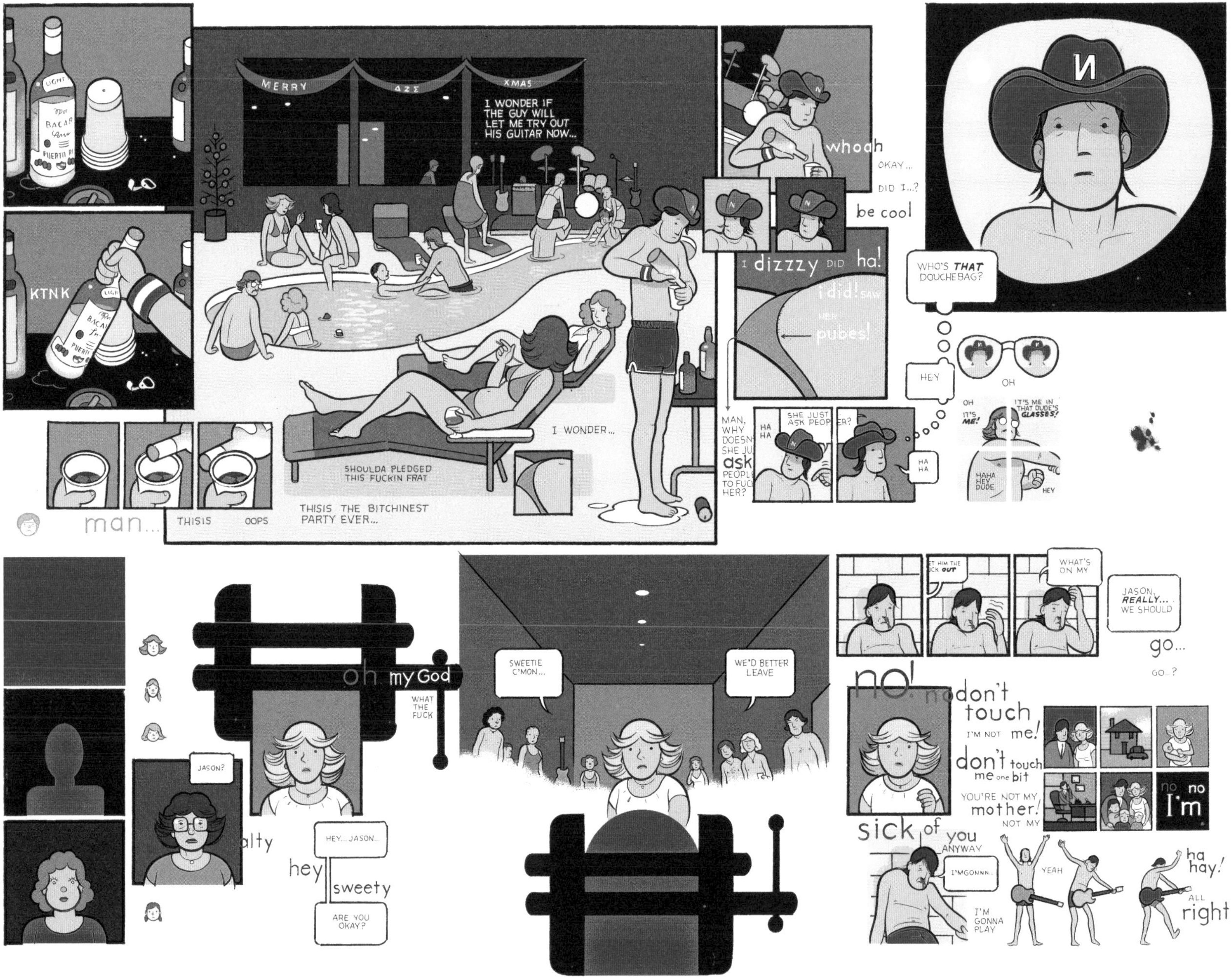

KTNK
MERRY
ΔΖΣ
XMAS
I WONDER IF THE GUY WILL LET ME TRY OUT HIS GUITAR NOW...
SHOULDA PLEDGED THIS FUCKIN FRAT
I WONDER...
THISIS THE BITCHINEST PARTY EVER...
man...
THISIS
OOPS
whoah
OKAY...
DID I...?
be cool
I dizzzy DID ha!
i did! SAW HER pubes!
MAN, WHY DOESN'T SHE JUST ask PEOPLE TO FUCK HER?
HA HA
SHE JUST ASK PEOPLE ...ER?
HA HA
WHO'S THAT DOUCHEBAG?
HEY
OH
OH IT'S ME!
IT'S ME IN THAT DUDE'S GLASSES!
HAHA HEY DUDE
HEY
oh my God
WHAT THE FUCK
JASON?
alty
HEY... JASON...
hey
sweety
ARE YOU OKAY?
SWEETIE C'MON...
WE'D BETTER LEAVE
...ET HIM THE ...CK OUT
WHAT'S ON MY
JASON, REALLY... WE SHOULD
go...
GO...?
no! no don't touch
I'M NOT me!
don't touch me one bit
YOU'RE NOT MY mother!
NOT MY
no no I'm
sick of you
ANYWAY
I'MGONNN...
I'M GONNA PLAY
YEAH
ha hay!
ALL right

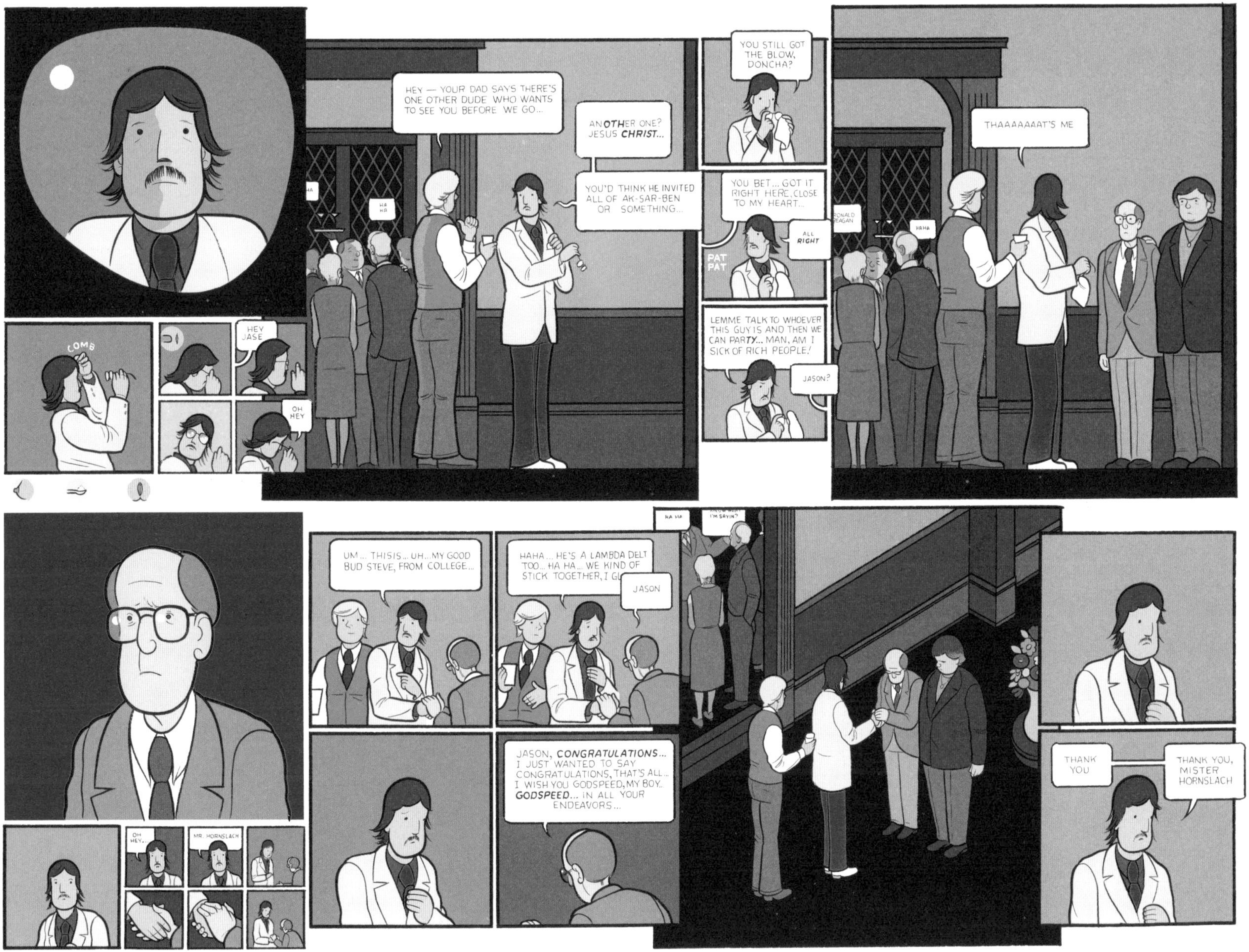
COMB
HEY JASE
OH HEY
HEY — YOUR DAD SAYS THERE'S ONE OTHER DUDE WHO WANTS TO SEE YOU BEFORE WE GO...
HA
HA HA
ANOTHER ONE? JESUS CHRIST...
YOU'D THINK HE INVITED ALL OF AK-SAR-BEN OR SOMETHING...
YOU STILL GOT THE BLOW, DONCHA?
YOU BET... GOT IT RIGHT HERE, CLOSE TO MY HEART...
PAT PAT
ALL RIGHT
LEMME TALK TO WHOEVER THIS GUY IS AND THEN WE CAN PARTY... MAN, AM I SICK OF RICH PEOPLE!
JASON?
RONALD REAGAN
HAHA
THAAAAAAAT'S ME
OH HEY...
MR. HORNSLACH
UM... THIS IS... UH... MY GOOD BUD STEVE, FROM COLLEGE...
HAHA... HE'S A LAMBDA DELT TOO... HA HA... WE KIND OF STICK TOGETHER, I GU
JASON
JASON, CONGRATULATIONS... I JUST WANTED TO SAY CONGRATULATIONS, THAT'S ALL... I WISH YOU GODSPEED, MY BOY... GODSPEED... IN ALL YOUR ENDEAVORS...
HA HA
I'M SAYIN?
THANK YOU
THANK YOU, MISTER HORNSLACH

hh hh hh
OH MAN OH YEAH OH YEAH
OH MAN YOU'RE GONNA MAKE ME CUM AGAIN, BABE
OH YEAH
OH SHIT
oh
YEAH
OH FUCK
OH
OH
oh God
ARE YOU HAPPY WITH THAT OR D'YOU WANNA PUNCH IT IN AGAIN?
OH MAN...
OH MAN THEY SHOULD LEAVE IT... I THINK IT FUCKING ROCKED
okay WELL ex cuuse me dude... then, fuck you, okay? fuck you
Y'KNOW I'm THE GUY PAYING YOUR FUCKING HOURLY RATE man ($95 × 10 = $950 + TAPE $25 + uh $45 usage fee... is... um... a lot...)
but Y'KNOW I can too! I'm not JUST SOME FUCKIN loser
Y'KNOW? I'm not JUST SOME FUCKIN money man
YOU JUST WAIT AND SEE, OKAY? Mister "Hotel California"...
okay, dude?
I DIDN'T MOVE HERE TO BE insulted, okay?
you just wait...
YOU JUST wait... WHEN THIS HITS STORES & SOARS TO #1 AND IT'S all over MTV...
then ARE YOU GONNA SNUB ME asswipe?
MAYBE A LITTLE LESS PREVERB ON THE SNARE, THOUGH
UH... LET KEEP IT A
OKAY
kof
dude, hellooo..
I'M TALKIN TO YOU...
'SCUSE ME
ROCK
PREVERB? HELLO?
okay...
ROLL
hhhKT
hhhKT
THERE... WHADDYA THINK?
hhhKT
HUH? ARE YOU TALKING TO ME?
YEAH... I CUT THE PREVERB LIKE YOU SAID... IS IT OKAY?
hhhKT
SOUNDS BETTER TO ME
DONCHA THINK?
YEAH...
snf
YEAH... AWESOME

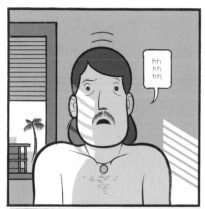

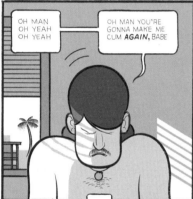

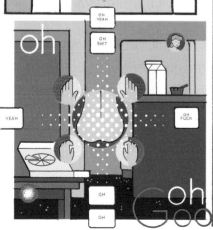

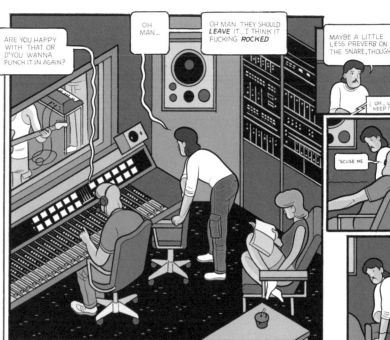

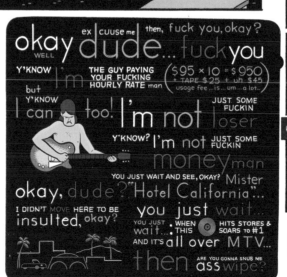

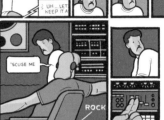

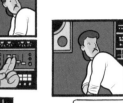

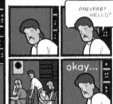

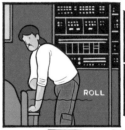

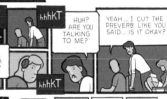

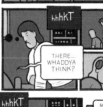

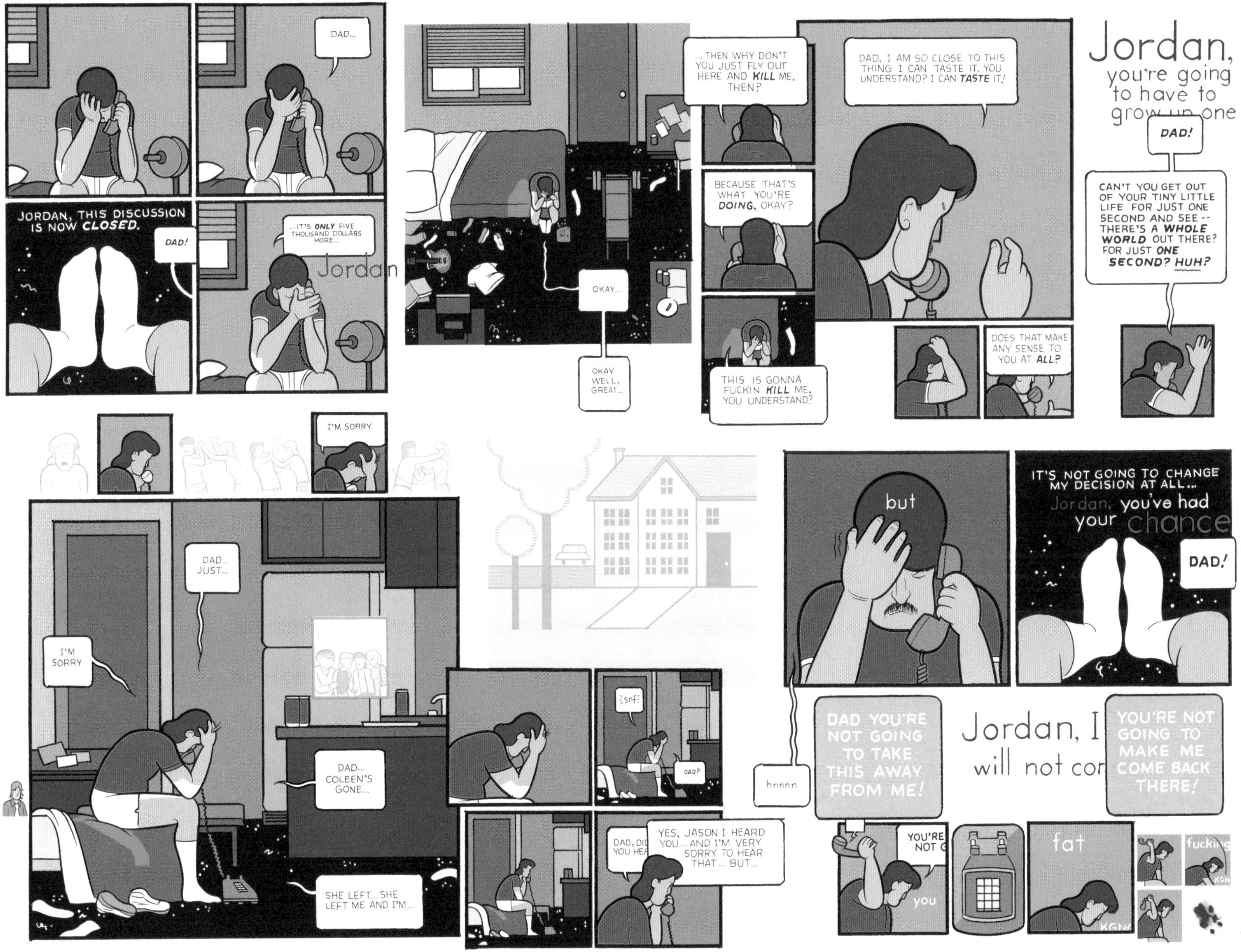
DAD...
JORDAN, THIS DISCUSSION IS NOW CLOSED.
DAD!
...IT'S ONLY FIVE THOUSAND DOLLARS MORE...
Jordan
OKAY...
OKAY WELL, GREAT...
...THEN WHY DON'T YOU JUST FLY OUT HERE AND KILL ME, THEN?
BECAUSE THAT'S WHAT YOU'RE DOING, OKAY?
THIS IS GONNA FUCKIN KILL ME, YOU UNDERSTAND?
DAD, I AM SO CLOSE TO THIS THING I CAN TASTE IT, YOU UNDERSTAND? I CAN TASTE IT!
DOES THAT MAKE ANY SENSE TO YOU AT ALL?
Jordan, you're going to have to grow up one
DAD!
CAN'T YOU GET OUT OF YOUR TINY LITTLE LIFE FOR JUST ONE SECOND AND SEE -- THERE'S A WHOLE WORLD OUT THERE? FOR JUST ONE SECOND? HUH?
I'M SORRY
DAD... JUST...
I'M SORRY
DAD... COLEEN'S GONE...
SHE LEFT... SHE LEFT ME AND I'M...
snf
DAD?
YES, JASON I HEARD YOU... AND I'M VERY SORRY TO HEAR THAT... BUT...
but
IT'S NOT GOING TO CHANGE MY DECISION AT ALL... Jordan, you've had your chance
DAD!
hnnnn
DAD YOU'RE NOT GOING TO TAKE THIS AWAY FROM ME!
Jordan, I will not co
YOU'RE NOT GOING TO MAKE ME COME BACK THERE!
YOU'RE NOT
you
fat
fucking

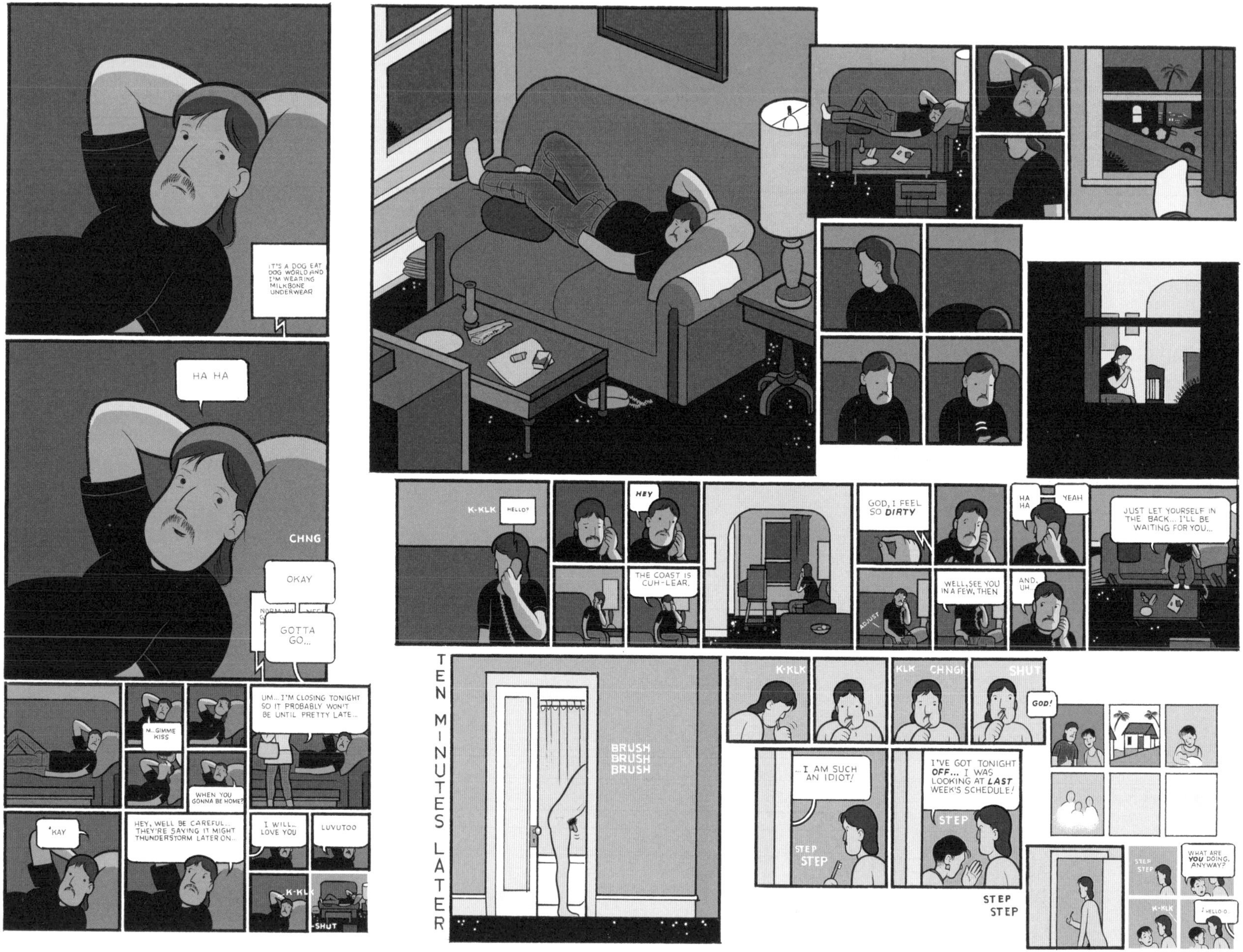
IT'S A DOG EAT DOG WORLD AND I'M WEARING MILKBONE UNDERWEAR
HA HA
CHNG
OKAY
GOTTA GO...
M...GIMME KISS
WHEN YOU GONNA BE HOME?
UM... I'M CLOSING TONIGHT SO IT PROBABLY WON'T BE UNTIL PRETTY LATE...
'KAY
HEY, WELL BE CAREFUL... THEY'RE SAYING IT MIGHT THUNDERSTORM LATER ON...
I WILL... LOVE YOU
LUVUTOO
K-KLK
SHUT
K-KLK
HELLO?
HEY
THE COAST IS CUH-LEAR.
GOD, I FEEL SO **DIRTY**
ADJUST
WELL, SEE YOU IN A FEW, THEN
HA HA
YEAH
AND, UH...
JUST LET YOURSELF IN THE BACK... I'LL BE WAITING FOR YOU...
TEN MINUTES LATER
BRUSH BRUSH BRUSH
K-KLK
KLK
CHNG!
SHUT
GOD!
...I AM SUCH AN IDIOT!
STEP STEP
I'VE GOT TONIGHT **OFF...** I WAS LOOKING AT **LAST** WEEK'S SCHEDULE!
STEP
STEP STEP
STEP STEP
WHAT ARE **YOU** DOING, ANYWAY?
K-KLK
♪ HELLO-O...

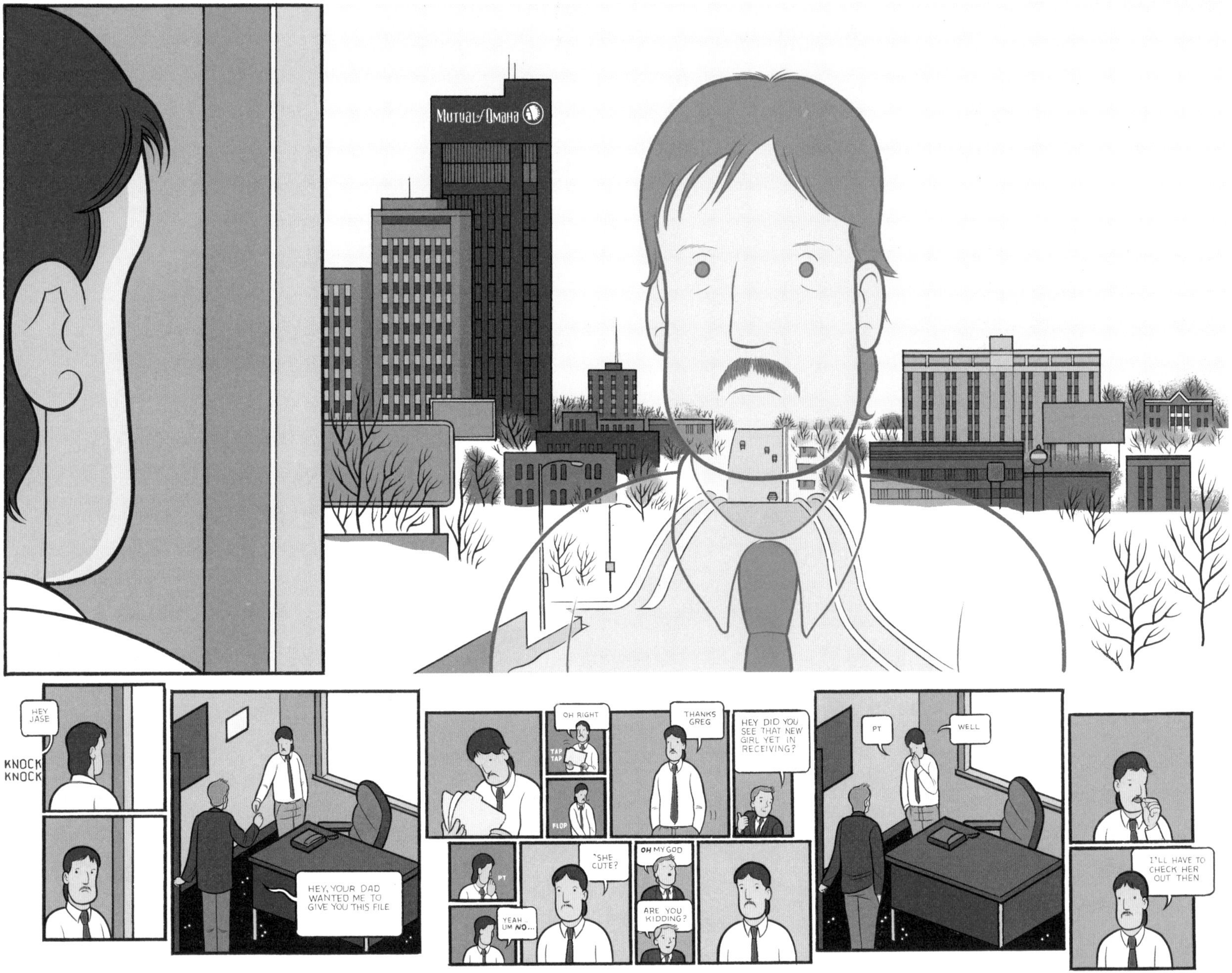
Mutual of Omaha
HEY JASE
KNOCK KNOCK
HEY, YOUR DAD WANTED ME TO GIVE YOU THIS FILE
OH RIGHT
TAP TAP
FLOP
THANKS GREG
HEY DID YOU SEE THAT NEW GIRL YET IN RECEIVING?
PT
YEAH... UM NO...
'SHE CUTE?
OH MY GOD
ARE YOU KIDDING?
PT
WELL
I'LL HAVE TO CHECK HER OUT THEN

I mean...
IT'S NOT LIKE I DON'T care ABOUT THE FIESTA BOWL...
Coors
Coors
I THINK IT'S great AND I'VE GOT GREAT FRIENDS, really...
DAMN THAT GUY'S BIG
HA HA
THIS JUST ISN'T me
...IT JUST ISN'T me ANYMORE...
I mean.
MAYBE I'M STILL RECOVERING FROM LAST NIGHT, TOO... BUT I JUST WANTED TO go...
I WANTED TO SEE you... I...
I COULDN'T STOP THINKING ABOUT you... your face...
snf
Y'KNOW?
THAT'S REALLY SWEET
REALLY, WHAT'S THE POINT OF SO MUCH PARTYING, ANYWAY? ISN'T ONE NIGHT ENOUGH?
I mean.
I THOUGHT, "I'VE GOT work TO DO TOMORROW."
AND...you know...
I ALMOST FOUND MYSELF looking forward TO IT, TOO...
IT'S CRAZY
HA HA
you know?
snf
YOU'VE HELPED ME SO MUCH, LESLIE...
you ...YOU DON'T EVEN WANT TO know WHAT I USED TO BE LIKE...
you I CAN'T begin TO TELL THE SORTS OF THINGS I'VE BEEN LETTING MYSELF THINK LATELY...
AND... UM... I...
Recovery: A Guide for Adult Children of Alcoholics
WHAT?
CHEW
UM... WELL...
I DON'T, UM, SPOSE I COULD, LIKE, stay TONIGHT, COULD I?
MINUTES LATER
TUNE TUNE
SONY
FINAL SCORE
NEBRASKA 23
OH MAN
FUCK
FUCK!

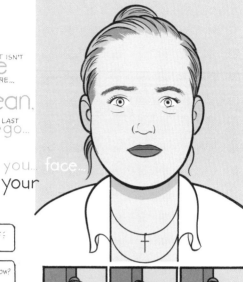

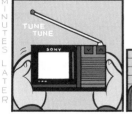

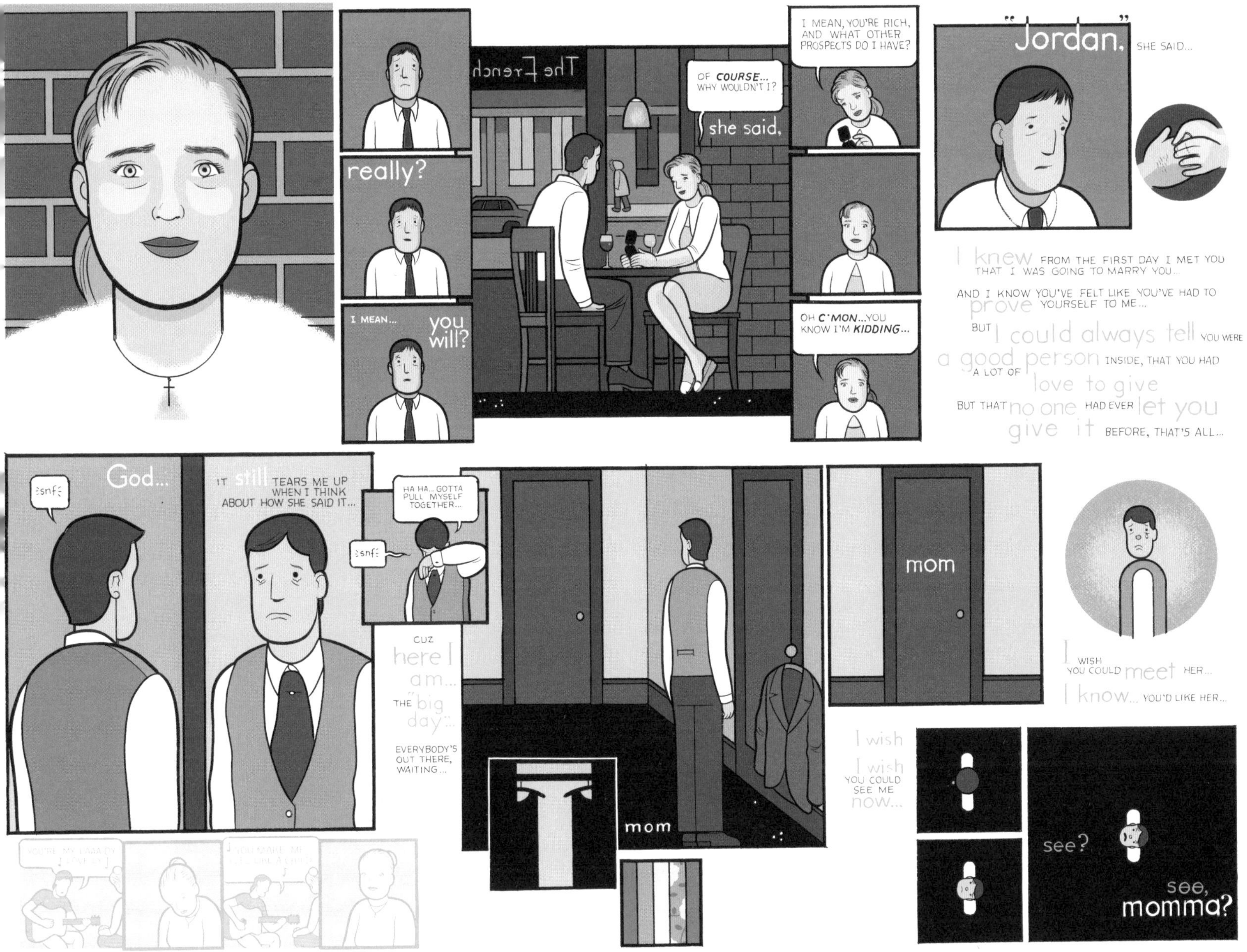
The French
really?
I MEAN...
you will?
OF COURSE... WHY WOULDN'T I?
she said,
I MEAN, YOU'RE RICH, AND WHAT OTHER PROSPECTS DO I HAVE?
OH C'MON...YOU KNOW I'M KIDDING...
"Jordan," SHE SAID...
I knew FROM THE FIRST DAY I MET YOU THAT I WAS GOING TO MARRY YOU...
AND I KNOW YOU'VE FELT LIKE YOU'VE HAD TO prove YOURSELF TO ME...
BUT I could always tell YOU WERE a good person INSIDE, THAT YOU HAD A LOT OF love to give
BUT THAT no one HAD EVER let you give it BEFORE, THAT'S ALL...
snf
God...
IT still TEARS ME UP WHEN I THINK ABOUT HOW SHE SAID IT...
HA HA... GOTTA PULL MYSELF TOGETHER...
snf
CUZ here I am... THE "big day"...
EVERYBODY'S OUT THERE, WAITING...
mom
mom
I WISH YOU COULD meet HER...
I know... YOU'D LIKE HER...
I wish
I wish YOU COULD SEE ME now...
see?
see, momma?

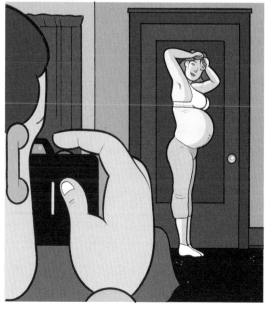
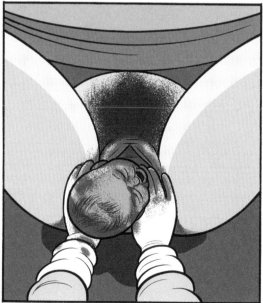

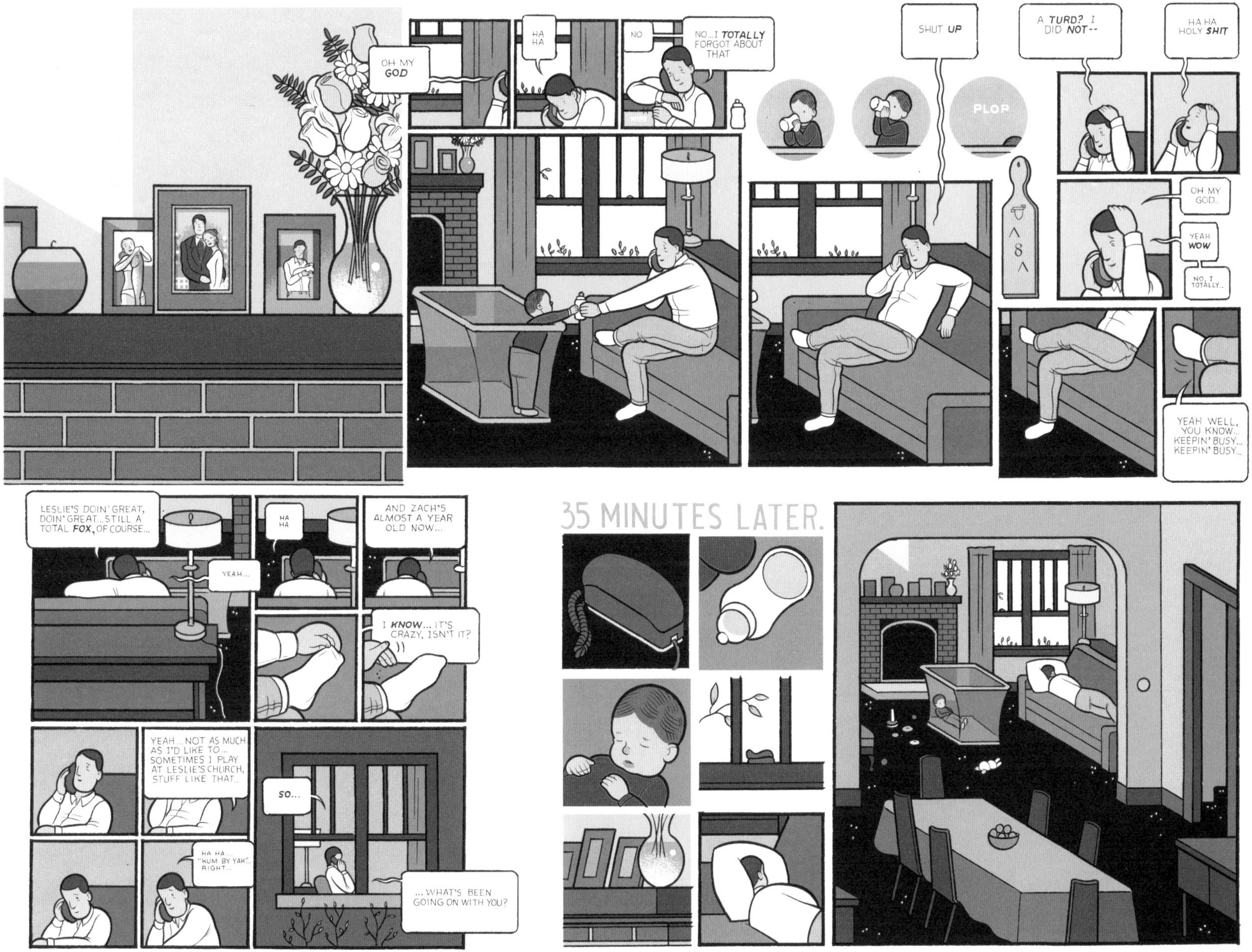

OH MY GOD
HA HA
NO
NO...I TOTALLY FORGOT ABOUT THAT
WIPE
PLOP
SHUT UP
A TURD? I DID NOT--
HA HA HOLY SHIT
OH MY GOD..
YEAH WOW
NO, I TOTALLY..
YEAH WELL, YOU KNOW... KEEPIN' BUSY... KEEPIN' BUSY...
LESLIE'S DOIN' GREAT, DOIN' GREAT...STILL A TOTAL FOX, OF COURSE...
YEAH...
HA HA
AND ZACH'S ALMOST A YEAR OLD NOW...
I KNOW... IT'S CRAZY, ISN'T IT?
YEAH... NOT AS MUCH AS I'D LIKE TO... SOMETIMES I PLAY AT LESLIE'S CHURCH, STUFF LIKE THAT..
HA HA... "KUM BY YAH"... RIGHT...
SO...
...WHAT'S BEEN GOING ON WITH YOU?
35 MINUTES LATER.

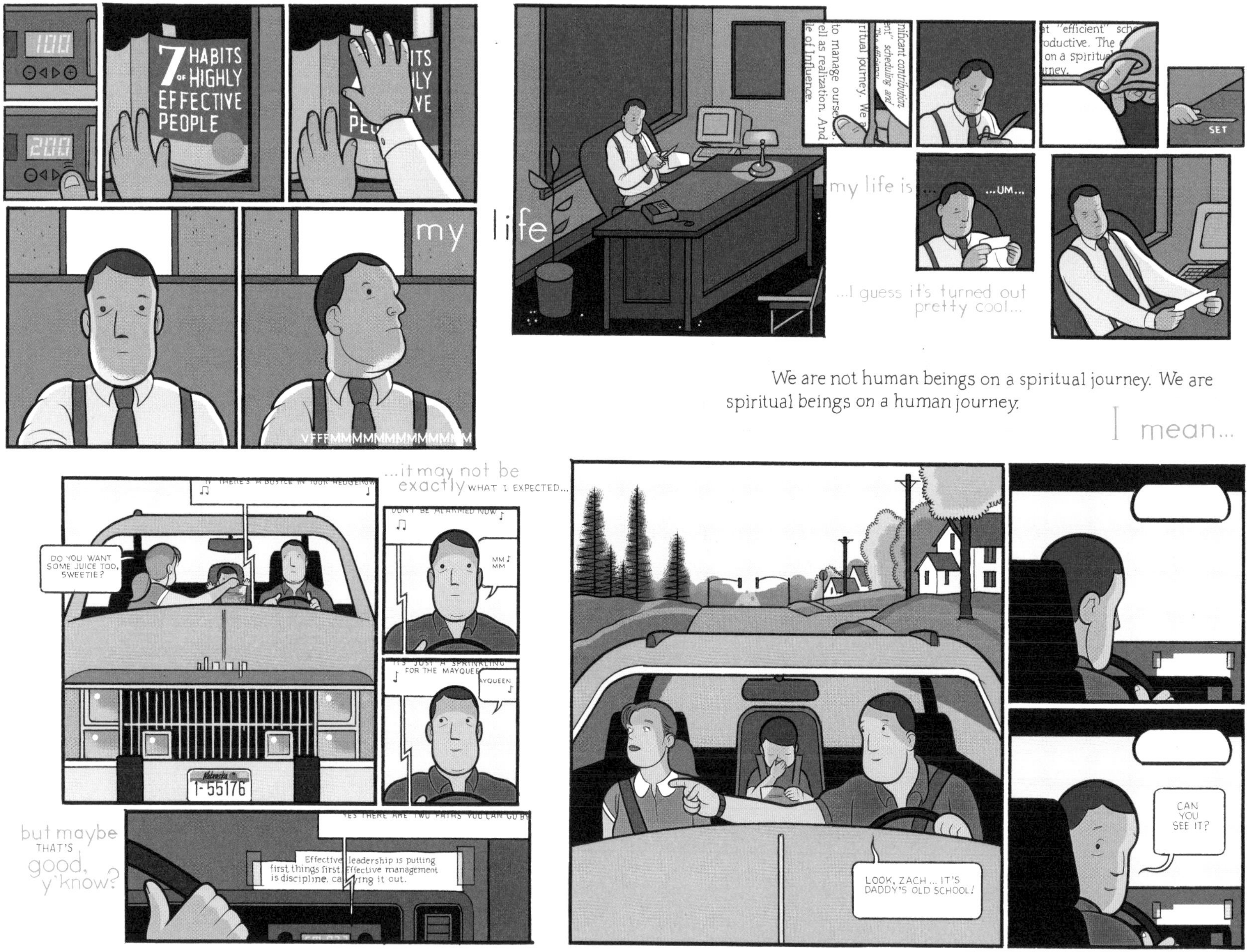
7 HABITS OF HIGHLY EFFECTIVE PEOPLE
VFFFMMMMMMMMMMMMM
my life
SET
my life is...
...UM...
...I guess it's turned out pretty cool...
We are not human beings on a spiritual journey. We are spiritual beings on a human journey.
I mean...
...it may not be exactly WHAT I EXPECTED...
IF THERE'S A BUSTLE IN YOUR HEDGEROW
DO YOU WANT SOME JUICE TOO, SWEETIE?
Nebraska
1-55176
DON'T BE ALARMED NOW
MM MM
IT'S JUST A SPRINKLING FOR THE MAYQUEEN
MAYQUEEN
but maybe THAT'S good, y'know?
YES THERE ARE TWO PATHS YOU CAN GO BY
Effective leadership is putting first things first. Effective management is discipline, carrying it out.
LOOK, ZACH ... IT'S DADDY'S OLD SCHOOL!
CAN YOU SEE IT?

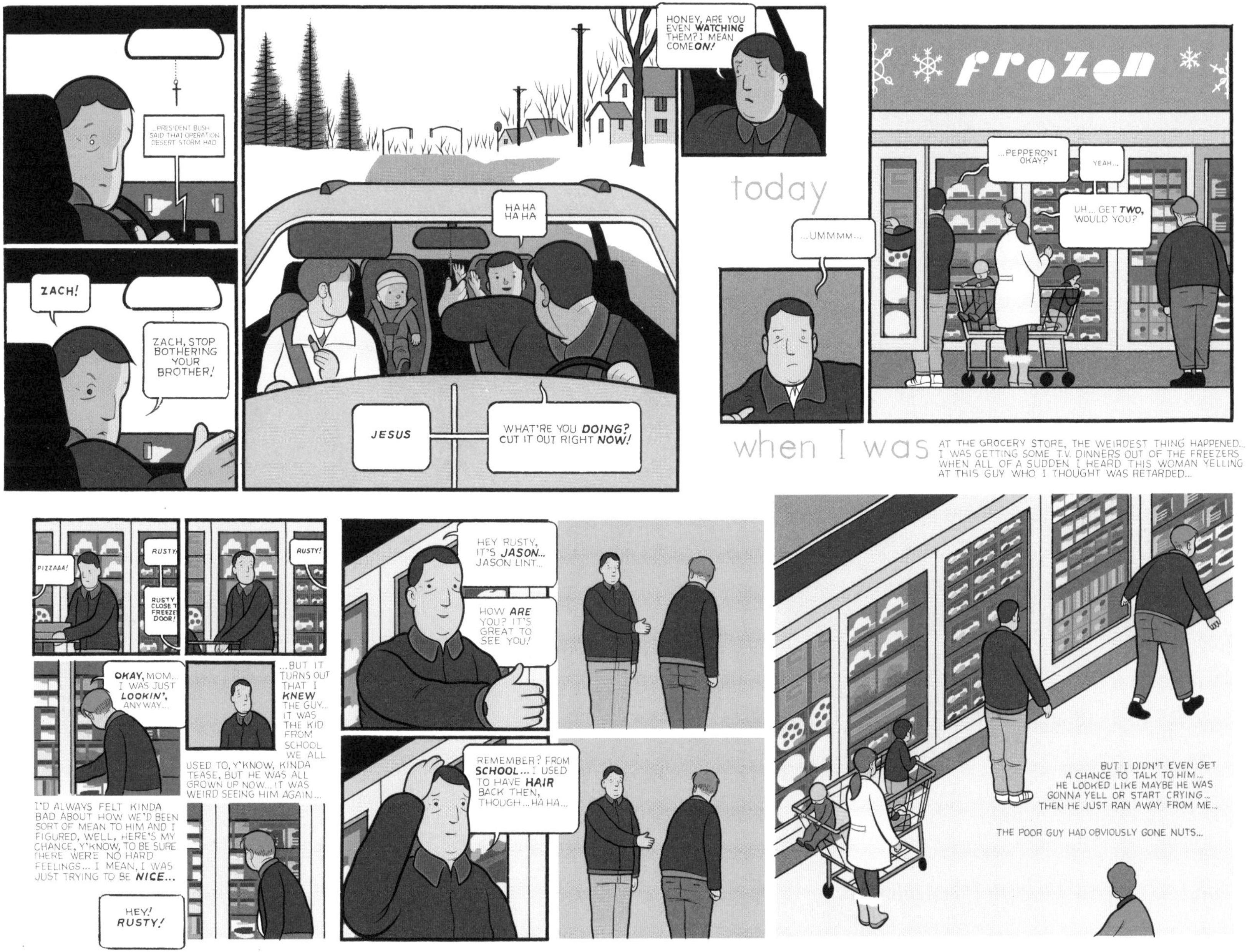
...PRESIDENT BUSH SAID THAT OPERATION DESERT STORM HAD
ZACH!
ZACH, STOP BOTHERING YOUR BROTHER!
HA HA HA HA
JESUS
WHAT'RE YOU DOING? CUT IT OUT RIGHT NOW!
HONEY, ARE YOU EVEN WATCHING THEM? I MEAN COME ON!
today
...UMMMM...
frozen
...PEPPERONI OKAY?
YEAH...
UH... GET TWO, WOULD YOU?
when I was
AT THE GROCERY STORE, THE WEIRDEST THING HAPPENED... I WAS GETTING SOME T.V. DINNERS OUT OF THE FREEZERS WHEN ALL OF A SUDDEN I HEARD THIS WOMAN YELLING AT THIS GUY WHO I THOUGHT WAS RETARDED...
PIZZAAA!
RUSTY!
RUSTY CLOSE T FREEZE DOOR!
RUSTY!
OKAY, MOM... I WAS JUST LOOKIN', ANYWAY...
...BUT IT TURNS OUT THAT I KNEW THE GUY... IT WAS THE KID FROM SCHOOL WE ALL USED TO, Y'KNOW, KINDA TEASE, BUT HE WAS ALL GROWN UP NOW... IT WAS WEIRD SEEING HIM AGAIN...
I'D ALWAYS FELT KINDA BAD ABOUT HOW WE'D BEEN SORT OF MEAN TO HIM AND I FIGURED, WELL, HERE'S MY CHANCE, Y'KNOW, TO BE SURE THERE WERE NO HARD FEELINGS... I MEAN, I WAS JUST TRYING TO BE NICE...
HEY! RUSTY!
HEY RUSTY, IT'S JASON... JASON LINT...
HOW ARE YOU? IT'S GREAT TO SEE YOU!
REMEMBER? FROM SCHOOL... I USED TO HAVE HAIR BACK THEN, THOUGH... HA HA...
BUT I DIDN'T EVEN GET A CHANCE TO TALK TO HIM... HE LOOKED LIKE MAYBE HE WAS GONNA YELL OR START CRYING... THEN HE JUST RAN AWAY FROM ME...
THE POOR GUY HAD OBVIOUSLY GONE NUTS...

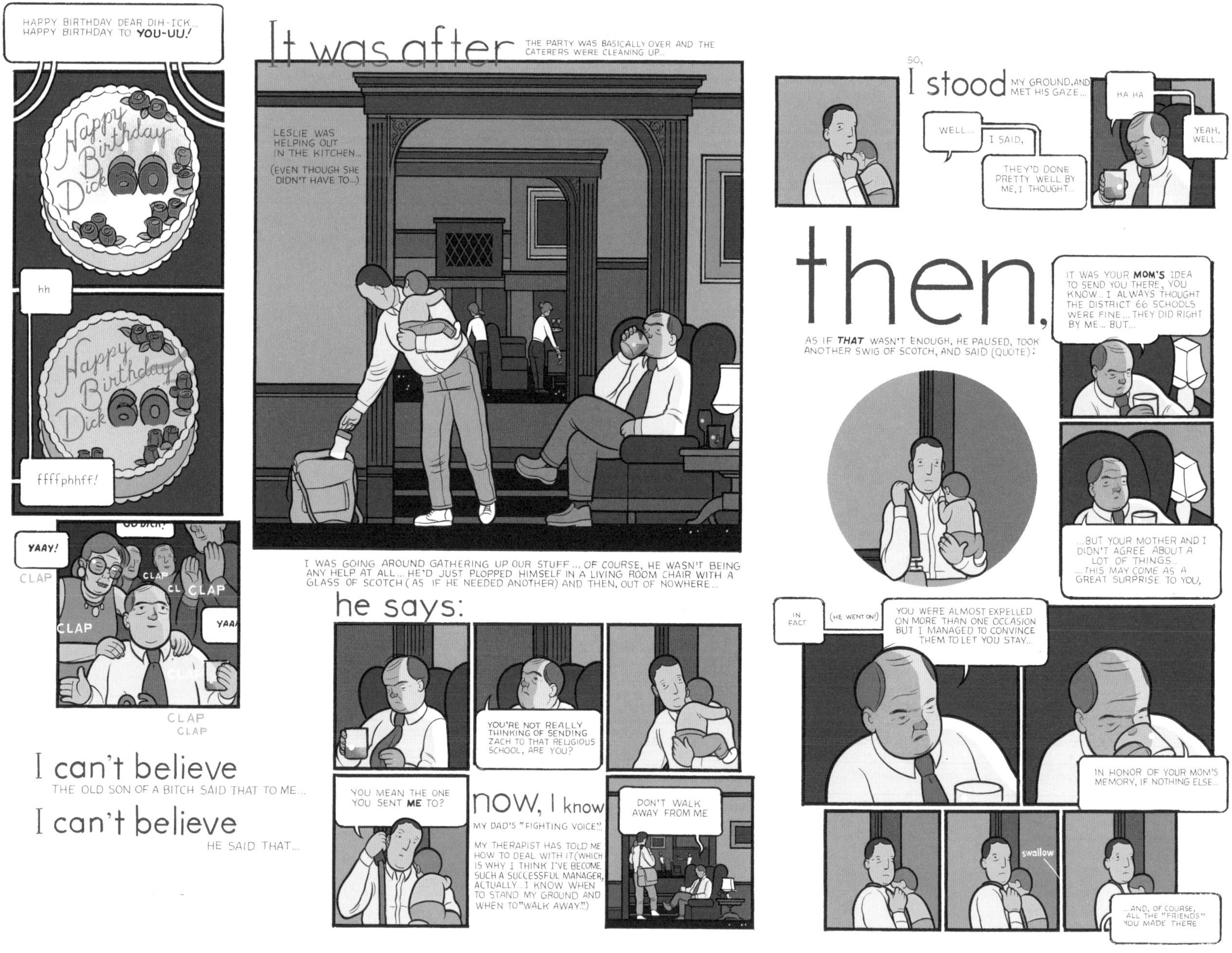
HAPPY BIRTHDAY DEAR DIH-ICK... HAPPY BIRTHDAY TO **YOU-UU!**
Happy Birthday Dick 60
hh
ffffphhff!
YAAY!
CLAP
CLAP
CL CLAP
CLAP
YAA
CLAP CLAP
I can't believe
THE OLD SON OF A BITCH SAID THAT TO ME...
I can't believe
HE SAID THAT...
It was after
THE PARTY WAS BASICALLY OVER AND THE CATERERS WERE CLEANING UP...
LESLIE WAS HELPING OUT IN THE KITCHEN...
(EVEN THOUGH SHE DIDN'T HAVE TO...)
I WAS GOING AROUND GATHERING UP OUR STUFF... OF COURSE, HE WASN'T BEING ANY HELP AT ALL... HE'D JUST PLOPPED HIMSELF IN A LIVING ROOM CHAIR WITH A GLASS OF SCOTCH (AS IF HE NEEDED ANOTHER) AND THEN, OUT OF NOWHERE...
he says:
YOU'RE NOT REALLY THINKING OF SENDING ZACH TO THAT RELIGIOUS SCHOOL, ARE YOU?
YOU MEAN THE ONE YOU SENT **ME** TO?
now, I know
MY DAD'S "FIGHTING VOICE".
MY THERAPIST HAS TOLD ME HOW TO DEAL WITH IT (WHICH IS WHY I THINK I'VE BECOME SUCH A SUCCESSFUL MANAGER, ACTUALLY... I KNOW WHEN TO STAND MY GROUND AND WHEN TO "WALK AWAY.")
DON'T WALK AWAY FROM ME
SO,
I stood
MY GROUND, AND MET HIS GAZE...
WELL...
I SAID,
THEY'D DONE PRETTY WELL BY ME, I THOUGHT...
HA HA
YEAH, WELL...
then,
AS IF **THAT** WASN'T ENOUGH, HE PAUSED, TOOK ANOTHER SWIG OF SCOTCH, AND SAID (QUOTE):
IT WAS YOUR **MOM'S** IDEA TO SEND YOU THERE, YOU KNOW... I ALWAYS THOUGHT THE DISTRICT 66 SCHOOLS WERE FINE... THEY DID RIGHT BY ME... BUT...
...BUT YOUR MOTHER AND I DIDN'T AGREE ABOUT A LOT OF THINGS... THIS MAY COME AS A GREAT SURPRISE TO YOU,
IN FACT
(HE WENT ON!)
YOU WERE ALMOST EXPELLED ON MORE THAN ONE OCCASION BUT I MANAGED TO CONVINCE THEM TO LET YOU STAY...
IN HONOR OF YOUR MOM'S MEMORY, IF NOTHING ELSE...
swallow
...AND, OF COURSE, ALL THE "FRIENDS" YOU MADE THERE

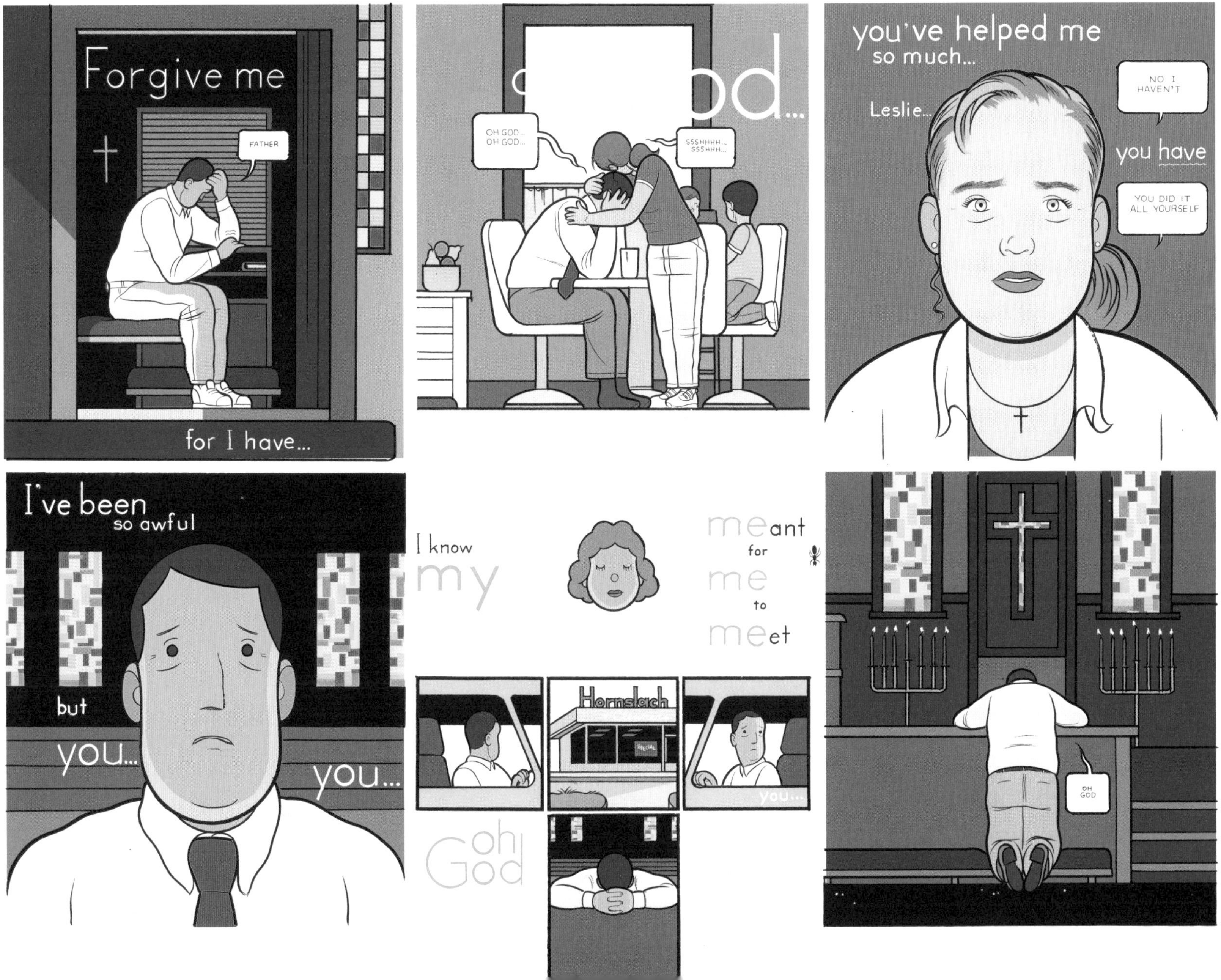
Forgive me
FATHER
for I have...
OH GOD... OH GOD...
od...
SSSHHHH... SSSHHH...
you've helped me so much...
Leslie...
NO I HAVEN'T
you have
YOU DID IT ALL YOURSELF
I've been so awful
but
you...
you...
I know my
meant for me to meet
Hornslach
SPECIAL
you...
oh God
OH GOD

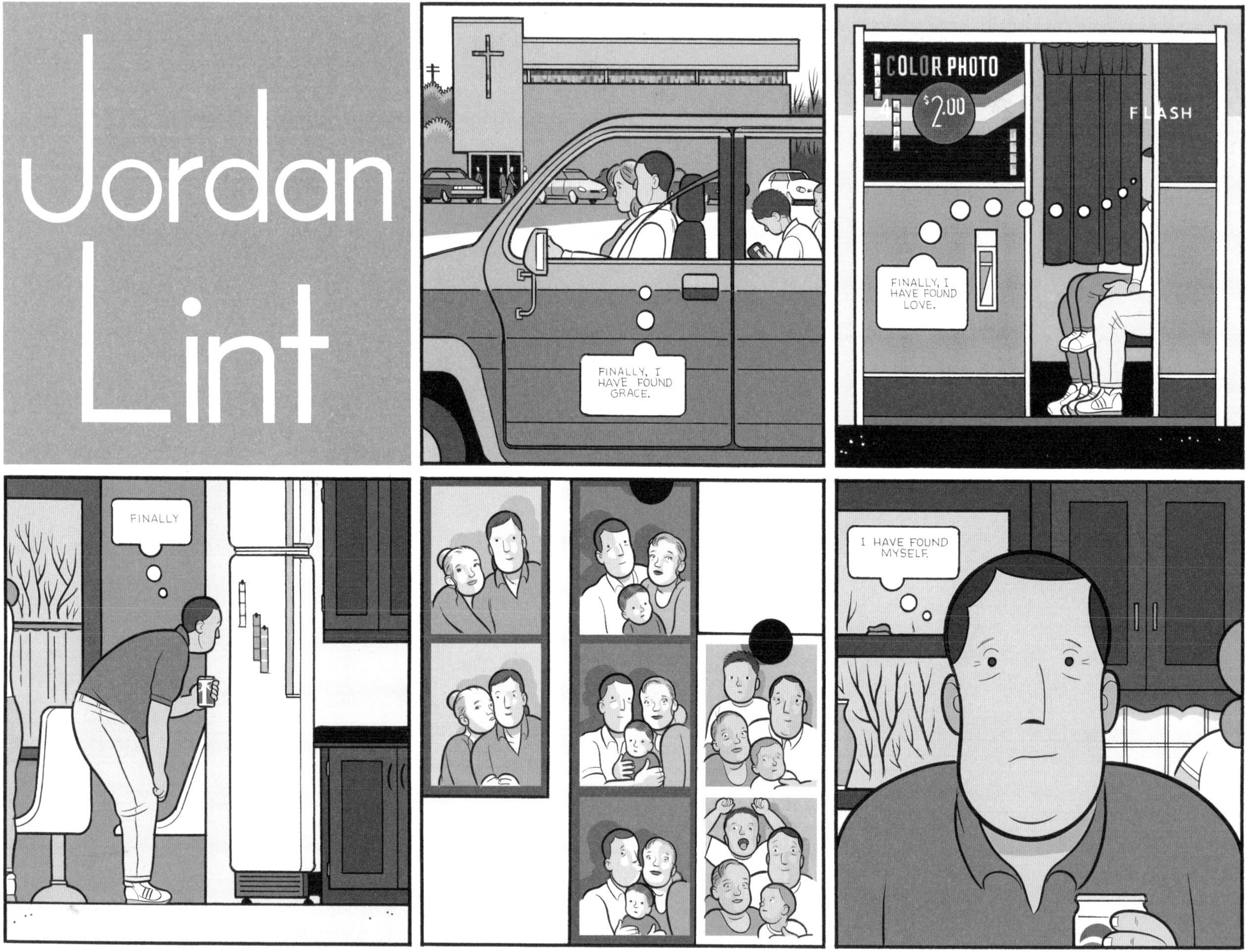
Jordan Lint
FINALLY, I HAVE FOUND GRACE.
COLOR PHOTO
4
$2.00
FLASH
FINALLY, I HAVE FOUND LOVE.
FINALLY
I HAVE FOUND MYSELF.

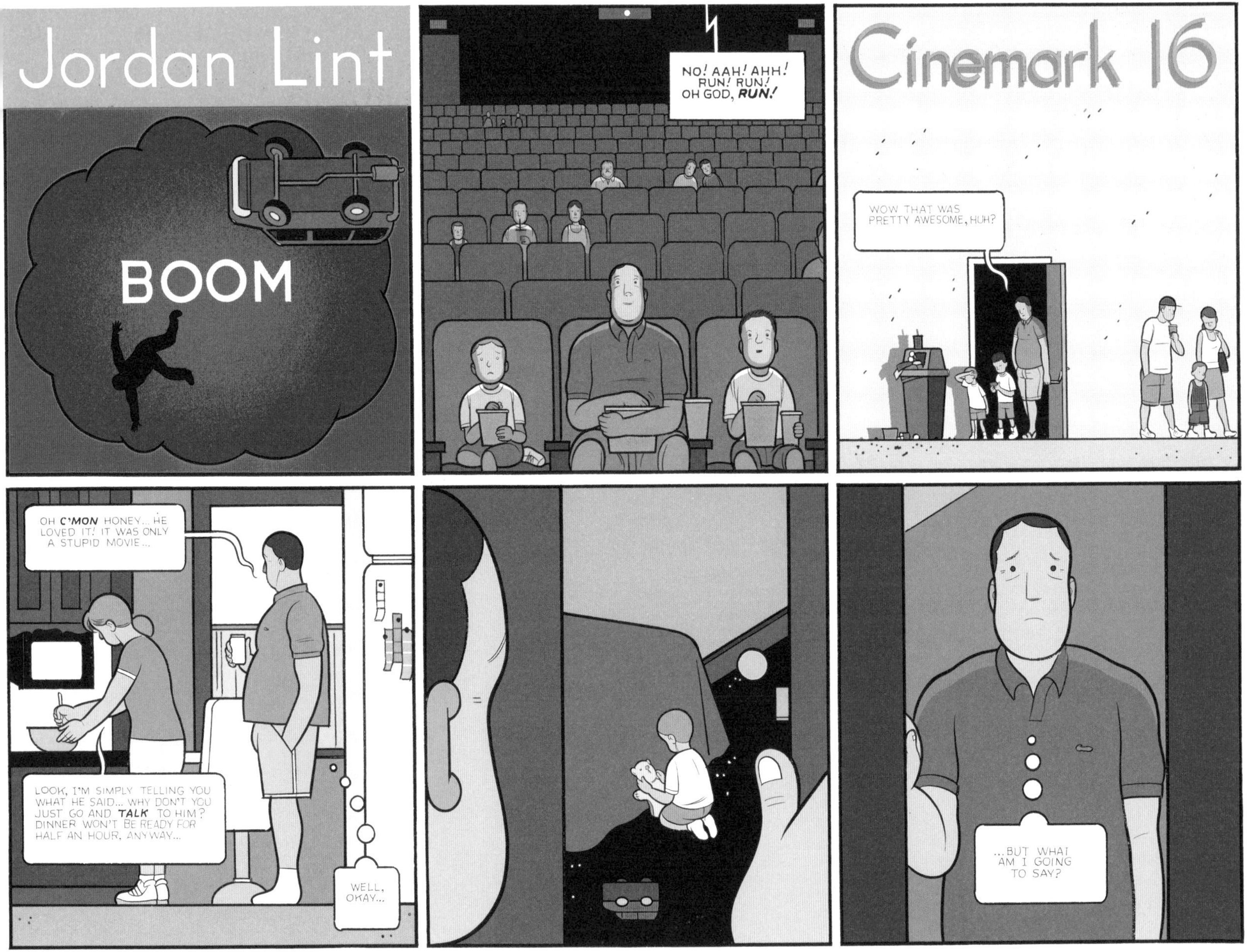
Jordan Lint
BOOM
NO! AAH! AHH! RUN! RUN! OH GOD, RUN!
Cinemark 16
WOW THAT WAS PRETTY AWESOME, HUH?
OH C'MON HONEY... HE LOVED IT! IT WAS ONLY A STUPID MOVIE...
LOOK, I'M SIMPLY TELLING YOU WHAT HE SAID... WHY DON'T YOU JUST GO AND TALK TO HIM? DINNER WON'T BE READY FOR HALF AN HOUR, ANYWAY...
WELL, OKAY...
...BUT WHAT AM I GOING TO SAY?

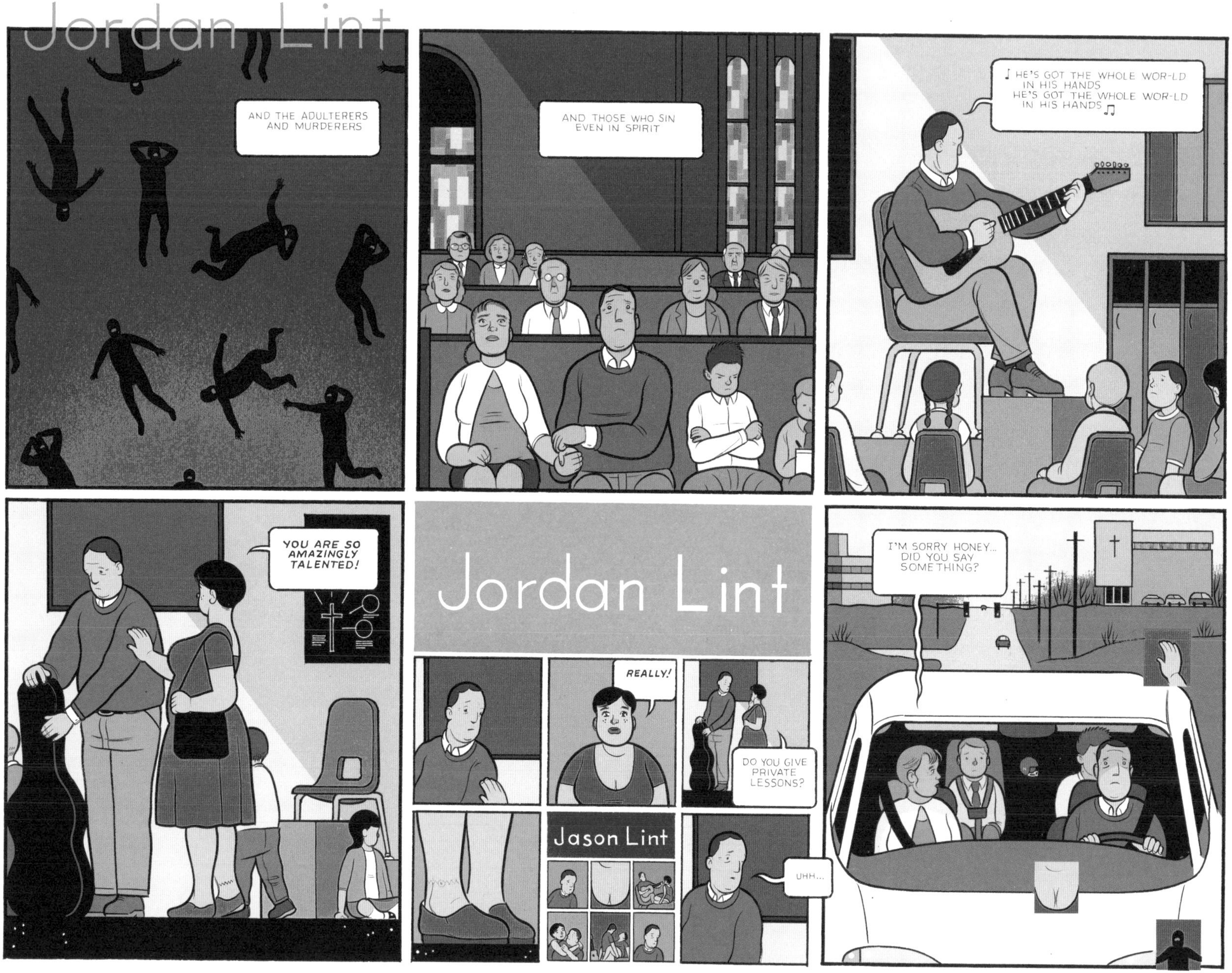
Jordan Lint
AND THE ADULTERERS AND MURDERERS
AND THOSE WHO SIN EVEN IN SPIRIT
HE'S GOT THE WHOLE WOR-LD IN HIS HANDS HE'S GOT THE WHOLE WOR-LD IN HIS HANDS
YOU ARE SO AMAZINGLY TALENTED!
Jordan Lint
REALLY!
DO YOU GIVE PRIVATE LESSONS?
Jason Lint
UHH...
I'M SORRY HONEY... DID YOU SAY SOMETHING?

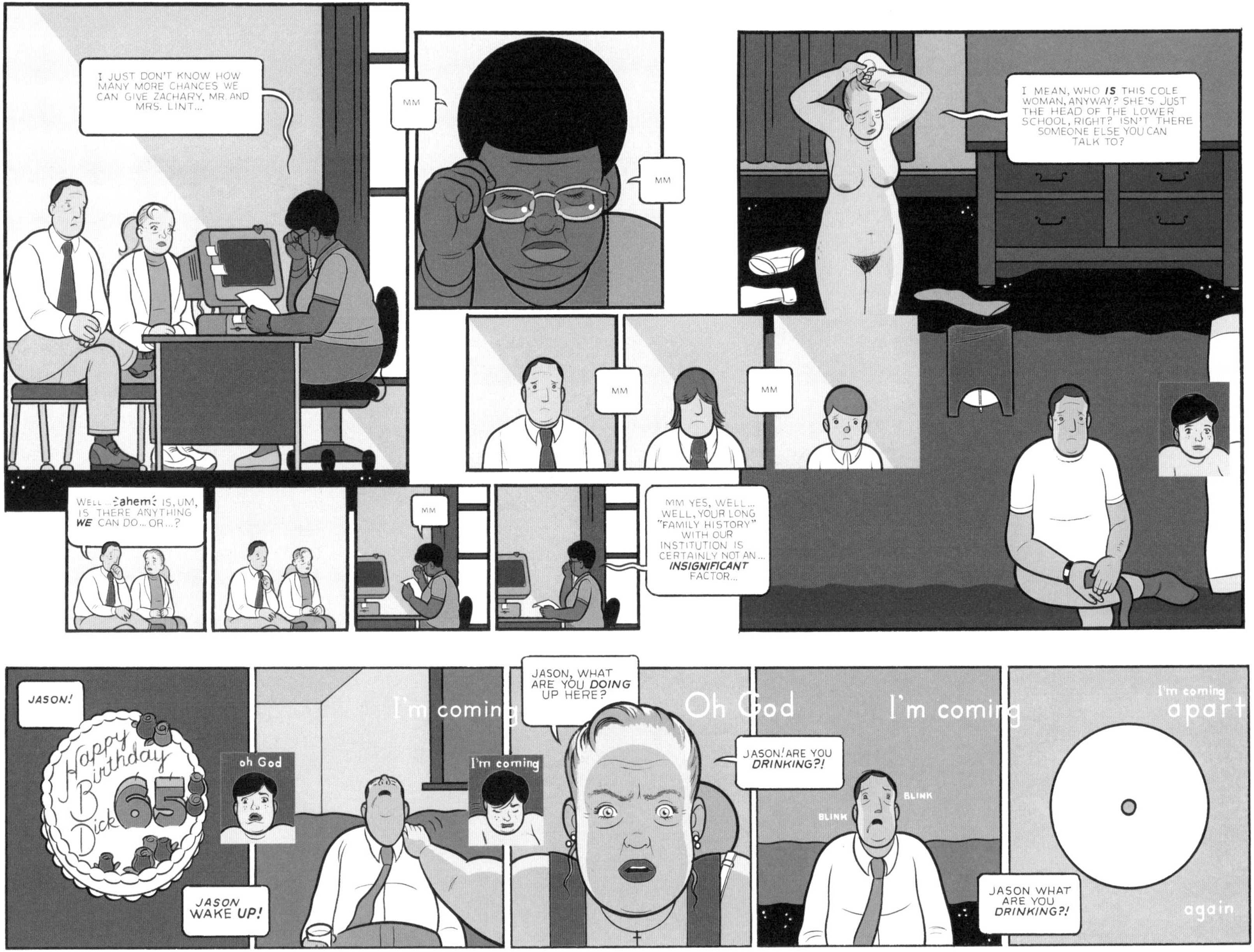
I JUST DON'T KNOW HOW MANY MORE CHANCES WE CAN GIVE ZACHARY, MR. AND MRS. LINT...
MM
MM
I MEAN, WHO IS THIS COLE WOMAN, ANYWAY? SHE'S JUST THE HEAD OF THE LOWER SCHOOL, RIGHT? ISN'T THERE SOMEONE ELSE YOU CAN TALK TO?
MM
MM
WELL ... ahem IS, UM, IS THERE ANYTHING WE CAN DO... OR...?
MM
MM YES, WELL... WELL, YOUR LONG "FAMILY HISTORY" WITH OUR INSTITUTION IS CERTAINLY NOT AN... INSIGNIFICANT FACTOR...
JASON!
Happy Birthday Dick 65
oh God
JASON WAKE UP!
I'm coming
I'm coming
JASON, WHAT ARE YOU DOING UP HERE?
Oh God
JASON! ARE YOU DRINKING?!
I'm coming
BLINK
BLINK
JASON WHAT ARE YOU DRINKING?!
I'm coming
apart
again

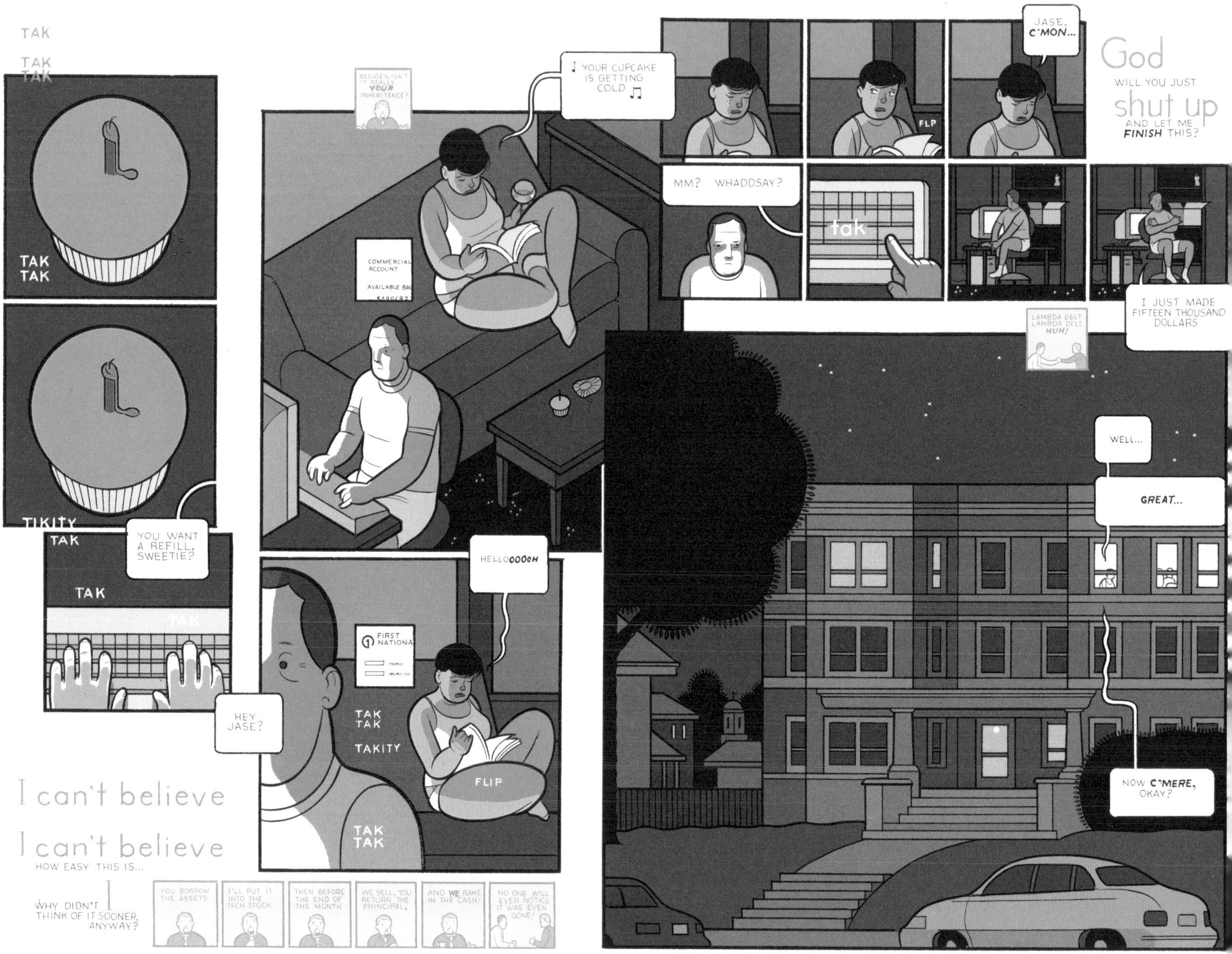

TAK
TAK
TAK
TAK
TAK
TIKITY
TAK
YOU WANT A REFILL, SWEETIE?
TAK
TAK
HEY JASE?
BESIDES, ISN'T IT REALLY YOUR INHERITANCE?
♪ YOUR CUPCAKE IS GETTING COLD ♫
COMMERCIAL ACCOUNT
AVAILABLE BAL
HELLOOOOOH
FIRST NATIONA
TAK
TAK
TAKITY
FLIP
TAK
TAK
I can't believe
I can't believe
HOW EASY THIS IS...
WHY DIDN'T I THINK OF IT SOONER, ANYWAY?
YOU BORROW THE ASSETS
I'LL PUT IT INTO THE TECH STOCK
THEN BEFORE THE END OF THE MONTH
WE SELL, YOU RETURN THE PRINCIPAL,
AND WE RAKE IN THE CASH!
NO ONE WILL EVER NOTICE IT WAS EVEN GONE!
FLP
JASE, C'MON...
God
WILL YOU JUST
shut up
AND LET ME FINISH THIS?
MM? WHADDSAY?
tak
I JUST MADE FIFTEEN THOUSAND DOLLARS
LAMBDA DELT LAMBDA DELT HUH!
WELL...
GREAT...
NOW C'MERE, OKAY?

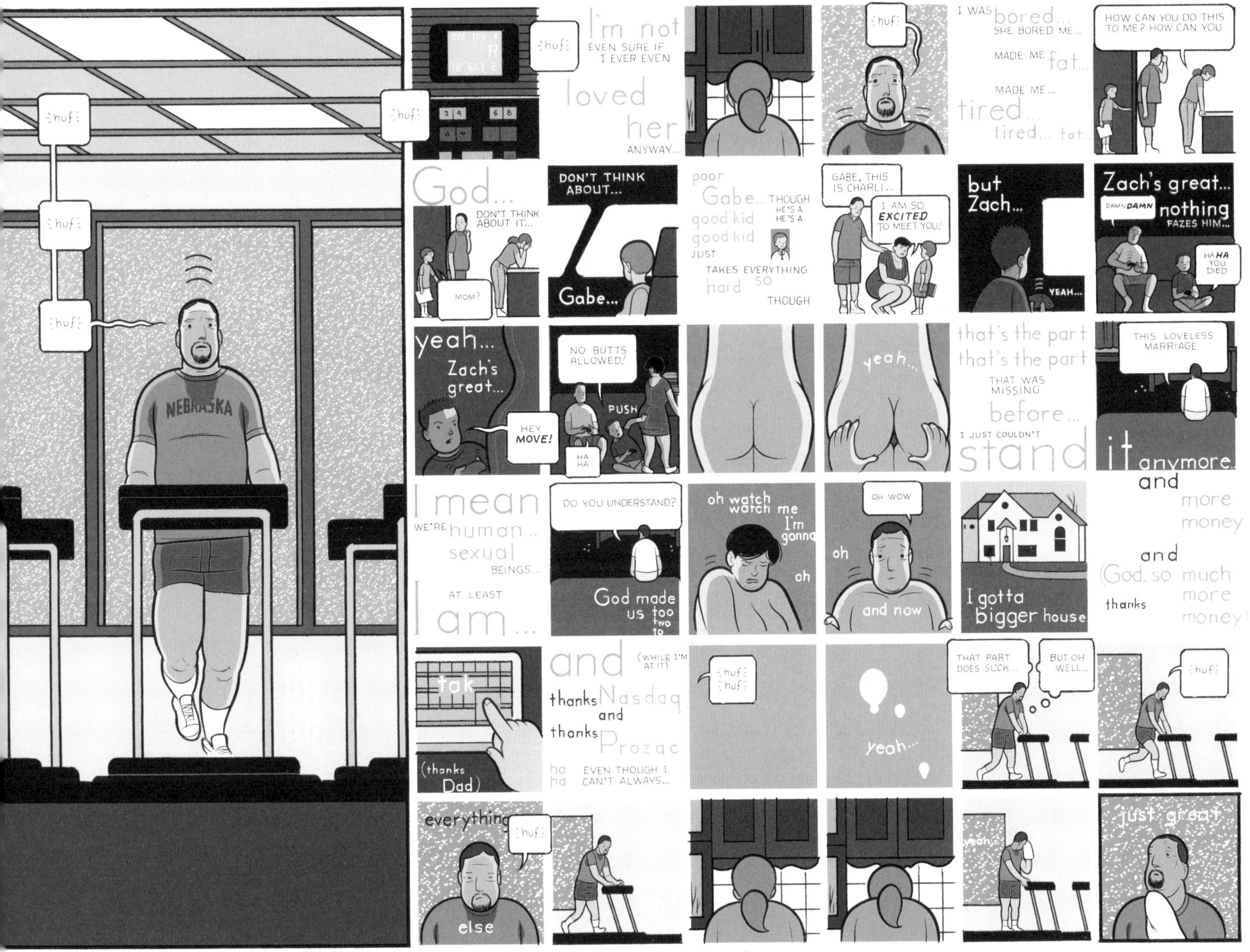

huf
huf
huf
huf
huf
I'm not EVEN SURE IF I EVER EVEN loved her ANYWAY...
huf
I WAS bored... SHE BORED ME... MADE ME fat... MADE ME... tired... tired... fat...
HOW CAN YOU DO THIS TO ME? HOW CAN YOU
God...
DON'T THINK ABOUT IT...
MOM?
DON'T THINK ABOUT...
Gabe...
poor Gabe... THOUGH HE'S A HE'S A good kid good kid JUST TAKES EVERYTHING SO hard THOUGH
GABE, THIS IS CHARLI...
I AM SO EXCITED TO MEET YOU!
but Zach...
YEAH...
Zach's great... nothing FAZES HIM...
DAMN DAMN
HA HA YOU DIED
yeah... Zach's great...
HEY MOVE!
NO BUTTS ALLOWED!
PUSH
HA HA
yeah...
that's the part that's the part THAT WAS MISSING before... I JUST COULDN'T stand it anymore.
THIS LOVELESS MARRIAGE
I mean WE'RE human... sexual BEINGS... AT LEAST I am...
DO YOU UNDERSTAND?
God made us too two to
oh watch watch me I'm gonna oh
oh oh
OH WOW
and now
I gotta bigger house
and more money and (God, so much more thanks money)
tak
(thanks Dad)
and (WHILE I'M AT IT) thanks Nasdaq and thanks Prozac ha ha EVEN THOUGH I CAN'T ALWAYS...
huf huf
yeah...
THAT PART DOES SUCK...
BUT OH WELL...
huf
everything else
huf
yeah
just great

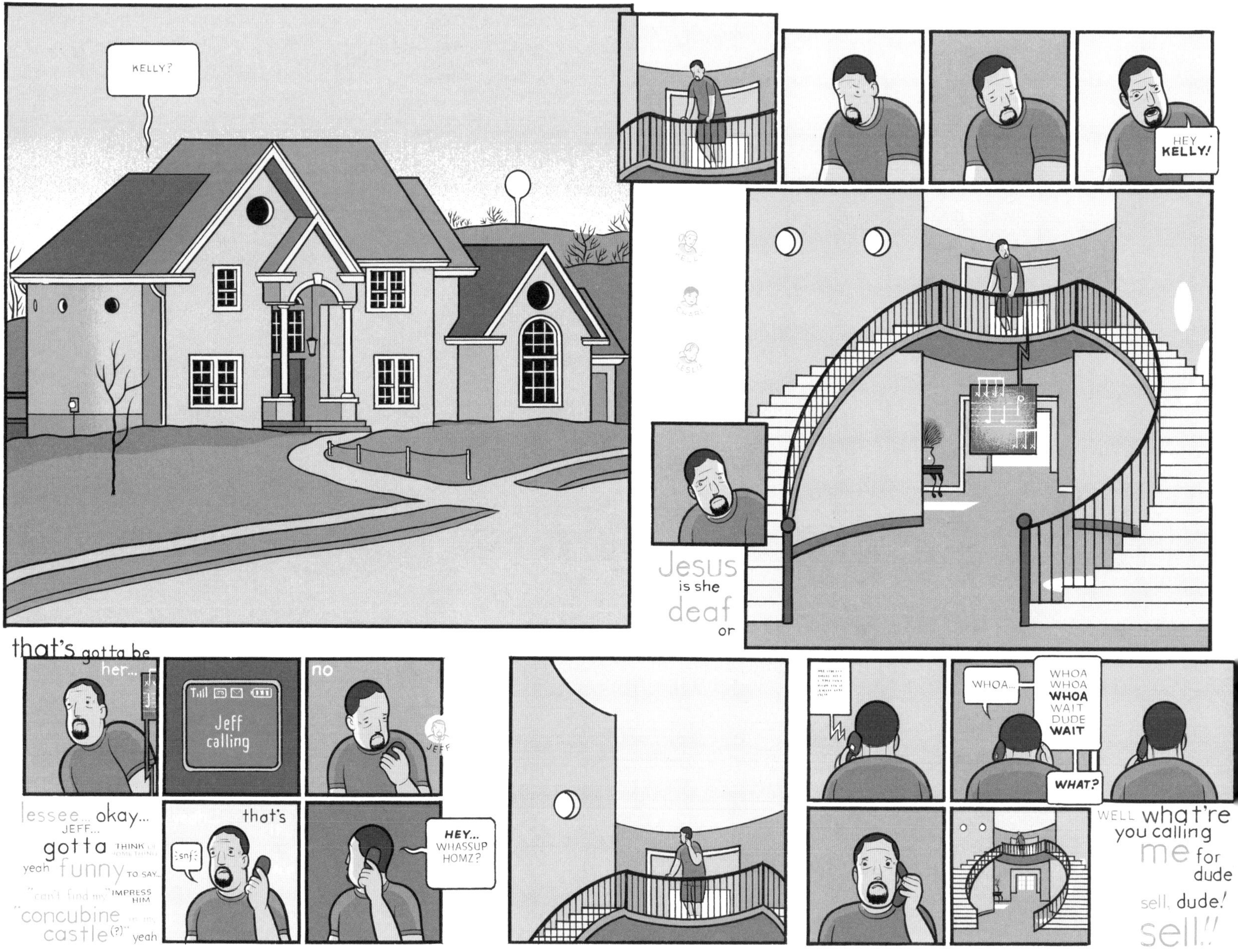

KELLY?
HEY KELLY!
Jesus is she deaf or
that's gotta be her...
Jeff calling
no
JEFF
lessee... okay... JEFF...
gotta THINK
yeah funny TO SAY...
"can't find my" IMPRESS HIM
"concubine
castle(?)" yeah
snf
that's
HEY... WHASSUP HOMZ?
WHOA...
WHOA WHOA WHOA WAIT DUDE WAIT
WHAT?
WELL what're you calling me for dude
sell, dude!
sell!!

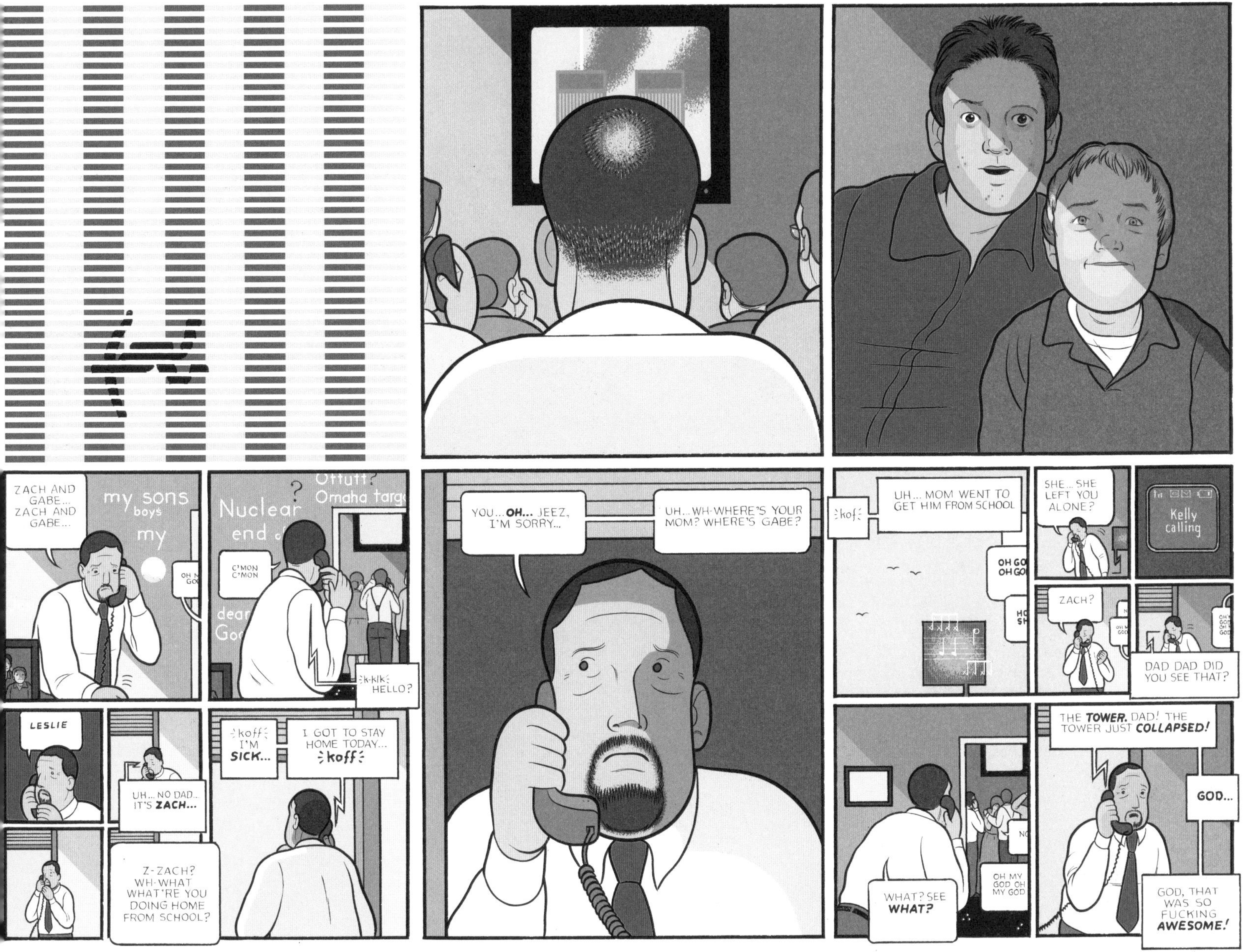

ZACH AND GABE... ZACH AND GABE...
my sons
boys
my
?
Nuclear
end
Omaha
dear
C'MON C'MON
k-klk HELLO?
LESLIE
UH... NO DAD.. IT'S ZACH...
Z-ZACH? WH-WHAT WHAT'RE YOU DOING HOME FROM SCHOOL?
koff I'M SICK...
I GOT TO STAY HOME TODAY... koff
YOU... OH... JEEZ, I'M SORRY...
UH... WH-WHERE'S YOUR MOM? WHERE'S GABE?
kof
UH... MOM WENT TO GET HIM FROM SCHOOL
SHE... SHE LEFT YOU ALONE?
Kelly calling
ZACH?
DAD DAD DID YOU SEE THAT?
WHAT? SEE WHAT?
OH MY GOD OH MY GOD
THE TOWER, DAD! THE TOWER JUST COLLAPSED!
GOD...
GOD, THAT WAS SO FUCKING AWESOME!

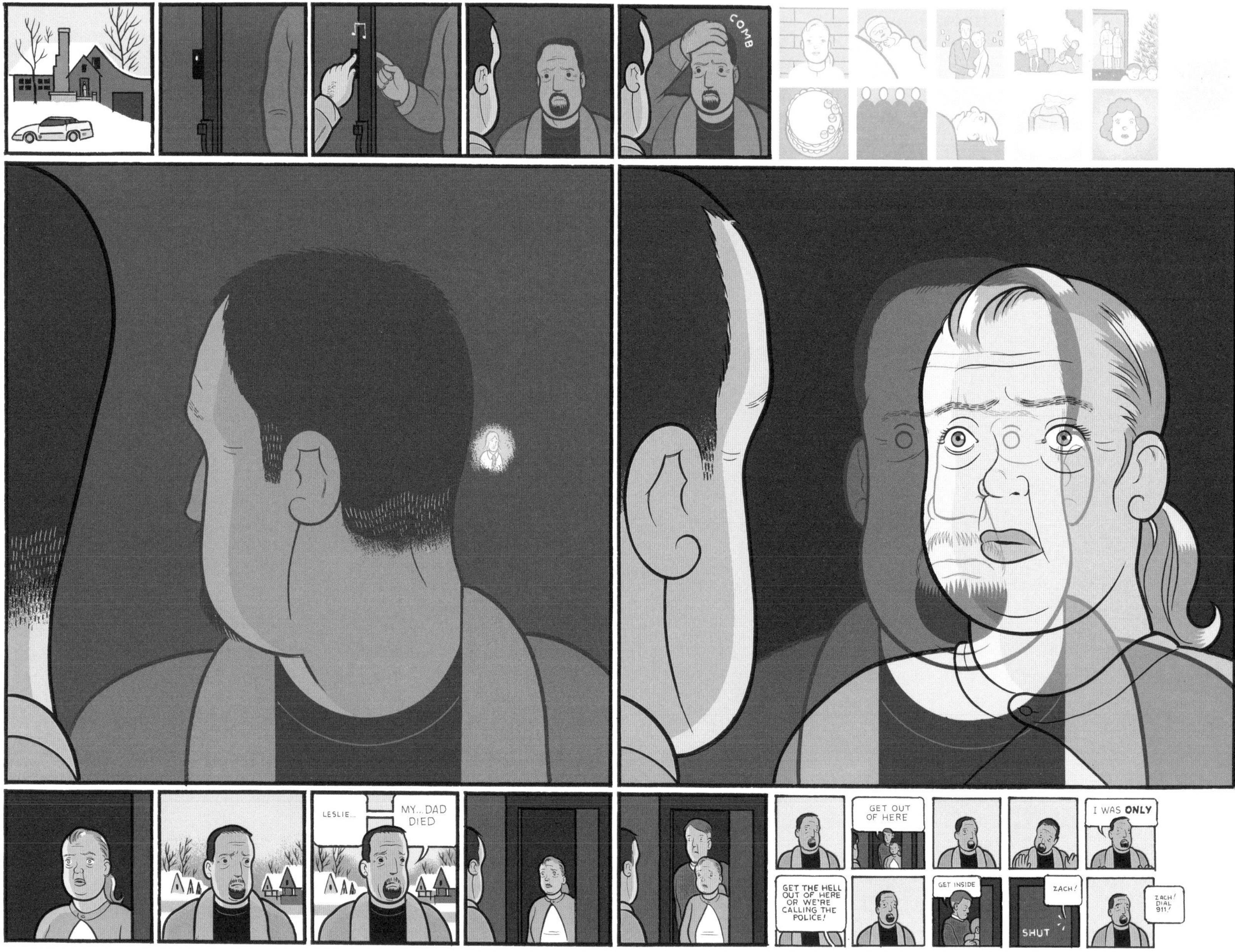
COMB
LESLIE...
MY...DAD DIED
GET OUT OF HERE
I WAS ONLY
GET THE HELL OUT OF HERE OR WE'RE CALLING THE POLICE!
GET INSIDE
ZACH!
SHUT
ZACH! DIAL 911!

...UM... CONTAINS AND MANAGES RISK...

...WHILE...

...WHILE INCENTING MAXIMIZED PROFITABILITY. IN SHORT...

...I THINK WE SHOULD MOVE ON IT.

ANY OBJECTIONS?

AND

GOD THAT SUCKED...

I SUCKED, DIDN'T I?

LATER

WE REALLY HAVE TO STOP DOING THAT AT THE OFFICE

WELL, THEN DO ME A LITTLE MORE AT HOME AND WE WON'T HAVE TO

I HAVE TO SAY, THIS IS THE FIRST TIME IN MY LIFE I'VE BEEN ACCUSED OF BEING UNDERSEXED...

GO EASY ON ME, OKAY? I'M PRACTICALLY OLD ENOUGH TO BE YOUR FATHER...

OOO STOP... YOU'LL GET ME HOT ALL OVER AGAIN

JESUS YOU ARE SICK, YOU KNOW THAT? YOU'VE GOT PROBLEMS!

WHAT? I LIKE FUCKING OLD GUYS AND I LIKE FUCKING AT WORK... WHAT'S SO WRONG WITH THAT?

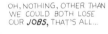
OH, NOTHING, OTHER THAN WE COULD BOTH LOSE OUR JOBS, THAT'S ALL...

WHAT -- YOU GONNA FIRE YOURSELF?

LOOK, IT'S JUST FUCKING... YOUR GENERATION HAS SO MANY HANGUPS, I SWEAR...

KGNLNG

KGNK

THERE'S A LOT MORE TO LIFE THAN SEX, Y'KNOW?

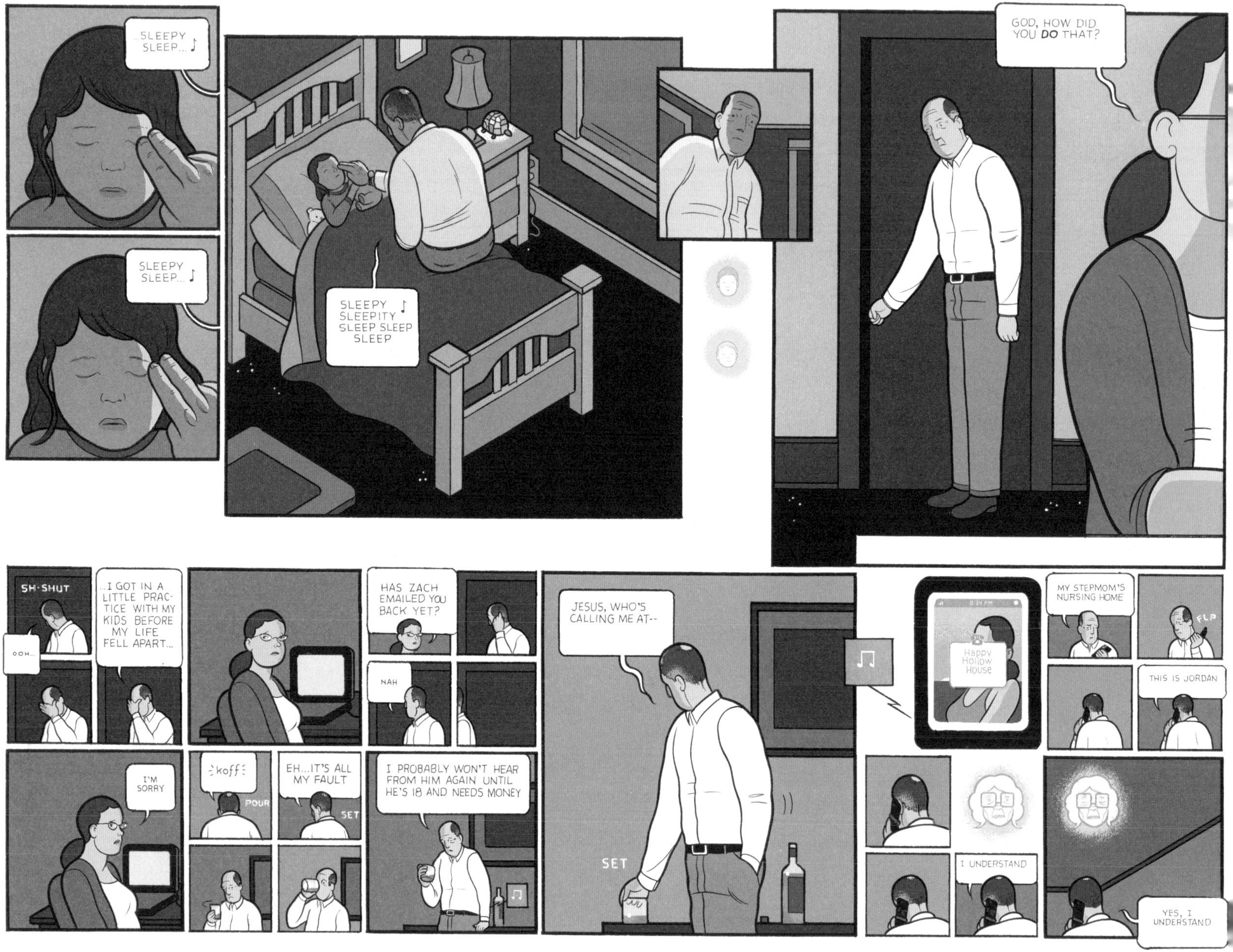
...SLEEPY SLEEP... ♪
SLEEPY SLEEP... ♪
SLEEPY SLEEPITY SLEEP SLEEP SLEEP ♪
GOD, HOW DID YOU DO THAT?
SH-SHUT
OOH...
...I GOT IN A LITTLE PRAC-TICE WITH MY KIDS BEFORE MY LIFE FELL APART...
HAS ZACH EMAILED YOU BACK YET?
NAH
I'M SORRY
koff
POUR
EH...IT'S ALL MY FAULT
SET
I PROBABLY WON'T HEAR FROM HIM AGAIN UNTIL HE'S 18 AND NEEDS MONEY
JESUS, WHO'S CALLING ME AT--
SET
Happy Hollow House
MY STEPMOM'S NURSING HOME
FLP
THIS IS JORDAN
I UNDERSTAND
YES, I UNDERSTAND

KRAK

SNAP
KRNCH

CHRIST

how could this all have gotten so... I mean, we're talking total renovation here ridiculous tens of thousands of

didn't she even...

plumbing...
electrical...
roofing...

MOMMA!

TUCKPOINTING...

MOMMA! LOOK!

KRNCH
KRNCH
SNAP

LOOK! LOOK, MOMMA!

A FLOWER, SEE?

♫ HAPPY BIRPDAY TO ME

I JUST DON'T SEE WHY, IF I HAVE A PRACTICALLY BRAND-NEW HOUSE IN A GOOD SCHOOL DISTRICT, WHY YOU'D WANT TO MOVE INTO ONE THAT'S BASICALLY FALLING DOWN...

HONEY, IT'S NOT...

LOOK...

I KNOW THERE ARE A LOT OF GHOSTS IN THIS HOUSE FOR YOU...

BUT...

HAPPY BIRPD

IT'S JUST SO... COOL, Y'KNOW?

HAPPY BIRPD DEAR

BESIDES, SHE LOVES IT... I MEAN, LISTEN TO HER...

HONEY?

HAPTY BIRPDA TO ME

OH, HONEY...

OH HONEY, I'M SORRY... WHAT DID I SAY?

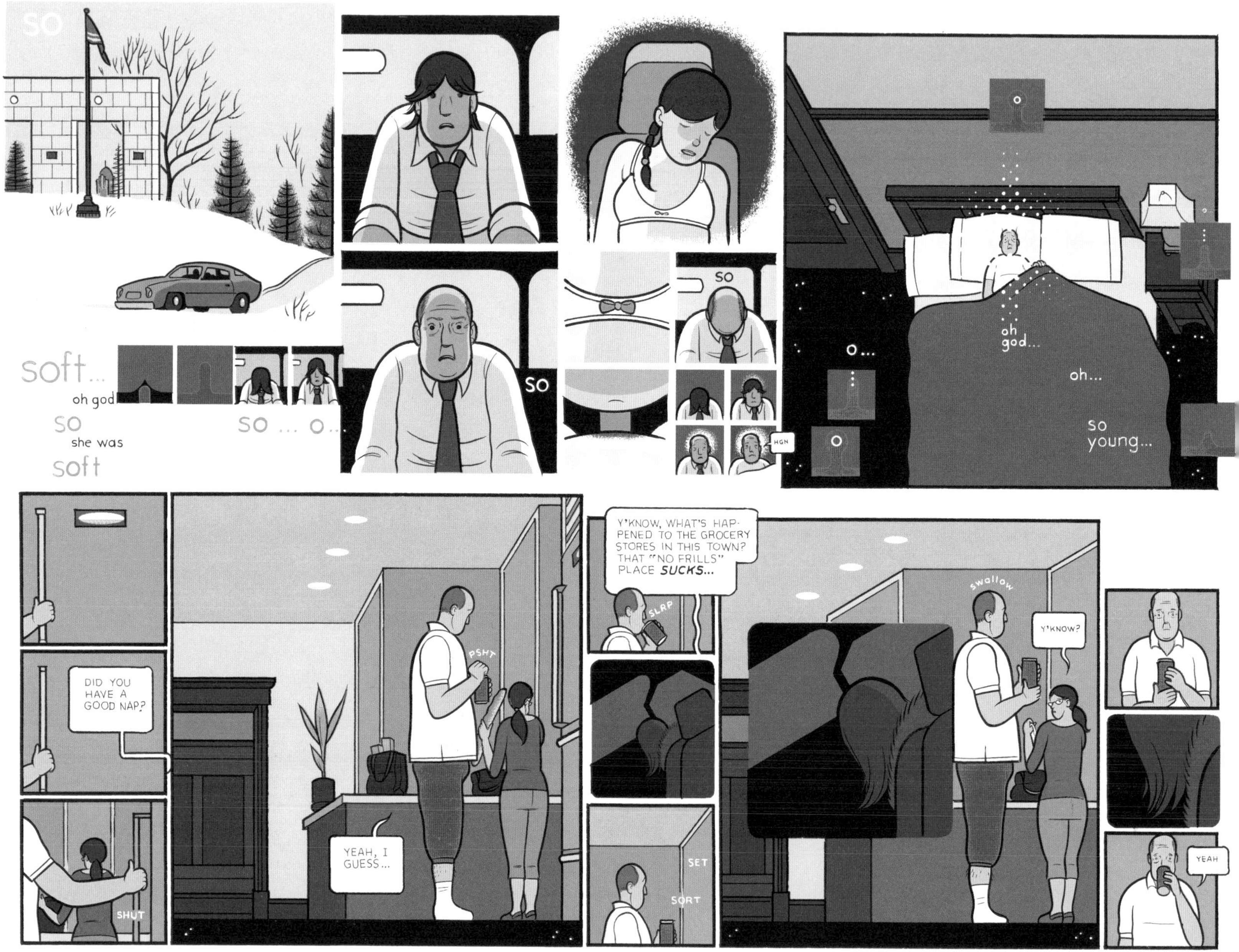
SO
soft...
oh god
so
she was
soft
so ... o...
SO
SO
HGN
o...
oh god...
oh...
so young...
DID YOU HAVE A GOOD NAP?
SHUT
PSHT
YEAH, I GUESS...
Y'KNOW, WHAT'S HAPPENED TO THE GROCERY STORES IN THIS TOWN? THAT "NO FRILLS" PLACE SUCKS...
SLRP
SET
SORT
swallow
Y'KNOW?
YEAH

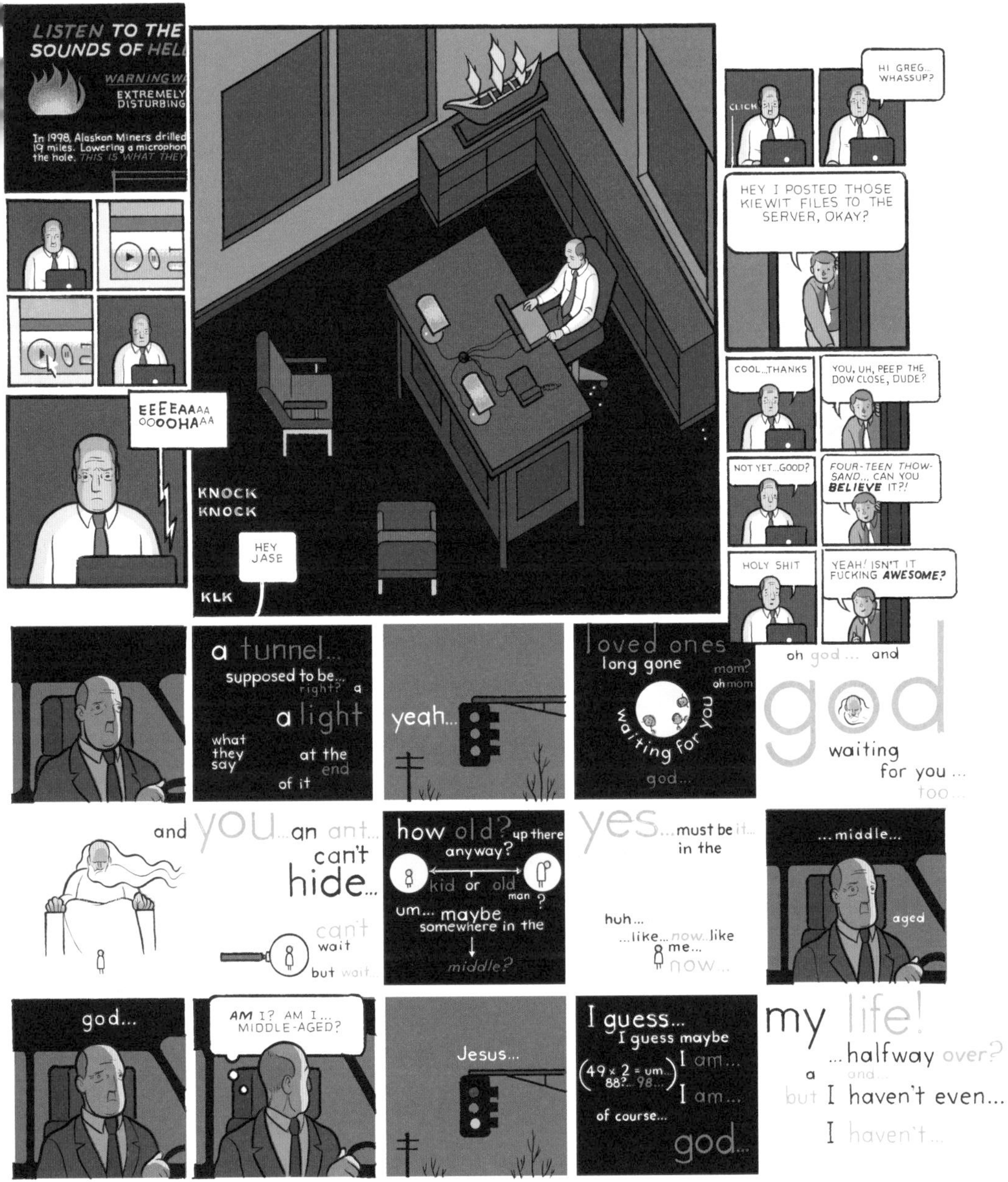

LISTEN TO THE SOUNDS OF HELL
WARNING
EXTREMELY DISTURBING
In 1998, Alaskan Miners drilled 19 miles. Lowering a microphone the hole. THIS IS WHAT THEY
EEEEAAAA OOOOHAAA
KNOCK KNOCK
HEY JASE
KLK
CLICK
HI GREG... WHASSUP?
HEY I POSTED THOSE KIEWIT FILES TO THE SERVER, OKAY?
COOL...THANKS
YOU, UH, PEEP THE DOW CLOSE, DUDE?
NOT YET...GOOD?
FOUR-TEEN THOW-SAND... CAN YOU BELIEVE IT?!
HOLY SHIT
YEAH! ISN'T IT FUCKING AWESOME?
a tunnel... supposed to be... right? a a light what they say at the end of it
yeah...
loved ones long gone mom? oh mom waiting for you god...
oh god... and god waiting for you... too...
and you... an ant... can't hide... can't wait but wait...
how old? up there anyway? kid or old man? um... maybe somewhere in the middle?
yes... must be it... in the
huh... ...like... now... like me... now...
...middle... aged
god...
AM I? AM I... MIDDLE-AGED?
Jesus...
I guess... I guess maybe I am... I am... of course... god...
(49 × 2 = um... 88?... 98...)
my life! ...halfway over? a and... but I haven't even... I haven't...

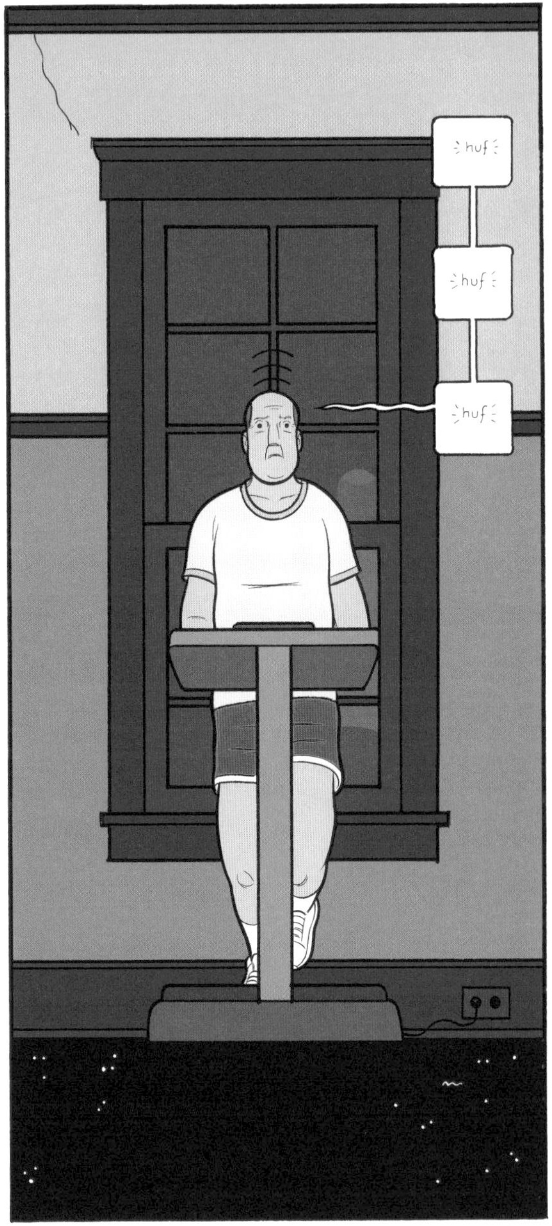

huf
huf
huf

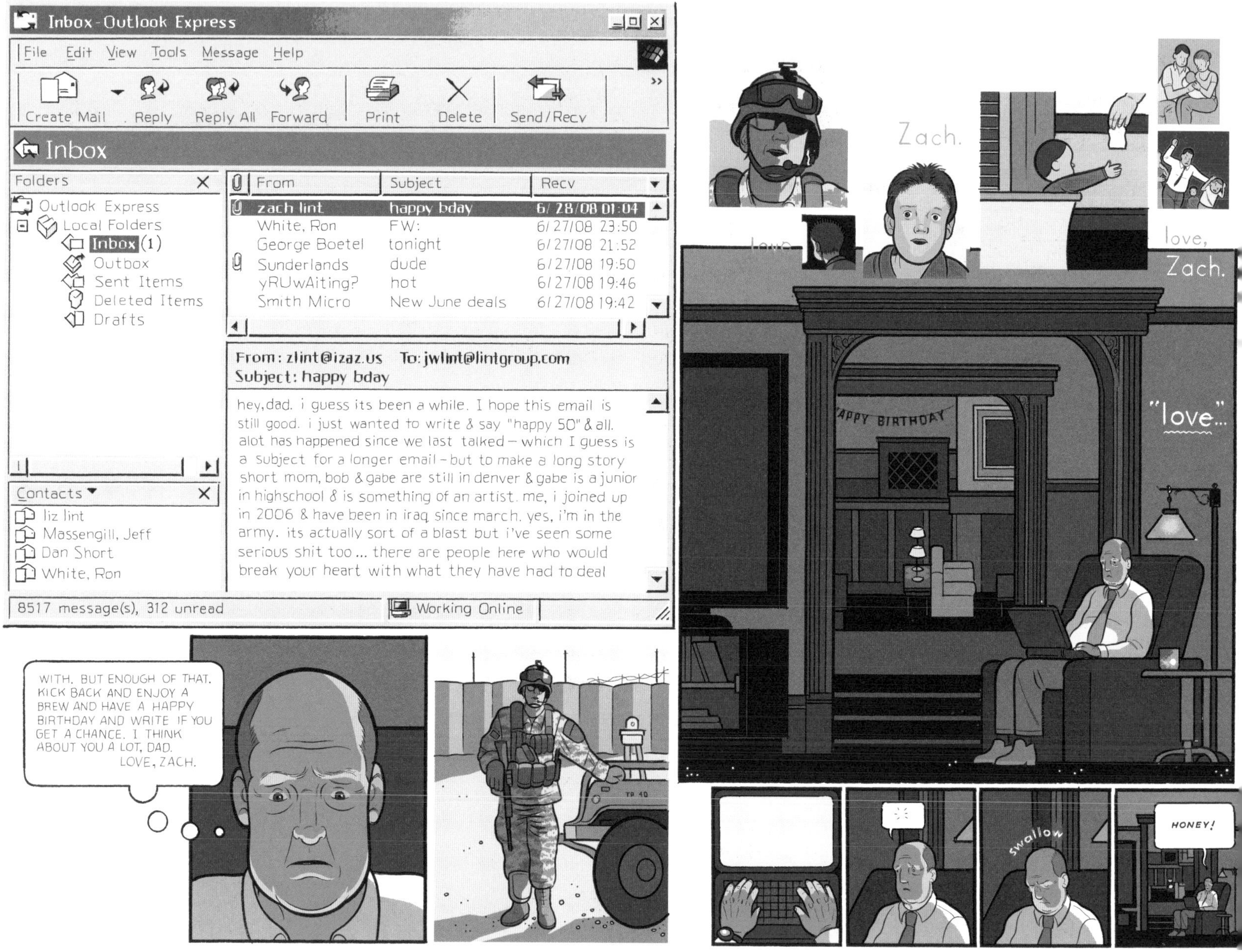
Inbox - Outlook Express
File Edit View Tools Message Help
Create Mail Reply Reply All Forward Print Delete Send/Recv
Inbox
Folders
Outlook Express
Local Folders
Inbox (1)
Outbox
Sent Items
Deleted Items
Drafts
From Subject Recv
zach lint happy bday 6/28/08 01:04
White, Ron FW: 6/27/08 23:50
George Boetel tonight 6/27/08 21:52
Sunderlands dude 6/27/08 19:50
yRUwAiting? hot 6/27/08 19:46
Smith Micro New June deals 6/27/08 19:42
From: zlint@izaz.us To: jwlint@lintgroup.com
Subject: happy bday
hey, dad. i guess its been a while. I hope this email is still good. i just wanted to write & say "happy 50" & all. alot has happened since we last talked – which I guess is a subject for a longer email – but to make a long story short mom, bob & gabe are still in denver & gabe is a junior in highschool & is something of an artist. me, i joined up in 2006 & have been in iraq since march. yes, i'm in the army. its actually sort of a blast but i've seen some serious shit too ... there are people here who would break your heart with what they have had to deal
Contacts
liz lint
Massengill, Jeff
Dan Short
White, Ron
8517 message(s), 312 unread
Working Online
WITH. BUT ENOUGH OF THAT. KICK BACK AND ENJOY A BREW AND HAVE A HAPPY BIRTHDAY AND WRITE IF YOU GET A CHANCE. I THINK ABOUT YOU A LOT, DAD. LOVE, ZACH.
Zach.
love,
Zach.
HAPPY BIRTHDAY
"love"...
swallow
HONEY!

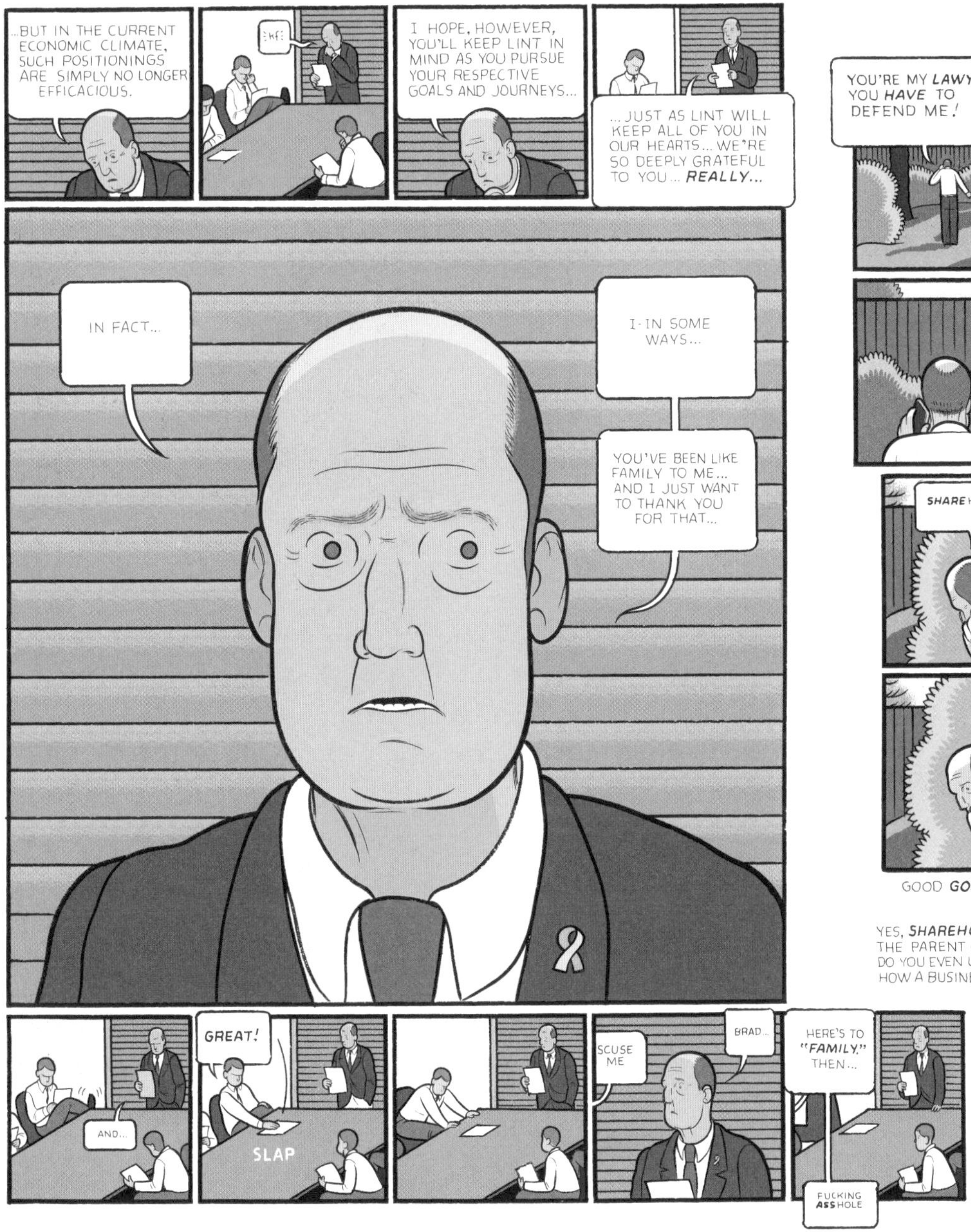
...BUT IN THE CURRENT ECONOMIC CLIMATE, SUCH POSITIONINGS ARE SIMPLY NO LONGER EFFICACIOUS.
I HOPE, HOWEVER, YOU'LL KEEP LINT IN MIND AS YOU PURSUE YOUR RESPECTIVE GOALS AND JOURNEYS...
...JUST AS LINT WILL KEEP ALL OF YOU IN OUR HEARTS... WE'RE SO DEEPLY GRATEFUL TO YOU... **REALLY...**
IN FACT...
I-IN SOME WAYS...
YOU'VE BEEN LIKE FAMILY TO ME... AND I JUST WANT TO THANK YOU FOR THAT...
AND...
GREAT!
SLAP
SCUSE ME
BRAD...
HERE'S TO "**FAMILY,**" THEN...
FUCKING **ASS**HOLE

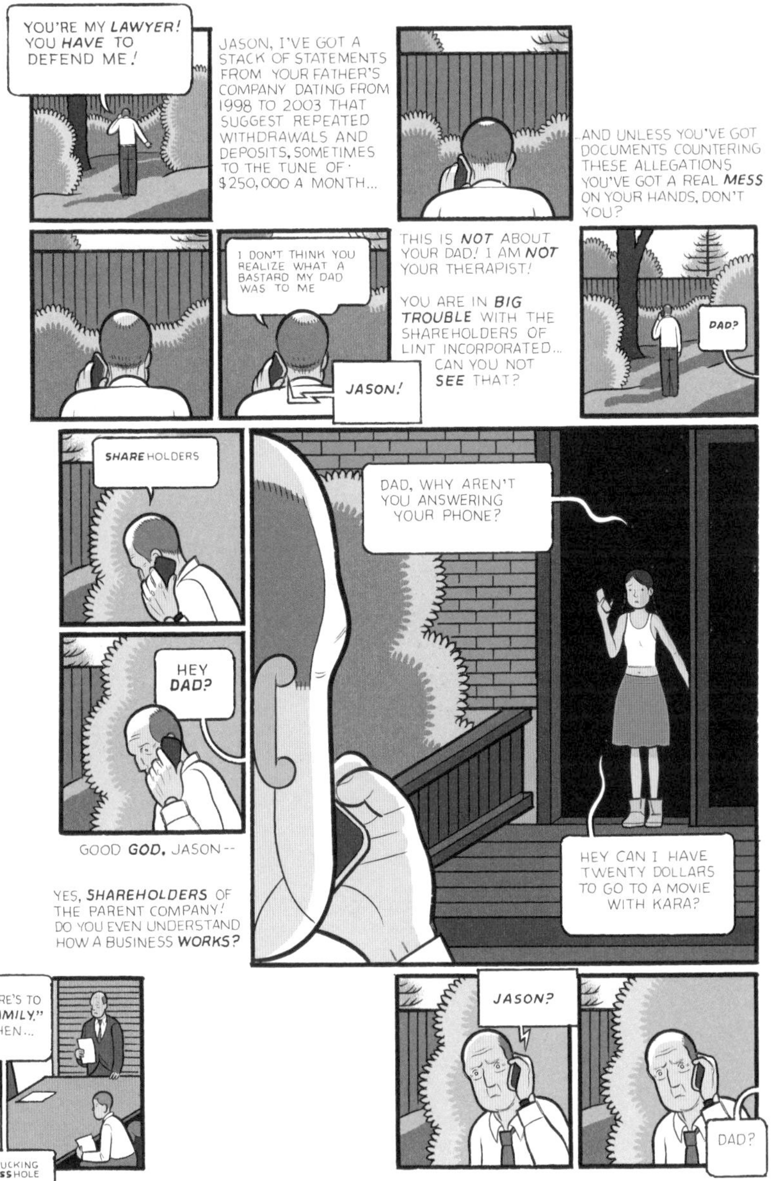
YOU'RE MY **LAWYER!** YOU **HAVE** TO DEFEND ME!
JASON, I'VE GOT A STACK OF STATEMENTS FROM YOUR FATHER'S COMPANY DATING FROM 1998 TO 2003 THAT SUGGEST REPEATED WITHDRAWALS AND DEPOSITS, SOMETIMES TO THE TUNE OF $250,000 A MONTH...
...AND UNLESS YOU'VE GOT DOCUMENTS COUNTERING THESE ALLEGATIONS YOU'VE GOT A REAL **MESS** ON YOUR HANDS, DON'T YOU?
I DON'T THINK YOU REALIZE WHAT A BASTARD MY DAD WAS TO ME
JASON!
THIS IS **NOT** ABOUT YOUR DAD! I AM **NOT** YOUR THERAPIST!
YOU ARE IN **BIG TROUBLE** WITH THE SHAREHOLDERS OF LINT INCORPORATED... CAN YOU NOT **SEE** THAT?
DAD?
SHAREHOLDERS
HEY **DAD?**
GOOD **GOD,** JASON--
YES, **SHAREHOLDERS** OF THE PARENT COMPANY! DO YOU EVEN UNDERSTAND HOW A BUSINESS **WORKS?**
DAD, WHY AREN'T YOU ANSWERING YOUR PHONE?
HEY CAN I HAVE TWENTY DOLLARS TO GO TO A MOVIE WITH KARA?
JASON?
DAD?

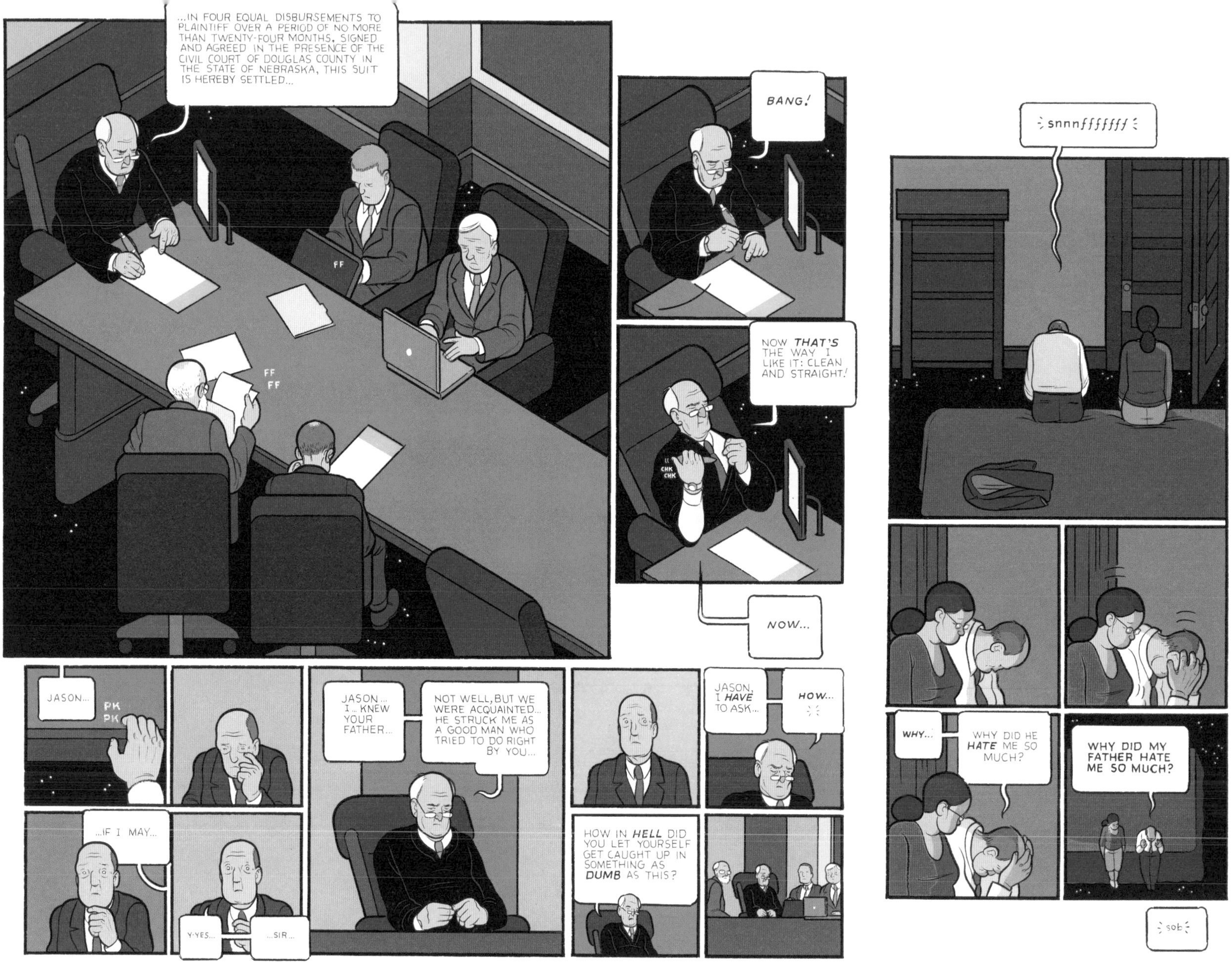

...IN FOUR EQUAL DISBURSEMENTS TO PLAINTIFF OVER A PERIOD OF NO MORE THAN TWENTY-FOUR MONTHS. SIGNED AND AGREED IN THE PRESENCE OF THE CIVIL COURT OF DOUGLAS COUNTY IN THE STATE OF NEBRASKA, THIS SUIT IS HEREBY SETTLED...
FF
FF
FF
BANG!
NOW THAT'S THE WAY I LIKE IT: CLEAN AND STRAIGHT!
CHK
CHK
NOW...
JASON...
PK
PK
...IF I MAY...
Y-YES...
...SIR...
JASON... I... KNEW YOUR FATHER...
NOT WELL, BUT WE WERE ACQUAINTED... HE STRUCK ME AS A GOOD MAN WHO TRIED TO DO RIGHT BY YOU...
JASON, I HAVE TO ASK...
HOW...
HOW IN HELL DID YOU LET YOURSELF GET CAUGHT UP IN SOMETHING AS DUMB AS THIS?
snnnfffffff
WHY...
WHY DID HE HATE ME SO MUCH?
WHY DID MY FATHER HATE ME SO MUCH?
sob

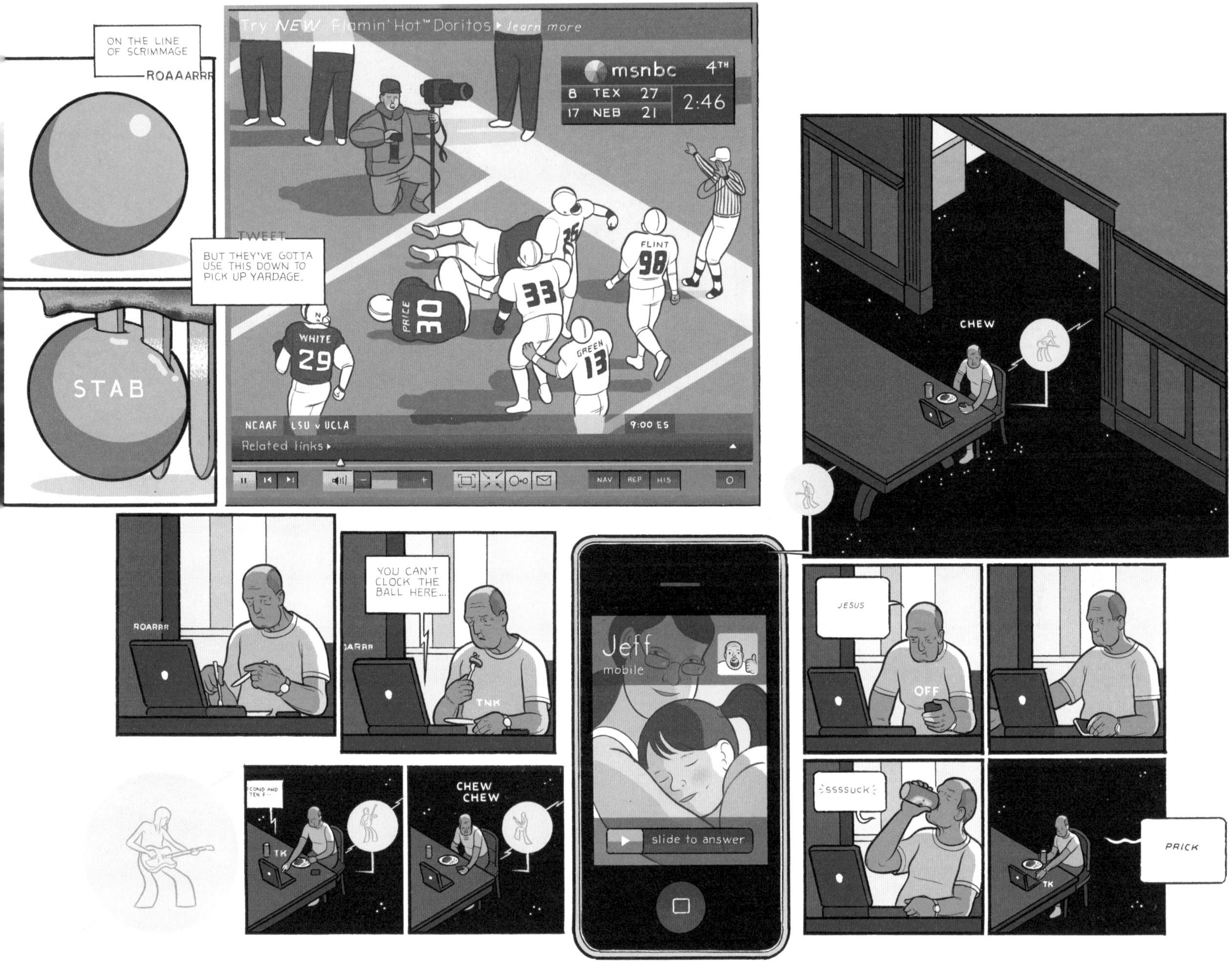

ON THE LINE OF SCRIMMAGE
ROAAARRR
STAB
Try NEW Flamin' Hot™ Doritos ▸ learn more
msnbc 4TH
8 TEX 27
17 NEB 21
2:46
TWEET
BUT THEY'VE GOTTA USE THIS DOWN TO PICK UP YARDAGE.
WHITE 29
PRICE 30
33
FLINT 98
GREEN 13
NCAAF
LSU v UCLA
9:00 ES
Related links ▸
NAV
REP
HIS
CHEW
ROARRR
YOU CAN'T CLOCK THE BALL HERE...
ARRR
TNK
Jeff
mobile
slide to answer
JESUS
OFF
ECOND AND TEN F--
TK
CHEW CHEW
SSSSUCK
TK
PRICK

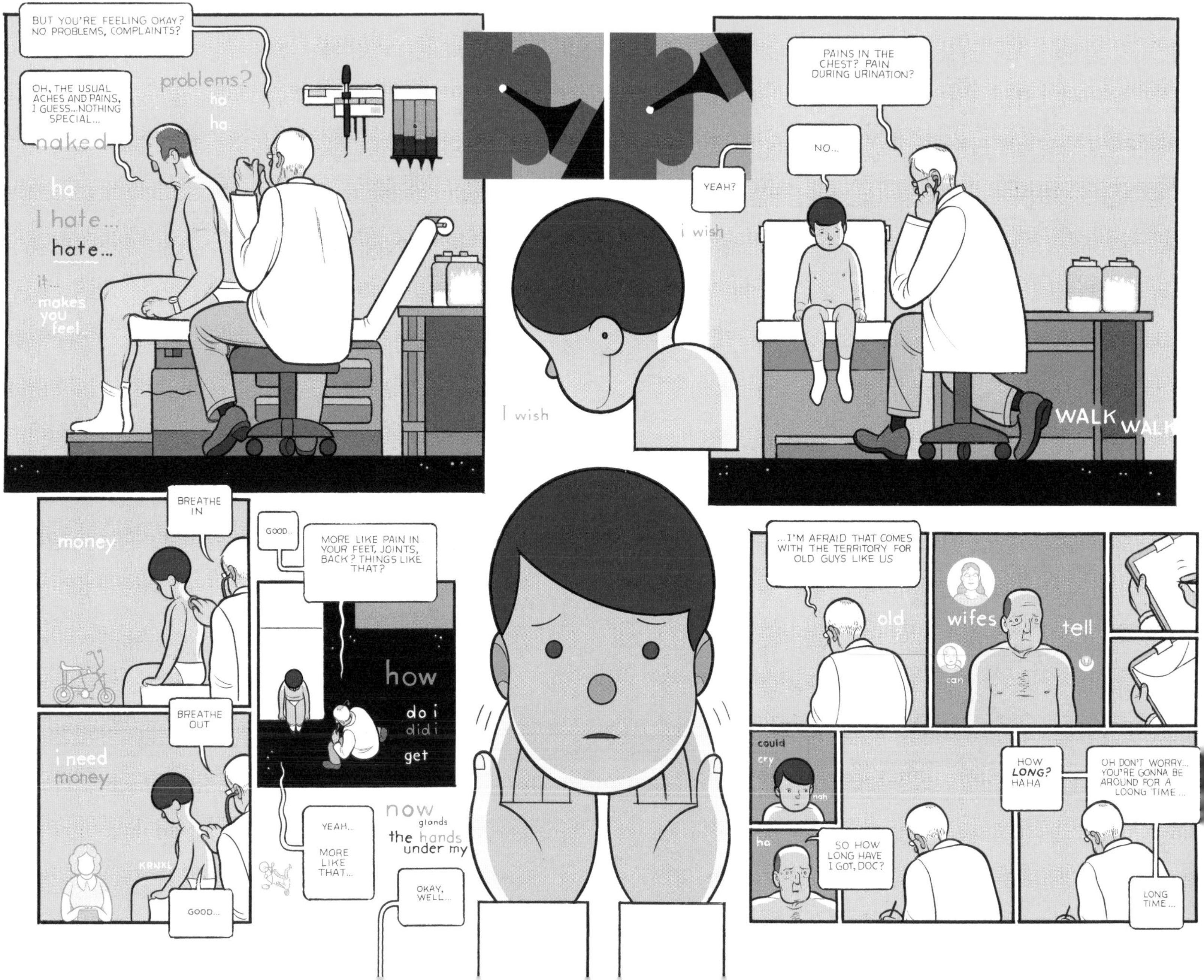
BUT YOU'RE FEELING OKAY? NO PROBLEMS, COMPLAINTS?
OH, THE USUAL ACHES AND PAINS, I GUESS...NOTHING SPECIAL...
problems?
ha
ha
naked
ha
I hate...
hate...
it...
makes you feel...
YEAH?
PAINS IN THE CHEST? PAIN DURING URINATION?
NO...
i wish
I wish
WALK
WALK
BREATHE IN
money
BREATHE OUT
i need money
KRNKL
GOOD...
GOOD...
MORE LIKE PAIN IN YOUR FEET, JOINTS, BACK? THINGS LIKE THAT?
how
do i
did i
get
YEAH...
MORE LIKE THAT...
now
glands
the hands
under my
OKAY, WELL...
...I'M AFRAID THAT COMES WITH THE TERRITORY FOR OLD GUYS LIKE US
old
?
wifes
tell
can
could
cry
nah
ha
SO HOW LONG HAVE I GOT, DOC?
HOW LONG? HAHA
OH DON'T WORRY... YOU'RE GONNA BE AROUND FOR A LOONG TIME...
LONG TIME...

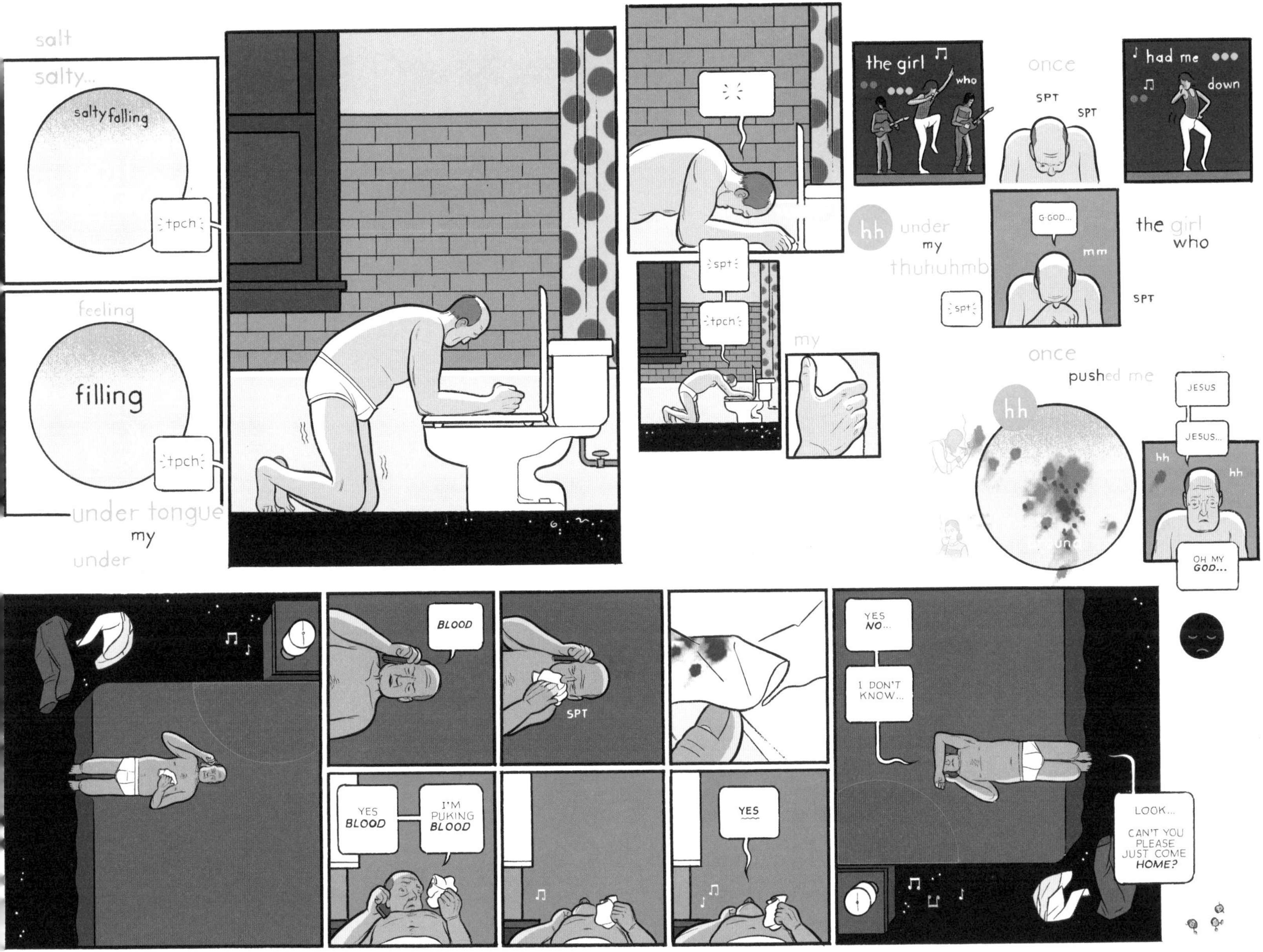
salt
salty...
salty falling
tpch
feeling
filling
tpch
under tongue
my
under
spt
tpch
my
the girl
who
once
SPT
SPT
had me
down
hh
under
my
thuhuhmb
spt
G GOD...
mm
the girl
who
SPT
once
pushed me
hh
JESUS
JESUS...
hh
hh
OH MY
GOD...
BLOOD
SPT
YES
BLOOD
I'M
PUKING
BLOOD
YES
YES
NO...
I DON'T
KNOW...
LOOK...
CAN'T YOU
PLEASE
JUST COME
HOME?

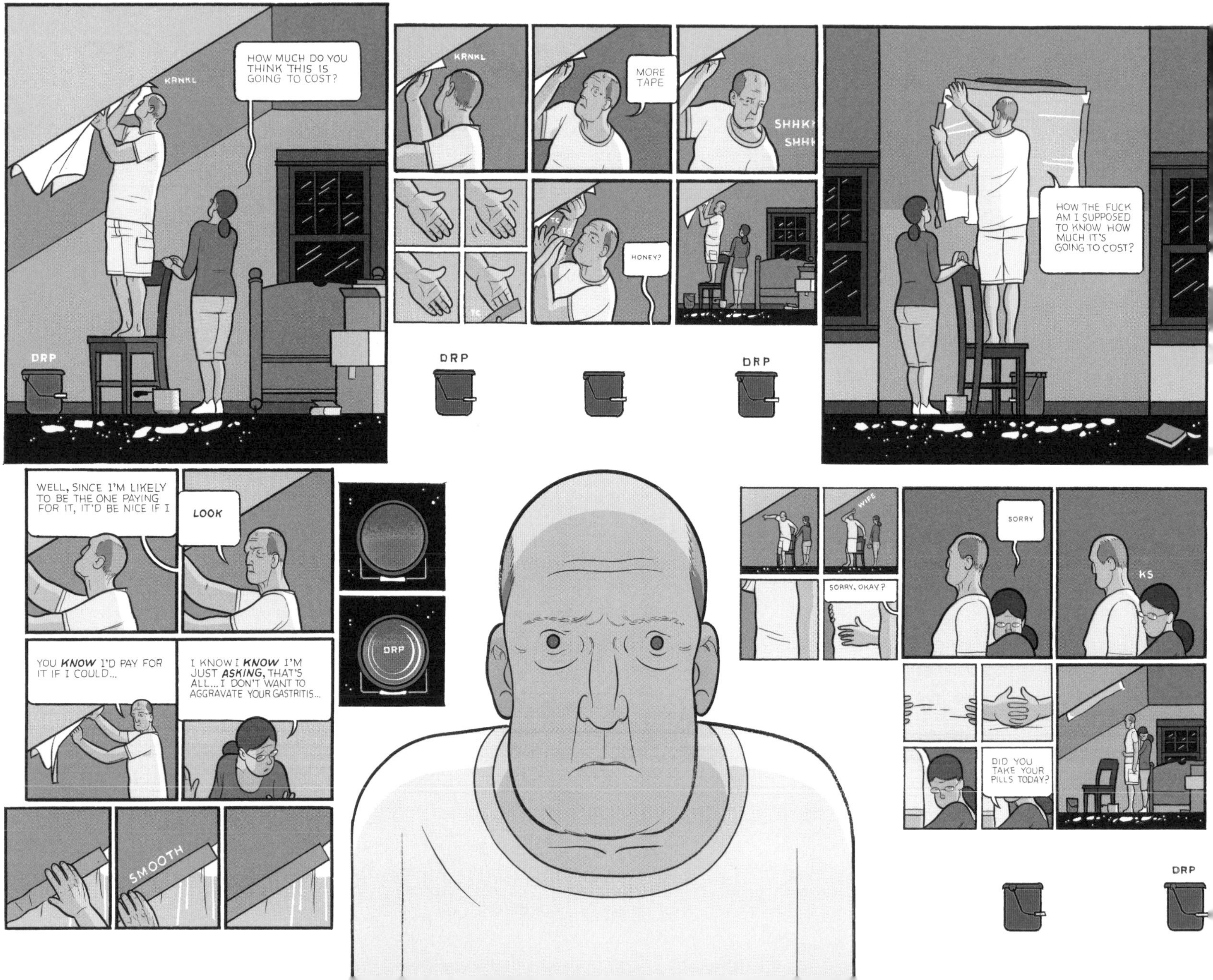

KRNKL
HOW MUCH DO YOU THINK THIS IS GOING TO COST?
DRP
KRNKL
MORE TAPE
SHHKK SHHK
TC
TC TC
HONEY?
DRP
DRP
HOW THE FUCK AM I SUPPOSED TO KNOW HOW MUCH IT'S GOING TO COST?
WELL, SINCE I'M LIKELY TO BE THE ONE PAYING FOR IT, IT'D BE NICE IF I
LOOK
YOU KNOW I'D PAY FOR IT IF I COULD...
I KNOW I KNOW I'M JUST ASKING, THAT'S ALL... I DON'T WANT TO AGGRAVATE YOUR GASTRITIS...
SMOOTH
DRP
WIPE
SORRY, OKAY?
SORRY
KS
DID YOU TAKE YOUR PILLS TODAY?
DRP

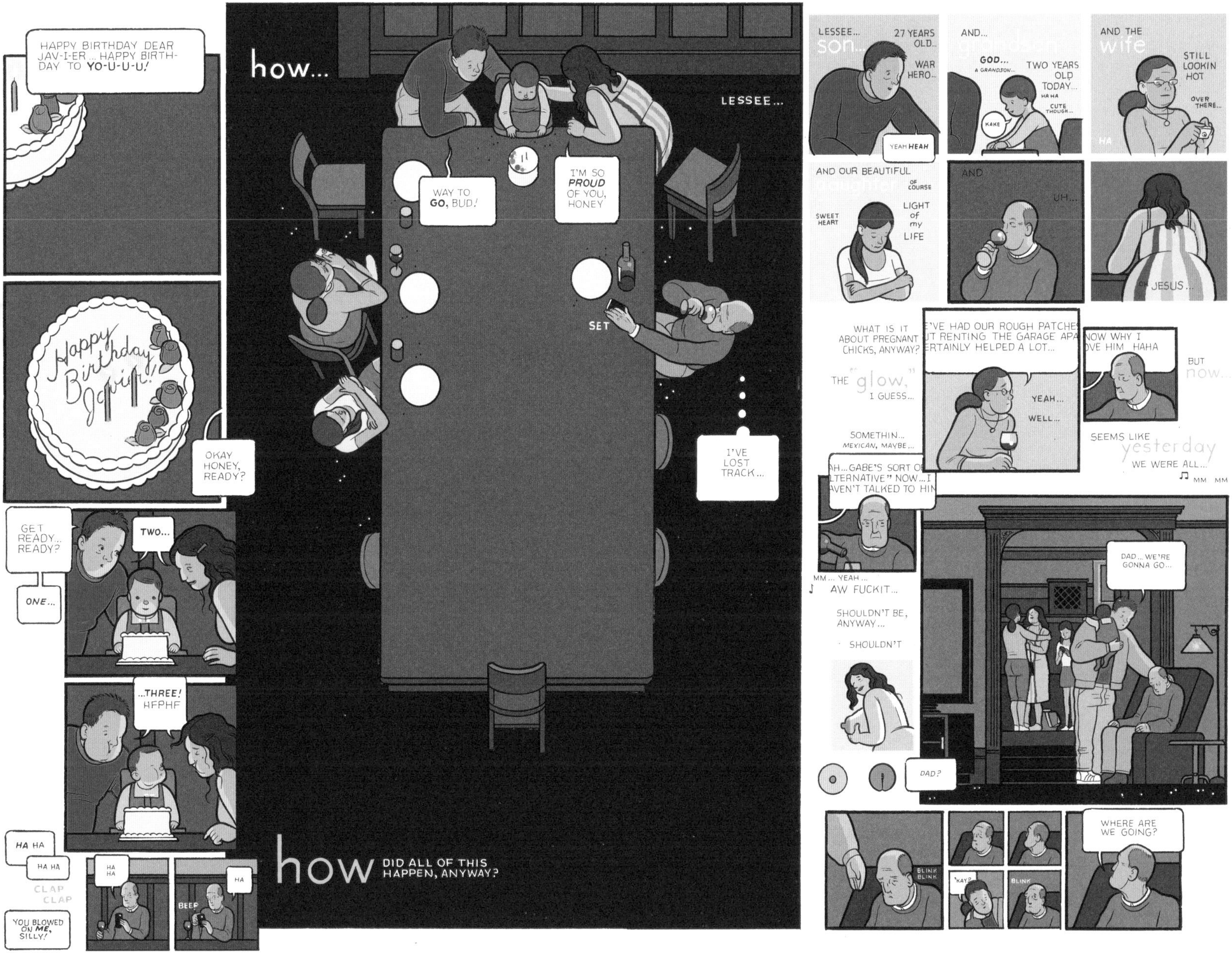

HAPPY BIRTHDAY DEAR JAV-I-ER... HAPPY BIRTH-DAY TO YO-U-U-U!
Happy Birthday Javier!
OKAY HONEY, READY?
GET READY... READY?
ONE...
TWO...
...THREE! HFPHF
HA HA
HA HA
CLAP
CLAP
YOU BLOWED ON ME, SILLY!
HA HA
BEEP
HA
how...
LESSEE...
WAY TO GO, BUD!
I'M SO PROUD OF YOU, HONEY
SET
I'VE LOST TRACK...
how DID ALL OF THIS HAPPEN, ANYWAY?
LESSEE... son...
27 YEARS OLD...
WAR HERO...
YEAH HEAH
AND... grandson
GOD... A GRANDSON...
TWO YEARS OLD TODAY...
HA HA
CUTE THOUGH...
KAKE
AND THE wife
STILL LOOKIN HOT
OVER THERE...
HA
AND OUR BEAUTIFUL daughter
OF COURSE
SWEET HEART
LIGHT of my LIFE
AND
UH...
OH JESUS...
WHAT IS IT ABOUT PREGNANT CHICKS, ANYWAY?
THE "glow," I GUESS...
SOMETHIN...
MEXICAN, MAYBE...
'VE HAD OUR ROUGH PATCHES UT RENTING THE GARAGE APA ERTAINLY HELPED A LOT...
YEAH...
WELL...
NOW WHY I VE HIM HAHA
BUT now...
SEEMS LIKE yesterday WE WERE ALL...
MM MM
AH... GABE'S SORT OF LTERNATIVE" NOW... I AVEN'T TALKED TO HIM
MM... YEAH...
AW FUCKIT...
SHOULDN'T BE, ANYWAY...
SHOULDN'T
DAD?
DAD... WE'RE GONNA GO...
BLINK BLINK
'KAY?
BLINK
WHERE ARE WE GOING?

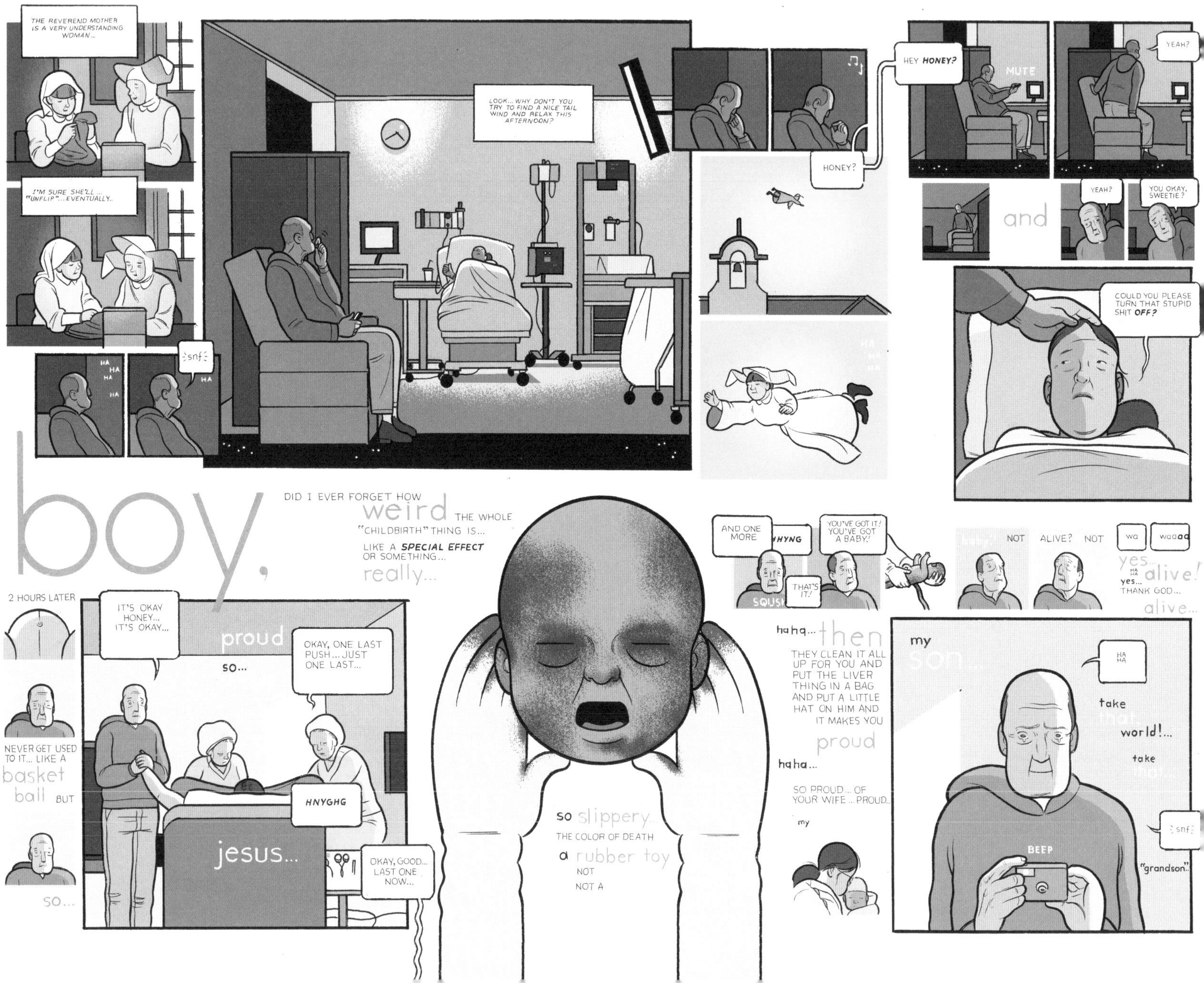
THE REVEREND MOTHER IS A VERY UNDERSTANDING WOMAN...
I'M SURE SHE'LL ... "UNFLIP"... EVENTUALLY..
HA HA HA HA
snf
HA
LOOK... WHY DON'T YOU TRY TO FIND A NICE TAIL WIND AND RELAX THIS AFTERNOON?
HONEY?
HEY HONEY?
MUTE
YEAH?
and
YEAH?
YOU OKAY, SWEETIE?
COULD YOU PLEASE TURN THAT STUPID SHIT OFF?
boy,
DID I EVER FORGET HOW weird THE WHOLE "CHILDBIRTH" THING IS...
LIKE A SPECIAL EFFECT OR SOMETHING...
really...
2 HOURS LATER
NEVER GET USED TO IT... LIKE A basket ball BUT
so...
IT'S OKAY HONEY... IT'S OKAY...
proud
so...
OKAY, ONE LAST PUSH... JUST ONE LAST...
HNYGHG
jesus...
OKAY, GOOD... LAST ONE NOW...
so slippery...
THE COLOR OF DEATH
a rubber toy
NOT
NOT A
AND ONE MORE
HYNG
THAT'S IT!
SQUSH
YOU'VE GOT IT! YOU'VE GOT A BABY!
NOT
ALIVE?
NOT
wa
waaaa
yes...
yes...
alive!
THANK GOD...
alive...
haha... then
THEY CLEAN IT ALL UP FOR YOU AND PUT THE LIVER THING IN A BAG AND PUT A LITTLE HAT ON HIM AND IT MAKES YOU
proud
haha...
SO PROUD... OF YOUR WIFE... PROUD...
my
my
son...
HA HA
take that world!...
take that
snf
BEEP
"grandson"

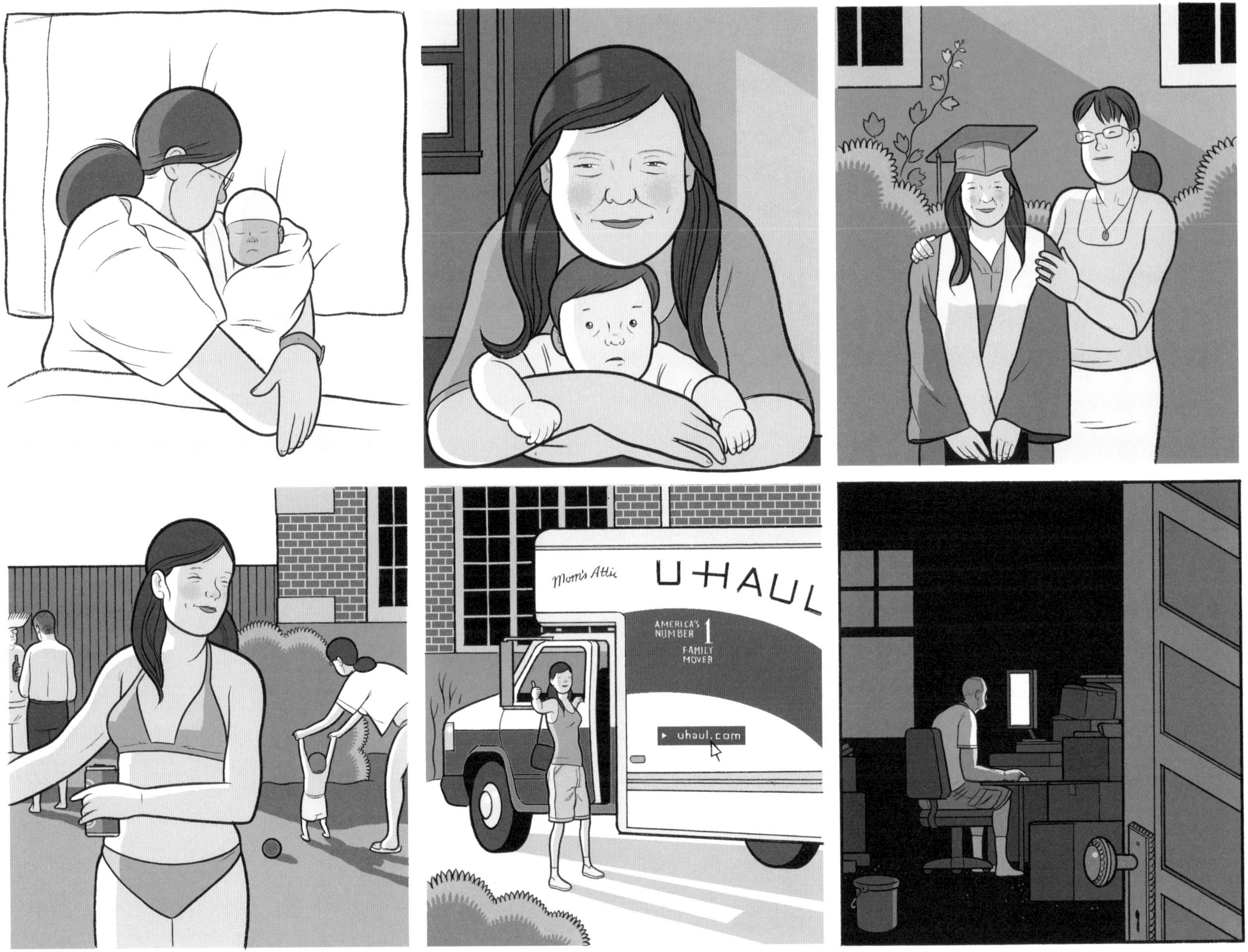

Mom's Attic
U-HAUL
AMERICA'S NUMBER 1 FAMILY MOVER
uhaul.com

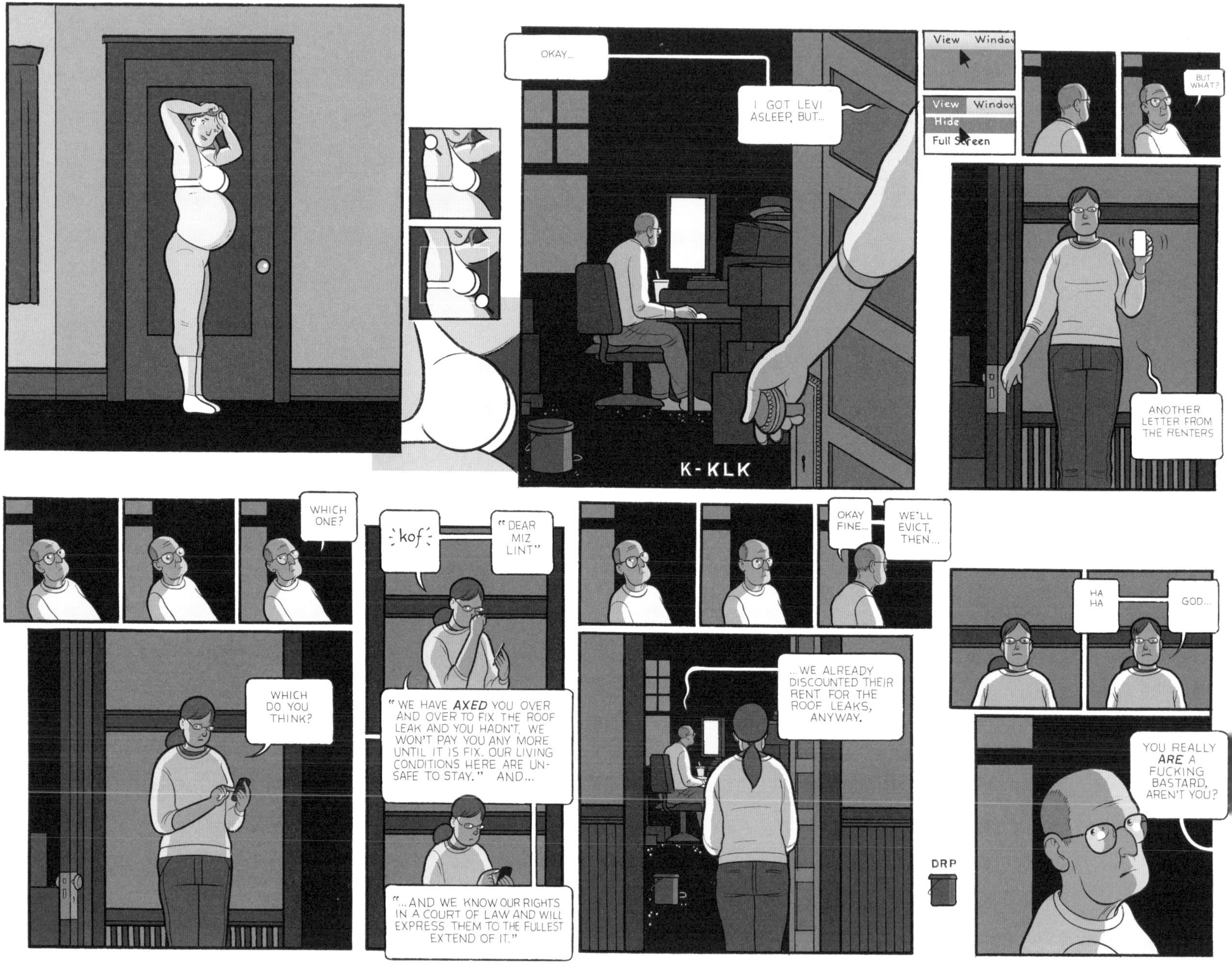

OKAY...
I GOT LEVI ASLEEP, BUT...
K-KLK
View Window
View Window
Hide
Full Screen
BUT WHAT?
ANOTHER LETTER FROM THE RENTERS
WHICH ONE?
WHICH DO YOU THINK?
kof
"DEAR MIZ LINT"
"WE HAVE **AXED** YOU OVER AND OVER TO FIX THE ROOF LEAK AND YOU HADN'T. WE WON'T PAY YOU ANY MORE UNTIL IT IS FIX. OUR LIVING CONDITIONS HERE ARE UN-SAFE TO STAY." AND...
"...AND WE KNOW OUR RIGHTS IN A COURT OF LAW AND WILL EXPRESS THEM TO THE FULLEST EXTEND OF IT."
OKAY FINE...
WE'LL EVICT, THEN...
...WE ALREADY DISCOUNTED THEIR RENT FOR THE ROOF LEAKS, ANYWAY.
DRP
HA HA
GOD...
YOU REALLY **ARE** A FUCKING BASTARD, AREN'T YOU?

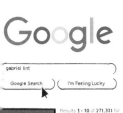

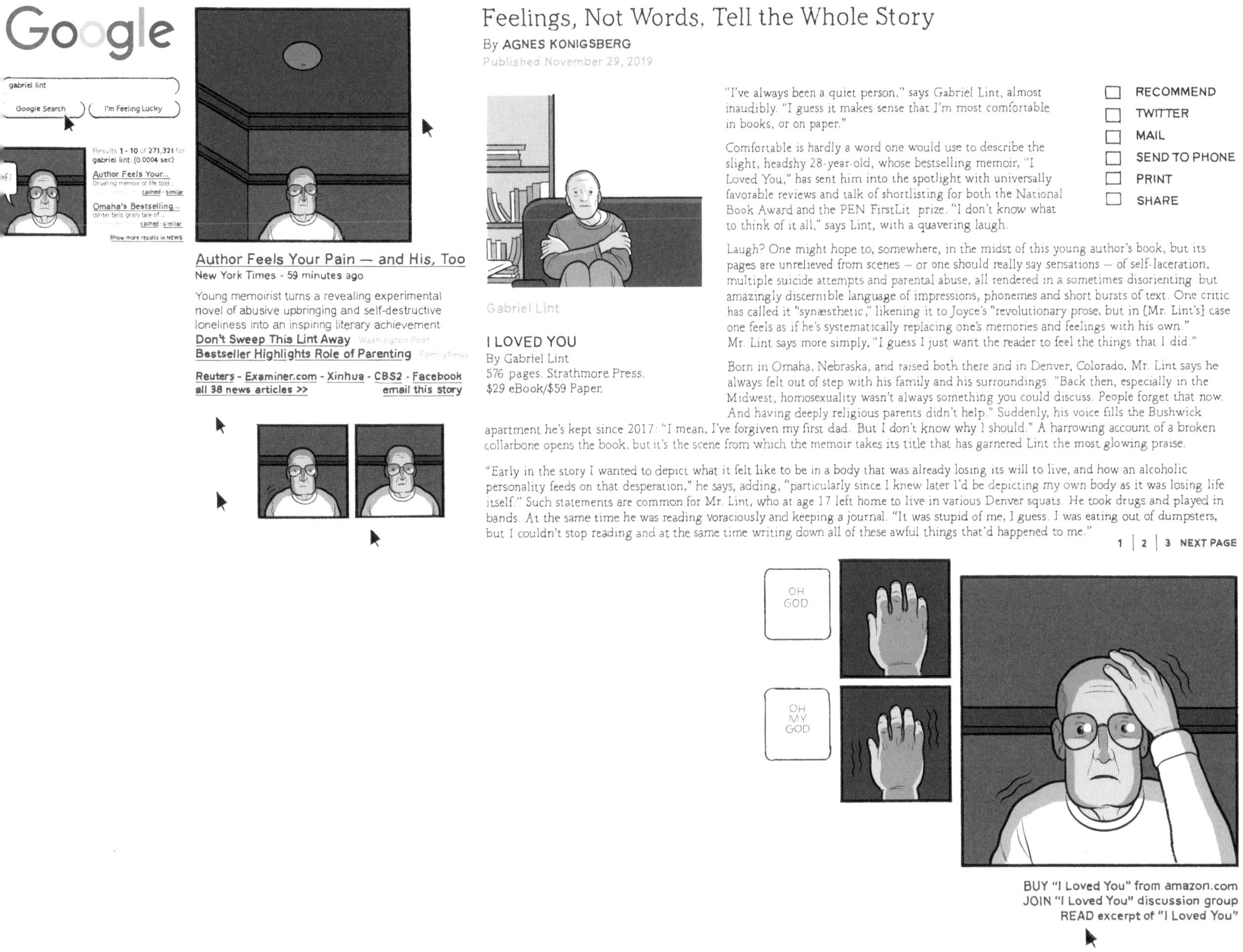

Google
gabriel lint
Google Search
I'm Feeling Lucky
Results 1 - 10 of 271,321 for gabriel lint. (0.0004 sec)
Author Feels Your...
Grueling memoir of life told...
cached - similar
Omaha's Bestselling...
Writer tells grisly tale of...
cached - similar
Show more results in NEWS
Author Feels Your Pain — and His, Too
New York Times - 59 minutes ago
Young memoirist turns a revealing experimental novel of abusive upbringing and self-destructive loneliness into an inspiring literary achievement.
Don't Sweep This Lint Away Washington Post
Bestseller Highlights Role of Parenting FamilyNews
Reuters - Examiner.com - Xinhua - CBS2 - Facebook
all 38 news articles >>
email this story
Feelings, Not Words, Tell the Whole Story
By AGNES KONIGSBERG
Published November 29, 2019
Gabriel Lint
I LOVED YOU
By Gabriel Lint
576 pages. Strathmore Press.
$29 eBook/$59 Paper.
RECOMMEND
TWITTER
MAIL
SEND TO PHONE
PRINT
SHARE
"I've always been a quiet person," says Gabriel Lint, almost inaudibly. "I guess it makes sense that I'm most comfortable in books, or on paper."
Comfortable is hardly a word one would use to describe the slight, headshy 28-year-old, whose bestselling memoir, "I Loved You," has sent him into the spotlight with universally favorable reviews and talk of shortlisting for both the National Book Award and the PEN FirstLit prize. "I don't know what to think of it all," says Lint, with a quavering laugh.
Laugh? One might hope to, somewhere, in the midst of this young author's book, but its pages are unrelieved from scenes – or one should really say sensations – of self-laceration, multiple suicide attempts and parental abuse, all rendered in a sometimes disorienting but amazingly discernible language of impressions, phonemes and short bursts of text. One critic has called it "synæsthetic," likening it to Joyce's "revolutionary prose, but in [Mr. Lint's] case one feels as if he's systematically replacing one's memories and feelings with his own." Mr. Lint says more simply, "I guess I just want the reader to feel the things that I did."
Born in Omaha, Nebraska, and raised both there and in Denver, Colorado, Mr. Lint says he always felt out of step with his family and his surroundings. "Back then, especially in the Midwest, homosexuality wasn't always something you could discuss. People forget that now. And having deeply religious parents didn't help." Suddenly, his voice fills the Bushwick apartment he's kept since 2017: "I mean, I've forgiven my first dad. But I don't know why I should." A harrowing account of a broken collarbone opens the book, but it's the scene from which the memoir takes its title that has garnered Lint the most glowing praise.
"Early in the story I wanted to depict what it felt like to be in a body that was already losing its will to live, and how an alcoholic personality feeds on that desperation," he says, adding, "particularly since I knew later I'd be depicting my own body as it was losing life itself." Such statements are common for Mr. Lint, who at age 17 left home to live in various Denver squats. He took drugs and played in bands. At the same time he was reading voraciously and keeping a journal. "It was stupid of me, I guess. I was eating out of dumpsters, but I couldn't stop reading and at the same time writing down all of these awful things that'd happened to me."
1 | 2 | 3 NEXT PAGE
OH GOD
OH MY GOD
BUY "I Loved You" from amazon.com
JOIN "I Loved You" discussion group
READ excerpt of "I Loved You"

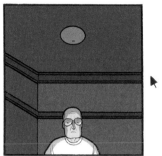

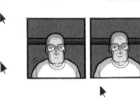

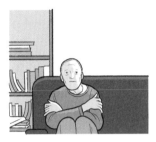

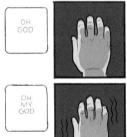

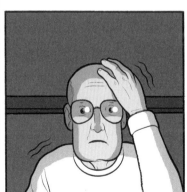

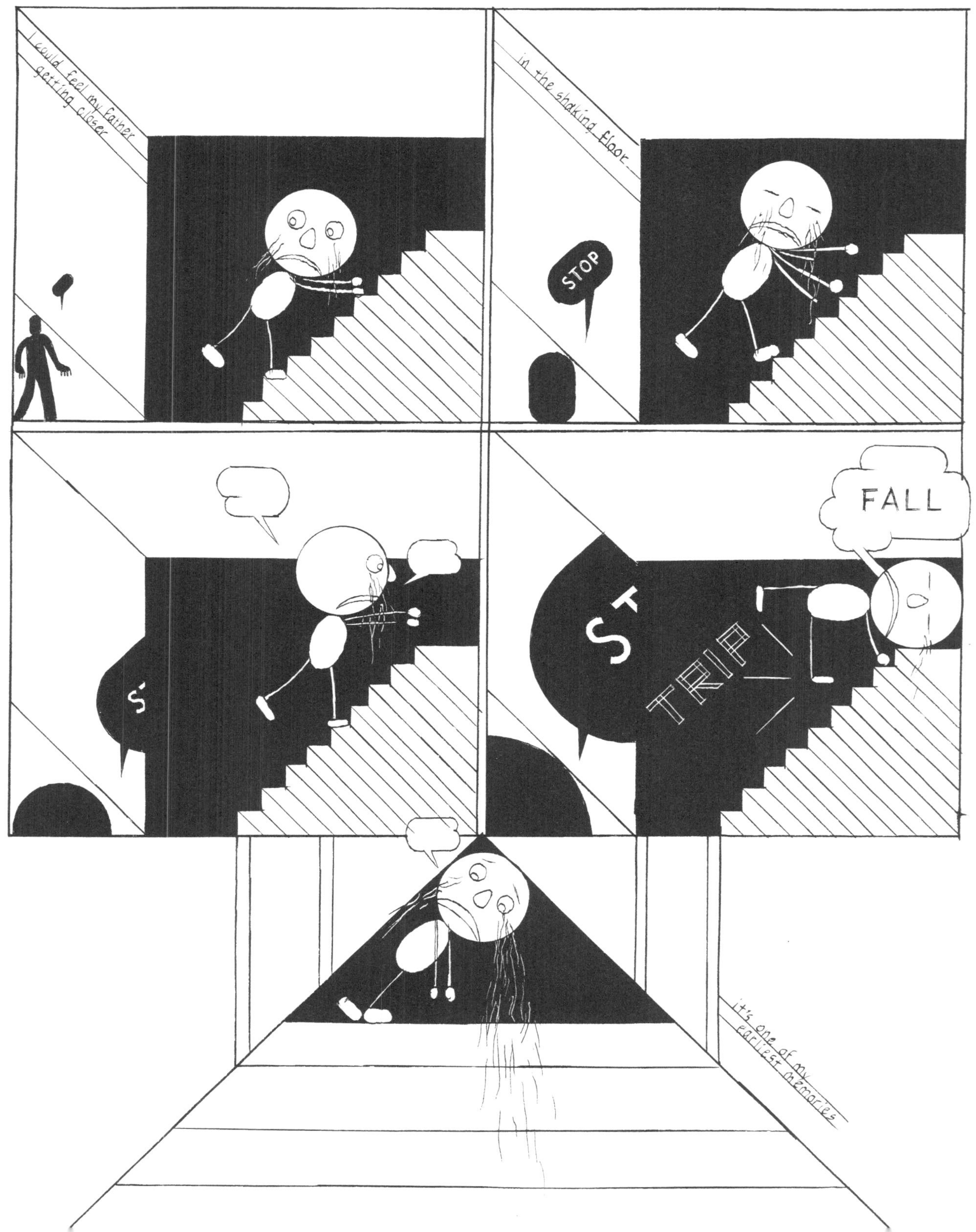
I could feel my father getting closer
in the shaking floor...
STOP
S'
S
T
TRIP
FALL
it's one of my earliest memories

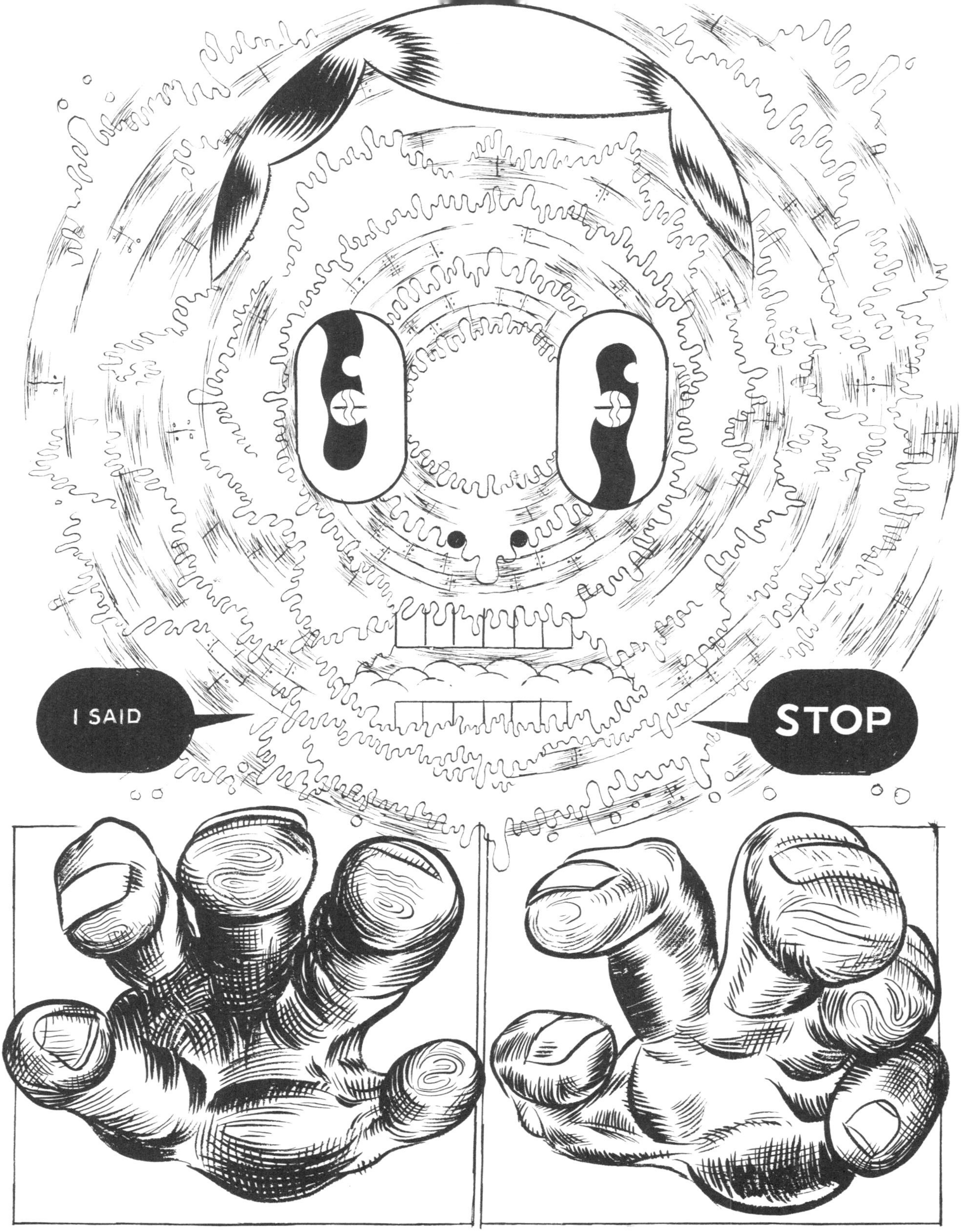
I SAID
STOP

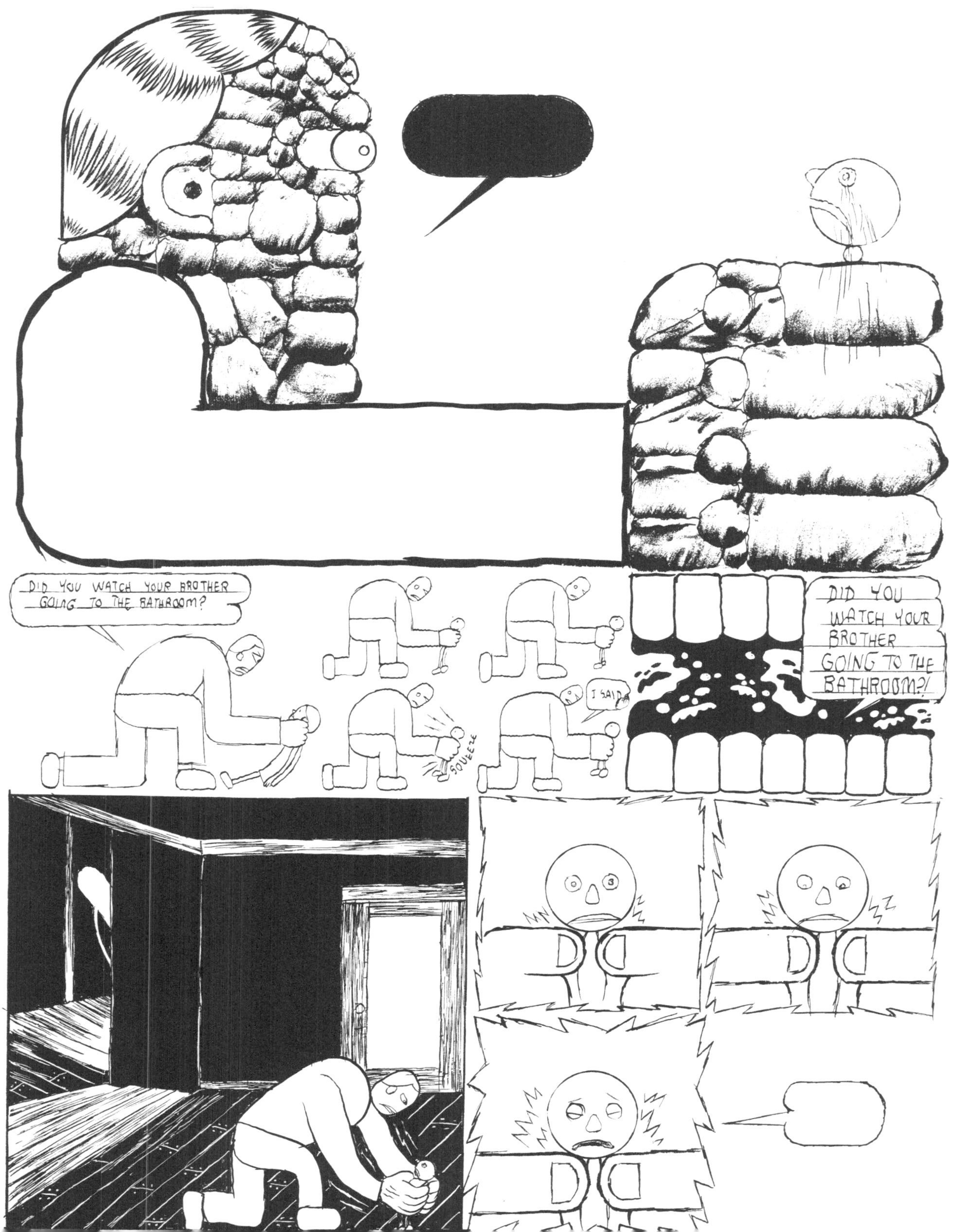
DID YOU WATCH YOUR BROTHER GOING TO THE BATHROOM?!
DID YOU WATCH YOUR BROTHER GOING TO THE BATHROOM?
SQUEEZE
I SAID

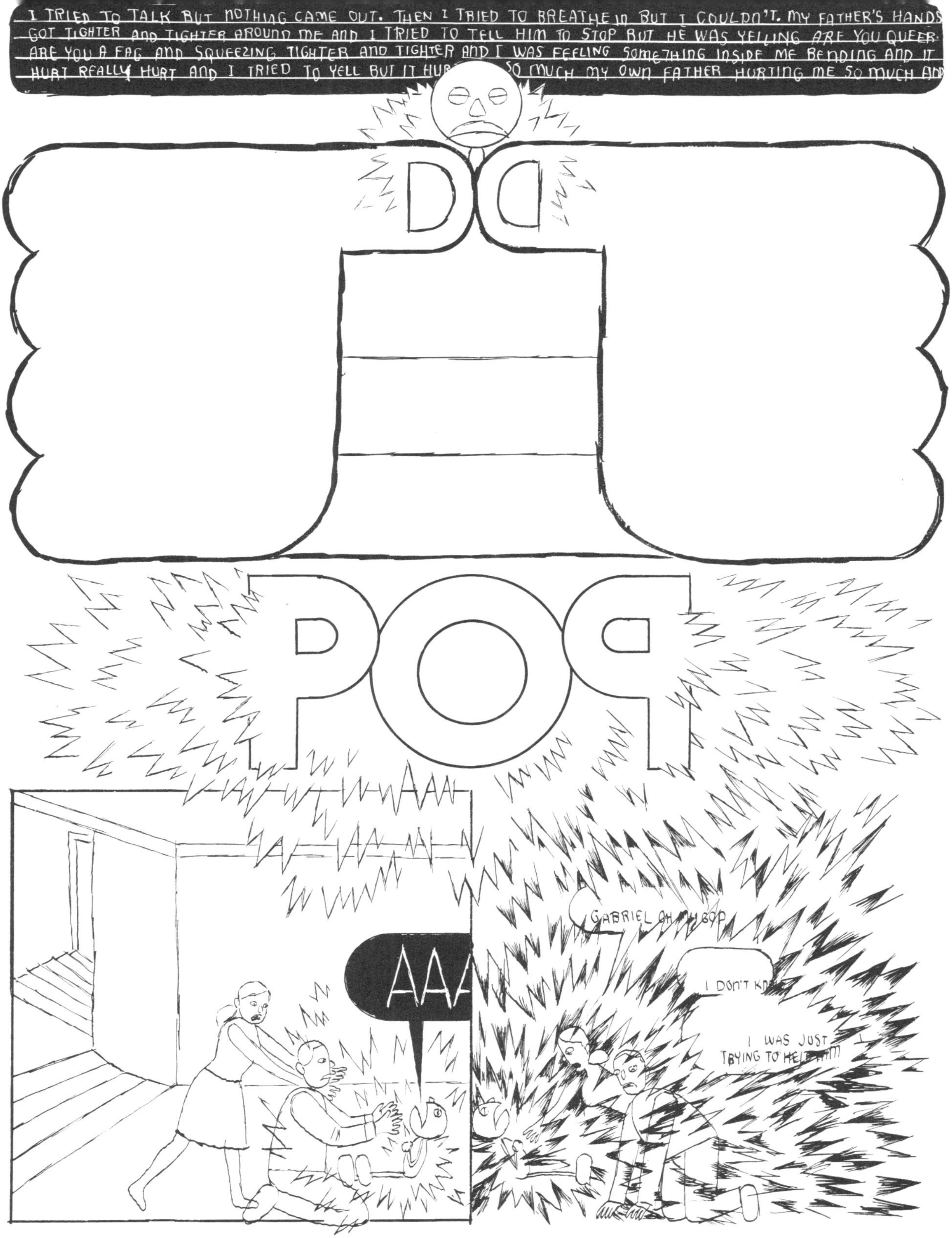
I TRIED TO TALK BUT NOTHING CAME OUT. THEN I TRIED TO BREATHE IN BUT I COULDN'T. MY FATHER'S HANDS GOT TIGHTER AND TIGHTER AROUND ME AND I TRIED TO TELL HIM TO STOP BUT HE WAS YELLING ARE YOU QUEER· ARE YOU A FAG AND SQUEEZING TIGHTER AND TIGHTER AND I WAS FEELING SOMETHING INSIDE ME BENDING AND IT HURT REALLY HURT AND I TRIED TO YELL BUT IT HUR SO MUCH MY OWN FATHER HURTING ME SO MUCH AND
POP
AAA
GABRIEL OH GOD
I DON'T KN
I WAS JUST TRYING TO

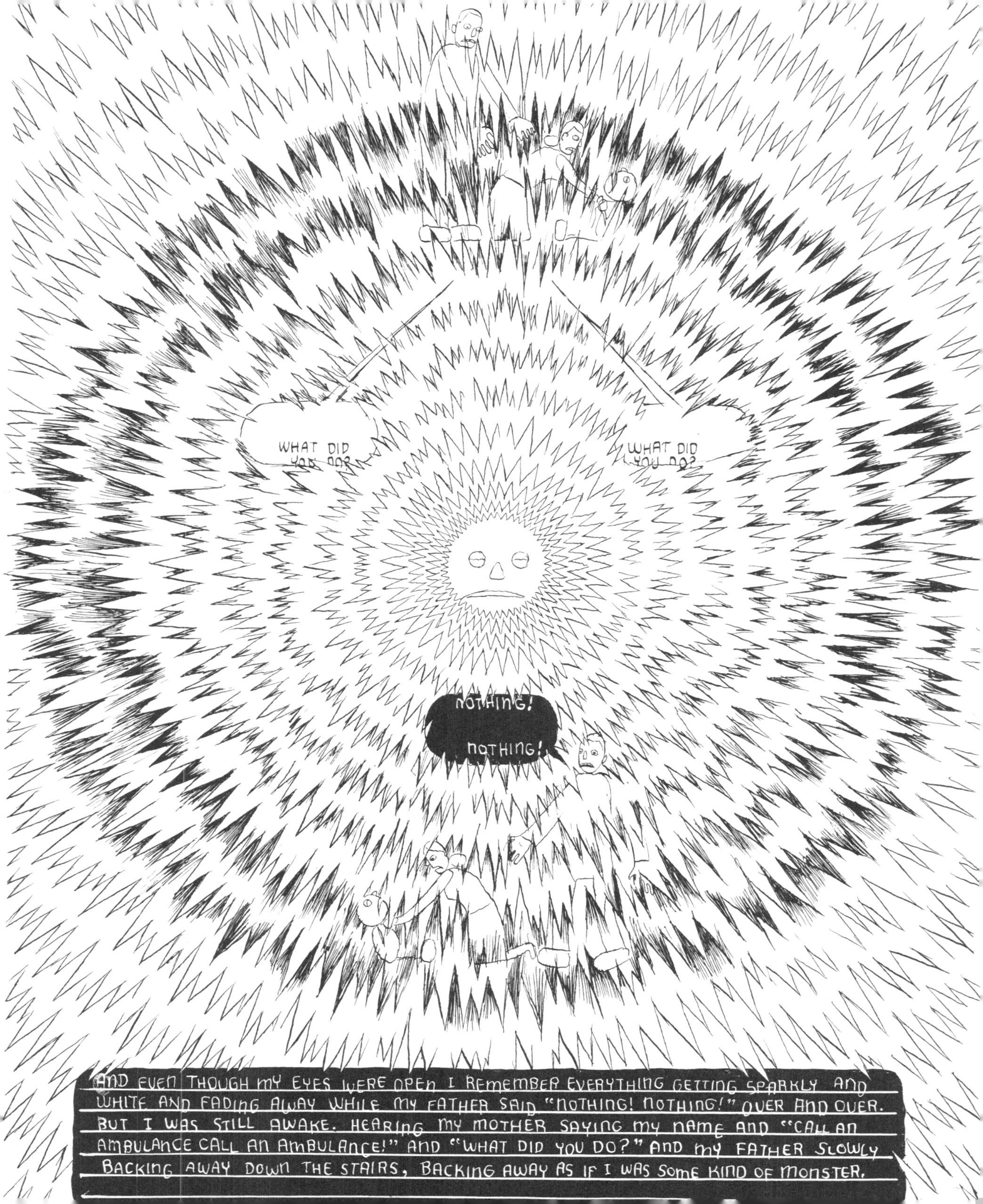
WHAT DID YOU DO?
WHAT DID YOU DO?
NOTHING!
NOTHING!
AND EVEN THOUGH MY EYES WERE OPEN I REMEMBER EVERYTHING GETTING SPARKLY AND WHITE AND FADING AWAY WHILE MY FATHER SAID "NOTHING! NOTHING!" OVER AND OVER. BUT I WAS STILL AWAKE. HEARING MY MOTHER SAYING MY NAME AND "CALL AN AMBULANCE CALL AN AMBULANCE!" AND "WHAT DID YOU DO?" AND MY FATHER SLOWLY BACKING AWAY DOWN THE STAIRS, BACKING AWAY AS IF I WAS SOME KIND OF MONSTER.

can an ambulance
t did you do?" and
y down the stairs,
kind of monster.
can an ambulance
t did you do?" and
y down the stairs,
kind of monster.
POPPA?
POPPA
POPPA WHERE'S MOMMA?
WHERE'S MOMMA, POPPA?

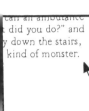

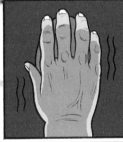

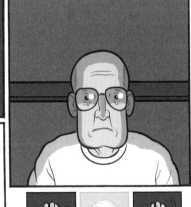

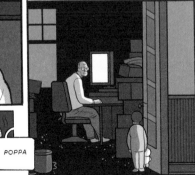

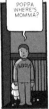

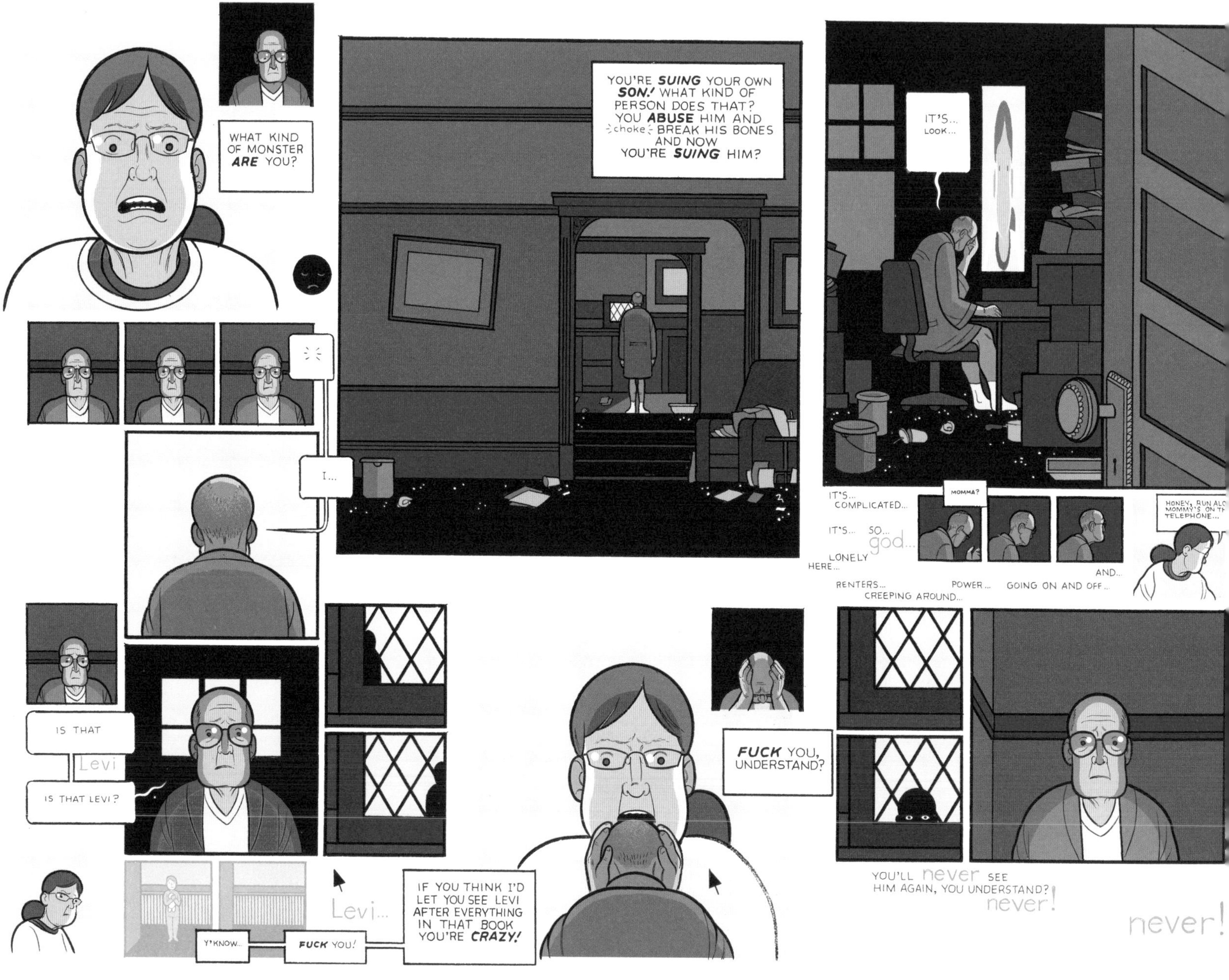

WHAT KIND OF MONSTER ARE YOU?
YOU'RE SUING YOUR OWN SON! WHAT KIND OF PERSON DOES THAT? YOU ABUSE HIM AND choke BREAK HIS BONES AND NOW YOU'RE SUING HIM?
I...
IS THAT
Levi
IS THAT LEVI?
Levi...
Y'KNOW...
FUCK YOU!
IF YOU THINK I'D LET YOU SEE LEVI AFTER EVERYTHING IN THAT BOOK YOU'RE CRAZY!
FUCK YOU, UNDERSTAND?
IT'S... LOOK...
IT'S... COMPLICATED...
IT'S... SO... god... LONELY HERE...
MOMMA?
HONEY, RUN ALO MOMMY'S ON TH TELEPHONE...
RENTERS... CREEPING AROUND...
POWER... GOING ON AND OFF... AND...
YOU'LL never SEE HIM AGAIN, YOU UNDERSTAND?
never!
never!

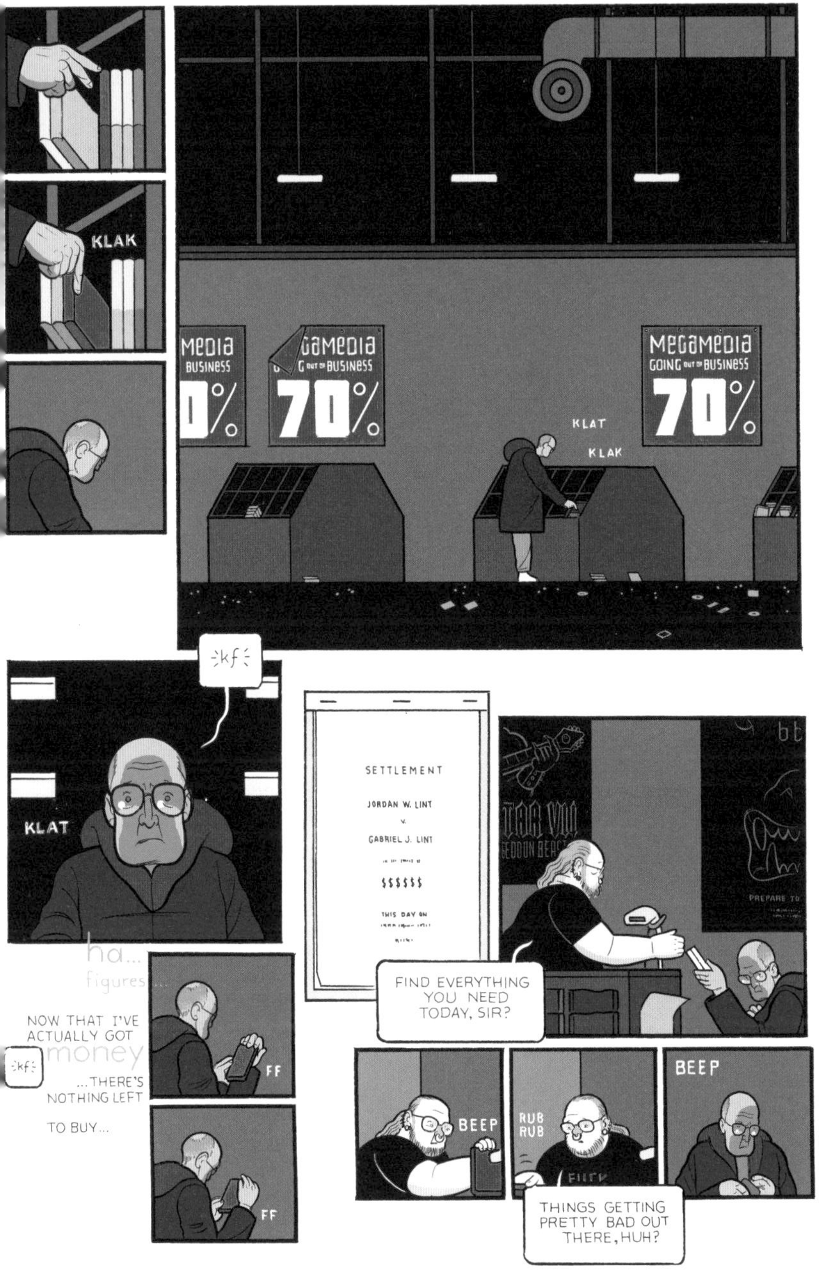
KLAK
MEDIA BUSINESS
70%
MEGAMEDIA GOING OUT OF BUSINESS
70%
KLAT
KLAK
kf
KLAT
SETTLEMENT
JORDAN W. LINT
V.
GABRIEL J. LINT
$$$$$$
THIS DAY ON
ha...
figures...
NOW THAT I'VE ACTUALLY GOT
money
kf
...THERE'S NOTHING LEFT TO BUY...
FF
FF
FIND EVERYTHING YOU NEED TODAY, SIR?
BEEP
RUB RUB
BEEP
THINGS GETTING PRETTY BAD OUT THERE, HUH?
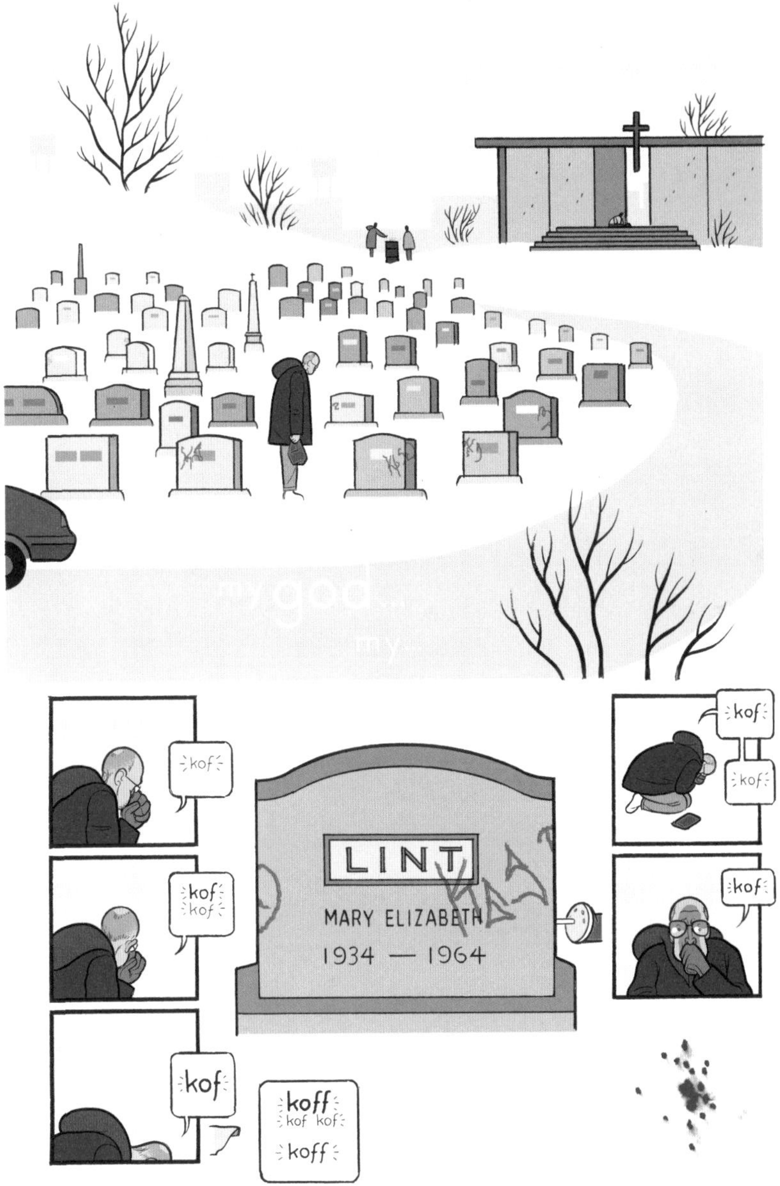
my god...
my
kof
kof kof
kof
LINT
MARY ELIZABETH
1934 — 1964
kof
kof
kof
koff kof kof koff

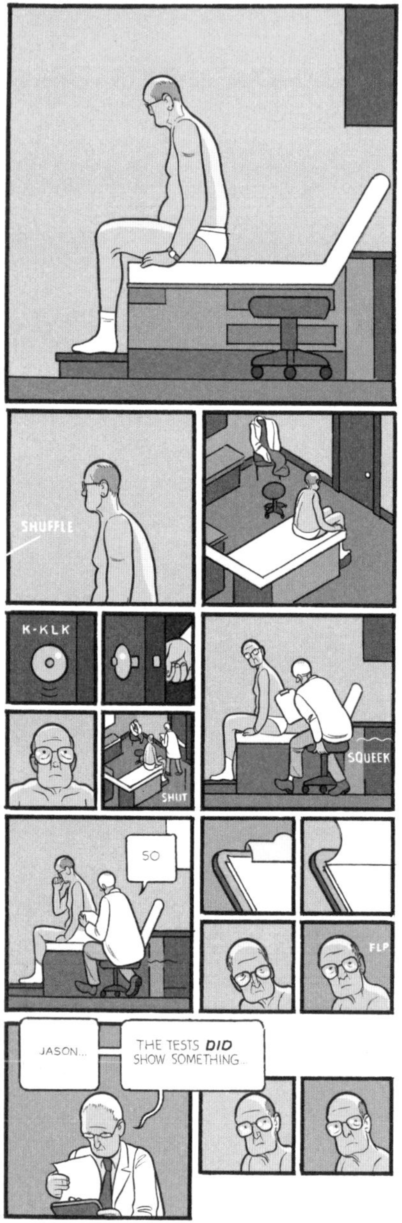
SHUFFLE
K-KLK
SHUT
SQUEEK
SO
FLP
JASON...
THE TESTS DID SHOW SOMETHING...

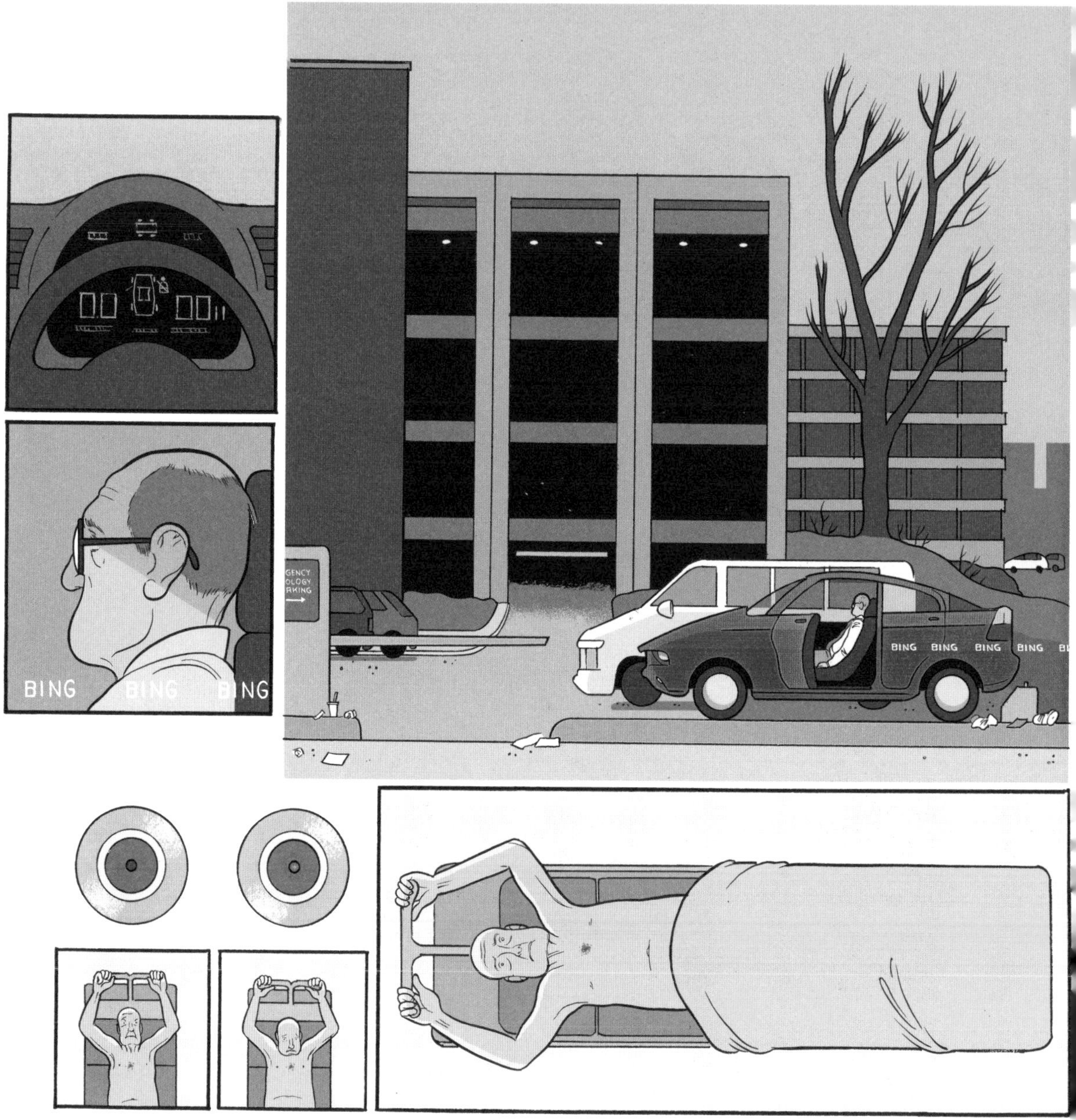
BING
BING
BING
GENCY
OLOGY
RKING
BING
BING
BING
BING

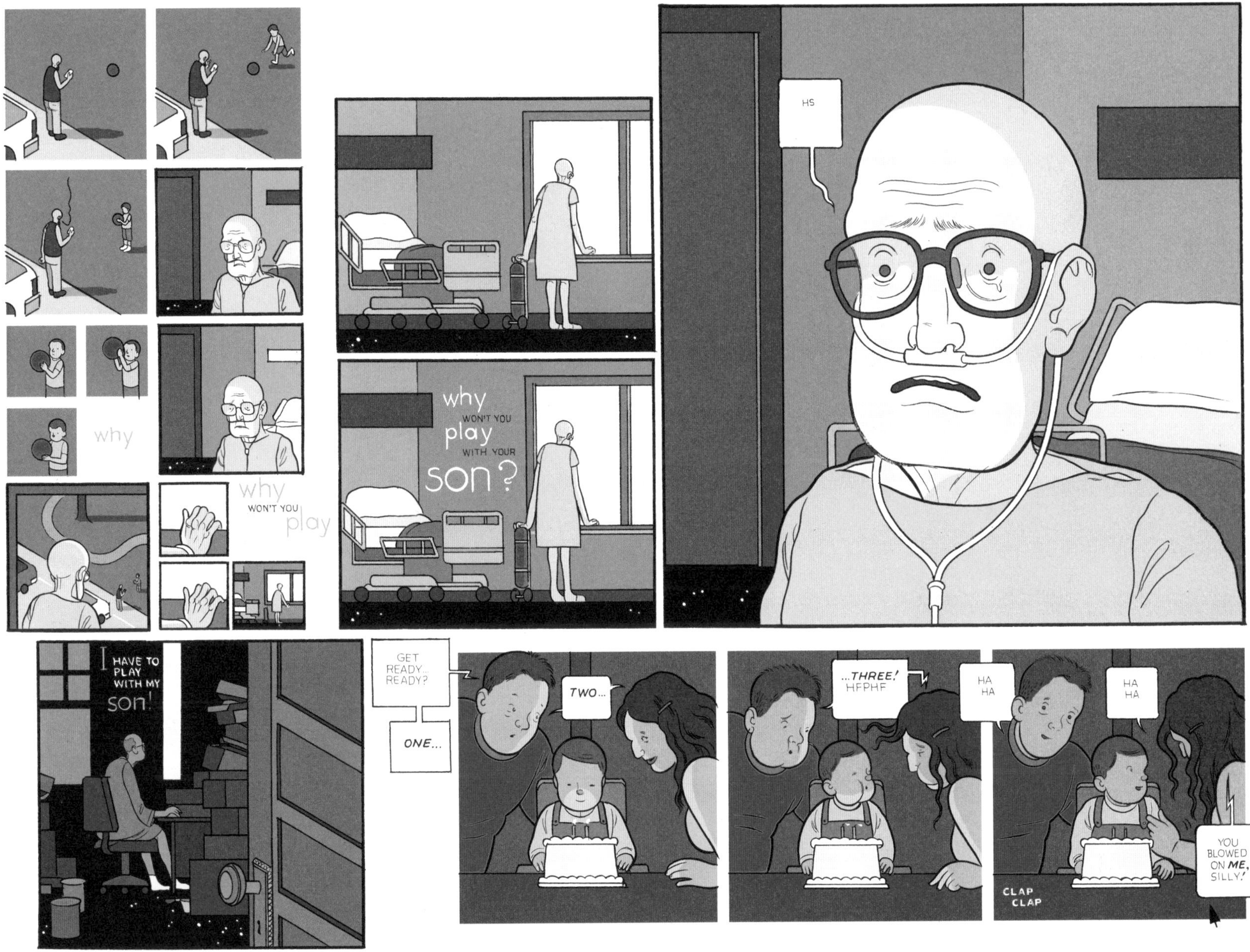

why
why
WON'T YOU
play
why
WON'T YOU
play
WITH YOUR
son?
HS
I HAVE TO PLAY WITH MY son!
GET READY... READY?
ONE...
TWO...
...THREE!
HFPHF
HA HA
HA HA
YOU BLOWED ON ME, SILLY!
CLAP CLAP

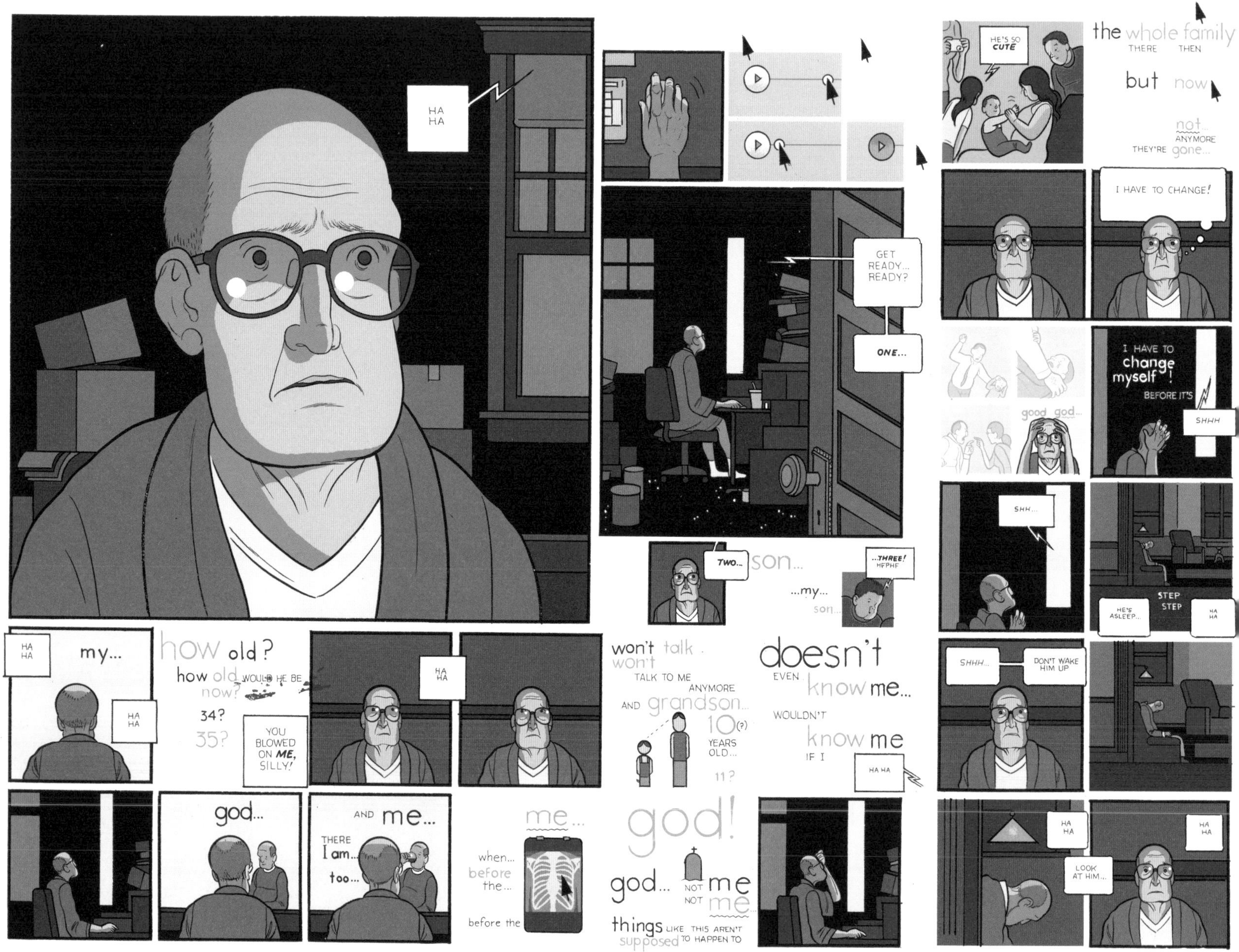

HA HA
GET READY... READY?
ONE...
TWO...
son...
...my...
son...
...THREE! HFPHF
HE'S SO CUTE
the whole family
THERE THEN
but now
not... ANYMORE
THEY'RE gone...
I HAVE TO CHANGE!
good god...
I HAVE TO change myself! BEFORE IT'S
SHHH
SHH...
HE'S ASLEEP...
STEP STEP
HA HA
SHHH...
DON'T WAKE HIM UP
HA HA
LOOK AT HIM...
HA HA
HA HA
my...
HA HA
how old?
how old WOULD HE BE now?
34?
35?
YOU BLOWED ON ME, SILLY!
HA HA
won't talk
won't TALK TO ME ANYMORE
AND grandson...
10(?) YEARS OLD...
11?
doesn't EVEN know me...
WOULDN'T know me IF I
HA HA
god...
AND me...
THERE I am... too...
me...
when... before the...
before the
god!
god... NOT me NOT me
things LIKE THIS AREN'T supposed TO HAPPEN TO

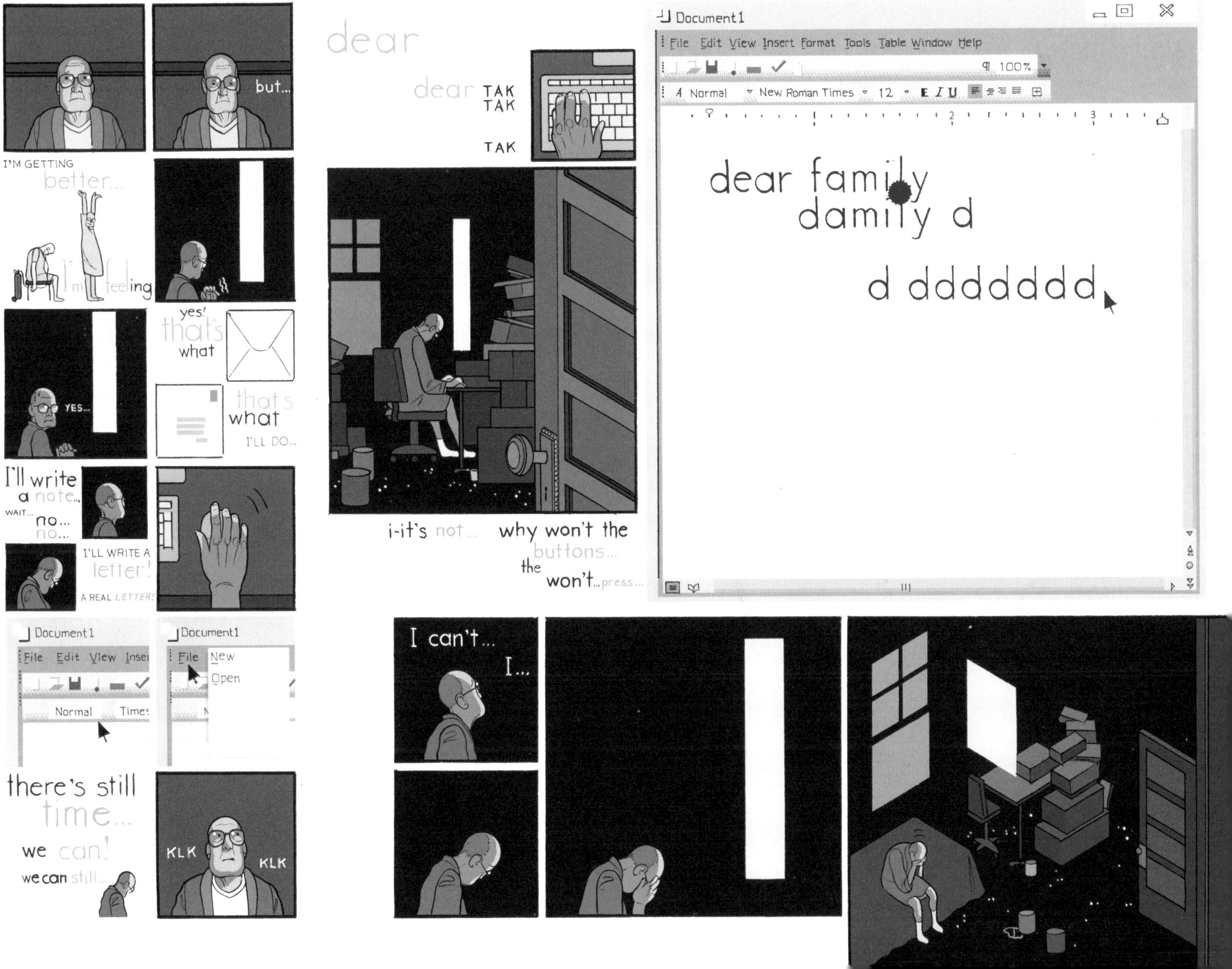
but...
I'M GETTING
better...
I'm feeling
yes!
that's
what
YES...
that's
what
I'LL DO...
I'll write
a note...
WAIT...
no...
no...
I'LL WRITE A
letter!
A REAL LETTER!
Document1
File Edit View Inser
Normal Times
Document1
File New
Open
there's still
time...
we can!
we can still...
KLK
KLK
dear
dear
TAK
TAK
TAK
i-it's not...
why won't the
buttons...
the
won't...press...
Document1
File Edit View Insert Format Tools Table Window Help
100%
Normal New Roman Times 12
dear family
damily d
d ddddddd
I can't...
I...

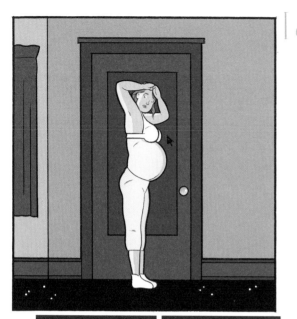

I didn't mean... TO EVER BE SO mean... god... BELIEVE...

YOU'RE THE ONLY ONE ... THE ONLY ONE WHO ...

oh I'm... god... I'm so...

WHO

I'm SO

WHO IS

WHO

SHE'S SHE'S SO...

OH GOD

SHE MAKES ME SO

SQSH

oh

OH MY POOR SWEETIE

oh

KRK

huf

FF

huf

KREK

I... I...

DON'T CRY...

DON'T CRY...

huf

I can't believe...
choke

snf

Y'KNOW,

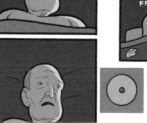

huf

I can't believe...

YOU'D FORGIVE ME...
sob

I didn't...

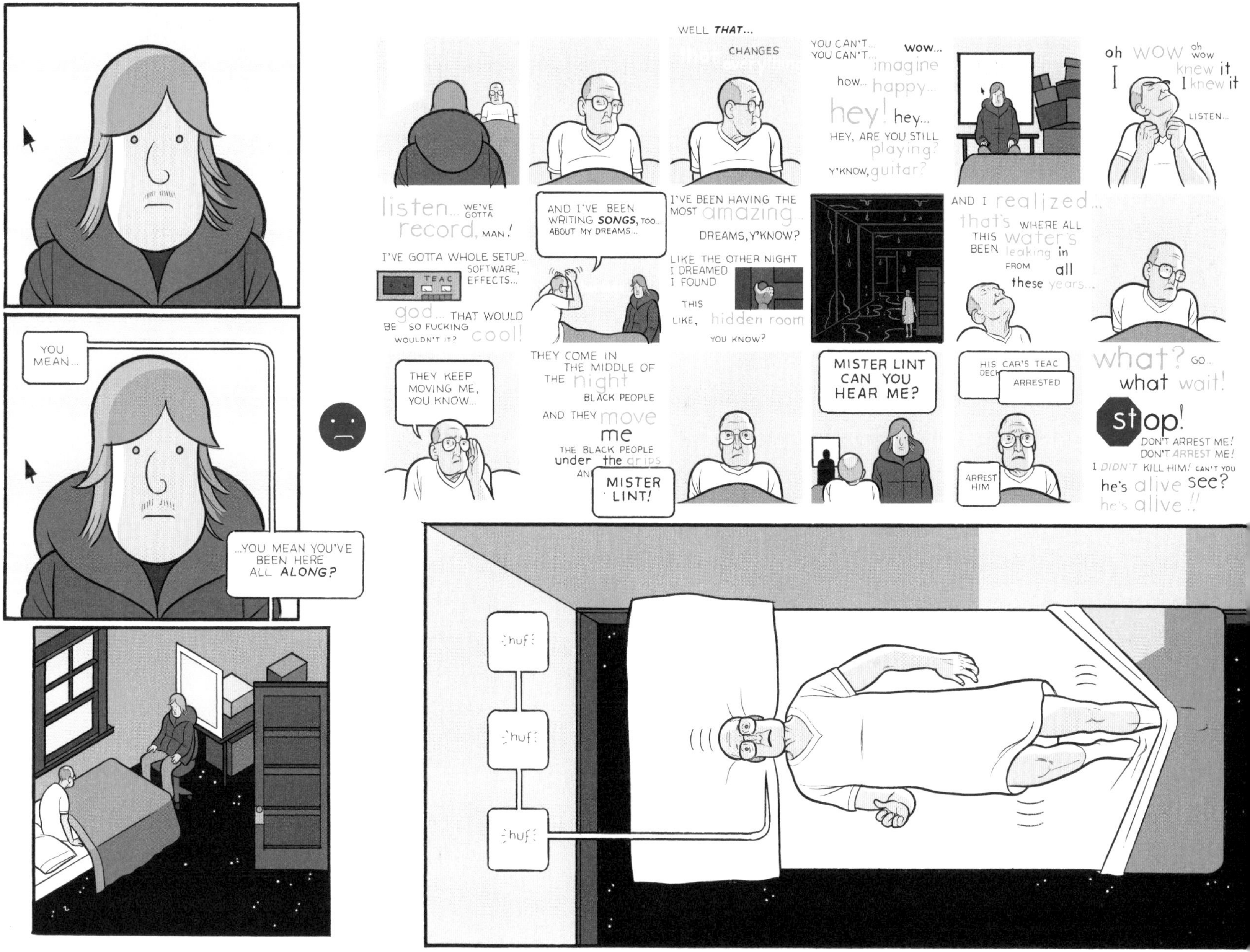

YOU MEAN...
...YOU MEAN YOU'VE BEEN HERE ALL ALONG?
WELL THAT...
CHANGES
YOU CAN'T... YOU CAN'T...
WOW...
imagine
how... happy...
hey! hey...
HEY, ARE YOU STILL playing?
Y'KNOW, guitar?
oh WOW oh wow
I
knew it
I knew it
LISTEN...
listen... WE'VE GOTTA record, MAN!
I'VE GOTTA WHOLE SETUP... SOFTWARE, EFFECTS...
TEAC
god... THAT WOULD BE SO FUCKING cool!
WOULDN'T IT?
AND I'VE BEEN WRITING SONGS, TOO... ABOUT MY DREAMS...
I'VE BEEN HAVING THE MOST amazing... DREAMS, Y'KNOW?
LIKE THE OTHER NIGHT I DREAMED I FOUND THIS LIKE, hidden room
YOU KNOW?
AND I realized...
that's WHERE ALL THIS water's BEEN leaking in FROM all these years...
THEY KEEP MOVING ME, YOU KNOW...
THEY COME IN THE MIDDLE OF THE night
BLACK PEOPLE
AND THEY move me
THE BLACK PEOPLE under the drips
MISTER LINT!
MISTER LINT CAN YOU HEAR ME?
HIS CAR'S TEAC DECK
ARRESTED
ARREST HIM
what? GO...
what wait!
stop!
DON'T ARREST ME!
DON'T ARREST ME!
I DIDN'T KILL HIM! CAN'T YOU see?
he's alive
he's alive!!
huf
huf
huf

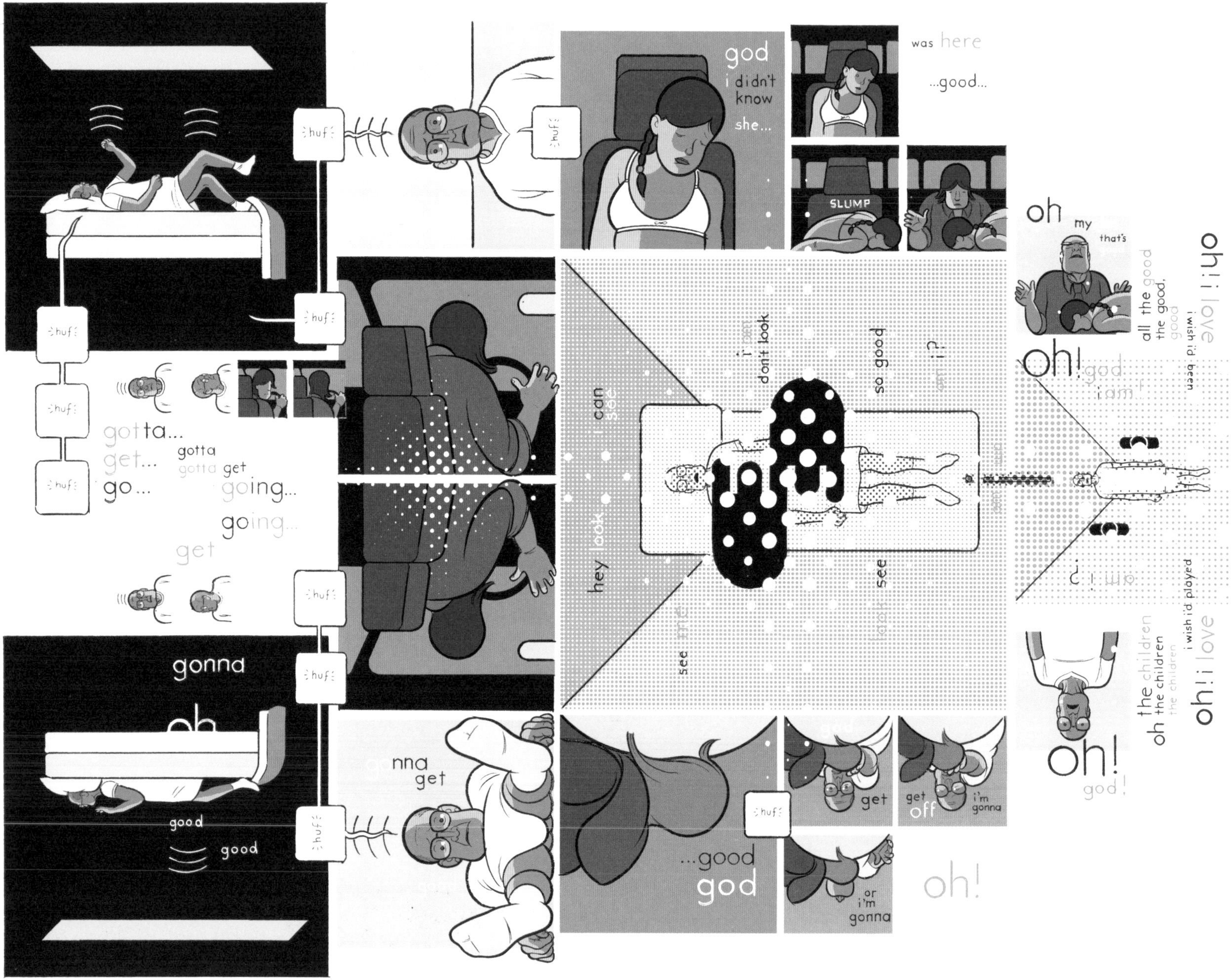
huf
huf
god
i didn't know
she...
was here
...good...
SLUMP
huf
huf
huf
huf
gotta...
get...
go...
gotta
gotta get
going...
going...
get
oh my
that's
Oh!
god
i am!
hey
i can see
i don't look
so good
see
see me
huf
huf
gonna
oh
good
good
huf
nna
get
huf
...good
god
get
get off
i'm gonna
or i'm gonna
oh!
Oh!
god!

━━ am   ∷∷∷ am   ·— am

AT THE THEATRES
LYRIC
Beginning Monday Evening, March 6
THE MAN ON THE BOX
NIGHTS at 8:30—15c, 25c, 35c, 50c
MATS. Wed. and Sat.—15c and 25c
OLIVER THEATRE
TODAY 2:30—TONIGHT 5:15
"PAID IN FULL"
Mat., 25c and 15c—Night, 15c to 50c
Tuesday Night, March 14
mer's Cafe
to 1:30
to 7:30 25c
ERIAN STYLE
Maple Syrup 10c
ING YOU WANT
Ordering Anywhere
nus, Announce-
at the Chicago uni-
or the Nebraska ex-
are much more de-
rly. The represent-
be chosen from the
e heavy gymnastic
horizontal bars, par-
rse, flying rings, and
events, such as club
, three classes of
ature the exhibition
in from the women's
ysical education will
a prominent feature
e. Demonstrations in
istic dancing will be
's gymnastic classes
ons in first year ap-
advanced apparatus
in both the wrestling
gts will size add vari-
tainment.
Class Play.
he senior class play
MARY MANNERING
March 13th Oliver Theatre
JOSEF HOFFMANN
"World's Greatest Pianist"
Prices $1.50, $1.00, 75¢, 50¢
SEATS NOW ON SALE
LINCOLN MATINEES (Except Monday) 3:30 EVENINGS AT 8:30
ORPHEUM
ADVANCED VAUDEVILLE
The Five Armanis
Covington & Wilbur
Polk & Hollier
INSTRUCTIONS:
1
2
Omaha World-Herald
February 1911
June 1911
Omaha World-Herald
June 1911
November 1911

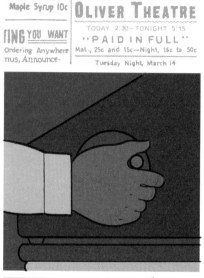

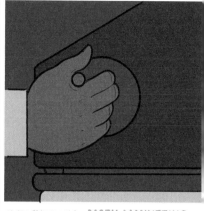

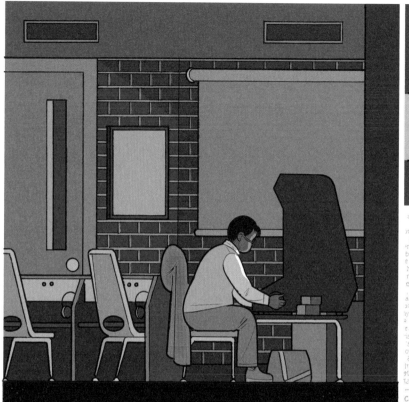

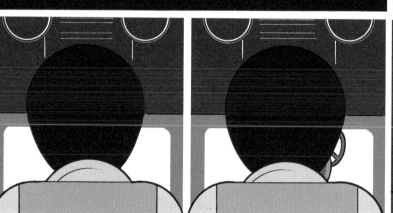

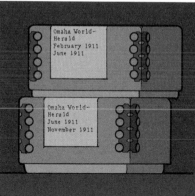

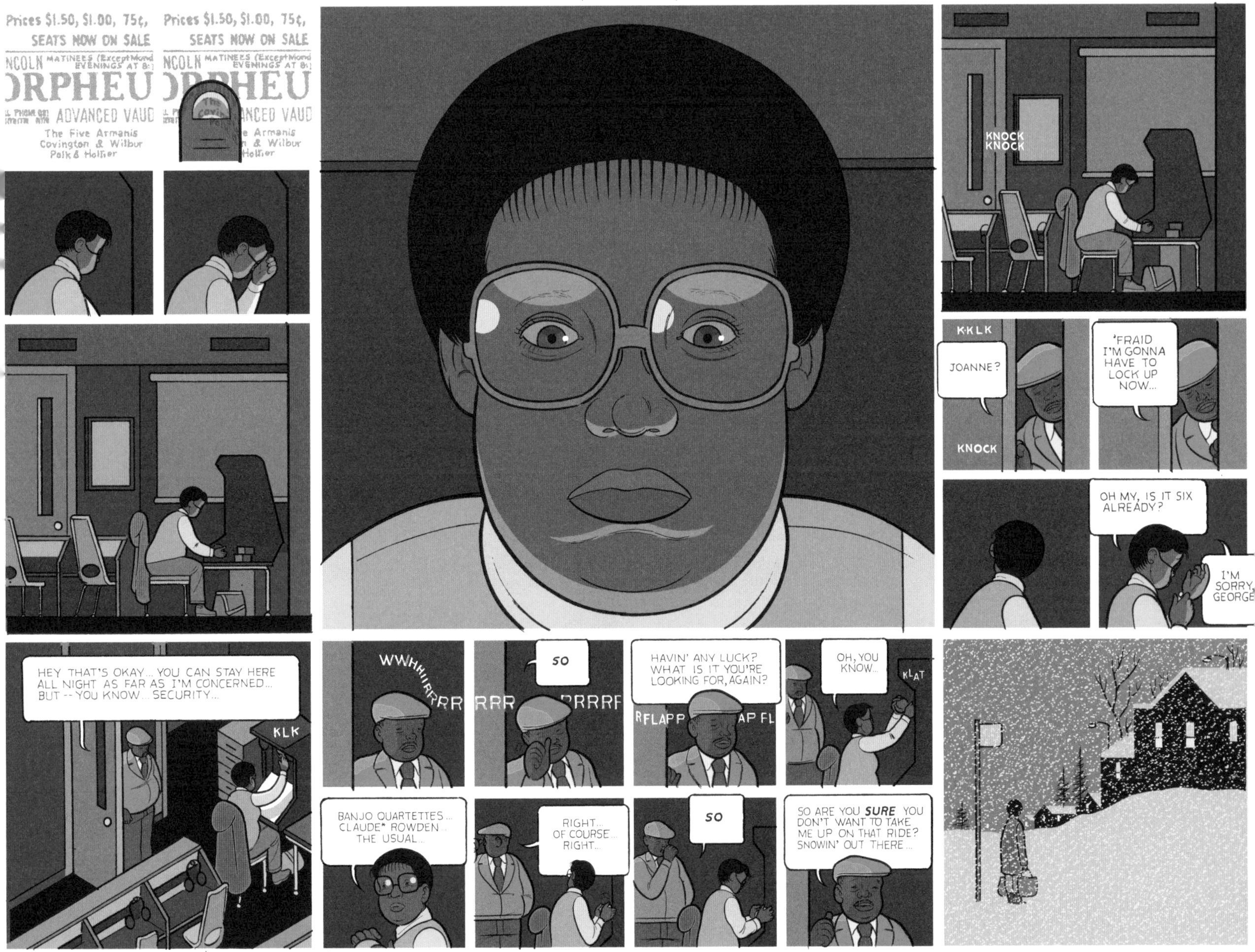

Prices $1.50, $1.00, 75¢,
SEATS NOW ON SALE
NCOLN MATINEES (Except Mond EVENINGS AT 8:
RPHEU
ADVANCED VAUD
The Five Armanis
Covington & Wilbur
Polk & Hollier
KNOCK KNOCK
K-KLK
JOANNE?
KNOCK
'FRAID I'M GONNA HAVE TO LOCK UP NOW...
OH MY, IS IT SIX ALREADY?
I'M SORRY, GEORGE
HEY THAT'S OKAY... YOU CAN STAY HERE ALL NIGHT AS FAR AS I'M CONCERNED... BUT -- YOU KNOW... SECURITY...
KLK
WWHHIIRRRR
RRR RRRRR
SO
HAVIN' ANY LUCK? WHAT IS IT YOU'RE LOOKING FOR, AGAIN?
RFLAPP AP FL
OH, YOU KNOW...
KLAT
BANJO QUARTETTES... CLAUDE* ROWDEN... THE USUAL...
RIGHT... OF COURSE... RIGHT...
SO
SO ARE YOU SURE YOU DON'T WANT TO TAKE ME UP ON THAT RIDE? SNOWIN' OUT THERE...

*sic--ed.

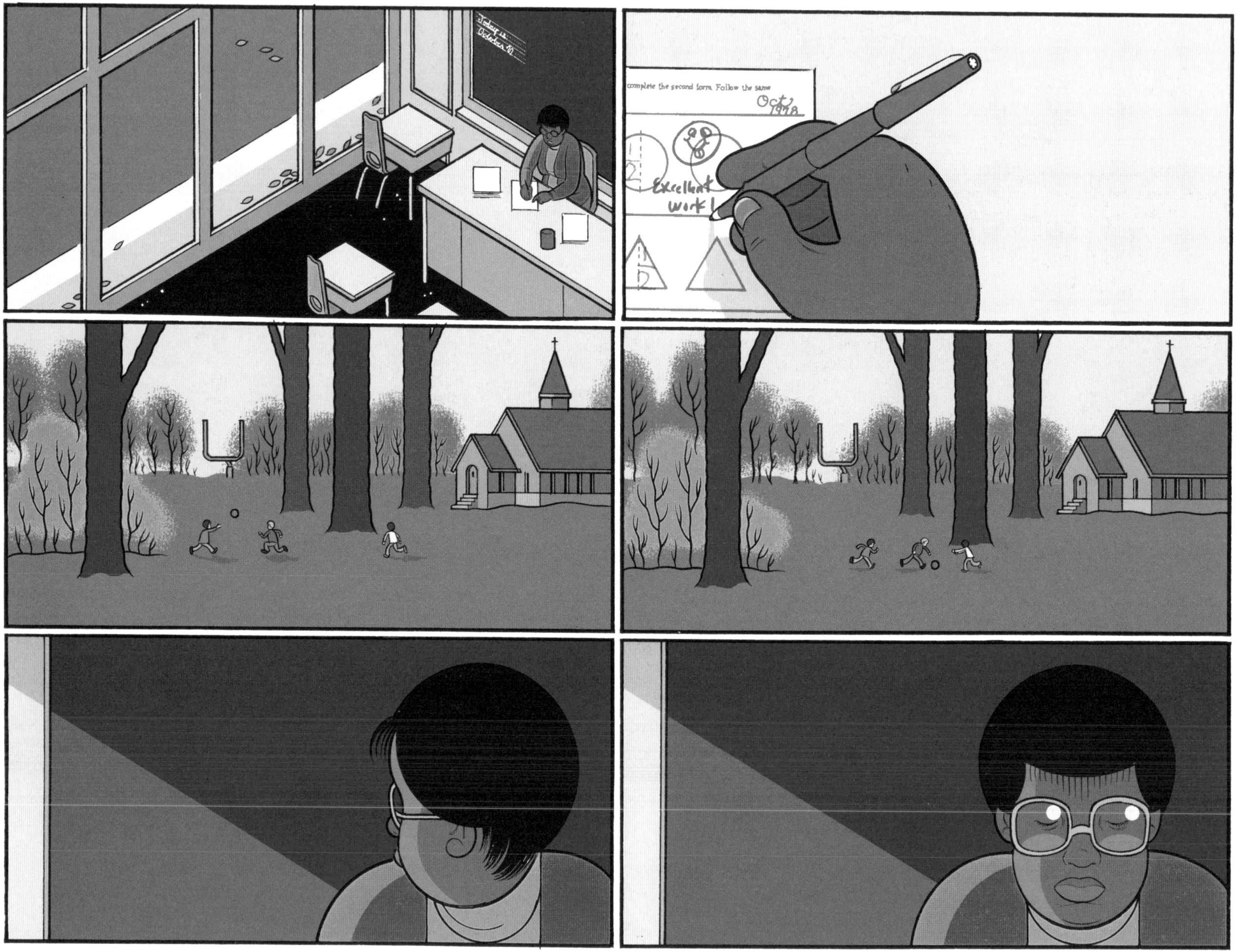
Today is:
complete the second form. Follow the same
Oct.
1998
Excellent work!

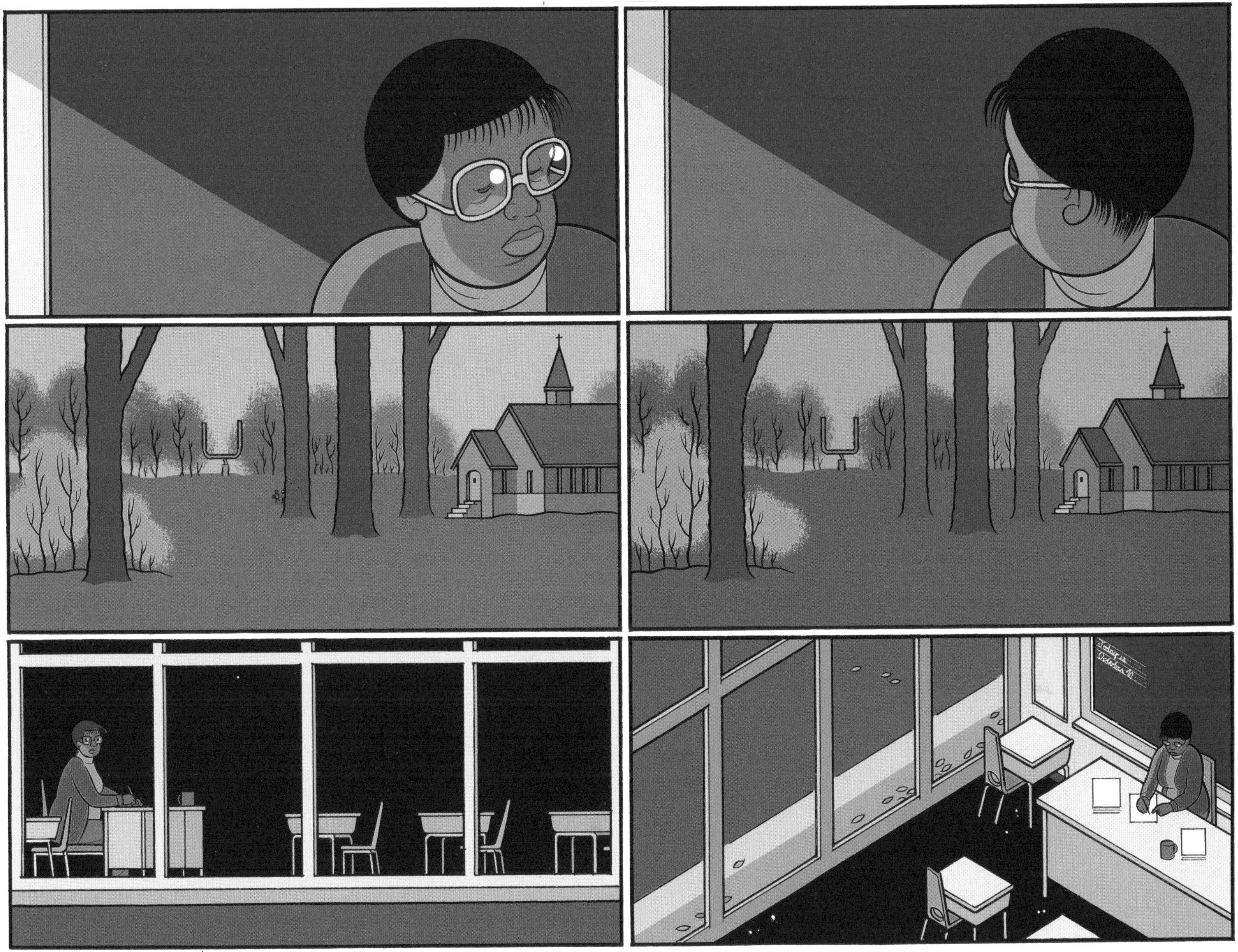
Today is
October

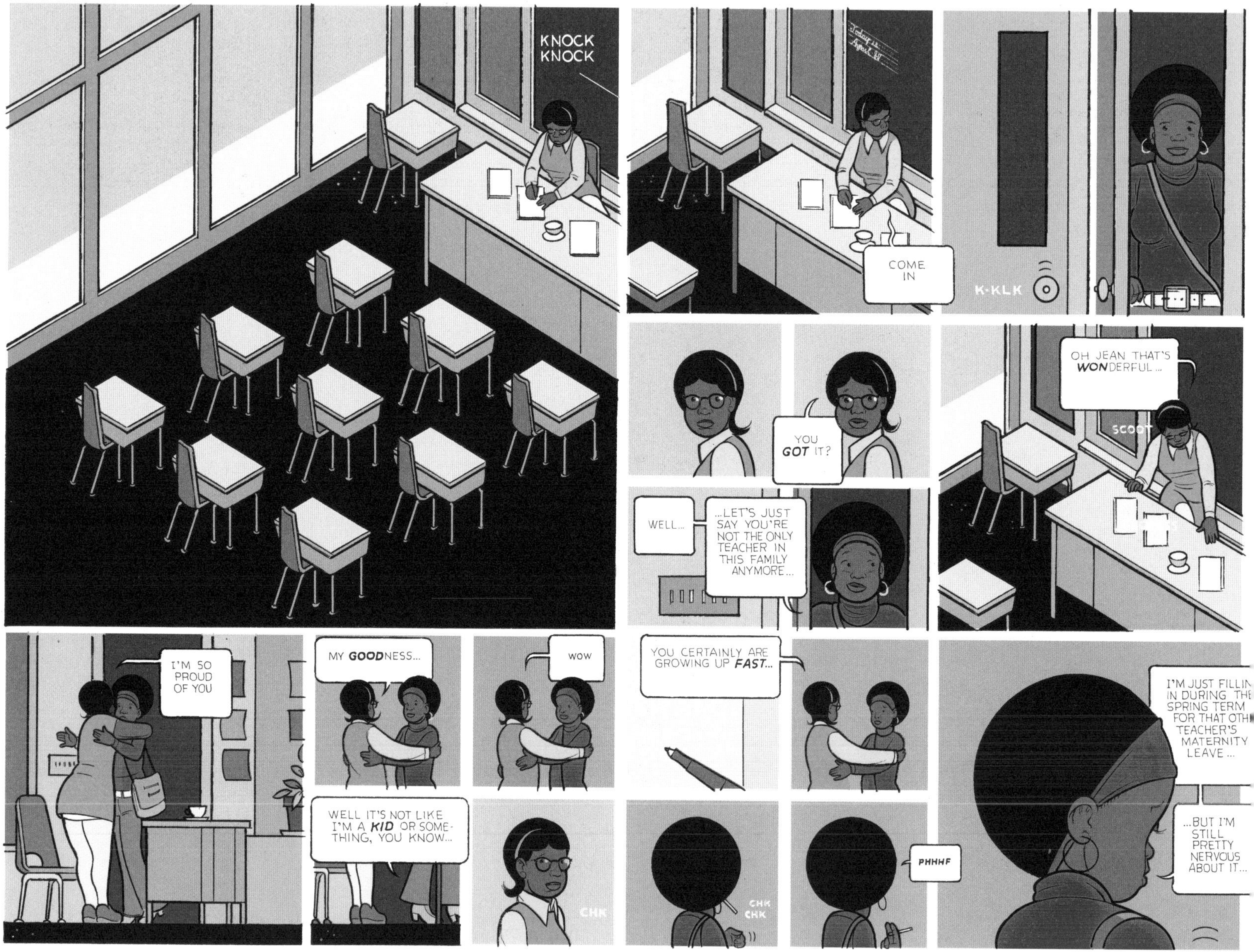
KNOCK KNOCK
COME IN
K-KLK
YOU GOT IT?
WELL...
...LET'S JUST SAY YOU'RE NOT THE ONLY TEACHER IN THIS FAMILY ANYMORE...
OH JEAN THAT'S WONDERFUL...
SCOOT
I'M SO PROUD OF YOU
MY GOODNESS...
WOW
WELL IT'S NOT LIKE I'M A KID OR SOMETHING, YOU KNOW...
CHK
YOU CERTAINLY ARE GROWING UP FAST...
CHK CHK
PHHHF
I'M JUST FILLIN IN DURING TH SPRING TERM FOR THAT OTH TEACHER'S MATERNITY LEAVE...
...BUT I'M STILL PRETTY NERVOUS ABOUT IT...

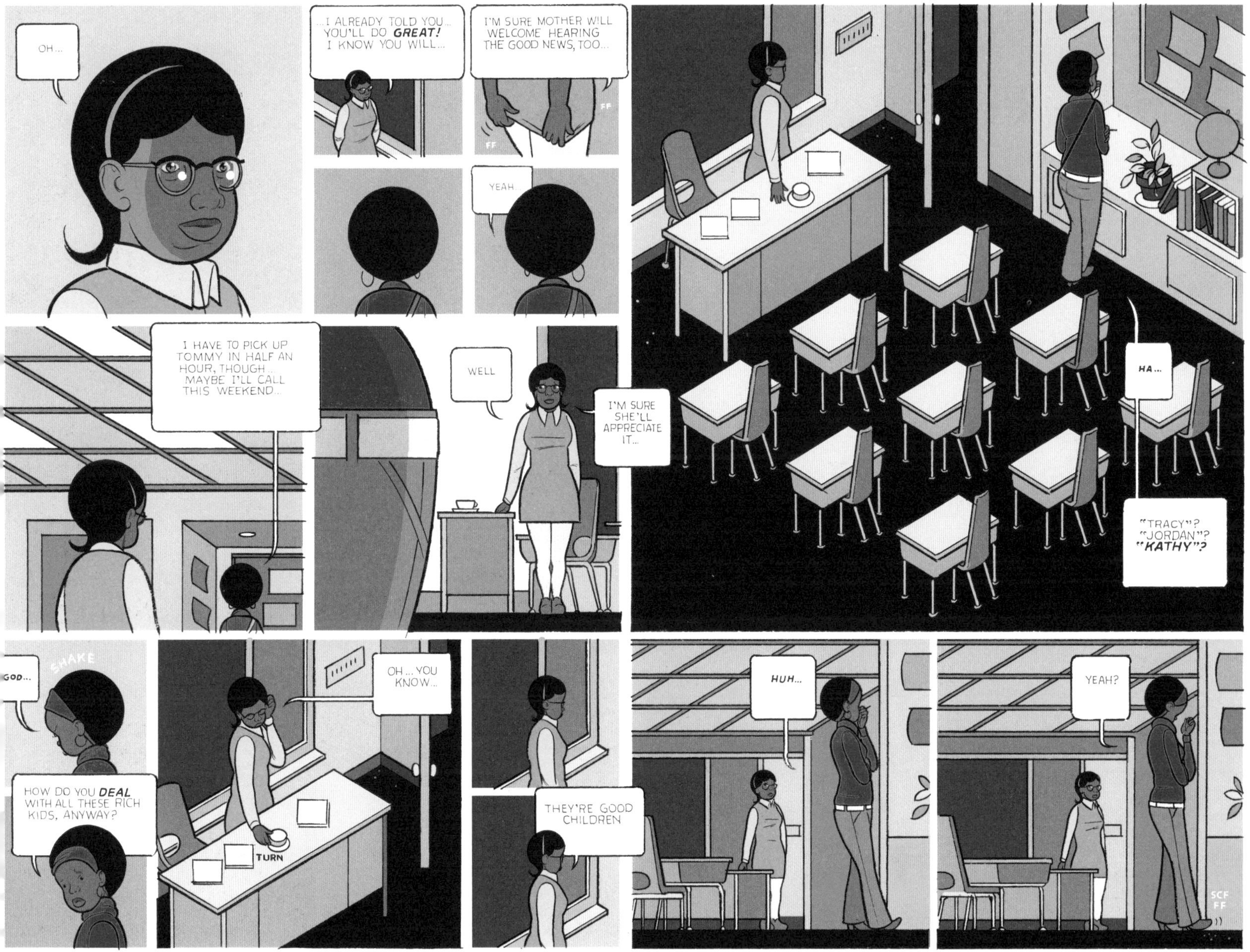
OH...
...I ALREADY TOLD YOU... YOU'LL DO **GREAT!** I KNOW YOU WILL...
I'M SURE MOTHER WILL WELCOME HEARING THE GOOD NEWS, TOO...
FF
FF
YEAH...
I HAVE TO PICK UP TOMMY IN HALF AN HOUR, THOUGH... MAYBE I'LL CALL THIS WEEKEND...
WELL
I'M SURE SHE'LL APPRECIATE IT...
HA...
"TRACY"? "JORDAN"? **"KATHY"?**
GOD...
SHAKE
HOW DO YOU **DEAL** WITH ALL THESE RICH KIDS, ANYWAY?
TURN
OH... YOU KNOW...
THEY'RE GOOD CHILDREN
HUH...
YEAH?
SCF
FF

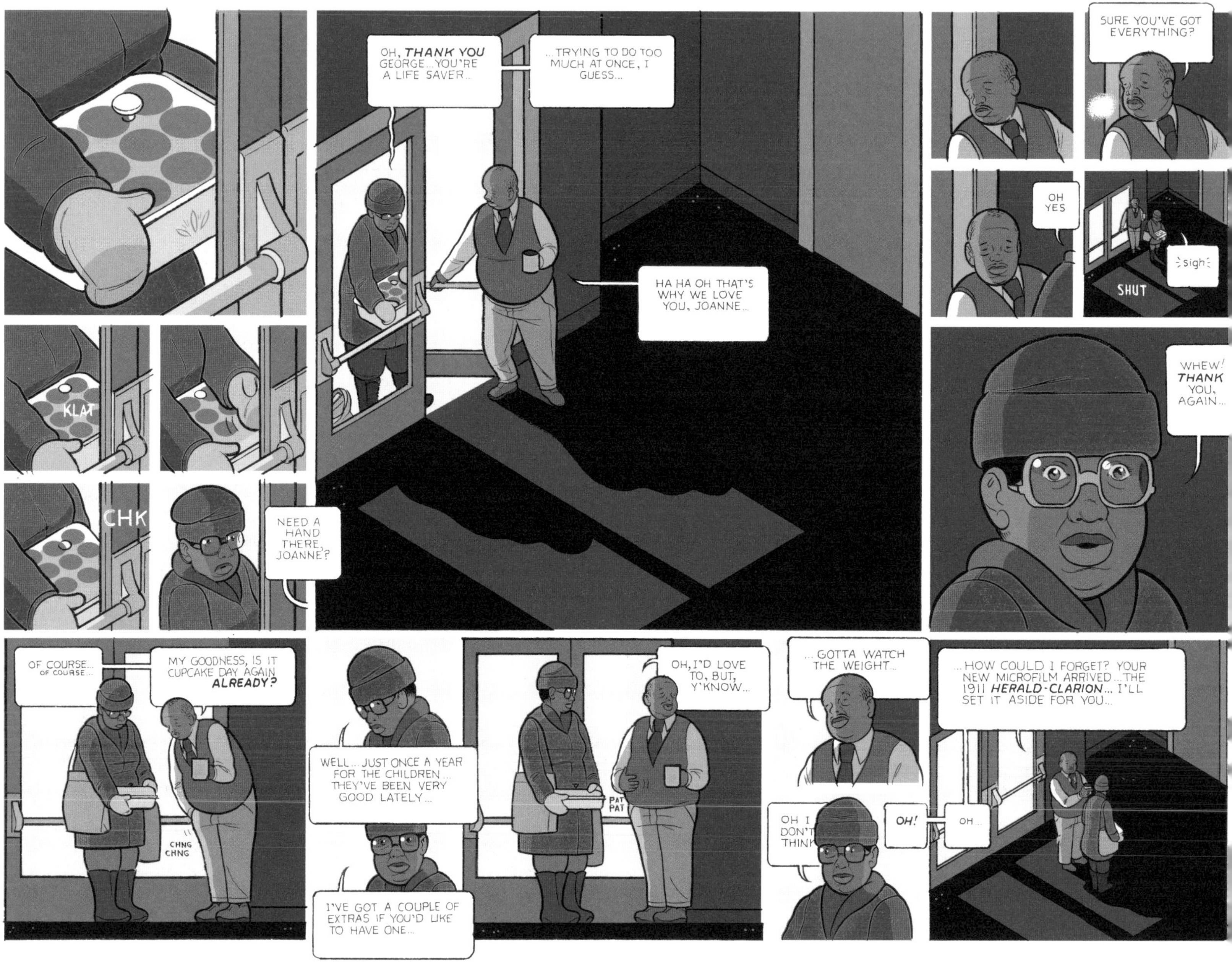

KLAT
CHK
NEED A HAND THERE, JOANNE?
OH, THANK YOU GEORGE... YOU'RE A LIFE SAVER...
...TRYING TO DO TOO MUCH AT ONCE, I GUESS...
HA HA OH THAT'S WHY WE LOVE YOU, JOANNE...
SURE YOU'VE GOT EVERYTHING?
OH YES
sigh
SHUT
WHEW! THANK YOU, AGAIN...
OF COURSE... OF COURSE...
MY GOODNESS, IS IT CUPCAKE DAY AGAIN ALREADY?
CHNG CHNG
WELL... JUST ONCE A YEAR FOR THE CHILDREN... THEY'VE BEEN VERY GOOD LATELY...
I'VE GOT A COUPLE OF EXTRAS IF YOU'D LIKE TO HAVE ONE...
PAT PAT
OH, I'D LOVE TO, BUT, Y'KNOW...
...GOTTA WATCH THE WEIGHT...
OH I DON'T THINK
OH!
OH...
...HOW COULD I FORGET? YOUR NEW MICROFILM ARRIVED... THE 1911 HERALD-CLARION... I'LL SET IT ASIDE FOR YOU...

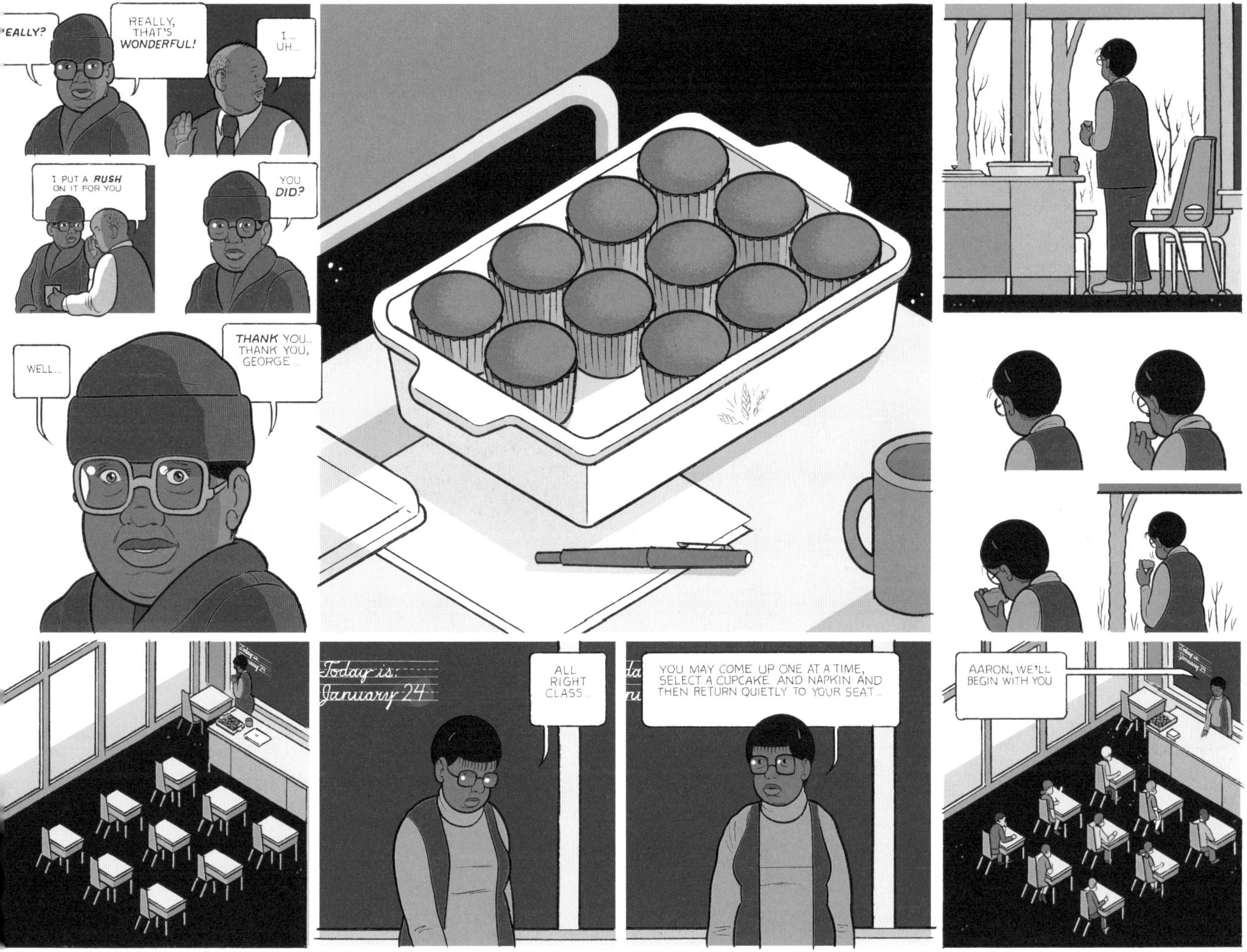
EALLY?
REALLY, THAT'S WONDERFUL!
I... UH...
I PUT A RUSH ON IT FOR YOU
YOU DID?
WELL...
THANK YOU... THANK YOU, GEORGE...
Today is: January 24
ALL RIGHT CLASS...
YOU MAY COME UP ONE AT A TIME, SELECT A CUPCAKE AND NAPKIN AND THEN RETURN QUIETLY TO YOUR SEAT...
AARON, WE'LL BEGIN WITH YOU

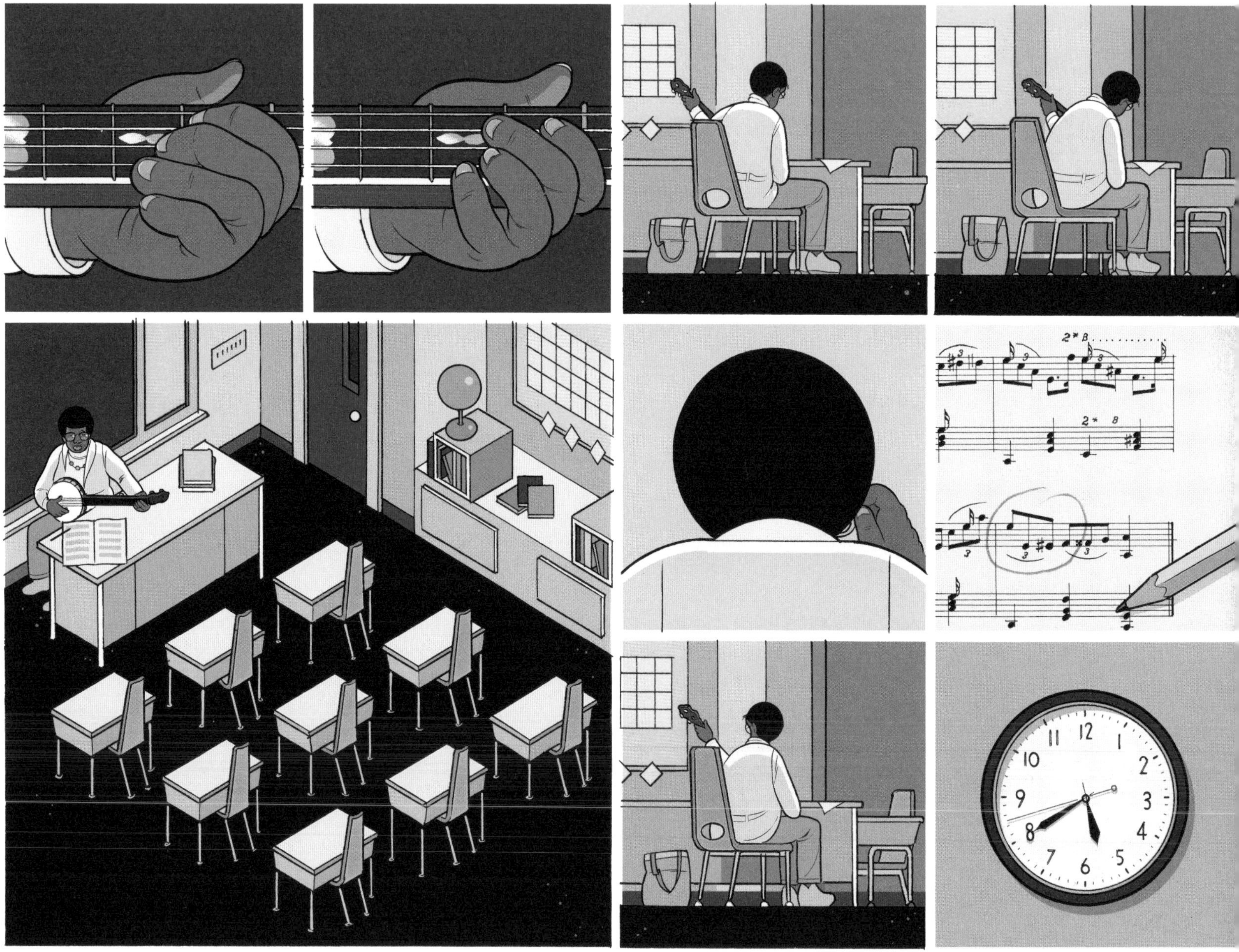

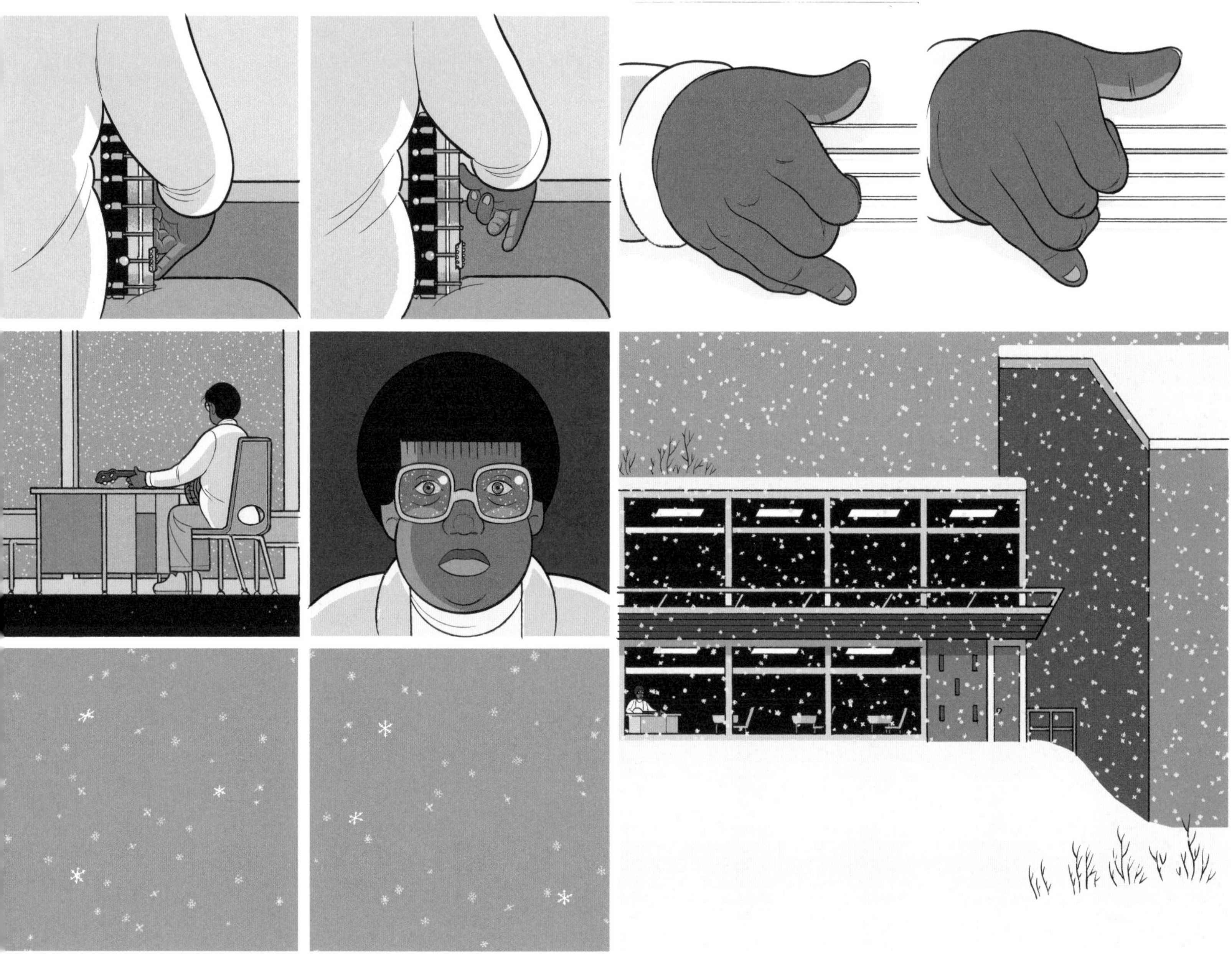

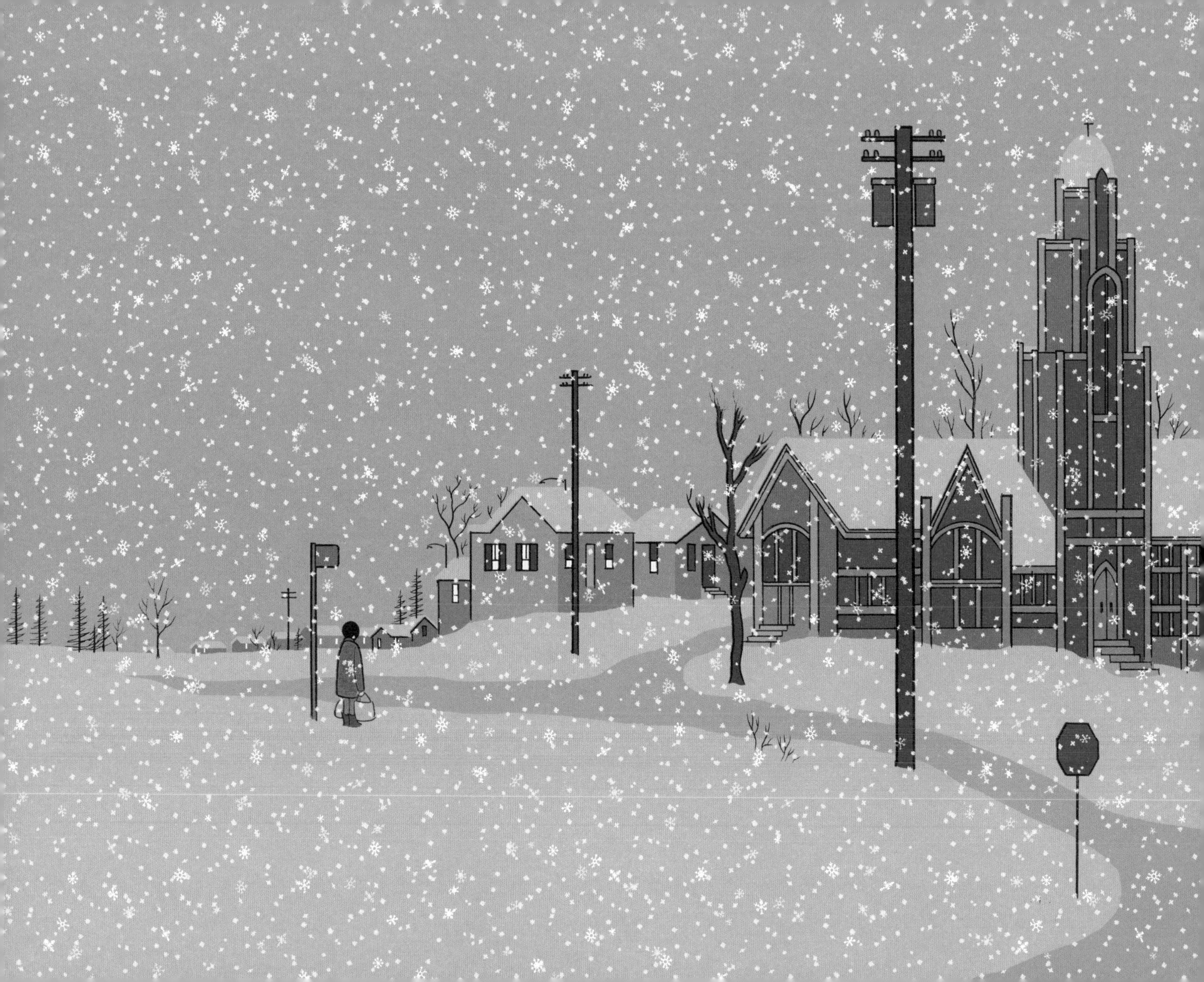

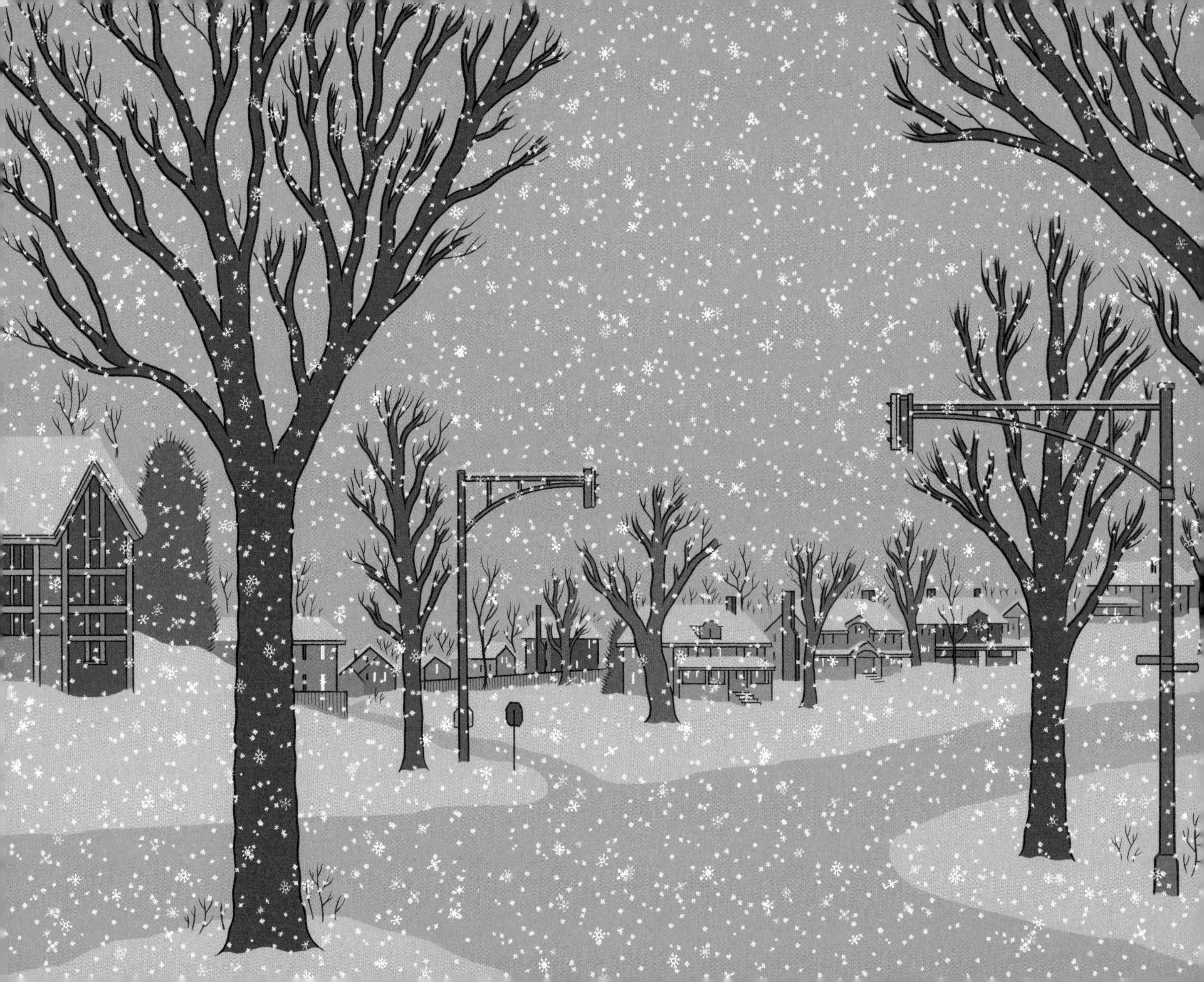

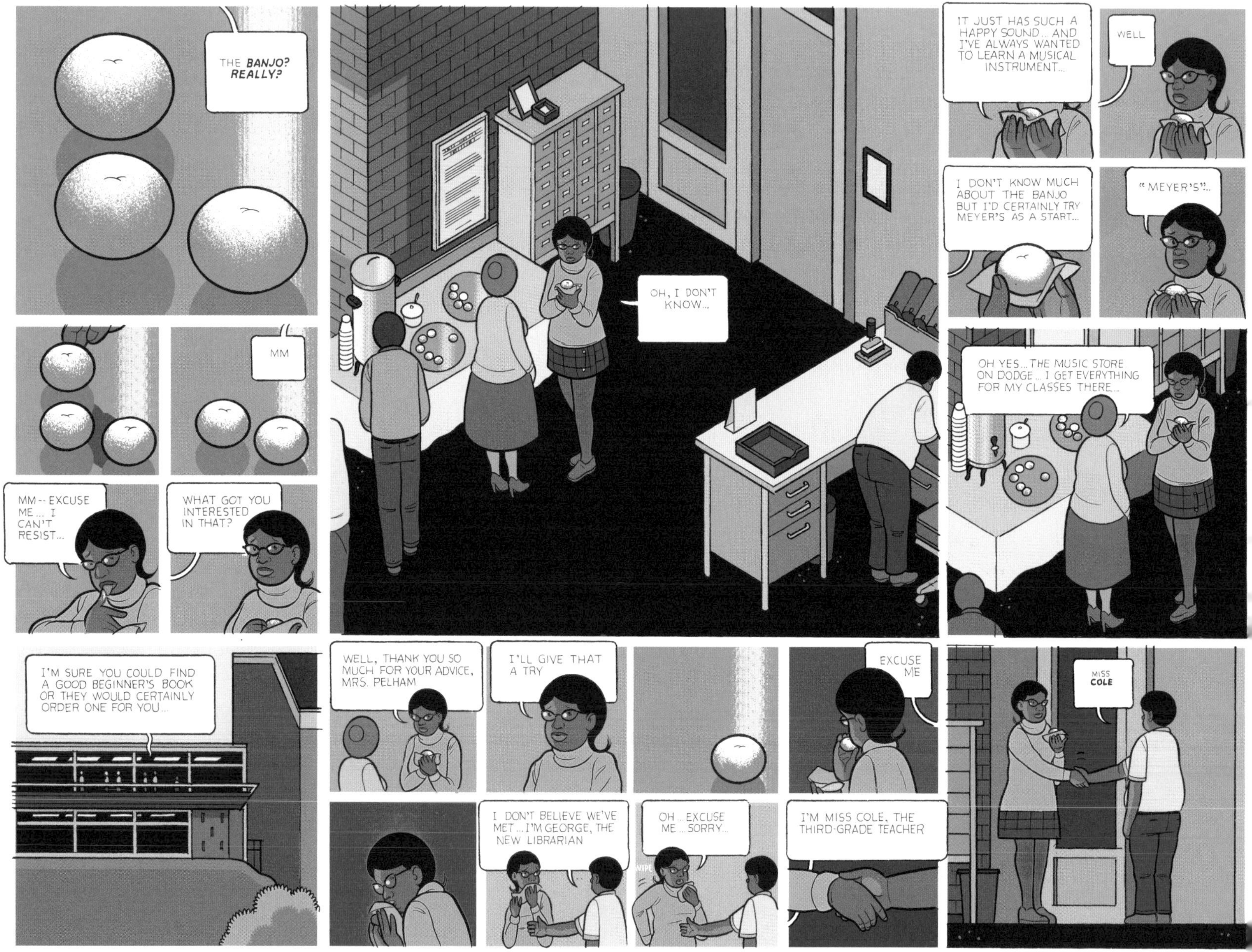
THE **BANJO? REALLY?**
MM
MM -- EXCUSE ME... I CAN'T RESIST...
WHAT GOT YOU INTERESTED IN THAT?
OH, I DON'T KNOW...
IT JUST HAS SUCH A HAPPY SOUND... AND I'VE ALWAYS WANTED TO LEARN A MUSICAL INSTRUMENT...
WELL
I DON'T KNOW MUCH ABOUT THE BANJO BUT I'D CERTAINLY TRY MEYER'S AS A START...
"MEYER'S"...
OH YES... THE MUSIC STORE ON DODGE... I GET EVERYTHING FOR MY CLASSES THERE...
I'M SURE YOU COULD FIND A GOOD BEGINNER'S BOOK OR THEY WOULD CERTAINLY ORDER ONE FOR YOU...
WELL, THANK YOU SO MUCH FOR YOUR ADVICE, MRS. PELHAM
I'LL GIVE THAT A TRY
EXCUSE ME
I DON'T BELIEVE WE'VE MET... I'M GEORGE, THE NEW LIBRARIAN
WIPE
OH... EXCUSE ME... SORRY...
I'M MISS COLE, THE THIRD-GRADE TEACHER
MISS **COLE**

UM

JOANNE

JO**ANNE**

WELL NICE TO MEET YOU, JOANNE

WELCOME TO "THE **LIBRARY**"...
BOW

...WHERE APPARENTLY ALL KNOWLEDGE ENDED WITH THE EISENHOWER ADMINISTRATION...

YOU'RE **TALL**, Y'KNOW THAT?

REMEMBER WHEN THEY WOULDN'T EVEN LET US CHECK **OUT** BOOKS?

HA HA

YES   HA HA

WELL

HA HA
HA HA

BECAUSE **I'M** NOT!

OH, I DON'T KNOW...
KRAK

OH, **I** KNOW... BELIEVE ME...

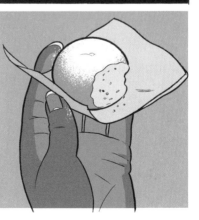

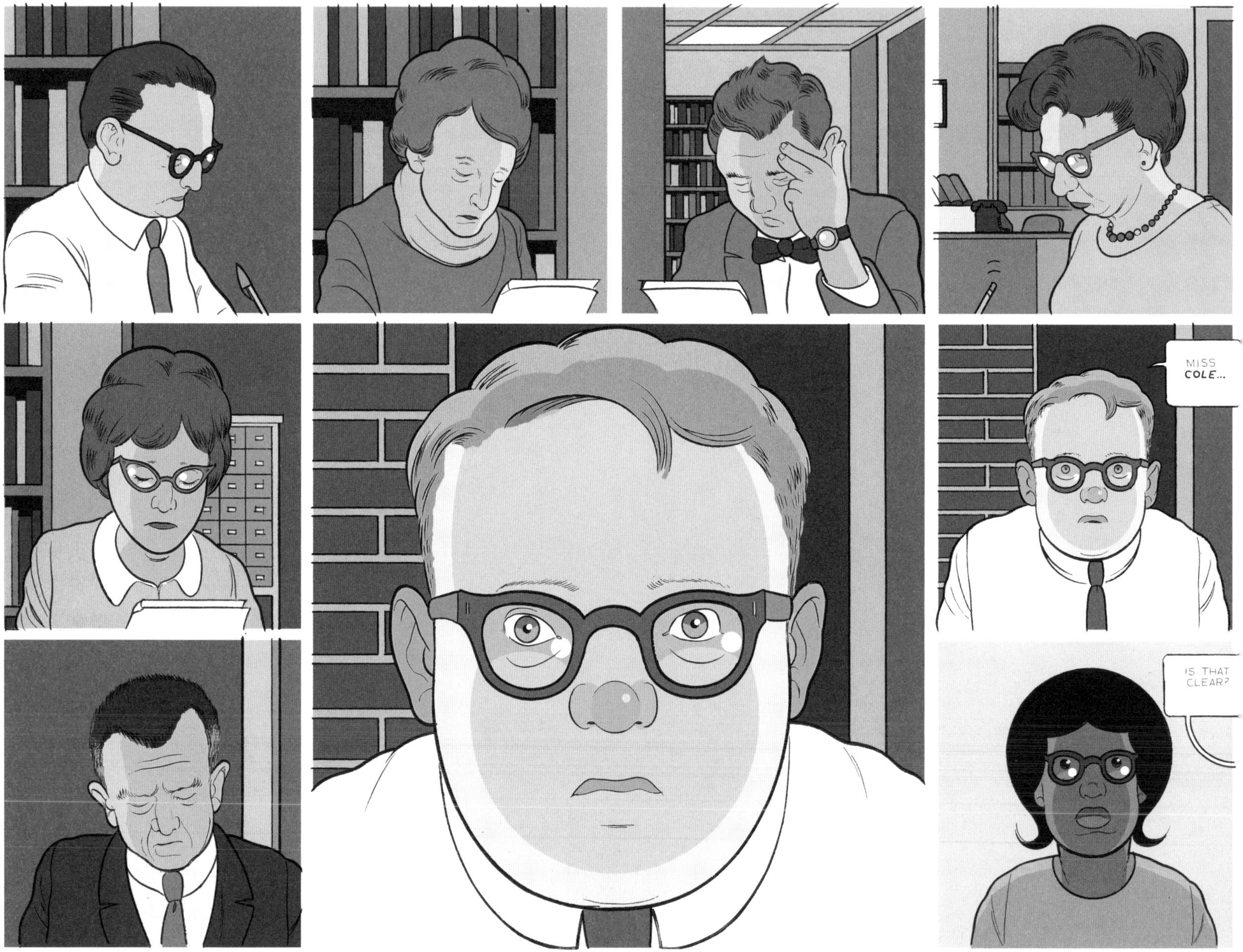
MISS
COLE...
IS THAT
CLEAR?

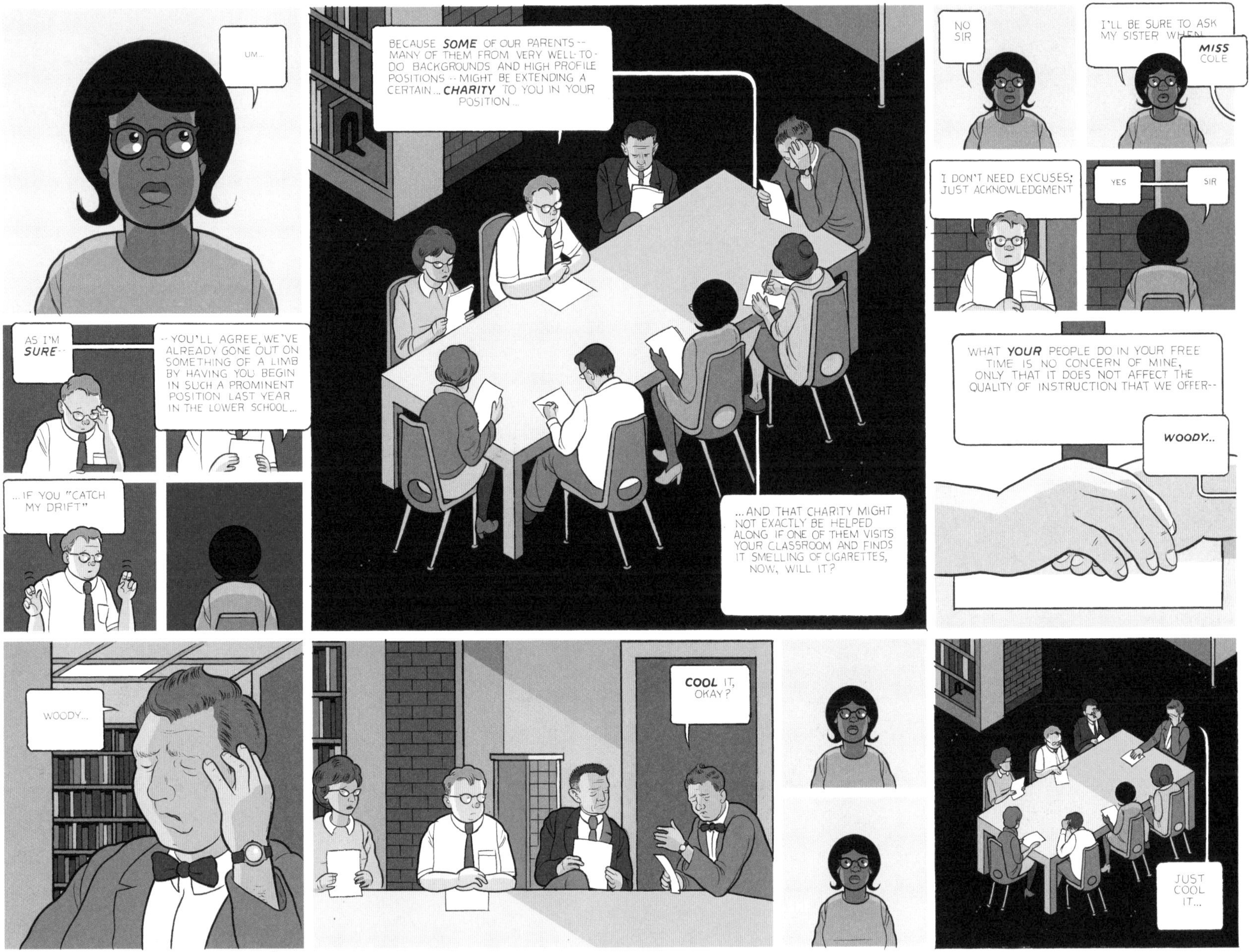
UM...
BECAUSE SOME OF OUR PARENTS -- MANY OF THEM FROM VERY WELL-TO-DO BACKGROUNDS AND HIGH PROFILE POSITIONS -- MIGHT BE EXTENDING A CERTAIN... CHARITY TO YOU IN YOUR POSITION...
...AND THAT CHARITY MIGHT NOT EXACTLY BE HELPED ALONG IF ONE OF THEM VISITS YOUR CLASSROOM AND FINDS IT SMELLING OF CIGARETTES, NOW, WILL IT?
NO SIR
I'LL BE SURE TO ASK MY SISTER WHEN-
MISS COLE
I DON'T NEED EXCUSES; JUST ACKNOWLEDGMENT
YES
SIR
AS I'M SURE--
-- YOU'LL AGREE, WE'VE ALREADY GONE OUT ON SOMETHING OF A LIMB BY HAVING YOU BEGIN IN SUCH A PROMINENT POSITION LAST YEAR IN THE LOWER SCHOOL...
...IF YOU "CATCH MY DRIFT"
WHAT YOUR PEOPLE DO IN YOUR FREE TIME IS NO CONCERN OF MINE, ONLY THAT IT DOES NOT AFFECT THE QUALITY OF INSTRUCTION THAT WE OFFER--
WOODY...
WOODY...
COOL IT, OKAY?
JUST COOL IT...

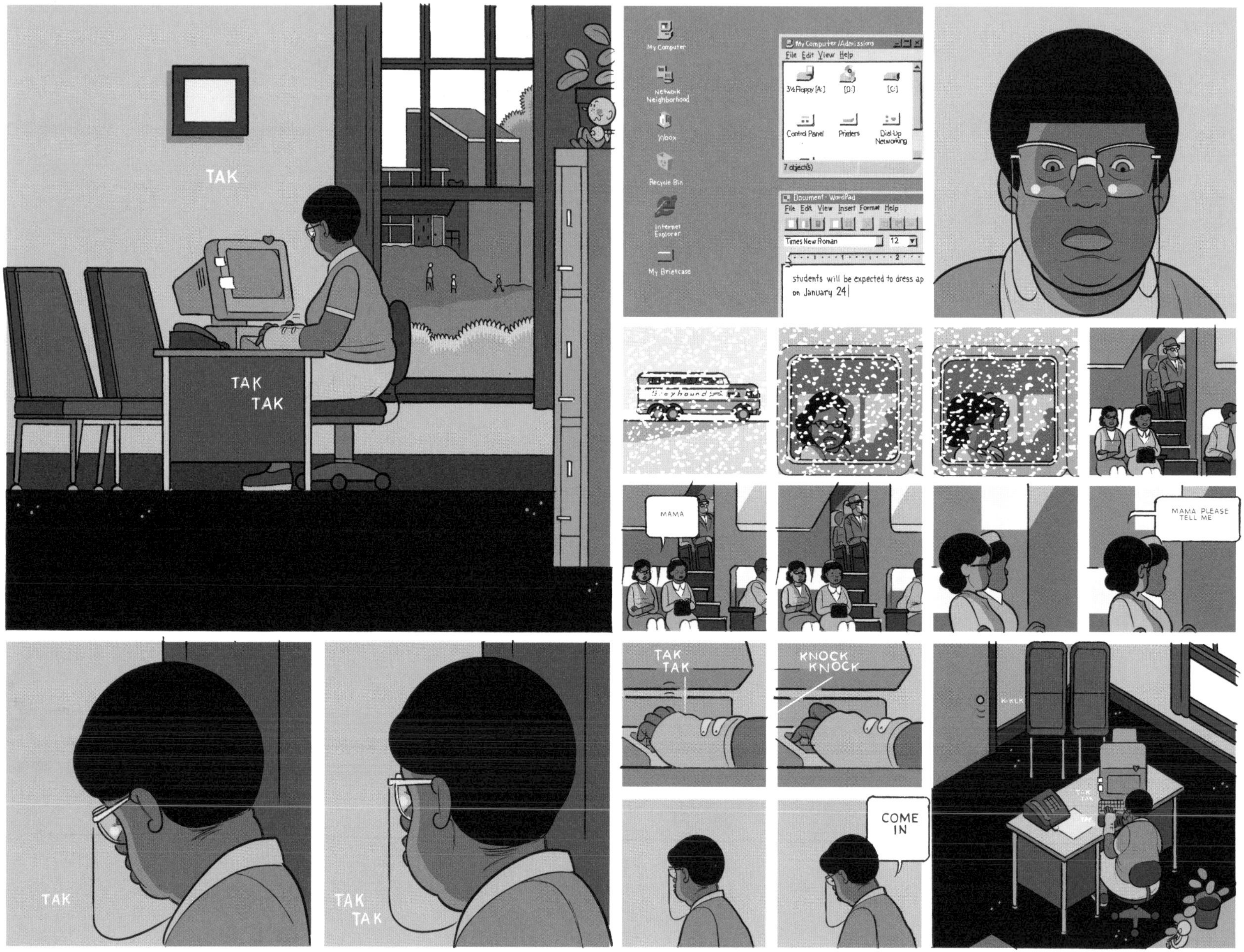
TAK
TAK TAK
My Computer
Network Neighborhood
Inbox
Recycle Bin
Internet Explorer
My Briefcase
My Computer /Admissions
File Edit View Help
3½ Floppy [A:]
[D:]
[C:]
Control Panel
Printers
Dial-Up Networking
7 object(s)
Document - WordPad
File Edit View Insert Format Help
Times New Roman
12
students will be expected to dress ap
on January 24
MAMA
MAMA PLEASE TELL ME
TAK
TAK TAK
TAK TAK
KNOCK KNOCK
COME IN
K-KLK
TAK TAK
TAK

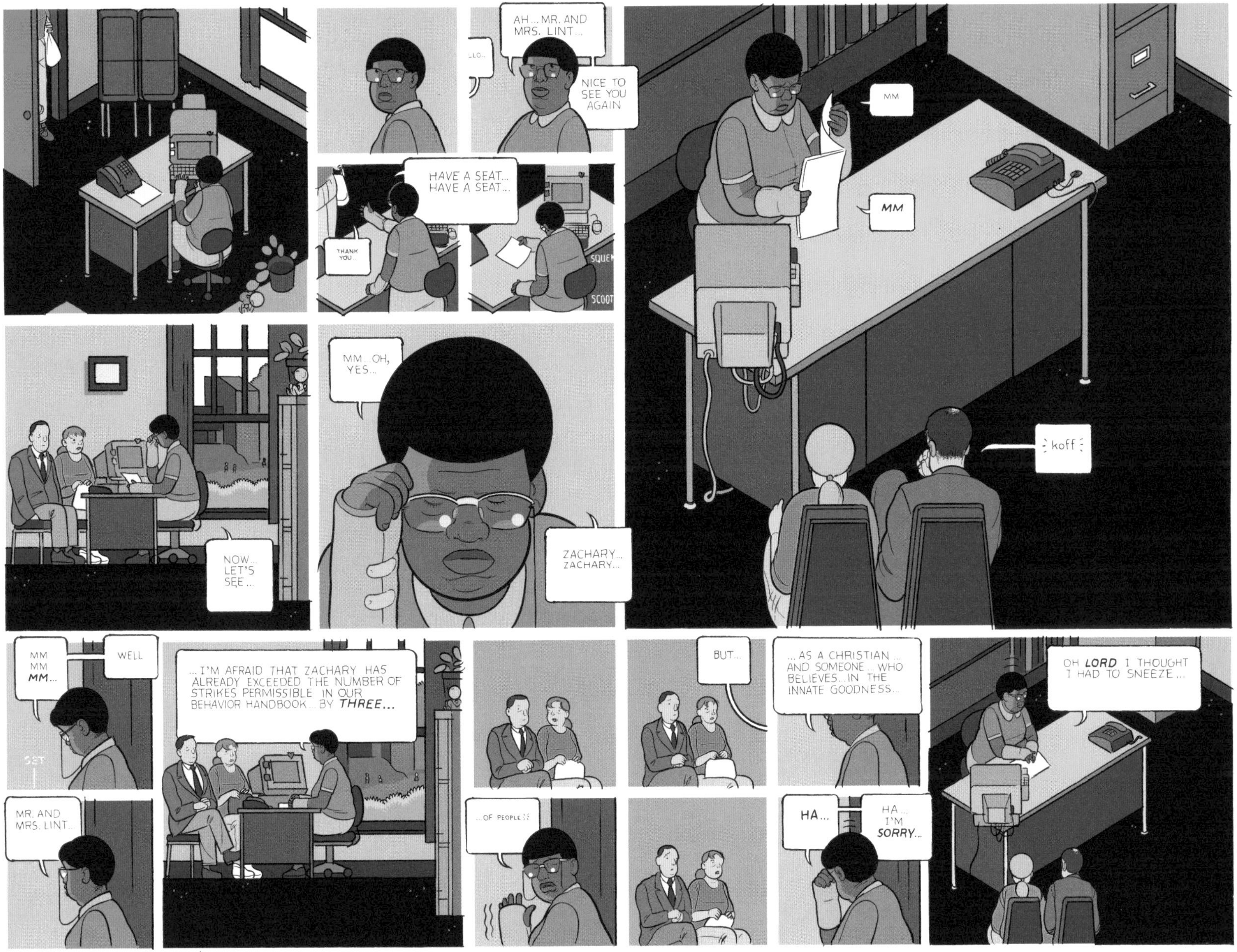
AH... MR. AND MRS. LINT...
NICE TO SEE YOU AGAIN
HAVE A SEAT... HAVE A SEAT...
THANK YOU...
NOW... LET'S SEE...
MM... OH, YES...
ZACHARY... ZACHARY...
MM
MM
koff
MM MM MM...
WELL
MR. AND MRS. LINT...
...I'M AFRAID THAT ZACHARY HAS ALREADY EXCEEDED THE NUMBER OF STRIKES PERMISSIBLE IN OUR BEHAVIOR HANDBOOK... BY THREE...
BUT...
...AS A CHRISTIAN... AND SOMEONE... WHO BELIEVES... IN THE INNATE GOODNESS...
...OF PEOPLE
HA...
HA... I'M SORRY...
OH LORD I THOUGHT I HAD TO SNEEZE...

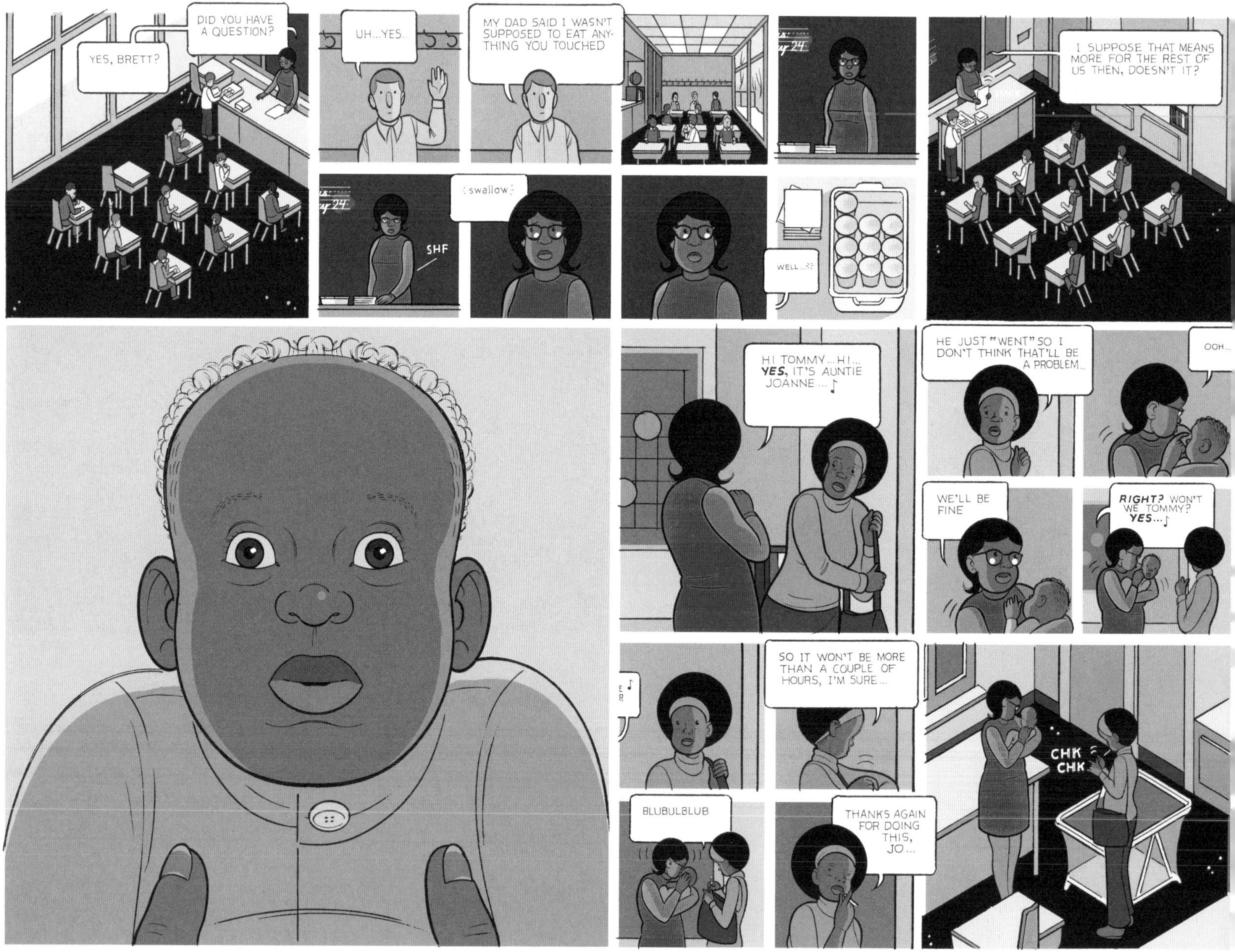
YES, BRETT?
DID YOU HAVE A QUESTION?
UH...YES...
MY DAD SAID I WASN'T SUPPOSED TO EAT ANY-THING YOU TOUCHED
swallow
WELL...
I SUPPOSE THAT MEANS MORE FOR THE REST OF US THEN, DOESN'T IT?
HI TOMMY... HI... YES, IT'S AUNTIE JOANNE ...
HE JUST "WENT" SO I DON'T THINK THAT'LL BE A PROBLEM...
OOH...
WE'LL BE FINE
RIGHT? WON'T WE TOMMY? YES...
SO IT WON'T BE MORE THAN A COUPLE OF HOURS, I'M SURE...
BLUBULBLUB
THANKS AGAIN FOR DOING THIS, JO...
CHK CHK

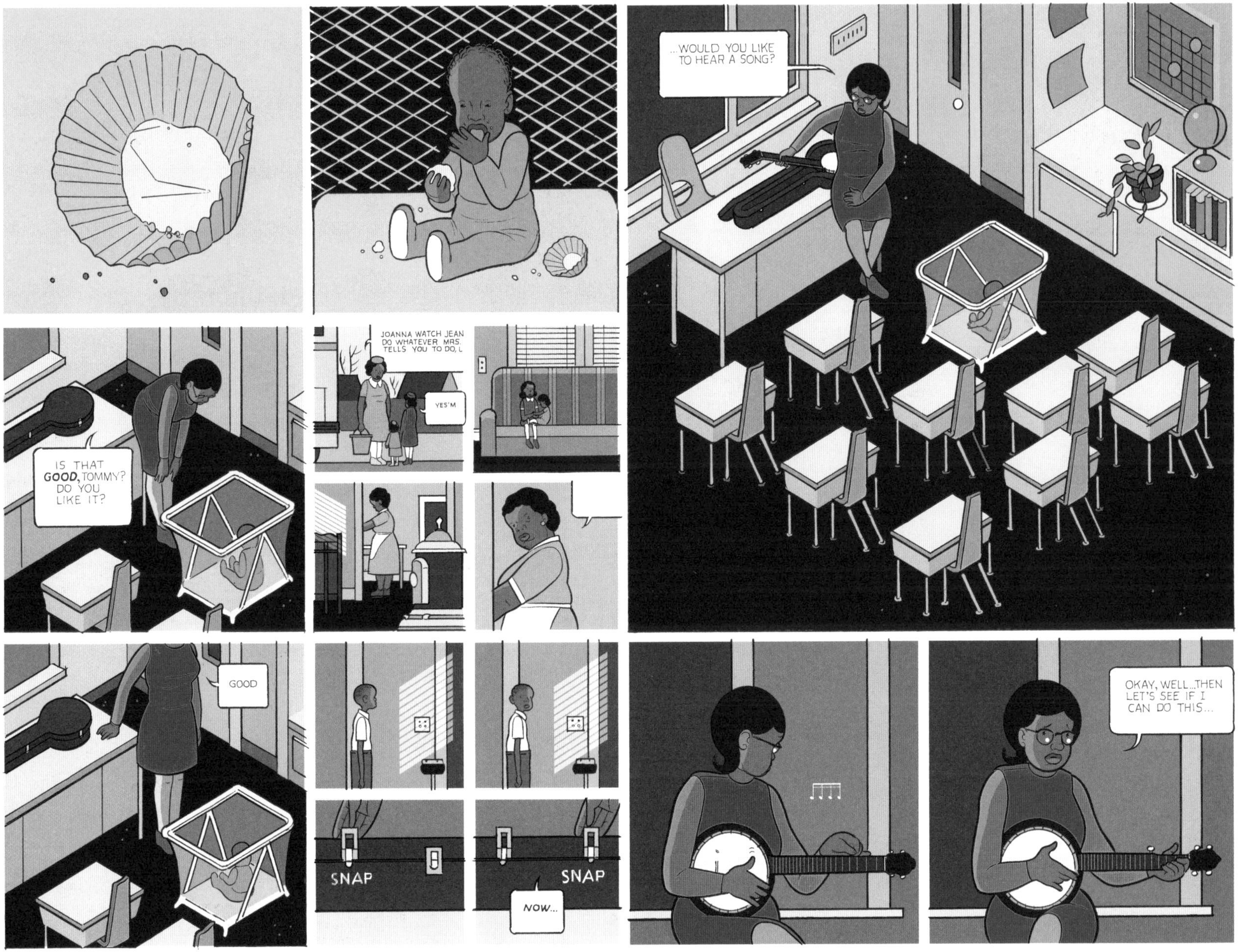

IS THAT GOOD, TOMMY? DO YOU LIKE IT?
JOANNA WATCH JEAN DO WHATEVER MRS. TELLS YOU TO DO, L
YES'M
GOOD
SNAP
SNAP
NOW...
...WOULD YOU LIKE TO HEAR A SONG?
OKAY, WELL...THEN LET'S SEE IF I CAN DO THIS...

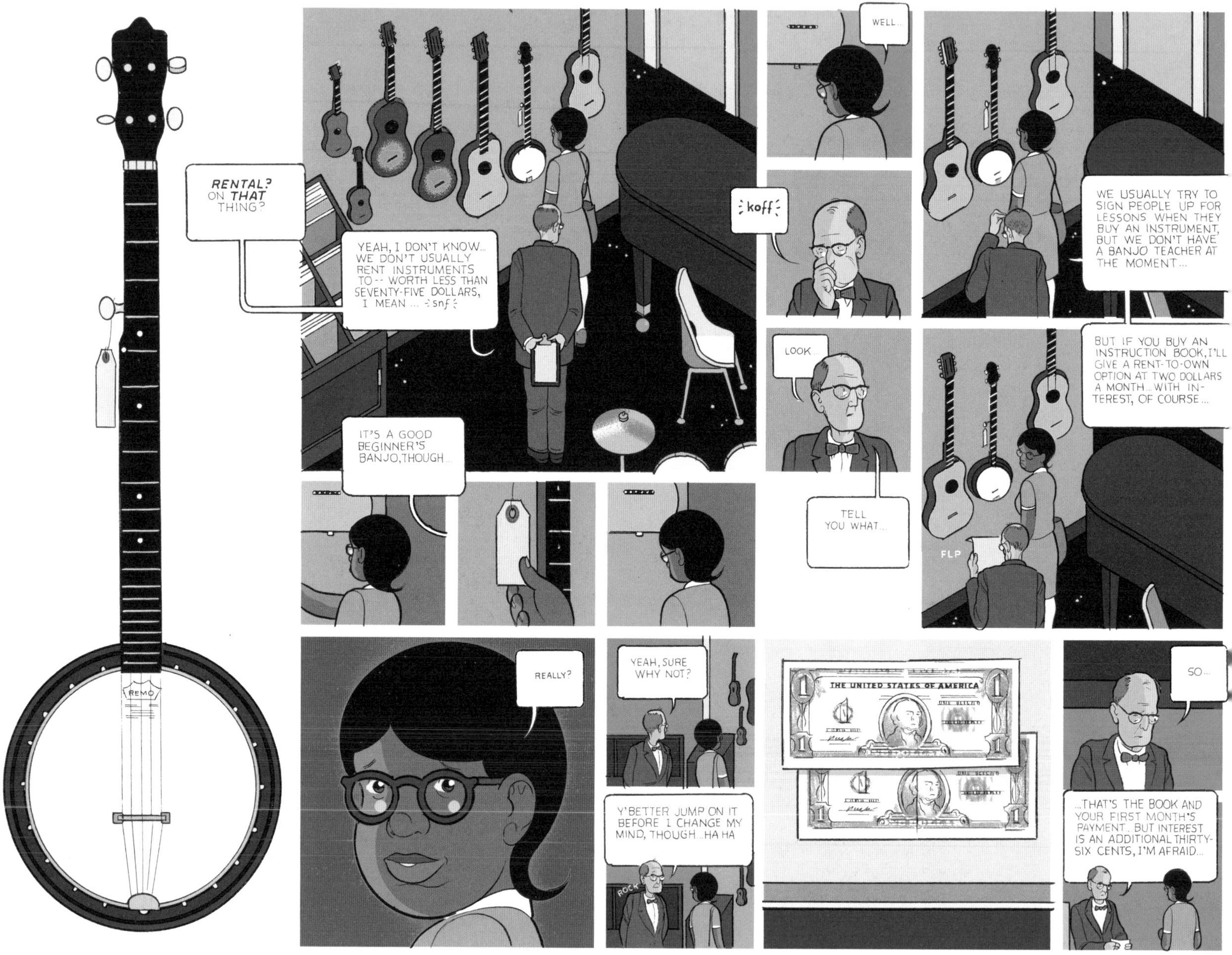
REMO
RENTAL? ON THAT THING?
YEAH, I DON'T KNOW... WE DON'T USUALLY RENT INSTRUMENTS TO -- WORTH LESS THAN SEVENTY-FIVE DOLLARS, I MEAN ... snf
IT'S A GOOD BEGINNER'S BANJO, THOUGH...
WELL...
koff
LOOK...
TELL YOU WHAT...
WE USUALLY TRY TO SIGN PEOPLE UP FOR LESSONS WHEN THEY BUY AN INSTRUMENT, BUT WE DON'T HAVE A BANJO TEACHER AT THE MOMENT...
BUT IF YOU BUY AN INSTRUCTION BOOK, I'LL GIVE A RENT-TO-OWN OPTION AT TWO DOLLARS A MONTH... WITH INTEREST, OF COURSE...
FLP
REALLY?
YEAH, SURE WHY NOT?
Y'BETTER JUMP ON IT BEFORE I CHANGE MY MIND, THOUGH... HA HA
ROCK
THE UNITED STATES OF AMERICA
SO...
...THAT'S THE BOOK AND YOUR FIRST MONTH'S PAYMENT... BUT INTEREST IS AN ADDITIONAL THIRTY-SIX CENTS, I'M AFRAID...

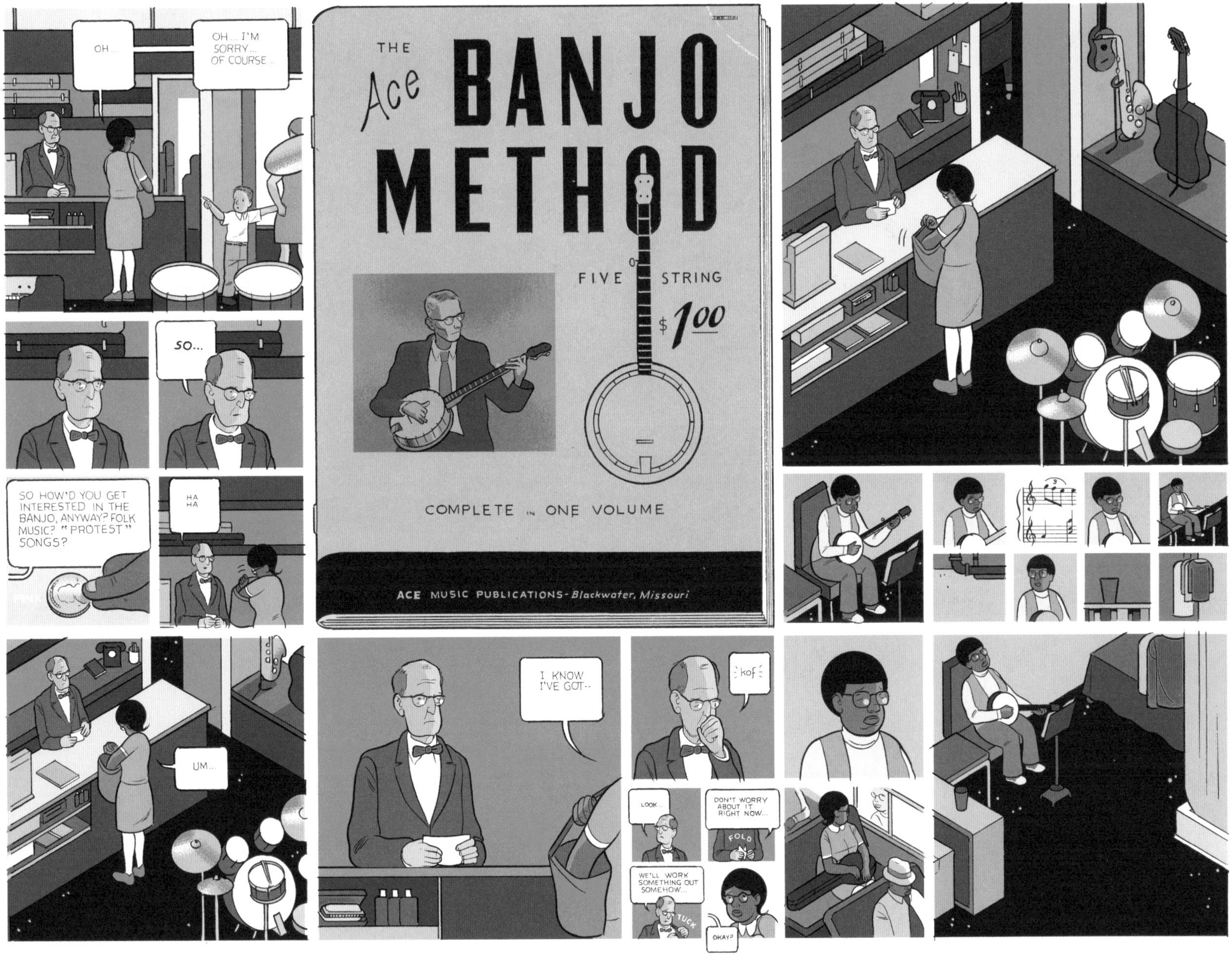
OH...
OH... I'M SORRY... OF COURSE...
SO...
SO HOW'D YOU GET INTERESTED IN THE BANJO, ANYWAY? FOLK MUSIC? "PROTEST" SONGS?
HA HA
THE Ace BANJO METHOD
FIVE STRING
$1.00
COMPLETE IN ONE VOLUME
ACE MUSIC PUBLICATIONS - Blackwater, Missouri
UM...
I KNOW I'VE GOT--
kof
LOOK...
DON'T WORRY ABOUT IT RIGHT NOW...
FOLD
WE'LL WORK SOMETHING OUT SOMEHOW...
TUCK
OKAY?

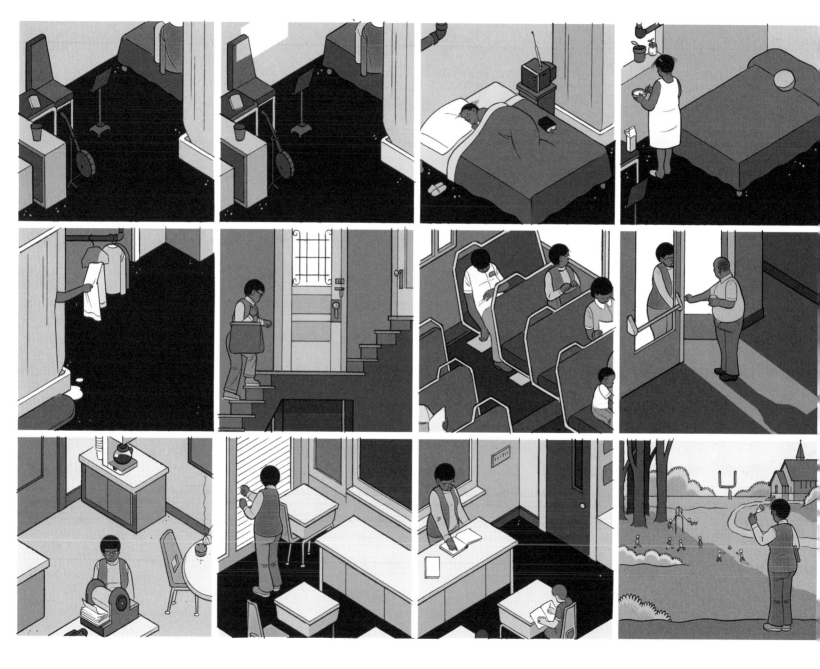

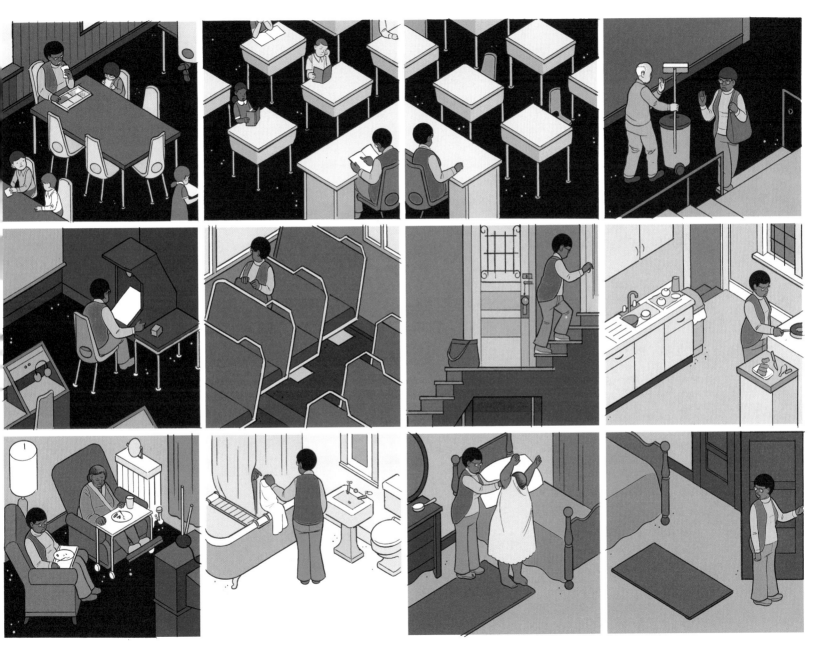

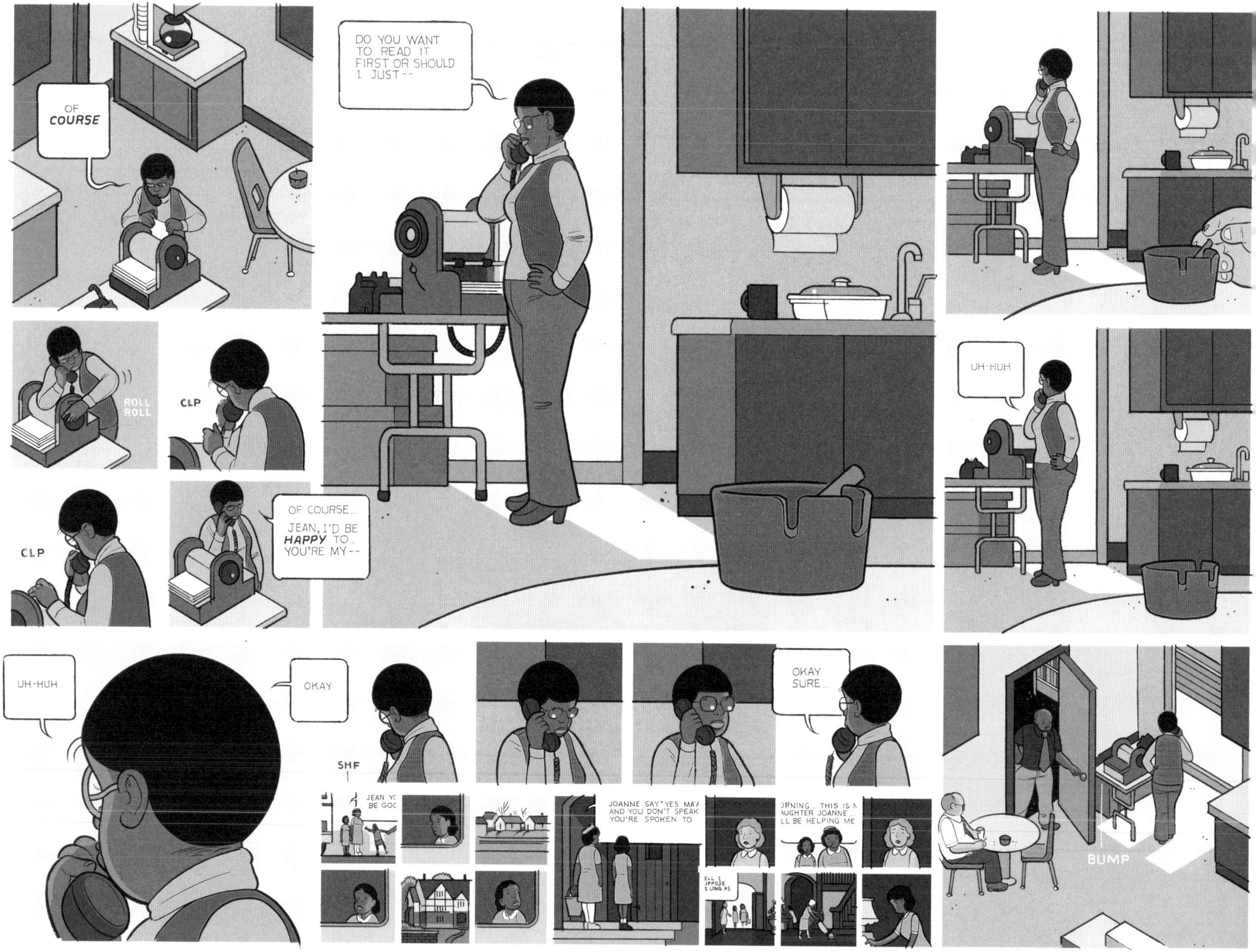
OF COURSE
DO YOU WANT TO READ IT FIRST OR SHOULD I JUST--
ROLL ROLL
CLP
CLP
OF COURSE... JEAN, I'D BE HAPPY TO... YOU'RE MY--
UH-HUH
UH-HUH...
OKAY
SHF
OKAY SURE...
BUMP

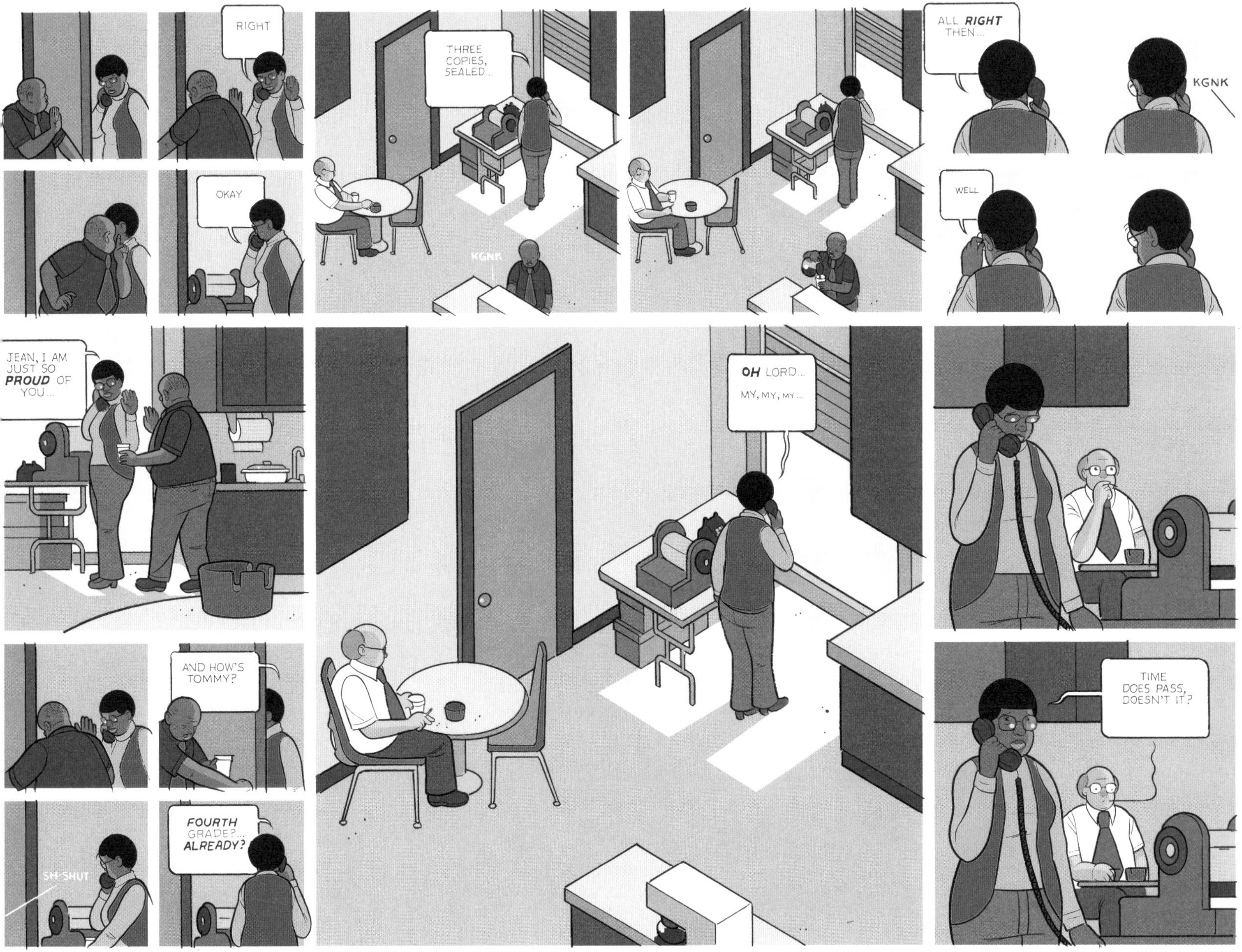
RIGHT
THREE COPIES, SEALED...
ALL RIGHT THEN...
KGNK
KGNK
OKAY
WELL
JEAN, I AM JUST SO PROUD OF YOU...
OH LORD...
MY, MY, MY...
AND HOW'S TOMMY?
TIME DOES PASS, DOESN'T IT?
SH-SHUT
FOURTH GRADE?... ALREADY?

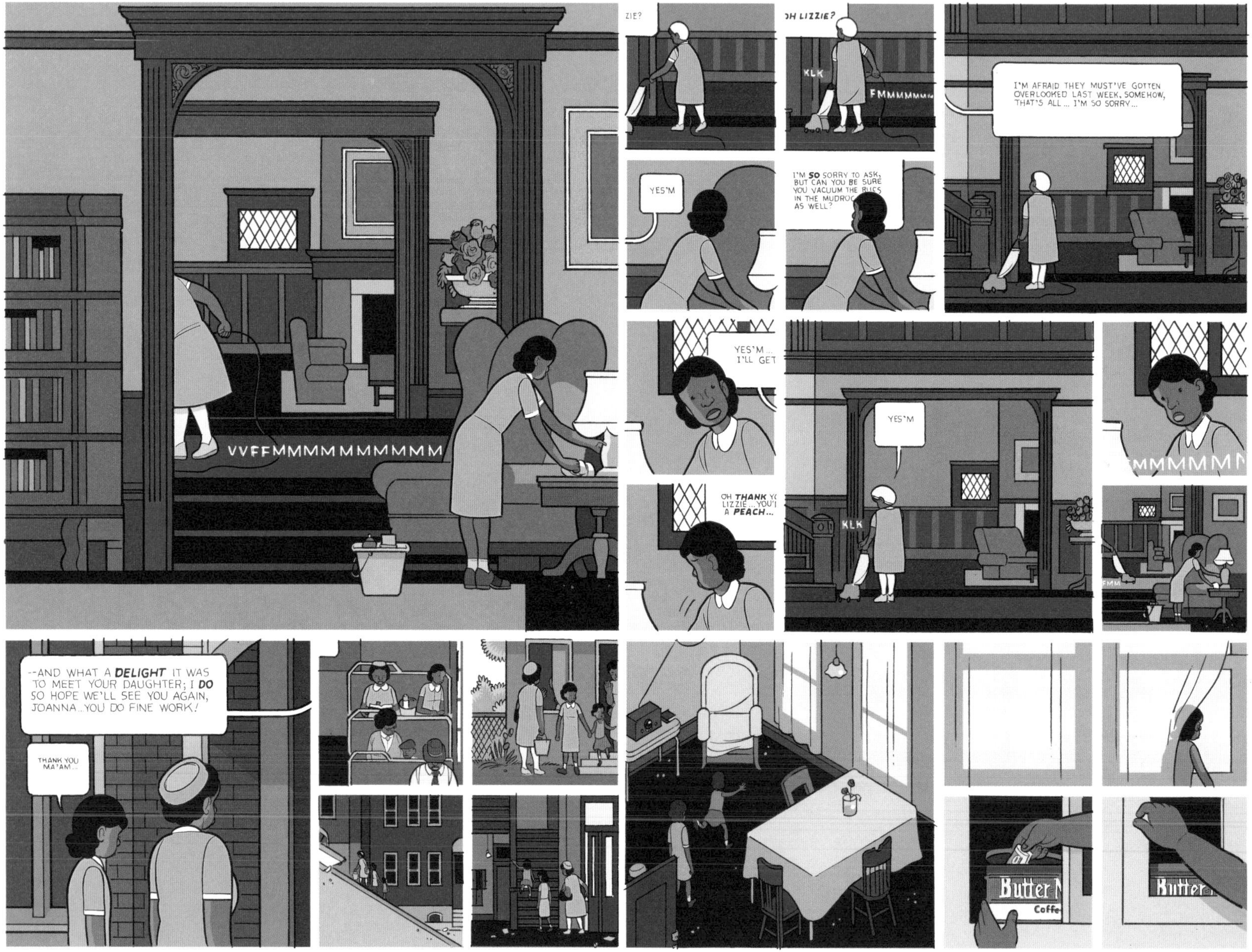

VVFFMMMMMMMMMMMM
ZIE?
OH LIZZIE?
KLK
FMMMMMM
YES'M
I'M **SO** SORRY TO ASK, BUT CAN YOU BE SURE YOU VACUUM THE RUGS IN THE MUDROO AS WELL?
I'M AFRAID THEY MUST'VE GOTTEN OVERLOOKED LAST WEEK, SOMEHOW, THAT'S ALL ... I'M SO SORRY...
YES'M ... I'LL GET
OH **THANK** YO LIZZIE... YOU'I A **PEACH**...
YES'M
KLK
MMMMMN
FMM
--AND WHAT A **DELIGHT** IT WAS TO MEET YOUR DAUGHTER; I **DO** SO HOPE WE'LL SEE YOU AGAIN, JOANNA...YOU DO FINE WORK!
THANK YOU MA'AM...
Butter-N
Coffe
Butter-

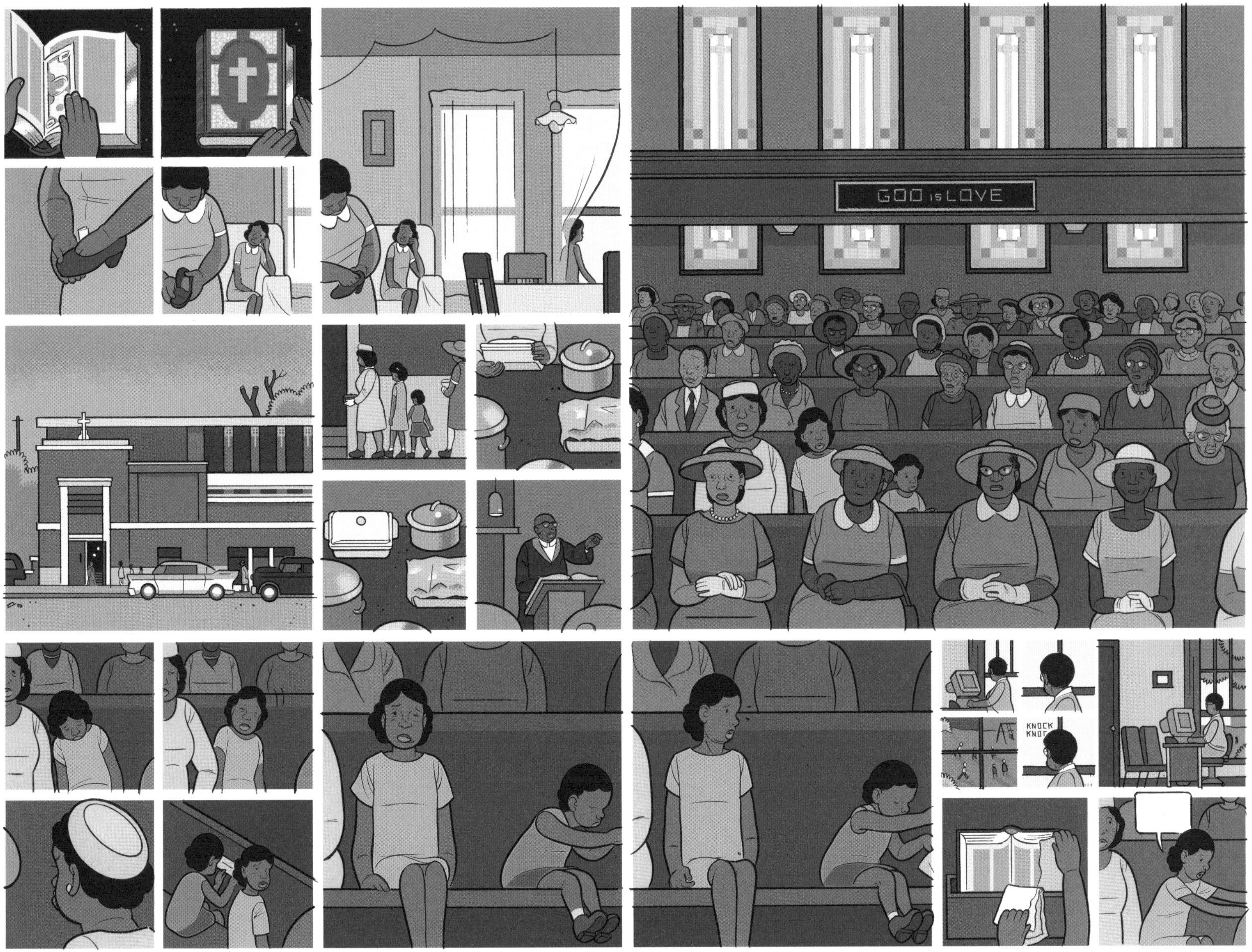
GOD is LOVE
KNOCK

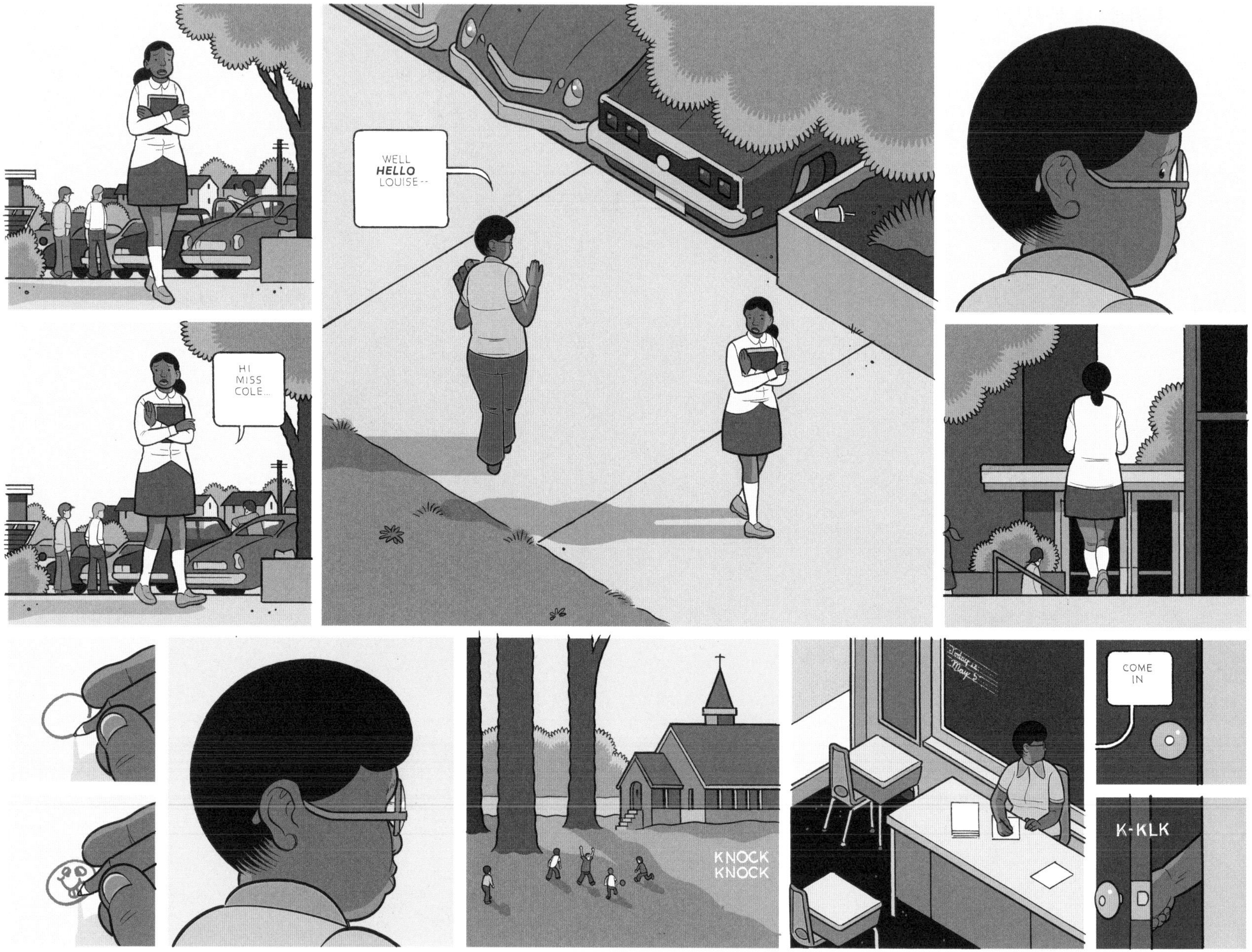
WELL HELLO LOUISE--
HI MISS COLE...
KNOCK KNOCK
Today is May 5
COME IN
K-KLK

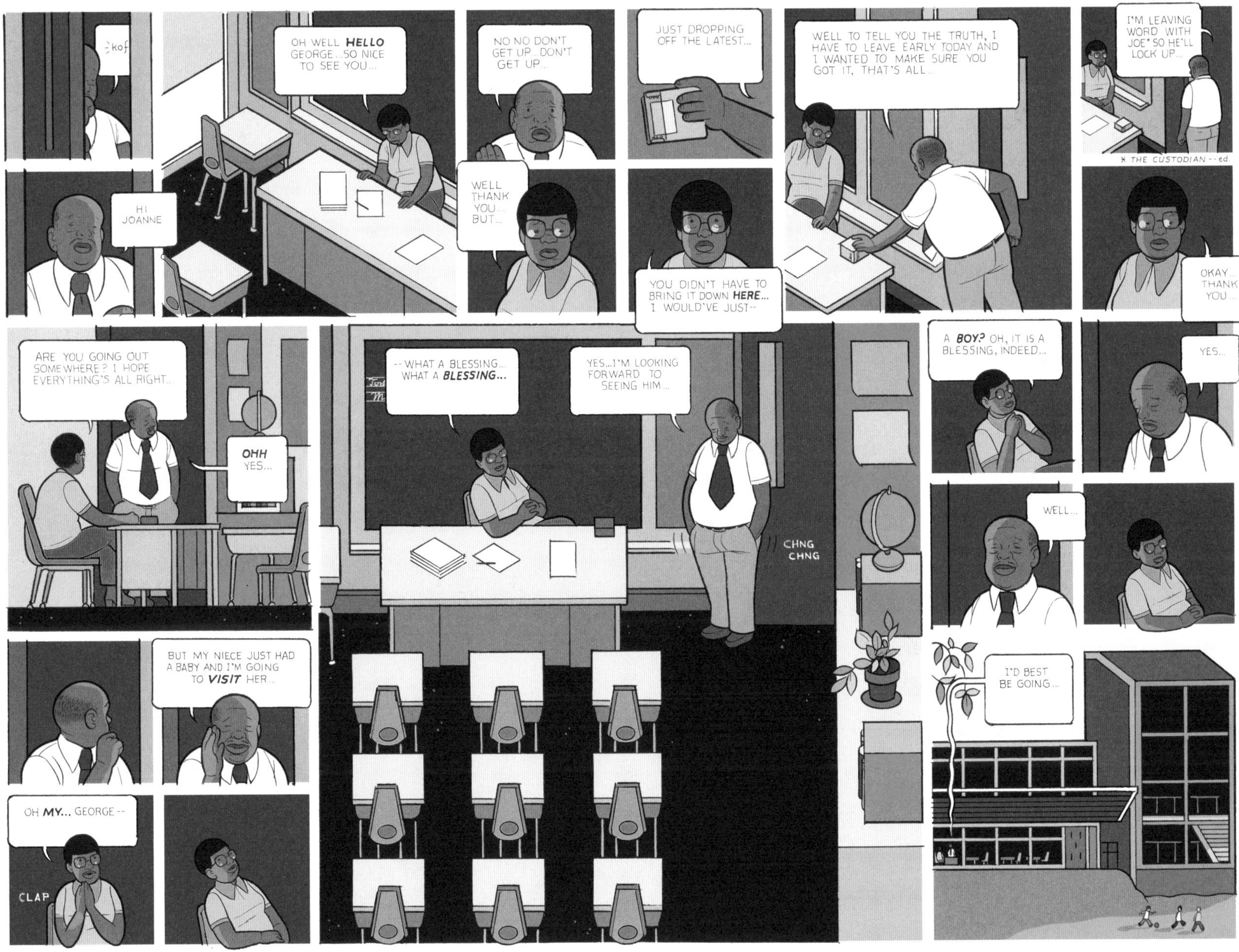

kof
HI JOANNE
OH WELL **HELLO** GEORGE...SO NICE TO SEE YOU...
NO NO DON'T GET UP...DON'T GET UP...
WELL THANK YOU... BUT...
JUST DROPPING OFF THE LATEST...
YOU DIDN'T HAVE TO BRING IT DOWN **HERE...** I WOULD'VE JUST--
WELL TO TELL YOU THE TRUTH, I HAVE TO LEAVE EARLY TODAY AND I WANTED TO MAKE SURE YOU GOT IT, THAT'S ALL...
I'M LEAVING WORD WITH JOE* SO HE'LL LOCK UP...
* THE CUSTODIAN --ed.
OKAY... THANK YOU...
ARE YOU GOING OUT SOMEWHERE? I HOPE EVERYTHING'S ALL RIGHT...
OHH YES...
BUT MY NIECE JUST HAD A BABY AND I'M GOING TO **VISIT** HER...
OH **MY...** GEORGE--
CLAP
--WHAT A BLESSING... WHAT A **BLESSING...**
YES...I'M LOOKING FORWARD TO SEEING HIM...
CHNG CHNG
A **BOY?** OH, IT IS A BLESSING, INDEED...
YES...
WELL...
I'D BEST BE GOING...

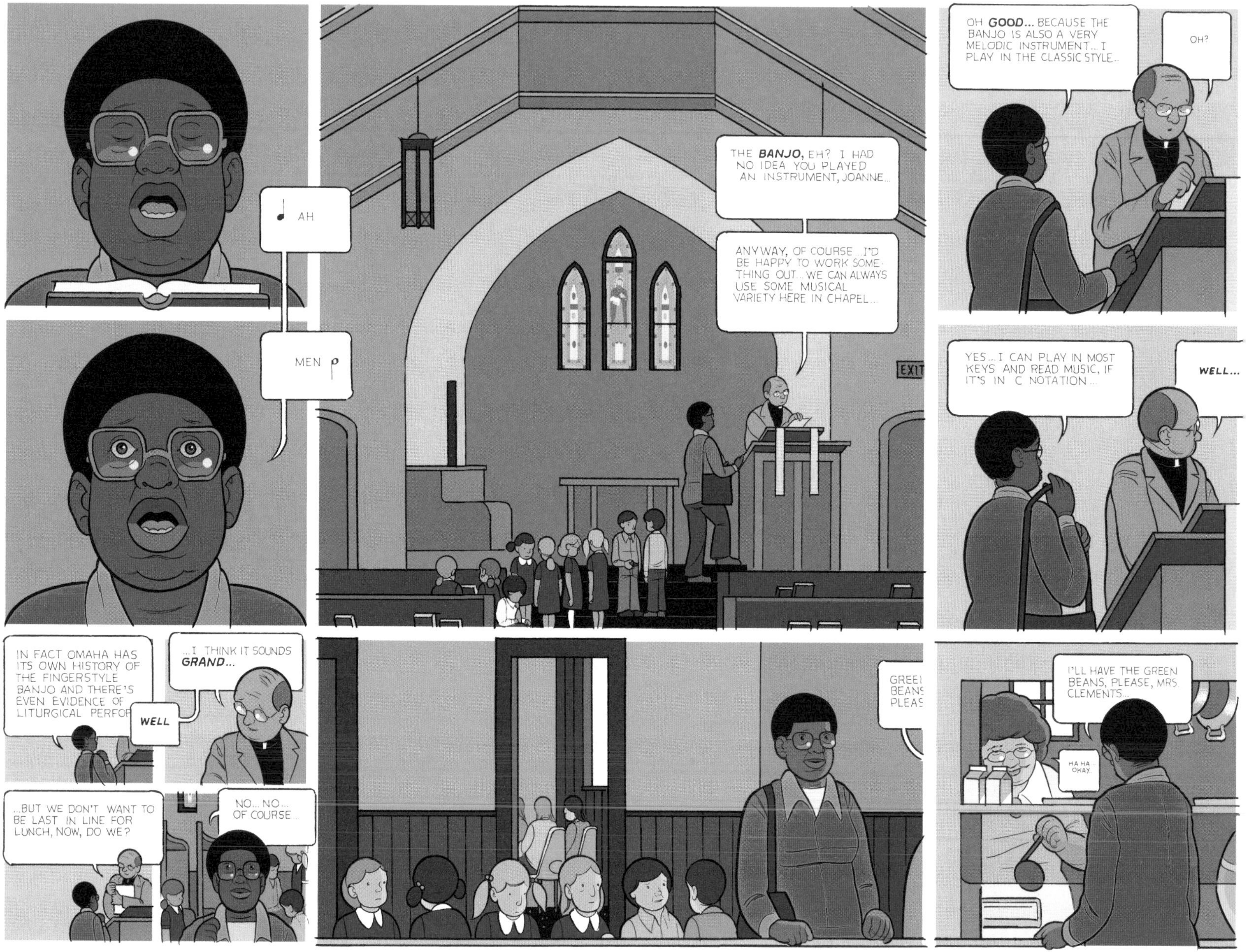
AH
MEN
THE **BANJO,** EH? I HAD NO IDEA YOU PLAYED AN INSTRUMENT, JOANNE...
ANYWAY, OF COURSE...I'D BE HAPPY TO WORK SOMETHING OUT... WE CAN ALWAYS USE SOME MUSICAL VARIETY HERE IN CHAPEL...
EXIT
OH **GOOD...** BECAUSE THE BANJO IS ALSO A VERY MELODIC INSTRUMENT... I PLAY IN THE CLASSIC STYLE...
OH?
YES... I CAN PLAY IN MOST KEYS AND READ MUSIC, IF IT'S IN C NOTATION...
WELL...
IN FACT OMAHA HAS ITS OWN HISTORY OF THE FINGERSTYLE BANJO AND THERE'S EVEN EVIDENCE OF LITURGICAL PERFOR
WELL
...I THINK IT SOUNDS **GRAND...**
...BUT WE DON'T WANT TO BE LAST IN LINE FOR LUNCH, NOW, DO WE?
NO... NO... OF COURSE...
GREE BEANS PLEAS
I'LL HAVE THE GREEN BEANS, PLEASE, MRS. CLEMENTS...
HA HA... OKAY.

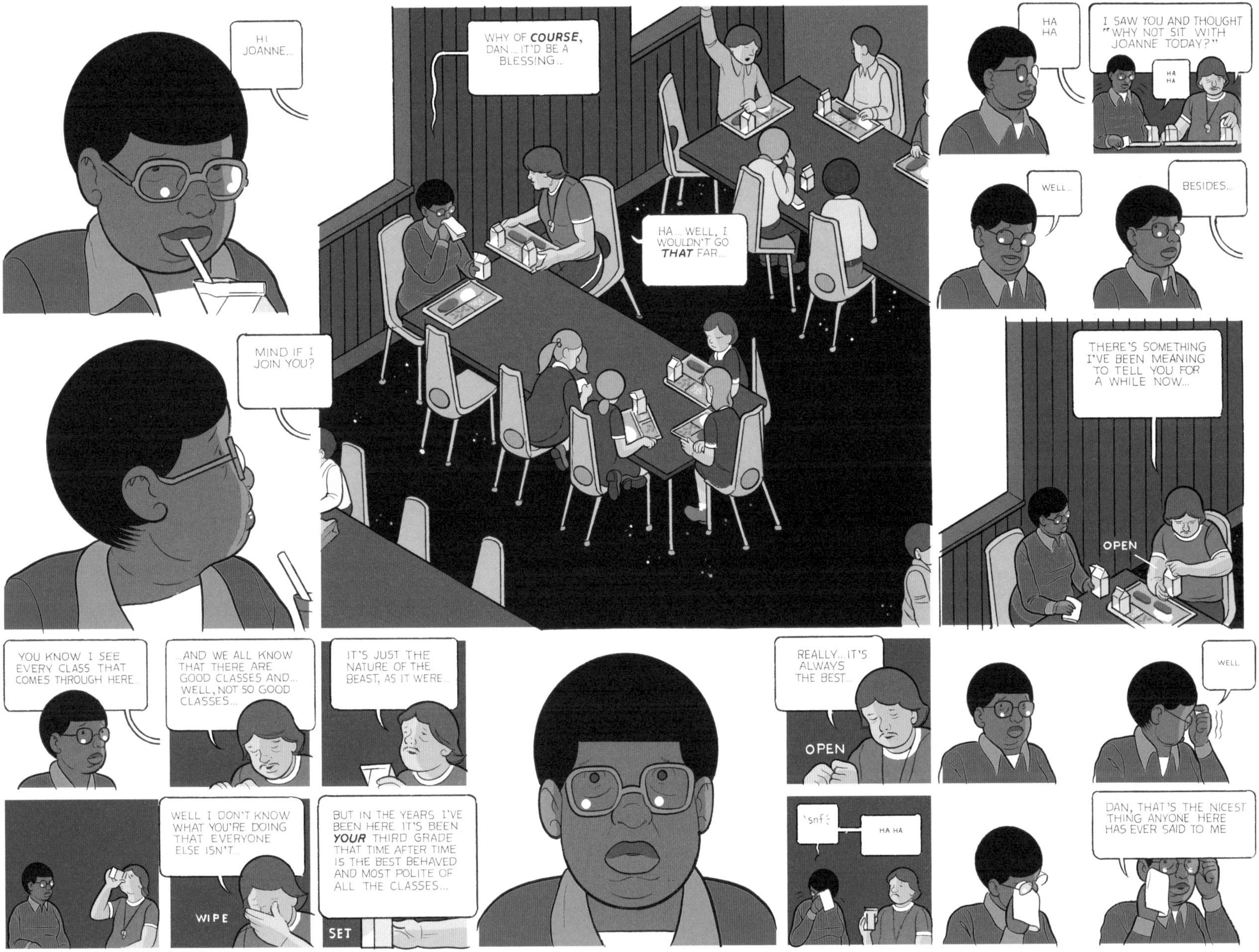
HI JOANNE...
MIND IF I JOIN YOU?
WHY OF COURSE, DAN... IT'D BE A BLESSING...
HA... WELL, I WOULDN'T GO THAT FAR...
HA HA
I SAW YOU AND THOUGHT "WHY NOT SIT WITH JOANNE TODAY?"
HA HA
WELL..
BESIDES...
THERE'S SOMETHING I'VE BEEN MEANING TO TELL YOU FOR A WHILE NOW...
OPEN
YOU KNOW I SEE EVERY CLASS THAT COMES THROUGH HERE...
...AND WE ALL KNOW THAT THERE ARE GOOD CLASSES AND... WELL, NOT SO GOOD CLASSES...
IT'S JUST THE NATURE OF THE BEAST, AS IT WERE...
REALLY... IT'S ALWAYS THE BEST...
OPEN
WELL
WELL I DON'T KNOW WHAT YOU'RE DOING THAT EVERYONE ELSE ISN'T...
WIPE
BUT IN THE YEARS I'VE BEEN HERE IT'S BEEN YOUR THIRD GRADE THAT TIME AFTER TIME IS THE BEST BEHAVED AND MOST POLITE OF ALL THE CLASSES...
SET
snf
HA HA
DAN, THAT'S THE NICEST THING ANYONE HERE HAS EVER SAID TO ME

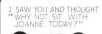

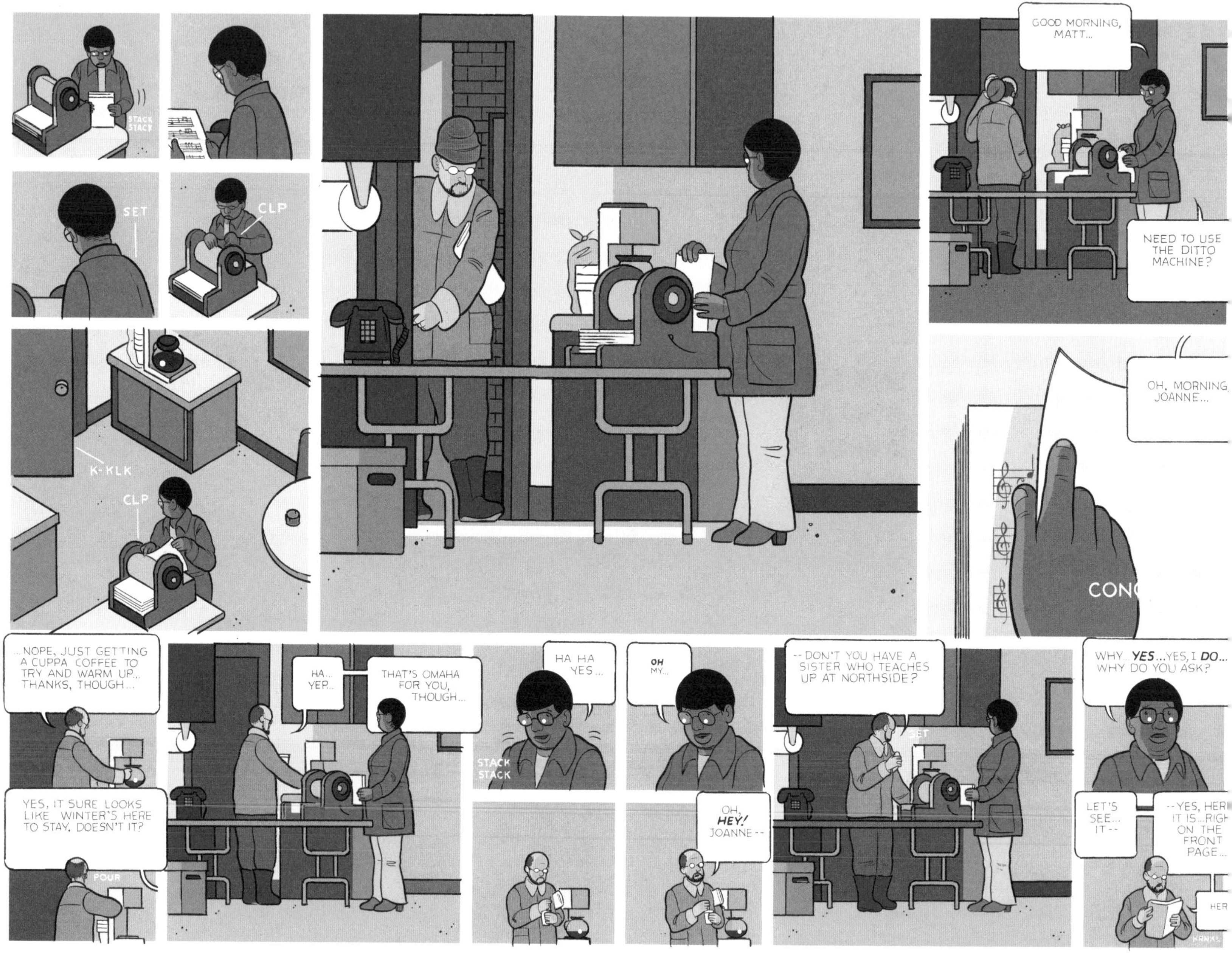
STACK STACK
SET
CLP
K-KLK
CLP
GOOD MORNING, MATT...
NEED TO USE THE DITTO MACHINE?
OH, MORNING, JOANNE...
CONC
...NOPE, JUST GETTING A CUPPA COFFEE TO TRY AND WARM UP... THANKS, THOUGH...
YES, IT SURE LOOKS LIKE WINTER'S HERE TO STAY, DOESN'T IT?
POUR
HA... YEP...
THAT'S OMAHA FOR YOU, THOUGH...
HA HA YES...
STACK STACK
OH MY...
OH, HEY! JOANNE--
--DON'T YOU HAVE A SISTER WHO TEACHES UP AT NORTHSIDE?
SET
WHY. YES...YES, I DO... WHY DO YOU ASK?
LET'S SEE... IT--
--YES, HER IT IS...RIGH ON THE FRONT PAGE...
HER

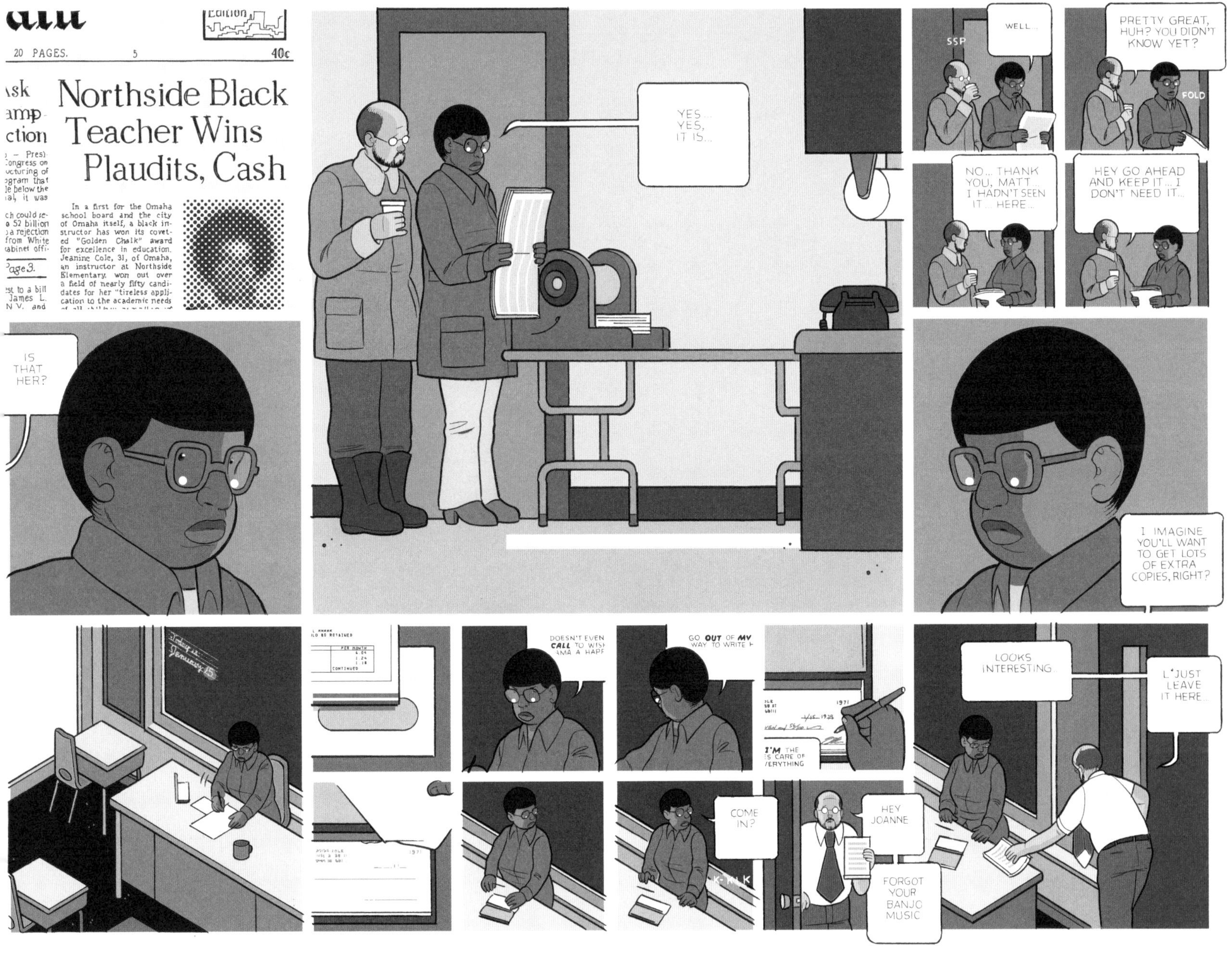

Edition
20 PAGES. 5 40¢
Northside Black Teacher Wins Plaudits, Cash
In a first for the Omaha school board and the city of Omaha itself, a black instructor has won its coveted "Golden Chalk" award for excellence in education. Jeanine Cole, 31, of Omaha, an instructor at Northside Elementary, won out over a field of nearly fifty candidates for her "tireless application to the academic needs
Page 3.
YES… YES, IT IS…
SSP
WELL…
PRETTY GREAT, HUH? YOU DIDN'T KNOW YET?
FOLD
NO… THANK YOU, MATT… I HADN'T SEEN IT… HERE…
HEY GO AHEAD AND KEEP IT… I DON'T NEED IT…
IS THAT HER?
I IMAGINE YOU'LL WANT TO GET LOTS OF EXTRA COPIES, RIGHT?
Today is: January 15
PER MONTH
CONTINUED
DOESN'T EVEN CALL TO WISH
GO OUT OF MY WAY TO WRITE
1971
I'M THE
CARE OF
COME IN?
K-KLK
HEY JOANNE
FORGOT YOUR BANJO MUSIC
LOOKS INTERESTING…
I…JUST LEAVE IT HERE…

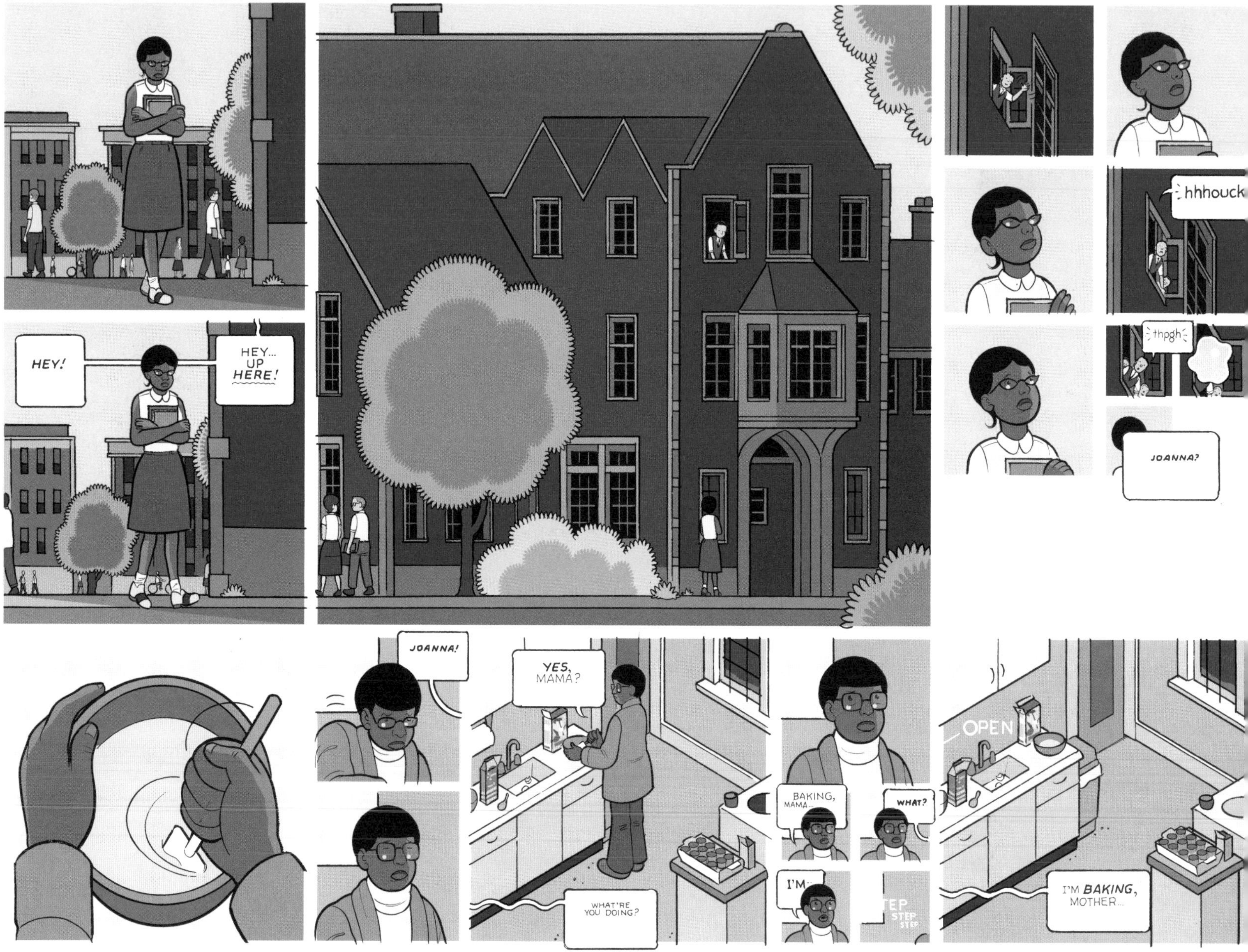
HEY!
HEY... UP HERE!
hhhouck
thpgh
JOANNA?
JOANNA!
YES, MAMA?
WHAT'RE YOU DOING?
BAKING, MAMA...
WHAT?
I'M-
STEP STEP STEP
OPEN
I'M BAKING, MOTHER...

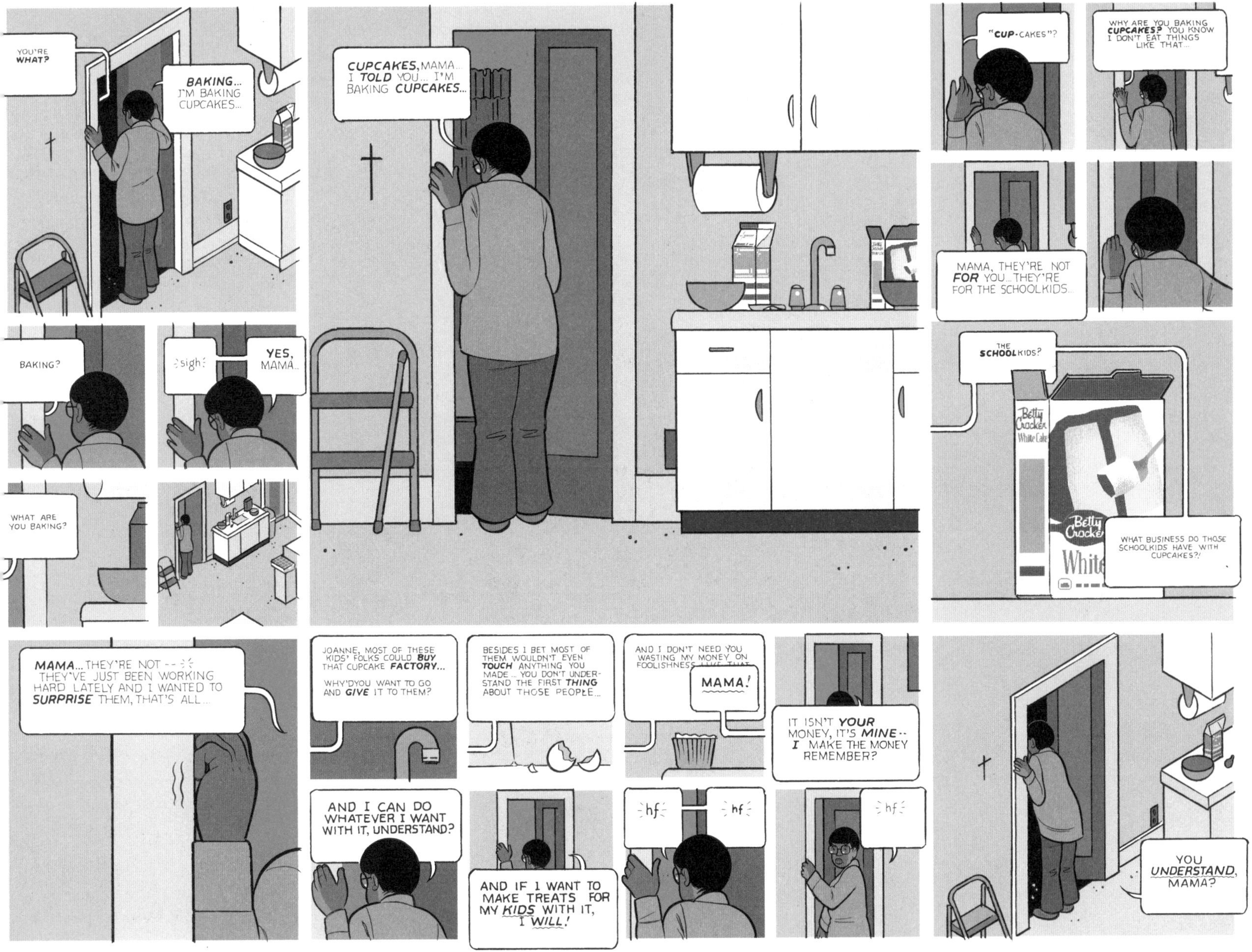

YOU'RE WHAT?
BAKING... I'M BAKING CUPCAKES...
BAKING?
sigh
YES, MAMA...
WHAT ARE YOU BAKING?
CUPCAKES, MAMA... I TOLD YOU... I'M BAKING CUPCAKES...
"CUP-CAKES"?
WHY ARE YOU BAKING CUPCAKES? YOU KNOW I DON'T EAT THINGS LIKE THAT...
MAMA, THEY'RE NOT FOR YOU... THEY'RE FOR THE SCHOOLKIDS...
THE SCHOOLKIDS?
Betty Crocker White Cake
Betty Crocker White
WHAT BUSINESS DO THOSE SCHOOLKIDS HAVE WITH CUPCAKES?!
MAMA... THEY'RE NOT -- THEY'VE JUST BEEN WORKING HARD LATELY AND I WANTED TO SURPRISE THEM, THAT'S ALL...
JOANNE, MOST OF THESE KIDS' FOLKS COULD BUY THAT CUPCAKE FACTORY...
WHY'D YOU WANT TO GO AND GIVE IT TO THEM?
BESIDES I BET MOST OF THEM WOULDN'T EVEN TOUCH ANYTHING YOU MADE... YOU DON'T UNDERSTAND THE FIRST THING ABOUT THOSE PEOPLE...
AND I DON'T NEED YOU WASTING MY MONEY ON FOOLISHNESS
MAMA!
IT ISN'T YOUR MONEY, IT'S MINE -- I MAKE THE MONEY REMEMBER?
AND I CAN DO WHATEVER I WANT WITH IT, UNDERSTAND?
AND IF I WANT TO MAKE TREATS FOR MY KIDS WITH IT, I WILL!
hf
hf
hf
YOU UNDERSTAND, MAMA?

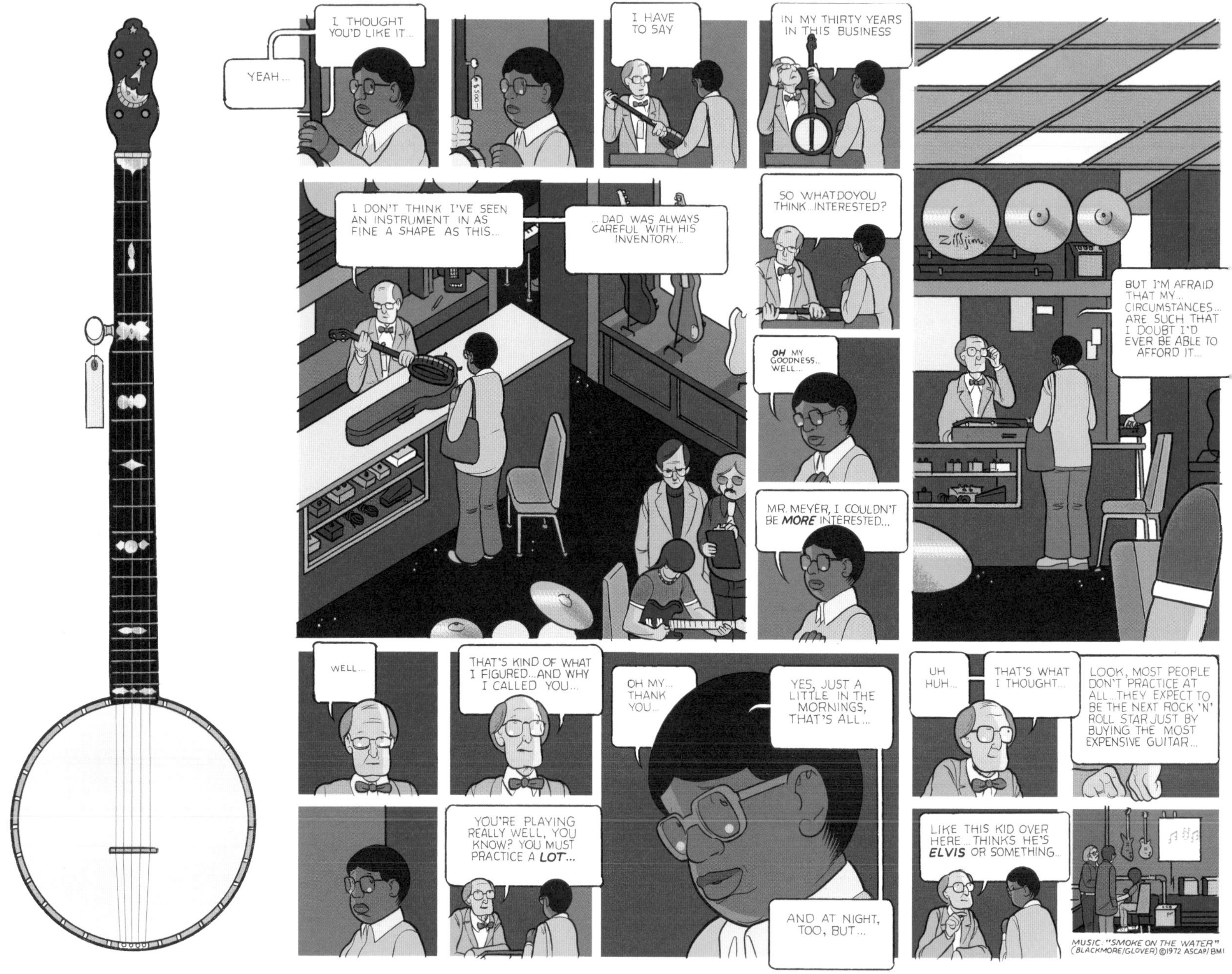

YEAH...
I THOUGHT YOU'D LIKE IT...
$500—
I HAVE TO SAY
IN MY THIRTY YEARS IN THIS BUSINESS
I DON'T THINK I'VE SEEN AN INSTRUMENT IN AS FINE A SHAPE AS THIS...
...DAD WAS ALWAYS CAREFUL WITH HIS INVENTORY...
SO WHATDOYOU THINK...INTERESTED?
OH MY GOODNESS... WELL...
MR. MEYER, I COULDN'T BE MORE INTERESTED...
Zildjian
BUT I'M AFRAID THAT MY... CIRCUMSTANCES... ARE SUCH THAT I DOUBT I'D EVER BE ABLE TO AFFORD IT...
WELL...
THAT'S KIND OF WHAT I FIGURED...AND WHY I CALLED YOU...
YOU'RE PLAYING REALLY WELL, YOU KNOW? YOU MUST PRACTICE A LOT...
OH MY... THANK YOU...
YES, JUST A LITTLE IN THE MORNINGS, THAT'S ALL...
AND AT NIGHT, TOO, BUT...
UH HUH...
THAT'S WHAT I THOUGHT...
LOOK, MOST PEOPLE DON'T PRACTICE AT ALL...THEY EXPECT TO BE THE NEXT ROCK 'N' ROLL STAR JUST BY BUYING THE MOST EXPENSIVE GUITAR...
LIKE THIS KID OVER HERE... THINKS HE'S ELVIS OR SOMETHING...
MUSIC: "SMOKE ON THE WATER" (BLACKMORE/GLOVER) ©1972 ASCAP/BMI

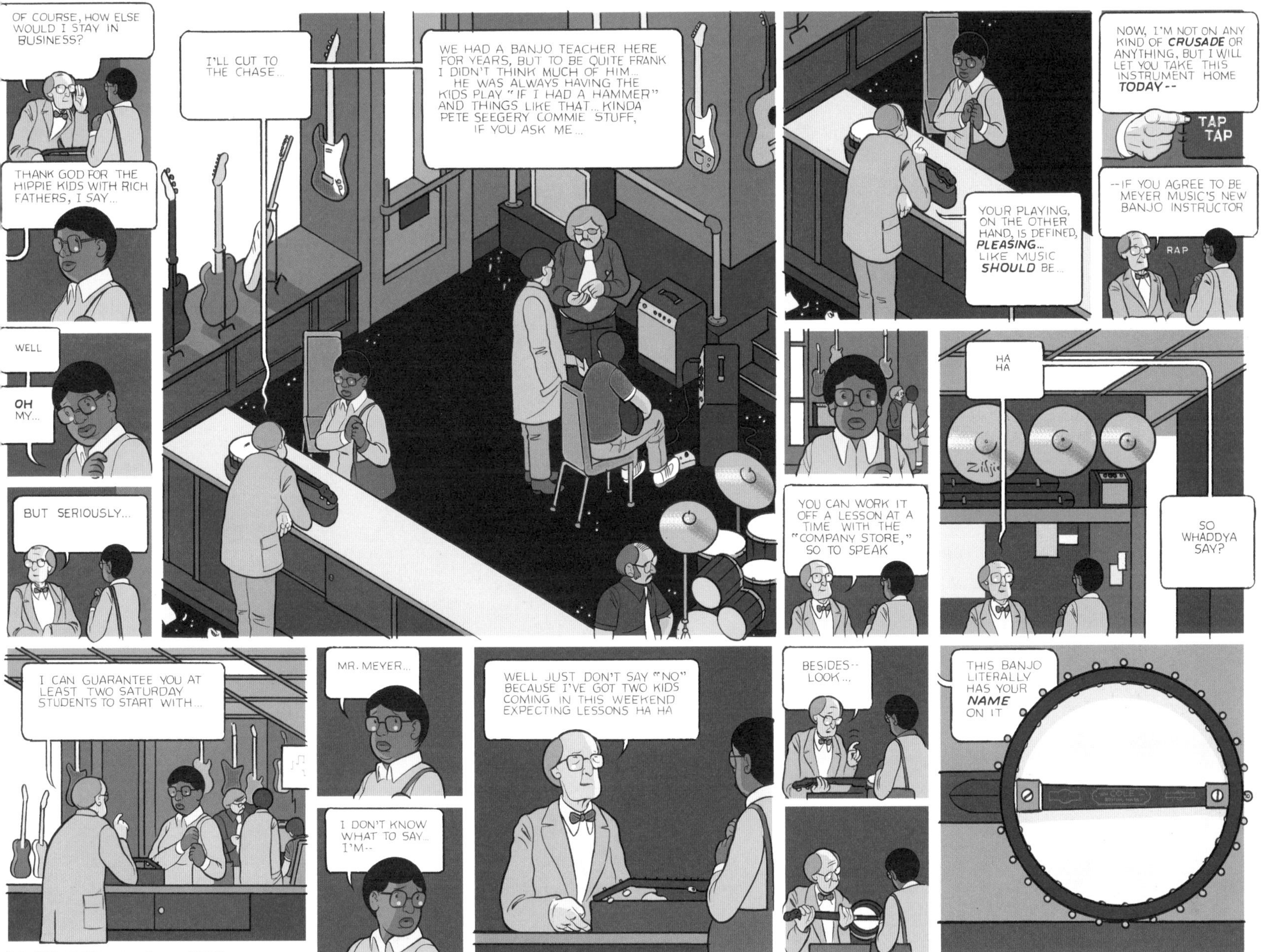

OF COURSE, HOW ELSE WOULD I STAY IN BUSINESS?
THANK GOD FOR THE HIPPIE KIDS WITH RICH FATHERS, I SAY...
WELL
OH MY...
BUT SERIOUSLY...
I'LL CUT TO THE CHASE...
WE HAD A BANJO TEACHER HERE FOR YEARS, BUT TO BE QUITE FRANK I DIDN'T THINK MUCH OF HIM... HE WAS ALWAYS HAVING THE KIDS PLAY "IF I HAD A HAMMER" AND THINGS LIKE THAT... KINDA PETE SEEGERY COMMIE STUFF, IF YOU ASK ME...
YOUR PLAYING, ON THE OTHER HAND, IS DEFINED, **PLEASING**... LIKE MUSIC **SHOULD** BE...
NOW, I'M NOT ON ANY KIND OF **CRUSADE** OR ANYTHING, BUT I WILL LET YOU TAKE THIS INSTRUMENT HOME **TODAY**--
TAP TAP
--IF YOU AGREE TO BE MEYER MUSIC'S NEW BANJO INSTRUCTOR
RAP
YOU CAN WORK IT OFF A LESSON AT A TIME WITH THE "COMPANY STORE," SO TO SPEAK
HA HA
SO WHADDYA SAY?
I CAN GUARANTEE YOU AT LEAST TWO SATURDAY STUDENTS TO START WITH...
MR. MEYER...
I DON'T KNOW WHAT TO SAY... I'M--
WELL JUST DON'T SAY "NO" BECAUSE I'VE GOT TWO KIDS COMING IN THIS WEEKEND EXPECTING LESSONS HA HA
BESIDES-- LOOK...
THIS BANJO LITERALLY HAS YOUR **NAME** ON IT

MUSIC: "RIDIN' THE STORM OUT" (RICHRATH) ©1973 ASCAP/EPIC

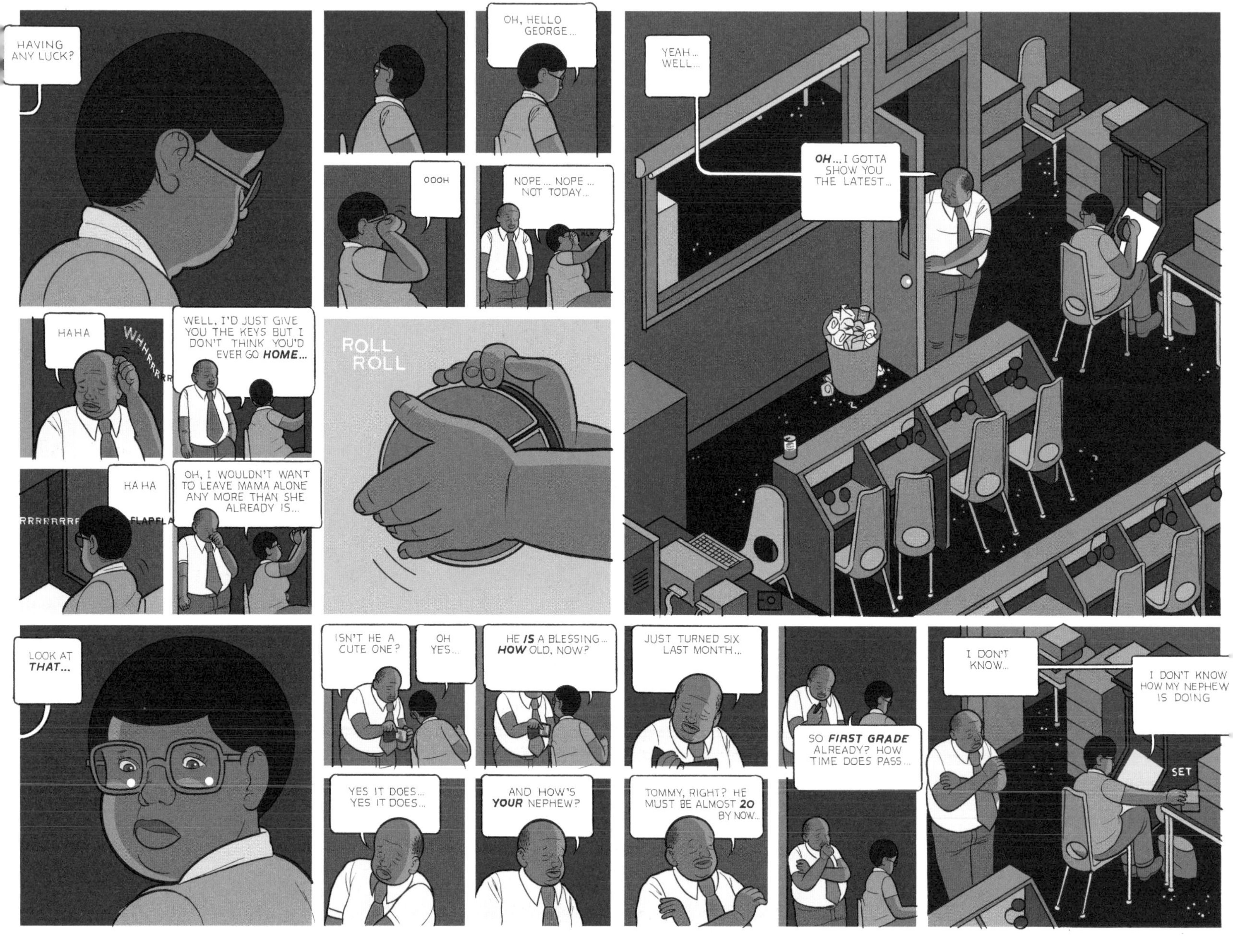

HAVING ANY LUCK?
OH, HELLO GEORGE...
OOOH
NOPE... NOPE... NOT TODAY...
HAHA
WELL, I'D JUST GIVE YOU THE KEYS BUT I DON'T THINK YOU'D EVER GO **HOME**...
HA HA
OH, I WOULDN'T WANT TO LEAVE MAMA ALONE ANY MORE THAN SHE ALREADY IS...
ROLL ROLL
YEAH... WELL...
OH... I GOTTA SHOW YOU THE LATEST...
LOOK AT **THAT**...
ISN'T HE A CUTE ONE?
OH YES...
HE ***IS*** A BLESSING... ***HOW*** OLD, NOW?
JUST TURNED SIX LAST MONTH...
SO ***FIRST GRADE*** ALREADY? HOW TIME DOES PASS...
YES IT DOES... YES IT DOES...
AND HOW'S ***YOUR*** NEPHEW?
TOMMY, RIGHT? HE MUST BE ALMOST ***20*** BY NOW...
I DON'T KNOW...
I DON'T KNOW HOW MY NEPHEW IS DOING
SET

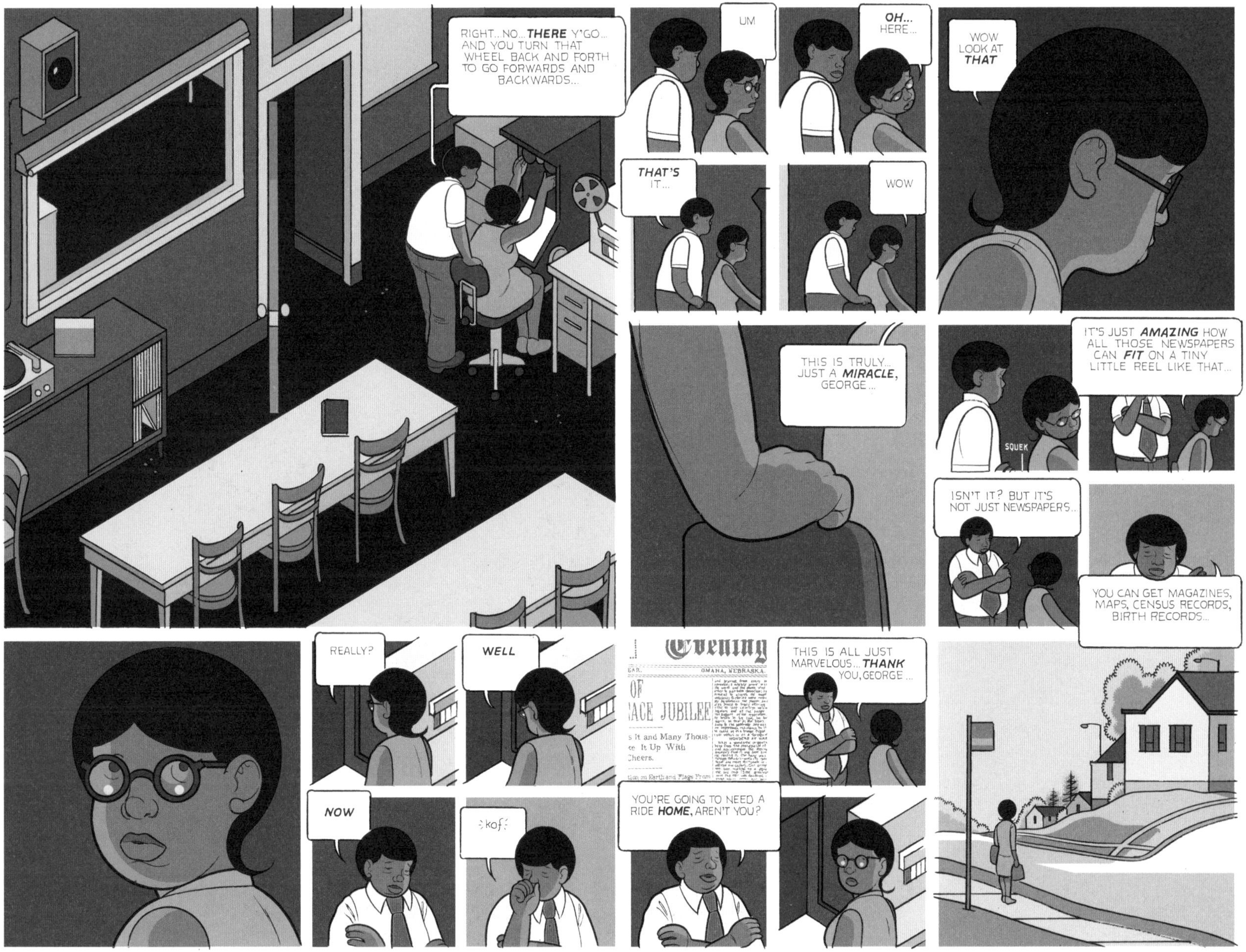
RIGHT...NO...**THERE** Y'GO... AND YOU TURN THAT WHEEL BACK AND FORTH TO GO FORWARDS AND BACKWARDS...
UM
OH... HERE...
THAT'S IT...
WOW
WOW LOOK AT **THAT**
THIS IS TRULY... JUST A **MIRACLE,** GEORGE...
SQUEK
IT'S JUST **AMAZING** HOW ALL THOSE NEWSPAPERS CAN **FIT** ON A TINY LITTLE REEL LIKE THAT...
ISN'T IT? BUT IT'S NOT JUST NEWSPAPERS...
YOU CAN GET MAGAZINES, MAPS, CENSUS RECORDS, BIRTH RECORDS...
REALLY?
WELL
NOW
kof
Evening
OMAHA, NEBRASKA.
JUBILEE
THIS IS ALL JUST MARVELOUS... **THANK** YOU, GEORGE...
YOU'RE GOING TO NEED A RIDE **HOME,** AREN'T YOU?

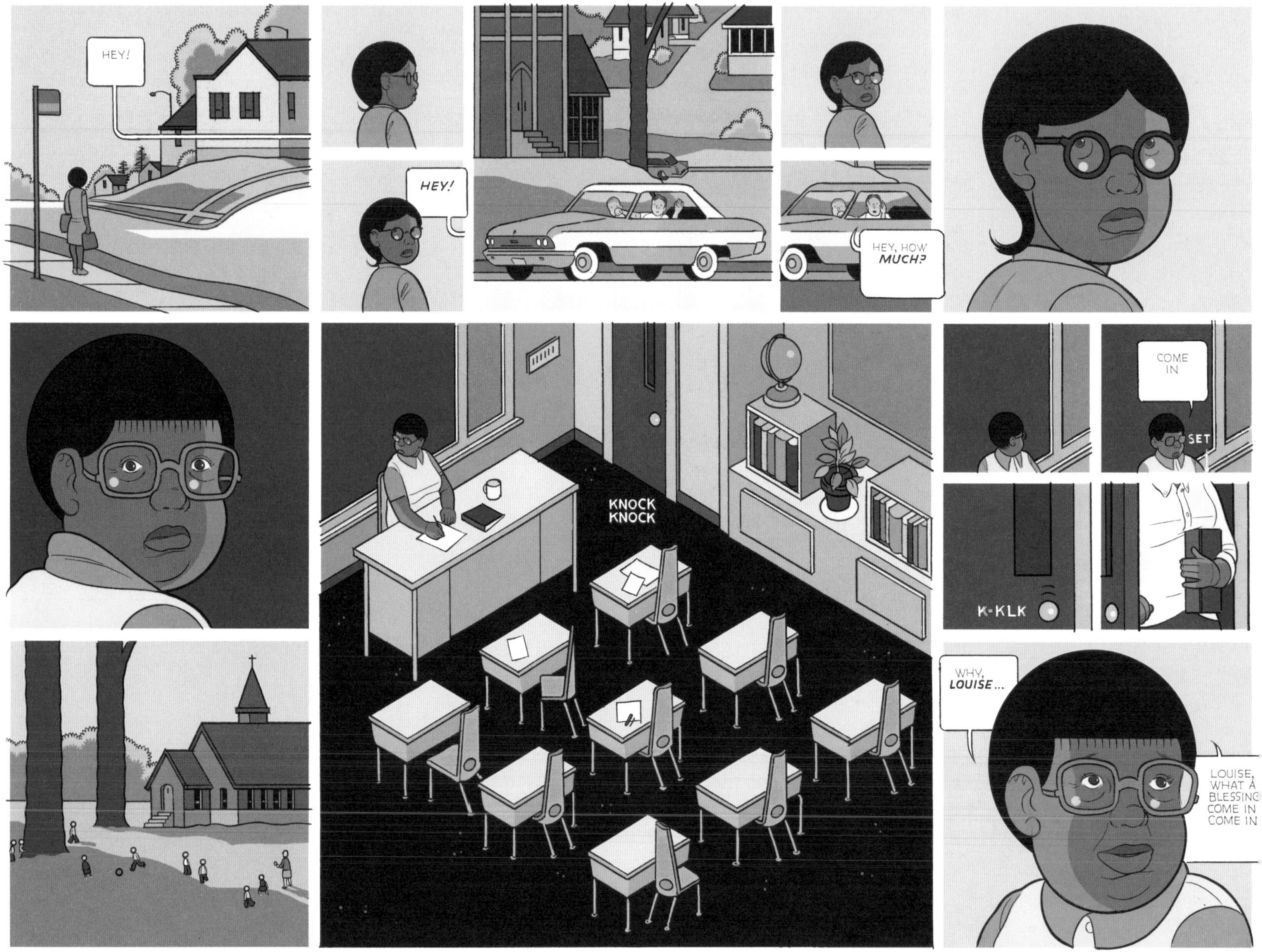
HEY!
HEY!
HEY, HOW MUCH?
KNOCK KNOCK
COME IN
SET
K-KLK
WHY, LOUISE...
LOUISE, WHAT A BLESSING COME IN COME IN

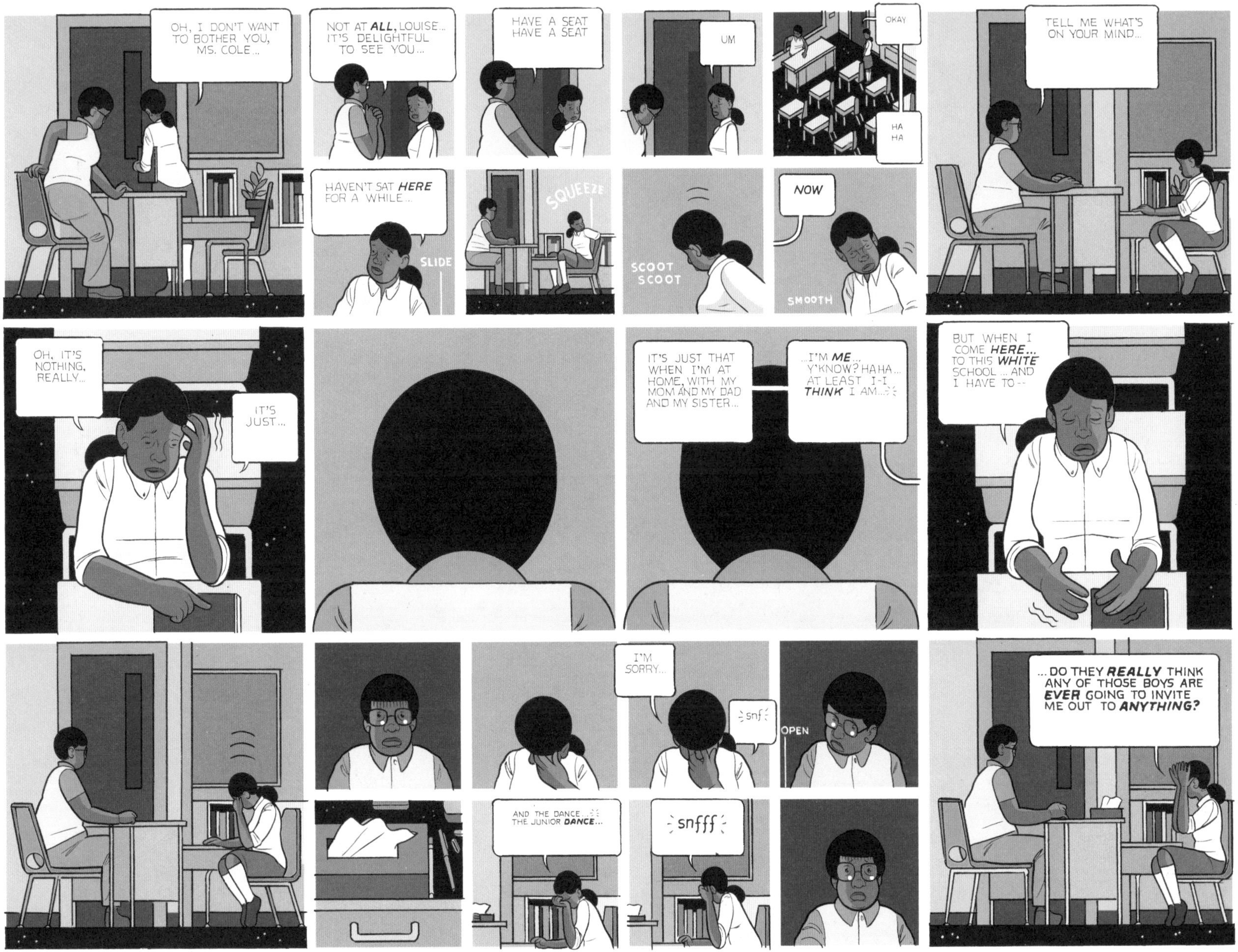

OH, I DON'T WANT TO BOTHER YOU, MS. COLE...
NOT AT ALL, LOUISE... IT'S DELIGHTFUL TO SEE YOU...
HAVE A SEAT HAVE A SEAT
UM
OKAY
HA HA
HAVEN'T SAT HERE FOR A WHILE...
SLIDE
SQUEEZE
SCOOT SCOOT
NOW
SMOOTH
TELL ME WHAT'S ON YOUR MIND...
OH, IT'S NOTHING, REALLY...
IT'S JUST...
IT'S JUST THAT WHEN I'M AT HOME, WITH MY MOM AND MY DAD AND MY SISTER...
...I'M ME... Y'KNOW? HA HA... AT LEAST I-I THINK I AM...
BUT WHEN I COME HERE... TO THIS WHITE SCHOOL ... AND I HAVE TO--
I'M SORRY...
snf
OPEN
AND THE DANCE... THE JUNIOR DANCE...
snfff
...DO THEY REALLY THINK ANY OF THOSE BOYS ARE EVER GOING TO INVITE ME OUT TO ANYTHING?

=swallow=

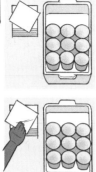

THANK YOU MISS COLE

THIS IS VERY KIND OF YOU

THANK YOU

THANK YOU, LOUISE

NOW **WHY** WOULD YOU WANT TO GO AND DO A CRAZY THING LIKE THAT?

YOU HOPED THAT I'D BE MORE THAN HAPPY TO LET ONE OF MY FINEST ADMINISTRATORS TAKE A HUGE PAY CUT AND GO BACK TO THE STRESSFUL GRIND OF TEACHING SIMPLY BECAUSE IT WOULD SAVE ME SOME MONEY, AND WHAT HEADMASTER DOESN'T WANT TO SAVE MONEY, ESPECIALLY THESE DAYS, RIGHT?

WELL...

YES... **RIGHT**, IS THAT ALL RIGHT?

WELL... FATHER... I-I'D HOPED... I-I MEAN...

JOANNE

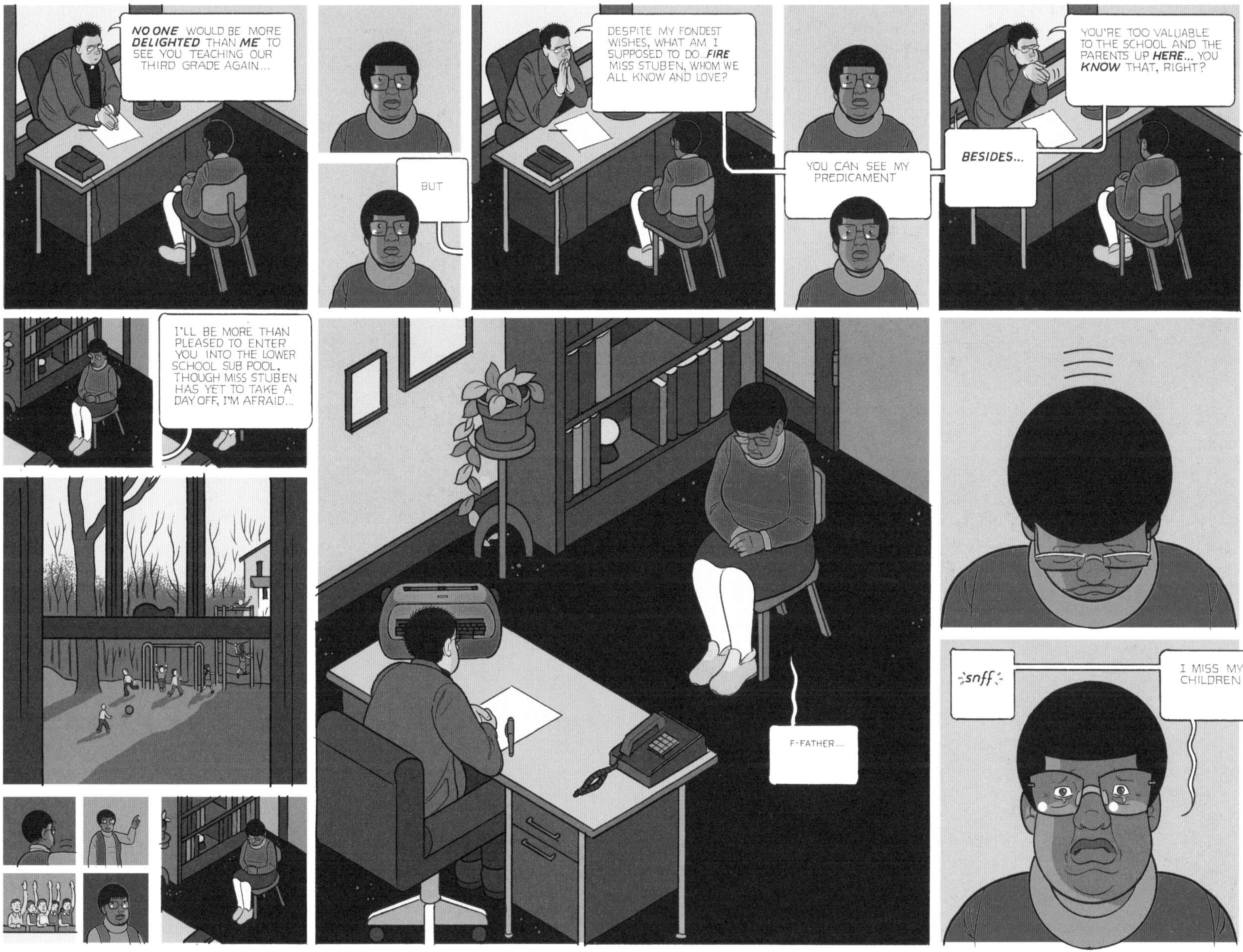
NO ONE WOULD BE MORE DELIGHTED THAN ME TO SEE YOU TEACHING OUR THIRD GRADE AGAIN...
BUT
DESPITE MY FONDEST WISHES, WHAT AM I SUPPOSED TO DO...FIRE MISS STUBEN, WHOM WE ALL KNOW AND LOVE?
YOU CAN SEE MY PREDICAMENT
BESIDES...
YOU'RE TOO VALUABLE TO THE SCHOOL AND THE PARENTS UP HERE... YOU KNOW THAT, RIGHT?
I'LL BE MORE THAN PLEASED TO ENTER YOU INTO THE LOWER SCHOOL SUB POOL, THOUGH MISS STUBEN HAS YET TO TAKE A DAY OFF, I'M AFRAID...
F-FATHER...
snff
I MISS MY CHILDREN

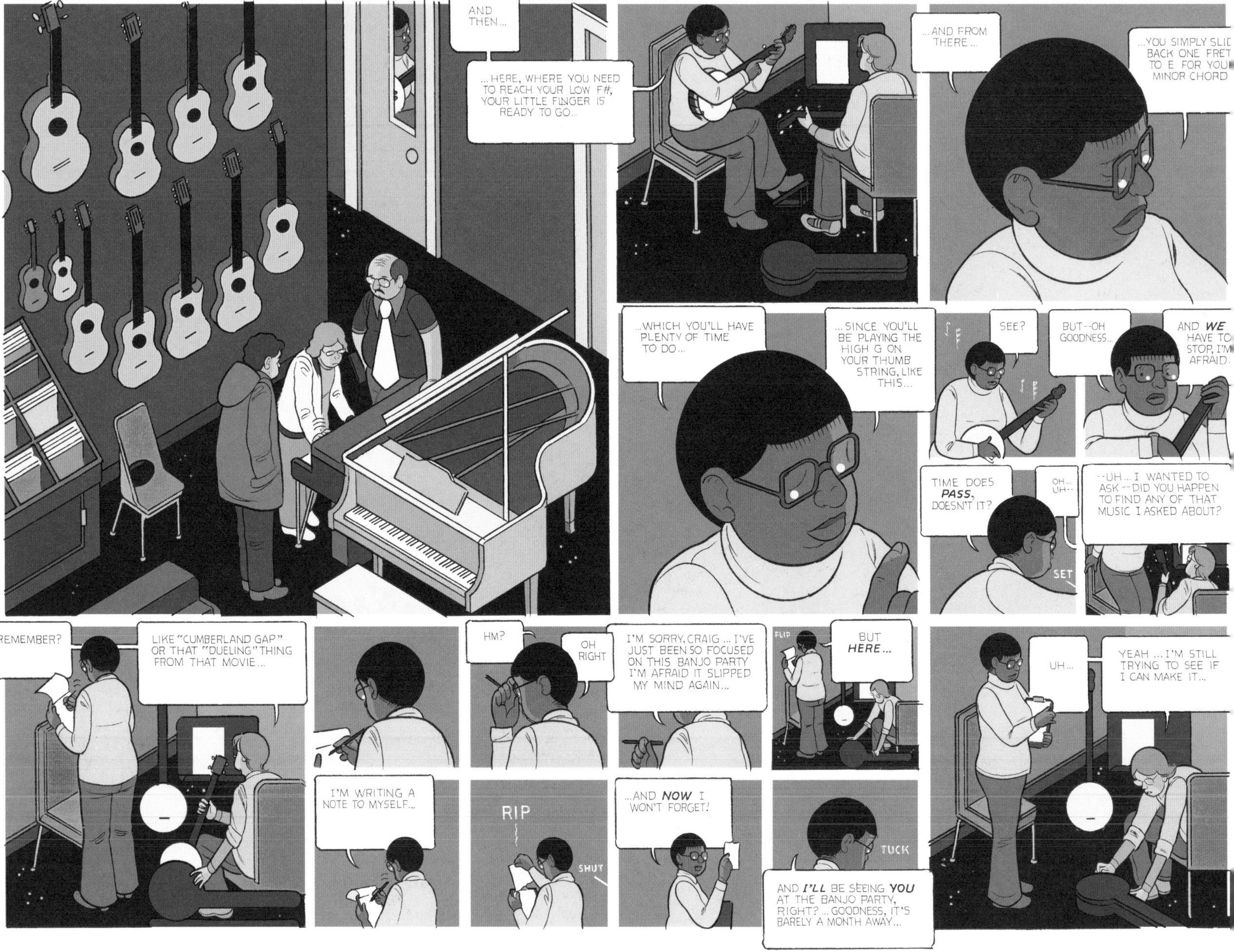
AND THEN...
...HERE, WHERE YOU NEED TO REACH YOUR LOW F#, YOUR LITTLE FINGER IS READY TO GO...
...AND FROM THERE...
...YOU SIMPLY SLID BACK ONE FRET TO E FOR YOU MINOR CHORD
...WHICH YOU'LL HAVE PLENTY OF TIME TO DO...
...SINCE YOU'LL BE PLAYING THE HIGH G ON YOUR THUMB STRING, LIKE THIS...
SEE?
BUT--OH GOODNESS...
AND *WE* HAVE TO STOP, I'M AFRAID.
TIME DOES **PASS**, DOESN'T IT?
OH... UH--
SET
--UH... I WANTED TO ASK --DID YOU HAPPEN TO FIND ANY OF THAT MUSIC I ASKED ABOUT?
REMEMBER?
LIKE "CUMBERLAND GAP" OR THAT "DUELING" THING FROM THAT MOVIE...
HM?
OH RIGHT
I'M SORRY, CRAIG... I'VE JUST BEEN SO FOCUSED ON THIS BANJO PARTY I'M AFRAID IT SLIPPED MY MIND AGAIN...
I'M WRITING A NOTE TO MYSELF...
RIP
SHUT
...AND **NOW** I WON'T FORGET!
FLIP
BUT **HERE**...
TUCK
AND ***I'LL*** BE SEEING **YOU** AT THE BANJO PARTY, RIGHT? ... GOODNESS, IT'S BARELY A MONTH AWAY...
UH...
YEAH ... I'M STILL TRYING TO SEE IF I CAN MAKE IT...

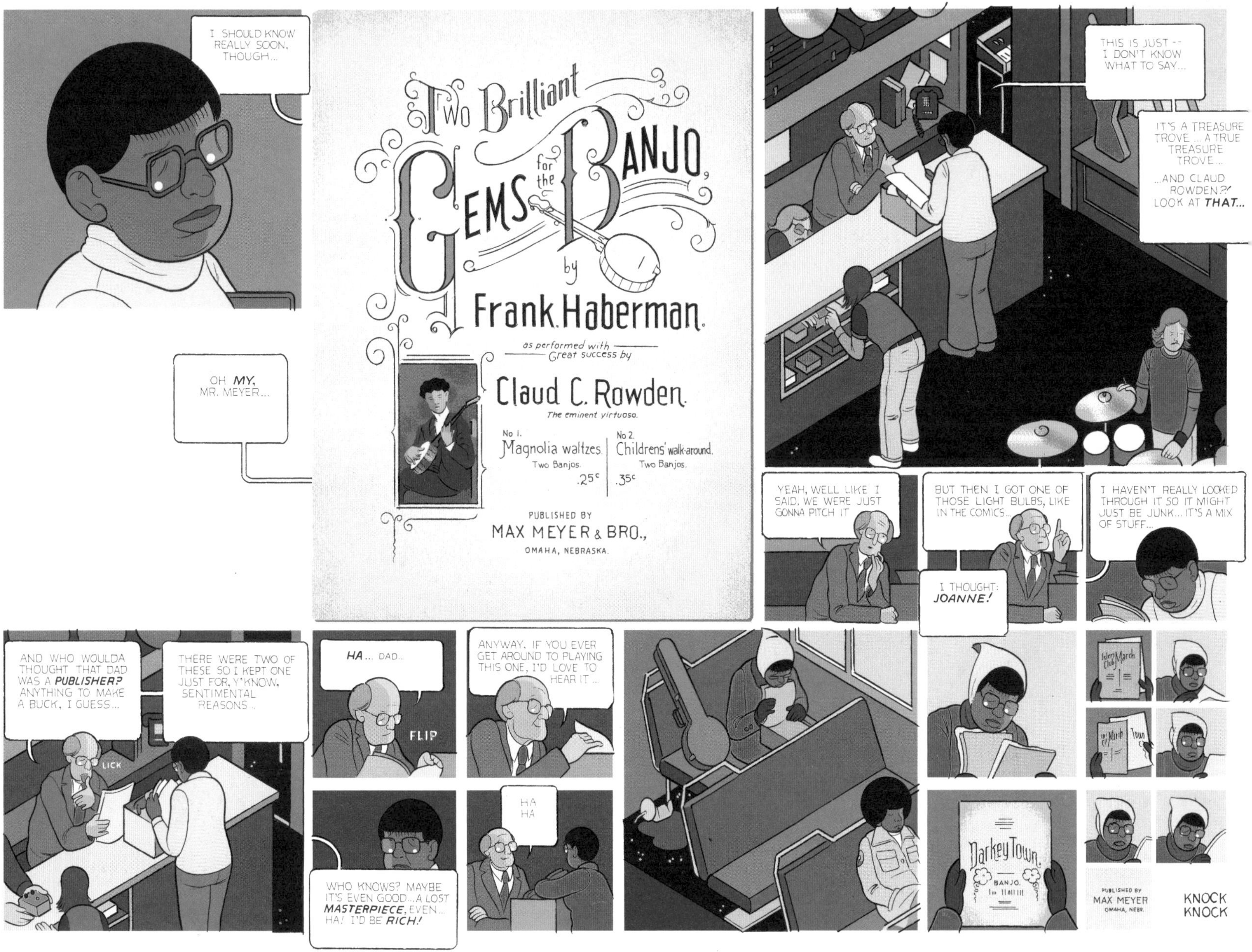

I SHOULD KNOW REALLY SOON, THOUGH...
OH MY, MR. MEYER...
Two Brilliant Gems for the Banjo,
by Frank. Haberman.
as performed with Great success by
Claud C. Rowden.
The eminent virtuoso.
No 1. Magnolia waltzes. Two Banjos. .25c
No 2. Childrens' walk-around. Two Banjos. .35c
PUBLISHED BY MAX MEYER & BRO., OMAHA, NEBRASKA.
THIS IS JUST -- I DON'T KNOW WHAT TO SAY...
IT'S A TREASURE TROVE... A TRUE TREASURE TROVE...
...AND CLAUD ROWDEN?! LOOK AT THAT...
YEAH, WELL LIKE I SAID, WE WERE JUST GONNA PITCH IT
BUT THEN I GOT ONE OF THOSE LIGHT BULBS, LIKE IN THE COMICS...
I THOUGHT: JOANNE!
I HAVEN'T REALLY LOOKED THROUGH IT SO IT MIGHT JUST BE JUNK... IT'S A MIX OF STUFF...
AND WHO WOULDA THOUGHT THAT DAD WAS A PUBLISHER? ANYTHING TO MAKE A BUCK, I GUESS...
LICK
THERE WERE TWO OF THESE SO I KEPT ONE JUST FOR, Y'KNOW, SENTIMENTAL REASONS...
HA... DAD...
FLIP
WHO KNOWS? MAYBE IT'S EVEN GOOD... A LOST MASTERPIECE, EVEN... HA! I'D BE RICH!
ANYWAY, IF YOU EVER GET AROUND TO PLAYING THIS ONE, I'D LOVE TO HEAR IT...
HA HA
Darkey Town.
BANJO.
PUBLISHED BY MAX MEYER OMAHA, NEBR.
KNOCK KNOCK

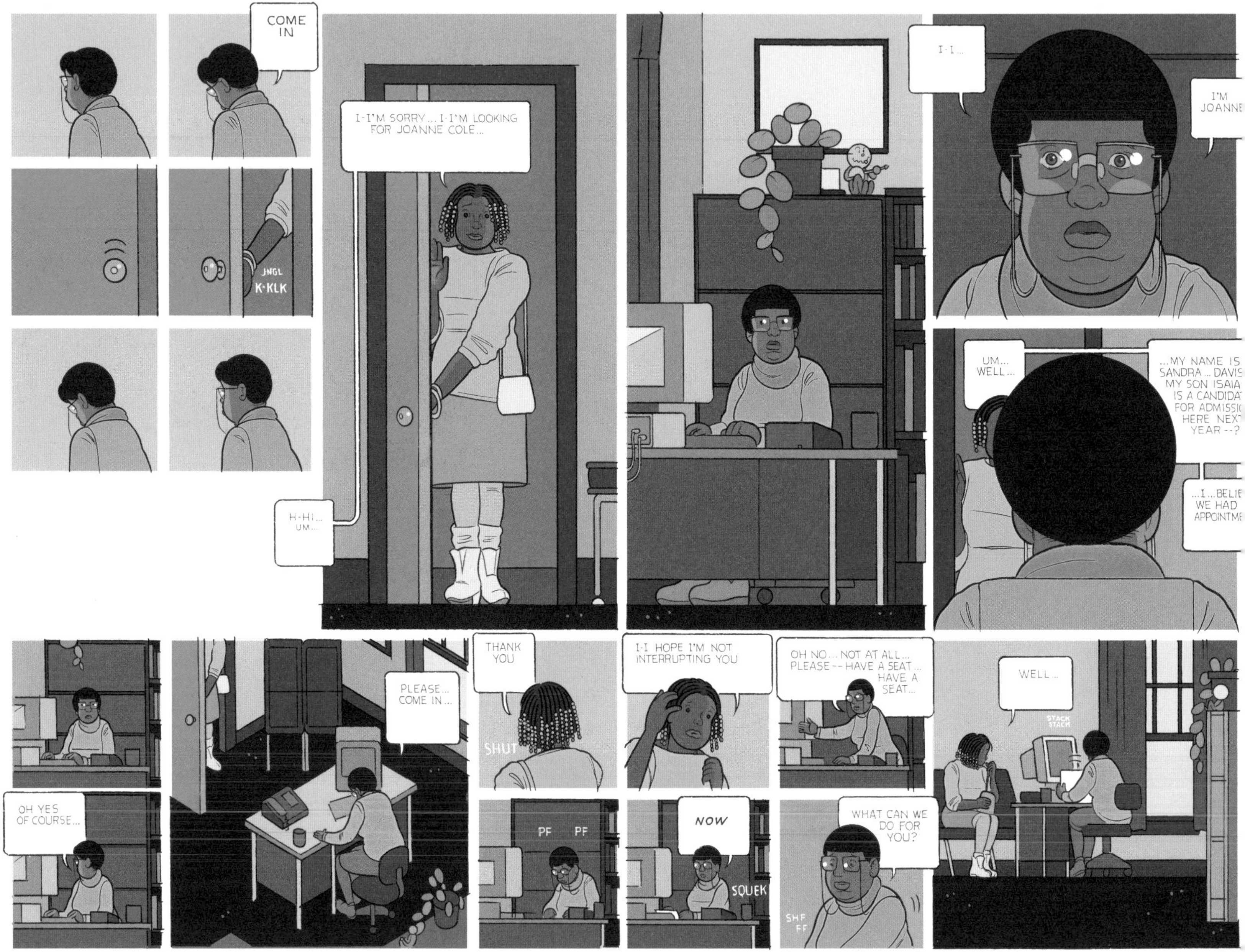
COME IN
JNGL
K-KLK
I-I'M SORRY... I-I'M LOOKING FOR JOANNE COLE...
H-HI... UM...
I-I...
I'M JOANNE
UM... WELL...
...MY NAME IS SANDRA... DAVIS MY SON ISAIA IS A CANDIDAT FOR ADMISSIO HERE NEXT YEAR --?
...I... BELIE WE HAD APPOINTME
OH YES OF COURSE...
PLEASE... COME IN...
THANK YOU
SHUT
I-I HOPE I'M NOT INTERRUPTING YOU
OH NO... NOT AT ALL... PLEASE -- HAVE A SEAT... HAVE A SEAT...
PF PF
NOW
SQUEK
WHAT CAN WE DO FOR YOU?
SHF FF
WELL...
STACK STACK

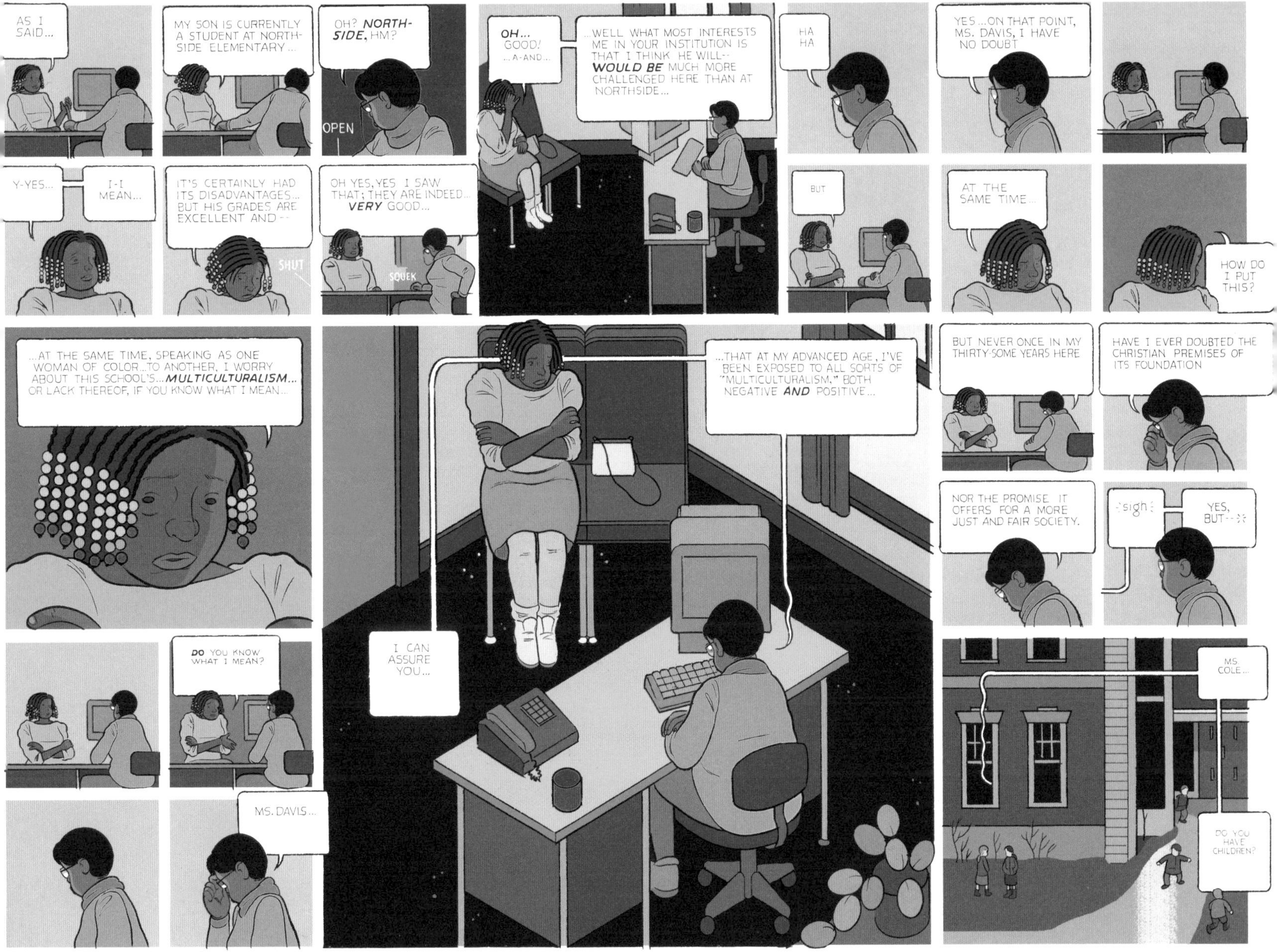

AS I SAID...
MY SON IS CURRENTLY A STUDENT AT NORTHSIDE ELEMENTARY...
OH? NORTHSIDE, HM?
OPEN
Y-YES...
I-I MEAN...
IT'S CERTAINLY HAD ITS DISADVANTAGES... BUT HIS GRADES ARE EXCELLENT AND--
SHUT
OH YES, YES I SAW THAT; THEY ARE INDEED... VERY GOOD...
SQUEK
OH... GOOD! ...A-AND...
...WELL WHAT MOST INTERESTS ME IN YOUR INSTITUTION IS THAT I THINK HE WILL-- WOULD BE MUCH MORE CHALLENGED HERE THAN AT NORTHSIDE...
HA HA
YES...ON THAT POINT, MS. DAVIS, I HAVE NO DOUBT
BUT
AT THE SAME TIME...
HOW DO I PUT THIS?
...AT THE SAME TIME, SPEAKING AS ONE WOMAN OF COLOR...TO ANOTHER, I WORRY ABOUT THIS SCHOOL'S... MULTICULTURALISM... OR LACK THEREOF, IF YOU KNOW WHAT I MEAN...
DO YOU KNOW WHAT I MEAN?
MS. DAVIS...
I CAN ASSURE YOU...
...THAT AT MY ADVANCED AGE, I'VE BEEN EXPOSED TO ALL SORTS OF "MULTICULTURALISM," BOTH NEGATIVE AND POSITIVE...
BUT NEVER ONCE IN MY THIRTY-SOME YEARS HERE
HAVE I EVER DOUBTED THE CHRISTIAN PREMISES OF ITS FOUNDATION
NOR THE PROMISE IT OFFERS FOR A MORE JUST AND FAIR SOCIETY.
sigh
YES, BUT--
MS. COLE...
DO YOU HAVE CHILDREN?

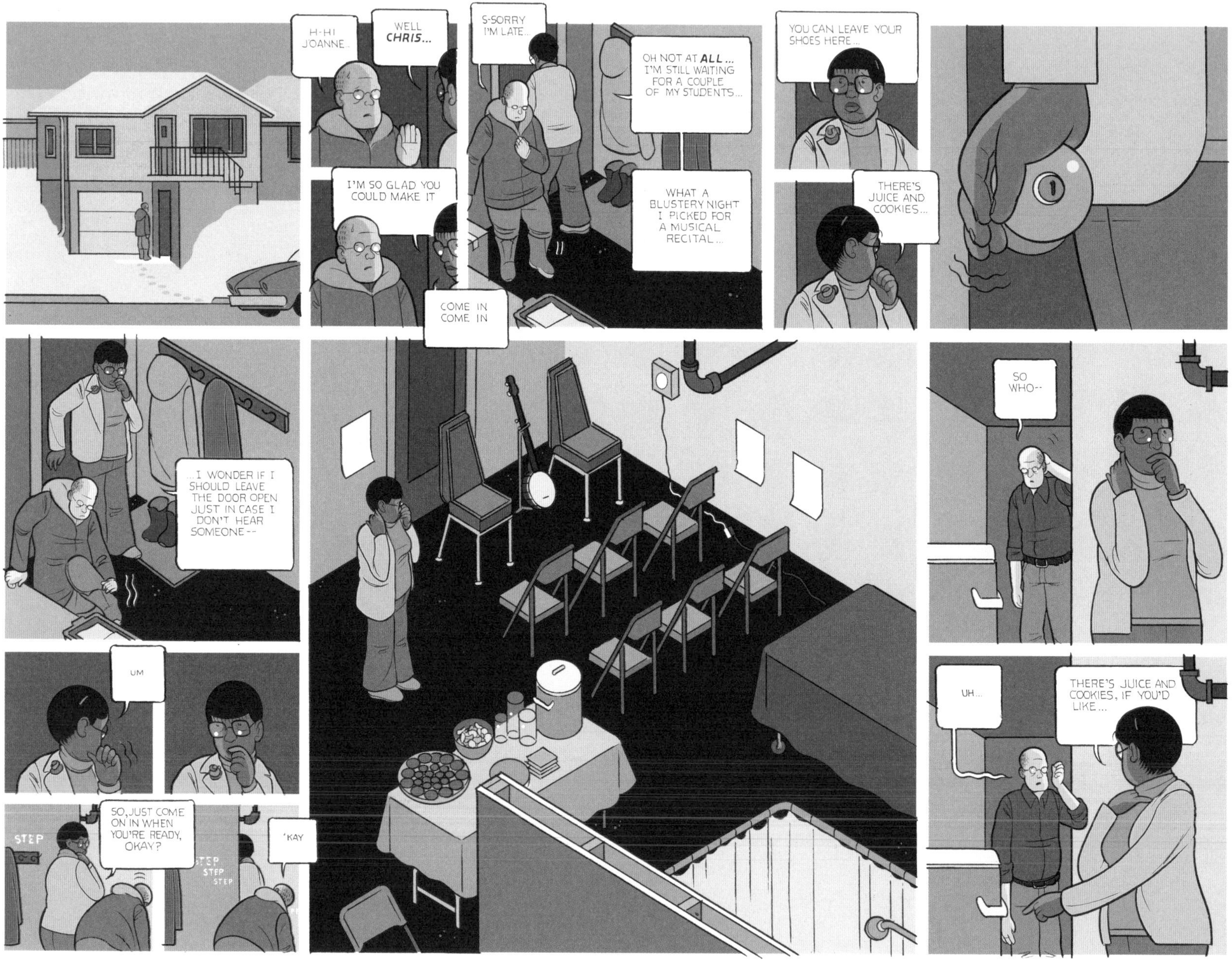
H-HI JOANNE...
WELL CHRIS...
I'M SO GLAD YOU COULD MAKE IT
COME IN COME IN
S-SORRY I'M LATE...
OH NOT AT ALL... I'M STILL WAITING FOR A COUPLE OF MY STUDENTS...
WHAT A BLUSTERY NIGHT I PICKED FOR A MUSICAL RECITAL...
YOU CAN LEAVE YOUR SHOES HERE...
THERE'S JUICE AND COOKIES...
...I WONDER IF I SHOULD LEAVE THE DOOR OPEN JUST IN CASE I DON'T HEAR SOMEONE--
UM
STEP
SO, JUST COME ON IN WHEN YOU'RE READY, OKAY?
STEP STEP STEP
'KAY
SO WHO--
UH...
THERE'S JUICE AND COOKIES, IF YOU'D LIKE...

SO...YOU SAID GEORGE IS OUT OF TOWN?

YES...

WELL

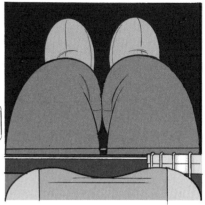

I GUESS NO ONE ELSE IS GOING TO MAKE IT

CRNCH CRNCH

IT'S REALLY A SHAME, THOUGH...SINCE ONE OF MY STUDENTS AND I *HAD* PLANNED --

CRNCH CRNCH CRNCH

MM †

†

WELL

I MIGHT AS WELL PLAY *ONE* SONG FOR YOU, SINCE YOU'RE HERE...

RIGHT?

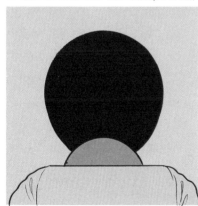

NOW

LET'S SEE...

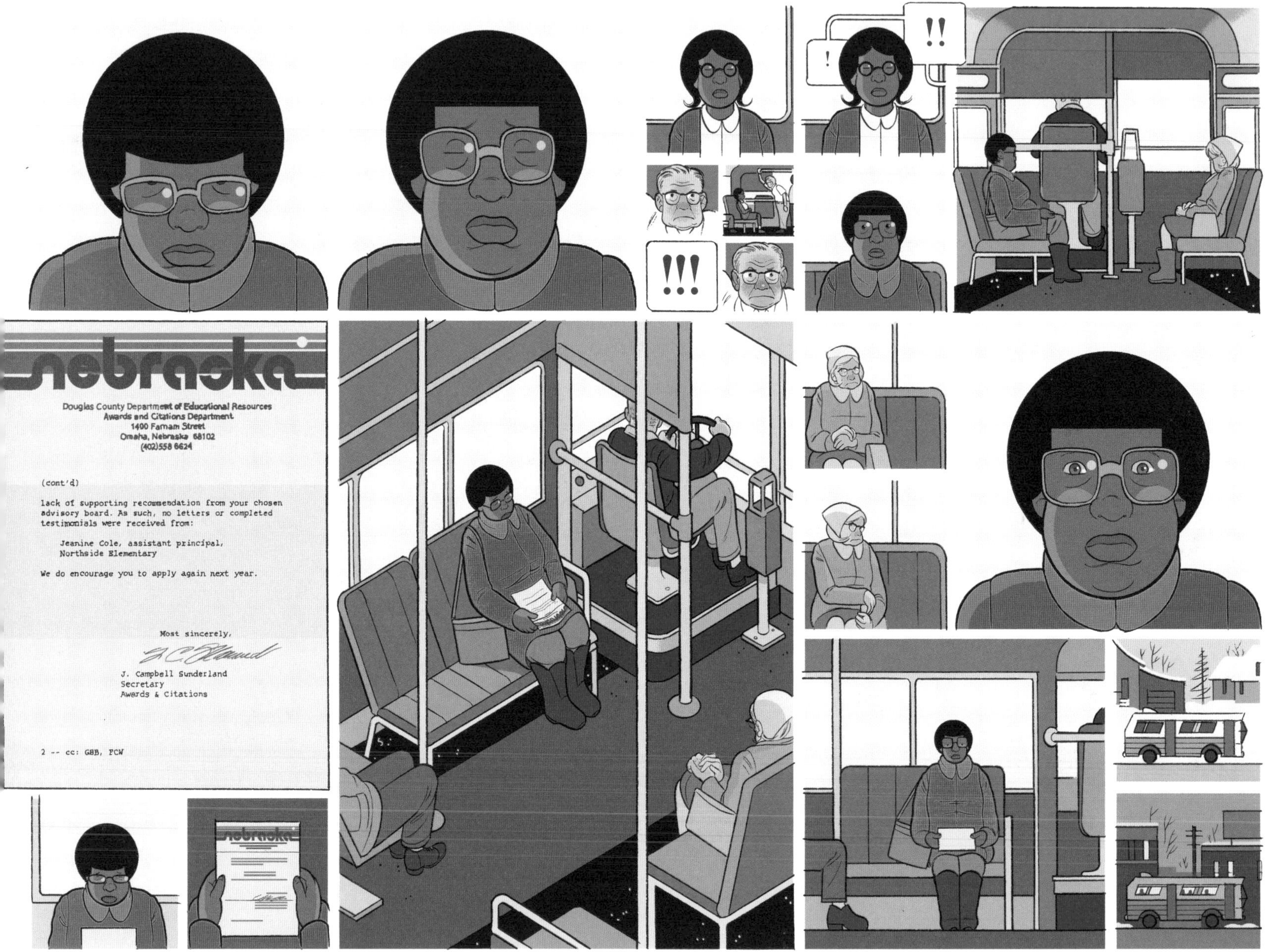
!!!
!
!!
nebraska
Douglas County Department of Educational Resources
Awards and Citations Department
1400 Farnam Street
Omaha, Nebraska 68102
(402)558 6624
(cont'd)
lack of supporting recommendation from your chosen advisory board. As such, no letters or completed testimonials were received from:
Jeanine Cole, assistant principal, Northside Elementary
We do encourage you to apply again next year.
Most sincerely,
J. Campbell Sunderland
Secretary
Awards & Citations
2 -- cc: GBB, FCW

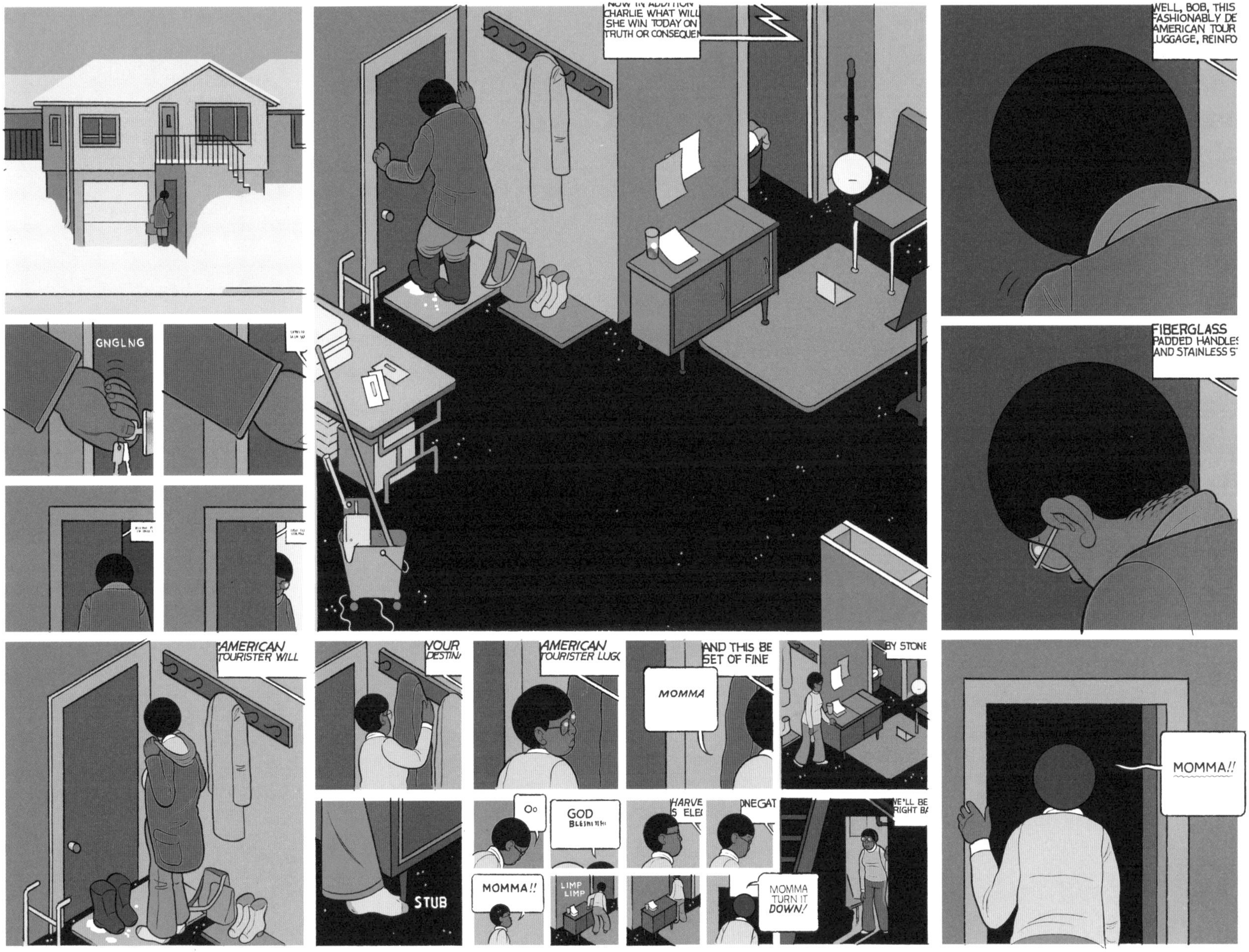
GNGLNG
NOW IN ADDITION
CHARLIE WHAT WILL
SHE WIN TODAY ON
TRUTH OR CONSEQUEN
WELL, BOB, THIS
FASHIONABLY DE
AMERICAN TOUR
LUGGAGE, REINFO
FIBERGLASS
PADDED HANDLES
AND STAINLESS S
AMERICAN
TOURISTER WILL
YOUR
DESTIN
AMERICAN
TOURISTER LUG
MOMMA
AND THIS BE
SET OF FINE
BY STONE
STUB
Oo
GOD
HARVE
S ELE
ONEGAT
WE'LL BE
RIGHT BA
MOMMA!!
LIMP
LIMP
MOMMA
TURN IT
DOWN!
MOMMA!!

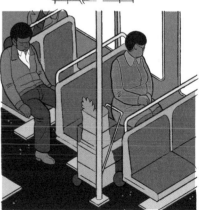

JOANNA!

JOANNA WHAT YOU *LOOKING*

DON'T YOU REMEMBER HOW I USED TO LOOK AFTER YOU?

HOW I USED TO BABYSIT YOU?

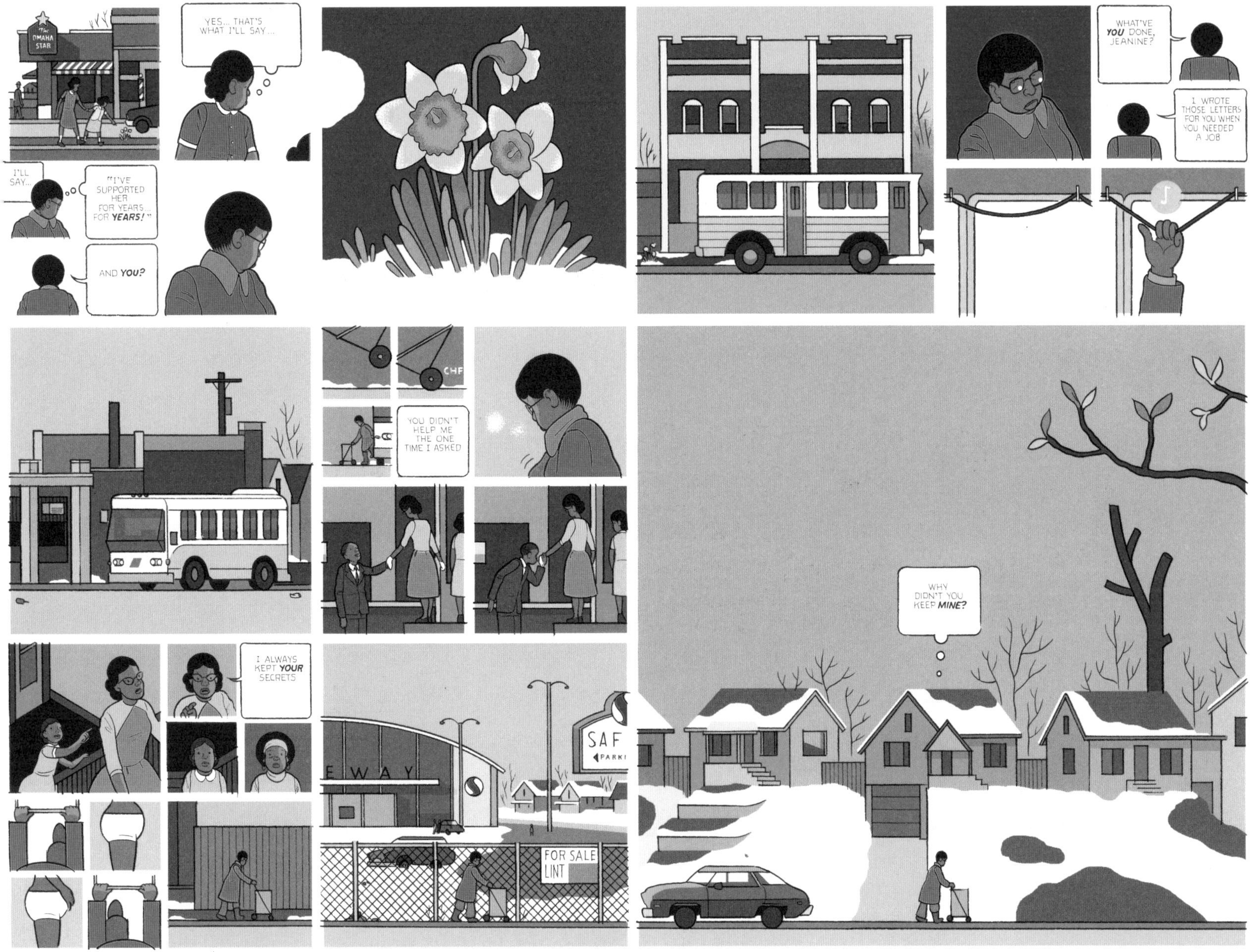

The OMAHA STAR
YES... THAT'S WHAT I'LL SAY...
I'LL SAY...
"I'VE SUPPORTED HER FOR YEARS... FOR **YEARS!**"
AND **YOU?**
WHAT'VE **YOU** DONE, JEANINE?
I WROTE THOSE LETTERS FOR YOU WHEN YOU NEEDED A JOB
CHF
YOU DIDN'T HELP ME THE ONE TIME I ASKED
I ALWAYS KEPT **YOUR** SECRETS
EWAY
SAF
PARK
FOR SALE
LINT
WHY DIDN'T YOU KEEP **MINE?**

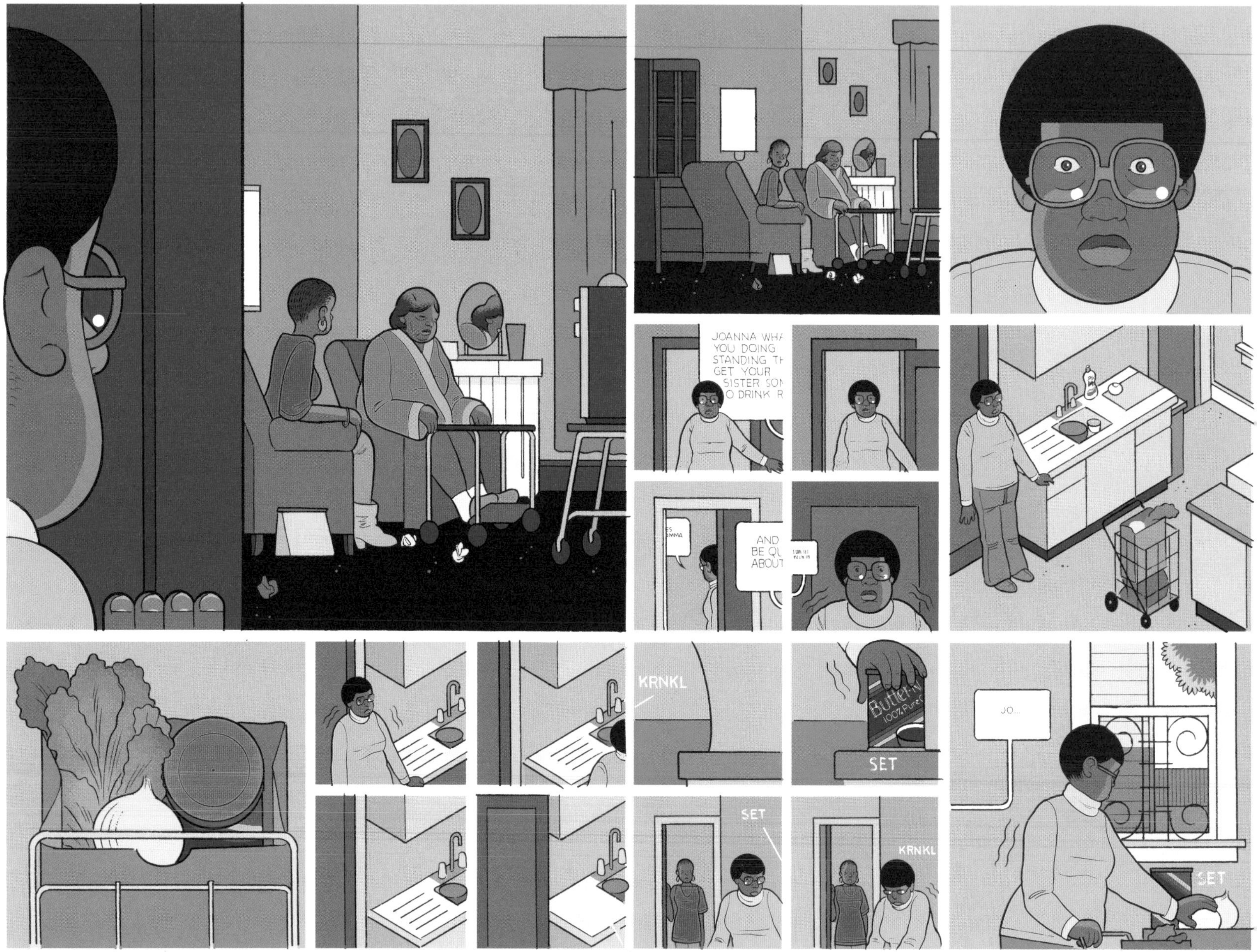

JOANNA WHA
YOU DOING
STANDING TH
GET YOUR
SISTER SOM
O DRINK R
AND
BE QU
ABOUT
KRNKL
SET
SET
KRNKL
JO...
SET

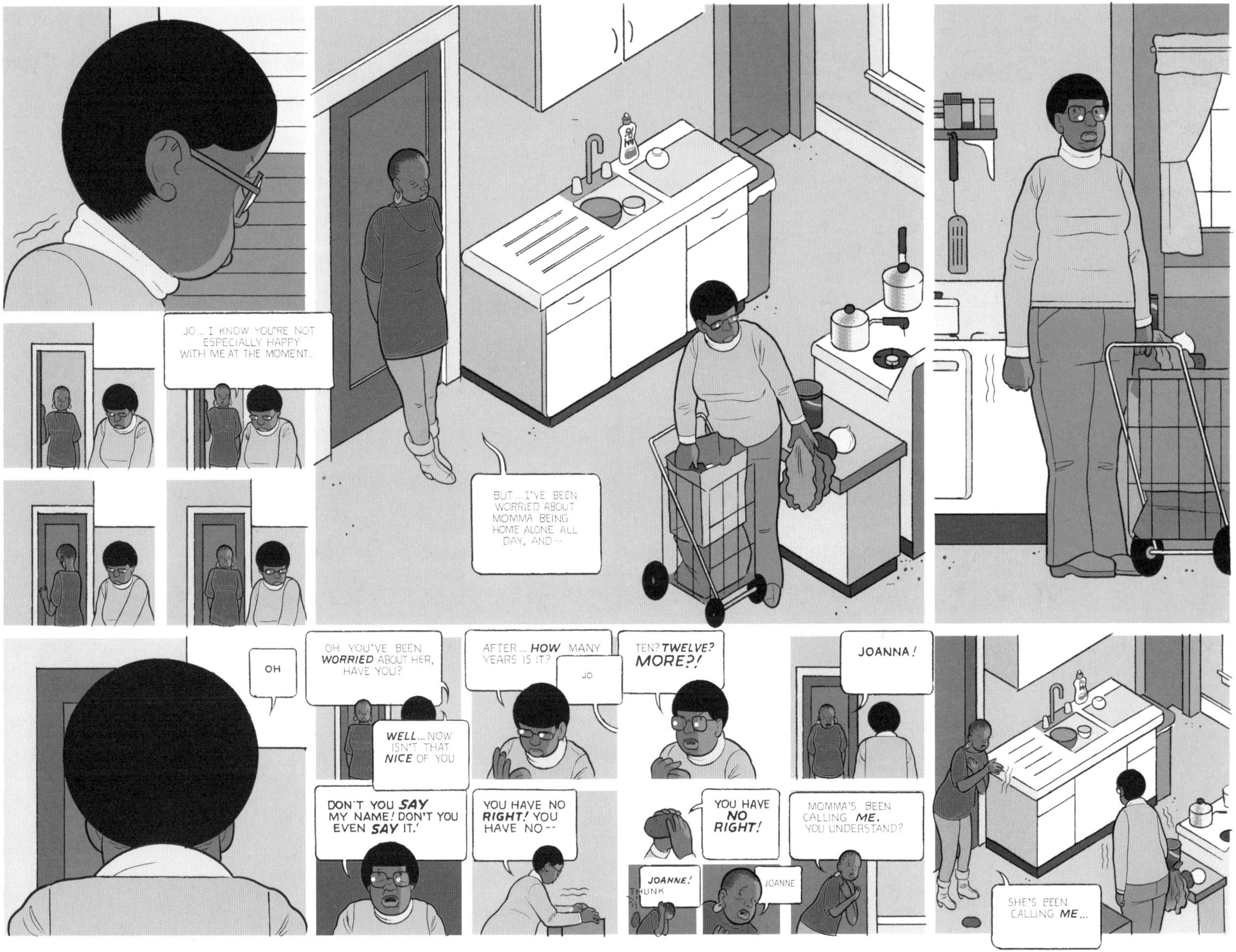

JO... I KNOW YOU'RE NOT ESPECIALLY HAPPY WITH ME AT THE MOMENT...
BUT... I'VE BEEN WORRIED ABOUT MOMMA BEING HOME ALONE ALL DAY, AND--
OH
OH YOU'VE BEEN WORRIED ABOUT HER, HAVE YOU?
WELL... NOW ISN'T THAT NICE OF YOU
AFTER... HOW MANY YEARS IS IT?
JO
TEN? TWELVE? MORE?!
JOANNA!
DON'T YOU SAY MY NAME! DON'T YOU EVEN SAY IT.'
YOU HAVE NO RIGHT! YOU HAVE NO--
YOU HAVE NO RIGHT!
JOANNE!
THUNK
JOANNE
MOMMA'S BEEN CALLING ME. YOU UNDERSTAND?
SHE'S BEEN CALLING ME...

OmahaPublicPowerDistrict
oppd
OMAHA PUBLIC POWER DISTRICT
1198
1071
A11
3 56
5 12
ELIZABETH J. COLE
2618 24TH STREET
13-1810
This Envelope is for Your Convenience...
1 — ENCLOSE CASH OR MONEY ORDER
2 — PAY AT ANY LOCAL AUTHORIZED STORE
NO POSTAGE NECESSARY!
7

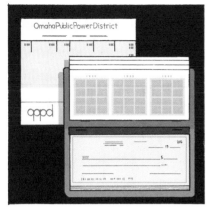

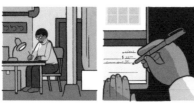

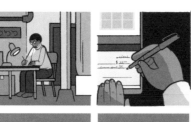

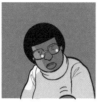

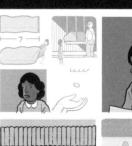

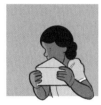

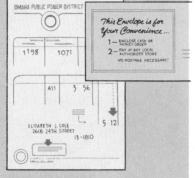

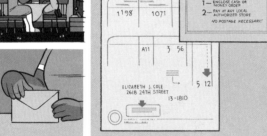

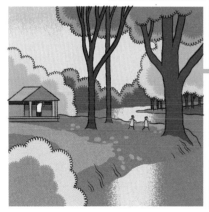

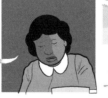

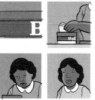

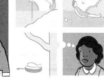

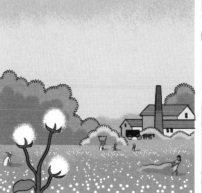

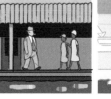

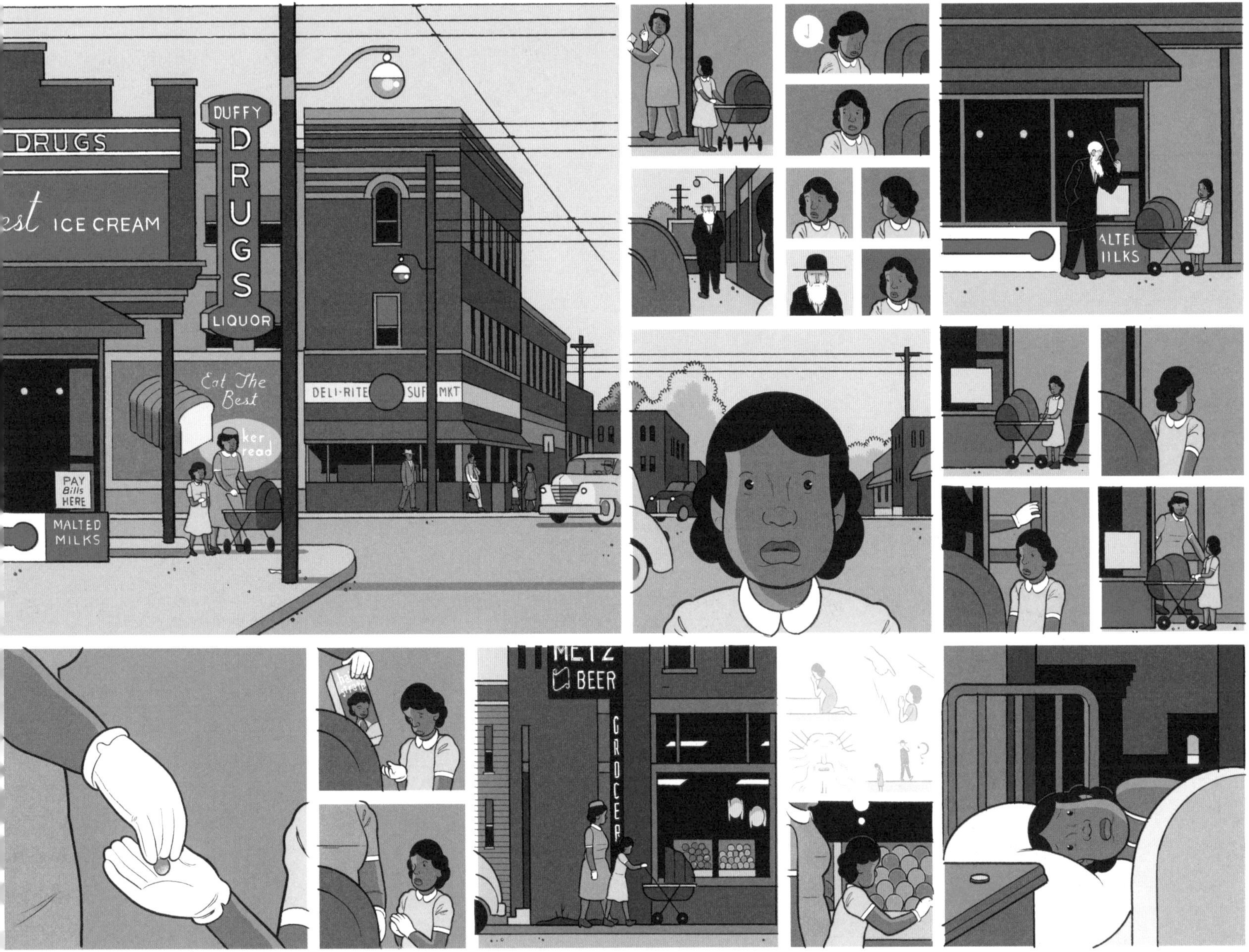
DRUGS
ICE CREAM
DUFFY
DRUGS
LIQUOR
Eat The Best
PAY Bills HERE
MALTED MILKS
DELI-RITE
BEER

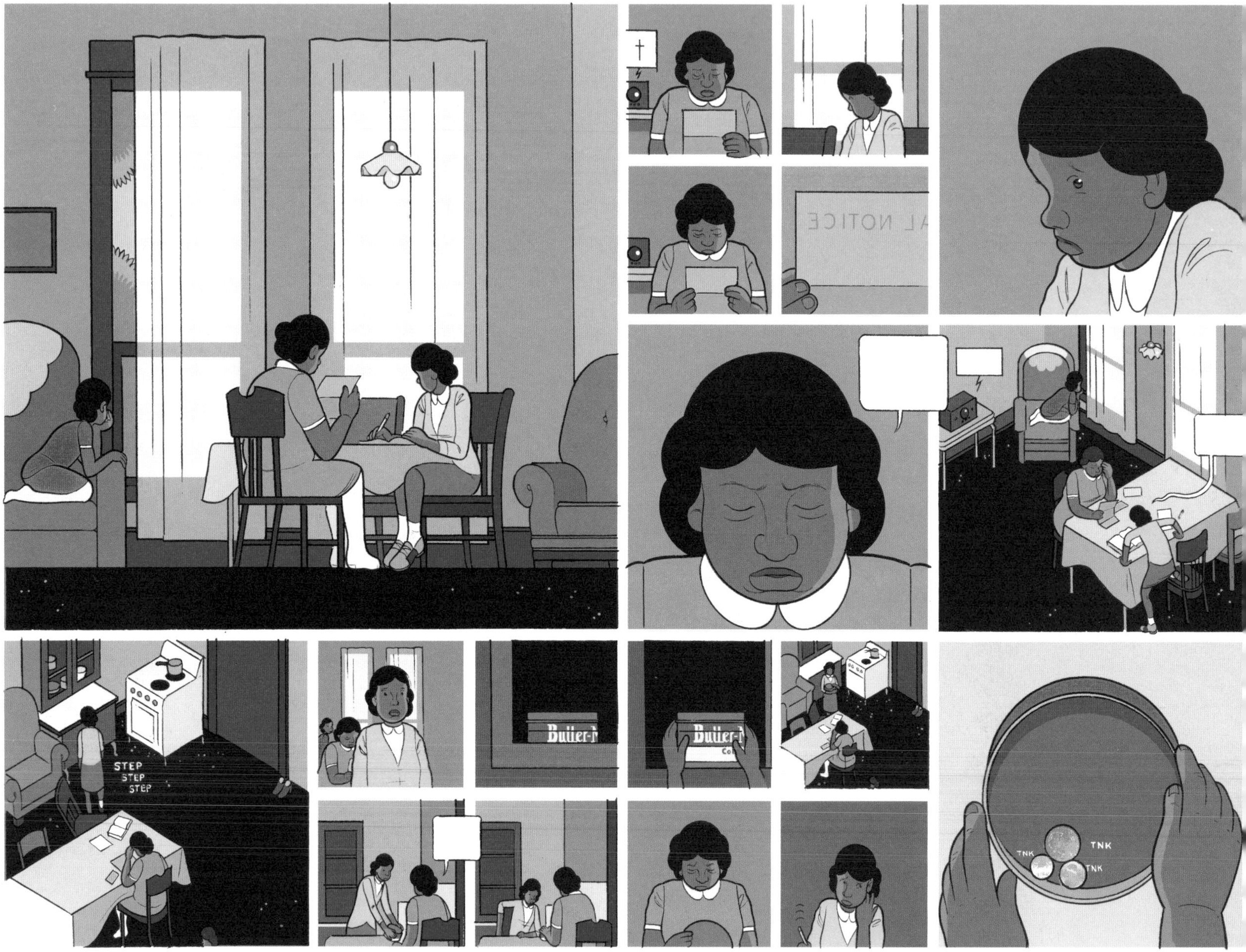
STEP
STEP
STEP
TNK
TNK
TNK

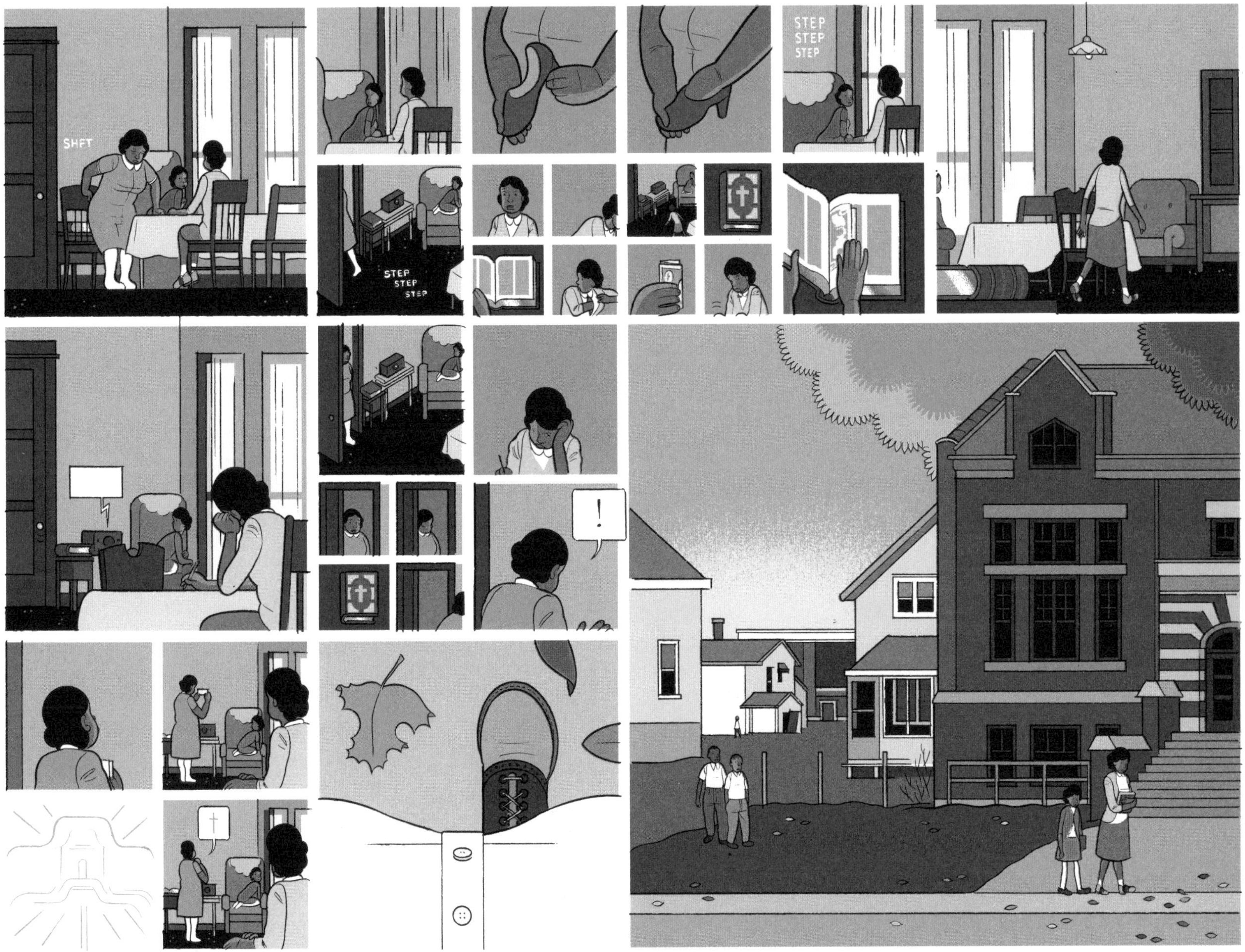
SHFT
STEP
STEP
STEP
STEP
STEP
STEP
!
†

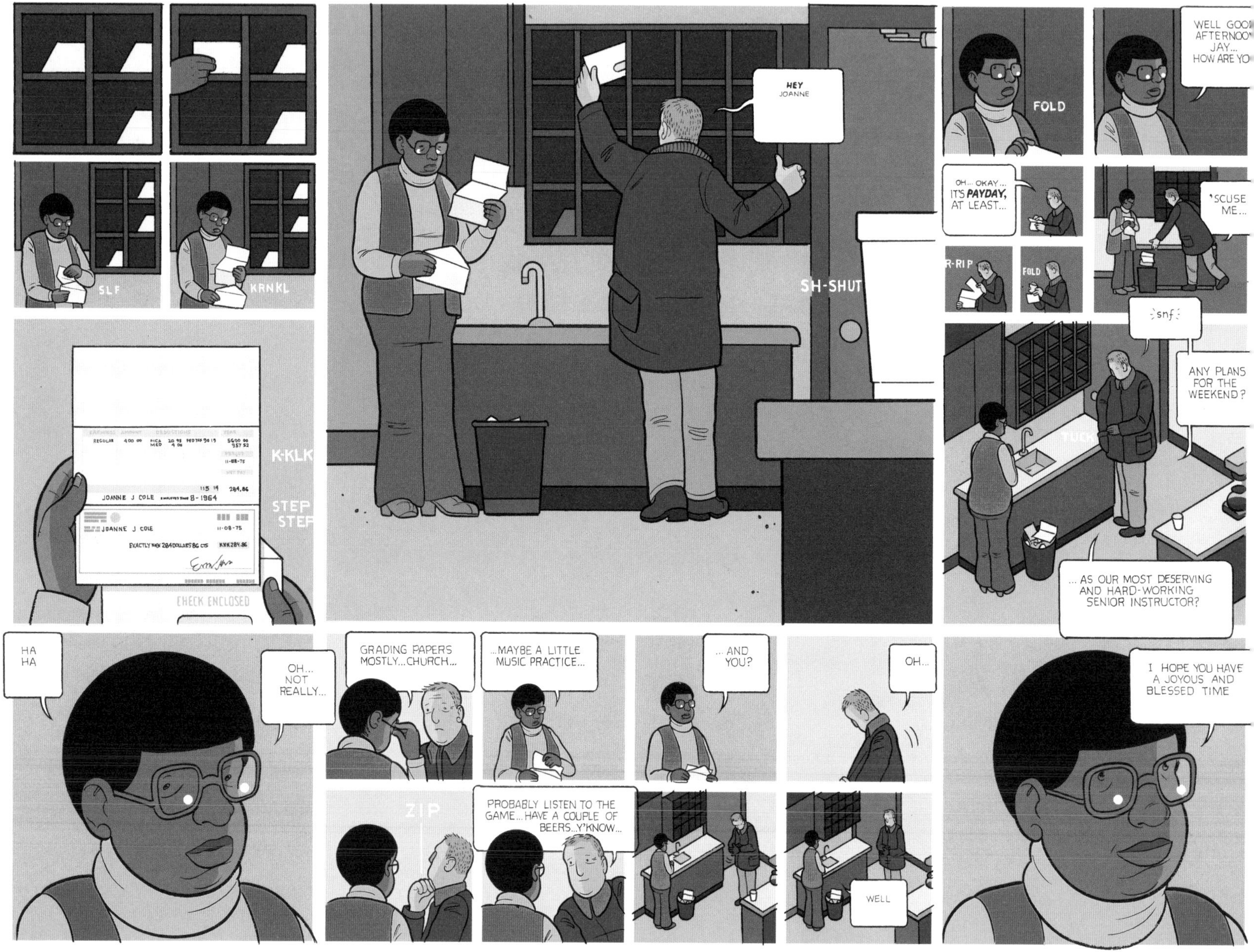

SLF
KRNKL
K-KLK
JOANNE J COLE
11-08-75
EXACTLY 284 DOLLARS 86 CTS
CHECK ENCLOSED
STEP STEP
HEY JOANNE
SH-SHUT
FOLD
WELL GOO AFTERNOO JAY... HOW ARE YO
OH... OKAY... IT'S **PAYDAY,** AT LEAST...
R-RIP
FOLD
'SCUSE ME...
snf
ANY PLANS FOR THE WEEKEND?
TUCK
... AS OUR MOST DESERVING AND HARD-WORKING SENIOR INSTRUCTOR?
HA HA
OH... NOT REALLY...
GRADING PAPERS MOSTLY...CHURCH...
...MAYBE A LITTLE MUSIC PRACTICE...
... AND YOU?
OH...
ZIP
PROBABLY LISTEN TO THE GAME... HAVE A COUPLE OF BEERS...Y'KNOW...
WELL
I HOPE YOU HAVE A JOYOUS AND BLESSED TIME

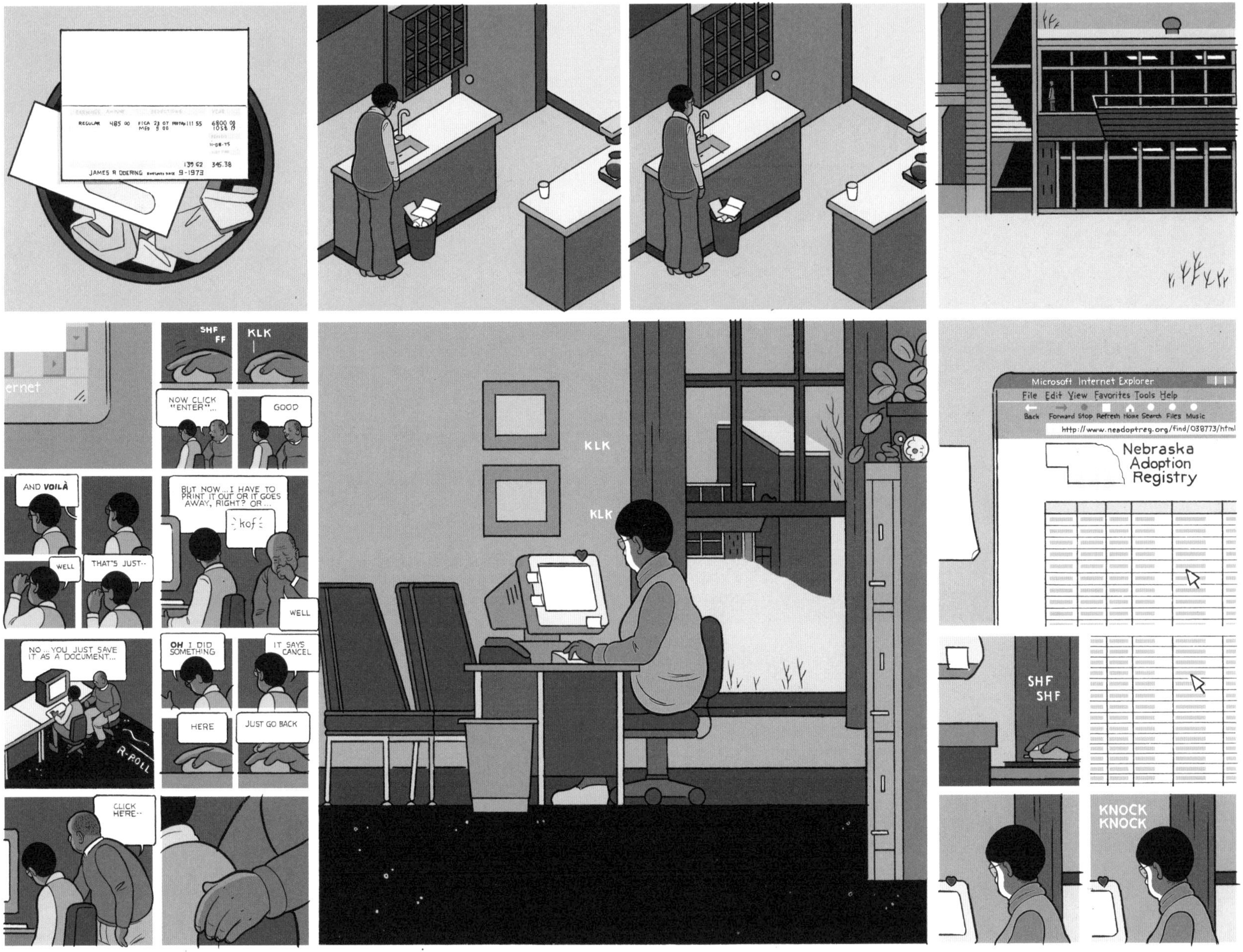
REGULAR 485 00
FICA 23 07
MED 5 00
111 55
6800 00
1058 19
11-08-75
139 62
345.38
JAMES R DOERING 9-1973
ernet
SHF FF
KLK
NOW CLICK "ENTER"...
GOOD
AND VOILÀ
WELL
THAT'S JUST--
BUT NOW... I HAVE TO PRINT IT OUT OR IT GOES AWAY, RIGHT? OR...
kof
WELL
NO... YOU JUST SAVE IT AS A DOCUMENT...
R-ROLL
OH I DID SOMETHING
IT SAYS CANCEL
HERE
JUST GO BACK
CLICK HERE--
KLK
KLK
Microsoft Internet Explorer
File Edit View Favorites Tools Help
Back Forward Stop Refresh Home Search Files Music
http://www.neadoptreg.org/find/038773/html
Nebraska Adoption Registry
SHF SHF
KNOCK KNOCK

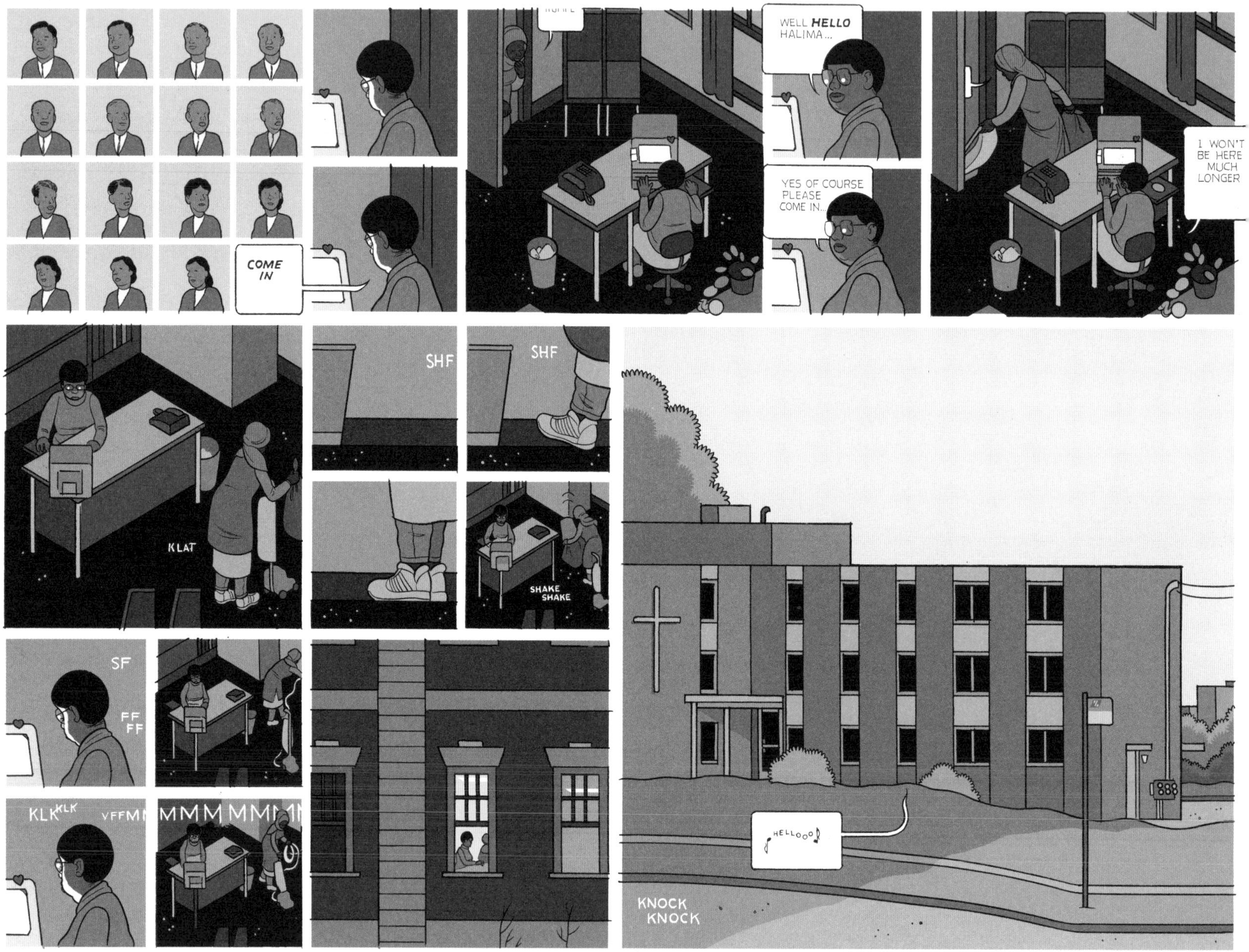
COME IN
WELL HELLO HALIMA...
YES OF COURSE PLEASE COME IN...
I WON'T BE HERE MUCH LONGER
KLAT
SHF
SHF
SHAKE SHAKE
SF
FF FF
KLK KLK
VFFMMMMMMMM
HELLOOO
KNOCK KNOCK

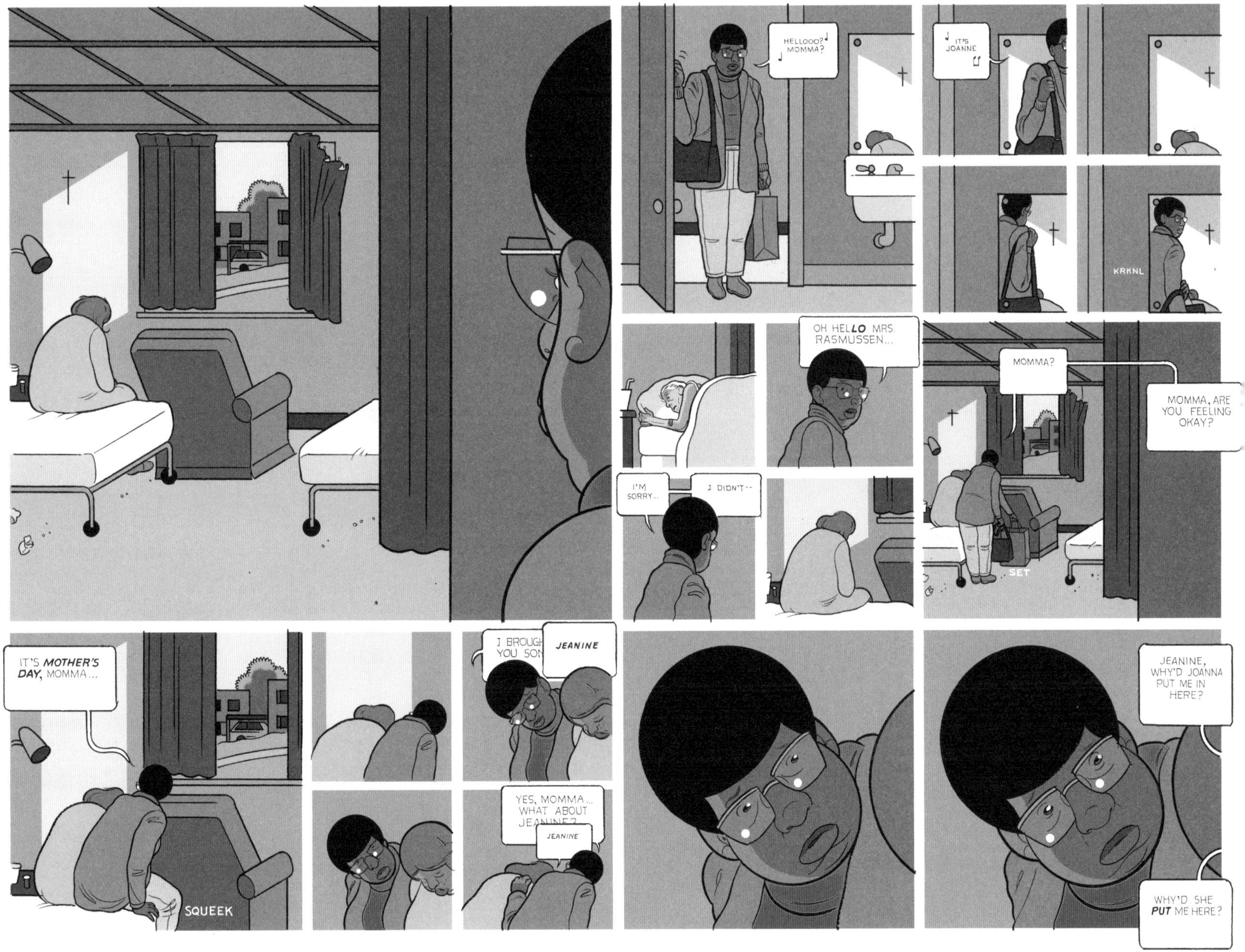

HELLOOO? MOMMA?
IT'S JOANNE
KRKNL
OH HELLO MRS. RASMUSSEN...
I'M SORRY...
I DIDN'T--
MOMMA?
MOMMA, ARE YOU FEELING OKAY?
SET
IT'S MOTHER'S DAY, MOMMA...
SQUEEK
I BROUGH
YOU SON
JEANINE
YES, MOMMA... WHAT ABOUT
JEANINE
JEANINE, WHY'D JOANNA PUT ME IN HERE?
WHY'D SHE PUT ME HERE?

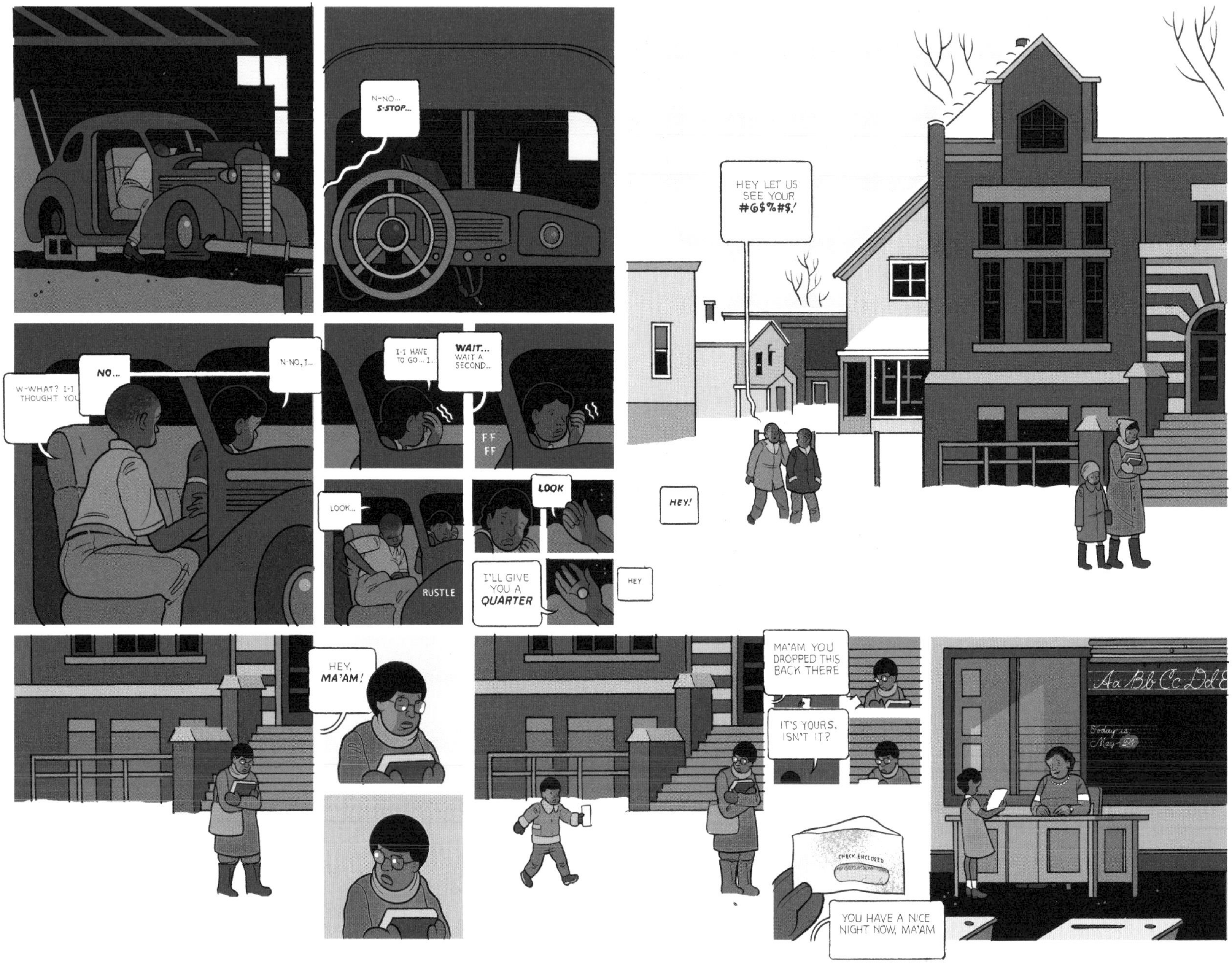
N-NO... S-STOP...
W-WHAT? I-I THOUGHT YOU
NO...
N-NO, I...
I-I HAVE TO GO... I...
WAIT... WAIT A SECOND...
FF FF
LOOK...
RUSTLE
LOOK
I'LL GIVE YOU A QUARTER
HEY
HEY LET US SEE YOUR #G$%#$!
HEY!
HEY, MA'AM!
MA'AM YOU DROPPED THIS BACK THERE
IT'S YOURS, ISN'T IT?
CHECK ENCLOSED
YOU HAVE A NICE NIGHT NOW, MA'AM
Aa Bb Cc Dd E
Today is: May 21

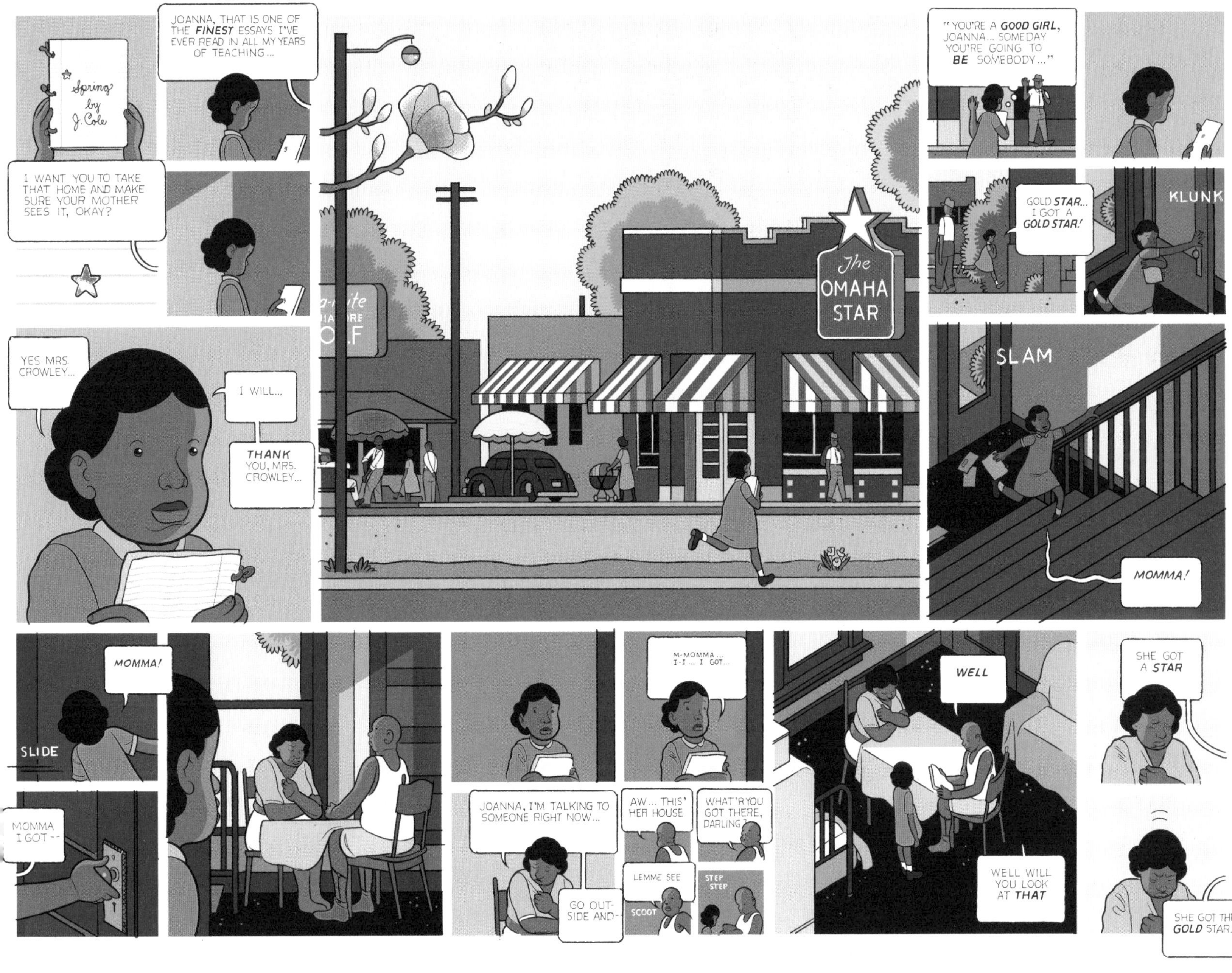
Spring by J. Cole
JOANNA, THAT IS ONE OF THE FINEST ESSAYS I'VE EVER READ IN ALL MY YEARS OF TEACHING...
I WANT YOU TO TAKE THAT HOME AND MAKE SURE YOUR MOTHER SEES IT, OKAY?
YES MRS. CROWLEY...
I WILL...
THANK YOU, MRS. CROWLEY...
The OMAHA STAR
"YOU'RE A GOOD GIRL, JOANNA... SOMEDAY YOU'RE GOING TO BE SOMEBODY..."
GOLD STAR... I GOT A GOLD STAR!
KLUNK
SLAM
MOMMA!
MOMMA!
SLIDE
MOMMA I GOT--
M-MOMMA... I-I... I GOT...
JOANNA, I'M TALKING TO SOMEONE RIGHT NOW...
GO OUT-SIDE AND--
AW... THIS' HER HOUSE
WHAT'R YOU GOT THERE, DARLING?
LEMME SEE
SCOOT
STEP STEP
WELL
WELL WILL YOU LOOK AT THAT
SHE GOT A STAR
SHE GOT THE GOLD STAR...

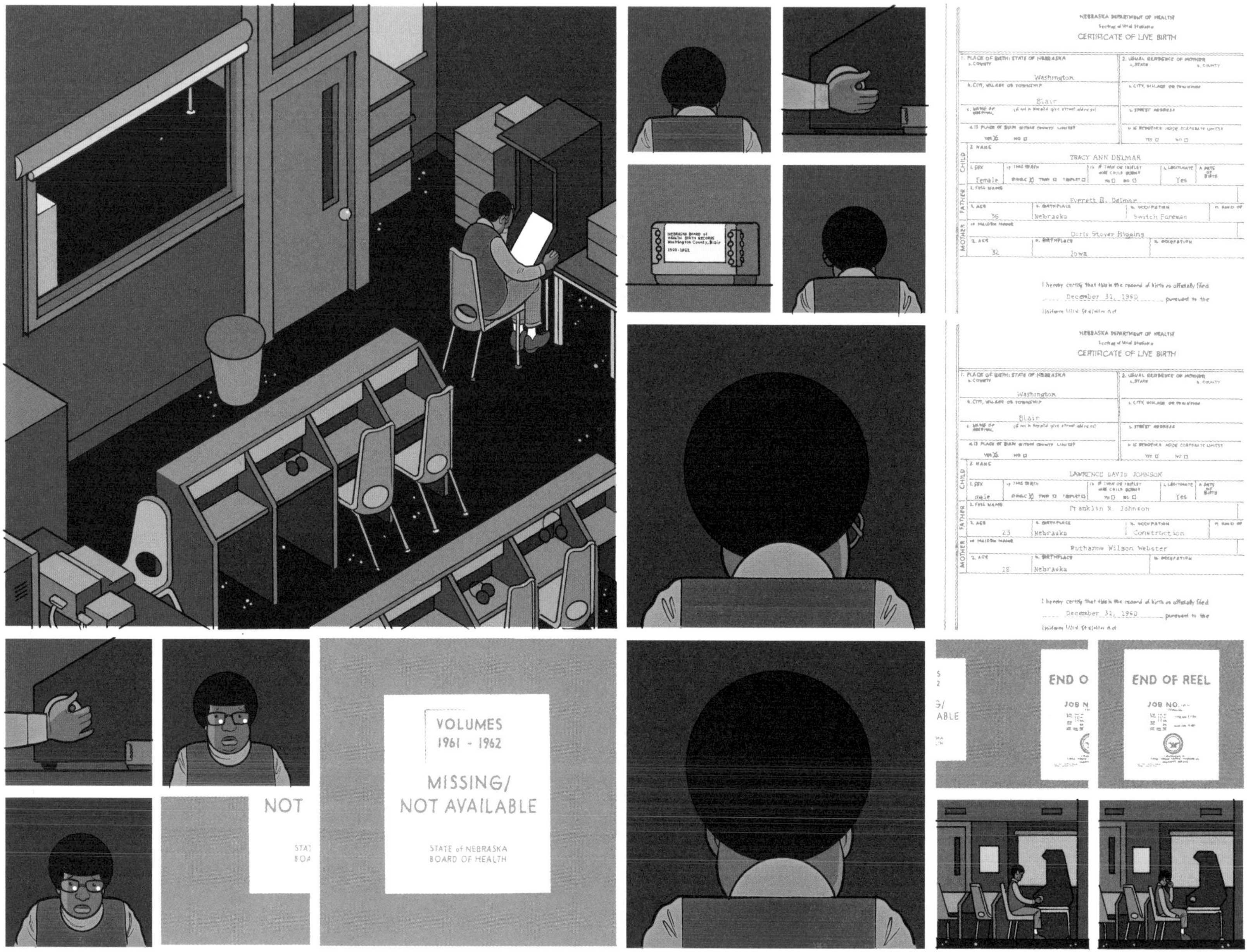
NEBRASKA BOARD of
HEALTH BIRTH RECORDS
Washington County, Blair
1960-1962
NEBRASKA DEPARTMENT OF HEALTH
CERTIFICATE OF LIVE BIRTH
1. PLACE OF BIRTH: STATE OF NEBRASKA
Washington
Blair
TRACY ANN DELMAR
Female
Yes
Everett B. Delmar
36
Nebraska
Switch Foreman
Doris Stover Higgins
32
Iowa
December 31, 1960
NEBRASKA DEPARTMENT OF HEALTH
CERTIFICATE OF LIVE BIRTH
1. PLACE OF BIRTH: STATE OF NEBRASKA
Washington
Blair
LAWRENCE DAVID JOHNSON
male
Yes
Franklin R. Johnson
23
Nebraska
Construction
Ruthanne Wilson Webster
18
Nebraska
December 31, 1960
VOLUMES
1961 - 1962
MISSING/
NOT AVAILABLE
STATE of NEBRASKA
BOARD OF HEALTH
NOT
END O
END OF REEL
JOB NO.

Springtime Waltz
Composed by
JOANNE COLE
1ST BANJO:
2nd BANJO:
pp
p
CHNK
THIS IS THE SECOND, OR ACCOMPANYING, BANJO PART TO "SPRINGTIME WALTZ"...
hgm
...AS PLAYED BY THE COMPOSER, JOANNE COLE, DECEMBER 16, 1975.

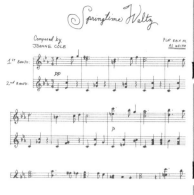

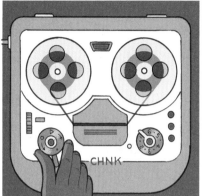

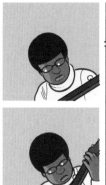

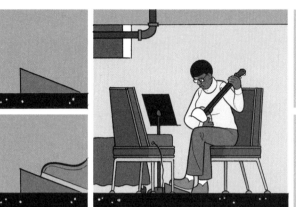

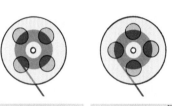

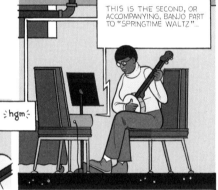

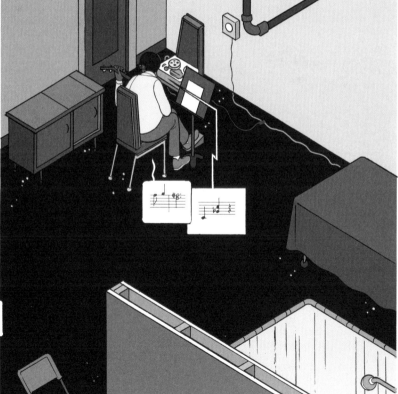

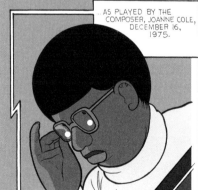

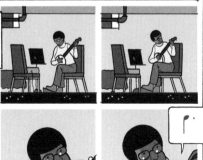

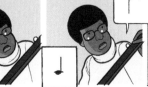

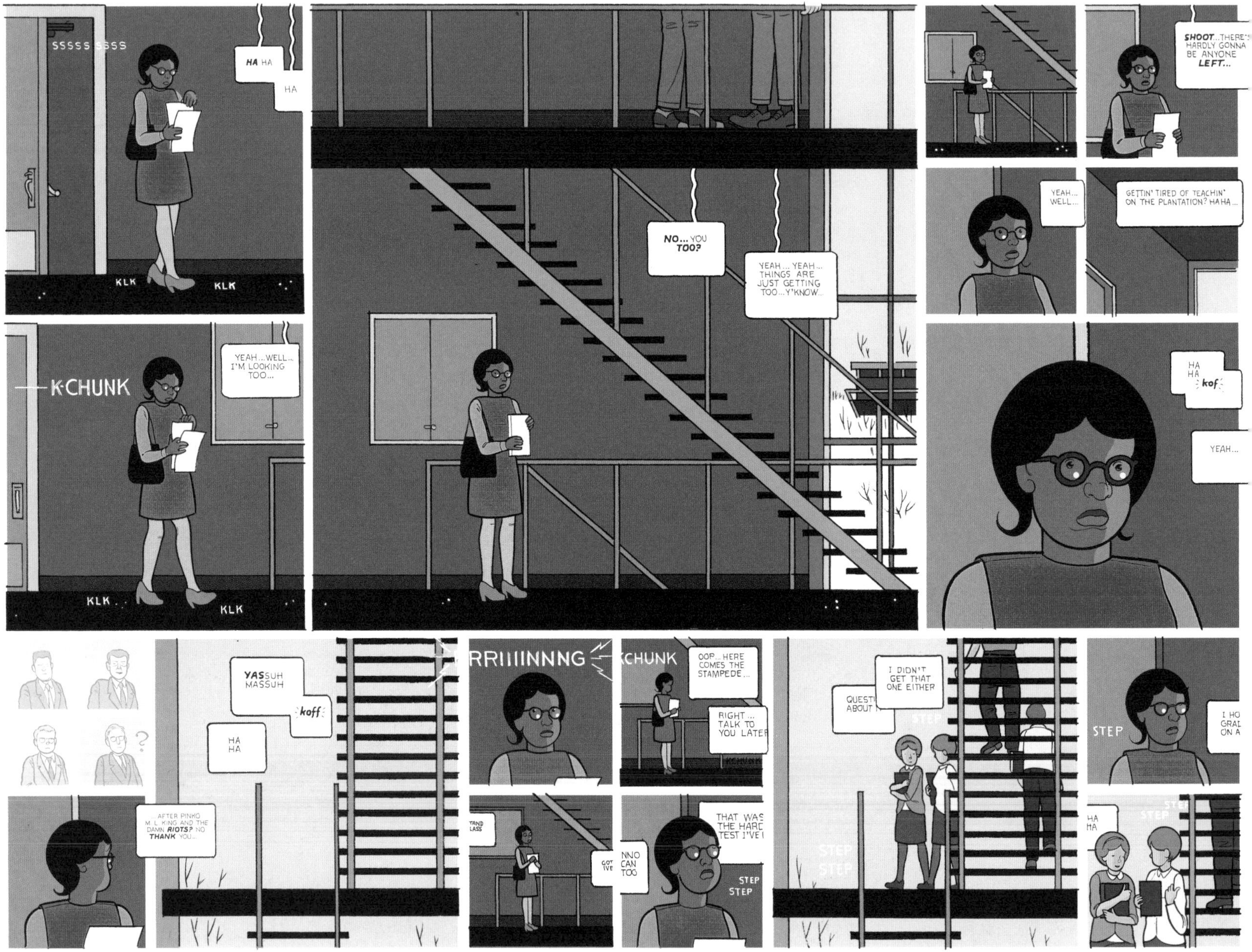
SSSSS SSSS
HA HA
HA
KLK
KLK
K-CHUNK
YEAH... WELL... I'M LOOKING TOO...
KLK..
KLK
NO... YOU TOO?
YEAH... YEAH... THINGS ARE JUST GETTING TOO... Y'KNOW...
SHOOT... THERE'S HARDLY GONNA BE ANYONE LEFT...
YEAH... WELL...
GETTIN' TIRED OF TEACHIN' ON THE PLANTATION? HA HA...
HA HA kof
YEAH...
YASSUH MASSUH
koff
HA HA
...AFTER PINKO M.L. KING AND THE DAMN RIOTS? NO THANK YOU...
RRIIIIINNNG
KCHUNK
OOP... HERE COMES THE STAMPEDE...
STEP STEP
I DIDN'T GET THAT ONE EITHER
STEP STEP
STEP
HA HA
STEP

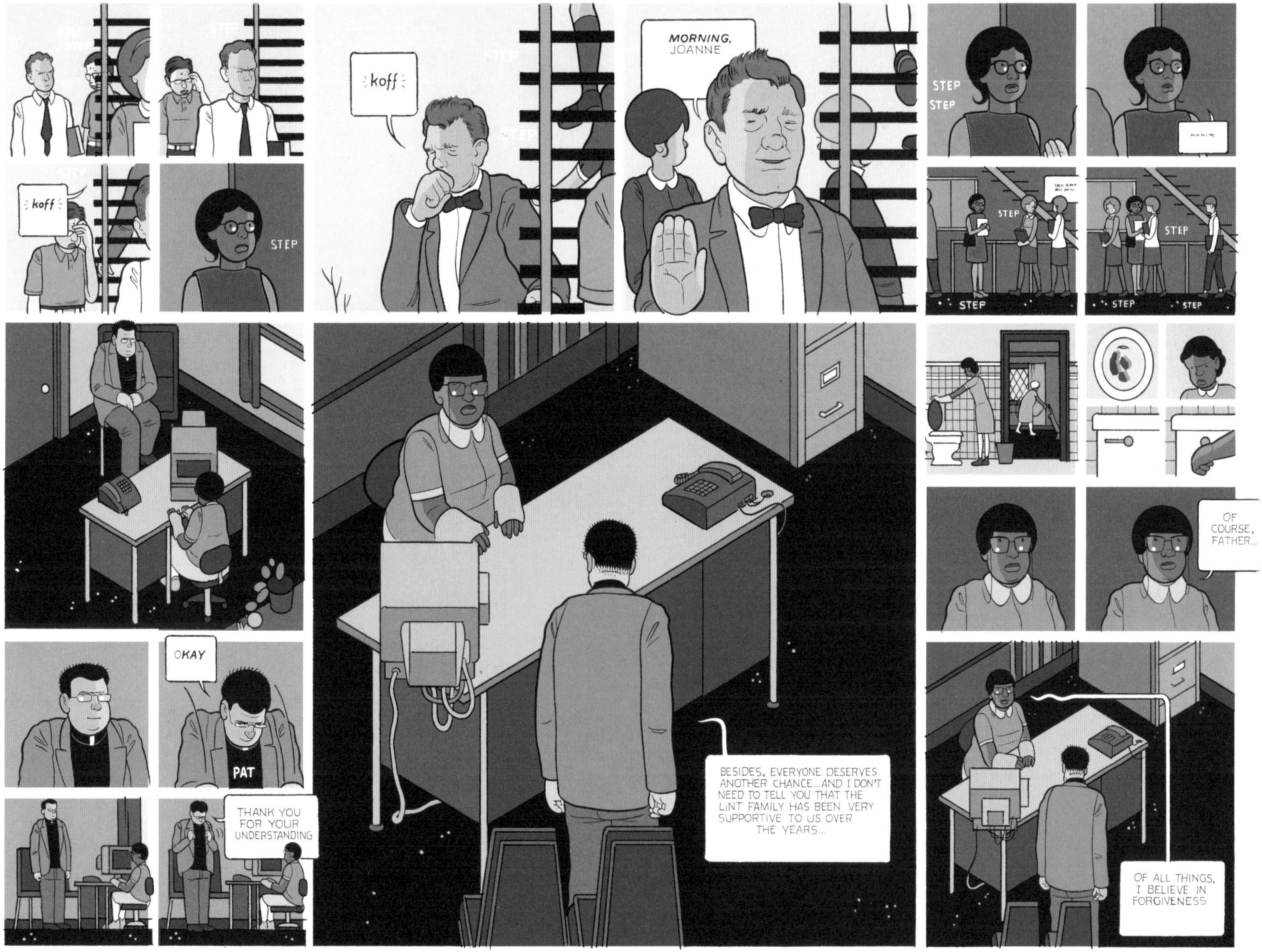
koff
STEP
koff
MORNING, JOANNE
STEP
STEP
STEP
STEP
STEP
STEP
STEP
OKAY
PAT
THANK YOU FOR YOUR UNDERSTANDING
BESIDES, EVERYONE DESERVES ANOTHER CHANCE...AND I DON'T NEED TO TELL YOU THAT THE LINT FAMILY HAS BEEN VERY SUPPORTIVE TO US OVER THE YEARS...
OF COURSE, FATHER...
OF ALL THINGS, I BELIEVE IN FORGIVENESS

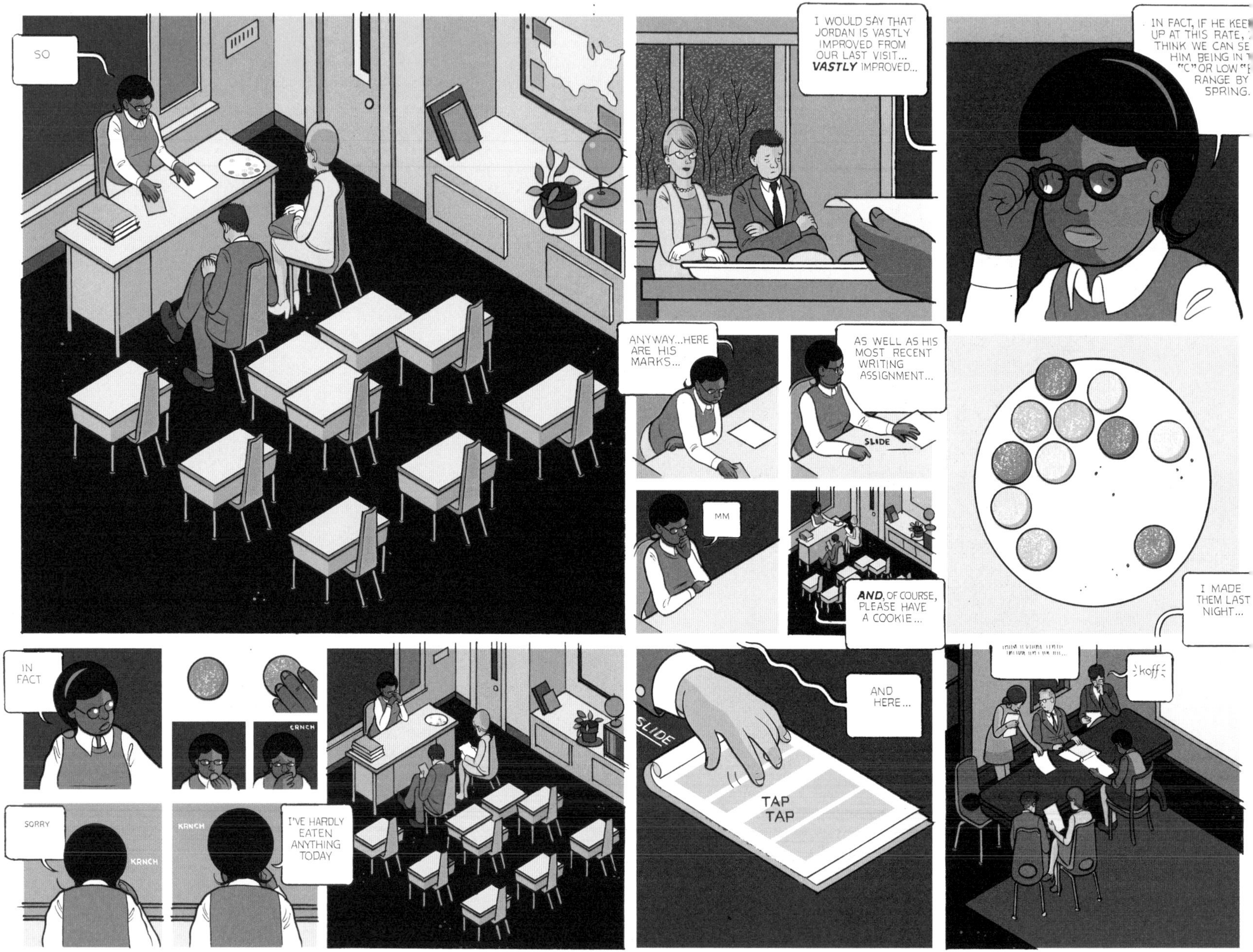
SO
I WOULD SAY THAT JORDAN IS VASTLY IMPROVED FROM OUR LAST VISIT... **VASTLY** IMPROVED...
IN FACT, IF HE KEE UP AT THIS RATE, THINK WE CAN SE HIM BEING IN "C" OR LOW " RANGE BY SPRING.
ANYWAY...HERE ARE HIS MARKS...
AS WELL AS HIS MOST RECENT WRITING ASSIGNMENT...
SLIDE
MM
AND, OF COURSE, PLEASE HAVE A COOKIE...
I MADE THEM LAST NIGHT...
IN FACT
KRNCH
SORRY
KRNCH
KRNCH
I'VE HARDLY EATEN ANYTHING TODAY
AND HERE...
SLIDE
TAP TAP
koff

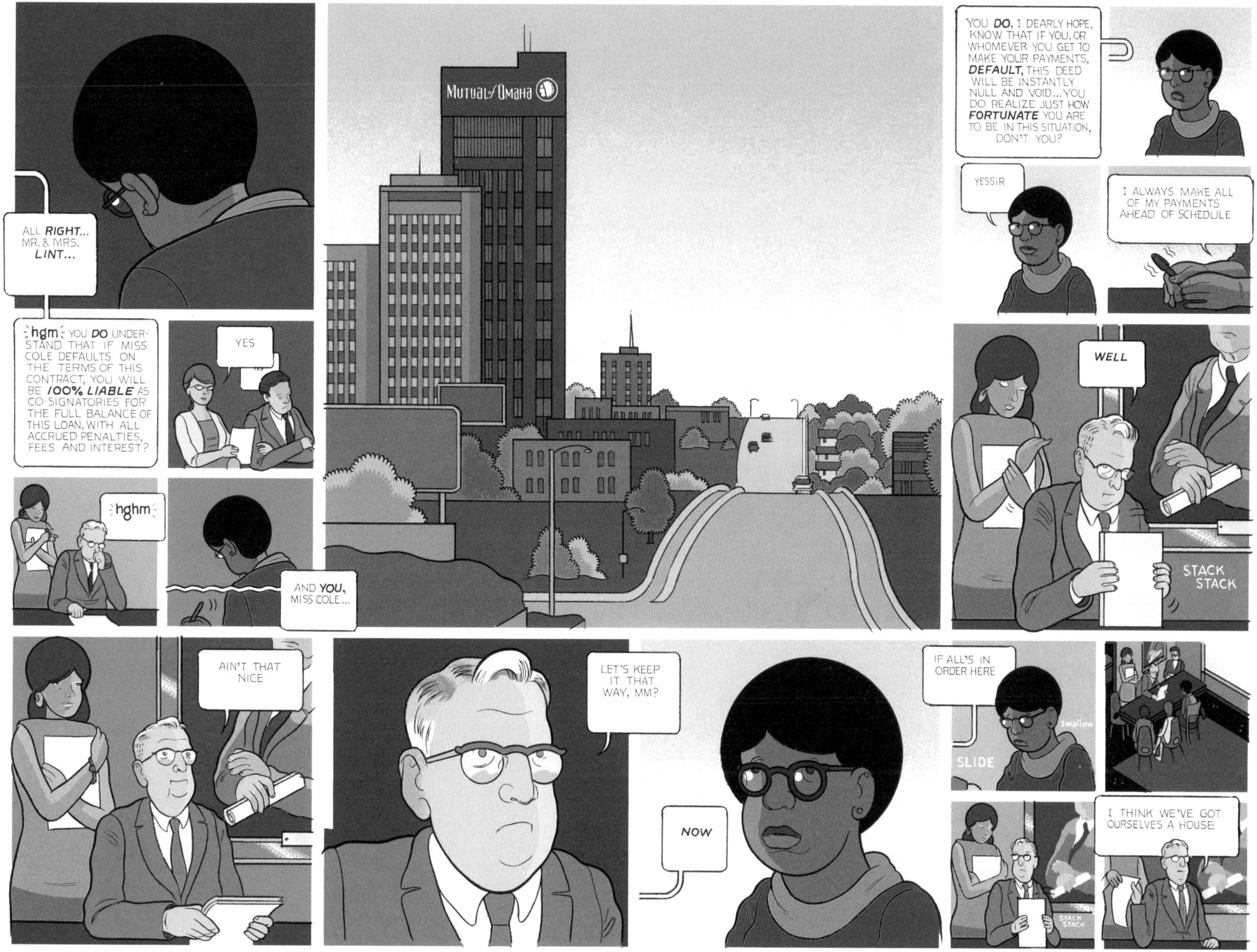

ALL **RIGHT**... MR. & MRS. **LINT**...
hgm YOU **DO** UNDERSTAND THAT IF MISS COLE DEFAULTS ON THE TERMS OF THIS CONTRACT, YOU WILL BE **100% LIABLE** AS CO-SIGNATORIES FOR THE FULL BALANCE OF THIS LOAN, WITH ALL ACCRUED PENALTIES, FEES AND INTEREST?
YES
hghm
AND **YOU**, MISS COLE...
MUTUAL of OMAHA
YOU **DO**, I DEARLY HOPE, KNOW THAT IF YOU, OR WHOMEVER YOU GET TO MAKE YOUR PAYMENTS, **DEFAULT**, THIS DEED WILL BE INSTANTLY NULL AND VOID... YOU DO REALIZE JUST HOW **FORTUNATE** YOU ARE TO BE IN THIS SITUATION, DON'T YOU?
YESSIR
I ALWAYS MAKE ALL OF MY PAYMENTS AHEAD OF SCHEDULE
WELL
STACK STACK
AIN'T THAT NICE
LET'S KEEP IT THAT WAY, MM?
NOW
IF ALL'S IN ORDER HERE
SLIDE
swallow
I THINK WE'VE GOT OURSELVES A HOUSE
STACK STACK

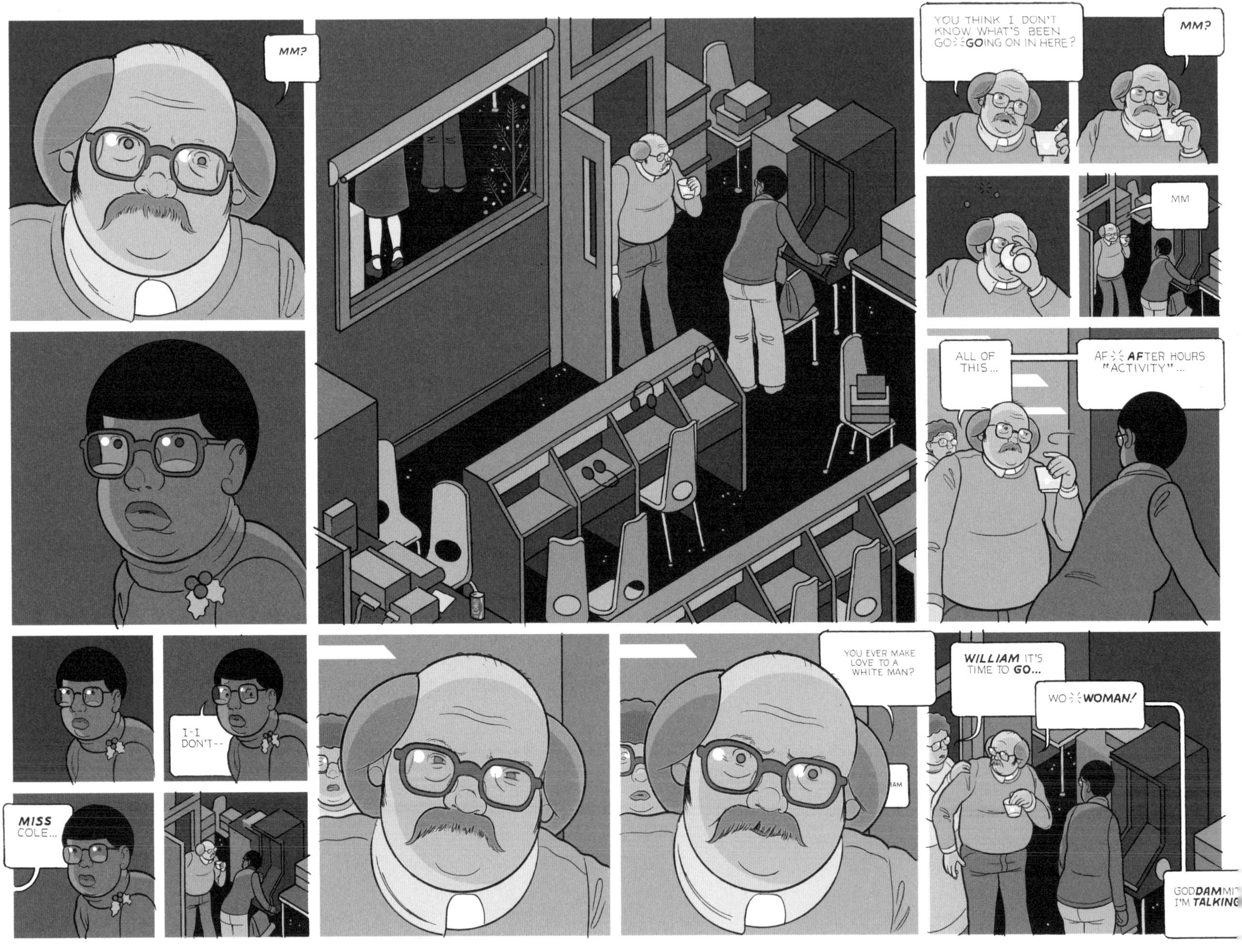
MM?
YOU THINK I DON'T KNOW WHAT'S BEEN GO GOING ON IN HERE?
MM?
MM
ALL OF THIS...
AF AFTER HOURS "ACTIVITY"...
I-I DON'T--
MISS COLE...
YOU EVER MAKE LOVE TO A WHITE MAN?
WILLIAM IT'S TIME TO GO...
WO WOMAN!
GODDAMMI
I'M TALKING

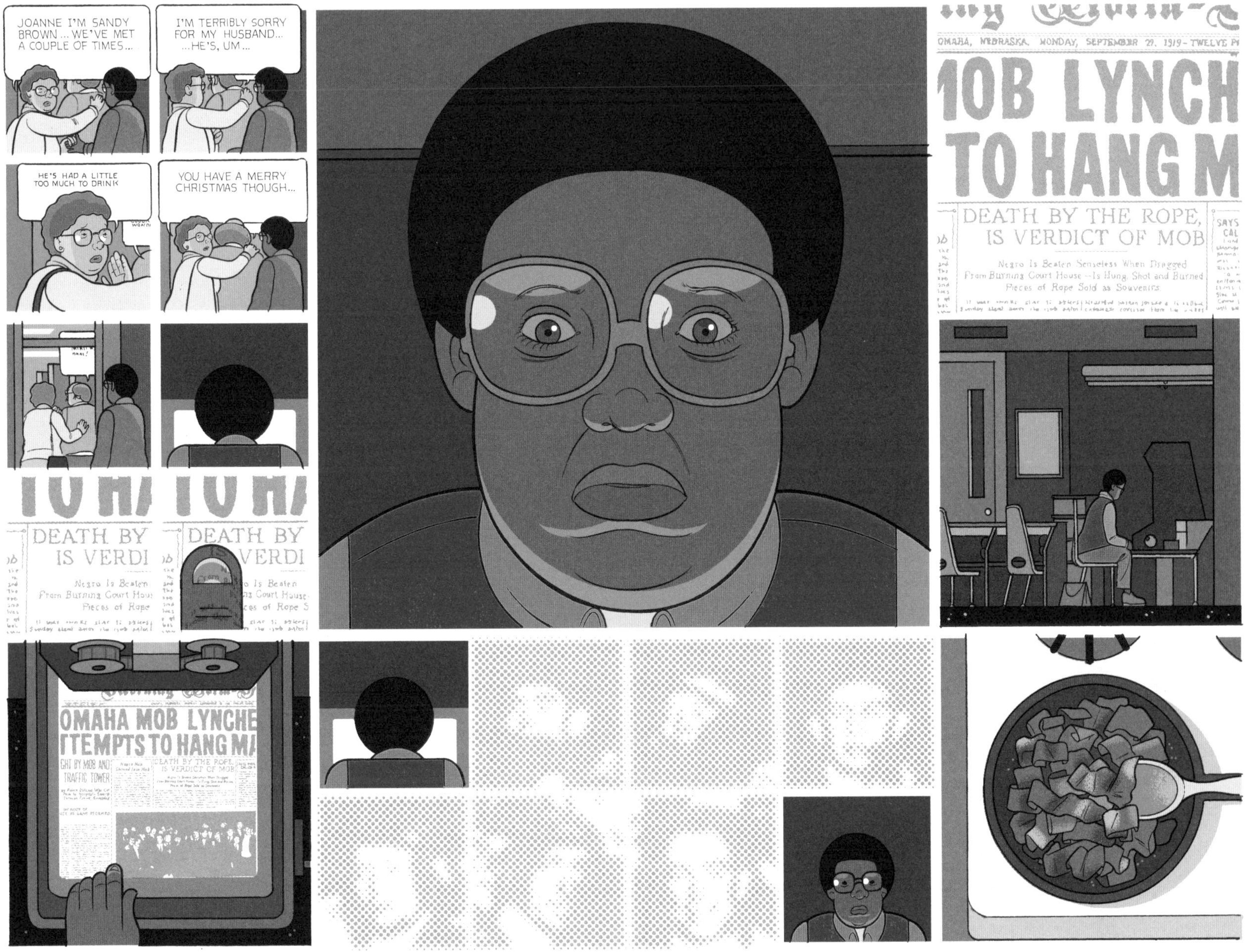

JOANNE I'M SANDY BROWN... WE'VE MET A COUPLE OF TIMES...
I'M TERRIBLY SORRY FOR MY HUSBAND... ...HE'S, UM...
HE'S HAD A LITTLE TOO MUCH TO DRINK
YOU HAVE A MERRY CHRISTMAS THOUGH...
OMAHA, NEBRASKA, MONDAY, SEPTEMBER 29, 1919 - TWELVE P
10B LYNCH
TO HANG M
DEATH BY THE ROPE, IS VERDICT OF MOB
Negro Is Beaten Senseless When Dragged From Burning Court House --Is Hung, Shot and Burned. Pieces of Rope Sold as Souvenirs
OMAHA MOB LYNCHE
TTEMPTS TO HANG MA

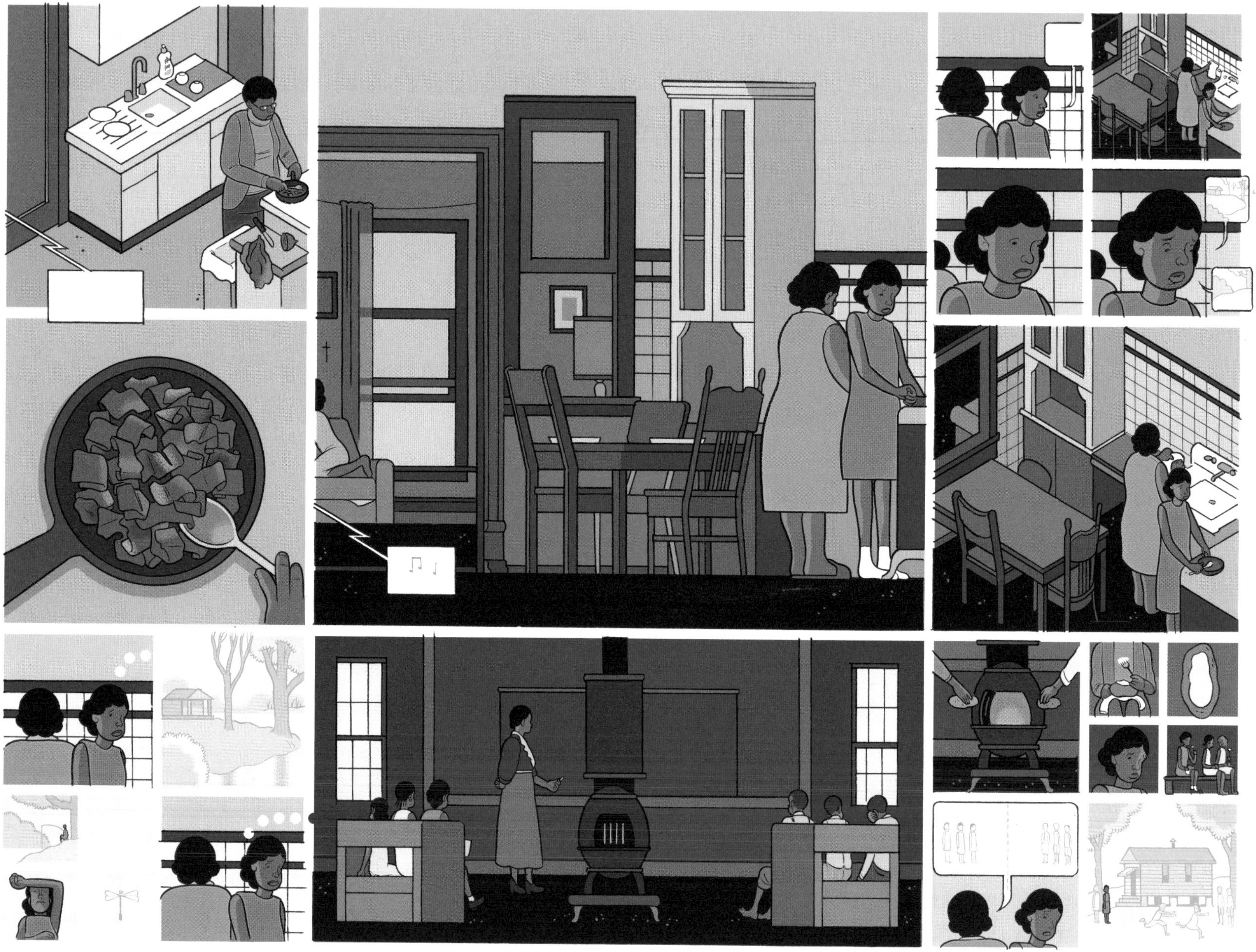

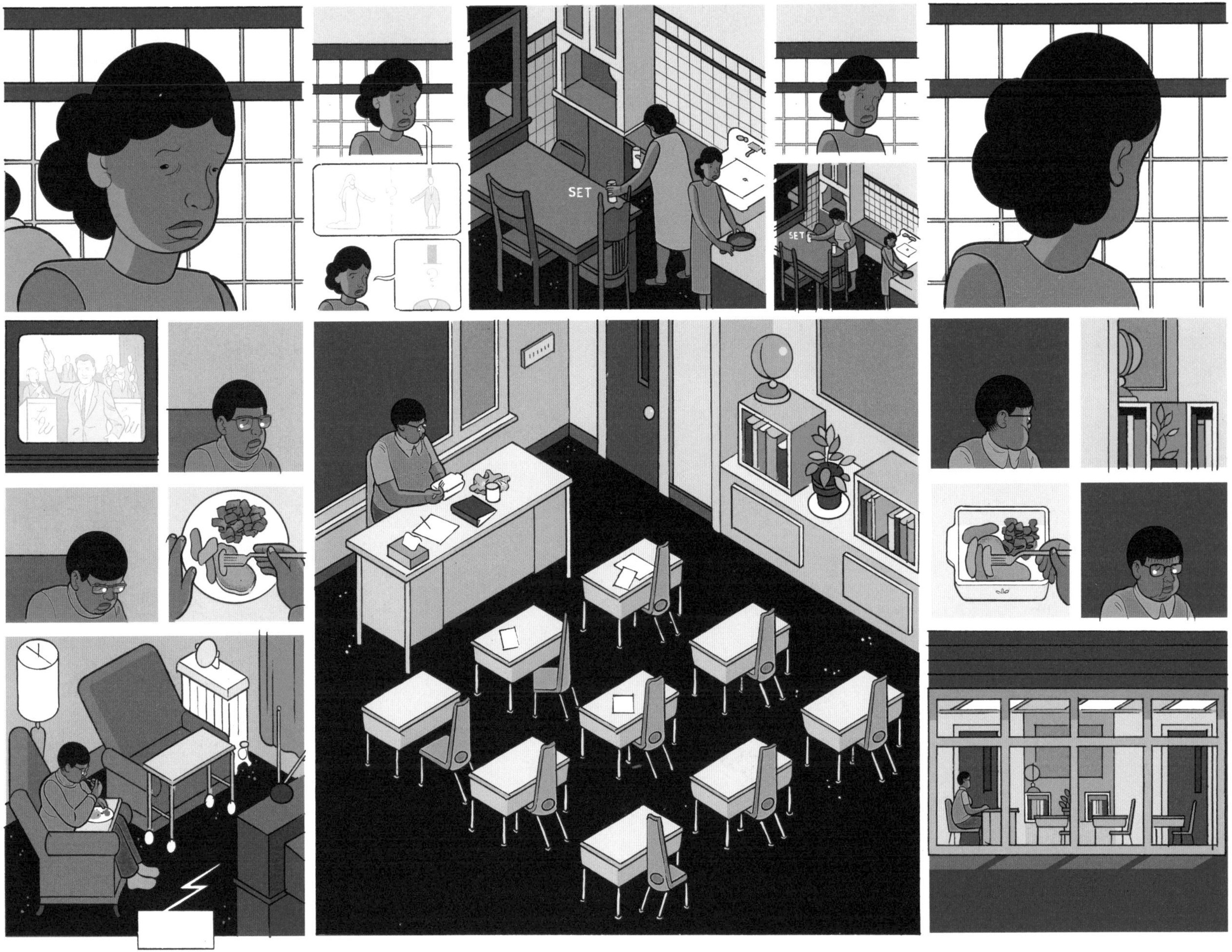
SET
SET

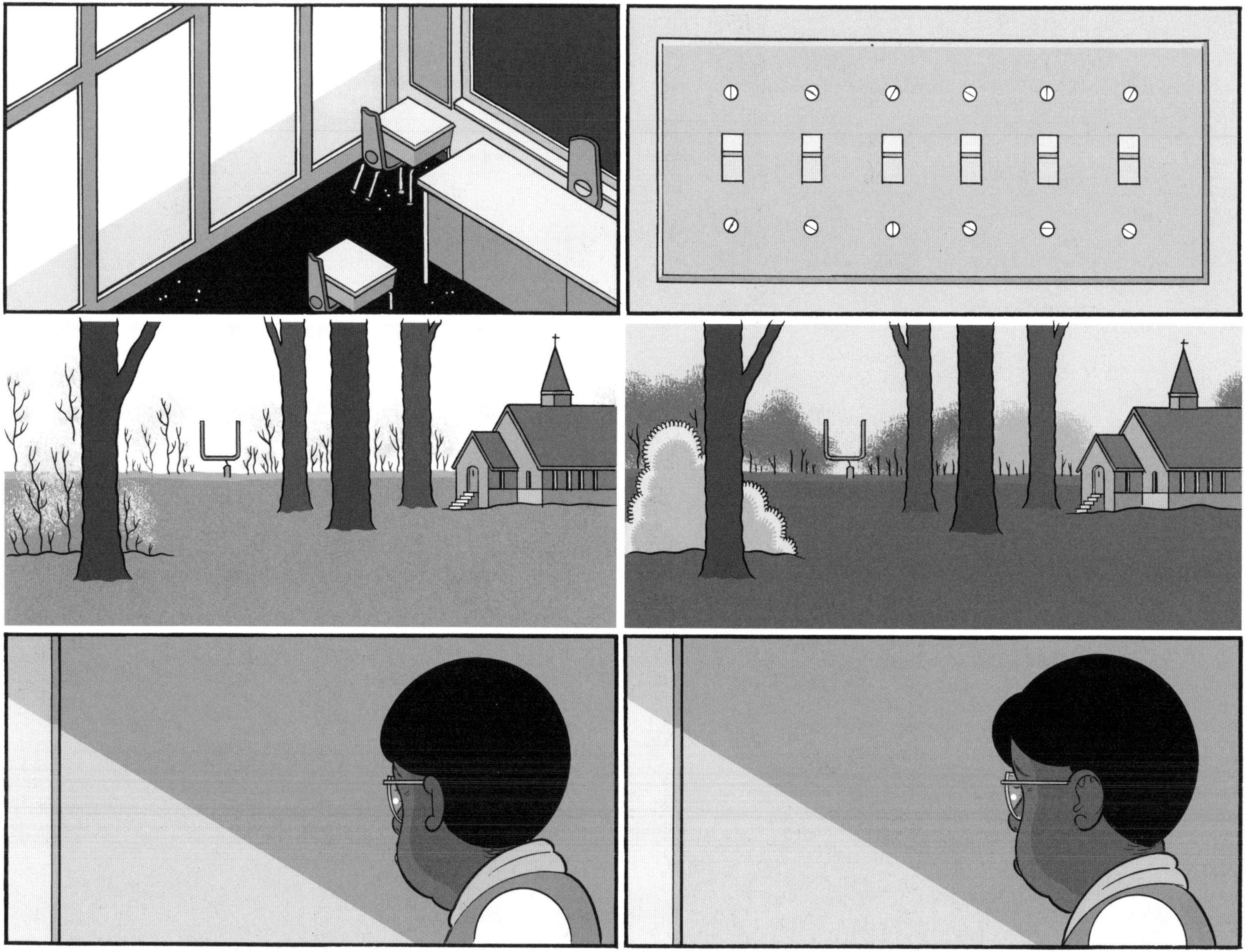

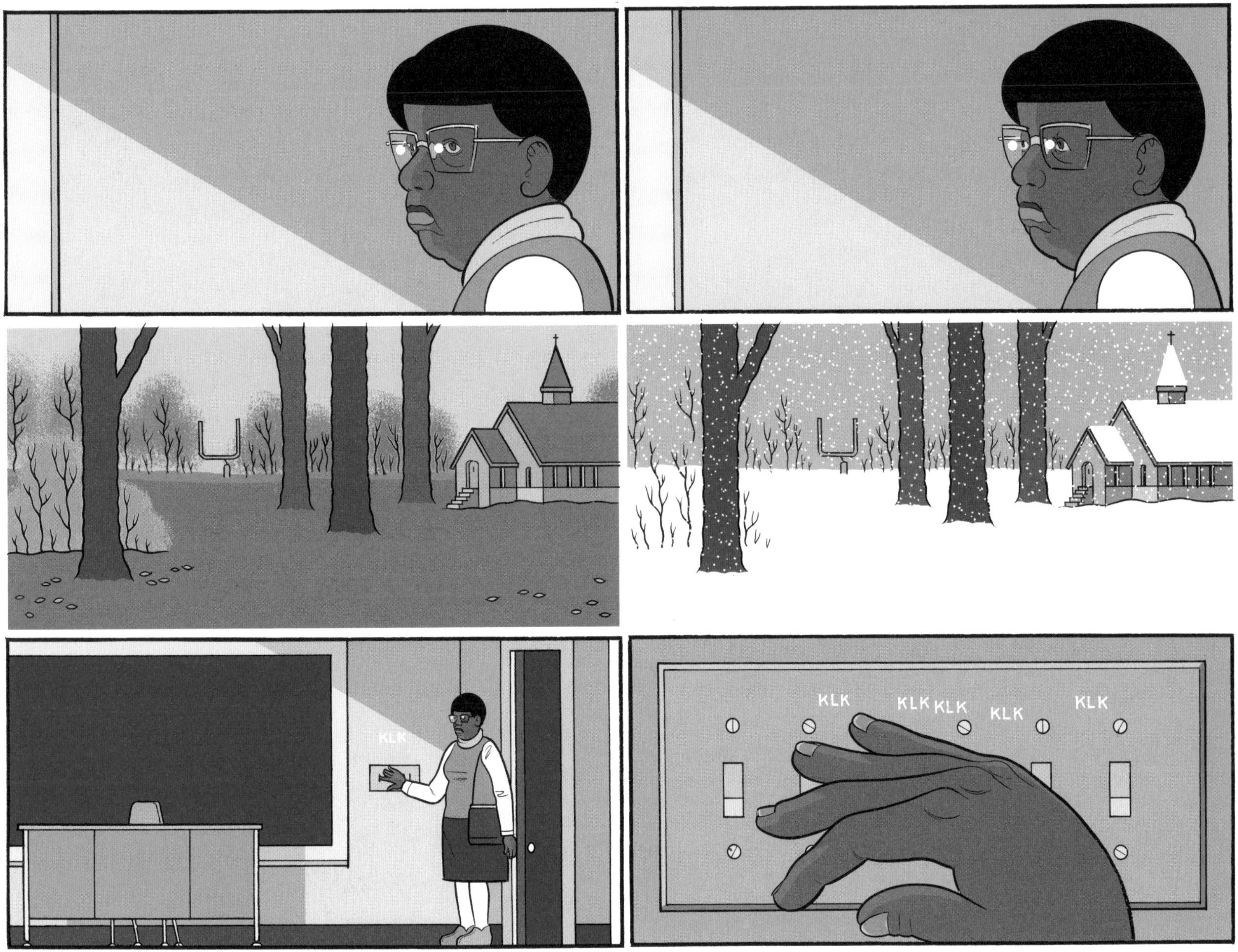
KLK
KLK
KLK
KLK
KLK
KLK

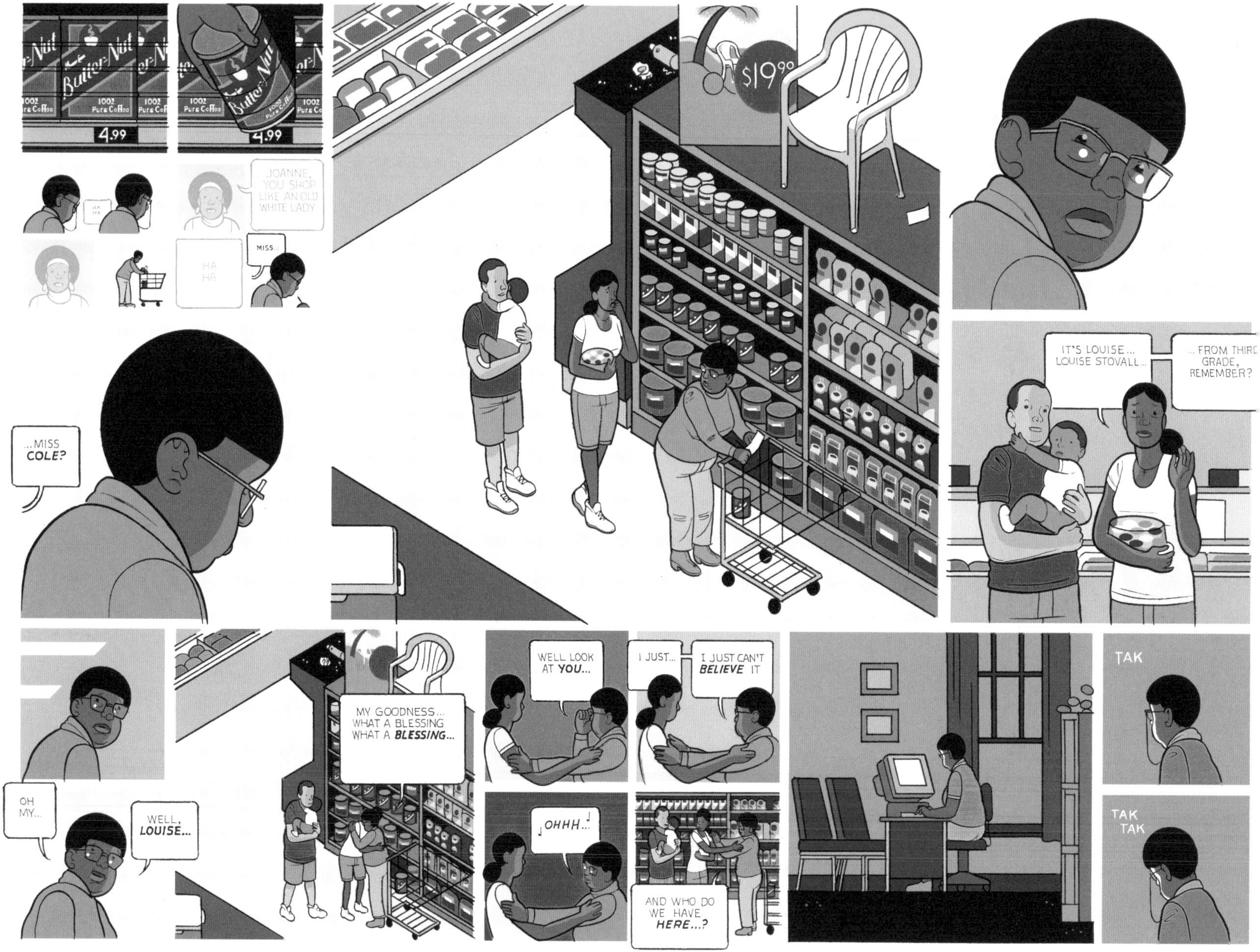
Butter-Nut
100% Pure Coffee
4.99
HA HA
JOANNE, YOU SHOP LIKE AN OLD WHITE LADY
HA HA
MISS...
...MISS COLE?
$19.99
IT'S LOUISE... LOUISE STOVALL...
... FROM THIRD GRADE, REMEMBER?
OH MY...
WELL, LOUISE...
MY GOODNESS... WHAT A BLESSING WHAT A BLESSING...
WELL LOOK AT YOU...
I JUST...
I JUST CAN'T BELIEVE IT
OHHH...
AND WHO DO WE HAVE HERE...?
TAK
TAK TAK

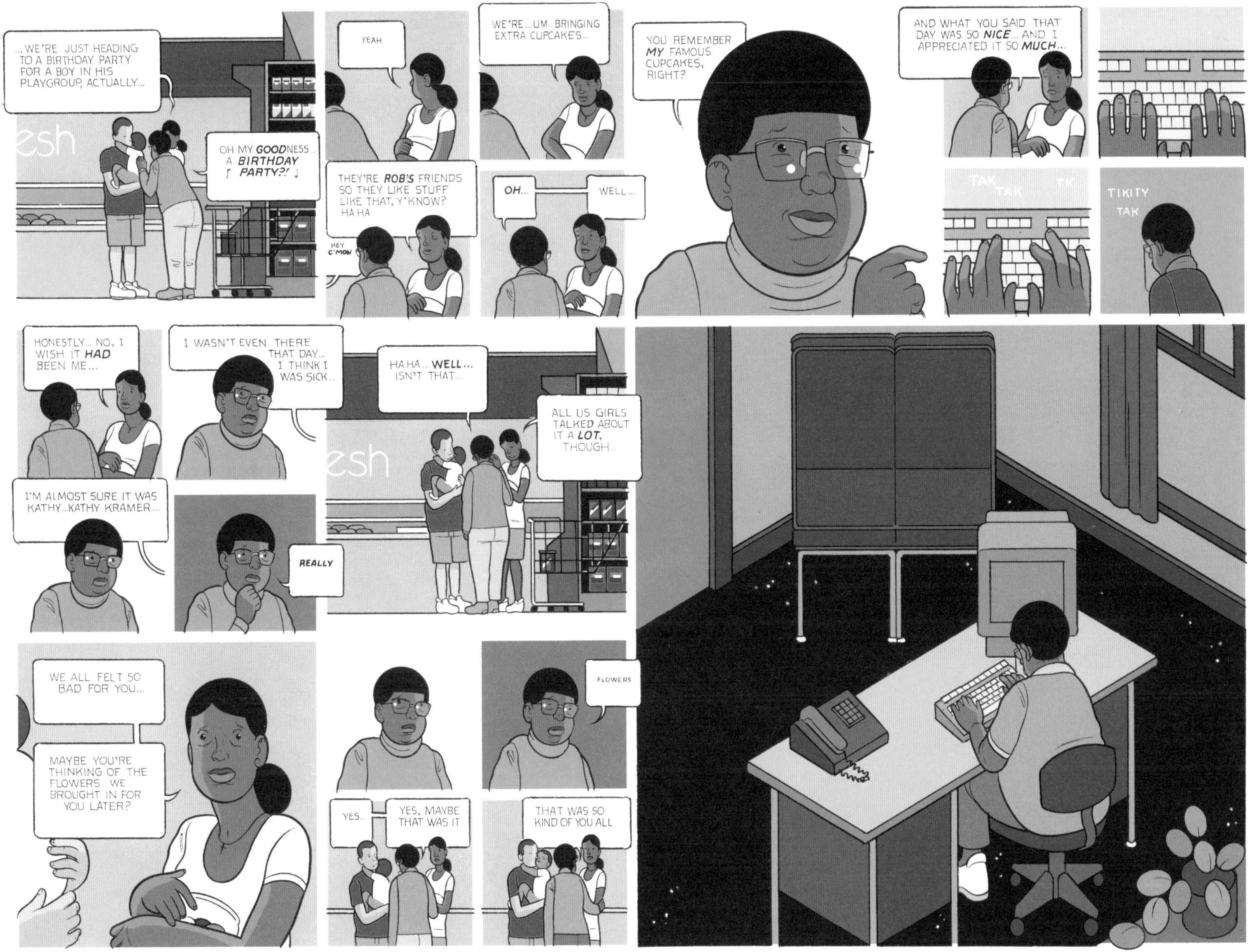

...WE'RE JUST HEADING TO A BIRTHDAY PARTY FOR A BOY IN HIS PLAYGROUP, ACTUALLY...
OH MY GOODNESS... A BIRTHDAY PARTY?!
YEAH
THEY'RE ROB'S FRIENDS SO THEY LIKE STUFF LIKE THAT, Y'KNOW? HA HA
HEY C'MON
WE'RE...UM...BRINGING EXTRA CUPCAKES...
OH...
WELL...
YOU REMEMBER MY FAMOUS CUPCAKES, RIGHT?
AND WHAT YOU SAID THAT DAY WAS SO NICE... AND I APPRECIATED IT SO MUCH...
TAK TAK TK
TIKITY TAK
HONESTLY... NO, I WISH IT HAD BEEN ME...
I WASN'T EVEN THERE THAT DAY... I THINK I WAS SICK...
I'M ALMOST SURE IT WAS KATHY...KATHY KRAMER...
REALLY
HA HA ... WELL... ISN'T THAT...
ALL US GIRLS TALKED ABOUT IT A LOT, THOUGH...
WE ALL FELT SO BAD FOR YOU...
MAYBE YOU'RE THINKING OF THE FLOWERS WE BROUGHT IN FOR YOU LATER?
FLOWERS
YES...
YES, MAYBE THAT WAS IT
THAT WAS SO KIND OF YOU ALL

KNOCK KNOCK
COME IN
Funeral
for
Mr. George
Sunrise:
May 16, 1939
esc
F1
tab
Q
W
KLK
TAK
T!K
TK
K-KLK

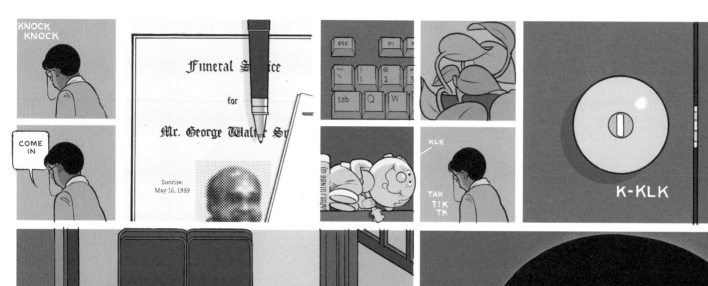

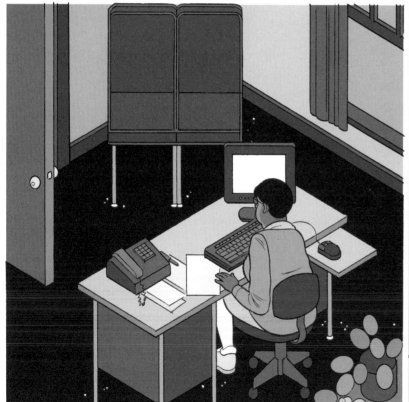

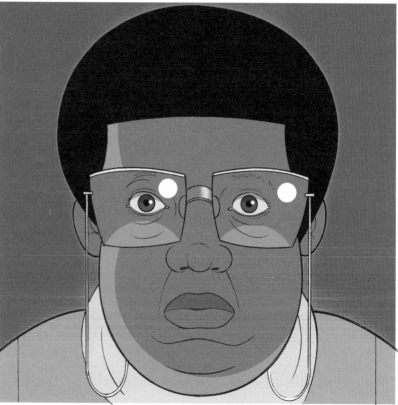

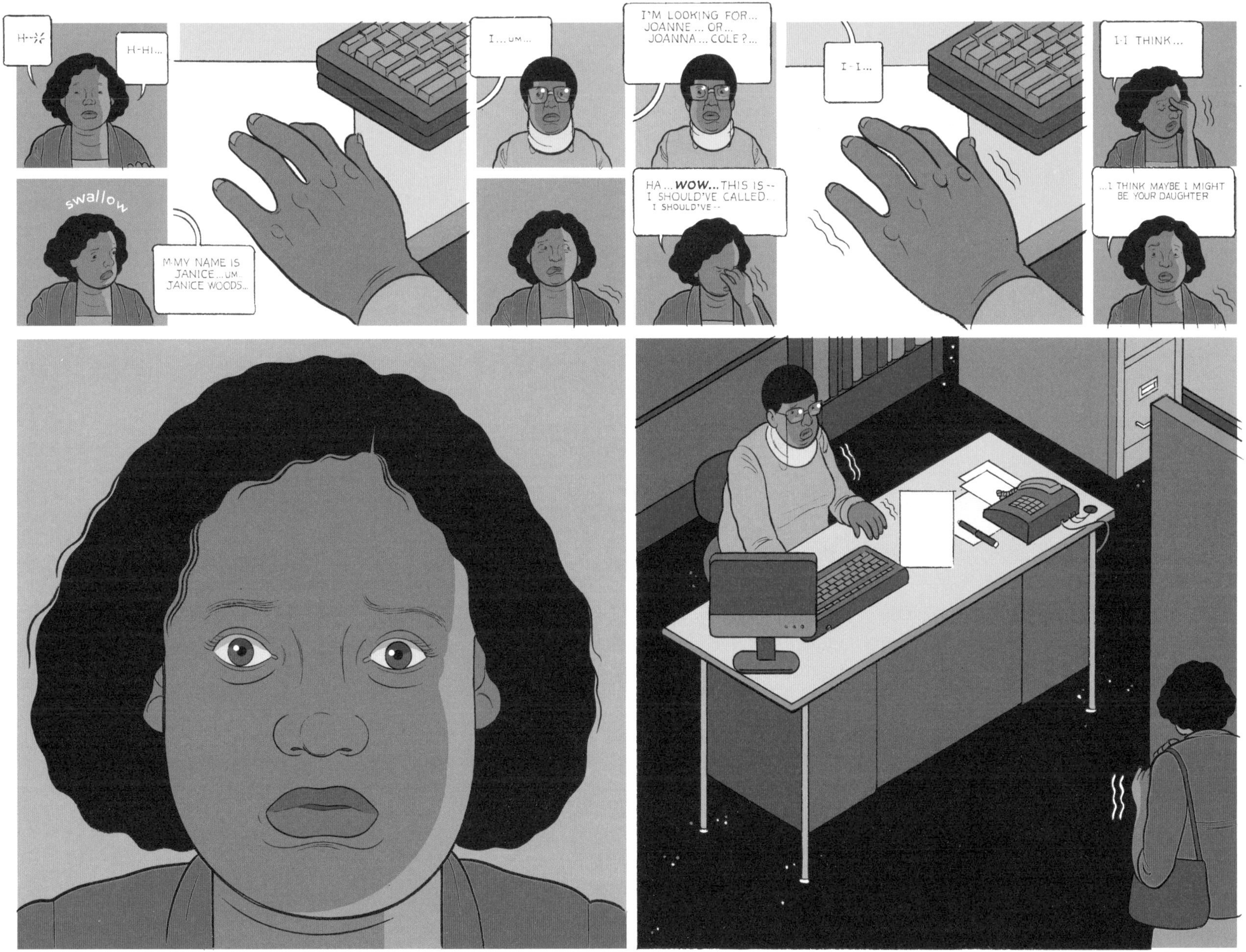

H--
H-HI...
swallow
M-MY NAME IS JANICE...UM.. JANICE WOODS...
I...UM...
I'M LOOKING FOR... JOANNE... OR... JOANNA... COLE?...
HA... WOW... THIS IS -- I SHOULD'VE CALLED... I SHOULD'VE --
I-I...
I-I THINK...
...I THINK MAYBE I MIGHT BE YOUR DAUGHTER

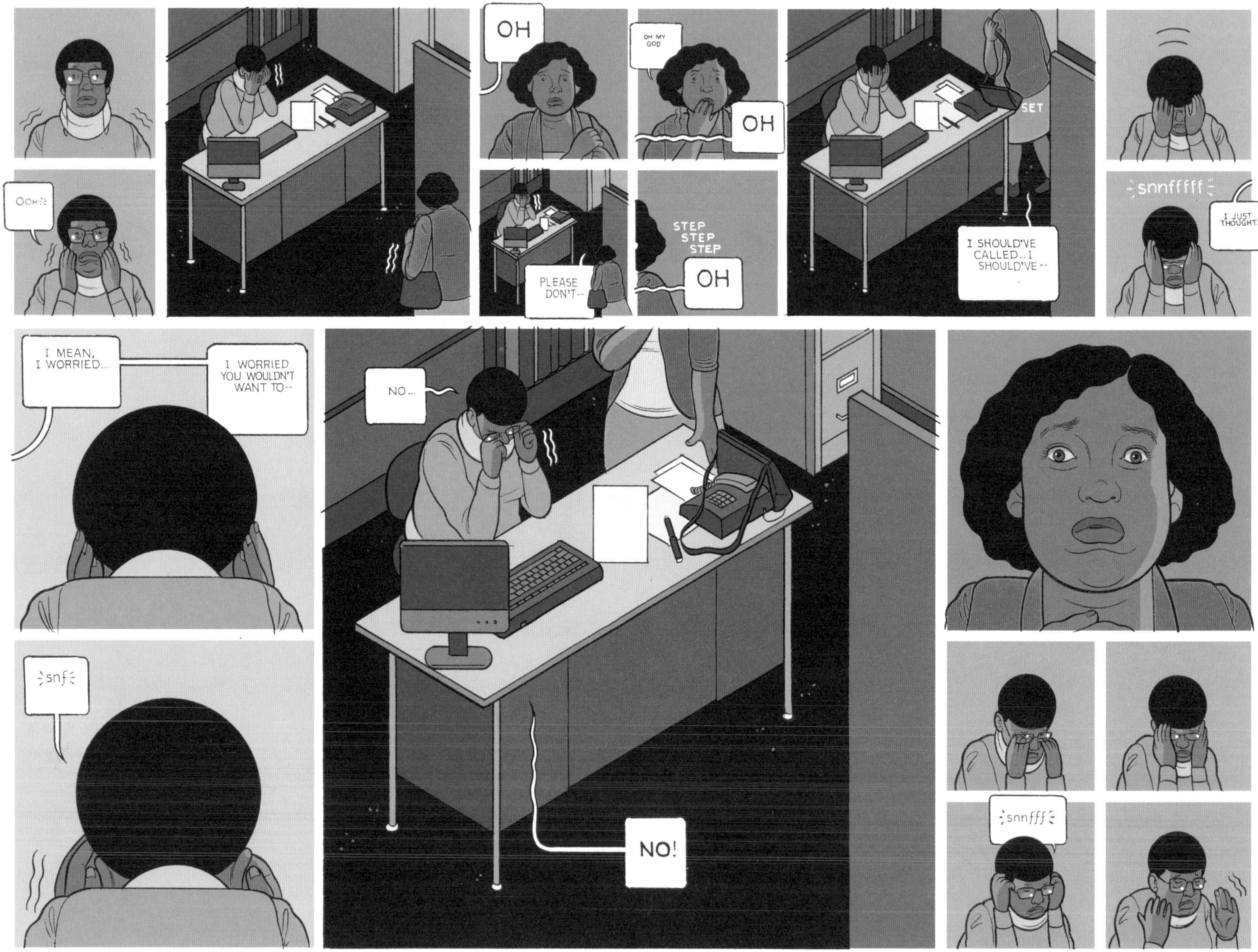

OOH
OH
OH MY GOD
OH
PLEASE DON'T--
STEP STEP STEP
OH
SET
I SHOULD'VE CALLED... I SHOULD'VE --
snnffffff
I JUST THOUGHT...
I MEAN, I WORRIED...
I WORRIED YOU WOULDN'T WANT TO--
snf
NO...
NO!
snnfff

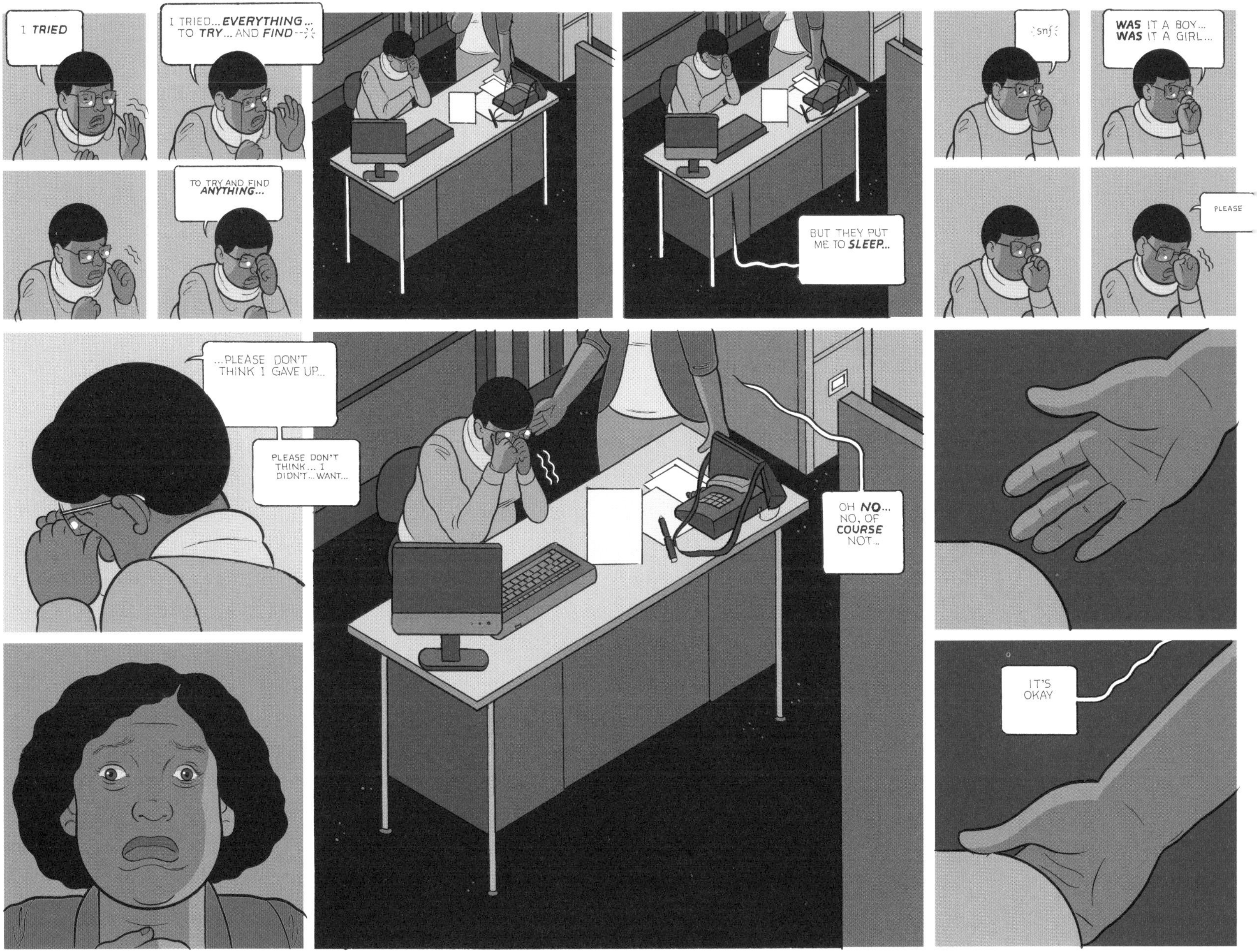
I TRIED
I TRIED... EVERYTHING... TO TRY... AND FIND--
TO TRY AND FIND ANYTHING...
BUT THEY PUT ME TO SLEEP...
snf
WAS IT A BOY... WAS IT A GIRL...
PLEASE
...PLEASE DON'T THINK I GAVE UP...
PLEASE DON'T THINK... I DIDN'T... WANT...
OH NO... NO, OF COURSE NOT...
IT'S OKAY

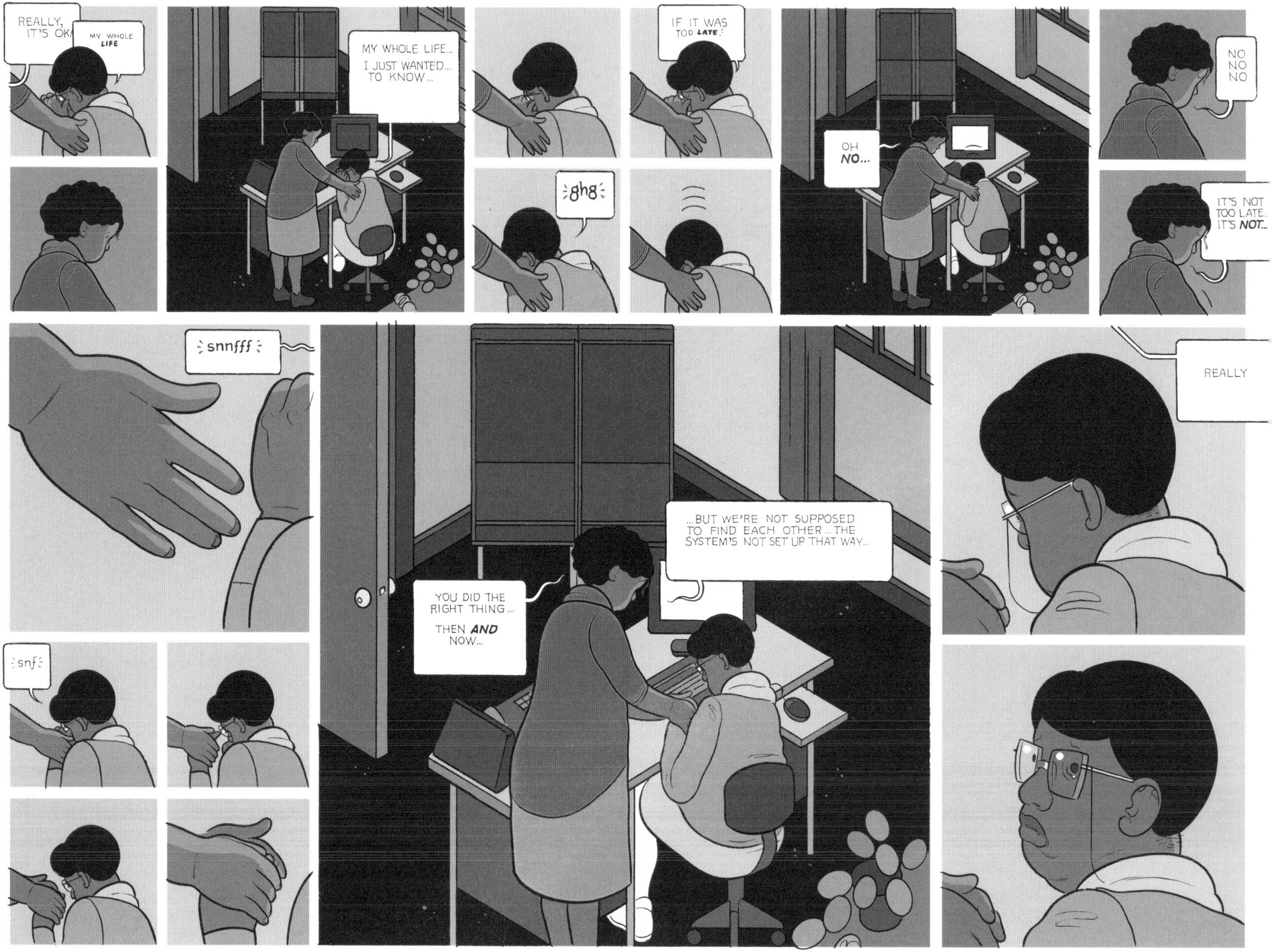
REALLY, IT'S OK
MY WHOLE LIFE
MY WHOLE LIFE... I JUST WANTED... TO KNOW...
ghg
IF IT WAS TOO LATE
OH NO...
NO NO NO
IT'S NOT TOO LATE.. IT'S NOT...
snnfff
snf
YOU DID THE RIGHT THING... THEN AND NOW...
...BUT WE'RE NOT SUPPOSED TO FIND EACH OTHER... THE SYSTEM'S NOT SET UP THAT WAY...
REALLY

AND I SHOULD KNOW...

I'M A NEONATAL NURSE

SO IT WAS PROBABLY A LOT EASIER FOR ME...

HA HA Y'KNOW?

THE BLAIR CHILDREN'S HOME AND AID SOCIETY?

BUT... I... I WAS IN TOWN... AND MY FRIEND AMY* MADE ME PROMISE I WAS GOING TO DO THIS. AND... AND I JUST THOUGHT "I HAVE TO DO THIS... I HAVE TO DO THIS *NOW*..."

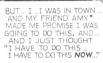

SO... 1961... RIGHT?

*CORRIGAN--ed.

JANUARY 24TH?

INTERM

ISSION

NOTES

The book's **Introduction** (pp. 1 – 113) was written between 2000 and 2003, originally appearing in *NewCity* and the *Chicago Reader;* for fears of consumer fatigue it was split between *The ACME Novelty Libraries 16* & *17* (2005-6) and here made æsthetically inhabitable via slight modifications and renovations. *Presidents:* William Jefferson Clinton, George Walker Bush. *Internet access:* Global Village TelePort 33.6 Mbps modem.

William Brown (pp. 114 – 182) was drawn between 2002 and 2004 and originally appeared in the *Chicago Reader,* with slight modifications in 2008 for his role in *The ACME Novelty Library 19.* *President:* George Walker Bush. *Internet:* ADSL 660 CenturyLink Series LAN.

The first sixteen pages of **Jordan Lint** (pp. 183 – 263) were written in 2006 for *The Book of Other People* (Zadie Smith, editor) with the remainder partially serialized in the *Chicago Reader* and the *Virginia Quarterly Review,* collecting in 2010 around the drain hole of *The ACME Novelty Library 20,* through which the entire blockage was then forcefully ejected. Ameliorations were added in 2018. *Presidents:* George Walker Bush, Barack Hussein Obama. *Internet:* Cable, with 3G and 4G cellular data for mobile queries and comedy videos.

Excepting the first four pages, which appeared in *Drawn & Quarterly: Twenty-Five Years of Contemporary Cartooning, Comics, and Graphic Novels* in 2014, **Joanne Cole** (pp. 264 – 351) is previously unpublished, being drawn and written between 2012 and 2018. *Presidents:* Barack Hussein Obama, Donald John Trump. *Internet:* Undefined, in response to precipitous and unquantifiable attacks upon previously reliable mnemonic biomass.

The charitable and perspicacious literary booster will note that the author, **F. C. Ware** (b. 1967, Omaha, Nebraska) employed himself fashioning other projects and artistic experiments over the previous 18 years, not just this single, sad, inexplicable work.

Thanks to: Nicole Aragi, Lynda Barry, Susan Betz, Ivan Brunetti, Charles Burns, Jackie Byers, Miss Cassette, Hillary Chute, Dave Cihla, Daniel Clowes, Patrick Doyle, Dave Eggers, Dan Frank, Kathleen Fridella, Ted Genoways, Ira Glass, Andy Hughes, Altie Karper, Dan Kelly, Chip Kidd, Alex Kotlowitz, Doris & David McCall, Françoise Mouly, Chris Oliveros, Mark Parker, Francesco Pacifico, Gary Panter, Peter Power, Daniel Raeburn, Seth, Sheila Sachs, Tim Samuelson, Zadie Smith, Art Spiegelman, Susan Stein and Adrian Tomine.

For **Marnie** and **Clara.**

1

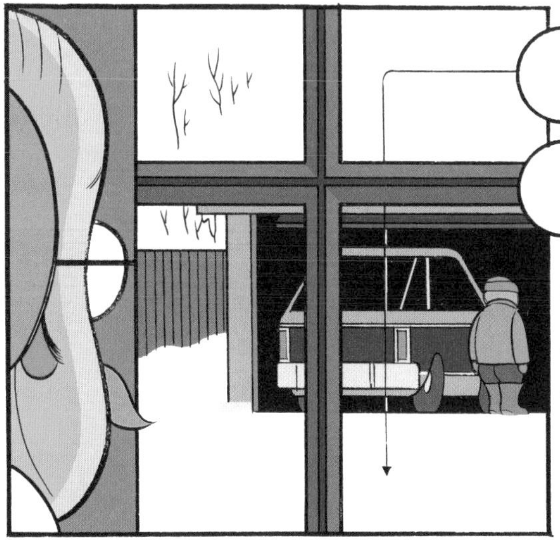

Compare/contrast with snow crystal highlighted on page 1. Explain.

2

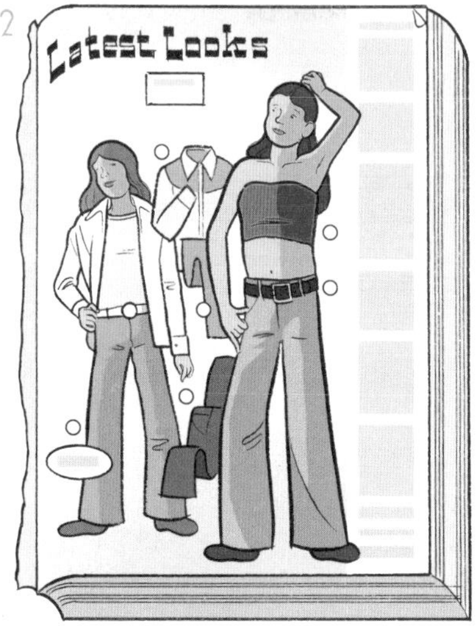
Latest Looks

3

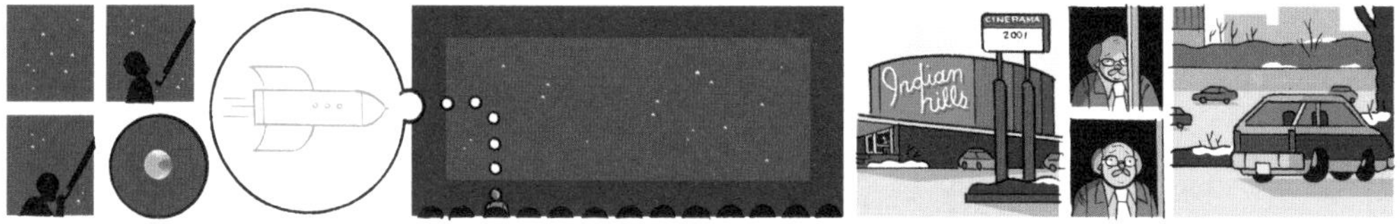
CINERAMA
2001
Indian hills

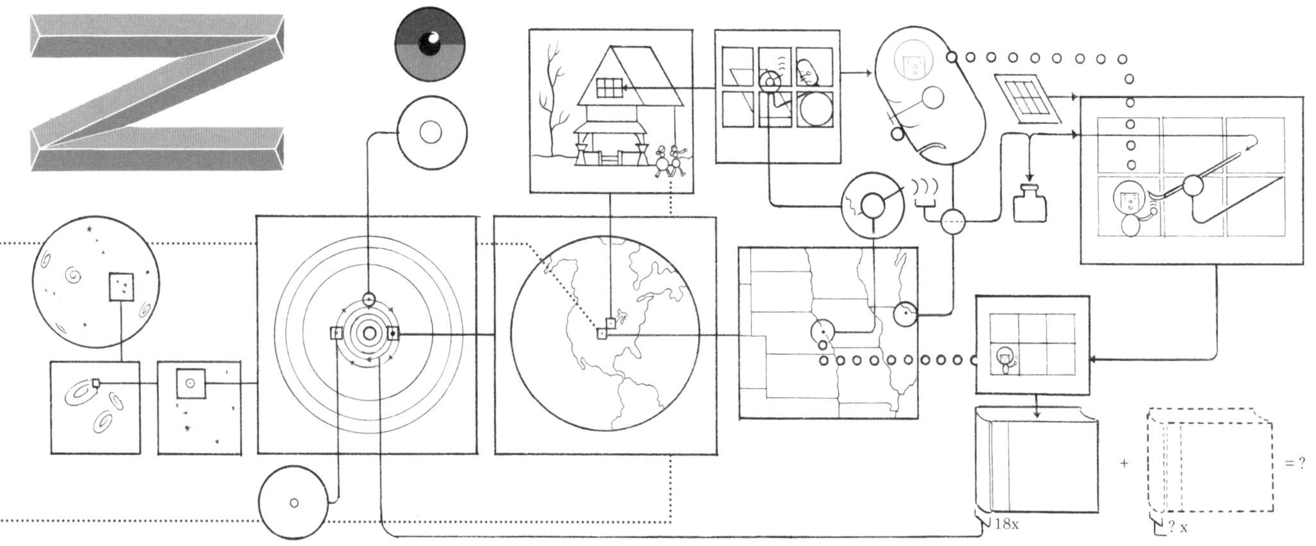
18x
+
= ?
? x

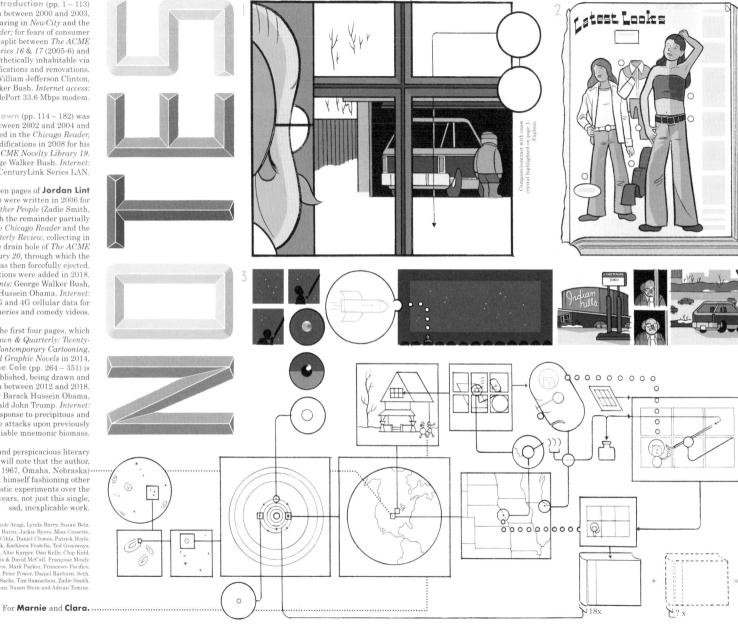